DR SPOCK'S BA… CHILD CA…

Dr Benjamin Spock practised paediatrics in New York City from 1933 to 1947. He then became a medical teacher and researcher at the Mayo Clinic, the University of Pittsburgh and Case Western Reserve University in Cleveland. The author of eleven books, he was a political activist for causes that vitally affect children: disarmament, day care, schooling, housing and medical care for all. He had two sons, a stepdaughter and four grandchildren. Dr Spock, who died on 15 March 1998, aged ninety-four, was married to Mary Morgan. *Dr Spock's Baby and Child Care* has been translated into thirty-nine languages and has sold fifty million copies worldwide since its first publication in 1946.

Dr Robert Needlman is Associate Professor of Pediatrics at Case Western Reserve University and co-founder of Reach Out and Read, a national organization that promotes reading aloud to young children. A practising paediatrician for more than twenty years, Dr Needlman has contributed to numerous magazines, textbooks and journals and is a widely featured speaker on early learning, literacy and child development. The author of *Dr Spock's Baby Basics* (also available from Simon & Schuster), Dr Needlman lives in Cleveland, Ohio, with his wife and daughter.

BOOKS BY DR BENJAMIN SPOCK

BABY AND CHILD CARE
(and Dr Steven J. Parker)

FEEDING YOUR BABY AND CHILD
(with Dr Miriam E. Lowenberg)

RAISING CHILDREN IN A DIFFICULT TIME

A TEENAGER'S GUIDE TO LIFE AND LOVE

ALSO FROM THE DR SPOCK COMPANY

DR SPOCK'S BABY BASICS
(Dr Robert Needlman)

DR SPOCK'S PREGNANCY GUIDE
(Dr Marjorie Greenfield)

Dr Spock's Baby and Child Care

9TH EDITION

by Dr Benjamin Spock

Revised and Updated by

Dr Robert Needlman

SIMON & SCHUSTER

London · New York · Sydney · Toronto · New Delhi

A CBS COMPANY

Dr Spock's Baby & Childcare 9th Edition
First published in the USA by Pocket Books, a division of
Simon & Schuster Inc., 2011
This anglicised edition published in Great Britain in 2012
by Simon & Schuster UK Ltd
A CBS COMPANY

1 3 5 7 9 10 8 6 4 2

Simon & Schuster UK Ltd
1st Floor
222 Gray's Inn Road
London WC1X 8HB

www.simonandschuster.co.uk

Simon & Schuster Australia, Sydney
Simon & Schuster India, New Delhi

A CIP catalogue record for this book
is available from the British Library.

ISBN: 978-0-85720-526-1

Illustrations by Grace Needlman

Printed and bound in Finland by Bookwell

ACKNOWLEDGMENTS

The book you are reading was first published more than sixty-five years ago. When it came out in 1945, *The Common Sense Guide to Baby and Child Care* by Dr Benjamin Spock revolutionized parenting and changed the lives of a generation. The children of that generation are the grandparents of this one. Maybe they are *your* parents. So, in a way, you might be 'a child of Spock'. I know I am.

Dr Spock's warm and wise advice still makes sense today. That is largely because the book changed with the times. When Gloria Steinem, the groundbreaking feminist, told Spock that he was a sexist, he listened and he changed. When the health risks of our high-cholesterol, high-fat diet became known, Spock embraced a vegetarian diet and went on to live to ninety-four.

Before he died, Spock worked on the seventh edition of *Baby and Child Care* with a gifted paediatrician, Steven Parker, who had been, by coincidence, one of my own most influential teachers. So when I revised *Baby and Child Care* for its eighth edition, I owed a huge debt to Dr Spock and to Dr Parker, and to all of the other doctors, parents and children who have made the book so rich, accurate, timely and wise. That debt still stands.

For the ninth edition, I turned for help to a team of

experts from many fields: Marjie Greenfield for pregnancy and childbirth; Mary O'Connor for breast-feeding; James Kozick for dental health; Abdulla Ghori and Nazha Abughali for infections; Leyla McCurdy for environmental health; Henry Ng for sexuality; and Erin Whipple for going to the hospital. They and a host of other friends and colleagues have greatly enriched this edition of *Baby and Child Care,* although, of course, the responsibility for the finished product is mine.

Special thanks are due to Micki Nuding and Maggie Crawford, my editors at Simon and Schuster, and to Robert Lescher, Dr Spock's agent for many years and now mine as well. Mary Morgan, who was married to Dr Spock for twenty-five years and who worked with him on multiple editions of *Baby and Child Care,* has been an enormous source of guidance and support. Writing a book, like raising a child, is an act of faith. Thanks, Mary, for having faith in me.

Finally, thanks to my family: to Grace for the joy and creativity you bring to life, and to Carol for your love, acceptance and good sense. Without you, I couldn't even start, let alone finish, a project like this book.

To Allen and Gloria Needlman, my first and best teachers

CONTENTS

SECTION II

FEEDING and NUTRITION

SECTION III
HEALTH and SAFETY

PREFACE

About This Ninth Edition of *Dr Spock's Baby and Child Care*

Baby and Child Care has always been a book about enduring principles and values, but it is also a book of its time. The first edition came in a time of rapid growth and optimism. This ninth edition comes at a time of economic dislocation and hardship. Families who have been hit with job losses or repossessions are shaken terribly; others dread losses that might be just around the corner. Like the economy, the global environment seems threatened; storm clouds darken the sky, and it isn't easy to see brightness ahead. Still, bringing up children is an intrinsically hopeful act. Parents want their children to grow up strong and healthy, and children want the same thing for themselves. These are powerful forces. They can change the world.

As you go about nurturing, protecting and preparing your children, I hope that this edition of *Baby and Child Care* will be a supportive partner. Rather than hard-and-fast rules, it offers reliable information about children, how they grow and develop, and their physical, intellectual and emotional needs at different ages. The whole book has been reviewed and revised, with up-to-date information on nutrition, immunizations, environmental health, autism, ADHD and many other topics. The Resource Guide has also been updated and expanded.

More and more, people are realizing that part of bringing up healthy children means creating a healthy world for them to grow up in. Thoughtless, wasteful consumption threatens the environment and isn't good for children either. Wherever possible, this book pushes back against materialism. You won't find many recommendations for the newest toys and gizmos, for example. In that spirit, you might notice that this edition is a little thinner than the one before. Don't worry: the important information is there and easier than ever to get at. The first edition of Dr Spock's book was a *pocket* book. This latest edition might not fit in your pocket, but it should slip into a backpack or handbag.

Like children, books change and also stay the same. On the change side, you may notice the new illustrations by Grace Needlman, a talented young artist who is also my daughter. As a very small child she would draw for hours. She never stopped, and has now completed her undergraduate degree in art at Yale. I am so delighted to be able to share her gift with you. Like the pictures, the language of the book has been modernized in places. Still, I hope these pages will talk to you in the same clear, warm and supportive voice that was Dr Spock's. The core message is the same as ever: what's most important is your love for your child; beyond that, if you listen to the advice that makes sense to you, you can't go too far wrong.

A word on wording. There are many places in this book where I suggest that you talk with your child's doctor. I mean to include not only paediatricians and family doctors but also health visitors where relevant; 'doctor' is just quicker to read. When talking about children I try to use 'he' and 'she' at random, except in those very few instances that apply only to one or the other (care of the penis, for example). By the same token, while I often refer to parents using 'she', I usually mean to include parents of both sexes, as well as stepparents, adoptive parents and others who are in the parenting role. You'll notice some sections set off under the heading 'Dr Spock Comments'. In other places when the word 'I' shows up, it refers to me, Robert Needlman.

TRUST YOURSELF *AND* YOUR CHILDREN

TRUST YOURSELF

You know more than you think you do. Your family is growing and changing. You want to be the best parent you can be, but it's not always clear what's best. Everywhere you turn there are experts telling you what to do. The problem is, they often don't agree with each other. The world is different from how it was twenty years ago, and the old answers might not work any more.

Don't take too seriously all that the neighbours say. Don't be overawed by what the experts say. Don't be afraid to trust your own common sense. Bringing up your child won't be a complicated job if you take it easy and trust your own instincts. The natural loving care that parents give their children is a hundred times more important than their knowing how to make a nappy fit tightly or just when to introduce solid foods. Every time you pick your baby up – even if you do it a little awkwardly at first – and change her, bathe her, feed her, smile at her, she's getting the feeling that she belongs to you and that you belong to her.

The more people have studied different methods of bringing up children, the more they have come to the conclusion that what good mothers and fathers instinctively feel like doing for their babies is usually best after all. All parents do their best job when they have a natural, easy confidence in themselves. Better to relax and make a few mistakes than to try too hard to be perfect.

If you don't always respond instantly when your baby cries, your baby has the opportunity to learn self-soothing. If you lose your patience with your toddler (and every parent does, sometimes), then your toddler learns that you have feelings, too, and has a chance to see how you get yourself back together. Children are driven from within themselves to grow, explore, experience, learn and build relationships with other people. A lot of good parenting lies in simply allowing your child to go with these powerful drives. So, while you are trusting yourself, remember also to trust your child.

How you learn to be a parent. Fathers and mothers don't really find out how to care for and manage children from books and lectures, though these may help by answering specific questions and doubts. They learn as children, from the way they themselves were brought up. That's what they were always practising when they played house and cared for their dolls. If a child is raised in an easygoing way, then he is likely to be the same kind of parent; likewise for a child raised by strict or controlling parents. We all end up at least somewhat like our parents, especially in the way we deal with our children. The moment will come when you are talking to your child and you hear your mother's or father's voice coming from your own lips with almost the same tone and maybe even the same words.

Think about your own parents. What did they do that you now see as positive and constructive? What did they do that you never want to repeat? Think about what made you the kind of person you are today and what kind of parent you would like to be. This sort of insight will help you understand and trust your own parenting instincts.

We learn how to be parents gradually, through the experience of caring for our children. With a baby, finding out that you can feed, change and bathe successfully, and that your baby responds contentedly, builds confidence and familiarity. These feelings grow in time; you probably won't feel this way right off the bat.

All parents expect to influence their children, but many are surprised to find that it's a two-way street. You may find, as many others have, that being a parent becomes the most important step in your own growth as a person.

WHAT ARE YOUR AIMS IN RAISING A CHILD?

Think about your goals. What kind of adults do you want your children to become? Is doing well in school your top objective for them? Is the ability to have close relationships important? Do you want them to be competitive in our dog-eat-dog society, or do you want them to learn to cooperate and sometimes defer to others?

Parenting is about choices. So many parents get so caught up in the difficult day-to-day issues of *how* they are parenting that they lose perspective about *why* they are parenting in the first place. I hope that bringing up your children will help you to clarify what's truly important to you, and that these insights will guide the choices you make.

PARENTS ARE HUMAN

Parents have needs, too. Books about child care, including this one, put so much emphasis on the child's needs – for love, for understanding, for patience, for consistency, for firmness, for protection, for comradeship – that parents sometimes feel physically and emotionally exhausted just from reading about what is expected of them. They get the impression that they are meant to have no life of their own apart from their children. They can't help feeling that any book that seems to be standing up for children all the time is going to be critical of parents when anything goes wrong.

To really be fair, this book should have an equal number of pages about the genuine needs of parents: their frustrations (both inside and outside the home), how tired they get, and their need to hear once in a while that they are doing a good job. An enormous amount of hard work goes along with child care: preparing food, washing clothes, changing nappies, cleaning up messes, stopping fights and drying tears, listening to stories that are hard to understand, joining in games and reading books that aren't very exciting to an adult, trudging around zoos and museums, responding to pleas for help with homework, being slowed down in housework and gardening by eager helpers, going to parent-teacher association meetings on evenings when you are tired, and so on.

The fact is that child rearing is a long, hard job, the rewards are not always obvious, the work is often undervalued, and parents are just as human and almost as vulnerable as their children.

Of course, parents don't have children because they want to be martyrs. They have them because they love children and want to bring up their very own, especially when they remember being loved so much when they were little. Taking care of their children, seeing them grow and develop, gives most parents – despite the hard work – their greatest satisfaction in life. It is a creative and generative act on every level. Pride in other accomplishments usually pales in comparison.

Needless self-sacrifice and excessive preoccupation. Many people facing the new responsibility of parenthood feel that they are being called on to give up all their freedom and all their former pleasures, not as a matter of practicality but almost as a matter of principle. Others simply become obsessed with parenting, forgetting all their other interests. Even if they do occasionally sneak off to have some fun, they feel too guilty to get full enjoyment. They come to bore their friends and each other. In the long run, they chafe at the imprisonment and can't help unconsciously resenting their babies.

Total absorption in a new baby is normal. But after a while, usually by two to four months, your focus needs to broaden again. In particular, pay attention to sustaining a loving intimate relationship with your partner. Carve out some quality time with your husband, wife or significant other. Remember to look at each other, smile at each other, and express the love you feel. Make an effort to find enough privacy and energy to continue your sexual relationship. Remember that a close, loving relationship between parents is the best way children learn about how to be loving with others. One of the best things you can do for your child, as well as for yourself, is to let your children deepen, not inhibit, your relationship with your partner.

NATURE AND NURTURE

How much control do you have? It's easy to get the impression that how your child turns out is entirely up to you. Do a good job, and you'll have a good child. If your child learns to talk later than other children or has more temper tantrums, then of course it's all your fault.

Except that it isn't. The truth is, some children are simply more difficult to soothe, more fearful, more reckless, more intense, or in other ways more challenging for parents. If you are lucky, your baby will have a temperament that fits well with your expectations and personal style. If not, then you may need to learn special skills in order to help your child thrive. For example, you may need to learn how to calm a colicky baby, or how to help an extracautious child begin to take small risks.

But special skills are not enough. First, you'll need to accept your child for who he is. As a parent, you can shape your child's developing personality, but you don't have anything near total control. Children need to feel accepted. Only after that can they work together with their parents to handle themselves in more and more effective ways.

Accepting the child you have. One gentle couple might be ideally suited to raise a boy with a sensitive nature but unprepared for an energetic, assertive one. Another couple may handle a spunky daughter with joy, but feel disappointed with a quiet, thoughtful one.

It doesn't really matter that the parents know they can't order the kind of child they wanted most. Parents have well-formed personalities, too, which they can't change overnight. Being human, they can't help feeling let down if their real child doesn't match the child of their dreams. What's more, as children become a little older they may remind us, consciously or unconsciously, of a brother, sister, father or mother who made life hard for us. A daughter may have traits like her mother's younger sister, who used to be always in her hair, and yet the mother may not realize that this is the cause of a lot of her irritation. A father may be excessively bothered by timidity in his son and never connect it with the fact that he himself had a terrible time overcoming his shyness as a child.

How well your expectations and aspirations for your children fit with the talents and temperament they were born with affects how well things go for you and your children. If, for example, you are chronically disappointed that your child is not a maths whiz or sports star, and if you push to make him what he is not, then trouble is brewing. On the other hand, if you accept your child for who he is, then your life together is bound to be a lot smoother, and your child will grow up accepting himself.

Can you make your baby cleverer? The short answer is yes . . . and no. Experts now agree that roughly half of a person's intelligence is determined by genes and half by other factors, such as nutrition and early experiences. Here we're talking about the kind of intelligence that is measured by standard IQ tests. There are other kinds of intelligence, such as interpersonal intelligence (for example, the ability to be a good listener), athletic intelligence or musical intelligence. These, too, almost certainly depend on both genes and experience.

A person's genes provide a rough blueprint for the brain, but the details are filled in by experience. Genes determine the main pathways that link different brain regions. Experience influences how the individual nerve cells form the minicircuits that are the physical basis for ideas and skills. For example, when a child learns to speak English, certain nerve circuits grow stronger. At the same time, circuits that are unique to other languages (Chinese, say) fade away.

Genes influence how easily or quickly a person can pick up certain types of knowledge or skills. In this way, genes may point an individual's talents in a particular direction (like being a 'numbers person' or a 'people person'). Genes also set limits for what a child can reasonably be expected to achieve. As a child, I spent a summer in Little League baseball and never once hit the ball. Maybe I could have learned with enough practice and coaching. But it would have taken a huge effort, and I doubt I'd ever have been really good. I had a much better time in music camp.

The experiences a child has (batting practice, for instance) determine the brain's wiring, but the brain plays a large role in determining what experiences a child seeks and enjoys. Wise parents help their children nurture their talents and respect their limitations.

Superbabies? Learning changes the brain. But that does not mean that we can create superbabies by relentless stimulation, nor should we try. The best learning occurs when a child is happy, relaxed and actively involved. Flash cards really have no place at all in an infant's education.

The best experiences for infants are those that make sense to them. You can tell that an experience is making sense when your baby smiles, laughs, coos, or gazes with bright, sparkly eyes. Little babies don't understand the words their parents are saying, but being talked to certainly makes sense to them!

Many products are marketed with the claim that they

are 'scientifically proven' to make babies smarter. These claims are all exaggerations, if not outright lies. Simple materials and human interactions are what truly nurture infant learning.

DIFFERENT FAMILIES, DIFFERENT CHALLENGES

There is no one right way to bring up children, and there is no one best kind of family. Children can thrive with a mother and father, with a mother or father alone, with grandparents or foster parents, with two mothers or two fathers, or as part of large extended families. I hope that this wonderful diversity is reflected throughout this book, although to save words I often just say 'mother and father'.

Families that don't fit the typical mum-and-dad mode may need to do some special planning. For example, in families with same-sex parents it may take planning to ensure that the children have a chance to develop close relationships with both men and women. In families with children adopted from overseas, parents may need to make special efforts to learn about their children's cultures of origin. When parents embrace different religious beliefs, they need to work out how their children can grow up with a connection to tradition and community. Good parenting means planning for your children's needs; that's true in *all* families.

Global mobility. Some parents find themselves in countries far from where they grew up. It's stressful to leave behind everything familiar – family, language, culture, land – particularly when it comes to bringing up children. So many things that were important in a parent's own childhood simply don't exist in this new place, and all the rules seem different. What was good parenting at home might even be considered neglectful or abusive here. No wonder parents often feel unsure of themselves, worried or angry.

The key to success is flexibility. Families need to hold on to their cultural values while at the same time taking part in mainstream society. Parents who cut off their cultural roots altogether often find themselves adrift without any values to anchor them. Parents who try to build a wall around their families may find that the larger culture breaks in or that their children break out. To be successful, children may need to learn to speak different languages at home and at school, and to switch back and forth between two sets of social rules. Parents need to find ways to support their children as they shuttle back and forth between worlds, to embrace tradition and newness at the same time.

Special challenges. Some children are more difficult to parent than others. Children with special health and developmental needs make special demands on parents (see page 912). Children who tend to react intensely and negatively require special parenting skills, as do children who have serious illnesses. Lack of money, safe housing, healthy food and good schools certainly weighs on parents and children. The past can also be an obstacle. It's natural to replay as adults the scenes we lived through as children. If you had a difficult time in your own childhood, if your parents were cruel or had to battle emotional problems or addiction, then you know how hard it is to learn a better way to parent.

You can make that choice. Parents from all kinds of backgrounds, facing all kinds of challenges, find the wisdom and courage to give their children what they need. In turn, their children give those qualities back to the world.

SECTION I

Your Child, Age by Age

BEFORE YOUR CHILD IS BORN

BABIES DEVELOP; PARENTS, TOO

Foetal development. Think of all the incredible changes that turn a fertilized egg into a baby! Most women realize they're pregnant about five weeks after their last menstrual period. By then, the embryo has an inner layer of cells that will become most of the internal organs, a middle layer of cells that will form muscles and bones, and an outer layer that will become the skin and brain. The major organs begin to form about five weeks later. The foetus is beginning to look human but only measures about 5 cm (2 in) long and weighs about 10 g (⅓ oz).

Four or five months into the pregnancy – just about halfway – is when you probably first feel your baby moving. Those little kicks and nudges are a constant reminder that there really is a baby in there – a thrilling moment!

During the third trimester, after about twenty-seven weeks, the baby's length doubles and the weight triples. The brain grows even more quickly, and new behaviours begin to appear. By twenty-nine weeks, a foetus will startle in response to a sudden loud noise. But if the noise repeats every twenty seconds or so, the baby learns to ignore it – a sign of very early memory.

If a pleasant sound is repeated, like the sound of your voice, your unborn baby remembers this, too. After birth, babies choose to listen to their mother's voice over that of a stranger. If you have a favourite piece of music that you play over and over, chances are your baby will love it, too. Learning starts before birth, but you don't need to break out the flash cards along with the maternity clothes. Natural stimuli – the sound of your voice and the rhythms of your body – are most nurturing to development.

Mixed feelings about pregnancy. We have an ideal about motherhood that says every woman is overjoyed when she finds that she is going to have a baby. She spends the pregnancy dreaming happy thoughts about the baby. Love is instantaneous, bonding like glue.

This is one side of the picture. Almost every pregnant woman has some negative feelings, too. Early on, nausea and vomiting can be mild or severe. Clothes that were loose become tight; clothes that were tight become unwearable. Athletic women find that their bodies don't move as they once did.

The first pregnancy spells the end of carefree youth; social life and the family budget have to be spread thinner. After you have had one or two, the arrival of one more child may not seem like such a drastic change. But a mother's spirit may rebel at times during any pregnancy. A certain pregnancy may be strained for obvious reasons: perhaps it came unexpectedly, or at a time of disharmony between the parents or serious illness in the family. Or there may be no apparent explanation.

A mother who truly wants another child may still be disturbed by sudden doubts about whether she will have the time, the physical energy or the unlimited reserves of love that she imagines will be called for. Or the inner doubts may start with the father, who feels somewhat neglected as his wife becomes more and more preoccupied with the children. In either case, one spouse's disquiet soon has the other one feeling dispirited also. Each parent may have less to give the other.

These reactions aren't inevitable, but they occur even in the very best of parents. They are part of the normal mixed feelings during pregnancy, and in the great majority of cases they are temporary. It may be easier to work through these feelings early, before the actual baby arrives. Parents who have had no negative feelings during pregnancy may have to face them for the first time after their babies are born, at a point when their emotional reserves are fully taken up in baby care.

Fathers' feelings during pregnancy. A man may react to his wife's pregnancy with various feelings: protectiveness of the wife, increased joy in the marriage, pride in his virility (that's one thing men always worry about to some degree). A certain amount of worry – 'Will I be able to be a good father to this baby?' – is very common, especially for men who remember their own childhoods as having been difficult.

There can also be, way underneath, a feeling of being left out, which may be expressed as crankiness toward his wife, wanting to spend more evenings with his men friends, or flirtatiousness with other women. These reactions are normal, but they are no help to his partner, who needs extra support at this stage of her life. It's very important for fathers to talk about all of their feelings. When they do, they often find that the negative emotions (fear, jealousy) shift aside, allowing the positive ones (excitement, connection) to come forward.

Sad to say, pregnancy leads some men to become emotionally or physically abusive. If you feel threatened or afraid, or if you have ever been hurt or forced to have sex, you owe it to yourself and your baby to get help. Talk to your doctor, or call 0808 2000 247, the National Domestic Violence Freephone Helpline. (For more on domestic violence, see page 772.)

The supportive father. The role of fathers has changed. In the past, a father wouldn't have dreamed of reading a book on child care. Now it almost goes without saying that fathers take some responsibility for child rearing (although women still do most of the work). Fathers also take a more active role before the baby is born. A father may go to antenatal appointments and attend childbirth classes. He may be an active participant in the labour. He no longer has to be the lonely, excluded onlooker.

Love for the baby may come gradually. Many parents who are pleased and proud to be pregnant still find it hard to feel a personal love for a baby they've never held. For some parents, love starts with the first ultrasound that shows a beating heart; for others, it's feeling the baby move for the first time; for others it's not until still later. There is no 'normal' time to fall in love with your baby. Love may come early or late, but it comes.

Even when feelings during pregnancy are primarily positive, there may be a letdown when the baby actually arrives. Parents may expect to recognize the baby immediately as their own flesh and blood, to respond with an overwhelming rush of maternal and paternal feelings, and to bond like epoxy. But in many cases, this doesn't happen on the first day or even in the first week. Completely normal negative feelings often pop up. A good and loving parent may have the sudden thought that having a baby has been a terrible mistake – and then feel instantly guilty for having felt that way. Instead of instant bonding, the process is often a gradual one that isn't complete until parents have had time to recover somewhat from the physical and emotional strains of labour and delivery. How long that takes varies from parent to parent.

Most of us have been taught that it's unwise to hope for a girl or a boy, in case it turns out to be the opposite. I wouldn't take this too seriously. It's hard to imagine a future baby without picturing it as being one sex or the other. Most expectant parents have a sex preference during each pregnancy. So enjoy your imaginary baby, and don't feel guilty if you learn that your baby is not the sex you had envisioned.

ANTENATAL PLANS AND DECISIONS

Before you conceive. It's a good idea to consult with a doctor before you start trying to become pregnant, especially if you have concerns about your health or questions about fertility or genetic disorders. As soon as pregnancy is even a possibility, start taking folic acid. A daily multivitamin or supplement with 400 microgrammes of folic acid, started three months or more before conception, lowers the risk of serious spinal cord defects.

This is also the time to limit your exposure to environmental hazards that can affect a growing foetus. Steer clear of secondhand cigarette smoke and industrial pollution. Instead of eating fish that tend to be high in mercury, such as sea bass and swordfish, choose farm-raised trout, wild Pacific salmon, sardines, anchovies, or fish fingers. Farm-raised salmon may contain other toxins and antibiotics, so it probably should not be part of your diet during pregnancy. If you work with chemicals, animals or young children, ask your doctor about possible risks during pregnancy. For more information to help you have the healthiest possible pregnancy, I suggest *Dr Spock's Pregnancy Guide*, by Dr Marjorie Greenfield.

Get good prenatal care. Going for antenatal checkups is one of the most important things you can do for your baby. Simple steps – taking folic acid, avoiding cigarettes and alcohol, and getting your blood pressure checked regularly – can make a huge difference in both your baby's health and your own. Routine tests can uncover problems such as infections that can be treated before they affect your baby. Even if you're nearing the end of your pregnancy, it's not too late for your baby and you to benefit from an antenatal appointment.

The schedule of antenatal appointments varies, but you will probably have seven to ten appointments overall, with their frequency increasing after 20–24 weeks, and going up to about once a week in the late weeks of pregnancy. The visits are an opportunity for you to get advice about common issues such as morning sickness, weight gain and exercise. Antenatal ultrasounds take place at 8–14 weeks and at 18–20 weeks. Even a grainy black-and-white ultrasound image can make the baby seem much more real, especially for fathers. And you'll have the option of learning your baby's sex at the second scan.

When it comes to choosing antenatal care, visit your doctor as soon as your pregnancy has been confirmed. He or she will be able to advise you on the types of antenatal care available in your area. If your doctor cannot give you all the information you need, contact your local hospital or talk to other women you know who are pregnant or have recently had babies. It is useful to ask yourself questions such as whether being cared for by the same person or team throughout pregnancy and labour is important to you, whether you would like your carers to be female, and who you would like to have for your antenatal care? A midwife, who you can get to know, or your GP, who may already be a friend? If, at any point, you feel that you have made the wrong choice, you are entitled to change your mind.

What kind of delivery do you want? Home or hospital? Natural childbirth or an epidural? Support during labour by a husband or partner, by a trained professional (a doula), or by a family member *and* a doula? Lying down or squatting? Visiting lactation consultant?

No one approach suits every woman, and no method is clearly superior from the baby's point of view. Childbirth is safer now than ever before, but it is still unpredictable. Think about what you want – your ideal delivery – while remaining flexible in case of unforeseen events. Plan to ask a lot of questions and do some more reading. The book by Marjorie Greenfield, mentioned above, covers all the most important issues.

Doulas. Doulas are women who are trained to provide continuous support throughout labour. They help mothers find the most comfortable positions and movements, and use massage and other time-tested techniques to reduce tension. A doula who has been through many deliveries can often reassure a woman who may be feeling panicky or overwhelmed.

Doulas can be good for fathers, too. It's the rare father who can soothe a labouring woman's pain and anxiety as well as a trained doula, especially when the father is anxious himself. By taking over these tasks, the doula frees up the father to be with his partner in a loving way rather than as a coach. Most fathers feel supported by the doula rather than replaced.

There have now been many good studies on the effects of doulas, and the results are powerful. Doulas have been shown to reduce the need for caesarean sections and epidural (spinal) anaesthesia. (Epidural anaesthesia, although often a godsend, does have some risks: for example, it increases the risk that the baby may run a fever and therefore need to be given antibiotics after delivery.) For more information about doulas, see www.doula.org.uk.

Emotional responses to labour and delivery. Every woman responds differently to the stresses of labour and delivery. Some take pride in receiving no medication at all. Others are certain from the start that an epidural is for them. For some women, labour is a painful experience to be endured and, they hope, forgotten; others consider it a profoundly moving rite of passage. Some will push with each contraction for endless hours; others will get discouraged and demand that the doctor pull the baby out. Some exhausted women scream at their well-meaning husbands to get out of the delivery room and never come back. Some new mothers feel immediate love and affection for their infant; others, after hearing their infant is fine, simply want to go to sleep. And most turn out to be wonderful, loving parents.

If your labour and delivery experience is not what you expected, it's normal to feel bad, even guilty. If you go in hoping for a natural birth and end up with a caesarean, it's natural that you might feel that somehow you were to blame (you weren't) or that your baby will be permanently harmed by the experience (almost never the case). Many parents fear that if they are apart from their baby for the first hours or days, bonding will be ruined. That also is not true. Bonding – the process of baby and parent falling in love with each other – develops over months, not hours.

Antenatal breast-feeding consultation. If you are unsure whether to breast-feed or bottle-feed, it can be helpful to discuss the issue with a lactation consultant or midwife. You may want to attend a breast-feeding class offered by many antenatal groups. Knowing more will help you feel comfortable with your decision. If you decide to breast-feed, an antenatal consultation can help you anticipate any problems and deal with them ahead of time. (See page 273 for more on breast-feeding.)

PLANNING THE HOMECOMING

Arranging for extra help in the beginning. If you can get someone to help you during the first few weeks, by all means do so. Trying to do everything yourself can be exhausting. Most expectant parents feel a little scared at the prospect of taking sole charge of a helpless baby for the first time. If you have this feeling, it doesn't mean that you won't be able to do a good job. But if you feel really panicky, you will probably handle things more comfortably with an agreeable relative by your side.

The baby's father may be a great support person, or he may be feeling too anxious or overwhelmed himself. Your mother may be the ideal helper, if you get along with her easily. If you feel she is bossy and still treats you like a child, it's probably better if she visits but doesn't stay. It helps to have a person who has taken care of babies before, but it's most important to choose someone you enjoy having around.

You might consider hiring a housekeeper, maternity nurse or doula for a few weeks. Doulas are professionals who support women during labour (see page 22), and many offer their services in the weeks after birth as well. You may be able to afford a person to come in once or twice a week to do the laundry, help you catch up on the housework, and perhaps watch your baby for a couple of hours. It makes sense to keep your helper around for as long as you need the help and can afford it.

Midwife home visits. A community midwife will make a home visit one or two days after you take your baby home. The visiting nurse can look for medical problems, such as jaundice, that may not show up in the first day or two, and can help deal with breast-feeding or other common issues. If all is well, you will be discharged to the care of a health visitor when your baby is about ten days old.

Visitors. The birth of a baby brings relatives and friends flocking. How much is too much? You're the best person to decide. It's normal to be tired during the first weeks with a new baby, and visitors can be a further drain on your energy. It makes sense to limit visits to the few people you really want to see. Everyone else should understand.

Most visitors want to hold the baby, waggle their heads at her, and keep up a blue streak of baby talk. Some babies can take a lot of this treatment, some can't take any, and most are in between. Pay attention to how your baby responds, and stop things if you think she may be feeling stressed or tired out. Relatives and friends who care about you and your baby won't be offended. Young children, in particular, often carry viruses that can make newborns quite ill. So keep young cousins and other relatives at a safe distance for the first three or four months, and if they do touch your baby, make sure they wash their hands well first.

Preparing your home. If your home was built before 1980, there's a good chance that it contains lead paint. While it makes sense to remove any loose paint chips and to paint over exposed, weathered patches, it isn't safe to use a scraper, sander or heat gun: the fine lead dust and vapours can raise your own lead level, which might affect your baby. Professional lead removal is safe. For more, see page 483. Have any mouldy walls repaired.

If you are using well water, it's important to have it tested for bacteria and nitrates before the baby arrives. Nitrate salts in well water can cause blueness of the baby's lips and skin.

HELPING SIBLINGS COPE

What to say while you're pregnant. It's good for a child to know ahead of time that he's going to have a baby brother or sister, if he's old enough to understand such an idea (around a year and a half). That way he can get used to the idea gradually. Of course, you have to gear your explanations to your child's developmental level, and no amount of explanation can truly prepare him for what's to come. Your job is just to begin the dialogue, try to answer your child's questions, and reassure him often that you love him as much as ever. Don't overdo your enthusiasm or expect him to be enthusiastic about the baby. A good time to begin these discussions is once your body shape begins to change and the risk of an early miscarriage has passed.

The arrival of the baby should change an older child's life as little as possible, especially if he has been the only child up to that time. Emphasize the concrete things that will stay the same: 'You'll still have your same favourite toys; we'll still go to the same park to play; we'll still have our special treats; we'll still have our special time together.'

Make changes ahead of time. If your older child is still breast-feeding, it will be easier to stop a few months *before* you deliver, and not when she is feeling displaced by the new baby. If her room is to be given over to the baby, move her to her new room a few months ahead so that she feels that she is graduating because she is a big girl, not because the baby is pushing her out. The same applies to advancing to a big bed. If she is to go to preschool, she should start well before the baby arrives, if possible. Nothing sets a child's mind against preschool as much as the feeling that she is being banished to it by an interloper. By contrast, a child who has friends at school often feels less threatened by the new arrival at home.

During and after delivery. Some parents hope to strengthen family togetherness by including the older sibling in the delivery itself if they are having a home birth. But watching one's mother go through labour can be very upsetting for a young child, who might think that something quite awful is happening. Older children can also be very disturbed by the stressful effort and the blood that are part of even the smoothest deliveries. From the mother's point of view, labour is tough enough all by itself without having to worry about how a child is handling it. Children can feel included by being nearby but not actually in the room.

After the delivery, when everyone is calmer, is a good time to show the baby to an older sibling. He can be encouraged to touch the baby, talk to her, and help out in some simple task, like going to get a nappy. He should get the feeling that he is an integral part of the family. He should visit as much as he wants, but not be forced to.

Bringing your baby home. It's usually a hectic moment when you come home after giving birth. You're tired and preoccupied. The father scurries about, being helpful. If the older child is there, he stands around feeling left out, thinking warily, 'So this is the new baby!'

It may be better for the older child to be away on an excursion, if this can be arranged. An hour later, when the baby and the luggage are in their place and the mother is at last relaxing on the bed, is a good time for the child to come in. His mother can hug him, talk to him and give him her undivided attention. Since children appreciate concrete rewards, it's nice to bring a present home for the sibling, like a baby doll of his own or a wonderful new toy. You don't have to keep asking him, 'So how do you like your new sister?' Let him bring up the subject of the baby when he is ready, and don't be surprised if his comments are unenthusiastic or hostile.

Actually, most siblings handle the first days of a new baby pretty well. It often takes several weeks before they realize that the competition is there to stay, and several months before the baby is old enough to start grabbing their toys and bugging them. The section on siblings (page 793) has more on how you can help siblings get along.

THINGS YOU'LL NEED

Buying things ahead of time. Some parents don't feel like buying anything until they have their baby. The idea that shopping for things ahead of time might cause the pregnancy to come to a bad end is common in many cultures. Parents may not want to tempt fate.

The advantage of arranging things ahead of time is that it lightens your burden later. Many parents feel exhausted after delivery, and a little chore like buying nappies can seem overwhelming. It can be comforting to know that you have the basics on hand.

What do you really need? The sections that follow should help you decide what to buy ahead of time and what you might buy later (or never). I'd suggest you check the most recent copies of magazines such as *Which?* for the latest information on safety, durability and practicality.

CHECKLIST

Things You'll Need Right from the Start

- ✓ A safety-approved car seat (see below).
- ✓ A cot, cradle, moses basket or co-sleeper – even if just for naps.
- ✓ Several snug-fitting cotton sheets and at least one waterproof, washable mattress cover.
- ✓ Several small cotton blankets for swaddling, and perhaps a heavier blanket for warmth.
- ✓ A few T-shirts or short-sleeved bodysuits as well as several babygros.
- ✓ Nappies, either disposable, cloth or a nappy service (see page 66) and wipes. Cloth nappies come in handy, even if you choose disposables for the baby's bottom.
- ✓ Nursing bras and probably a breast pump (page 312) if you plan to breast-feed.
- ✓ Two or three plastic bottles and nipples; more bottles and a supply of formula if you plan to bottle-feed.
- ✓ A cloth sling or front-pack baby carrier.
- ✓ A nappy bag, with compartments for nappies, wipes, ointment, a folding plastic changing mat and nursing supplies.
- ✓ A digital thermometer and a child's nose syringe with bulb suction.

Car seats. Babies need to be in car seats any time they ride in a car. The trip home from the hospital is no exception.

The safest place is the rear seat, in the middle. The front passenger seat is especially dangerous, because an inflating airbag can seriously injure or even kill an infant or small child.

There are two basic kinds of infant car seats. One kind doubles as a baby carrier. The other kind can be turned around to face forward once your baby is large enough (current guidelines recommend that babies stay rear-facing until the age of two). Either way, be sure that the seat has a label showing that it meets government safety standards. Choose a seat with a harness to hold the child, rather than a shield or bar. Try to buy your car seat new from the store; one that has been in the family for years may not provide adequate protection, because plastic weakens over time. A seat that has been through one crash, even if it looks fine, might not hold up in a second one.

Which? frequently updates its ratings of car seats. I also suggest you check think.direct.gov.uk for the latest advice.

It's hard to put a car seat in correctly (I took a week-long course to learn how) so, if you can, have a certified child safety seat inspector show you how. Your local council will be able to put you in touch with garages that are part of the Fit Safe Sit Safe scheme. You'll find more detailed information on car seats on page 452.

A place to sleep. You may long for a beautiful cradle lined with silk, but your baby won't care. All she needs is a firm mattress with sides to keep her from rolling off. Firmness is important, because babies can more easily suffocate if they lie face down on a very soft mattress (even though babies *should* sleep on their backs to prevent cot death, sometimes they end up face down anyhow). A simple moses basket is convenient for the first few weeks.

A co-sleeper is a three-sided box that sits alongside your bed, with the opening facing you. It's wonderful to be able to reach your baby without getting up, especially if you are breast-feeding. It's important that the co-sleeper attaches firmly to the bed, so that there isn't a gap that a baby could be caught in. A co-sleeper is probably safer than having your baby sleep in bed with you, although many families choose this option (see page 58 for pros and cons).

Many parents, however, start with a cot. For safety, a cot should have slats less than 6 cm (2⅜ in) apart and any cut-out openings on the ends should also be less than 6 cm (2⅜ in) across. It should have a snug-fitting mattress, child-proof side locking mechanisms, and at least 66 cm (26 in) from the top of the rail to the mattress set at its lowest level. Look out for sharp edges and for corner posts that stick up more than 2 mm (1⁄16 in), high enough to snag an article of clothing, which could then trap or strangle a baby. Cots should be sturdy, with the mattress support firmly attached to the headboard and footboard. Before 1980, many cots were painted with lead-containing paints; they aren't safe unless all of the old paint has been stripped off. If you're buying a new cot, look on the box to see that it meets government safety standards. For used cots, hand-me-downs and family heirlooms, *you* have to be the safety inspector.

Your baby doesn't need a pillow for her head, and you should not use one. Likewise, it's best to keep stuffed animals out of your baby's cot or cradle: little babies don't care much about them, and they may pose a suffocation risk. For more on sleep and sleep safety, see page 59.

Equipment for bathing and changing. Babies can be bathed in the kitchen sink, a plastic tub (get one with a wide edge to rest your arm on), a dishpan, or a washstand. A spray tap that works like a mini shower is great for rinsing the baby's hair and for keeping him warm and happy. Moulded plastic bathing tubs with contoured pads or liners are useful and generally inexpensive.

A bath thermometer is not necessary but can be a comfort to the inexperienced parent. Always test the water temperature with your hand anyway. Water should never be hot, always lukewarm. Never run warm water into the tub or sink while the baby is in it unless you are sure that the temperature is constant. To prevent scalding, the temperature setting on your hot water heater should be 49°C (120°F) or lower.

You can change and dress your baby on a low table or bathroom counter or on the top of a bureau. Changing tables with a waterproof pad, safety straps and storage shelves are convenient, though expensive, and may not be adaptable for other uses later. Some types fold; some have an attached bath. Wherever you change your baby (except on the floor) it's important to keep one hand on him at all times: safety straps are nice, but don't trust them.

Seats, swings and walkers. An inclined plastic seat with safety straps and a handle is a most useful accessory. You can carry your baby and set her down almost anywhere, and let her watch the world go by. Some infant car seats can be used for this purpose, too. Make sure the base is larger than the seat, so that your baby can't tip it over when she gets active. A cloth seat can be inexpensive, light and equally comfortable. Be careful about placing your baby in any kind of seat on countertops and tables, as his movements could inch the seat off the edge.

Baby seats are often overused. A baby needs contact with people. Hold your baby for feeding, comforting, dancing and playing. Plastic baby seats are also not the best things for carrying babies: your baby will be happier and more secure in a cloth sling or front-pack baby carrier, and you will have both arms free, with less strain on your shoulders.

Young babies usually love motion, and a swing can be wonderfully calming. A cloth baby sling does the same thing, of course. I don't think that babies actually become 'addicted' to swinging, but too many hours of the same hypnotizing motion probably isn't best for them.

Infant walkers, especially those with inbuilt seats, are a major cause of injury (see page 127). Other than providing temporary amusement, they offer no benefits and they are dangerous. It only takes an instant for a baby to drive his walker down a flight of stairs. Manufacturers now make stationary walkers that bounce, swivel or rock. They come with toys attached for entertainment and are much safer for children. If you already have a wheeled walker, take off the wheels or throw it away.

Pushchairs, prams and backpacks. Pushchairs are best for babies who can hold their heads up steadily. Newborns and little infants do better in a cloth sling or front pack, where they can look up into their parent's face and listen to her heartbeat. A folding umbrella pushchair can be easily carried on a bus or in a car, but be sure it's a sturdy one. Products that combine a car seat and pushchair make it easy to go from car to pushchair without having to wake up a sleeping infant. When you use your pushchair, be sure to strap your child in for safety.

A pram is like a cot on wheels; it's nice to have for the first few months if you plan on taking long strolls with your baby, but hardly necessary. An alternative, after your baby has outgrown the soft front-pack carrier, is a backpack, preferably with a metal frame and padded hip belt so you can carry a large baby or toddler without much strain. Your baby can look over your shoulder, chat with you, play with your hair, and fall asleep with her head nestled into your neck.

Playpens. Some parents and psychologists fear that imprisoning a child in a playpen may stifle the child's spirit. Children deprived of human contact for hours on end do suffer, but an hour here and there in a playpen gives a baby a chance to learn to entertain himself, which is a good thing. A young infant can be left safely in her cradle or cot, but once your baby starts crawling, it's very helpful to have a confined place where she can play safely while you take care of other business. There are playpens designed to fold into compact travel-size cases, which are great for going on visits. They are recommended for children up to 13.5 kg (30 lb) or up to 87 cm (34 in) tall.

If you are going to use a playpen, you should start putting your baby in it each day starting around three months. Some babies tolerate playpens well, some poorly. If you wait until a baby starts to crawl (six to eight months), the playpen will surely seem like a prison and will be met with persistent howls.

Bedding. Blankets made of acrylic or a polyester-cotton combination are easy to wash and nonallergenic. A knitted shawl is a particularly convenient form of blanket for babies because it wraps around them so easily when they are up and stays tucked in when it's over them in bed. Make sure there are no long threads for the baby to wrap around fingers or toes or large holes that a baby can get caught in. Blankets should be large enough to tuck well under a cot mattress. A baby wearing a fleece sleepsuit probably doesn't also need a blanket, unless the room is chilly. Babies should to be comfortable, not overheated.

Cotton swaddling blankets, which furnish little warmth, are useful for wrapping around a baby who would otherwise kick off the bed coverings or for tightly wrapping the young baby who is comfortable and secure and can sleep only when held immobile.

You'll probably want a plastic mattress cover. The plastic cover that comes on most new mattresses is not sufficient by itself; sooner or later urine gets into the air holes and makes it smell. A cloth mattress pad lets air circulate under the sheet; you'll need three to six pads, depending on how often you do laundry. Waterproof sheeting that has a flannelette covering serves the same purpose. A thin plastic bag such as one from a dry cleaner should *never* be used in a cot, because of the danger of suffocation if the baby's head gets tangled in it.

You will need three to six sheets. They should fit snugly so that they don't come undone and pose a suffocation risk. The best sheets are made of cotton knit. They are easy to wash, quick to dry, spread smoothly without ironing and do not feel clammy when wet.

Clothing. Remember that your baby will be growing very rapidly during the first year, so buy her clothing to fit loosely. Except for nappy covers, it's generally better to begin with three- to six-month-size clothes instead of newborn-size clothing.

A baby or child doesn't need more in the way of clothing or covering than an adult; if anything, she needs less.

Vests come in three styles: pullover, side-snap closing and a one-piece type that slips over the head and snaps around the crotch. The last type stays in place easily. The type with side snaps is slightly easier to put on a small baby. Medium weight and short sleeves should be fine unless your home is unusually chilly. The most comfortable fabric for children is 100 per cent cotton. Start with the one-year-old size or, if you are fussy about fit, the six-month size. Buy at least three or four. If you cut or pull off the tags, they won't irritate your baby's neck.

Babygros can work for day or night. Check the insides of the feet regularly. They can collect threads, which can wind painfully around your baby's toes. Sweaters are useful for extra warmth. Be sure that the neck opening has sufficient give or that there are shoulder snaps, well-secured buttons, or zippers up the back.

Knitted acrylic or cotton caps are all right for going outdoors in the kind of weather that makes grown-ups put on caps, or for sleeping in an equally cold room. At night avoid using caps that are too large, because they could cover your baby's face as she moves around while sleeping. For milder weather, caps are unnecessary; most babies don't like them anyway. You don't need booties and stockings, at least until your baby is sitting up and playing in a cold house. Dresses make a baby look pretty but are otherwise a bother to babies and parents. A sun hat with a chin strap to keep it on is useful for the baby who will tolerate it. See page 124 about shoes.

Some parents find that quality used clothes or hand-me-downs are a good choice for rapidly growing children. Watch for scratchy lace close to the face and arms: it can make even an adult irritable. Headbands are cute, but if they're too tight or itchy (or if a ponytail or braids are too tight), they can cause the head to hurt. Most important, be on the lookout for any loose buttons or decorations that could pose a choking hazard, and for ribbons and cords that could get wrapped around a baby's arms or neck.

Toiletries and medical supplies. Any mild soap will do for the bath. Avoid liquid baby soaps and deodorant soaps: they may cause rashes. For all but the most soiled body parts, plain water works fine. There are no-tears shampoos that are gentle on babies' eyes. Cotton balls are useful at bath time for wiping the baby's eyes. Baby lotion is not really necessary unless your child's skin is dry, but it's pleasant to rub it on, and babies love a massage. Look for creams and lotions with no added scent or colour.

Baby oils, most of which are made of mineral oil, are fine for dry or normal skin or for nappy rash. But mineral oil itself may cause a very mild rash in some babies.

Don't use baby talcum powder, because it can damage the lungs if inhaled. Cornstarch-based powders are safer.

An ointment containing lanolin and petroleum jelly protects the skin when there is nappy rash. Pure petroleum jelly also works well, but it can be messy.

Infant nail scissors have blunted ends, though many parents find infant nail clippers easier to use. I prefer using a nail file: there's no chance of drawing blood, and files don't leave sharp edges that can cause scratches.

You'll need a fever thermometer. Digital thermometers are quite cheap and are fast, accurate, easy to use and safe. High-tech ear thermometers are less accurate and much more expensive. Old-style thermometers that contain mercury aren't safe. If you have one already, don't just throw it in the bin; call the local council for information about proper disposal.

A child's nose syringe with bulb suction is helpful to remove mucus during colds, if the mucus is interfering with feeding.

Feeding equipment. If you're planning to breast-feed, you may not need any equipment other than yourself. Many nursing mothers, however, find that it is helpful to have a breast pump (see page 312). Hand-operated pumps are slow and tiring to use; good motorized pumps are expensive but can be rented. If you pump, you'll need at least three or four bottles (look for BPA-free plastic bottles or, to be safest, glass) to store the milk, and nipples to go with them. Breast pads, nursing bras, nipple shields and other items are described in the breast-feeding section (page 273).

If you know ahead of time that your baby is going to bottle-feed, buy at least nine of the 250 ml (8 fl oz) bottles. You'll need to have a bottle brush, too. For water and juice (not needed in the first months), some parents prefer to use smaller bottles. Buy a few extra nipples, in case you are having trouble making the nipple holes the right size. There are all kinds of specially shaped nipples, but no proof for the claims made by their manufacturers. Some nipples withstand boiling and wear and tear better than others. Be sure to follow instructions as to when to replace old nipples. See page 322 for information on washing and sterilization.

You don't have to warm a baby's bottle. Cold formula is fine if your baby likes it that way, although most babies prefer their formula at least room temperature. Test the milk temperature on the underside of your wrist. *Never* warm a baby's bottle in a microwave oven; hot spots in the milk can be scalding even when the bottle feels cool, and plastic bottles may release BPA, a toxic chemical (see page 903), especially when microwaved.

Small round bibs help keep drool off the baby's clothes.

For the mess that babies or children always make with their solid food, they need a large bib of plastic, nylon, or terry (or a combination), preferably with a pocket along the lower edge to catch drips. A formed plastic bib with a food-catcher on the bottom is easily rinsed; it just looks uncomfortable to the adult. A terry bib works for wiping the face if you can find a dry corner.

Dummies. If you decide to use them, three or four will do (see page 62). The practice of blocking up a baby bottle nipple with cotton or paper and using it as a dummy is dangerous, because the contraption tends to fall apart, leaving little pieces that are easy to choke on.

YOUR NEWBORN, BIRTH TO ABOUT THREE MONTHS

ENJOY YOUR BABY

Challenges of the first three months. Once the awe, shock, relief, and exhaustion of delivery have worn off a bit, you'll probably find that caring for your new baby is a lot of work; wonderful, but still work. The main reason for this is that newborn babies rely on their parents to manage all of their basic life functions – eating, sleeping, eliminating and keeping warm. Your baby can't tell you what she needs from moment to moment; it's up to you to figure out what to do.

Many parents find that all of their energy is focused on fine-tuning their babies: helping them eat when they're hungry and stop when they're full, stay awake more during the day and sleep more at night, and feel comfortable in a bright, buzzing world that is so much more stimulating than the womb. Some babies seem to take these challenges in their stride. Others have a harder time adjusting. But by two or three months, most babies (and their parents) have the basics figured out, and it's time to start exploring.

Relax and enjoy your baby. From what some people – including some doctors – say about babies demanding attention, you'd think that they come into the world determined to get their parents under their thumbs by hook or by crook. This isn't true. Your baby is born to be a reasonable, friendly – though occasionally demanding – human being.

Don't be afraid to feed her when you think she's truly hungry. If you are mistaken, she'll simply refuse to take much. Don't be afraid to love her and enjoy her. Every baby needs to be smiled at, talked to, played with and fondled gently and lovingly just as much as she needs vitamins and calories. That's what will make her a person who loves people and enjoys life.

Don't be afraid to respond to her other desires as long as they seem sensible to you and you don't become a slave to her. When she cries in the early weeks, it's because she's uncomfortable for some reason: maybe it's hunger or indigestion, fatigue or tension. The uneasy feeling you have when you hear her cry, the feeling that you want to comfort her, is meant to be part of your nature, too. Being held, rocked or walked may be what she needs.

Spoiling doesn't come from being good to a baby in a sensible way: it happens when parents are too afraid to use their common sense, or when they really want to be slaves and encourage their babies to become slave drivers.

All parents want their children to turn out to be healthy in their habits and easy to live with. Children want the same thing. They want to eat at sensible hours and later learn good table manners; to develop a regular pattern of sleep that meets their needs; to move their bowels according to their own healthy pattern, which may or may not be regular. Most children will sooner or later fit into the family's way of doing things, with only a minimum of guidance from you.

Babies aren't frail. 'I'm so afraid I'll hurt her if I don't handle her just right,' a parent may say about her first baby. You don't have to worry: there are many ways to hold her. If her head falls backward by mistake, it won't hurt her. The soft spot on her skull (the fontanel) is covered by a tough membrane that isn't easily injured.

The system to control body temperature works quite well in most babies if they're covered sensibly. They inherit good resistance to most germs. During a family cold epidemic, the baby is apt to have it the mildest of all. If a baby gets her head tangled in anything, she has a strong instinct to struggle and yell. If she's not getting enough to eat, she will probably cry for more. If the light is too strong for her eyes, she'll blink and fuss, or just close them. She knows how much sleep she needs, and takes it. She can care for herself pretty well for a person who can't say a word and knows nothing about the world.

TOUCH AND BONDING

Babies thrive on touch. Before birth, not only are babies enveloped, warmed and nourished by their mothers, but they participate in every bodily movement their mothers make. After birth, babies in many parts of the world are held against their mothers all day long in slings. They continue to share in all their mothers' activities – food gathering and preparing, tilling, weaving, house care – and they sleep in the same bed at night. These babies are breast-fed the moment they whimper. They not only hear but feel the vibrations of their mothers' words and songs. As they get a little older, they may be carried on the hips or backs of their older sisters. Babies in these cultures don't cry much, and spitting up and fretfulness are rare.

Our society has thought up a dozen ingenious ways to put distance between mothers and their babies. They are given commercial formulas from bottles and put to sleep on flat, firm mattresses. We strap them into infant seats so that they don't have to be held. There are even car seats that can be snapped right onto the pushchair, so parents never need to touch their babies at all. Compare this treatment to the best cure for the hurts, slights and sadness of infants, children and adults – a good hug.

The urge for bodily contact is strong. Physical touch releases hormones in the brain – both the baby's and the parent's – that heighten feelings of relaxation and happiness and reduce pain. When babies have their heels pricked for routine blood tests, they cry much less if their mother is holding them skin to skin; premature infants who have daily skin-to-skin time grow faster.

Early contact and bonding. It's fascinating to watch mothers with their new babies. They spend a lot of time touching their baby's limbs and bodies and faces with their fingers. As a group, mothers who have ample opportunity to touch their babies in this way have easier relations with their babies even months later, and their babies are more responsive, too.

Observations like this led paediatricians John Kennell and Marshall Klaus to use the term 'bonding' to describe the process by which parents connect naturally with their newborn infants. One marvellous result of such research has been that it is now standard practice for newborns straight from the womb to be dried and placed on their mothers' chests, where they snuggle in and often begin to nurse.

But bonding has also been widely misunderstood. Parents and even professionals often seem to think that if bonding hasn't taken place in the first twenty-four or forty-eight hours, it never will. The truth is, bonding occurs over time, and there is no deadline. Parents bond with children they adopt at any age. Bonding – the sense of connection and belonging between parents and children – is a very strong force. Bonding happens *despite* child-rearing practices that separate parents from their infants. Premature babies often spend the first months of life isolated in incubators, but their parents still manage to reach in through the portholes.

DR SPOCK COMMENTS

I think that parents in our society can get a better perspective on our methods by comparing them with what comes naturally in less technological societies. How to be natural? I'd draw the following conclusions:

- Natural childbirth should be available for all who want it.

- Mothers and fathers should have their baby to hold and fondle for an hour after the baby is born.
- Breast-feeding should be encouraged, especially by midwives, health visitors, doctors and families.
- Bottle-propping should be avoided except when there's no choice – as when a mother of twins has no help and has to prop for one baby, at least, at each feeding.
- Mothers and fathers should try to use a sling more than the infant seat, when they are at home or out and about. Slings that hold babies against their mother or father's chest are best.

Bonding and early return to a job. These days, many mothers return to their paid jobs within six months of having their babies. Financial necessity and demanding careers put huge pressure on women. Mothers often grieve because they feel they are losing precious time with their baby. And they worry about the effects of early separation on their babies.

Babies will form strong emotional bonds with mothers and fathers even when they are cared for by others during the day. Loving care provided in the mornings and evenings, at weekends and (of course) in the middle of the night is enough to cement the bond from the child's side. But many new mothers pull back emotionally because they are already getting ready for the time, all too soon, when they will have to say goodbye. This is a natural self-protective response, but it can place great strain on a mother and on her relationship with her child.

As you make the decision about when to return to your job, try to listen to your heart. If there is any way you can stretch your maternity leave, even if it means a loss of income, you may end up glad you made that choice. By leaving it a little later, most mothers feel much better about heading back to their jobs, having had a chance to truly connect with their babies.

EARLY FEELINGS

Being scared. Many new parents find that they are anxious and just plain exhausted. They worry about the baby's crying and fretful spells, about every sneeze and spot of rash. They tiptoe into the baby's room to see whether she is still breathing. It's probably instinctive for parents to be overly protective at this period. It's nature's way of being sure that new parents take their job seriously. A little overconcern might be a good thing; fortunately, it wears off.

The blue feeling. You may find yourself feeling discouraged early on. It's a common feeling, especially with the first baby. You may not be able to put your finger on anything that is definitely wrong. You just weep easily. Or you may feel bad about certain things.

A feeling of depression may come on soon after the baby is born or several weeks later. The commonest time is when a mother comes home from the hospital. It isn't just the work that gets her down. It's the feeling of being responsible for the household, plus the entirely new responsibility of the baby's care and safety. A woman who was used to going to work every day is bound to miss the companionship of colleagues. Then there are all the physical and hormonal changes at the time of birth, which can alter the mother's mood to some degree.

If you begin to feel blue or discouraged, try to get some relief. Go for a walk or workout. Work on some new or unfinished project such as writing, painting, sewing, building – something creative and satisfying. Visit a good friend, or get your friends to come and see you. Activities like these can help lift your mood. At first you may not feel like doing anything. But if you make yourself take action, you will feel better.

Talk with your partner about how you are feeling, and be prepared to listen, too. It's pretty common for a new father to feel strangely down when he thinks he ought to be the happiest person in the world. A natural response – although not a helpful one – is for the father to withdraw emotionally or to become whiny and critical just when the mother needs support the most. Feeling unsupported, a mother might become angry, sad or depressed, and of course this just makes the whole situation worse. Talking together is essential if couples are going to avoid this kind of problem.

If your mood does not lift in a few days or if it is getting worse, you may be suffering from postnatal depression. The 'baby blues' almost always pass by two months, but postnatal depression can go on and on. True depression happens after as many as one in five pregnancies. Rarely, it is so severe that there is even a risk of suicide. If you or your partner has a severe mood change at any time, but especially after pregnancy, get medical help right away. No one knows exactly what causes postnatal depression, but women who have faced depression before are more vulnerable to it.

This is not the sort of problem you can simply talk yourself out of; you need to get professional help. You can start by talking with your doctor, who might refer you to a mental health professional. The good news about postnatal depression is that it is *treatable.* Both talk therapy and antidepressant medication can be very helpful. No new mother should have to suffer with this problem alone.

The father's feelings in the early weeks at home. A father shouldn't be surprised if he finds that he has mixed feelings at times toward his wife and baby. These feelings can arise during the pregnancy, during all the commotion of the labour and delivery stage, or after they are all home again. He can remind himself that his feelings are probably not nearly so churned up as his wife's, especially after the homecoming. She has been through an intense physical change. If it's her first baby, she can't help feeling anxious. Any baby will make great demands on her strength and spirits at first.

What all this adds up to is that most women need a great deal of support from their partners at this time. They need help with care of the baby and any other children, and with housework. Even more, they need patience, understanding, appreciation and affection. The father's job may be complicated by the fact that if his wife is tired and upset, she might not thank him for his efforts. In fact, she may be critical or complaining. Even so, when fathers understand how much they are needed, they can put their negative responses aside and instead choose to play their crucial supporting role.

PARENTS' SEXUAL RELATIONS AFTER DELIVERY

The process of pregnancy, labour and delivery usually interferes with parents' sexual relations. Near the end of pregnancy, intercourse may become uncomfortable or at least physically challenging. Following delivery there is a normal period of discomfort, readjustment of the body to its prepregnancy state, hormonal shifts, and the hard work, sleep deprivation and fatigue of caring for a newborn. Sex may be crowded out for days, weeks, even months.

This can also be a difficult time for a man's libido. He may be tired. For some men, the shift in perspective of their partner from lover to mother is difficult to reconcile with sexual feelings. All manner of emotional contradictions may arise.

If you recognize that sexual intercourse may be slow in returning, you won't be too alarmed at its temporary absence. Taking a break from sexual intercourse doesn't mean stopping all sexual relations. Cuddling, hugging, kissing and romantic words and glances are as meaningful and important as ever, maybe even more so.

Most parents get sexually back on track after a while. What makes the biggest difference is that, in the tumult of caring for a new baby, they don't lose sight of how much they love and care for each other, and that they make a conscious effort to express that love by word and by touch. You might enjoy reading poetry aloud to each other, going for walks together, exchanging warm oil massages, meditating together, having quiet meals together, and sharing lots of hugs and kisses.

CARING FOR YOUR BABY

Being companionable with your baby. Be quietly friendly with your baby whenever you are with him. All the time that you're feeding him, burping him, bathing him, dressing him, changing his nappy, holding him or just sitting in the room with him, he's getting a sense of how much you mean to each other. When you hug him or make noises at him, when you show him that you think he's the most wonderful baby in the world, it makes his spirit grow, just the way milk makes his bones grow. That must be why we grown-ups instinctively talk baby talk and waggle our heads when we greet a baby, even grown-ups who are otherwise dignified or unsociable.

I don't mean that you need to entertain your baby all the time he's awake, constantly joggling or tickling him. That would tire him out, and in the long run might make him tense. You can be quiet much of the time you are with him. Gentle, easygoing companionship is good for him and good for you. It's the comfortable feeling of your arms when you hold him, the fond, peaceful expression on your face when you look at him, and the gentle tone in your voice.

Your newborn's senses. All of your baby's senses work at birth (and, indeed, were working *before* birth), although to different degrees. Touch and motion are already well developed, which may explain why holding, swaddling and rocking have such a calming effect. Smell is also well developed. Babies detect odours in the amniotic fluid before birth, and very early on, they prefer the smell of their mothers' bodies.

Newborns can hear, but their brains process sound slowly. If you whisper in a baby's ear, it may take several seconds before the baby responds by looking for the source of the sound. Because of the way the inner ear develops, babies hear higher-pitched sounds better and prefer speech that is slow and musical – the way parents seem to naturally talk to them.

Babies also can see, but they are very shortsighted. Their eyes focus best at 23–30 cm (9–12 in), about the distance to the mother's face when nursing at the breast. You can tell when a baby catches you with his eyes: if you slowly move your face from side to side, his eyes follow you. Babies prefer looking at faces. Their eyes are sensitive, so they tend to keep them closed in normal light but open them when the lights go down.

Your baby is an individual. Newborn babies have their own personalities. Some are very calm; others are more excitable. Some are regular in their eating, sleeping and bowel habits; others are more erratic. Some can handle lots of stimulation; others need a quieter environment. When babies have their eyes open and a look of concentration on their faces, they are taking in information about the world around them. One baby may stay in this alert, receptive mode for several minutes; another baby may shift in and out, alternating with periods of drowsiness or fussing. As you take care of your baby, you'll begin to figure out how to provide enough talking, touching and playing to keep the alert state going, but not so much that your baby gets stressed. Your baby will also become more skilful in letting you know when he wants more and when he has had enough. Over weeks and months, you begin to work as a team.

FEEDING AND SLEEPING

Breast or formula? This is your first feeding decision, and it's worth thinking about carefully before making it. Breast-feeding is clearly better for babies' health, and probably for their brain development as well. You also need to do what feels comfortable to you. Don't let fear – either of failure or of disapproval from family or friends – hold you back. Many women choose formula because they plan to return to work soon. But even a short period of breast-feeding is better, medically, than none at all. And breast-feeding often can continue during hours at home, even after work resumes. Women who love breast-feeding talk about a unique sense of closeness that comes from nourishing a baby from your own body. I know many women who bottle-feed yet wonder about that feeling or perhaps yearn for it. If you find yourself moved in this direction, then by all means follow your heart. There is so much to say about the hows and whys of breast-feeding and formula-feeding that each has its own chapter (starting on page 273).

What feeding means to your baby. Think of the baby's first year this way: she wakes up and cries because she's hungry and wants to be fed. She is so eager when the nipple goes into her mouth that she may shudder. When she nurses, you can see that it is an intense experience. Perhaps she breaks into a sweat. If you stop her in the middle, she may cry furiously. When she has had as much as she wants, she is usually groggy with satisfaction and falls asleep.

Even when she is asleep, she sometimes looks as if she is dreaming of nursing. Her mouth makes sucking motions, and her whole expression looks blissful.

This all adds up to the fact that feeding is her great joy. She gets her first ideas about people from those who feed her, and she gets her early ideas about life from the way feeding goes. When you feed your baby, hold her, smile at her, and talk with her; you are nurturing her body, mind and spirit. When it's working well, feeding feels good for your baby and you. Some babies feed well right from the start; others take several days before they begin to catch on. When feeding problems last longer than one or two weeks, even with help from family members and experienced friends, it's wise to get professional help (see page 940). There is much more on feeding – getting to a regular schedule, knowing how much to give, and so on – beginning on page 247.

Sorting out day and night. Many babies like to sleep more during the day and have their wakeful hours at night. Your baby couldn't care less if it's night or day, so long as he's fed, cuddled and kept warm and dry. This shouldn't be too surprising. In the womb it was pretty dark, and he was probably more active during the hours that you were quietest, at night.

How do you turn this around? Talk and play with your baby more during the daytime. After dark, feed him efficiently and without much fanfare; don't wake him to feed unless there's a medical reason to. Let him learn that daytime is fun time and night time is kind of low-key and boring. By two to four months, most babies have begun to sort out day and night.

How much should a baby sleep? The baby is the only one who can answer this question. One baby needs eighteen hours of sleep, another only about twelve. As long as babies feed well, get plenty of fresh air, and sleep in a cool place, you can trust them to take the amount of sleep they need.

Most babies in the early months sleep from feeding to feeding if they are getting enough to eat and not having indigestion. There are a few babies, though, who are unusually wakeful right from the beginning, and not because anything is wrong. If you have this kind of baby, try to let some of the awake times be more stimulating – talking, playing, looking at things together – and let other periods be calm ones.

As babies get older, they gradually stay awake longer and take fewer naps during the day. You're apt to notice more wakefulness first in the late afternoon. Each baby develops a personal pattern of wakefulness and tends to be awake at the same times every day.

Sleep habits. Many babies get used to the idea that they always go to sleep right after a meal; others are ready to socialize. You can choose which routine fits best with the schedule of your family.

Newborns sleep wherever they are. But by about three or four months, it's a good idea for them to get used to falling asleep in their own beds, without company (unless you plan to have your baby sleep with you for a long time). This is one way to prevent later sleep problems. A baby who gets used to being held and rocked to sleep tends to need the same attention for months or even years; when she awakens in the night, she expects the same treatment.

Babies can get accustomed to either a silent home or a noisy one, so there is no point in tiptoeing and whispering around the house. An infant who is used to ordinary household noises usually sleeps right through a visit by talking, laughing friends or a radio or TV turned to a reasonable volume. Some infants, however, appear to be hypersensitive to sounds. They startle easily at the least noise and appear to be happiest when it's quiet. If your baby is like this you'll probably need to keep the house quiet while she sleeps, or else she will constantly wake and fuss.

Sleeping with your baby. Experts often have strong opinions about this, pro and con. I think it is a matter of personal choice. Parents and babies sleep together all around the world. A parent who is an unusually deep sleeper or who is under the influence of medications, drugs or alcohol might roll over and smother her baby. But for most parents, the risk of this happening is extremely small. A much bigger risk is that the parent sleeps poorly because she's always aware of the baby next to her. There is no evidence that sleeping together – or *not* sleeping together – affects babies' physical or emotional health, so it makes sense to do what feels right and comfortable for you. If you do sleep with your baby, it's important to follow all of the other safety precautions below.

The current advice from the NHS and FSID (Foundation for the Study of Infant Deaths) is that babies sleep in a cot in the same room as their parents until they are six months old. After that, they can sleep in a room on their own. An inexpensive baby monitor can help, unless you are near enough to always hear them cry. If you leave it much after six months, it is harder to move a child to her own room, although never impossible.

On back or stomach? Today everyone agrees that 'back to sleep' is the way to go. All infants should be put to sleep on their backs (face up) unless there's a medical reason to do otherwise. Sleeping face up has cut the number of deaths from sudden infant death syndrome (SIDS, also called 'cot death') by 50 per cent. Most babies easily take to sleeping on their backs if they've never got used to sleeping the other way. Sleeping on the side isn't as safe as sleeping on the back, since side-sleeping babies often roll face down. Babies who spend all of their time lying face up sometimes develop flat spots on the back of their head, so it's a good idea to give your baby time lying on her stomach *when she is awake and you are watching her.*

CHECKLIST

Sleep Safety Tips

✓ Always put babies to sleep on their backs (face up), unless advised otherwise by a doctor.

- ✓ Remove soft, fluffy blankets, pillows and other cloth items – they increase the risk of suffocation.
- ✓ Use a safety-approved moses basket, cradle, co-sleeper or cot. If in doubt, look for the British Standards Institution (BSI) kitemark, or check with the Royal Society for the Prevention of Accidents (ROSPA) at www.rospa.co.uk.
- ✓ Avoid overdressing or overbundling your baby: overheating increases the risk of SIDS.
- ✓ Protect your baby from secondhand cigarette smoke, which has many harmful effects, including increasing risk of SIDS.

CRYING AND COMFORTING

What does all that crying mean? This is an important question, especially with a first baby. As the baby's main form of communication, crying has many meanings, not just pain or sadness. As babies grow older, crying is much less of a problem because older babies cry less and parents worry less. But in the first weeks, baffling questions pop into your mind: is she hungry? Is she wet? Is she uncomfortable? Is she sick? Does she have indigestion? Is she lonely? Parents are not apt to think of fatigue, but it's one of the commonest causes of crying.

Quite often, none of these explanations seems to apply. By the time they are a couple of weeks old, most babies have fretful periods for no apparent reason. When they cry mainly in the late afternoon or evening, we call it colic. If they fuss off and on throughout the day, we say that they're fretful. If they're unusually tense and jumpy, we may call them hypertonic (different from the 'hyperactive' label that is often used for older children).

Fussy crying is common in healthy babies all over the world. It usually increases over the first six weeks of life, then fades away around three months of age. During the first three months of life, the baby's immature nervous system and digestive system have to adjust to life in the outside world. A smooth adjustment is harder for some babies than for others. Compared to babies in industrialized countries, babies in developing countries cry as often but tend to stop sooner, probably because they are held close to their mothers all day.

Few things are more upsetting to a parent than a little baby who cries and cannot be comforted. So it's important to remember that excessive crying in the early weeks is usually temporary and not a sign of anything serious. If you're concerned (and who wouldn't be?), ask for a medical assessment, more than once if need be. The other key thing to remember – and it bears repeating – is that it is *never* safe to shake a baby to make the fussing stop. For more on babies who cry and can't be comforted, see page 104.

Sorting out the causes. We used to think that mothers could learn to recognize their baby's different cries. In reality, even excellent parents generally can't tell cries apart by their sounds. Instead, they figure out the cause by trying different things. Here are some possibilities to consider:

- Is it hunger? Whether you're feeding your baby on a regular schedule or according to her desire, you may get an idea of her pattern of hunger. (A few babies never develop a regular pattern, which makes it harder to figure out what they need at any given moment.) If your baby took less than half her usual amount at her last feeding, it may be the reason she's awake and crying an hour later, instead of after the usual three hours. If she cries soon after a full feeding, however, it's less likely that she's hungry.
- Does she crave sucking? Sucking is calming for babies, even when they're not hungry. If your baby is fussy but you think she's well fed, you can offer a dummy or encourage her to find her own fingers. Most babies suck for pleasure in the early months and stop on their own sometime in the first or second year of life. Early sucking does not cause long-term dummy addiction.
- Could she have outgrown her formula or the breast milk supply, or is the supply decreasing? A baby doesn't outgrow the milk supply all of a sudden. She will have been breast-feeding for a longer time or have been polishing off every bottle for several days and then looking around for more. She begins to wake and cry a little earlier than usual. In most cases, it's only after she has been waking early from hunger for a number of days that she begins crying after a feeding.

- Does she need to be held? Young babies often need the physical sensations of being held and rocked in order to calm down. Some are comforted by being wrapped up snugly in a blanket. It may be that swaddling and rocking are comforting because they re-create the familiar sensations of being in the womb. White noise – the sound of a vacuum cleaner, a radio turned to static, or a parent going 'Shhhh' – often has a similar calming effect.
- Is she crying because she's wet or has had a bowel movement? Most babies don't seem to care if they're wet, but some seem more sensitive. Check the nappy and try changing her. If she wears cloth nappies, check the safety pins: one may be poking her. Also check for hair or threads wrapped around a finger or toe.
- Is it indigestion? The occasional baby who has a hard time digesting milk may cry an hour or two after a feeding. If this becomes an early pattern while you are breast-feeding, you should consider changing your own diet – cutting down on cow's milk or caffeine, for example. If you are bottle-feeding, ask your doctor if a formula change is worth a try. Some studies have found that switching to a hypoallergenic formula reduces crying in many babies; other experts disagree with this tactic, unless there are other signs of allergy such as rash or a family history of food allergies.
- Is it heartburn? Most babies spit up without even noticing. A few of them experience pain when

stomach acid irritates the oesophagus (the tube from the mouth to the stomach). Babies with heartburn usually cry soon after feeding, when the milk is still in the stomach. You can try burping your baby again, even though you got a burp before. If this kind of crying happens often, talk with your doctor about gastro-oesophageal reflux disease, or GORD (for more, see page 130).

- Is the baby sick? Sometimes babies cry because they just aren't feeling well. Irritability may be an early symptom, followed later by fever, rash, diarrhoea or vomiting. If your baby is crying inconsolably and has other symptoms of illness, take her temperature and consider calling her doctor.
- Is she spoiled? Though older babies can be spoiled, you can be sure that in the first few months your baby is not crying because she's spoiled. Something is bothering her.
- Is it fatigue? Some young babies seem to be made in such a way that they can't drift peacefully into sleep. Their fatigue at the end of every awake period produces a tension that is a sort of hump they must get over before falling asleep. They have to cry. Some of them cry frantically and loudly. Then gradually or suddenly the crying stops and they are asleep.

  When young babies have been awake an unusually long while or when they have been stimulated more than usual, they may react by becoming tense and irritable. Instead of it being easier for them to fall asleep, it may be harder. If the parents or strangers then try to comfort them with more play or more talk, it only makes matters worse. So if your baby is crying at the end of a wakeful period and after she has been fed and her nappy changed, you can assume that she's tired, and put her to bed. If she continues to cry, you can try leaving her on her own for a few minutes (or as long as you can stand) to give her a chance to settle down on her own.

Another baby who has become overfatigued may relax sooner if kept in gentle motion, by being pushed back and forth in a rocking cradle, rocked in the pram, or held in your arms or in a sling and walked quietly, preferably in a darkened room. A baby swing is sometimes very helpful for this purpose. Some parents put their babies in a baby seat on top of the dryer; the sound and vibration can be comforting. (If you try this, make sure your baby is securely belted in, and use duct tape to make sure the seat cannot vibrate off the dryer onto the floor.) But you might not want to always put your baby to sleep this active way. She might become more and more dependent on it and continue to demand it later on; then you're stuck. (See page 104 for more on colicky, hard-to-comfort infants.)

CHECKLIST

Tips for Comforting a Crying Baby

- ✓ Offer a feeding or a dummy.
- ✓ Change the nappy.
- ✓ Hold, swaddle and rock or vibrate (never shake).
- ✓ Play white noise (vacuum cleaner, radio static or 'shhhh').
- ✓ Darken the room and reduce stimulation.
- ✓ Reassure yourself that your baby is fine and you've done all you can. Then take a break and give your baby time to calm down on her own.

NAPPY CHANGING

Cleaning your baby. It isn't necessary to wash your baby when changing a wet nappy, but it's nice to let the skin air-dry. After a bowel movement, you can use plain water on cotton balls or a washcloth, baby lotion and tissues, or baby wipes. Premoistened, shop-bought wipes are handy, but some contain perfumes and other chemicals that can irritate the skin. With girls, always wipe from front to back. For boys, put a spare nappy loosely over the penis until you're ready to fasten the nappy. This way you won't be sprayed if he happens to urinate before you're done. Always wash your hands with soap and water after changing a nappy.

When to change. If children have sufficient covers over them, the wet nappy doesn't feel cold. Most parents change the nappy when they pick their baby up for feeding and again before they put him back down. Parents who are very busy have found they can save time and laundry by only changing after a feeding, because babies often have a bowel movement while eating. Most babies don't mind being wet, but a few are extrasensitive and have to be changed more often.

Disposable nappies. Most parents choose disposable nappies for convenience, and because they absorb more fluid. Disposables may seem dry, but they still need changing about as often as cloth. The costs of cloth and disposable

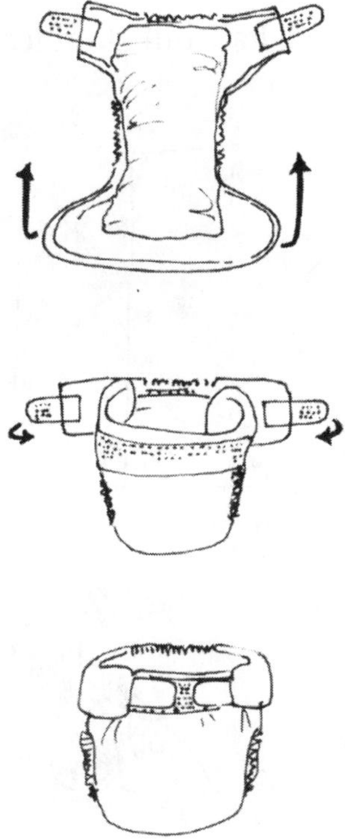

nappies are similar when a nappy service is used. Cloth nappies washed at home cost less but take a lot more work. Cloth nappies reduce the consumption of wood pulp and the clogging of landfills. Not surprisingly, the manufacturers of disposables have promoted the idea that disposables aren't any worse for the environment than cloth, but their arguments have never made sense to me.

Occasionally a superabsorbent nappy splits open, releasing some of its gelling material (the stuff that soaks up the fluid). Some parents mistake this material for insects or even for a rash, but it's not dangerous at all.

Cloth nappies. If you use a nappy service, you'll get a bag of clean nappies delivered each week. Washing your own cuts the cost in half but doubles the work. Many

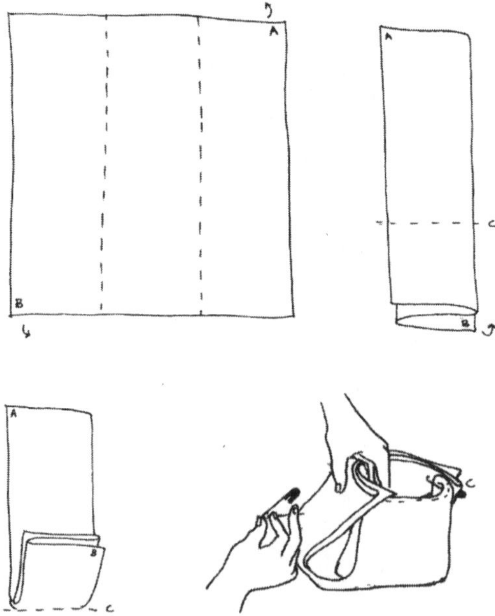

parents choose prefolded cloth nappies that close with Velcro. For a full-size newborn baby, you can fold a usual rectangular or square nappy as in the pictures: first fold lengthwise so that there are three thicknesses. Then fold about one-third of the end over. Half of the folded nappy now has six layers; the other half has three layers. A boy needs the double thickness in front. A girl needs the thickness in front when she's lying on her belly (not to sleep, of course, but for playing), and in the back when she lies on her back to sleep. When you put in the pins, slip two fingers of your other hand between the baby and the nappy to prevent sticking the child. The pins slide through the cloth more easily if you keep them stuck into a bar of soap.

In the past, parents put their babies in waterproof plastic pants to protect the sheets (and themselves). Modern nappy wraps made out of high-tech, breathable materials allow more air to circulate around the baby's bottom, a real help in reducing moisture and the resulting rashes. But they tend to leak a bit. An alternative is to use two nappies. The second one can be pinned around the waist like an apron, or folded into a narrow strip down the middle.

Washing nappies. Put used nappies into a covered bucket partially filled with water, with 120 ml (4 fl oz) of borax or bleach per 4 litres (7 pints) of water to help remove stains. Before you put a soiled nappy in the bucket, scrape the bowel movement off into the toilet with a knife, or rinse the nappy by holding it in the toilet while you flush it (hold tight). A high-pressure sprayer that attaches to the toilet makes rinsing faster and easier; you can buy these online. Clean the nappy bucket each time you do a nappy wash. (If you use a nappy service, of course, you just toss the nappy and all its contents into the plastic bucket supplied by the nappy company; the company picks up the bucket and leaves you a big bag of nice, clean nappies.)

Wash the nappies with mild soap or detergent in a washing machine or washtub (dissolve the soap well first), and rinse two or three times. The number of rinsings depends on how soon the water gets clear and on how delicate the baby's skin is. If your baby's skin isn't sensitive, two rinsings may be enough. (For more on nappy rash, see page 132.)

If the nappies are becoming hard, nonabsorbent and grey with soap deposit, you can soften them by using a water conditioner. Don't use a fabric softener: these leave a coating that makes nappies less absorbent.

BOWEL MOVEMENTS

Meconium. For the first day or so after birth, the baby's bowel movements are a greenish-black, sticky substance called meconium. After that they change to brown or yellow. If a baby hasn't had a movement by the end of the second day, the doctor should be told.

The gastrocolic reflex. Filling the stomach stimulates the intestinal tract all the way down. This hookup is called the gastrocolic reflex (gastro = stomach, colic = intestines). It's very active in the early months of life, especially in breast-fed babies, who may have a bowel movement after every feeding. Some begin to strain almost as soon as they start nursing; they produce nothing, but keep straining so hard as long as the nipple is in their mouths that they can't nurse. You have to let their intestines quiet down for fifteen minutes and try again.

Breast-fed babies. A breast-fed baby may have many or few bowel movements daily. Most have several a day in the early weeks. They are usually of a light yellow colour and may be watery, pasty or seedy, or they may have the consistency of thick cream soup. They are practically never too hard.

Many breast-fed babies change from frequent to infrequent bowel movements by the time they are two or three months old. This occurs because breast milk is so well digested that there is too little residue to make up a good-sized bowel movement. A breast-fed baby may have one bowel movement every day, every other day, or even less often. Don't let this pattern alarm you: there is nothing to worry about as long as your baby is comfortable. The breast-fed baby's bowel movements stay just as soft when they are passed infrequently.

Bottle-fed babies. The baby who is fed commercially prepared formula usually has between one and four movements a day at first, though an occasional baby has as many as six. As he grows older, the number tends to decrease to one or two a day. Movements in babies fed formula are most often pasty and of a pale yellow or tan colour. However, some young babies always have movements that are more like soft scrambled eggs (curdy lumps with looser material in between). The number and colour is not important if their consistency is soft but not watery and your baby is comfortable and gaining well.

The commonest disturbance of the bowel movements in a baby on cow's milk is a tendency to hardness. See page 583 for constipation. A very few bottle-fed babies have a tendency to loose, green, curdy movements in the early months. If the movements are always just a little loose, this can be ignored provided your baby is comfortable and gaining well and the doctor finds nothing wrong.

Straining with stools. A baby may push and strain a lot, with lots of grimacing and grunting, but then produce a soft bowel movement. This isn't constipation, which always goes with hard stools. Rather, the problem is poor coordination. The baby is pushing out with one group of muscles and holding back with another. The net result is that nothing happens. Finally the holding-back muscles relax, and things go well after that. The problem goes away as the baby's nervous system matures.

Sometimes adding two to four teaspoons of pureed and strained prunes to the daily diet helps make the baby's bowels more regular, even though the baby doesn't otherwise need solid food yet. There is no call for shop-bought laxatives in this kind of difficulty. I think it is better not to use suppositories or enemas, for fear that the baby's intestines will come to depend on them. Try to solve the problem with prunes or prune juice.

Changes in the movements. You can see that it doesn't matter if one baby's movements are always a little different from another's, as long as each is doing well. It's more apt to mean something when a baby's movements undergo a real change. For example, green movements can occur with both breast-fed and bottle-fed babies. If the movements are always green and the baby is doing fine, there is nothing to be concerned about. If they were previously pasty and then turn lumpy, slightly looser and slightly more frequent, it may be a spell of indigestion or a mild intestinal infection. If they become definitely loose, frequent and greenish and the smell changes, this is almost certainly due to an intestinal infection, whether mild or severe. Generally speaking, changes in the number and consistency of the movements are more important than changes in colour. A bowel movement exposed to the air may turn brown or green. This is of no importance.

Mucus in the bowel movements is common when a baby has diarrhoea, and it just means that the intestines are irritated. Similarly, it may occur in indigestion. It can also come from higher up – from the throat and bronchial tubes of a baby with a cold or a healthy newborn baby. Some babies form a great deal of mucus in the early weeks.

When a new vegetable is added to the diet (less frequently in the case of other foods), part of it may come through looking the same as it went in. If there are signs of irritation, such as looseness and mucus, give much less the next time. If there is no irritation, you can keep on with the same amount or increase slowly until the baby's intestines learn to digest it better. Beets can turn the whole movement red.

Small streaks of blood on the outside of a bowel movement usually come from a crack, or fissure, in the anus, caused by hard bowel movements. The bleeding is not serious in itself, but the doctor should be notified so that the constipation can be treated promptly.

Larger amounts of blood in the movement are rare and may come from malformations of the intestines, from severe diarrhoea, or from intussusception (see page 582). The doctor should be called or the child taken to a hospital promptly.

THE BATH

When to bathe. Most babies, after a few weeks' experience, have a wonderful time in the bath. Take your time and enjoy it with your baby. It's often convenient in the early months to give a bath before the midmorning feeding. Before any feeding is all right, but after a feeding is when you want your child to sleep. By the time your baby is on three meals a day, you may want to give a bath before lunch or supper. As your child gets older still and stays up for a while after supper, it may work out better to give the bath after supper, especially if she needs her supper early. Bathe her in a reasonably warm room; the kitchen often works well.

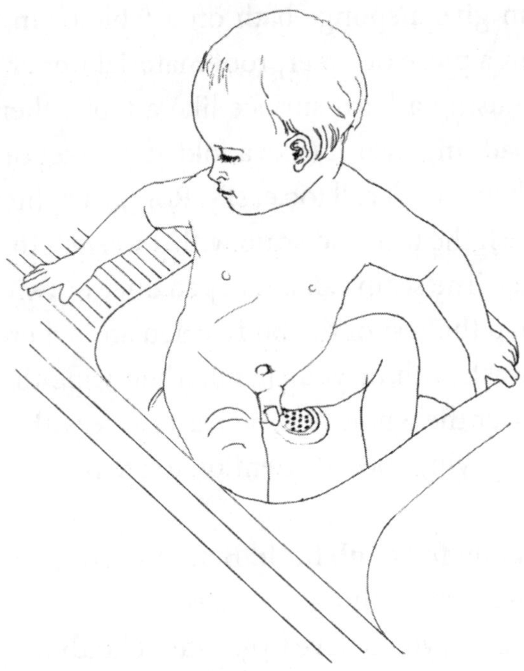

Sponge baths. Though it's the custom in most Western countries to give a complete tub or sponge bath every day, it isn't necessary more than once or twice a week. On days when you don't do a full bath, give a sponge bath in the nappy area, and clean around your baby's mouth and nose. The tub bath is apt to be frightening at first to the inexperienced parent – the baby seems so helpless, limp and slippery, especially after having been soaped. Babies may feel uneasy in the tub at first, because they can't be well supported there. You can give a sponge bath for a few weeks until you and your baby feel more secure, or even for months, if you prefer. Most doctors advise avoiding tub baths until the navel is dried up. But nothing awful happens if the navel gets wet; just dry it off.

You can give a sponge bath on a table or in your lap. You'll want a piece of waterproof material under the baby. If you are using a hard surface like a table, there should be some padding over it (like a folded blanket or quilt) so that your baby won't roll too easily. Rolling frightens young babies. Wash the face and scalp with a washcloth and clear warm water. The scalp can be soaped once or twice a week. Lightly soap the rest of the body when and where needed, with the washcloth or your hand. Then wipe the soap off by going over the whole body at least twice with the rinsed washcloth, paying special attention to creases.

Getting ready for a tub bath. Before starting the bath, be sure you have everything you need close at hand. If you forget the towel, you'll have to go after it holding a dripping baby in your arms. Take off your wristwatch. An apron protects your clothes. Have at hand:

- Soap
- Washcloth
- Towel
- Absorbent cotton for nose and ears if necessary
- Lotion
- Nappies, pins, vest, babygro

The bath can be given in a washbowl, dishpan, kitchen sink or plastic tub. Some tubs have sponge cutouts to support and position the baby properly. The regular bathtub is hard on a parent's back and legs. For your own comfort, you can put a dishpan or tub on a table or on something higher like a dresser. You can sit on a stool at the kitchen sink.

The water should be about body temperature (32–38°C; 90–100°F). A bath thermometer is a comfort to the inexperienced parent but is not necessary. Always test the water temperature with your wrist. It should feel comfortably warm but not hot. Use only a small amount of water at first, a few centimetres deep, until you get the knack of holding your baby securely. A tub is less slippery if you line it with a towel or cloth nappy each time.

Giving a tub bath. Hold your baby so that her head is supported on your wrist, and the fingers of that hand hold her securely in the armpit. Wash the face first, with a soft washcloth without soap, then the scalp. The scalp needs to be soaped only once or twice a week. Wipe the soap suds off the scalp with a damp washcloth, going over it twice (if the washcloth is too wet, the soapy water may get into the eyes and sting). Then you can use the washcloth or your hand to wash the rest of your baby. Wash lightly between the outer lips of the vagina. (See page 82 about washing the circumcised or uncircumcised penis.) When you use soap, it's easier to soap your hand than a washcloth. If the skin gets dry, try omitting soap except for once or twice a week.

If you feel nervous at first, for fear you'll drop your baby in the water, you can soap her while she is on your lap or on a table. Then rinse her off in the tub, holding her securely with both hands. Use a soft bath towel for drying, and blot rather than rub. If you begin giving the tub bath before the navel is completely healed, dry it well after the bath with cotton balls.

Lotion. It's fun to apply lotion to a baby after a bath, and your baby will like it, too, but it's rarely necessary. Lotion may be helpful when the skin is dry or there is a mild nappy rash. Baby oils and mineral oil work the same, but sometimes they cause a mild rash. Avoid baby powder containing talcum, because it is harmful to the lungs if inhaled. Cornstarch-based powder works almost as well and is safer.

BODY PARTS

Skin. Newborn babies develop all sorts of spots and rashes, most of which fade or disappear on their own. Rashes *may* be signs of a serious medical condition, however, so it's sensible to ask the doctor to look at any new rash. For more on rashes and birthmarks, see page 87.

Ears, eyes, mouth, nose. You need to wash only the outer ear and the entrance to the canal, not inside. Use a washcloth, not a cotton bud (which just pushes the wax further in). Wax is formed in the canal to protect and clean it.

The eyes are bathed by tears constantly, not just when your baby is crying. This is why it is unnecessary to put any drops into healthy eyes.

The mouth ordinarily needs no extra care.

The nose has a beautiful system for keeping itself clear. The cells lining the nose are covered with a fringe of whip-like projections that beat constantly, moving the mucus down toward the front of the nose. The mucus collects on the nose hairs, tickling the baby until she sneezes or rubs it away. When you are drying your baby after the bath, you can first moisten and then gently wipe out any balls of dried mucus with the corner of the washcloth. Don't fuss at this too long if it makes your baby angry.

Sometimes, especially when the house is heated, enough dried mucus collects in the nose to interfere with a baby's breathing. You can tell if this is happening because each time she breathes in, the lower edges of the chest are pulled inward. An older child or adult would breathe through the mouth, but most babies can't do this. See page 39 and 540 for ways to clear a plugged-up nose.

Nails. The nails can be cut easily while your baby sleeps. Clippers may be easier than nail scissors. Or try a nail file: if you file the nails smooth, there are no sharp edges to scratch your baby's face when she waves her hands around, and there is no risk of pinching or clipping her fingertips. Sing a song while you file, and nail care can become a pleasant part of your routine.

The soft spot (fontanel). The soft spot on the top of a baby's head is where the bones of the skull have not yet grown together. The size of the fontanel at birth is different in different babies. A large one is nothing to worry about, although it's bound to be slower to close than a small one. Some fontanels close as early as nine months; slow ones can take as much as two years. The average is twelve to eighteen months.

Parents worry unnecessarily about the danger of touching the soft spot. It is covered by a membrane as tough as canvas, and there is no risk of hurting a baby there with ordinary handling. If the light is right, you can see that the fontanel pulsates at a rate between the breathing rate and the beat of the heart.

The navel. Right after birth, the doctor or midwife clamps the umbilical cord and cuts it off. The stump that's left dries up and eventually drops off, usually in about two or three weeks, though it may take longer.

When the cord falls off, it leaves a raw spot, which takes a number of days or weeks to heal over. The raw spot should be kept clean and dry. A scab covers it until it is healed; it doesn't need a dressing and will stay drier without one. Once the cord falls off, your baby can have tub baths. Just dry the navel afterward. There may be a little bleeding or drainage a few days before the cord falls off and until the healing is complete. If the scab on the unhealed navel gets pulled by clothing, there may be a drop or two of blood. Don't worry about this.

It's best to keep the nappy below the level of the unhealed navel, so that it doesn't keep the navel wet. If the unhealed navel becomes moist and produces a discharge, it should be protected from constant wetting by the nappy, and cleaned each day with a cotton ball dampened with surgical spirit, used in the skin fold around the cord. If healing is slow, the raw spot may become lumpy with what's called granulation tissue, but this is of no importance. The doctor may apply a chemical that will hasten drying and healing.

If the navel and the surrounding skin become red or there is a smelly discharge, infection may be present. You should get in touch with your doctor right away, because these infections can be serious.

The penis. The foreskin is a sleeve of skin that covers the head (glans) of the penis. The opening of the foreskin is large enough to let the baby's urine out, but small enough to protect the tip of the penis from nappy rash. (See page 604 about sores on the end of the penis.) As the baby grows, the foreskin normally separates from the glans and becomes retractable. By age three or four, most foreskins can be pulled back to expose the glans all the way, but some boys take longer, even into their teen years. This is no cause for concern. Routine washing without retracting the foreskin is enough to keep the penis clean and healthy.

At the end of your baby's foreskin you may see a white, waxy material (smegma). This is perfectly normal. Smegma is secreted by the cells on the inside of the foreskin as a natural lubricant between the foreskin and the glans.

Circumcision. When a penis is circumcised, the foreskin is cut off. This operation is at least four thousand years old. For Jewish and Muslim people, it has religious significance. In some other cultures it's a puberty rite, marking a boy's passage into adulthood.

Uncircumcised boys tend to get more bladder or kidney infections during childhood, but circumcised boys also get these infections. Many experts believe that men who are circumcised are less likely to spread HIV, genital herpes and other serious infections, a very important benefit from the view point of public health. Risks include bleeding or infection, both usually easy to treat. Circumcision is painful, although many doctors now use injections to numb the area; others give babies sugar water, which relieves the pain at least a little. In the Jewish tradition, babies suck on a cloth soaked with wine.

Babies usually recover from the stress of the operation in about twenty-four hours. If your baby seems to be uncomfortable for longer than this, or if there is persistent oozing of blood or swelling of his penis, tell the doctor. A spot of blood or several spots on successive nappy changes merely means that a small scab has been pulled off.

Penis care. Good genital hygiene is important from birth on, whether the penis is circumcised or not. It's part of children learning general habits of personal cleanliness. If your baby isn't circumcised, the penis should be washed whenever you give him a bath. You don't have to do anything special to the foreskin; just wash gently around the outside to remove any excess accumulation of smegma. If you want, you can clean beneath the foreskin by pushing it back very gently, just until you meet resistance. Never forcibly retract the foreskin. This hurts, and could lead to infections or other complications. In time, the foreskin normally becomes looser.

If your baby is circumcised, change his nappy often

while the wound is healing. This will lessen the chance of irritation. A simple petroleum jelly ointment helps to keep the healing skin from sticking. It's bound to be quite sensitive for a week or so. After the wound has healed, you can wash the penis just as you do the rest of your baby, during the bath.

Boy babies often have erections, especially when the bladder is full or during urination, or for no apparent reason. It's normal.

TEMPERATURE, FRESH AIR AND SUNSHINE

Room temperature. A room temperature of 18–20°C (65°F–68°F) for eating and playing is right for babies weighing over 2.25 kg (5 lb), just as it is for older children and adults. Smaller babies have a harder time controlling their body temperature, and may need to be kept warmer and dressed in extra layers. Very small babies control their body temperature best when they're right next to their parents, ideally skin to skin. Avoid cold or hot draughts, in front of an air conditioner or a heat vent.

In cold weather, the air outside tends to contain very little moisture. When this dry air is taken into a house and warmed up, it acts like a dry sponge, sucking up moisture from the skin and nose. Dried mucus can make it hard for babies to breathe and may lower children's resistance to infections. Any source of moisture can help: house plants, pans of water on the radiators or humidifiers (see page 540). The warmer the room temperature, the more drying the air becomes.

Inexperienced parents sometimes feel that they need to keep their baby overly warm. They keep the room too hot and the baby too wrapped up. Under these conditions, some babies even develop heat rash in winter. Overheating also increases the risk of cot death (see page 608).

How much clothing. A normal baby has as good an internal thermostat as an adult as long as he isn't put into so many layers of clothing and covering that his thermostat doesn't work properly. Babies and children who are reasonably plump need less covering than adults. More babies are overdressed than underdressed. This isn't good for them. If a person is always too warmly dressed, the body loses its ability to adjust to changes and is more likely to become chilled. So, in general, put on too little rather than too much, and then watch your baby. Don't put on enough to keep the hands warm; most babies' hands stay cool when they are comfortably dressed. Feel the legs or arms or neck. The best guide is the colour of the face. Babies who are getting cold lose the colour from their cheeks, and they may begin to fuss, too.

In cold weather, a warm cap is essential, because babies lose lots of body heat from their heads. A cap in which to sleep in very cold weather should be of knitted acrylic, so that if it slips over the face the baby can breathe through it.

When putting on sweaters and shirts with small openings, remember that a baby's head is more egg-shaped than ball-shaped. Gather the sweater into a loop, slip it first over the back of your baby's head, then forward, stretching it forwards as you bring it down past the forehead and nose. Then put your baby's arms into the sleeves. When taking it off, pull your baby's arms out of the sleeves first. Gather the sweater into a loop as it lies around the neck. Raise the front part of the loop up past the nose and forehead while the back of the loop is still at the back of the neck, then slip it off towards the back of the head.

Practical coverings. It is better to use all-acrylic blankets or bags when a baby is sleeping in a cool room (15.5–18°C/60–65°F). They have the best combination of warmth and washability. Knitted shawls tuck and wrap more easily than woven blankets, especially when your baby is up, and because they are thinner you can adjust the amount of covering to the temperature more exactly than you can with thick blankets. Avoid coverings that are heavy, such as solid-feeling quilts. In a warm room (over 22°C/72°F) or in warm weather, a baby really needs only cotton coverings. All blankets, quilts and sheets should be large enough to tuck securely under the mattress, so that they will not work loose and pose a suffocation hazard.

Fresh air. Changes of air temperature help tone up the body's system for adapting to cold or heat. A bank clerk is much more likely to become chilled staying outdoors in winter than a lumberjack, who is used to such weather. A baby living continuously in a warm room usually has a pasty complexion and may have a sluggish appetite. A baby weighing 3.6 kg (8 lb) can certainly go out when it's 15.5°C (60°F) or above. The temperature of the air is not the only factor. Moist, cold air is more chilling than dry air of the same temperature and wind is the greatest chiller. Even when the temperature is cooler, a baby weighing 5.4 kg (12 lb) may be comfortable in a sunny, sheltered spot if dressed appropriately.

If you live in a city and have no garden to park your baby in, you can push the child in a pram. If you get in the habit of carrying the baby in a sling on your chest or back, you will be wonderfully conditioned as the baby gets bigger. Your baby will love riding in close contact with you and will be able to look around or sleep. If you enjoy being out and can afford the time, the more the better.

DR SPOCK COMMENTS

It's good for a baby (like anyone else) to get outdoors for two or three hours a day, particularly during the season when the house is heated. I grew up and practised paediatrics in the northeastern part of the United States, where most conscientious parents took it for granted that babies and children should be outdoors two or three hours a day. Children love to be outdoors and it gives them pink cheeks and good appetites. So I can't help but believe in the tradition.

Sunshine and sunbathing. The body needs sunlight to make vitamin D. But even if babies can't spend time in a sunny room or outside, they can still get all the vitamin

D they need from their formula and from vitamin drops (see page 269). Sunlight also exposes children to ultraviolet (UV) rays, which can result in skin cancer years later. Infants are especially vulnerable, because their skin is thin and contains relatively little melanin, the pigment that protects against UV damage. Babies with dark skin are safer; those with pale skin and blond or red hair are most at risk. Beaches, pools and boats are especially hazardous, because the UV rays are reflected up from the water as well as coming down from above.

Skin specialists recommend that children and adults use sunscreen, either cream or lotion, with a sun protection factor (SPF) of at least 15, and higher for those with more sun-sensitive skin. For babies under six months of age, sunscreens tend to irritate the skin. A baby who will be in the sun for more than a few minutes should be covered up: a hat with a wide brim, made out of a material that will block the sun's rays, and long-sleeved trousers and top. Even with those precautions, a fair-skinned baby should not sit poolside for a long time, since the reflected rays are also damaging. (See page 467 for more on sun protection.) Sunbathing – exposure to UV light for the purpose of getting a tan – is unhealthy at any age.

COMMON NEWBORN CONCERNS

Birthmarks. It's the rare newborn who does not have one or more birthmarks. Doctors, who see these all the time, may not remember to reassure parents about spots that have no medical significance and are destined to fade in time. So if you have questions, be sure to ask them.

Stork bites and angel's kisses. Many babies have a collection of red, irregularly shaped spots on the nape of the neck (stork bites), upper eyelids (angel's kisses), or between the eyebrows when they are born. These birthmarks are nests of little blood vessels that have grown because of exposure to the mother's hormones in the womb. Most disappear gradually (stork bites may persist) and nothing needs to be done for them.

Port wine stains. Areas of skin that are flat with a deep purplish-red colouring may occur on the temples and cheeks or other parts of the body. Some of these birthmarks do fade, particularly the lighter ones; others are permanent. Laser treatments are now used for some of the larger permanent port-wine stains. Occasionally such birthmarks are associated with other problems.

Hyperpigmented spots. These slate-blue patches used to be called Mongolian spots, but they occur in babies of all nationalities, especially those with darker skin. They often occur around the buttocks but may be scattered anywhere. They are simply areas of increased pigment in the top layer of the skin and almost always disappear completely in the first two years.

Moles. Moles can be of all sizes and be smooth or hairy. All moles should be checked by your doctor or nurse practitioner, especially if the mole starts to grow or change colour. Most are entirely benign, though a few have the potential for cancerous transformation later in life. They can be removed surgically if they are potentially dangerous, disfiguring or irritated by clothing.

Strawberry marks and cavernous haemangiomas. Strawberry marks are fairly common though they usually show up later in the first year of life. They start as pale areas, then over time change to raised marks of an intense, deep-crimson colour that look very much like the outside of a shiny strawberry. These marks usually grow for a year or so, then stop and shrink until they disappear. Generally, half are completely gone by age five, 70 per cent by age seven, and 90 per cent by nine years. Medical treatment with lasers or surgery is occasionally necessary, but it's best if you can just let nature take its course. Cavernous haemangiomas are fairly large blue-and-red marks caused by a collection of distended veins deep in the skin. They may disappear completely on their own. They can be removed if necessary.

Sucking blisters. Some babies are born with blisters on their lips, hands or wrists. They are caused by finger-sucking in the womb. Other babies develop white dry blisters in the middle part of their lips from sucking. Sometimes the blisters peel. Sucking blisters clear up with no special treatment.

Blue fingers and toes. The hands and feet of many newborns look blue, especially if they are at all cool. Some babies with pale skin also show a bluish mottling all over their bodies when undressed. These colour changes are caused by slow blood circulation in the skin and are not a sign of illness. Babies often have bluish lips. Blueness of the gums or the skin around the mouth sometimes signals low blood oxygen, especially if there is also difficulty breathing or feeding. If you see this, call your doctor.

Jaundice. Many newborn babies develop jaundice, a yellow tinge of the skin and eyes. The yellow colour is from a substance called bilirubin, which is produced when red blood cells are broken down. Usually the bilirubin is taken up by the liver and passed in the stools (giving them their brownish-yellowish colour). The liver of newborn babies, however, is still immature and the intestines may not be very active for the first few days, so the bilirubin remains in the blood and makes the skin yellow.

A little jaundice is very common. It goes away over the first few days and causes no problems whatsoever. In rare cases, when the production of bilirubin is especially rapid or the liver is especially slow to respond, the bilirubin level can climb to dangerous levels. It's easy to measure bilirubin levels in a drop of blood and treatment with special lights (that cause the bilirubin to break down) keeps the bilirubin in the safe range. If your baby seems yellow in the first week of life, have the doctor or nurse practitioner take a look.

Sometimes jaundice persists beyond the first week or two. This usually occurs in a baby who is breast-feeding. Some doctors recommend stopping breast-feeding altogether for a day or two. Others recommend continuing or even increasing breast-feeding. In either case, the baby almost always does well. When jaundice doesn't respond as expected, special laboratory testing may reveal a rare medical cause.

Breathing problems. New parents usually worry a little about a new baby's breathing because it is irregular and may be so shallow that they can't hear it or see it. They may worry, too, the first time they hear their baby snoring faintly. These things are normal, but if anything at all concerns you about your baby's breathing, it's always right to ask the doctor.

Umbilical hernia. After the skin of the navel heals, there is often still a weak area in the deeper layer of the abdomen where the umbilical cord ran. When the baby cries, a small part of the intestine may push through this area (the umbilical ring), causing the navel to puff out. This is called an umbilical hernia. Usually the ring is small and closes completely in a few weeks or months. When the weak spot is larger, it may take months or even years to close, and the protrusion can be quite large.

It used to be thought that the closing of the umbilical ring could be hastened by putting a tight strap of adhesive and a coin across the navel; actually, that doesn't make any difference. Keeping your baby from crying is impossible, and also doesn't help. Umbilical hernias almost never cause any trouble, and time almost always does the trick. If an umbilical hernia is still large at six or eight years and shows no decrease, minor surgery may be recommended. Very, very rarely, a loop of bowel can become trapped in the hernia. If this happens, the hernia mass becomes very hard and tender, and the baby looks very sick indeed. This condition is a medical emergency.

Swollen breasts. Many babies, both boys and girls, have swollen breasts for some time after birth. In some cases a little milk runs out (this used to be called 'witches' milk', although I can't imagine why). The breast swelling and milk are the result of hormones that passed from the mother to the baby in the womb. Nothing needs to be done for this condition, as the swelling will normally disappear in time. The breasts should not be massaged or squeezed, since this is likely to irritate them and may lead to infection.

Vaginal discharge. Girl babies often have a vaginal discharge at birth, with white, thick, sticky mucus. This condition is caused by the mother's hormones (the same ones that can cause a baby to have swollen breasts) and goes away on its own without treatment. At a few days of age, many girl babies have a little bit of bloody discharge, caused by the dropping off of maternal hormones after delivery. It usually lasts only a day or so. If a bloody discharge persists after the first week, have it checked out by the doctor.

Undescended testicles. In a certain number of newborn boys, one or both testicles are not in their usual place in the scrotum, but are farther up in the groin or even inside the abdomen. Many of these undescended testicles come down into the scrotum soon after birth.

The testicles are originally formed inside the abdomen and move down into the scrotum only shortly before birth. There are muscles attached to the testicles that can jerk them back up into the groin or even back into the abdomen. This reflex protects the testicles, and there are lots of boys whose testicles withdraw on the slightest provocation. Even chilling of the skin from being undressed may be enough to make them disappear into the abdomen. Handling the scrotum in an examination frequently makes them disappear. Therefore, a parent shouldn't decide that the testicles are undescended just because they are not usually in sight. A good time to look for them is when the boy is in a warm bath. Testicles that have been seen at any time in the scrotum, even if only rarely, need no treatment; they will surely settle into place during puberty.

If one or both testicles have never been seen in the scrotum by the time a boy is nine to twelve months old, he should be examined by a paediatric surgeon. If one or both are truly undescended, the surgeon may recommend watchful waiting, a trial of medication to bring the testicles down, or an operation. The goal is to avoid potential damage to the undescended testicle.

Startles and jittery movements. Newborn babies are often startled by loud noises and sudden change in position. Some are more sensitive than others. When you put babies on a flat, hard surface and they jerk their arms and legs, it's likely to rock the body a little. This unexpected motion is enough to make sensitive babies nearly jump out of their skins and cry with fright. They may hate the bath because they are held so loosely. They need to be washed in their parent's lap and then rinsed in the tub while held securely in both hands. They gradually get over this uneasiness as they grow older.

The trembles. Some babies have trembly or jittery

moments in the early months. The chin may quiver, or the arms and legs may tremble, especially when the baby is excited or just after being undressed. This trembling is usually nothing to be disturbed about. It is just one of the signs that the baby's nervous system is still young. The tendency passes away in time.

Twitching. Some babies twitch occasionally in their sleep, and once in a while there is one who twitches frequently. This, too, usually disappears as the baby grows older. Twitching that continues even while you are holding the limb is more concerning, as it could be a sign of a seizure (see page 511); be sure to tell the doctor or nurse practitioner.

THE FIRST YEAR, FOUR TO TWELVE MONTHS

A TIME OF FIRSTS

Discoveries in the first year. The first three months of life are about getting basic systems working smoothly. Months four to twelve are all about discovery. Infants discover their own bodies and gain control of muscles large and small. They explore the world of things and begin to figure out the fundamentals of cause and effect. And they learn to read other people's feelings and predict how their own actions will affect those feelings. These momentous discoveries take infants to the very threshold of language. Some cross that threshold before their first birthday; others cross it some time later.

The meaning of milestones. Doctors tend to focus on easy-to-see milestones: rolling over, sitting up, standing, walking. It's true that a baby who is very late with these may have developmental problems. But many healthy children are early and many are late, and the timing turns out not to be too important. More meaningful are the milestones that mark the child's connection with other people: smiling in response to being smiled at, listening when talked to, paying close attention to a parent's face to see if a new situation is safe, and noticing whether a parent is pleased or not. Parents are usually tuned into these social milestones, even though they may not keep track of them the way they do the sitting-standing-walking ones.

Along with timing, pay attention to the *quality* of your baby's behaviour. One child prefers to sit and watch, taking everything in but doing relatively little; another is constantly active, impatient to move, and quick to lose interest. One seems constantly alert to every small change; another is blissfully unaware. One is serious, another bubblier. These are all perfectly fine ways for a baby to be, but they call for different input from parents. (See page 617 for more on temperament.)

There are developmental timetables you can consult to see if your child is doing exactly what she is 'supposed' to be doing at each age. Such charts have never been part of this book. First off, every child's pattern of development is unique. One may be very advanced in her strength and coordination, a sort of infant athlete, yet she may be slow in doing skilful things with her fingers or in talking. Children who turn out later to be good at schoolwork may have been very slow to talk in the beginning. Likewise, children of average talent may have shown advanced early development.

It's a mistake to compare your baby to an average timetable. Development is bumpy. There are often small backward slides just before forward moves. You don't need to push for forward progress or worry too much about small regressions. There is no evidence that making a concerted effort to teach a child to walk or talk or read early has any real long-term benefit. Children need an environment that allows for the next developmental achievement but doesn't push them into it.

Autism. The rate of autism and autism spectrum disorders among UK children is approximately one in a hundred and may be climbing. Every young parent has heard of autism, and many know a child with the condition. You can find more on autism beginning on page 930. Here you'll want to know the red flags that signal the need for more evaluation. At four months, your baby should love 'talking' with you – that is, looking at your face, listening to your voice and responding with noises and excited facial expressions of his own. By nine months, he should be babbling, making a variety of wordlike sounds. By one year, he should be pointing with one finger to show you something interesting, and by fifteen months he should have at least one meaningful word. If you are concerned, talk with your baby's doctor or health visitor. With early identification, more and more children with autism are growing up connected, communicating and much more content.

CARING FOR YOUR BABY

Companionship without spoiling. During his play periods, it's good for a baby to be somewhere near his parents (and brothers and sisters, if any) so that he can see them, make noises at them, hear them speak to him, and now and then have them show him something. But it isn't necessary or sensible for him to be in a parent's lap or arms or to have someone amusing him the majority of the time. He can enjoy being around people and still learn how to occupy himself. When new parents are so delighted with their baby that they hold him or make up games for him all day long, he may become quite dependent on these attentions and demand more and more of them.

Things to watch and things to play with. Beginning around three or four months, babies enjoy looking at bright-coloured things and things that move, but mostly they enjoy looking at people and their faces. Outdoors, they are delighted to watch leaves and shadows. Indoors, they study their hands and shadows and pictures on the wall. There are bright-coloured cot toys that you can suspend between the top rails of the cot. Place them just within arm's reach – not right on top of your baby's nose – for when he begins reaching. You can make mobiles yourself – cardboard shapes covered with coloured paper that hang from the ceiling or from a lighting fixture and rotate in slight draughts – or you can hang suitable household objects within reach, such as spoons or plastic cups. (Be careful to keep any strings short, however, so they can't become strangulation hazards if your baby pulls them down.) All of these toys are nice, but never forget it is human companionship, above all else, that babies love and that particularly fosters their development.

A word about TV: if a television is on, an infant will stare at it. This is not a sign of advanced development. TV entertains at a cost. Young children easily become dependent on the TV for stimulation and lose some of their natural drive to explore. A child with a plastic cup and spoon, a few wooden blocks and a board book can think up fifty creative ways to use those objects; a child in front of a TV can only do one thing.

Remember that eventually everything goes into the mouth. Toward the middle of her first year, a baby's greatest joy is handling and mouthing objects: collections of plastic objects linked together (made for this age), rattles, teething rings, animals and dolls of cloth, household objects that are safe in the mouth. Don't let your child have objects or furniture that may be covered in paint containing lead, small glass beads and other small objects that can be choked on, or thin plastic toys that can be chewed into small, sharp pieces.

FEEDING AND GROWTH

Feeding decisions. Feeding in the first year is a big enough topic that it has its own chapter (starting on page 247). Here I'll just mention some of the main themes. The NHS urges mothers to breast-feed for the first six months at least. Six months is probably long enough to give your baby most of the biological benefits of breast milk, but *any* amount of time is better than none.

If you do decide to stop breast-feeding, switch to infant formula made from either cow's milk or soyabeans. There's no clear-cut advantage of one over the other, although experts disagree on this point. Homemade formulas and low-iron formulas generally don't provide adequate nutrition. Regular cow's milk isn't safe for babies under twelve months, and there is debate about the value of cow's milk at all (see page 318 for formulas, and page 319 for dairy foods).

Most parents introduce solid foods around four to six months of age, starting with iron-fortified cereals, and gradually adding vegetables, fruits, and meats. The NHS recommends you wait until around six months. It's reasonable to wait a week or so before adding a new food, to reassure yourself that your baby has tolerated the last item without stomach upset or a rash. There's no rush, but babies are more likely to accept new foods that are introduced during the first year or so of life.

Mealtime behaviour. This can be difficult for many parents because babies love to play with food. Slinging squash and poking peas is an important way babies find out about the physical world; teasing and provoking parents is an important way they learn about the world of relationships. Parents need to share in the fun but also set appropriate limits ('You can pick up your mashed potatoes, but if you throw them, dinner is over'). You know that feeding is going well if both you and your baby come away feeling happy. If mealtimes regularly leave you tense, worried or angry, it's time to make a change. A good place to start is by talking with your baby's doctor or nurse practitioner.

Around nine months, a baby may start showing signs of independence in feeding. He wants to hold the spoon himself and he turns his head to the side if you try to do it for him. This behaviour is often the first sign that the baby is developing a will of his own, a development that will continue full force in the coming years. (A good way to handle the spoon issue, by the way, is to give your baby one spoon to hold and use as best he can while you use a second spoon to actually get some food in his mouth.)

Growth. Babies roughly double their birth weight by about four months and triple it by a year. Doctors usually plot children's weight, length and head size on growth charts that give the average and normal range for each age. These charts can be reassuring: a healthy growth pattern is a good sign that your baby is getting enough food (but not too much) and that other body systems are working well. Occasionally I feel I have to discourage a parent from focusing too much on the numbers. Bigger is not necessarily better and while a growth curve at the 95th percentile means that a child is likely to be one of the largest in his preschool class, it doesn't mean much more than that.

SLEEPING

Bedtime rituals. Many of us have our own bedtime habits. We like our pillow just right and the covers to fit a certain way. Babies are the same. If they learn to fall asleep while being held by Mummy or Daddy, this can become the *only* way for them to nod off. Then, when they wake up in the middle of the night, Mummy or Daddy has to wake up, too.

If, on the other hand, your baby learns to fall asleep while lying alone in his cot, then he can do the same thing in the middle of the night (and you can keep on sleeping). So, once your baby is three or four months old, try to put her to bed while she's awake and let her learn to get herself to sleep. You may hear her awaken in the middle of the night (all babies do this), but she won't have to cry until you get up and rock her: she'll just fall back asleep. For more on babies who refuse to go to sleep, see page 104.

Early waking. Some parents like to get up with the sun and enjoy early mornings with their babies. But if you prefer to sleep, you probably can train your baby to sleep later or to be happy in bed in the morning. In the middle part of the first year, most babies become willing to sleep a little later than the uncivilized hour of 5 or 6 am. However, most parents develop a habit of listening for their babies in their sleep and jumping out of bed at the first murmur, so they never give the children a chance to go back to sleep. As a result, parents may find themselves still getting up before 7 am when the child is two or three years old. And a child who has been used to early company for so long will demand it.

Sleeping bags. By six months, when babies can move about in their cots, most parents find it more practical to put them to bed in sleeping bags than to try to keep blankets over them. (They simply crawl out from under their covers.) The bags are shaped like long nighties and cover the feet. They come in different sizes to fit your child as they grow.

Sleeping bags are available in a range of togs, or weights,

to suit different room temperatures. If a baby or child is going to sleep in a room warm enough that you would be comfortable wearing a cotton shirt or sleeping under a cotton blanket, your baby's bag should not be warmer than cotton blanketing. If the room is cold enough that an adult would require a good wool or acrylic blanket for covering, your baby will need a heavier bag. Check the advice that came with the sleeping bag when you bought it.

Changes in sleep. By about four months, most babies are sleeping mainly at night, perhaps waking up once or twice, with two or three naps during the day. Toward the end of the first year, most are down to two naps a day. The total amount of sleep varies from baby to baby. Some sleep as little as ten or eleven hours total, others as much as fifteen or sixteen hours. Total sleep time gradually decreases during the first year.

Around nine months of age, many babies who have been good sleepers start waking up in the middle of the night and demanding attention. This change occurs at about the same time that babies are discovering that a toy or other object that disappears under a cloth actually still exists. Psychologists call this intellectual breakthrough 'object permanence'. From your baby's point of view, it means that out of sight is no longer out of mind. (You know your baby is developing object permanence when you can't simply take things away any more: you hide them behind your back, but your baby keeps reaching for them.)

The same thing happens in the middle of the night. When your baby wakes up and finds herself alone, she now knows that you are nearby, even though out of sight, so she cries for company. Sometimes a simple 'Go to sleep' will be enough to resettle your baby; at other times you might need to pick her up to reassure her that you really are there. If you put her back down before she is completely asleep, she has the chance to practise falling back to sleep on her own.

Sleep problems. Many babies develop problems falling asleep or staying asleep. These problems often start with a minor illness, such as a cold or ear infection, but may last long after the infection has cleared up. The first step is to reestablish the baby's habit of falling asleep in her own bed, at first with Mummy or Daddy right there, and then gradually more and more independently. A comforting ritual – stories, prayers, kisses – helps a great deal.

Parents who are away at work all day sometimes find it hard to say good night in the evening. I often hear, 'When I get home at seven, and she goes to sleep at eight, we don't have any time together.' In these cases, it strikes me that the baby's sleeplessness is not so much a problem as a solution, a way to have time together with parents. A change in the parent's schedule, if possible, may be a better answer.

CRYING AND COLIC

Normal crying versus colic. All babies cry and fret sometimes, and it's usually not too hard to work out why. The section on crying in newborns (starting on page 60) also applies to babies through the first year of life. Crying tends to increase until a baby is about six weeks old and then, mercifully, begins to diminish. By three or four months, most babies fuss for a total of about an hour a day.

For some babies, however, the crying just goes on and on, hour after hour, week after week, no matter what the well-meaning and frantic parents do. A standard definition of colic is inconsolable crying for more than three hours a day, more than three days a week, and lasting more than three weeks. In reality, any crying or fussing that lasts much longer than expected in an otherwise healthy baby who has no apparent reason to cry qualifies as colic. Colic means pain from the intestines, but there are probably other causes for crying and fussing as well.

There seem to be two distinct patterns of crying in infants with colic. For some, the crying is generally limited to one period in the evening, typically 5 pm to 8 pm. The infant is contented and easy to soothe for most of the day, but when evening rolls around, the trouble begins. He cries, sometimes inconsolably, for the next few hours. This raises a question: what is happening in the early evening that makes him so fretful? If it were indigestion, for example, he would have it at any time of day, not just in the evening. Other infants cry at any and all times of day or night. Some of these infants also seem to be generally somewhat tense and jumpy. Their bodies don't relax well. They startle easily or cry at slight noises or on any quick change of position.

Responding to colic. It's hard to be the parent of a fretful, hypertonic, colicky, irritable baby. Your baby may be soothed when you first pick her up, but after a few minutes she's apt to be screaming harder than ever. She thrashes with her arms and kicks with her legs. Not only does she refuse to be comforted, but she acts as if she were angry at you for trying. As the minutes go by and she acts angrier and angrier, you feel that she is spurning you as a parent and you can't help feeling angry with her underneath. But getting angry at a tiny baby makes you ashamed of yourself, and you try hard to suppress the feeling. This makes you tenser than ever.

There are various things you can try to help the situation, but first I think you have to come to terms with your feelings. All parents feel anxious, upset, fearful and incompetent if they can't calm their infant. Most feel guilty, especially if it is their first baby, as if the baby is crying because they are doing something wrong (which is not true). And most parents also get angry at their babies. This is quite normal. Give yourself a break. It isn't your fault that your baby is crying and that you're reacting emotionally. It just means that you truly love your baby; otherwise you wouldn't be so upset.

Never shake a baby. Feelings of desperation and anger drive some parents to shake their babies in a last-ditch effort to get them to stop crying. But the result – a real tragedy – is often severe, permanent brain damage, or even death. Before you get to the point where shaking seems to be a solution, get help. Your baby's doctor is a good place to start. Alternatively, ring Cry-sis (08451 228669), a charity that offers support to families with excessively crying babies. It's important to make sure that *all* of the adults who take care of your child – including grandparents, babysitters and friends – know that it is *never* safe to shake a baby.

Medical evaluation. If you have a baby with colic, the first thing to do is have her examined to make sure there is no obvious medical cause for the crying. It can be very reassuring if a baby is growing and developing normally; sometimes repeated doctor visits are necessary. (A colicky baby who is *not* growing normally deserves a very thorough medical evaluation.)

Once you know that your baby just has colic, you can rest assured that colicky babies don't grow up to be any more or less happy, clever or emotionally healthy than other babies. The trick for you is to get through the next few months with your confidence and good spirits intact.

Help for your baby. First, look again at the list of remedies for crying on page 60. In consultation with your doctor, there are several other things you can try for a colicky infant, as well as the following ideas. All of these approaches work some of the time, but none works all of the time: offer a dummy between feedings; swaddle your baby snugly in a swaddling blanket; rock her in a cradle or pram; use a sling for long walks; take her for a ride in the car; try an infant swing (although most infants get bored and start crying again after a few minutes); play music, soothing or raucous. Hypertonic babies often do best on a quiet regime: quiet room, few visitors, low voices, slow movements in handling them, a firm hold in carrying them, a big pillow (with a waterproof cover) to lie on while being changed and sponge-bathed so that they won't roll, or being swaddled in a swaddling blanket most of the time.

Give your baby a tummy massage with lubricating lotion. Place a warm-water bottle on her tummy. (Make sure it is not too hot: you should be able to rest the inside of your wrist against the warm-water bottle without discomfort. As an extra precaution, wrap it in a cloth nappy or towel.) Lay your baby across your knees or across a warm-water bottle and massage her on the back.

Change what she drinks: try a formula change (this may help as often as half the time), or chamomile or mint tea. If you're breast-feeding, stop drinking milk, coffee, and tea with caffeine, and stop eating chocolate (which also contains caffeine) and foods that cause gas, such as cabbage.

If none of these methods works and if your baby is not hungry, wet or sick, then what? I think it's best to put your baby down in his cot, let him cry for a while, and see if he can calm himself. It's hard to listen to a crying infant without trying to do something, but realistically, what else is there for you to do? Some parents can go out for a little walk while they let their baby cry (as long as there is another adult to watch the baby); others can't bear to leave the room. Do whatever feels right for you, because there is simply no right or wrong way to handle this situation. Many babies fall asleep within ten to twenty minutes. If your baby is still crying after this time, pick her up and try everything again.

Help for yourself. Many parents get worn out and frantic listening to a baby cry, especially when it's their first and they're with their baby constantly. It can really help to get away from home and your baby for a few hours at least twice a week, more often if it can be arranged. It's often best if the parents can go out together. Hire a sitter or ask a friend or neighbour to come in and relieve you.

If you're like many parents, you may hesitate to do this: 'Why should we inflict the baby on somebody else? Besides, we'd be nervous being away for so long.' But you shouldn't think of time off like this as just a treat for you. It's very important for you, your baby and your whole family that you do not get exhausted and depressed. If you can't get anyone to come in, take turns with your partner one or two evenings a week to go out to visit friends or see a film. Your baby doesn't need two parents at a time to listen to her. Invite friends to come in and visit you. Remember that everything that helps you keep a sense of balance, everything that keeps you from getting too preoccupied with your baby, also helps your baby in the long run. (Also, even though it may seem awkward, remember to make sure that whoever watches your baby is aware of the dangers of shaking.)

SPOILING

Can you spoil a baby? This question comes up naturally in the first few weeks at home if a baby is fussing a lot between feedings instead of sleeping peacefully. You pick him up and walk him around and he stops crying, at least for the time being. Lay him down, and he starts all over again. It might feel like your baby is running the show, but it's more likely that such a young baby is simply feeling miserable. If he stops fussing when picked up, it's probably because the motion and distraction and perhaps the warm pressure on his abdomen from being held make him forget his pain or tension at least temporarily.

The answer to the spoiling question really depends on what lessons you think babies are learning in the first months of life. They aren't yet capable of learning to expect their every whim to be attended to twenty-four hours a day; that's what being spoiled would mean. Young infants can't anticipate the future; they live entirely in the here and now. They also can't formulate the thought 'I'm going to make life miserable for these people until they give me everything I want' – another key component of the spoiled child.

What infants are learning during this period is a sense of basic trust in the world. If their needs are met promptly and lovingly, they come to feel that good things generally happen and unhappiness passes, with the help of special people they come to know as parents. The famous psychologist Erik Erikson felt that this sense of basic trust – or the lack of it – forms the core of a person's character, a generally positive approach to people and to life's challenges. So the answer to the question 'Can a young baby be spoiled?' is no, not until six to nine months of age. A better question is, how can you help your baby develop a sense of basic trust? The answer is to try to work out his needs, and meet them.

Spoiling after six months. You can be a little more suspicious by six or seven months. By then, colic and other causes of physical discomfort are usually done. Naturally, some of these babies who were held and walked a great deal during their colicky period have become accustomed to constant attention. They want their walking and their company to continue.

Take the example of a mother who can't stand to hear her baby fret, even for a minute, and who carries him most of the time he's awake. By the age of six months, the baby cries immediately and holds out his arms to be picked up as soon as his mother puts him down. Housework has become impossible. The mother can't help resenting her enslavement, but she can't tolerate the indignant crying, either. The baby is likely to sense the parent's anxiety and resentment and may respond by becoming even more demanding.

This situation is quite different from that of a mother who willingly picks up her baby at the slightest whimper or carries him in a sling all day even if he doesn't fret. In many cultures, babies are rarely left alone until they are walking; these babies aren't spoiled. But it's also fine to leave a baby of six to twelve months to play by himself for a few minutes, and to allow him to wait a bit for your attention. With a very young baby, you try hard to meet his needs; with an older baby, toddler and child, you help him to understand that needs and wants are different things – needs get met, wants *sometimes* get met.

How do you unspoil? It takes willpower and a little hardening of the heart to say no to your baby. To get yourself in the right mood you have to remember that, in the long run, being unreasonably demanding and excessively dependent is worse for babies than for you, and gets them off-kilter with themselves and with the world. So you are reforming them for their own good.

Make out a schedule for yourself, on paper if necessary, that requires you to be busy with housework or anything else while your baby is awake. Go at it with a great bustle – to impress your baby and to impress yourself. Say you are the mother of a baby boy who has become accustomed to being carried all the time. When he frets and raises his arms, explain to him in a friendly but very firm tone that this job and that job must get done this afternoon. Though he doesn't understand the words, he does understand the tone of voice. Stick to your busy work. The first hour of the first day is the hardest.

One baby accepts the change better if his mother stays out of sight a good part of the time at first and talks little. This helps him to become absorbed in something else. Another adjusts more quickly if he can at least see his mother and hear her talking to him, even if she won't pick him up. When you bring him a plaything or show him how to use it, or when you decide it's time to play with him, sit down beside him on the floor. Let him climb into your arms if he wants, but don't get back into the habit of walking him around. If you're on the floor with him, he can crawl away when he eventually realizes you won't walk. If you pick him up and walk him, he'll surely object noisily just as soon as you start to put him down again. If he keeps on fretting indefinitely when you sit with him on the floor, remember another job and get busy again.

What you are trying to do is to help your baby begin to build frustration tolerance – a little at a time. If she does not begin to learn this gradually between six and twelve months, it is a much harder lesson to learn later on.

PHYSICAL DEVELOPMENT

A baby learns to control his body. He starts with his head and gradually works down to his hands, trunk and legs. A lot of early movements are preprogrammed. At birth a baby knows how to suck, and if something touches his cheek – your finger, for example – he tries to reach it with his mouth. After a few days he's more than ready to do his part in nursing. If you try to hold his head still, he becomes angry right away and twists to get it free. (Probably he has this instinct to keep from being smothered.) All on his own, he follows objects with his eyes, usually by about one month if not before, and begins to reach for things.

Using their hands. Some babies can put their thumbs or fingers in their mouths from day one. Ultrasounds during pregnancy show they were doing it in the womb. But most can't get even their hands to their mouths with any regularity until they are two or three months old. And because their fists are still clenched tight, it usually takes them longer still to get hold of a thumb separately.

At about two or three months, many babies will spend

hours just looking at their hands. They bring them up until, surprised, they bang themselves in the nose – only to stretch their arms out and start all over again. This is the beginning of eye-hand coordination.

The main business of hands is to grab things. A baby seems to know ahead of time what he's going to be learning next. Weeks before he can actually grab an object, he looks as if he wants to and is trying. At this stage, if you put a rattle into his hand, he holds on to it and waves it.

Around the middle of the first year, he learns how to grab something that's brought within arm's reach, and how to transfer an object from one hand to the other. Gradually he handles things more expertly. Starting around nine months, he loves to pick up tiny objects, especially those you don't want him to (like a speck of dirt), carefully and deliberately.

Right- and left-handedness. The subject of handedness in children is somewhat confusing. Most babies use either hand equally well for the first year or two and then gradually become right- or left-handed. It's unusual for a baby to prefer the right or left hand in the first six to nine months. About 10 per cent of all people are left-handed. Handedness tends to run in families, so some families will have several lefties and others may have none. Since handedness is an inborn trait, it's a mistake to try to force a left-handed child to become right-handed. This is confusing to the brain, which has been set up to work by a different scheme. Handedness also applies to a preference for the right or left leg and eye.

Rolling over and falling off. The age when babies roll over, sit up, crawl, stand up or walk is more variable than the age when they get control of their head or arms. A lot depends on temperament and weight. A wiry, energetic baby is in a great rush to get moving. A plump, placid one may be willing to wait until later.

A baby should never be left unguarded on a table for even as long as it takes you to turn your back. Since you can't be sure when that first roll will happen, it's safest to always keep a hand on your baby when she's up high. Once she can roll, it's not safe to leave her even in the middle of an adult's bed. It is amazing how fast a baby can reach the edge, and many do fall from an adult bed to the floor, which makes a parent feel very guilty.

If a baby cries immediately after a fall from a bed, then stops crying and regains his normal colour and activities within a few minutes, he probably has not been injured. If you notice any change in behaviour in the next hours or days (fussier, sleepier or not eating, for example), call your doctor and describe the event; in most cases, you will be reassured that your baby is well. If you child has lost consciousness, even for a short time, you need to call the doctor promptly.

Sitting up. Most babies learn to sit steadily without support after being helped up at seven to nine months. But before babies have the coordination to succeed, they want to try. When you take hold of their hands, they attempt to pull themselves up. This eagerness always raises the question in a parent's mind: 'At what age can I prop my baby up in the pushchair or high chair?' In general, it's better not to prop babies straight up until they can sit steadily by themselves for many minutes. This doesn't mean that you can't pull them up to a sitting position for fun, or sit them in your lap, or prop them on a slant in the pushchair, just as long as the neck and back are straight. It's a curled-over position that's not good for long periods.

This brings up the question of high chairs. They're great for letting your baby eat meals with the rest of the family, but falling out of one is bad news. If you are going to use a high chair, get one with a broad base so that it doesn't tip over easily, and always use the strap to buckle your baby in. Don't ever leave a baby alone in a high or low chair.

Squirming while being changed. Babies rarely lie still while being changed or dressed. It goes completely against their nature. From the time they learn to roll over until about one year, when they can be dressed standing up, they may struggle against lying down or cry indignantly as if they have never heard of such an outrage.

There are a few things that can help. One baby can be distracted by a parent who makes funny noises, another by a small bit of biscuit. You can have an especially fascinating toy, like a music box or a special mobile, that you offer at dressing time only. Distract your baby just before you lay her down, not after she starts yelling.

Creeping and crawling. Creeping, when your baby begins to drag himself across the floor, can begin any time between six months and one year. Crawling on hands and

knees usually starts a few months later. Occasionally, some perfectly normal babies never creep or crawl at all; they just sit around until they learn to stand up.

There are a dozen different ways of creeping and crawling, and babies may change their style as they become more expert. One first learns to creep backward, another sideways, like a crab. One wants to crawl on her hands and toes with her legs straight, another on his hands and knees, still another on one knee and one foot. The baby who learns to be a speedy creeper may be late in walking, and the one who is a clumsy creeper, or who never learns to creep at all, has a good reason for learning to walk early.

Standing. Standing usually comes in the last quarter of the first year, but an ambitious and advanced baby may stand as early as seven months. Occasionally you see one who doesn't stand until after one year but seems to be bright and healthy in all other respects. Some of these are plump, easygoing babies. Others just seem to be slow getting coordination in their legs. These children almost always turn out just fine. It's reassuring if the doctor finds them healthy and they seem bright and responsive in other ways.

Quite a number of babies get themselves into a jam when they first learn to stand up, because they don't yet know how to sit down again. One poor thing stands until she is frantic with exhaustion. The parents take pity on their baby, unhitch her from the railing of her playpen, and sit her down. But instantly she forgets all about her fatigue and pulls herself to her feet again. This time she is crying within a few minutes. The best a parent can do is to give her especially interesting things to play with while she's sitting, wheel her in the pushchair longer than usual, and take comfort in the fact that she'll probably learn how to sit down within a week. One day she tries it. Very carefully she lets her behind down as far as her arms reach and, after a long moment of hesitation, plops down. She finds that it wasn't such a long drop and that her seat is well padded.

As the weeks go by, she learns to move around while hanging on, first with two hands, then with one. This is called cruising. Eventually she has enough balance to let go altogether for a few seconds when she is absorbed and doesn't realize what a daring thing she's doing. She is getting ready for walking.

Walking. Babies walk alone when they're ready to; lots of factors come into play. Inheritance probably plays the largest role, followed by ambition, boldness, heaviness and how well they can get places by crawling. A baby who is just beginning to walk when an illness lays her up for two weeks may not try again for a month or more. One who is just learning and has a fall may refuse to let go with her hands again for many weeks.

Most babies learn to walk between twelve and fifteen months. A few start as early as nine months, some as late as eighteen. In otherwise healthy babies, the age of walking doesn't have much to do with other developmental attainments. A late walker is no more likely to be slow intellectually than an early one. You don't have to do anything to teach your child to walk. When her muscles, her nerves and her spirit are ready, you won't be able to stop her. (The devices called 'walkers' don't help babies learn to walk sooner, and they're dangerous; see page 127.)

DR SPOCK COMMENTS

I remember a mother who got herself into a jam by walking her baby around a great deal before he was able to do it by himself. He was so delighted with this suspended walking that he demanded it all day long. Needless to say, she was tired and bored long before he was.

Bowlegs, toeing in, toeing out. A parent of an early walker may worry that it's bad for the baby's legs. For the most part, though, children's physiques are able to stand whatever they're ready to do by themselves. Babies sometimes become bowlegged or knock-kneed in the early months of walking, but this happens with late walkers as well as with early walkers. Most babies toe out to some degree when they start to walk and then gradually bring the front part of the feet in. One baby starts with the feet sticking right out to the sides, like Charlie Chaplin, and ends up toeing out only moderately. The average baby starts toeing out moderately and ends up with the feet almost parallel. The baby who starts out with feet almost parallel is more apt to end up toeing in. Toeing in and bowlegs often go together.

The straightness of legs, ankles and feet depends on several factors, including a baby's inborn pattern of development. Some babies seem to have a tendency to knock-knees and ankles that sag inward. The heavy child is more apt to develop these conditions. Other babies – especially active, athletic ones – seem to be born with a tendency to bowlegs

and toeing in. Another factor may be the position babies keep their feet and legs in. For instance, you occasionally see a foot that becomes turned in at the ankle because the baby always sits with that foot tucked under him.

You can ask your doctor to examine hips, knees, ankles and feet regularly; if weak ankles, knock-knees, bowlegs or toeing in develop, corrective measures may be recommended, but most of these conditions resolve themselves over time.

LEARNING ABOUT PEOPLE

Changing reactions to strangers. You can get an idea of how your baby goes from phase to phase in development by watching his reaction to strangers at different ages. This is how it goes in a doctor's office for a typical baby until he's about a year old: at two months he doesn't pay much attention to the doctor. As he lies on the examining table, he keeps looking over his shoulder at his mother. The four-month-old is the doctor's delight. He breaks into a body-wiggling smile just as often as the doctor is willing to smile and make noises at him. By five or six months, the baby may have begun to change his mind; by nine months he is certain that the doctor is a stranger and therefore to be feared. When the doctor approaches, he stops his kicking and cooing. His body freezes as he eyes the doctor intently, even suspiciously, maybe for twenty seconds. Finally his chin puckers and he begins to shriek. He may get so worked up that he cries long after the appointment is over.

Stranger anxiety. The nine-month-old baby isn't only suspicious of the doctor; anything new and unfamiliar makes him anxious, even a new hat on his mother or his father's clean-shaven face if he usually has a beard. This behaviour is called stranger anxiety, and it's very interesting to think about what has changed to make your baby go from loving everyone to being a suspicious worrywart.

Before about six months of age, babies can recognize when they have seen something before (we know, because they tend to stare longer at such things), but they don't seem to really *think* about things as being either strange or familiar. This is probably because in a four-month-old the thinking part of the brain – the outer layer, or cortex – is not yet fully online. By six months, the cortex is much more functional. One result is that babies now have much better memory skills. They clearly recognize the difference

between what is familiar and what is strange, and they seem to have the ability to understand that strange things might be dangerous. You can almost watch this thought process take place as your baby first stares at the stranger, then back at you, then back to the stranger, and finally several seconds later bursts into tears.

At six to nine months babies are much cleverer, but they still aren't good at predicting what is likely to happen next based on past experience. A six-month-old lives pretty much in the present. So when there is a stranger right in front of him, he can't understand why it's not a familiar person, and he can't figure out any good that will come of this situation. He also can't do much about the situation except protest and cry. By twelve to fifteen months, when stranger anxiety is generally on the way out, the infant is better at learning from the past and anticipating the future: 'Maybe I don't know who this person is, but nothing awful has happened in the past, so I can handle this stranger without panicking.'

Some babies (about one in seven) become particularly anxious in response to strange things and people. Even as small infants, their hearts beat faster when they see something unexpected, and all through childhood they tend to be extracautious. As toddlers, for example, they often hang back for a long time in a new situation before joining in. This temperament trait is often called 'slow to warm up,' a very appropriate name. It is inborn, a result of the way the child's brain works, not the result of early parenting practices. Most importantly, it is not an illness, and it is not something that needs to be fixed.

If your baby seems especially sensitive about new people and new places in the middle of the first year, it's sensible to protect him from too much fright by making strangers keep at a little distance until he gets used to them. Don't keep him from seeing strangers, though. In time, through repeated exposure, things that were strange become more familiar, and even children who are slow to warm up become more comfortable.

CLOTHES AND EQUIPMENT

Shoes: when and what kind? In most cases, there's no need to put anything on your baby's feet until he walks outdoors. Indoors, babies' feet stay cool just the way their hands do, so they aren't uncomfortable barefoot. In other words, there's no necessity for knitted booties or soft shoes in the first year unless the floor is unusually cold.

After a baby is standing and walking, there's a real value in leaving the child barefoot most of the time when conditions are suitable. The arches are relatively flat at first. The baby gradually builds the arches up and strengthens the ankles by using them vigorously in standing and walking. Walking on an uneven or rough surface also fosters the use of the foot and leg muscles.

Of course, a child who is walking needs shoes outdoors in cold weather and when walking on pavements and other surfaces that are hazardous. But it's good for a child to continue to go barefoot (or with socks) indoors till the age of two or three and outdoors, too, in warm weather at the beach, in the sandpit, and in other safe places.

Semisoft-soled shoes are best at first, so that your child's feet have a better chance to move. Shoes with fancy supports are pretty much a waste of money. The important thing is to have the shoes big enough so that the toes aren't cramped but not so big that they almost slip off.

Small children outgrow their shoes at a discouragingly fast rate, sometimes in two months, and parents should form the habit of feeling the shoes every few weeks to make sure they are still large enough. There must be more than just enough space for the toes because as the child walks, the toes are squeezed forwards into the front of the shoe with each step. There should be enough empty space in the toe of the shoe as the child stands that you can get about half your thumbnail, about 6 mm (¼ in), onto the tip of the shoe before running into the child's toe. You can't judge while the child is sitting down, since the feet fill more of the shoe when a person is standing. Naturally, the shoes should be comfortably wide, too. There are soft, adjustable shoes that can be let out a full size. It's helpful to have a nonskid sole so that your child learns to walk before he learns to skate. You can rough up a smooth sole with coarse sandpaper.

Choose inexpensive shoes as long as they fit well. Canvas shoes are just fine as long as they don't cause excessive sweating. The feet are pudgy the first couple of years; as a result, low shoes sometimes do not stay on as well as high-top shoes. There isn't any other reason for ankle-high shoes; the ankles don't need extra support.

Playpens. A playpen can be a great help, especially for the busy parent, from about three months on. A playpen in the lounge, kitchen or home office lets a baby be near the action without the danger of being stepped on or spilled on. When babies are old enough to stand up, the playpen gives them a railing to hold onto and a firm foundation under their feet. In good weather they can sit safely in the playpen on the patio.

If you are going to use a playpen, it's best if your baby gets accustomed to it at three or four months, before he has learned to sit and crawl and before he has had the freedom of the floor. Otherwise he might consider it a prison from the start. By the time he can sit and crawl, he has fun going after things that are a metre or so away and handling larger objects, like cooking spoons, saucepans and strainers. When he becomes bored with the playpen, he can sit in a bouncing chair or a chair-table arrangement. It's good for him to have some free crawling time, too.

Even if they are willing, babies should not be kept in playpens all the time. They need time for explorative crawling – with an adult watching. Every hour or so they should be played with, hugged and perhaps carried around in a sling for a spell. Between twelve and eighteen months, the period of time for which most babies will tolerate the playpen grows increasingly shorter.

Swings. Swings are useful after babies have learned to sit and before they learn to walk. Some swings are for indoors or out, some have motors, some are for use in doorways, and others have springs so your baby can bounce. The springs should have covers to prevent finger injury, or the coils should not be more than 3 mm

(⅛ in) apart. One baby is happy swinging for a long time, while another grows bored fairly soon. Swings keep babies from getting into as much trouble as they would crawling, but babies shouldn't spend their whole days in swings. They need lots of opportunities to crawl, explore, stand and walk.

Walkers. You might think that walkers would help babies walk. Actually, they interfere with learning to walk because all babies have to do to get around is to thrash their legs; they don't have to balance. This is particularly the case with walkers with an inbuilt seat. Different skills are needed to walk, and the baby who uses a walker may be less motivated to learn them. After all, she gets around fine under her own steam. Why learn something new, like walking, that is more difficult?

Walkers, especially those with an inbuilt seat, injure babies. They raise the baby's height so that she can reach objects that may hurt her; they raise her centre of gravity so that it's easier for her to tip over; and they allow her to move forward at an amazingly fast rate. Terrible injuries have come from babies falling down flights of stairs in their walkers. Baby walkers should not be produced. If you already own one, the safest course is to take the wheels off so it can't roll, or just throw it out.

COMMON PHYSICAL ISSUES IN THE FIRST YEAR

It's best to consult your doctor or nurse practitioner promptly about any change in your baby's health. Don't try to diagnose it yourself – there is too much chance of error. There are many other causes of the problems mentioned here. This discussion is mainly to help you to deal with a few common types of mild physical concerns of early infancy, after the doctor has made a diagnosis.

Hiccups. Most babies hiccup pretty regularly after meals in the early months. In fact, many babies can be seen hiccupping on the antenatal ultrasound and can be felt hiccupping during the last stages of pregnancy. It doesn't seem to mean anything, and there is nothing that you need to do, aside from seeing if they have to burp. If you want to try something, a drink of warm water occasionally stops the hiccups.

Spitting up and vomiting. When a small amount of curdled milk spills gently out of the baby's mouth, that's spitting up. When the stomach contents are ejected in large quantity with enough force to propel them several centimetres, that's vomiting.

Babies spit up because the muscle that closes off the entrance to the stomach hasn't fully developed. Anything that increases the pressure in the stomach – joggling, squeezing too tightly, laying the baby down, or just the digestive motions of the stomach itself – causes stomach contents to flow in the wrong direction. Most babies do a lot of spitting up during the early months. Some spit up several times after every feeding. Others do it only occasionally. Milk sometimes comes out of their noses; this isn't a sign of anything dire, merely that the nose and the mouth are connected. (Milk stains come out of sheets, nappies and clothing more easily if they are first soaked in cold water.)

The tendency to spit up is usually greatest in the early weeks and months. Most babies have stopped by the time they can sit up; some continue until they're walking. Once in a while babies only start spitting up when they are several months old. Sometimes teething seems to make it worse for a while. Spitting up is messy and inconvenient but not important if the baby is gaining weight well, isn't bothered by coughing or gagging, and is happy.

Vomiting is different. It alarms new parents when their baby first vomits a large amount of milk. But this is not serious as long as it doesn't happen often and the baby seems otherwise happy and healthy and is gaining weight well. There are a few babies who vomit a large amount as often as once a day, especially in the early weeks. It's worthwhile taking extra care to burp the baby, but in most cases the spitting up or vomiting goes right on, no matter how you change the formula, decrease the quantity or burp him.

If a baby vomits what seems like a whole feeding and seems happy enough, don't feed her until she acts very hungry. The stomach may be a little upset, and it is better to give it a chance to quiet down. Remember that the amount vomited usually looks larger than it actually is. There are babies who you would swear are vomiting most of every feeding but who still go on gaining weight satisfactorily.

Whether or not the spit-up or vomited milk is sour and curdled is not important. The first step in digestion in the stomach is the secretion of acid. Any food that has been in the stomach for a while is acidified, and the effect of acid on milk is to curdle it.

Spitting up after feedings or occasional vomiting are nothing to worry about. When should you call the doctor?

- Spitting up along with irritability, crying, gagging, arching of the back, coughing or poor weight gain. These can be signs of gastro-oesophageal reflux (see page 64).
- New onset of vomiting (more than one or two episodes), especially if the vomiting is forceful or if what comes up looks yellowish or greenish, a sign that there is bile in it.
- Vomiting along with fever or a change in activity (sleepier, less playful, irritable), or other signs of illness.
- Vomiting or spitting up that is concerning to you for any reason. Even if it turns out to be plain old spitting up, it's never wrong to seek reassurance from your doctor.

Changes in the colour of the stool. Brown, yellow or green – it simply doesn't matter. Bowel movements come in many colours, and none is healthier than the next. You should be concerned if the bowel movement turns black (this could indicate lots of blood, which turns black and tarry-looking as it goes down the intestines), red or chalk white, which can indicate a problem with the bile. Beets and some red juices can turn the stool red, too.

Constipation. Constipation refers to hard, dry stools that are difficult to pass. It's not the number of movements each day that determines whether or not a baby has constipation. Passing hard stools can cause small streaks of red blood on the stool; it's usually not serious, but ask the doctor.

Constipation sometimes starts when the older breastfed baby is first begun on solid foods. It seems as though his intestine has had such an easy time with the breast milk, it doesn't know what to do with different foods. The baby develops firm, infrequent stools and seems uncomfortable. You can offer a little sugar water (one teaspoon of granulated sugar to 60 ml/2 fl oz of water), prune, apple or pear juice (start with 60 ml/2 fl oz; ask the doctor before giving more than 120 ml/4 fl oz), or stewed prunes (start with two teaspoons a day). Some babies get cramps from prunes, but most don't. If constipation lasts longer than a week, check with the doctor.

Formula-fed babies can also become constipated. Adding 120 ml (4 fl oz) a day of water or prune juice often loosens things up. If this doesn't work, or if constipation is severe, it's important to ask the doctor. Some parents feel that the iron in infant formula causes constipation, but studies have not found this to be the case, and the iron is needed for brain growth, so low-iron formula is not a good cure for constipation.

Diarrhoea. A baby's intestines are sensitive during the first year or two and may be upset not only by infections but also by a new food or by too much fruit juice. Fortunately, this kind of upset is usually mild: a couple of extra stools that are looser than usual, greenish and unusually smelly. Most important, the baby acts well or almost well. He is playful and active, urinates as often as usual, and doesn't have more in the way of illness than perhaps a slightly stuffy nose or a mild decrease in appetite. In a couple of days, without any special treatment, the symptoms usually disappear.

Doctors used to tell parents to take these babies off solids and formula and instead give a lot of liquids that are high in sugar (such as apple juice). But this strategy actually makes diarrhoea worse. It's better to simply offer breast milk or formula and the baby's regular diet (except for any new food you think might have triggered the diarrhoea) and let him eat as much as he seems hungry for. If the diarrhoea lasts more than two or three days, consult the doctor, even if your baby continues to act healthy. For more on diarrhoea and dehydration, see page 422.

Rashes in general. It's always reasonable to show an unidentified rash to your baby's doctor. Rashes are often hard to describe in words, and while most rashes aren't too serious, some are signs of illnesses that need prompt medical attention.

Common nappy rash. Most babies have sensitive skin. The nappy region often suffers because the skin there stays moist, even with the most absorbent nappies. That's why the best treatment for almost any nappy rash is to go nappy-free for a few hours a day. A good time is right after a bowel movement, since there is less likelihood of action in the near future. Fold a nappy underneath your baby or put him on a large waterproof pad (boys are apt to spray, so keep some paper towels handy). Almost all babies develop a few spots of nappy rash from time to time. If it is slight and goes away as fast as it came, no special treatment is necessary except air drying.

Don't wash the nappy area with soap while there is a rash, because soap can be irritating. Use plain water instead of baby wipes. You can give the skin a protective coating by slathering on petroleum jelly or any of the nappy ointments. Some nappy services use special rinses in the case of nappy rash. If you wash the nappies at home, try adding half a cup of white vinegar to the last rinse.

A nappy rash caused by yeast (also called candida) will have bright red spots that often come together to form an area that is solidly red, bordered by the red spots. Treatment is with a prescription anti-yeast cream. A rash with blisters or pus (especially with fever, but even without) is likely to be caused by bacteria and should be seen by a doctor.

Rash from diarrhoea. Irritating bowel movements during an attack of diarrhoea sometimes cause a very sore rash around the anus or a smooth, bright red rash on the buttocks. The treatment is to try to change the nappy just as soon as it is soiled – which is no small task. Then clean the area with oil, or if the area is too sore to wipe, hold the baby's bottom under warm water from a running tap, pat him dry, and apply a thick covering of a protective ointment (one brand is as good as another). If this doesn't work, the nappy should be left off and the nappy area exposed to the air. Sometimes it seems that while the baby has diarrhoea, nothing helps very much. Fortunately, this rash cures itself as soon as the diarrhoea is over.

Rashes on the face. There are several mild face rashes that babies have in the first few months that aren't definite enough to have names but are very common. Milia are minute shiny white spots without any redness around them. They look like tiny pearls in the skin. In this case, the oil glands in the skin are making oil but they haven't opened up to the skin yet, so the oil packets just sit there. Over the next weeks or months, the oil ducts open up and let the oil out.

Some babies have collections of a few small red spots or smooth spots on the cheeks and forehead. They look like acne, and that's exactly what they are. They are caused by exposure to the mother's hormones in the womb. These may last a long time and get a parent quite upset. At times they fade and then get red again. Different ointments don't seem to do much good, but these spots always go away eventually.

Erythema toxicum consists of splotchy red patches that are 6–13 mm (¼–½ in) in diameter, some of them with a tiny white pimple head. In darker-skinned infants, the splotches can be purplish in colour. They come and go on different parts of the face and body. We don't know what causes this common rash, but once it goes away, it doesn't come back. Larger, pus-filled blisters or spots could be infections and should be reported promptly to the doctor.

An irritated rash with scaling and flaking on the cheeks may be eczema; it often runs in families. See page 570.

Rashes on body and scalp. *Prickly heat* is very common in the shoulder and neck region of babies when hot weather first begins. It looks like clusters of very small pink spots surrounded by blotches that are pink in light-skinned babies and may be dark red or purplish in dark-skinned ones. Tiny blisters form on some of the spots. When they dry up they can give the rash a slightly tan look. Prickly heat usually starts around the neck; it may spread down onto the chest and back and up around the ears and face, but it seldom bothers a baby. You can pat this rash several times a day with a bicarbonate of soda solution (one teaspoon bicarbonate of soda to 250 ml/8 fl oz water) on absorbent cotton. Another treatment is dusting with cornstarch powder (avoid talcum powder because it can irritate the lungs). Most prickly heat goes away on its own without any special treatment. It is more important to try to keep the baby cool. Don't be afraid to take off the baby's clothes in hot weather.

Cradle cap (seborrhoea) appears as patches on the scalp that look like greasy yellow or reddish crusts. It can also occur on the face, in the nappy area and elsewhere on the body. Try oiling the patches to soften them and then washing with a mild dandruff shampoo and brushing out the scales. Don't leave the oil on for too long before shampooing it out, however. Medicated shampoos and prescription medication can also help. Cradle cap rarely persists beyond the first six months.

Impetigo is a bacterial infection of the skin. It's not generally serious, but it is contagious. It starts with a very delicate small blister that contains yellowish fluid or white pus and is surrounded by reddened skin. The blister is easily broken and leaves a small raw spot. It does not develop a thick crust in infants as it does in older children. It's apt to start in a moist place, such as at the edge of the nappy or in the groin or armpit. New spots may develop. Over-the-counter antibacterial ointments and air drying can help. Arrange the clothing and bedclothes so that they do not cover the spot or spots, and keep the room warmer than usual if necessary. During impetigo, disinfect the nappies, sheets, underclothing, babygros, towels and washcloths, using ordinary bleach in the wash, according to the directions on the bottle. If the problem doesn't clear up promptly, call the doctor. Prescription antibiotics may be needed.

Mouth troubles. *Thrush* is a very common mild yeast infection. It looks like patches of milk scum stuck to the cheeks or tongue or roof of the mouth. But, unlike milk, it does not wipe off easily. If you do rub it off, the underlying skin may bleed slightly and look inflamed. Thrush can make babies' mouths sore and they may fuss when nursing. A prescription medication applied inside the mouth several times a day usually cures the problem, although it may come back later. If there is a delay in getting medical advice, it is helpful to have your baby drink 15 ml (½ fl oz) of water after the milk. This washes the milk out of the mouth and gives the thrush fewer nutrients to live on. Don't be fooled by the colour of the inner sides of the gums where the upper molar teeth are going to be. The skin colour here is normally very pale and is sometimes mistaken for thrush by mothers who are on the lookout for it.

Cysts on the gums and the roof of the mouth. Some babies have one or two little pearly white cysts on the sharp edge of their gums. They may remind you of teeth, but they are too round and they don't make a click on a spoon. Similar cysts can often be seen on the roof of the mouth, along the ridge that runs from front to back. They have no importance and eventually disappear.

Teething is discussed on page 522.

Eye troubles. Many babies develop a mild redness of the eyes a few days after birth. This is probably caused by an immature tear duct that may be partially obstructed. It doesn't require any treatment, as it usually clears up by itself.

Blocked tear duct. Another kind of very mild but chronic infection of the eyelids develops off and on in the early months in many babies, often in only one eye. The eye waters and tears excessively, particularly in windy weather. White matter collects in the corner of the eye and along the edges of the lids. This discharge may keep the lids stuck together when your baby first wakes up. The cause is a blocked tear duct. The tear duct is a tiny tube that carries tears from the inner corner of the eye into the nose. When this duct is blocked, tears can't drain off fast enough; they well up in the eye and run down the cheek. The lids keep getting mildly infected because the eye is not being cleansed well by the tears. The usual treatment is gentle massage of the tear ducts to try to open them up; your doctor will show you how to do this. Antibiotic drops or ointments may be needed, too.

Blocked tear ducts are not serious, but the condition may last for months. If it hasn't gone away by one year of age, an eye doctor may open up the duct with a small metal probe (this procedure sounds worse than it is). When the lids are stuck together, you can soften the crust and open the eye by gently applying warm water (not hot – the eyelid skin is very sensitive to temperature) with your washed fingers or a clean washcloth.

Conjunctivitis. A transparent tissue lines the eyelids and covers the whites of the eyes. Conjunctivitis, an infection of that tissue, causes the whites of the eyes to look bloodshot or even pink. Usually there is a discharge of yellow or white pus from the eye. The doctor should be called promptly. See also page 597.

Crossed eyes. It's never normal for eyes to be fixed in a crossed position, but it is normal for them to cross now and then, up until three or four months of age. After that, even fleeting crossed eyes should be reported to the doctor. Another reason babies' eyes sometimes appear crossed is that when they are looking at something in their hands they have to converge (cross) the eyes a lot to focus on it, because babies' arms are so short. They are only converging their eyes normally, the way we adults do to a lesser extent. Their eyes won't get stuck that way. Parents often ask whether it is safe to hang toys over the cot, since the baby sometimes is cross-eyed looking at them. Don't hang a toy right on top of a baby's nose; hang it a foot away or more. (See page 98 for safety considerations.)

Sometimes parents think their baby's eyes are crossed when they are really straight, an illusion caused by the base of the nose being wider in babies; a doctor will know what to look for. It's also not uncommon in a newborn baby for the lid of one eye to droop a little lower than the other or for one eye to look smaller. In most cases, these differences become less and less noticeable with time.

It is important for infants' eyes to be examined promptly if there is a question about whether they are straight, in order to preserve the child's vision. When the two eyes do not converge on an object, each eye sees a somewhat different scene. In response, the brain suppresses the vision of one eye, a condition known as lazy eye. In time, the brain loses the capacity to process visual information from that eye.

The eye doctor's job is to promptly put the lazy eye back to work, usually by having the child wear a patch over the good eye for long periods of time. The eye doctor may also prescribe glasses to further encourage the coordinated use of both eyes. Occasionally one or more operations have to be performed to get the eyes pointing in the same direction.

Breathing troubles. Babies sneeze easily. Sneezing is most often caused by dust and dried mucus that has collected in the front of the nose and tickles; it doesn't mean a cold unless the nose begins to run, too.

Chronic noisy breathing is common and usually not serious; still, every baby with noisy breathing should be examined by a doctor. Many babies make a soft snoring noise in the back of the nose. It's just like a grown-up snoring, except that babies do it while they are awake. It seems to be caused by the fact that they haven't yet learned to control their soft palates, and they will outgrow it.

A common type of chronic noisy breathing is caused by underdevelopment of the cartilage around the larynx (voice box). As the baby inhales, the cartilage flops together and rattles, causing the noise, which doctors call *stridor*. It sounds as if the baby is choking, but she can breathe that way indefinitely. In most cases the stridor occurs only when the baby is breathing hard, especially during a cold. It usually goes away when she is quiet or asleep. It may be better when she lies face down. If your baby has stridor, by all means talk with your doctor. The new onset of stridor is always important, because it can be due to something the baby choked on. Mild stridor goes away as the baby grows older.

Noisy breathing that comes on suddenly in an infant or child may be due to croup, asthma or other infection, and requires prompt medical attention (see page 406).

Breath-holding spells. Some babies get so furiously angry when they are frustrated that they cry and then hold their breath and turn blue. When this first happens, it's bound to scare the wits out of the parents. (It's often a baby who's quite happy at other times.) You should be reassured that no one can hold her breath to death. In the worst-case scenario, the baby holds her breath for so long that she blacks out; at that point, the body assumes control and starts breathing again. The occasional baby holds her breath so long she not only blacks out but also has seizure-like movements. This is terrifying to watch but not actually dangerous. A different sort of breath-holding spell occurs when a baby is startled or suddenly in pain, cries once, then passes out.

Talk with your doctor about any breath-holding episodes. Once you're reassured that there's nothing medically wrong, there isn't much else to do. If there's low iron, iron drops can help. You can try to divert your baby's attention when she starts to fuss, by encouraging another activity. But this won't work all the time. It also helps to remember that breath-holding spells aren't truly dangerous and usually go away by the time the child starts preschool.

YOUR TODDLER, TWELVE TO TWENTY-FOUR MONTHS

WHAT MAKES THEM TICK?

Feeling their oats. One year is an exciting age. Babies are changing in lots of ways – in their eating, in how they get around, in how they understand the world, in what they want to do, and in how they feel about themselves and other people. When they were little and helpless, you could put them where you wanted them, give them the playthings you thought suitable, and feed them the foods you knew were best. Most of the time they were willing to let you be the boss. It's more complicated now that they are around a year old. They seem to realize that they're not meant to be baby dolls the rest of their lives, that they're human beings with ideas and wills of their own.

By fifteen to eighteen months, your child's behaviour makes it clear that she's heading for what is often called the 'terrible twos' – a slanderous term, because two years is a marvellous and exciting, if challenging, age. When you suggest something that doesn't appeal to her, she feels she must assert herself. Her nature tells her to. It's the beginning of the process called individuation, when she begins to become a person in her own right. The honeymoon with you is over, at least partly, because to become her own person she needs to push back against your control.

So she may begin to say no in words or actions, even about things that she likes to do. Some call this negativism, but stop and think what would happen if she never disagreed with you. She'd never learn anything through trial and error, which is the best way to learn; she'd just have to memorize everything you said. She'd never learn to think for herself and make her own decisions.

The process of separating from you begins at this stage. While you may feel rejected sometimes, and it's surely hard to give up control, this process is part of your child's growth as a human being. So say good-bye to that special bond of unquestioning, unconditional love that your infant once gave you, and say hello to a more complicated relationship with this newly emerging person.

Independence and outgoingness. A baby grows more dependent and more independent at the same time. This sounds contradictory, but that's how babies are. A parent complains about a one-year-old boy, 'He's begun to cry every time I go out of the room.' This doesn't mean that he is developing a bad habit. Rather, he's growing up and realizing how much he depends on his parents. It's inconvenient, but it's a good sign. Yet at this very age he is also becoming more independent: he is developing the urge to be on his own, discover new places and befriend unfamiliar people.

Watch a baby at the crawling stage when his parent is washing the dishes. He plays contentedly with some pots and pans for a while. Then he gets a little bored and decides to explore in the dining room. He creeps around under the furniture there, picking up little pieces of dust and tasting them. After a while he feels the need for company again and suddenly scrambles back into the kitchen. At one time you see his urge for independence getting the upper hand; at another, his need for security. He satisfies each in turn.

As the months go by, he becomes bolder and more daring in his experiments and explorations. He still needs his parents, but not as often. He is building his independence, but part of his courage comes from knowing he can get security when he needs it.

Independence comes from security as well as from freedom. A few people get that twisted around backward. They try to train independence into children by leaving them in a room by themselves for long periods, even though they are crying for company. But when parents force the issue this hard, a child is learning that the world is a mean place, which makes him even more dependent in the long run.

At around a year old, your baby is at a fork in the road. Given a chance, she will gradually become more independent: more sociable with outsiders (both grown-ups and children), more self-reliant and more outgoing. Stranger anxiety, so intense at nine months, begins to wane. If she's confined a great deal, kept away from others, and used to having only her parents around, it may take longer for her to become sociable outside of the home. The most important thing is for a one-year-old to have a strong attachment to consistent caregivers. With a solid foundation of emotional security, outgoingness will eventually come.

The passion to explore. One-year-olds are determined explorers. They poke into every nook and cranny, shake a table or anything else that isn't nailed down, want to take every single book out of the bookcase, climb onto anything they can reach, fit little things into big things, and then try to fit big things into little things. In short, they are into everything.

Like everything else, their curiosity is a two-edged sword. On the one hand, it's the way your child learns. He has to find out about the size and shape and movableness of everything, and test his own skill before he can advance to the next stage. His endless exploration is a sign that he's bright in mind and spirit.

On the other hand, this can be a physically exhausting and trying time for you, requiring your constant attention to allow him to explore but at the same time make sure that he is safe.

HELP YOUR TODDLER EXPLORE SAFELY

Exploration and risk. When a baby has learned to walk, it's time to let her out of her pushchair on her daily outings. Never mind if she gets dirty; she should. Try to go to a place where you don't have to be after her every minute and where she can get used to other children. If she picks up cigarette butts, you have to jump up, take them away and show her something else that's fun. You can't let her eat handfuls of sand or earth, because it will irritate her intestines. If she puts everything in her mouth, try giving her a hard biscuit or some clean object to chew on to keep her mouth busy.

Such are the ordinary risks of independence at this age. Keeping an able-bodied walking baby tucked in her push-chair may keep her out of trouble, but it also hinders her development and dampens her spirit.

Avoiding injuries. One year is a dangerous age. Parents cannot prevent all injuries. If they were careful enough or worried enough to succeed, they would only make a child timid and dependent. All children will get some cuts and bruises as a natural part of their active, healthy play. But if you keep your guard up and take a few simple precautionary measures, you can protect your children from serious injury. See pages 448–92, 'Preventing Injuries'.

Let them out of the playpen. One child is willing to stay in the playpen, at least for short periods, as late as a year and a half. Another thinks it's a prison by the time she's nine months. Most accept it well enough until they learn to walk. Let your baby out of the playpen when she feels unhappy there, but not necessarily at the first whimper. If you give her something new to play with, she may be content for another hour. Outgrowing the pen is a gradual process. At first she gets sick of it only after a long spell. Gradually she gets impatient earlier. It may be months before she objects to being put in at all. In any case, let her out each time she's sure she's had enough.

Harness or wrist lead? Many toddlers naturally stay close to a parent when out in a supermarket or shopping mall, but some very active and adventurous ones are apt to wander off, giving their parents heart attacks. For these children, a harness that ties around the upper body or a wrist lead can be very practical. Will some people give you disapproving stares for leashing your child? Possibly. Should that worry you? No. Safety is the main objective, and anything that helps your child to feel safe while exploring and at the same time allows you to relax and enjoy your child is a good thing.

DR SPOCK COMMENTS

When I tell parents that their toddler has outgrown the playpen and that they ought to let her on the floor, they are apt to look unhappy and say, 'But I'm afraid she'll hurt herself. At the least, she'll wreck the house.'

Sooner or later she must be let out to roam around, if not at ten months, at least by fifteen months, when she's walking. And she's not going to be any more reasonable or easier to control then. At whatever age you give her the freedom of the house, you will have to make adjustments, so it's better to do it when she is ready.

Arranging the house for a wandering baby. How do you keep a one-year-old baby from hurting herself? First of all, you can arrange the rooms where she'll be so that she's allowed to play with most of the things she can reach. Then you'll rarely have to tell her she can't play with something. If there are plenty of things she *can* do, she's not going to bother so much about the things she can't do.

Practically speaking, this means taking breakable vases and ornaments off low tables and shelves and putting them up high. It means taking the valuable books off the lower shelves of the bookcases and putting the old magazines there instead, or jamming the good books in tight so that your baby can't pull them out. In the kitchen, put the pots and pans and wooden spoons on the shelves near the floor and put the china and packages of food out of reach. Put a lock on the cabinet under the sink, where cleaning supplies are, and lock up all true poisons far from anywhere your baby can reach. Fill a lower bureau drawer with old clothes, toys and other interesting objects and let the baby explore it, empty it and fill it to her heart's content.

Setting limits. Even after you babyproof, there will always be a few things that your toddler will have to leave alone. After all, there have to be lamps on tables: she mustn't pull them off by their cords or push the tables over. She mustn't touch the hot stove, turn on the gas or crawl out of a window.

You can't stop a toddler just by saying no, at least not in the beginning. Even later it will depend on your tone of voice, how often you say it, and whether you really mean it. It's not a method to rely on heavily until she has learned from experience what it means – and that you mean it. Don't say no in a challenging voice from across the room. This gives her a choice. She says to herself, 'Shall I be a wimp and do as she says, or shall I be mature and grab this lamp cord?' Remember that her natural instinct is egging her on to try things and to balk at directions. Chances are she'll keep on approaching the lamp cord with an eye on you to see how angry you get. It's much wiser, the first few times she goes for the lamp, to go over promptly and whisk her to another part of the room. You can say no at the same time to begin teaching her what it means. Then quickly give her a magazine or an empty box, anything that is safe and interesting.

What if she goes back to the lamp a few minutes later? Remove her and distract her again, promptly, definitely, cheerfully. Say, 'No, no,' at the same time that you remove her. Sit down with her for a minute to show her what she can do with the new plaything. If necessary, put the lamp out of reach this time, or even take her out of the room. You are cheerfully but firmly showing her that you are absolutely sure in your own mind that the lamp is not the thing to play with. You are keeping away from choices, arguments, cross looks and scoldings – which may not do the job and which are likely to make her irritable.

You might say, 'But she won't learn unless I teach her it's naughty.' Oh, yes, she will. In fact, she can accept the lesson more easily if it's done in this matter-of-fact way. When you disapprovingly waggle a finger from across the room at babies who haven't yet learned that no really means no, your crossness rubs them the wrong way. It makes them want to take a chance on disobeying. And it's no better if you grab them, hold them face-to-face and give them a talking-to. You're not giving them a chance to give in gracefully or forget. Their only choice is to surrender meekly or to defy you.

Take the example of a baby who is getting close to a hot stove. A parent doesn't sit still and say 'No-o-o' in a disapproving voice; he jumps up and gets the baby out of the way. This is the method that comes naturally if a parent is really trying to keep a child from doing something, and not just engaging in a battle of wills.

DR SPOCK COMMENTS

I think of a Mrs T who complained bitterly that her sixteen-month-old daughter was 'naughty'. Just then Suzy toddled into the room – a nice girl with a normal amount of spunk. Instantly Mrs T looked disapproving and said, 'Now, remember, don't go near the radio.' Suzy hadn't been thinking of the radio at all, but now she had to. She turned and moved slowly toward it. Mrs T gets panicky just as soon as each of her children in turn shows signs of developing into an independent person. She dreads the time when she won't be able to control them. In her uneasiness, she makes an issue when there doesn't need to be any. It's like the boy learning to ride a bicycle who sees a rock in the road ahead. He is so nervous about it that he keeps steering right for it.

FEARS AT AROUND ONE YEAR

Fear of separation. Many healthy children develop a fear of being separated from their parents beginning at around the age of one year. This is probably the same instinct that makes the young of sheep and goats follow close after their mothers and bleat when separated. Without this instinct, a newborn lamb might wander away and be lost.

In humans, separation anxiety also kicks in at about the time that children develop the ability to wander away, at around one year. Some bold, busy children show very little separation anxiety; others show a lot. This difference is not so much a matter of parenting as it is a reflection of inborn temperament. You can't change a timid child into a bold one, but you can help such a child to feel gradually more and more confident, by giving patient acceptance and gentle encouragement.

At around eighteen months or so, many children who have been happy explorers develop a new, heightened clinginess. They now have the ability to imagine being apart from their parents, and the image is frightening. This period of anxious clinging usually fades away some time around age two or two and a half, as children learn that separations are always followed by reunions.

Frightening sounds and sights. Your baby at one year may become fascinated with one thing for several weeks on end – the telephone, for instance, or planes overhead or electric lights. Remember that he learns best by touching, smelling and tasting things, and that as a little scientist, he needs to conduct his experiments over and over again. Let him touch and become familiar with objects that are not dangerous or disturbing.

But the hardy explorer also begins to develop fears of certain things at this time. He may be frightened by strange objects that move suddenly or make a loud noise, such as folded pictures that pop up from a book, the opening of an umbrella, a vacuum cleaner, a siren, a barking dog, a train, even rustling branches. All children have fears; this is a normal element of the developmental process. We all fear what we don't understand. In the second year of life, that covers a lot of territory. I'd suggest simply avoiding as much as possible these startling things until he figures them out. If the vacuum cleaner bothers him, tell him when you're about to turn it on, let him see how you do it, and allow him to do it himself a few times. If he's still scared, try not to use the vacuum for a while while he's nearby. Always be comforting and sympathetic. Don't try to convince him it's a ridiculous fear; his terror makes perfect sense to him at his level of understanding.

Fear of the bath. Between one and two years, your child may become frightened of the bath. She may fear slipping underwater, getting soap in her eyes or even seeing and hearing the water go down the drain. She has to have a bath, so you need to work out how to help her to come to terms with it. To avoid soap in the eyes, soap her face with a washcloth that is not too wet and rinse several times with a damp but not dripping washcloth. Use baby shampoo that won't sting her eyes. Babies who are afraid to get into the bathtub shouldn't be forced to. You can try using a dishpan, but if she is afraid of that, too, give her sponge baths for several months until her courage returns. Then start with just a couple of centimetres of water and remove her before you let the water out.

Leeriness around strangers. At this age, a baby's nature tells her to be leery and suspicious of strangers until she has had a chance to look them over. But then she wants to get closer and eventually make friends – in one-year-old fashion, of course. She may just stand close and gaze, or solemnly hand something to the newcomer and then take it back, or bring everything movable in the room and pile it in the person's lap.

Many adults don't know that a small child should be let alone while she sizes them up. They rush up to her, full of talk and enthusiasm, while she beats a hasty retreat to her parent for protection. Then it takes longer for her to work up her courage to be friendly. It helps for a parent to tell a visitor in the beginning, 'It makes her shy when you pay attention to her right away. If you ignore her for a while, she'll try to make friends sooner.'

When your baby is old enough to walk, give her plenty of chances to get used to seeing strangers. Take her to the supermarket a couple of times a week. As often as you can, take her to some place where other small children play. She won't be very interested in actually playing with them, but at times she'll want to watch. As she gets used to seeing others play, she will be more ready for cooperative play when the time comes, between two and three.

CHALLENGING BEHAVIOURS

Dawdling. The mother of an eighteen-month-old boy walks with him every day to the newsagent. But she complains that instead of walking right along, he wanders across the pavement and climbs the front steps of every house they pass on the way. The more she calls to him, the more he lingers. When she scolds him, he runs in the opposite direction. She is afraid he is developing a behaviour problem.

This baby doesn't have a behaviour problem, though he may be made to have one. He's not at an age when he can keep the newsagent in mind. His natural instincts say to him, 'Look at that pavement to explore! Look at those stairs!' Every time his mother calls to him, it reminds him of his newly felt urge to assert himself. What can the mother do? If she has to get to the shop promptly, she can take him in his pushchair. But if she's going to use this time for his outing, she should allow four times longer than if she were going alone, and let him make his side trips. If she keeps moving slowly, he'll want to catch up to her every once in a while.

Trouble stopping fun activities. It's time to go in for lunch, but your small daughter is digging happily in the mud. If you say, 'Now it's time to go in,' in a tone of voice that means, 'Now you can't have any more fun,' you will get resistance. But if you say cheerfully, 'Let's go climb the stairs,' you may give her a desire to go.

But suppose she's tired and cranky that day, and nothing that's indoors has any appeal. Just pick her up casually and carry her indoors, even if she's squealing and kicking. Do this in a self-confident way, as if you were saying to her, 'I know you're tired and cross, but when we have to go in, we have to.' Scolding her won't make her see the error of her ways. Arguing with her won't change her mind: you will only get yourself frustrated. A small child who is feeling miserable and making a scene is comforted underneath by sensing that the parent knows what to do without getting angry.

Young children are very distractible, and that's a big help. They are so eager to find out about the whole world that they don't much care where they begin or where they stop. If they're absorbed in a ring of keys, you can make them drop it by giving them an empty plastic cup. If your baby fights against having the food washed off his face and hands with a cloth after meals, set a pan of water on the tray and let him dabble his hands while you wash his face with your wet hand. Distractibility is one of the handles by which wise parents guide their children.

Dropping and throwing things. Around the age of one year, babies learn to drop things on purpose. They solemnly lean over the side of the high chair and drop food on the floor, or toss toys, one after the other, out of the cot. Then they cry because they haven't got them. Are these babies deliberately trying to annoy their parents? No. They aren't even thinking about their parents. They are fascinated by a new skill and want to practise it all day long, the way an older child wants to ride a new two-wheeler. If you pick up the dropped object, they realize it's a game that two can play and are even more delighted.

Unless you want to play this game *a lot*, it's better not to get in the habit of picking up dropped toys right away. Instead, simply put your baby on the floor when he gets in this dropping mood. If you don't want him throwing food off the high chair, take the food away promptly when he starts dropping, and put him down to play. You can say, 'Food is for eating, toys are for playing,' but there's no need to raise your voice. Trying to scold a baby out of dropping things leads to nothing but frustration.

Temper tantrums. Between one and three years, almost all children have temper tantrums; some start as early as nine months. They've developed a sense of their own desires and individuality. When they're thwarted, they know it and feel angry. A temper tantrum once in a while doesn't mean anything. Many tantrums are a result of fatigue or hunger, or of putting a child into a situation that is too stimulating. (Most shopping trip tantrums fall into this category.) If the tantrum is of this sort, a wise parent addresses the underlying problem: 'You're tired and hungry, aren't you? Let's get you home and fed and to bed, and you'll feel a lot better.' Some tantrums arise out of fear. This happens all the time at the doctor's office. The best thing to do in these situations is to be calm and reassuring. No good comes from scolding a scared child.

Tantrums happen more frequently in children who tend to be easily upset by changes or who are especially sensitive to sensory input (noises, motion or the feel of clothing against the skin, for instance). Tantrums often last longer in children who tend to be very persistent. Once they get started it's hard for them to stop, whether they're playing, practising walking or screaming at the top of their lungs. Excessive tantrums – for example, more than three a day, lasting more than ten or fifteen minutes each – are sometimes a sign of illness or stress, so it's reasonable to ask your child's doctor. See page 809 for more on tantrums and other acting-out behaviours.

SLEEP ISSUES

Nap hours are changing. Nap times are shifting in most babies around the age of a year. Some who were taking a nap at about 9 am may refuse it altogether or show that they want it later in the morning. If they take it late, they are unready for their next nap until the middle of the afternoon. This probably throws off their bedtime after supper. Or they may refuse the afternoon nap altogether. A baby may vary a lot from day to day at this period, even going back to a 9 am nap after two weeks of refusing it.

So don't come to a final conclusion too soon. Put up with these inconveniences as best you can, realizing that they are temporary. With some babies who are not ready to sleep in the first part of the morning, you can remove the need for the before-lunch nap by putting them in their beds anyway, around nine in the morning, if they are willing to sit or lie quietly for a while. Of course, another kind of baby only gets in a rage if put to bed when she's not sleepy, so nothing is accomplished.

If a baby becomes sleepy just before noon, it's the parent's cue to move lunch up to 11.30 or even 11 for a few days. The long nap will come after lunch, but for a while, cutting down to one nap a day, whether morning or afternoon, may make the baby frantically tired before suppertime.

Don't get the idea from this section that all babies give up their morning nap in the same way or at the same age. One is through with it at nine months; another craves it and benefits from it as late as two years. There is often a stage in a baby's life when two naps are too many and one is not enough! You can help babies through this period by giving them supper and putting them to bed for the night a little earlier for the time being.

Bedtime routines. Though you need to be a little flexible around sleep issues, it's also very helpful to have a bedtime routine. When things happen in the same way every day, it gives a young child a comforting sense of control. Bedtime routines can include stories, songs, prayers, hugs and kisses. What's important is that the same things happen in roughly the same order. Television or videos and roughhouse play tend to keep children excited and awake, so these activities are best left out of the bedtime routine. For more on sleep issues, see pages 101–4.

DR SPOCK COMMENTS

Keep bedtime agreeable and happy. Remember that it is delicious and inviting to the tired child, if you don't turn it into an unpleasant duty. Have an air of cheerful certainty about it.

EATING AND NUTRITION

Changes around one year. Around twelve to fifteen months, growth normally slows down and a toddler's appetite is likewise apt to level off. Some actually eat *less* than they did a few months before, causing their parents to worry. But if a child's growth plots out okay on the standard growth curve at the baby clinic, you can be assured that he is getting enough. If you make the mistake of showing your toddler that you want him to eat more, chances are he'll reward you by eating less, just to show you who's in charge. A better strategy is to give your baby small helpings, so he can enjoy demanding more, and not to pay much attention to how much goes in. Instead, watch your baby to see whether he is happy and full of energy and pay attention to the growth chart.

Early in the second year, many parents wean their babies from the breast or the bottle (see pages 313 and 335). Unless you are giving your toddler a nondairy diet (page 374), the drink of choice should be whole cow's milk.

Toddlers need the high fat content of whole milk (or full fat soya milk) to build their brains. After age two, it's sensible to switch to semi-skimmed milk to lower the risk of heart disease as an adult. See page 269 for more on vitamins, vegetables and other nutritional issues. For picky eating, food fads, and other worrisome eating aspects, see page 886.

Eating is a learning experience. For children to approach eating in a reasonable and healthy manner, they need to learn to pay attention to the body signals that tell them when they are hungry and when they've had enough. They need confidence that food will be there when they're hungry and that they won't be forced to eat when they're not hungry. You help your toddler learn these important lessons by making good food available and leaving it up to your child to decide how much to eat.

Table manners are also important. Every toddler experiments with mixing and smearing, testing the limits of what is acceptable. When your toddler crosses the line – throwing mashed potatoes, for instance – all you need to do is tell her firmly but calmly that food is for eating. Then remove her from the table and find her a ball or a cloth toy to throw. When eating turns to playing and it's clear that your child isn't hungry any more, it's time for the meal to end. Twenty minutes or so is usually long enough.

TOILET TRAINING AND LEARNING

Readiness to train. Before about eighteen months, most toddlers aren't ready for toilet training. They don't yet have the body awareness to recognize when they have to go, nor the control to hold everything in and then let it out at just the right time. Mostly they don't really understand why they should sit on the potty instead of just filling up their nappies. Toddlers typically find their bodily productions interesting, not disgusting. They don't see what all the fuss is about if the contents of their nappy get smeared around a bit.

Of course, there are some toddlers who train early and make all the *other* parents think that their children are behind. But for most children, training much before age eighteen months is bound to be difficult and unsatisfying. My advice to most parents is to wait with training until your child is two or two and a half. At that age, most can master the potty without a fuss. If you do start earlier and things don't go well, you haven't caused long-term psychological damage (assuming you didn't use harsh punishment or abuse). But the training process may involve more upset and take longer in the end. See page 857 for more on toilet training.

Toilet learning. While most one-year-olds aren't ready for *training*, they can certainly *learn* about the potty. If you let your child into the bathroom with you and there happens to be a child-size potty there, your toddler might sit on it or even pretend to use it, just as she mimics vacuuming and other adult activities. This early interest doesn't necessarily mean she's ready to take the next step. If you pressure her or even overdo the praise, there's a good chance she'll balk.

Part of using the toilet is hand-washing afterward, and

many toddlers are happy to have an excuse to get their hands wet and soapy. It's helpful if you talk about what you're doing as you do it, so your child learns the words. I favour simple, factual terms like 'pee' and 'poo' rather than cutesy baby talk or euphemisms ('wee-wee' or 'number two', for example). By talking in a straightforward way, you let your child know that toileting is simply a fact of life – not something secret, shameful, exciting or mysterious.

YOUR TWO-YEAR-OLD

BEING TWO

A tumultuous time. Some refer to this period as the 'terrible twos', but it's really a terrific time. It's a time when your child is beginning to come into her own and learning what it's like to be an independent person, when her language skills and imagination are increasing at a breathtaking pace. But her understanding of the world is still so limited that many things can seem scary.

Two-year-olds live in contradictions. They are both independent and dependent, loving and hateful, generous and selfish, mature and infantile. They stand with one foot in the warm, cozy, dependent past and the other in an exciting future full of autonomy and discovery. With so much excitement going on, it's no wonder that two is a challenging age for parents and children alike. But terrible it isn't. It's really pretty amazing.

Two-year-olds learn by imitation. In a doctor's surgery, a two-year-old girl solemnly places the stethoscope bell on different spots on her chest. Then she pokes the otoscope in her ear and looks a little puzzled because she can't see anything. At home she follows her parents around, sweeping with a broom when they sweep, dusting with a cloth when they dust, and brushing her teeth when they do. It's all done with great seriousness. She is making giant strides forward in skill and understanding by means of constant imitation.

Young children also imitate their parents' behaviour. For example, when you treat others politely, your two-year-old learns to be polite. It's okay to tell a two-year-old to say 'please' and 'thank you', but it's much more effective to let him hear *you* use those words in appropriate circumstances. (Don't expect to see politeness right away, but by four or five your early investment in politeness is bound to begin to pay off.) In the same way, young children who see parents using hurtful language or threats often develop similar troublesome behaviours. That doesn't mean that parents can't ever argue or disagree. But a steady diet of angry conflict is harmful to children, even if they are just bystanders.

Communication and imagination. At two, one child speaks in three- and four-word sentences, while another is just beginning to link two words together. A two-year-old who only says a few isolated words probably should have a hearing test and developmental evaluation, even though chances are good the child will simply be a late talker.

Imagination and language grow together. It's wonderful to watch a young child's imagination unfold over the year from twenty-four to thirty-six months. What starts out as simple imitation and experimentation becomes rich make-believe play. As a spur to imagination, let your child experience blocks, dolls, musical instruments, old shoes, dough, water for splashing and pouring, and as many other interesting objects as you can think of. Expose your child to nature, even if it's just the local park. Look at picture books together (see page 965), and let your child use paper and crayons. Scribbling is the first step on the path to writing.

One thing I'd strongly recommend *against* is television. Even high-quality children's TV can limit a child's imagination, because it does all the work and requires so little effort from the child. At all ages TV teaches children to become passive consumers of entertainment, rather than learning how to amuse themselves. (For more on TV, see page 723.)

Parallel play and sharing. Two-year-olds don't play cooperatively with each other very much. Mostly they enjoy playing alongside each other in what is called parallel play. There is no point in trying to teach a two-year-old to share; he simply isn't ready. In order to share, a child first has to understand that something *belongs* to him – that he can give it away and expect to get it back. Refusing to share at age two says nothing about how generous a person he will become when he is older.

Still, a two-year-old can begin to learn good play skills. When your child grabs a toy from his companion, you can firmly but cheerfully take the toy away from him, return it to its rightful owner, and quickly try to distract him with another object of interest. Long harangues about why he should share things are wasted breath. He will start to share when he understands the concept of sharing, usually around three or four, and not before.

WORRIES AT AROUND TWO

Separation fears. By age two, some children have got over their toddler clinginess, but others haven't yet (see page 777). A two-year-old seems to realize clearly who gives her a sense of security, and she shows it in different ways. A mother complains, 'My two-year-old seems to be turning into a mummy's girl. She hangs on to my skirt when we're out of the house. When someone speaks to us, she hides behind me.' Two is a great age for whining, which can be a kind of clinging (see page 839). She may be timid about being left anywhere by her parents. She's apt to be upset if a parent or other member of the household goes away for a number of days or if the family moves to a new house. It's wise to take her sensitivity into account when changes in the household are being considered.

Here's what can happen when a sensitive, dependent child of two years, particularly an only child, is separated abruptly from the parent who has spent the most time with him. Perhaps his mother has to go out of town unexpectedly for a couple of weeks, or she has to go to work outside the home and arranges for a stranger to come in and take care of him during the day. He may not make a fuss while his mother is away, but when she returns, he hangs on to her like Velcro. He becomes panicky whenever he thinks his mother may be leaving again.

Bedtime separations. Separation anxiety is worst at bedtime. The terrified child fights against being put to bed. If his mother tears herself away, he may cry in fear for hours. If she sits by his cot, he lies down only as long as she sits still. Her slightest move toward the door brings him instantly to his feet.

If your two-year-old child has become terrified about going to bed, the soundest advice, but the hardest to carry out, is to sit by her cot in a relaxed way until she goes to sleep. Don't be in a hurry to sneak away: that will alarm her again and make her more wakeful. This campaign may take weeks, but it should work in the end. If your child was frightened because one of you left town, try to avoid going away again for many weeks.

Give her this special care the way you'd give special consideration to a sick child. Look for signs of your child's readiness to give up her dependence, step by step, and encourage her and compliment her. Your attitude is the most powerful factor in getting her over her fear – that and the maturational forces that, with time, will allow the child to better understand and master her fears.

Making the child more tired by keeping her up later or omitting her nap may help a little but usually won't do the whole job. A panicky child can keep herself awake for hours even though she's exhausted. You need to take away her worry.

DR SPOCK COMMENTS

A child who is frightened by separation – or anything else – is very sensitive to whether her parents feel the same way about it. If they act hesitant or guilty every time they leave her side, if they hurry into her room at night when she cries, their anxiety reinforces her fear that there really is great danger in being apart from them.

Concern about wetting the bed. Sometimes when a two-year-old has bedtime anxieties, there is also worry about urinating. The child keeps saying 'go wee' – or whatever word he uses. His mother takes him to the bathroom, he does a few drops, and then he cries 'go wee' again just as soon as he is back in bed. You might say that he uses this as an excuse to keep her there. This is true, but there is more to it. Children like this one are really worried that they might wet the bed.

They sometimes wake every two hours during the night thinking about it. This is the age when the parents are apt to be showing disapproval when there is an accident. Maybe the child thinks that if he wets the bed, his parents won't love him so much and will therefore be more likely to go away. If so, he has two reasons to fear going to sleep. If your child is worried about wetting, keep reassuring her that it doesn't matter if she needs a change of sheets – that you'll love her just the same.

Children may use separation anxiety to control. A child clings to his mother because he has developed a genuine fear of being separated from her. But if he finds that she is so concerned about his fear that she will always do anything he wants for reassurance, he may begin to use this as coercion. There are three-year-olds, for instance, who are anxious about being left at preschool and whose parents not only stay at school for days but stay close to the children and do whatever they ask, to reassure them. After a while you begin to see that such children are exaggerating their uneasiness because they have learned to use it to boss their parents around. A parent can say, 'I think you are grown-up now and aren't afraid to be in preschool. You just like to make me do what you want. Tomorrow I won't need to stay here any more.'

How to help a fearful two-year-old. When it comes to the management of children's fear, a lot depends on how important it is for them to get over it in a hurry. There's no great necessity for anxious children to be hurried into making friends with dogs or going into deep water in the lake. They'll want to do these things as soon as they dare.

On the other hand, children should not be allowed to come into the parents' bed every single night (unless you've decided that co-sleeping is for you; see page 58). They should be comforted and soothed in their own bed, so that sleeping with the parents doesn't become a pleasant habit that the child has no motivation to stop.

Once children have started nursery, it's better for them to go regularly unless they're deeply terrified. A skilful teacher can help a child become engaged in play, so that the separation becomes easier (see page 984). A child with a nursery-refusal problem must get back to nursery sooner or later; the longer it is put off, the harder it becomes to get back. Parents are wise to consider whether overprotectiveness is playing a part in these various separation fears. This is a tough task, and parents often need help from a doctor or other professional.

Some causes of overprotectiveness. Overprotective feelings often occur in devoted parents who are inclined to feel worried or guilty when there is no realistic need for it. There may have been an incident, long ago, when the child truly was in danger: a serious infection, for example, or an injury. The dread that something horrible could occur is hard for many parents to shake. A steady diet of horrific and graphic TV news reports further stokes parents' fears. (In fact, statistics show, children are actually *safer* in many ways now than at any time in the recent past.)

Overprotection sometimes comes from hidden anger and guilt. It is normal for parents to feel anger toward their children at times, and even to harbour negative wishes – for example, that the child had never been born. These thoughts make some parents feel so guilty that they suppress them and instead exaggerate dangers in the world outside, such as kidnappers. When parents can admit that they do sometimes have wishes that they would never act on, the guilt disappears, along with the sense that the outside world is terribly dangerous.

You might also see that your anger isn't always entirely fair. Yes, your child may have done something naughty or selfish, but perhaps you also feel frustrated with yourself because you haven't been able to correct your child's behaviour, and perhaps worried that you are failing as a parent. Feelings like this can easily fuel anger at your child that is more intense, perhaps, than your child deserves. Even this kind of misplaced anger is okay if you can own it and accept it. Nothing says that a good parent has to be fair all the time.

If your angry feelings have led you to act toward your child in ways you wish you hadn't – for instance, yelling when it really wasn't necessary – then it's helpful to talk with your child about how you were feeling. Talking about angry feelings helps a child understand and take control of his own emotions. Try to use simple words. You might say, 'I know how angry you feel toward me when I have to say no to you. Sometimes I feel angry, too.'

CHALLENGING BEHAVIOURS

Negativism. In the period between age two and age three, children are apt to show signs of negativism and other inner tensions. Your baby probably began to be balky way back when she was fifteen months old, so this is nothing new. But negativism reaches new heights and takes new forms after two. One-year-old Petunia contradicts her parents. Two-and-a-half-year-old Petunia even contradicts herself. She has a hard time making up her mind, and then she wants to change it. She acts like a person who feels she is being bossed too much, even when no one is bothering her and even when she tries to boss others. She insists on doing things just so, exactly as she has always done them. It makes her furious to have anyone interfere in one of her jobs or rearrange her possessions.

The child's nature urges her to decide things for herself and resist pressure from other people. Trying to fight this battle without much worldly experience seems to get her tightened up inside.

You can help by letting your child work at his own pace when possible. Let him dress and undress himself (with just a little help from you) when he has the urge. Start his bath early enough that he has time to dawdle. At meals, let him feed himself without urging. When he is stalled in his eating, let him leave the table. When it's time for bed, going outdoors, or coming in, steer him while talking about pleasant things. Get things done without raising issues. Your goal is not to let him be a little tyrant, but not to sweat the small stuff either.

Two-year-olds behave best when parents set firm, consistent and reasonable limits. The key is to choose those limits carefully. If you find yourself saying no a lot more than yes, you're probably setting too many arbitrary limits. A battle of wills with a two-year-old is tiring, so save the battles for issues that are truly important. Safety issues, such as sitting in the car seat, are clearly important. Wearing mittens on a cold day may not be so very important. After all, you can always stuff the mittens in your coat pocket and pull them out when your two-year-old's hands get cold.

Temper tantrums. Nearly every two-year-old has tantrums now and then, and some healthy children have many. Tantrums usually start around age one (see page 809) and peak around age two to three. There are many causes:

frustration, fatigue, hunger, anger and fear. Children who show their emotions intensely have more tantrums (and they also have more outbursts of joyful laughing). Children who are less flexible and more sensitive to changes also have more tantrums. Sometimes you'll be able to see a tantrum brewing and head it off by distracting your child, offering a well-timed snack or leaving a situation that is just too stimulating. At other times the tantrum blows up in an instant and all you can do is wait for the storm to pass.

During a tantrum, it's helpful to stay nearby so that your child doesn't feel alone. It doesn't help to yell at your child, threaten punishment, plead for calm or try too hard to 'make everything better'. Any of these responses just tends to make tantrums last longer and occur more often. Afterward, it's best to move on to a positive activity and put the upset in the past. A quick word of praise along the lines of 'Nice job pulling yourself together' can let your child salvage some self-esteem and learn to recover faster the next time. Remember to praise yourself, too, for staying calm and rational – not easily done when your two-year-old is having a meltdown.

Whining. It's normal for young children to whine (puppies whine, too), but it's still annoying. Early on, you have no choice but to try to work out what your child needs. Once your child can use words, however, it's best to insist that she do that. A firm, unemotional 'Use your words; I don't listen to whining' is all it usually takes, although you may have to repeat this message over many months before it sinks in fully. Be aware, though, that if you give in to whining now and then – and the temptation is strong – it can become much harder to put a stop to it. See page 839 for more on whining and what to do.

Favouritism toward one parent. Sometimes a young child can get along with either parent alone but flies into a rage when the other parent comes onto the scene. It may be partly jealousy, but at an age when she's sensitive about being bossed around and trying to do a little bossing herself, a child might just feel outnumbered when she has to take on two important people at once.

It's more often the father who is particularly unpopular at this period; he sometimes gets the feeling he's pure poison. He shouldn't take the child's reaction too seriously or feel hurt. It will help if he regularly cares for her by himself, doing things that are fun, as well as everyday things such as feeding and bathing. That way she gets to know him as an enjoyable, loving and important person, not just an intruder. If a child objects at first when her father takes over, the father should cheerfully but firmly carry on, and the mother should have the same firm and cheerful attitude as she leaves.

Taking turns this way can give each parent one-on-one time with the child, and time alone as well. But there is also value in time all together, even if the two-year-old acts cranky. It's good for a child (particularly a first child) to learn that her parents love each other, want to be with each other and will not be bullied by her.

DIET AND NUTRITION

Changes in the diet. A two-year-old can eat pretty much what the family does. You still need to be aware of choking hazards – small, hard foods such as peanuts, whole grapes, carrots and hard sweets – and keep these out of your child's diet. If you've been giving your toddler whole milk, you can switch to semi-skimmed. Brain growth slows down after age two, so a high-fat diet isn't needed, and getting used to a lower-fat diet early in childhood lowers the risk of heart disease years later. Young children can't usually wait five or six hours between meals. Three meals and three snacks is a good schedule. The best snacks are simple foods such as cut-up fruit or whole-grain toast, not highly processed items, whether or not they claim to be healthy.

Food choices. Most two-year-olds handle cups and spoons with ease but may still need help with forks and knives. Since many young children resent getting help, even if they need it, you may want to focus on foods that can be eaten with a spoon or just fingers. Young children need practice making food choices. Peas or carrots? Peanut butter sandwich or ham? It's enough to make one or two small choices. More and bigger choices can be overwhelming and may lead to tantrums. Wise parents offer a small selection of attractive foods at each meal, so that any choice the child makes is a healthy one.

Food choices start with what you bring home from the shop. Choose fresh vegetables instead of chips and other high-fat snacks, fruits instead of biscuits and cakes, and semi-skimmed milk or water instead of fizzy drinks. If you want your child to eat healthily, the best strategy is to keep the house stocked with healthy foods and keep the junk food out. See page 365 for more on nutrition and health.

Food fads and fights. One two-year-old wants only grilled cheese at every meal; another demands noodle soup. Usually such fads last a few days, then fade away, only to be replaced by other food obsessions. In the interest of peace and harmony, you may want to give in to some extent. Five days in a row of peanut butter on toast for lunch isn't harmful, and if there's milk, fruit or some green vegetable at other meals, chances are your child is getting a reasonably balanced diet. If you think about what your child eats not just in one day but over the course of a week or so, you might see that the diet is pretty balanced after all.

Many two-year-olds get locked into power struggles with their parents around food. Concerning behaviours include extreme pickiness, constant demands for special foods, gagging or tantrums. On the parent's side, it may be nagging, cajoling, threatening or outright force-feeding. See page 886 for ways to deal with these common problems.

TOILET TRAINING

One step towards independence. By twenty-four to thirty-six months, when most children learn how to use the toilet, most parents can't wait to see their last dirty nappy. But in their hurry to have the process over with, many parents push, prod or pester, with the result that training takes longer and is more stressful than it needs to be. Toilet training is part of a learning process that begins in the first year (see page 161) and ends several years later with a child who handles toileting independently, including wiping and hand-washing, who feels comfortable about bodily processes, and who has adopted her parents' views about privacy and modesty. If you take this long view, you might feel more comfortable allowing toilet training to move forward at its own pace. For more on toilet training, including specific suggestions for how and when to start and what to do, see page 857.

YOUR PRESCHOOLER, THREE TO FIVE YEARS

DEVOTION TO THE PARENTS

A less rebellious age. Boys and girls around three have reached a stage in their emotional development when they feel that their fathers and mothers are wonderful people, and they want to be like them. The automatic resistance and hostility that were just below the surface in the two-year-old seem to lessen after three in most children.

The feelings towards the parents aren't just friendly now; they are warm and tender. However, children are not so devoted to their parents that they always obey them and behave well. They are still real people with ideas of their own. They want to assert themselves, even if it means going against their parents' wishes at times.

While most children between three and five are delightful, four-year-olds can be the exception. A lot of assertiveness, cockiness, loud talk and provoking behaviours appear around four years in many children, when they come to the realization that they know everything – a realization that mercifully soon fades.

Striving to be like the parents. At two years old children eagerly imitate their parents' activities. If they are playing at mopping the floor or hammering a pretend nail, their focus is on the use of the mop or the hammer. By three years old the quality of their imitation changes. Now they want to be totally like their parents as people. They play at going to work, keeping house (cooking, cleaning, doing the washing) and caring for children (using a doll or a younger child). They pretend to go for a drive in the family car or to step out for the evening. They dress up in their parents' clothes and mimic their conversation, their manners and their mannerisms.

All of this playing has a serious purpose: it's how a child develops his or her character. This process depends more on what children perceive in their parents than on what the parents try to teach them in words. Basic ideals and attitudes – towards work, towards people, towards themselves – all get their start this way. This is how children learn to be the kind of parents they're going to turn out to be twenty or thirty years later. You can hear their future parent voices if you listen to the affectionate or scolding way they care for their dolls.

Gender awareness. It's at this age that a girl becomes more aware of the fact that she's female and will grow up to be a woman. She watches her mother with special attentiveness and tends to mould herself in her mother's image: how her mother feels about her husband and about the male sex in general, about other women, about girl and boy children, and about work and housework. The little girl is not about to become an exact replica of her mother, but she will surely be influenced by her in many ways.

A boy at this age realizes that he is on the way to becoming a man and attempts to pattern himself mainly after his father: how his father feels towards his wife and the female sex generally, towards other men, towards his boy and girl children, and toward work and housework.

Of course, girls also learn a great deal from observing their fathers, and boys from their mothers. This is how the two sexes come to understand each other well enough to be able to live together. And children partly model themselves on other important grown-ups in their lives as well. But in the very early years, parents (especially parents who are the child's same sex) play a special role.

Fascination with babies. Boys and girls now become fascinated with all aspects of babies. They want to know where babies come from. When they find out that babies grow inside their mothers, they are eager to carry out this amazing act of creation themselves – boys as well as girls. They want to take care of babies and love them, the way they realize they were cared for and loved. They will press a younger child into the role of a baby and spend hours acting as father and mother to him, or they'll use a doll.

It's not generally recognized that little boys are as eager as girls to grow babies inside themselves. When their parents tell them that this is impossible, they are apt to refuse to believe it for a long time. 'I *will* grow a baby,' they insist, really believing that if they wish something hard enough, they can make it come true. In a similar way, a preschool girl might announce that she is going to grow a penis. Ideas of this kind are not signs of dissatisfaction with being one sex or another. Instead, they come from the young child's belief that he or she can do everything, be everything and have everything.

ROMANTIC AND COMPETITIVE FEELINGS

Wishes and worries. Up to this age, a boy's love for his mother has been predominantly of a dependent kind, like that of a baby. But now it also becomes increasingly romantic, like his father's. These feelings aren't sexual, of course, in the same way an adolescent or adult feels a hormone-driven attraction, but they are possessive. By the time he's four, he's apt to insist that he's going to marry his mother when he grows up. He isn't clear just what marriage consists of, but he's absolutely sure who is the most important and appealing woman in the world. The little girl who is growing in her mother's pattern develops the same kind of love for her father.

These romantic urges help children to grow spiritually; they form the deep roots of the feelings that will later bear fruit in strong adult relationships. But there is another side to the picture that creates unconscious tension in most children at this age. As a little boy of three or four or five becomes more aware of his possessive devotion to his mother, he also becomes aware of how much she already belongs to his father. This irritates him, no matter how much he loves and admires his father. At times he secretly wishes his father would get lost, and then he feels guilty about having such disloyal feelings. Reasoning as a child does, he imagines that his father has the same jealous and resentful feelings toward him.

The little girl develops a similar possessive love for her father. She wishes at times that something would happen to her mother (whom she loves so much in other respects) so that she could have her father for herself. She may even say to her mother, 'You can go away for a long trip, and I'll take good care of Daddy.' But then she imagines that her mother is jealous of her, too – a frightening thought! If you think about classic fairy tales like Snow White, you can see these fantasies and worries brought to life in the figure of the wicked stepmother.

Children try to push these scary thoughts out of their minds, but they often come to the surface in their make-believe play. These mixed feelings towards the parent of the same sex – feelings of love, jealousy and fear – also come out in the bad dreams that little children are so apt to have. Dreams of being chased by monsters, robbers and other frightening figures often draw their power from angry or jealous feelings that are a part of the normal struggles at this age.

Moving past possessiveness. What happens to all of these powerful, conflicting feelings? When things work as they should, by age six or seven children become quite discouraged about the possibility of having a parent all to themselves. The unconscious fears about the parent's supposed anger turn their pleasure in dreaming about romance into an aversion. Now they shy away from kisses by the parent of the opposite sex. Their interests turn with relief to impersonal matters such as schoolwork and sport. More and more they try to model themselves after other children of their own sex, and after adults other than their parents.

How parents can help. Parents can help children through this romantic but jealous stage by gently keeping it clear that they do belong to each other, that a boy can't ever have his mother to himself and a girl can't have her father to herself, but that the parents aren't shocked to realize that their children are mad at them sometimes on this account.

When a girl declares that she is going to marry her father, he can act pleased with the compliment, but he can also explain that he's already married and that when she grows up she'll find a man her own age to marry.

When parents are being companionable together, they needn't and shouldn't let a child break up their conversation. They can cheerfully but firmly remind her that they have things to talk over, and they can suggest that she get busy, too. Their tactfulness will keep them from prolonged displays of affection in front of her, just as it would if other people were present, but they don't need to spring apart guiltily if she comes into the room unexpectedly when they're hugging or kissing.

When a boy is being rude to his father because he's feeling jealous, or to his mother because she's the cause of his jealousy, the parent should insist on politeness. The converse is equally true if a girl is being rude. But at the same time the parents can ease the child's feelings of anger and guilt by saying that they know the child is cross at them sometimes.

A father who realizes that his young son sometimes has unconscious feelings of resentment and fear towards him does not help the boy by trying to be too gentle and permissive. It's no help, either, for the father to try to avoid making his son jealous by pretending that he (the father) doesn't really love his wife very much. In fact, if a boy becomes convinced that his father is afraid to be a firm father and a normally possessive husband, the boy will sense that he is having his mother too much to himself and will feel really guilty and frightened. And he will miss the inspiration of a confident father, which he must have in order to develop his own self-assurance.

In the same way, a mother best helps her daughter to grow up by being a self-confident mother who doesn't let herself be pushed around, who knows how and when to be firm, and who isn't at all afraid to show her affection and devotion to her husband.

It complicates life for a boy if his mother is a great deal more permissive and affectionate towards him than his father is. The same is true if she seems to be closer to her son than she is to her husband. Such attitudes have a tendency to alienate a boy from his father and to make him too fearful of him. In the same way, the father who is putty in his daughter's hands and is always undoing the mother's discipline, or the father who acts as if he enjoys his daughter's companionship more than his wife's, is being unhelpful not only to his wife but to his daughter as well.

This interferes with the good relationship that a daughter should have with her mother in order to grow up to be a happy woman.

Incidentally, it is entirely normal for a father to be a bit more lenient towards his daughter and a mother towards her son, because there is naturally less rivalry between male and female than between two males or two females. In most families there is a healthy balance among the feelings of father, mother, sons, and daughters that guides them through these stages of development without any special effort.

CURIOSITY AND IMAGINATION

Intense curiosity. At this age, children want to know about everything they encounter. Their imagination is rich. They put two and two together and draw their own conclusions. They connect everything with themselves. When they hear about trains, they want to know right away, 'Will I go on a train some day?' When they hear about an illness, it makes them think, 'Will I have that?'

A gift for imagination. Preschool children are virtuosos of imagination. When children of three or four tell a made-up story, they aren't lying in our grown-up sense. Their imagination is vivid to them. They're not sure where the real ends and the make-believe begins. That is why they love to hear stories, and why they are scared of violent TV programmes and films and shouldn't see them.

You don't need to scold your child or make him feel

guilty for making up stories occasionally. You can simply point out that what he said isn't actually so, although he may *wish* it were so. In this way, you're helping your child learn the difference between reality and make-believe.

An imaginary friend who shows up now and then, perhaps to help with a particular adventure – daring to go to the bottom of the garden alone, for example – is a sign of a normal, healthy imagination. But sometimes a child who feels lonely will spend hours each day telling about imaginary friends or adventures, not as a game but as if he believes in them. When you help such a child to make friends with real children, the need for fantasy playmates lessens.

SLEEP ISSUES

Most children give up their naps some time before age four but may still need quiet time in the afternoon. If they sleep much less than ten hours a night, they're bound to be overtired (although there is a wide range of normal sleep needs at this age, from about eight hours to as many as twelve or thirteen). Sleep problems that began earlier in life, such as excessive bedtime stalling or frequent waking, often continue through the preschool years (see page 101), and new sleep problems may arise, even for children who have been good sleepers. Nightmares and night terrors are common at this age (see page 883).

Sleep problems can develop out of the normal feelings of possessiveness and jealousy described above. The child wanders into the parents' room in the middle of the night and wants to get into their bed because (without putting these thoughts into words) he doesn't want them to be alone together. If he is allowed to stay, he might end up literally kicking his father out of the bed. It's much better for everyone if his parents promptly and firmly, but not angrily, take him back to his own bed. (See page 883.)

FEARS AT AROUND THREE, FOUR AND FIVE

Imaginary worries. New types of fear crop up fairly often around the age of three and four – fear of the dark, of dogs, of fire engines, of death, of disabled people. Children's imaginations have now developed to the stage where they can put themselves in other people's shoes and picture dangers that they haven't actually experienced. They want to know not only the cause of everything but also what these things have to do with them. They overhear something about dying, and they want to know what dying is. As soon as they get a dim idea they ask, 'Do I have to die?'

Some children are born with a tendency to respond to anything new or unexpected with anxiety or fear. Fears are also more common in children who have been made tense from battles over such matters as feeding and toilet training, in children whose imaginations have been overstimulated by scary stories or films, in children who haven't had enough opportunity to develop their independence and outgoingness, or in children whose parents have overplayed warnings about the dangers 'out there'. The uneasiness accumulated before now seems to crystallize into definite dread.

This is not to say that every child who develops a fear has been handled mistakenly in the past. The world is full of things young children do not understand, and no matter how lovingly they have been raised, they recognize their own weakness and vulnerability.

Helping your child cope with fears. It is not your job as a parent to banish all fears from your child's imagination. Your job is to help your child learn constructive ways to cope with those fears. You can help your child deal with particular fears, whether about dogs or insects or monsters, by lowering the level of tension in general. Avoid scary films and TV programmes. Call off any battle that you might be engaged in about eating or staying dry at night. Keep her behaving well by firm guidance rather than by letting her misbehave and then making her feel guilty about it afterward. Never threaten her with monsters or policemen: she is afraid enough of her own mental creations. Arrange to give her a full, outgoing life with other children. The more she is absorbed in games and plans, the less she will worry about her inner fears.

In the end, your child is the one who needs to overcome her fears; you can support her, but you can't do the work for her. Still, your confidence that she'll be able to do it eventually is very important. One of the most powerful ways a young child combats fear is through make-believe play. You might see her pretending to give her doll an injection or beating up a pretend monster. You'll know when she's conquered the fear, because her playing will shift to other topics. Sometimes a child will become stuck in a particular fear, and her playing about it only makes her more and more anxious. In these cases, guidance from a child mental health professional can help (see page 940). For more on fears, see page 830.

Fear of the dark. If your child develops a fear of the dark, try to reassure her. This is more a matter of your manner than your words. Don't make fun of her or try to argue her out of her fear. If she wants to talk about it, as a few children do, let her. Give her the feeling that you want to understand but that you are absolutely certain that nothing bad will happen to her. Leave her door open at night if that is what she wants, or leave a dim light on in her room. It's a small price to pay to keep the goblins out of sight. The light, or the conversation from the living room, won't keep her awake as much as her fears will. When her fear subsides, she will be able to stand the dark again.

Fear of animals. Preschool children often develop a fear of certain animals, even if they have never had a bad experience with them. It doesn't help to drag a scared child towards a dog to prove that nothing bad happens. The more you pull, the more the child will feel he has to pull in the opposite direction. As the months go by, the child will try to get over his fear and approach a dog, and he'll do it faster by himself than you can ever persuade him.

Fear of the water. It's almost always a mistake to pull a child, screaming, into the ocean or a pool. It is true that occasionally a child who is forced in finds that it is fun and loses the fear abruptly, but in more cases it works the opposite way. Remember that the child is longing to go in, despite the dread she feels.

Fear of talking. Young children are often quiet around strangers until they feel more comfortable. A child who talks normally at home but refuses to say a word at preschool, even after days or weeks, may have *selective mutism* – see page 833.

Questions about death. Questions about death are apt to come up at this age. Try to make your first explanation matter-of-fact in tone. You might say, 'Everybody has to die some day. Most people die when they get very old and sick, and their body just stops working completely.' Remember that behind your young child's question about death in general, there is almost always a very specific concern that *you*, Mum or Dad, could die. Since time flows differently for a child than for an adult, saying that you'll be alive for a long, long time may not give much reassurance; for a child, 'a long time' could mean 'until tomorrow'. Instead, you can reassure your child that you will be very old and your child will be old and grown-up, with children of his own, and only then will it be time for you to die.

Choose your words carefully. For example, 'We lost Uncle Archibald' can strike terror into the heart of any child who himself has got lost. This is the age when children take everything quite literally. One child I know became terrified of flying after hearing death spoken of as 'going to our home in the sky'. It's especially important not to refer to death as 'going to sleep', because many children will become terrified of bedtime; or they'll wonder why somebody doesn't just wake Uncle Archibald up.

It's much better to explain as simply as possible – and without sugarcoating the facts – that death is what happens when the body 'stops working completely'. Children who spend time in nature have a chance to see many examples of things that die; they can begin to understand death as part of the larger pattern of the world.

It's important, too, to convey your family's beliefs about death, religious or otherwise. With this and other sensitive topics, it's important to be open to questions and answer them simply and truthfully, but don't give more information than your child is asking for. Children have a way of knowing when they have heard enough; it's best to honour that intuition. No important topic gets talked about all at once; there are always other opportunities. Remember to hug your child and remind her that you're going to be together for a very, very long time. (See page 773 for more on helping children cope with death.)

WORRIES ABOUT INJURY AND BODY DIFFERENCES

Why these worries arise. Children at this age want to know the reason for everything. If they see a disabled person, they first want to know what happened to that person; then they put themselves in the person's place and wonder if that injury might happen to them.

They have a great interest in physical abilities of all kinds (hopping, running, climbing), which makes body intactness very important and being 'broken' very upsetting. This explains why a young child can get so upset about a broken biscuit, refusing a biscuit that's in two pieces and demanding a whole one.

Body differences. Some young children also worry about the differences between boys and girls. If a boy around the age of three sees a girl undressed, it may strike him as odd that she hasn't got a penis like his. He's apt to say, 'Where is her wee-wee?' If he doesn't receive a satisfactory answer right away, he may jump to the conclusion that some accident has happened to her. Next comes the anxious thought, 'That might happen to me, too.' The same misunderstanding may worry the little girl when she first realizes that boys are made differently. First she asks, 'What's that?' Then she might want to know, 'Why don't I have one? What happened to it?' That's the way a three-year-old's mind works.

Children may be so upset that they're afraid to ask their parents.

This worry about why boys are different from girls shows up in different ways. Here are some examples: a boy just under three who, with an anxious expression, keeps watching his baby sister being bathed and telling his mother, 'Baby is boo-boo,' his word for hurt; at about the same time he begins to hold on to his own penis in a worried way. A little girl becomes worried after she finds out about boys, and keeps trying to undress different children to see how they are made. A boy of three and a half first becomes upset about his younger sister's body and then begins to worry about everything in the house that is broken, such as a broken toy. Everything that is damaged seems to remind him of his fears about himself.

It's wise to realize ahead of time that normal children between two and a half and three and a half are likely to wonder about things like bodily differences. It's no use waiting for them to say, 'I want to know why a boy isn't made like a girl,' because they won't be that specific. They may ask some kind of question, or they may hint around, or they may just wait and get worried. Don't think of this as an unwholesome interest in sex. To them it's just like any other important question at first. You can see why it would work the wrong way to shush them, scold them or blush and refuse to answer. That would give them the idea they are on dangerous ground, which is not what you want to convey.

On the other hand, you don't need to be solemn, as if you were giving a lecture. It's easier than that. It helps, first of all, to bring the child's fear out into the open by saying that he probably thinks a girl had a penis but something happened to it. Then you try to make it clear, in a matter-of-fact, cheerful tone, that girls and women are made differently from boys and men; they are meant to be that way. A small child understands an idea more easily from examples. You can explain that Johnny is made just like Daddy, Uncle Harry, David and so on, and that Mary is made like Mummy, Mrs Jenkins and Helen (listing all the individuals that the child knows best).

A little girl needs extra reassurance because it's natural for her to want to have something that she can see. (One little girl complained to her mother, 'But he's so fancy and I'm so plain.') It will help her to know that her mother likes being made the way she is, and that her parents love her just the way she is. This may also be a good time to explain that girls when they are older can grow babies of their own inside them and have breasts with which to nurse them. That's a thrilling idea at three or four.

SCHOOL AGE: FIVE TO ELEVEN YEARS

FITTING INTO THE OUTSIDE WORLD

After about five or six, children turn into kids. Parents are still important, but kids are usually more concerned with what other kids say and do. They are very aware of how they measure up and where they fit within the group. They are interested in impersonal subjects like arithmetic and computers; they develop skills in art, music and sport. They begin to notice world events and issues – wars, the economy, global warming – and some develop strong opinions. In little ways at first, and increasingly over time, they become independent of their parents, even impatient with them. In short, they're beginning the job of emancipating themselves from the family and taking their places as citizens of the outside world.

Self-control. Children after five or six become strict about some things. Think of the games children enjoy at this age. They're no longer so interested in make-believe without any plan. They want games that have rules and require skill. In hopscotch, skipping and video games, you have to do things in a certain order, which becomes harder as you progress. If you miss, you must penalize yourself, go back to the beginning and start over again. It's the very strictness of the rules that appeals to children.

This is the age for starting collections, whether it's stamps or cards or stones. The pleasure of collecting is in achieving orderliness and completeness. At this age children have the desire to put their belongings in order. Suddenly they neaten their desk, put labels on the drawers, or arrange their piles of comic books. They don't keep their things neat for long, but you can see that the urge must be strong just to get them started.

Independence from parents. Children of primary school age go on loving their parents deeply underneath, but they usually don't show it so much on the surface. They're often cooler toward other adults, too. They no longer want to be loved as a possession or as an appealing child. They're gaining a sense of dignity as individuals and want to be treated as such.

They turn to trusted adults outside the family for ideas and knowledge. If they mistakenly get the idea from an admired science teacher that red blood cells are larger than white blood cells, there's nothing their parents can say that will change their minds. The ideas of right and wrong that their parents taught them have not been forgotten. In fact, they have sunk in so deeply that kids now think of them as their own creations. Children are impatient when their parents keep reminding them of what they ought to do, because they know already and want to be considered responsible.

Bad manners. Kids often pick up a little tough talk, and they also want the style of clothes and haircut that other kids have. They may wear torn jeans with the same conviction with which people wear political party badges during a political campaign. They may lose some of their table manners, come to meals with dirty hands, slump over their plates and stuff too much food into their mouths. Perhaps they kick the leg of the table absentmindedly. They throw their coats on the floor. They slam doors or leave them open.

Without realizing it, they are accomplishing three things at once. First, they're looking to children of their own age as models of behaviour. Second, they're declaring their right to be more independent of parents. Third, they're keeping square with their own conscience, because they're not doing anything that's morally wrong.

These bad manners and bad habits are apt to make their parents unhappy. They imagine that children are forgetting all that they so carefully taught. Actually, these changes are proof that the children have learned what good behaviour is – otherwise they wouldn't bother to rebel against it. When they feel they have established their independence, they will probably start following their family's standards of behaviour again.

Not every kid has to be a troublemaker. One who gets along happily with easygoing parents may show no open rebelliousness at all. But if you look carefully, you will see signs of a change of attitude.

What do you do? After all, children must take a bath once in a while and get neatened up on special occasions. You may be able to overlook some of the minor irritating ways, but you should be firm in matters that are important to you. When you have to ask them to wash their hands, try to be matter-of-fact. A lighthearted, humorous approach can help, too. It's the nagging tone, the bossiness, that they find irritating and that spurs them on to rebel even more.

SOCIAL LIVES

Importance of peers. For kids, being accepted by peers is a matter of greatest importance. Ask the children in any classroom and they all can tell you who is popular and who is 'weird'. For kids with negative reputations, school is often a lonely and demoralizing place. It's no wonder, then, that school-age children often seem to go to great lengths to fit in, even if it means breaking some family rules.

Success fitting in and getting along is important for kids and for the adults they grow up to be. Children who can't be part of a group often grow up to be adults who have difficulties with colleagues, friends and family members. This doesn't mean that you ought to force your child to conform, but neither should you insist that your child always stands apart from the herd. Instead, your job is to find groups that share your core values – whether these are teams, clubs or less structured groups of other kids – so that the group reinforces the values you've taught your child.

Helping children to be sociable and popular. These are some of the early steps in bringing up children to be sociable and popular: not fussing over them in their first years; letting them be around other children their size from the age of one year; allowing them freedom to develop independence; making as few changes as possible in where the family lives and where the children go to school; letting

them, as far as possible, associate with, dress like, talk like, play like and have the same allowance and other privileges as the other average children in the area. Of course, that doesn't mean letting them take after the town's worst scoundrel. And you don't have to take your child's word about what the other children are allowed to do.

If a boy is having trouble making friends, it helps most if he can be in a school and in a class where the programme is flexible. Then the teacher can arrange things so that he has chances to use his abilities to contribute to class projects. This is how the other children learn to appreciate his good qualities and to like him. A good teacher who is respected by the class can also raise a child's popularity in the group by showing that she appreciates that child. It even helps to put him in a seat next to a very popular child, or to let him be partners with that child in activities, going on errands around the school and so on.

There are things that the parents can do at home, too. Be friendly and hospitable when your child brings others home to play. Encourage him to invite friends to meals and then serve the dishes that they consider fantastic. When you plan weekend trips, picnics, excursions, films, and other shows, invite another child with whom your child wants to be friends – not necessarily the one you would like him to be friendly with. Children, like adults, have a mercenary side and they are more apt to feel friendly towards a child whose parents provide treats for them.

Naturally, you don't want your child to have only bought popularity; that kind won't last anyway. What you are after is to prime the pump, to give him a chance to break into a group that may be shutting him out because of the natural clannishness of this age. Then, you hope, he can take over from that start and build real friendships of his own.

Clubs and cliques. This is the age for the blossoming of clubs. A number of kids who are already friends decide to form a secret club. Given a chance, they sit together at lunch, play with each other at break time, and go over to each other's houses after school. If they have the chance, they might fix up a secret meeting place and develop their own rules for governing themselves. Or they might use mobile phones or social networking sites to connect with each other.

It seems to help children, when they're trying to be grown-up, to get together with others who feel the same way. Often the group tries to bring outsiders into line by making them feel left out or by picking on them. This might sound conceited and cruel, but that's because we grown-ups are accustomed to using more refined methods of disapproving of each other. The children are only feeling the instinct to get community life organized. This is one of the forces that make our civilization click. However, the natural tendency to form groups can become destructive, leading to cruel teasing or even physical attacks. Then parents and teachers need to step in.

As children reach around age ten or eleven, the pressure to belong can be intense. Tight-knit groups, or cliques, make their own rules for who's in and who's out. Physical attractiveness, athletic or academic ability, money, the right clothes, the right talk: all are tickets in. A child who has none of these desirable traits might find herself left out altogether – a lonely and often miserable predicament. A sympathetic and skilful teacher or guidance counsellor can sometimes help turn things around; at other times, a psychologist or other professional can help a child learn the social skills she needs.

Bullies. There was a time when bullying was considered normal, one of those unpleasant parts of childhood, like injections, that kids just have to put up with. Now we know that bullying causes real harm. Children who are bullied often develop stomachaches, headaches and other signs of stress or depression. They might withdraw to their room or act out in angry ways. Bullies tend to target the most vulnerable kids, those with few friends. For these children, being bullied adds fear and humiliation to their everyday experience of loneliness – a terribly destructive mix.

In the short term, bullies can seem to be on top of the world, but in the long term they often suffer, too. Having learned to prosper through intimidation, they have a hard time finding other ways to get along. As a result, they often have difficulty keeping relationships and jobs, and keeping out of trouble with the law.

The answer to bullying is not to tell a child to ignore the attacks or to fight back, although some children benefit from exercise or martial arts training. The idea is not to make the child a better fighter but to build her self-confidence so that she is less easy to intimidate. In most cases, however, the first line of defence against bullying is adult supervision in the places where it typically takes place – hallways, toilets, the playground.

In the long run, the key to preventing bullying is education. With adult leadership, children learn to identify bullying and understand how it hurts everyone. It is now compulsory for schools to institute policies that say bullying is not okay and that children who witness bullying are expected to stand up for the victim, not give their silent approval by acting as an audience. Headteachers, parents and teachers have to make prevention a priority, because bullying undermines the security of all the children in the school, and children need to feel secure in order to learn.

AT HOME

Work and housework. In many societies school-age children work in farms or businesses, workshops or factories. In the United Kingdom, school has become

the main or only occupation expected of most children. But children also need to feel that they can contribute meaningfully to their family's well-being. If a child can't work in the family business, it's good for him to have chores that allow him to feel that he is truly helping out. A six-year-old can help set and clear the table; an eight-year-old can help with cleaning or pulling weeds; a ten-year-old can do simple cooking.

Chores teach children about doing their share in the household, just as they will later participate in the larger society. Although chores often conform with stereotyped sex roles – cooking for girls, lawn work for boys – it's better to let children experience a full range of jobs. That way, chores can help children take a broader view of their capabilities.

The best way to get your child to do chores is to be consistent and matter-of-fact about his responsibilities. Don't make lots of exceptions or let him get away without finishing his tasks. Assign chores that are simple and well within your child's abilities, and take the attitude that they will be done every day.

Pocket money. Children learn about handling money (like most other things) mainly through watching their parents. If you're thoughtful about how you spend and you talk about how you make money decisions, your child is apt to try to follow your lead. Most kids begin to understand about saving and spending at about age six or seven, so that's a good time to start giving a weekly allowance. Pocket money permits a child to make small decisions about money. For these decisions to be meaningful, parents need to resist the temptation to simply buy their children things when they feel generous, or when their children plead extra hard. Children need the opportunity to experience the consequences of their choices. Of course, parents still get to set limits on how pocket money is spent. If your child wants to spend his saved-up allowance on a toy gun, your rule against such toys still holds. The size of the allowance is less important than the expectations – both for decision making and for limits – that go with it.

Money shouldn't be used as payment for routine chores. Chores are a way that family members contribute to the work of the family. The reason to do chores is 'because everyone in the family helps out'. However, refusal to do chores might result in a loss of some privileges, including the privilege to control pocket money.

Homework. Early on, homework can help a child learn to work independently. Later on, it allows children to practise what they've learned at school. Children who do more homework tend to do better academically, but more is not always better. Homework should take no more than an hour a week in Years 1 and 2, one and a half in Years 3 and 4, thirty minutes a night in Years 5 and 6, forty-five minutes to ninety minutes in Years 7 and 8, building to one to two hours in Year 9. Sometimes a school simply assigns too much. In other cases, a child who has learning difficulties manages to get the work done, but only by putting in much more time than her classmates. When homework is tougher than it should be, teachers and parents can work together to find out why, and provide the right help. See page 999 for more on homework.

COMMON BEHAVIOUR CONCERNS

Lying. Younger children often lie simply to escape the consequences of their misdeeds. Did they take those biscuits? Well, they didn't really *mean* to, they just sort of did it, so in a way, perhaps the answer is no – or so the child may think. Children need to learn that saying something is so does not *make* it so. They also need to learn that it's better to own up early, rather than make things worse by lying. They learn through moral stories told by parents and teachers, and also through experience.

Why does an older child lie? Everyone, grown-up or child, gets in a jam occasionally when the only tactful way out is a small lie, and this is no cause for alarm. But if your child tells a lie to deceive, the first question to ask yourself is: 'Why does my child feel she has to lie?'

Children aren't naturally deceitful. A child who often lies is under too much pressure of some kind. As the parent, your job is to find out what is wrong and help find a better solution. You might say gently, 'You don't have to lie to me. Tell me what the trouble is and we'll see what we can do.' Often, though, a child won't be able to tell you right away. For one thing, she may not understand the situation well enough to explain in words. But even if she knows some of her worries, she may not feel comfortable talking about them. Helping her to express her feelings and worries takes time and understanding. Sometimes you'll need the help of a teacher, school psychologist, guidance counsellor or other professional.

For stealing, an issue that often goes along with lying, see page 960.

Cheating. Young children cheat because they don't like losing. A six-year-old thinks that the point of playing is to win. He's gleeful as long as he's on top, miserable if he starts to fall behind. Learning to lose gracefully takes years. Eventually most kids work out that everyone has more fun when everyone plays fair. They don't learn this from grown-ups as much as from each other.

A group of eight-year-olds is likely to spend more time arguing about *how* to play a game than they do actually playing it. A tremendous amount of learning takes place during these debates. At first, children see the rules as something fixed and unchangeable. Later, as their concepts of right and wrong become more mature and flexible, they realize that rules can be changed, as long as all the players agree.

Of course, children can also enjoy games where no one loses and everyone wins. More and more of these noncompetitive games are available in shops or over the Internet. Playing noncompetitive games may help a child realize that the object of playing a game is to have fun, not to beat your opponent.

Compulsions. The tendency toward strictness becomes so strong in many children around eight, nine and ten that they develop nervous habits. You might remember them from your own childhood. The commonest is stepping over cracks in the pavement. There's no sense to it; you just have a superstitious feeling that you ought to. Other examples are touching every third post in a fence, making numbers come out even in some way, and saying certain words before going through a door. If you think you have made a mistake, you must go way back to where you were absolutely sure that you were right, and start over again.

Compulsions may be a response to anxious feelings. One source of anxiety might be hostile feelings towards parents. Think about the childhood saying, 'Step on a crack, break your mother's back.' Everyone has hostile feelings at times towards the people who are close to him, but his conscience would be shocked at the idea of really harming them and warns him to keep such thoughts out of his mind. And if a person's conscience becomes excessively stern, it keeps nagging about such unacceptable thoughts even after he has succeeded in hiding them away in his subconscious mind. He still feels guilty, though he doesn't know what for. It eases his conscience to be extracareful and proper about such a senseless thing as how to navigate a crack in the pavement.

Mild compulsions are so common around the ages of eight, nine and ten years that they shouldn't be a concern, particularly in a child who is happy, outgoing and doing well in school. On the other hand, if a child has compulsions that occupy a lot of his time, such as excessive handwashing, or if he is tense, worried or unsociable, then it's sensible to seek professional help. Severe compulsiveness, like many other anxiety-related disorders, often has a genetic cause. A strong family history of anxiety problems should be a tip-off to consult a doctor or mental health professional sooner rather than later.

Tics. Tics are nervous habits such as eye blinking, shoulder shrugging, grimacing, neck twisting, throat clearing, sniffing or dry coughing. Like compulsions, tics occur most commonly around the age of nine, but they can begin at any age after two. The motion is usually quick, repeated regularly, and always in the same form.

A tic may last off and on for a number of weeks or months and then go away for good or be replaced by a new one. Blinking, sniffing, throat clearing and dry coughing often start with a cold but continue after the cold is gone. Shoulder shrugging may begin when a child has a new loose-fitting garment that feels as if it were falling off. Children may copy a mannerism from another child with a tic, especially from a child they look up to, but these mannerisms don't last long.

The main cause of tics seems to lie in the development of the brain. But psychology also plays a role. Tics tend to get worse when a child is tense or under a lot of pressure. Sometimes the problem is a parent who is overly critical or controlling, sets standards that are too high, or fills a child's days with too many planned activities. If the child were bold enough to fight back, he might be less tightened up inside.

A child's tics are out of his control, even if he can suppress them for a short time. Scolding a child for his tics only makes the problem worse; instead, parents' whole effort should go into making home life relaxed and agreeable, with the least possible nagging, and making school and social life satisfying. About one child in ten has mild tics like this; these almost always go away with benign neglect. Maybe one out of a hundred children will continue to have multiple tics that persist for over a year. Such a child may have *Tourette's Syndrome*, and should be checked by the doctor.

Posture. Some children seem to be born with a relaxed set of muscles and ligaments. Poor posture can be a reflection of wider health problems, most often a lack of physical activity and too many hours hunched in front of a video screen. Being overweight or obese can exaggerate swayback, knock-knees and flat feet. There are also rare diseases that affect posture. And chronic illness and chronic fatigue (from any cause) can cause children to slump and sag. A child with poor posture should have a thorough medical evaluation.

Many children slouch because of a lack of self-confidence. This may result from too much criticism at home, from difficulties in school, or from an unhappy social life. People who are buoyant and sure of themselves show it in the way they sit, stand and walk. The natural impulse of parents is to keep after posture: 'Remember the shoulders' or 'For goodness' sake, stand up straight'. But children who are stooped over because they feel beaten down won't be improved by more nagging.

Instead, children often do better with posture work

through dance or other body movement classes, or from a physical therapist. In these places the atmosphere is more businesslike than at home. The parents may be able to help a boy greatly in carrying out his exercises at home, if he wants help and if they can give it in a friendly way. But their main job is to help the child's spirit by aiding his school adjustment, fostering a happy social life and making him feel adequate and self-respecting at home.

ADOLESCENCE: TWELVE TO EIGHTEEN YEARS

A TWO-WAY STREET

Teenagers and their parents need to work out how to let go of each other. In some families, this happens smoothly; in others, there are struggles. The process is more comfortable when parents remember that their teenagers aren't really out to get them, but in fact are just trying to establish their own adult identities.

Adolescents have a lot to cope with. Puberty reshapes their bodies in ways that change how they feel about themselves and how the rest of the world responds to them. Sexual urges exhilarate and terrify at the same time. Our culture adds to the turmoil by sending mixed messages about adolescent sexuality, on the one hand idolizing it (just think of all the ads featuring young, sexy bodies) and on the other hand treating it as a dangerous force that needs to be quelled and controlled. School is a welcome haven for many teens but feels like a prison to others. The ability to think abstractly leads many teens to question the adult society that they are preparing to join. Idealism can be a powerful force for good, but it also can lead to acts of violence.

Faced with challenging or worrisome teen behaviour, it helps for parents to remind themselves that the fundamental values they taught their children have not disappeared. Most teens hold to their family's core beliefs, even if they dye their hair a colour never seen in nature. Yet there are real dangers, too. Risky sexual behaviour, alcohol use and drugs can all have long-term, even permanent consequences, and many mental health problems make their first appearance in the teen years. So, you need to trust your teen to make it through the maze of adolescence, but you must also keep alert to the pitfalls along the way. By focusing on the long-term goal – a healthy, well-functioning young adult – you may be better able to sort out behaviours that are truly concerning from those that are merely annoying.

Being a wise parent to an adolescent has always been a difficult job. Some unknown parent once said, 'Oh, to be only half as wonderful as my child thought I was, and only half as stupid as my teenager thinks I am.'

PUBERTY

The physical changes of puberty play out over two to four years of rapid growth and body changes, leading up to the ability to reproduce. The timing of these changes varies widely. Most girls start with breast development around age ten and have their first period at about thirteen. But some healthy girls begin at age eight, or even earlier, and others as late as twelve or thirteen; in the latter case the first menstrual period may not come until fourteen or fifteen. Most boys start puberty two years after the girls, at around twelve, but some healthy boys start as late as fourteen or fifteen. If puberty starts very early or very late, it's important to make sure that there is no medical condition causing the unusual timing.

The earliest changes of puberty occur in the brain. Hormones flowing from the brain's pituitary gland rev up the testicles and ovaries, which in turn make testosterone and oestrogen, the hormones that trigger all of the rest of puberty. What exactly sets the brain into action in the first place, no one knows for sure. Heredity, nutrition and general health all play a role. In the United Kingdom, better nutrition during childhood has lowered the age of puberty considerably over the last fifty years. Some experts also point to other factors such as pesticides and other chemicals that might mimic the brain's internal signals.

Puberty in girls. Let's trace what happens to the average girl who starts puberty at age ten. When she was seven years old, she was growing 5 to 6.5 cm (2 to 2½ in) a year. When she was eight, her rate of growth slowed down to perhaps 4.5 cm (1¾ in) a year. Nature seemed to be putting on the brakes. Suddenly, at about ten, the brakes let go and she begins to shoot up at the rate of 7.5 to 9 cm (3 to 3½ in) a year. Instead of putting on 2.25 to 3.6 kg (5 to 8 lb) a year, as she used to, she now gains from 4.5 to 9 kg (10 to 20 lb) a year. Her appetite increases significantly to make this gain possible.

But other things are happening, too. Her breasts begin to develop. A hard lump forms under one nipple, sometimes raising worries about breast cancer, until the other breast also declares itself. The breasts are cone-shaped for the first year or two, rounding out into hemispheres as the first menstrual period approaches. Occasionally one breast begins to develop months before the other. This is nothing to worry about, although the earlier-developing breast tends to stay larger throughout puberty and sometimes beyond.

Pubic hair starts to appear soon after the first breast changes, followed by armpit hair and changes in skin texture. The hips widen, and extra fat rounds out the body. Menarche – the first menstrual period – usually comes around the thirteenth birthday. After that, growth in height slows down. In the year after menarche, the average girl gains about 4 cm (1½ in), and perhaps 2 cm (¾ in) in the year after that. Many girls have irregular and infrequent periods for the first year or two. This is not a sign that something is wrong: it only means that full maturity was not reached by the first period. There are other normal variations: in some, pubic hair appears months before breast buds, and once in a while armpit hair is the earliest sign of change.

We have been talking about the average girl. The fact that a girl starts puberty much earlier or later usually just means that she is on a faster or slower timetable. Parents who were late developers are more apt to have children who are late developers, and vice versa. A thirteen-year-old who has shown no signs of pubertal development doesn't need to worry, just wait.

It can be upsetting if the onset of puberty is later or earlier than average. The girl who begins puberty at eight may feel awkward and self-conscious when she finds herself the only girl in her class who's shooting upward and growing breasts. The responses of teachers, parents and peers can also be confusing. Also bothered is the girl who's on a slow timetable. A girl who hits fourteen without any signs of puberty, or who has been physically mature for over two years without having a period, should be evaluated by her physician.

Puberty in boys. The average boy begins two years later than the average girl, at twelve in contrast to her ten. Early developers may begin as young as ten or younger still. Plenty of slow developers start as late as fourteen, and there are a few who wait longer.

Pubic hair appears, the testicles enlarge, and finally the penis begins to grow first in length and then in diameter. All these changes start before the growth spurt, so that early on the boy himself may be the only one who notices. (Body odour, alas, often announces puberty to the world; boys, for some reason, seem less interested in dealing with it than girls.) Boys are often very aware of their more frequent erections and are certain that everyone around them notices as well.

During puberty, boys often grow twice as fast as before. Height usually increases first, along with arm length and shoe size, creating a gangly, uncoordinated look. The muscles fill in later. The hair in the armpits and on the face grows thicker and longer; the voice cracks and deepens. Some boys notice changes in their breasts, with a small area under one or both nipples swelling and becoming tender; this is normal. The breasts themselves may enlarge, especially in obese boys, often causing great shame. Weight loss and exercise help; sometimes breast reduction surgery is necessary.

After about two years the transition is nearly complete. Boys keep on growing, more slowly, until around age eighteen. Late-developing boys may grow into their early twenties.

Early pubertal development in boys is seldom upsetting. For a couple of years, an early-developing boy may be the tallest and strongest in the class (very early development, before about age ten, should be evaluated medically). Late development, on the other hand, can be very upsetting. The boy who is on a slow timetable, who is still a 'shrimp' at fourteen when most of his friends have turned almost into grown men, usually needs reassurance, and sometimes counselling, to help him cope. Size, physique and athletic ability count for a lot at this age.

Some parents, instead of reassuring their son that he will start developing in time and will grow 20 or 22 cm (8 or 9 in) in the process, hunt for a doctor who will give him growth hormone treatment. This convinces him that something is really wrong with him. True, there are hormone preparations that bring on the signs of puberty at whatever age they are given. However, there is no evidence that long-term psychological benefits will follow, and these treatments may cause a boy to end up shorter than he normally would have been by stopping his bone growth prematurely. For the rare occasion when there might be too little or too much growth hormone production, a paediatric endocrinologist (hormone specialist) should be consulted before any decision is made about giving hormones.

OTHER HEALTH ISSUES

Body odour. One of the earliest changes of adolescence is more profuse and stronger-smelling perspiration. Some children (and parents, too) are unaware of the odour, but it can cause unpopularity with schoolmates. Daily washing with soap and perhaps the regular use of deodorant become important.

Acne. With puberty, the skin becomes coarser and the pores enlarge and secrete more oil. Some of the pores may become clogged with a combination of oil and old skin cells. When this plug of cells and oil comes into contact with the air, it turns black, making a blackhead. Bacteria that normally live on the skin may get into these enlarged, plugged pores and cause a spot, which is a small infection.

Nearly everyone has acne during puberty. It's not caused by dirt. Sexual fantasies and masturbation, which are nearly universal in teens, don't cause acne; neither does eating chocolate or fried foods. However, oil applied to the hair can set off acne on the forehead, and oil misting up from deep fryers often triggers spots in fast-food workers. Squeezing spots – a temptation many teens find hard to resist – really does tend to make them worse. Most spots are small and near the surface, but there is a deeper, scarring type of acne that tends to run in families and calls for medical treatment.

What can you do about acne? Vigorous daily exercise, fresh air and direct sunshine (wearing a suitable sunscreen to avoid sunburn) seem to improve many complexions. And it's generally a good idea to wash the face with a mild soap or soap substitute and warm water in the morning and again at bedtime. There are soaps and topical medications that contain 5 to 10 per cent benzoyl peroxide that can be purchased without a prescription. And there are many water-based cosmetic preparations (the oil-based ones should be avoided) available for covering up spots and blemishes while nature takes its course.

If these measures fail, medical intervention makes sense. Children are entitled to all the help they can get with spots, for the sake of improving their present appearance and spirits, and to prevent permanent scars. Prescription treatments include ointments or creams containing benzoyl peroxide, tretinoin or related compounds. Antibiotics can be either applied to the skin or taken daily. Hormones, the same ones found in birth control pills, can help, and there are even more powerful treatments for the worst cases.

Diet in adolescence. Now more than ever, the best way to encourage healthy eating is to make good food available as part of regular, pleasant meals, but let your child decide what and how much to eat. Teens who are active and growing quickly can eat huge portions and need every calorie. You can also assume that there will be a certain amount of eating whatever their peers are eating, just to fit in.

This is not the time to micromanage your child's intake. If you try, your teen may feel compelled to score points by eating whatever you say she shouldn't. In fact, most teens care about their bodies and are eager to understand the connections between what they eat and how they feel. If food is not a battleground for control, a teenager may enjoy learning about different foods with and from her parents. You may find that the best approach is to keep healthy food in your house, and keep your mouth closed when your teen opens hers.

Adolescent idealism often focuses on diets. Many teens experiment with vegetarianism, for ethical or environmental reasons, if not for health. All of these reasons are valid, and vegetarian diets that include dairy and eggs can easily provide complete nutrition without any special supplements. Vegetarian diets offer many advantages, both in long-term health and for the health of the planet. Of course, if you've brought your child up in a vegetarian household, there's a pretty good chance that, as a teen, he'll have a fling with a hamburger or two. It's not the end of the world, as long as you don't make it so. (For more on plant-based diets, see page 374.)

For the most part, a healthy mix of grains, vegetables, fruits and, if you choose, lean meats is all a teen needs to thrive. Fast-growing teens need an adequate intake of milk or (for vegans) nondairy sources of calcium.

At times, diets change in potentially negative ways. Sharp increases in consumption, especially of sweets and salty snacks, sometimes follow stress or depression, and can lead to jumps in weight that compound the emotional upset. On the other hand, a loss of appetite and preoccupation with being 'fat' can signal anorexia nervosa (particularly in a tense or driven teen); laxative abuse and binge eating followed by vomiting are other reasons to go for professional help (see page 886).

Sleep. Along with the adolescent growth spurt comes an increased need for sleep. The average ten-year-old can get by with eight hours a night, but the average teen needs nine or ten. Teens also naturally go to bed later and tend to wake later in the morning. But school interferes, forcing teens to get up early even though they stayed up late. A teen who gets sleepier and sleepier (or crankier) through the week and then catches up by sleeping fourteen hours is sleep-deprived. The consequences of too little sleep can include poor school performance, irritability with parents and siblings, symptoms of depression, and excessive weight gain. It can be difficult to help a busy teen get enough sleep. But one of the main culprits, late-night television, is fairly easy to deal with: just say no! Television and other sources of video entertainment really don't belong in the bedroom.

Exercise. Even though they're busy, many teens don't get enough exercise. Regular exercise, through sport, dance, martial arts or other pursuits, helps teens maintain energy, avoid obesity and prevent depression, and it may even boost IQ. More is not always better, however. Constant exercise can be a sign of anorexia nervosa (see page 906).

PSYCHOLOGICAL TASKS

Even though billions have gone before, each adolescent charts his own journey. Some sail through; others crash into rocks along the way. All face a unique set of challenges shaped by personality, family, school, neighbourhood, religion and culture. Still, certain psychological tasks are universal in early, middle and late adolescence. As you go about the tough job of parenting a teen, understanding these tasks can help you to decide when to step in and when to step aside.

PSYCHOLOGICAL TASKS OF ADOLESCENCE

- ✓ Coming to terms with their new physical selves
- ✓ Developing a new male or female emotional identity
- ✓ Reconciling the values of their peers and those of their parents
- ✓ Finding and expressing their own moral convictions
- ✓ Taking responsibility for themselves
- ✓ Charting a path to financial self-sufficiency

A central problem for adolescents and young adults is to figure out what kind of people they are going to be, doing what work, living by what principles. This is partly a conscious process and partly an unconscious one. In groping to create their identities, adolescents may try out a variety of roles: dreamer, cosmopolitan, cynic, politician, entrepreneur and so on. Some adolescents seem to find themselves early and fairly directly; others head down many side roads before they find their paths.

Adolescents have to separate themselves emotionally from their parents in order to find out who they are and what they want to be. Yet they are basically made from their parents – not only because they have inherited their genes from them but also because they have been patterning themselves after them all their lives. So they must now pry themselves apart.

Taking risks. Teens tend to see themselves as invulnerable. It's hard to talk teens out of this perception, because it is based on the fact that most likely they always *have* been fine and therefore expect they always *will* be. Appeals to logic often fall on deaf ears: teens live in the real present, not the hypothetical future.

Not all risks are bad. A teen who bicycles through the countryside or spends hour after hour practising skateboard jumps is gaining skills, building self-esteem and learning to exercise judgment. Mistakes, as long as they are not too serious, are great teachers.

Some risks, however, can be costly. The child who experiments with cigarettes may end up addicted to nicotine. Teen drinking is a form of risk-taking that can end in tragedy when a drunk teen gets behind the wheel of a car. Drug use often progresses to abuse and addiction in troubled teens, but also in adolescents from stable homes. Irresponsible sex is another way teens tempt fate.

The challenge for parents is to help teens take risks

sensibly. Education about risks and risky behaviour needs to start before the teen years. Many primary schools teach about cigarettes, drugs and sex. Parents need to be involved, too. Effective parents find many opportunities to talk with their children about values; even more important, they teach by example. They also avoid putting their children in situations where the temptations are too great. Allowing a sixteen-year-old to stay late working on the school newspaper conveys trust and encourages responsibility. Leaving a fourteen-year-old at home alone for a weekend invites risky behaviour.

Parents often ask what they should tell their children about their own histories of risk taking – usually drugs or sex – when they were teens. There's a fear that the kids might rationalize, 'Well, it didn't seem to hurt my mum and dad, so why not try it myself?' Of course, parents are under no obligation to confess everything to their children, but lying is not the answer. Ultimately the truth comes out, and when a child learns he has been lied to, he loses his ability to trust what his parents tell him; he can't rely on their guidance when he really needs it. A parent's lie is also a powerful vote of no confidence in a teen, as if to say, 'I'm going to manipulate you, rather than trust that you'll respond reasonably.' In a sense, lying to a child cuts him off from his most important source of support. It's much better that your child trusts you than that he sees you as a paragon of virtue. If your child asks you about something that you really don't feel comfortable talking about, it's best to say just, 'I really don't feel comfortable talking about it.'

Even though many teens push back against their parents' values, they almost all do care what their parents think. Let your teen know that what you care about most is that he or she is safe. Above all, he must never get into a car driven by someone who is drunk or less than completely awake, because the consequences can be sudden and permanent. After that, you expect him to stay away from alcohol, cigarettes and drugs, because these too could be harmful. Your messages about risky behaviours will ring true, and your teen will listen, especially if you have been talking with your child all along about keeping safe and healthy.

EARLY ADOLESCENCE

Changing bodies and minds. From twelve to about fourteen, the main psychological challenge is to come to terms with rapidly changing bodies – one's own and one's peers'. These years also see the widest variations in physical development. The average girl is nearly two years ahead of the average boy, towering over him in height and more sophisticated in her interests. She may be interested in going to discos and being treated as if she were glamorous, while he is still an uncivilized little boy who thinks it would be shameful to pay attention to her. Social functions that include a range of age groups may work more smoothly, because kids can find peers of different ages whose interests match their own.

Early adolescents are acutely self-conscious about their bodies. They exaggerate and worry about any defects, and think that everyone else is focused on them, too. If a girl has freckles, she may think they make her look horrible. A boy whose body is shorter, taller, rounder or thinner than most may easily conclude that he is abnormal.

Early adolescents may not be able to manage their new bodies with as much coordination as they used to, and the same is true of their new feelings. They are apt to be touchy and easily hurt when criticized. At one moment they feel like grown-ups and want to be treated as such. The next moment they feel like children again and expect to be cared for.

Friendships. Adolescents often become ashamed of their parents for a few years, particularly around their friends. They feel an intense need to be just like their friends and to be accepted totally by them. They fear that they could face ridicule and rejection by their friends if their parents deviate in any way from the social ideal.

In trying to establish their own identity, early adolescents often turn away from their parents and make intimate ties with friends of the same age. Close friendships support teens while they work on creating identities of their own.

Sometimes a teen finds himself through finding a similarity in his friend. He mentions that he loves a certain song, hates a certain teacher or craves a certain article of clothing. His friend exclaims with amazement that he has always felt the very same way. Both are delighted and reassured. Each has lost a degree of his feeling of aloneness and gained a sense of belonging. This is one reason teens spend so much time talking with each other, not to mention texting and posting on social networking sites. A great benefit of the digital revolution is that teens can connect with like-minded comrades anywhere in the world.

The importance of appearance. Many adolescents help to overcome their feelings of aloneness by slavishly conforming to the styles of their classmates – in clothes, hair, language, reading matter, songs and entertainers. These styles have to be different from those of their parents' generation. If they irritate or shock their parents, so much the better. That's why it rarely works for a parent to simply express revulsion or distaste. You can issue a simple ban ('No navel rings in my house!'), but you're probably asking for a fight, one you may well lose. Instead, if you can get past your gut reaction, you might actually be able to speak reasonably with your teen. You might point out, for example, that a certain style in hair or clothes proclaims an association with a subgroup – skinheads, for example – that your child actually does not endorse. You might point out a real-life constraint, such as 'They won't let you into school wearing that miniskirt.' If you can persuade your teen rather than simply overrule her, you can both win.

On the other hand, if you have an open discussion with your teenager, you might end up being persuaded yourself. We adults tend to be slow to accept new styles. What horrifies or disgusts us one day may later become quite acceptable for us as well as for our children. This was true with the long hair and blue jeans introduced by youths in the 1960s, the trousers for girls that so upset school authorities at one time, fluorescent hair colours and tattoos. The challenge is to hold on to your core values while you keep an open mind.

Early teen sexuality. Most kids fantasize about sex in the early teen years. Many experiment with kissing and petting. A minority experience actual intercourse. Masturbation, a nearly universal teen behaviour, may be a simple fact of life or a source of shame and self-reproach. Erections, either spontaneous or in response to sexual fantasies, make many boys who are already quite self-conscious even more uncomfortable. Most boys also experience ejaculation of semen during sleep (wet dreams). One boy takes these in his stride; another worries there might be something wrong with him.

Sexual feelings and experimentation don't always involve the opposite sex. Homosexuality can be confusing and frightening, but there is seldom any confusion about

alcohol but regularly get drunk themselves – this relieves them of the moral duty to conform and offers a welcome opportunity to reproach their parents. At the same time, however, it may undermine their sense of safety.

Jobs and work. Middle adolescence is when many teens first take on serious jobs besides occasional babysitting or gardening. In moderation, paid work can build self-esteem, responsibility and independence. Work also allows teens to widen their social contacts and explore fields that may eventually lead to careers. Some teens, however, spend so much time on the job that they don't have time to relax or do homework, and they are chronically overtired and cranky. Also, many jobs carry significant health and safety risks. Parents may need to step in to keep work from getting out of hand.

Sexual experimentation. Middle adolescence is when many teens try sex of various sorts. Kissing and petting are almost universal, oral-genital sex happens frequently (although many teens don't think of this as 'real' sex) and in the middle teen years many adolescents experience sexual intercourse. Dating often happens in groups, or sometimes one-on-one. Romances are often brief, with relationships taking a backseat to attraction and experimentation. This is not to say that middle-adolescent romances are all superficial or of no consequence. The emotions – joy and misery, elation and dejection – often have an intensity rarely rivalled in later, more settled periods of life.

Realistically, parents are limited in their ability to control their middle adolescents' sexual behaviour. Educational programmes stressing abstinence as the only choice have obvious appeal to parents but don't actually reduce teen pregnancy, according to most studies. If teens are intent on sexual experimentation, the rules laid down by parents may not stop them; they might even make sex seem more exciting and attractive because it is off-limits. It's more effective for parents to keep communication open, let their children know how they feel about sexual relationships, limit tempting situations (for example, no unchaperoned sleep-overs) and trust their teens to act responsibly. Feelings, freedoms and limits need to be a regular topic of conversation. Parents should talk with their teens about sex, rather than having 'the talk'. A trusted doctor can often help open these lines of communication. For more on talking about sex, see page 708.

Homosexuality. Adolescence is a time of experimentation, and many teens try out homosexual behaviour. A smaller number identify themselves as mostly or completely homosexual in their orientation. Homosexuality is more visible and accepted than ever, but homosexual teens still often feel terribly isolated. A very high rate of suicide and attempted suicide gives dramatic evidence of their pain.

Heterosexual parents might not know where to begin talking to a teenager about sexual orientation. Remember, it's likely that your child is as afraid of the subject as you are and might feel threatened if confronted abruptly. It's best to make the subject of sexual orientation something that comes up naturally, ideally long before your child's teen years. Take notice of insulting jokes and prejudiced comments made by friends or relatives, and speak out against them. Talk about homophobia and why it's as wrong as racism or any other form of discrimination. Introduce into your family collection books, films and music that are created by openly gay, lesbian or bisexual artists, or that deal with those themes. All of these actions send the message that it is safe for your teen to talk about his own sexual identity. Parents who convey intolerance only close off the conversation and risk adding to their children's isolation.

Some gay and lesbian adolescents recognize and accept their sexual orientation early on; others go through a phase of uncertainty. Parents might seek professional counselling, not to change their teen's orientation but to help the boy or girl work through the issue with a minimum of anxiety and shame. A trusted family doctor would be a good place to start. Organizations such as Stonewall Youth (www.youngstonewall.org.uk) and the Lesbian and Gay Switchboard, which has groups throughout the UK, provide information and advice and can put you in touch with local support groups. For more, see page 1054.

LATE ADOLESCENCE

Tasks of the age. By age eighteen to twenty-one, conflicts between adolescents and their parents are beginning to subside. The major tasks during this period involve choosing a career direction and beginning to make more meaningful and lasting emotional relationships.

In the past, the general expectation was that older teens would be preparing to go off to university or to a job that would allow them to live independently. More recently, many older teens have either chosen or felt compelled to continue living in their parents' homes. As society and the economy continue to change, the challenges of late adolescence will change, too.

Idealism and innovation. With increased knowledge and independence comes the desire to make discoveries, create new art forms, displace tyrants and right wrongs. A surprising number of scientific advances have been made and masterpieces of art created by individuals just on the threshold of adulthood. They were not cleverer than the older people in their fields, and they were certainly less experienced. But they were critical of traditional ways, biased in favour of the new and the untried, and willing to take risks, and that was enough to do the trick.

Finding their way. It sometimes takes young adults several years to create their own positive identities. They may decline to take ordinary jobs like their parents did and instead adopt unconventional dress, grooming and acquaintances. These decisions might seem like evidence of vigorous independence to them, but they don't add up to a positive stand on life or a constructive contribution to the world. They are essentially a negative protest against the parents' lifestyle. Even when the striving to be independent shows up only in the form of eccentricities of appearance, it should be recognized as an attempted step in the right direction, which may later lead to a constructive, creative stage.

Other young people who are idealistic and altruistic in character may take a sternly radical or purist view of things for a number of years – in politics, the arts, or other fields. Various tendencies of this developmental stage operate together to draw them into these extreme positions: a heightened need to criticize, cynicism about hypocrisy, intolerance of compromise, courage and a willingness to sacrifice.

A few years later, having achieved a satisfactory degree of emotional independence from parents and having found out how to be useful in their chosen field, they are more tolerant of the frailties of their fellow human beings and more ready to make constructive compromises. Many remain progressive, some remain radical, but most become easier to live and work with.

GENERAL STRATEGIES FOR DEALING WITH TEENS

Make rules. Most adolescents are bound to feel rebellious at least some of the time, whether or not the parent is being reasonable. The first and most important point, by far, is that adolescents need and want guidance – and even consistent limits – from their parents, no matter how much they argue against them. Their pride won't let them admit the need openly, but in their hearts they often think, 'I wish my parents would make definite rules for me, like my friends' parents do.' They sense that it is one aspect of parents' love to want to protect their children from misunderstandings and embarrassing situations out in the world, from giving the wrong impression and gaining an unfortunate reputation, from getting into trouble through inexperience.

Show respect, and expect it in return. This doesn't mean that parents can be arbitrary, inconsistent or overbearing. Adolescents have too much dignity and indignation for that. They want to discuss the issues on what they feel is an adult-to-adult basis. If the argument ends in a draw, though, the parents shouldn't be so scrupulously democratic that they assume the child is as likely to be right as they are. The parents' experience should be presumed to count for a lot. In the end, the parents should confidently express their judgment and, if appropriate, their explicit request. They owe their child this clarity and certitude. Parents should indicate, without necessarily saying so in words, that they realize the young person will be out of their sight most of the time and will therefore comply because of her conscience and respect for her parents, not because the parents can make her obey or because they can watch her at all times.

Parents need to discuss with their young adolescent

children the hour at which they are expected to come home from parties and dates, where they are going and with whom, and what is the mode of transport. If the child asks why they want to know, they can answer that good parents feel responsible for their children. 'Suppose there is an accident,' parents can say. 'We ought to know where to inquire or to search.' Or the parents can say, 'If there were a family emergency, we would want to be able to reach you.' Parents should tell their children where they're going and when they expect to be home, for the same reasons. Incidentally, if there is a delay or a change in plan, adolescents (and parents) should call home to explain before they are overdue. With the agreement of their children, the parents can set a certain hour and be waiting for them. This reminds children that the parents are genuinely concerned with their conduct and safety. When children have a party at home, the parents should be there.

Parents can't dictate to their adolescent children or talk down to them. But they can have mutually respectful, adult-to-adult discussions. Young people never have been willing to be guided beyond a certain point by their parents, but that doesn't mean that they haven't benefited from discussions. Many parents conceal their own opinions and refrain from criticizing adolescent tastes and manners for fear of seeming old-fashioned or oppressive. It's more helpful, however, for parents to talk freely about their views and their own experiences growing up, but to do so as if they are talking to a respected adult friend, not as if they are laying down the law or as if they think their opinions are right simply because they are older.

Deal with defiance. But, parents ask, what if the child openly defies a request or quietly disobeys? In the early years of adolescence, if the child-parent relationship is sound and the rules or limits are reasonable, few children defy or disobey when it comes to serious matters, although they may protest loudly. Parents who feel out of control on key issues of safety or behaviour should seek help from a doctor or other professional, in order to take control appropriately.

In the later years, the parents may choose to back their teen's decision, even if it goes against the parents' best judgment. For example, a seventeen-year-old might have her heart set on becoming a chef, but her parents think law school is a better direction. In such cases, an older teen needs support to follow her own path even if it turns out to be a mistake. When parents know and accept their children, they are better able to see the world through their eyes. They may then come to embrace their children's choices, or succeed in persuading them to rethink their decisions.

Even when an older adolescent defies or disobeys a parental direction, this does not mean that the direction did no good. It certainly helps inexperienced people to hear all sides. If they decide not to take their parents' direction, they may of course be making a reasonably sound decision, perhaps being in possession of knowledge or insights that the parents lack. Certainly as they progress into adulthood, they must be prepared to reject advice on occasion and to take responsibility for their decisions. If young people reject their parents' direction and get into trouble, they'll gain greater respect for their parents' judgment, though they may not admit it.

Take the stance of a concerned parent (which you are). If your teen is doing something that seems dangerous or unwise, it's more effective to let her know that you are concerned than simply to criticize or lay down the law. 'You always seem unhappy after you go on a date with Jim' is likely to be more effective than 'Jim's a stinker!'

Contract for safety. Let your teen know that you'll pick him up any time, from anywhere, no questions asked. As unpleasant as this sounds, it is far better than having to deal with injuries or legal problems that result from driving intoxicated, for example. Teens also need access to confidential medical care so that they are free to discuss any questions that they may not feel comfortable sharing with their parents. Good medical care doesn't make teens promiscuous; just the opposite.

Take reasonable precautions against suicide. If your teen seems sad, down or distant, if he loses interest in things that he used to love, or if his grades drop off suddenly, keep the possibility of depression in mind and seek help.

Use your best judgment. Suppose you don't know what to say or think about some issue. For example, your teen wants to go to a concert that's scheduled to last until 2 am. You can discuss it with other parents, but don't feel bound in advance to follow their advice. In the long run, you can do a good job only if you are convinced you are doing the right thing. And what is right for you is what you feel is right, after hearing the arguments.

Some questions to ask yourself when deciding whether or not to allow a specific behaviour: is it safe? Is it legal? Does it undermine a core moral principle? Has your child considered the consequences? Is your child acting freely, or is someone else (a teacher, a peer) exercising undue influence? By focusing on such questions, you may be able to chart your own best course of action, and may also be able to help your teen make a wise decision.

Expect civil behaviour and participation. Individually and in groups, adolescents should be expected to behave civilly to people and to be cordial to their parents, family friends, teachers and the people who work with them. At times it is natural for youths to have at least a mildly hostile attitude towards adults. But it does them no harm, and much good, to have to control this hostility and be polite anyway. Adolescents should also have serious obligations in helping their families by doing regular housework and special additional jobs.

This benefits them by giving them a sense of dignity, participation, responsibility and happiness, and it helps the family as a whole.

You can't enforce these rules, but you are entitled to express them in discussions with your children. It helps adolescents to hear their parents' principles, even if they don't conform.

SECTION II

Feeding and Nutrition

FEEDING IN THE FIRST YEAR

Feeding decisions. You want to feed your baby, and your baby wants to be fed. Both of you come with strong instincts about how to get the job done. There are also plenty of other people – friends and family, the media and of course doctors – telling you what to do. It's fine to listen to everybody, but in the end, you have to do what your heart, or your gut, tells you is best. Perhaps the most important person to listen to is your baby.

A baby knows a lot about diet. She knows how many calories her body needs and what her digestion can handle. If she's not getting enough, she'll probably cry for more. If there's more in the bottle than she feels like eating, she'll probably stop. Take her word for it. Feeding usually works best when you follow your baby's cues: let her fill up when she feels empty and stop when she feels full. That way, you'll be nurturing her self-confidence, her joy in life and her love of people, as well as her body.

Your main job, then, is to understand your baby's hunger cues. Some babies are fairly easy to read. They feel hungry on a predictable cycle and feel comfortable once full. Other babies are more difficult. They cry at odd intervals, sometimes from hunger, sometimes from other discomforts. Babies like this put parents' patience and self-confidence to the test. If it feels like you can't make sense of your baby's signals, don't blame yourself, but do ask for help from experienced friends and family members and from your baby's doctor.

The important sucking instinct. Babies nurse eagerly for two reasons: first, because they're hungry, and second, because they love to suck. If you feed them but don't give them enough chance to suck, their craving for sucking will go unsatisfied and they will try to suck something else – their fists, thumbs or clothes. Some babies feel this urge more than others. Bottle-fed babies sometimes end up overeating because they just keep on sucking and the formula keeps on flowing. When they overfill their stomachs, they spit up (it can seem like an awful lot) or pass large watery stools. Less often, breast-fed babies have the same problem. It's reasonable, in these cases, to let your baby take in what seems like a reasonable amount, then offer a dummy to satisfy the need for more sucking.

WHEN TO FEED

Strict schedules. A hundred years ago, experts told parents to feed their babies every four hours by the clock. This plan, which was supposed to prevent diarrhoea, worked well enough for many babies. But there were always some babies who had trouble adjusting to a regular schedule: babies whose stomachs couldn't seem to hold four hours' worth of milk, babies who went to sleep halfway through feedings, restless babies, colicky babies. They would cry miserably, but their mothers dared not feed them – or even pick them up – off schedule. This was hard on the babies *and* on their parents. With the availability of pasteurized milk and safe tap water, severe diarrhoea became much less of a problem for babies. But it took many more years before doctors began experimenting with flexible schedules.

Self-demand feeding. In 1942, a psychologist and a new mother decided to see what would happen if a baby was allowed to nurse on his own schedule. They called this 'self-demand feeding'. The baby awoke rather infrequently for the first few days; then, starting about the time the milk began to come in during the second week, he awoke surprisingly often, about ten times a day. After two weeks he settled down to six or seven feedings a day, at rather irregular intervals. By ten weeks he had arrived at approximately a two- to four-hour schedule. He did fine.

That brave experiment inspired a general relaxation in infant feeding schedules. We now know that breast-fed babies in the first two weeks of life nurse more or less every two hours. That means that some nurse every three hours and some as often as every hour and a half. All of these patterns are normal, and it's normal for feeding frequency to change over time.

What good is regularity? From a baby's point of view, the most important thing is to be fed more or less right away. I say more or less, because most babies can wait a little now and then. But when they have to scream with hunger for long periods – and even a few minutes is long to a little baby – they don't learn to trust in the people who provide for them, and they can come to feel helpless and alone. Rigid schedules don't work for babies who have very unpredictable hunger cycles. Most babies, however, can adjust their hunger cycles to fit the regular times that feedings occur.

A regular schedule also helps parents to conserve their strength and spirits. This usually means getting down to a reasonable number of feedings at predictable hours and giving up the night feeding as soon as the baby is ready. If parents prefer to feed their baby on an irregular, self-demand schedule for many months, there will be no harm done to the baby's nutrition. But parents shouldn't get the idea that the more they give up for the baby the better it is for the child, or that they have to prove that they are good parents by ignoring their own convenience. These attitudes tend to create difficulties in the long run. Instead, parents can work with their babies to shape a schedule that meets everyone's needs.

Scheduling: the baby's part. A baby approaching her first birthday usually sleeps through the night, though she may awaken early for a feeding. She eats three meals and a couple of snacks, has a nap or two, and goes to sleep at a reasonable hour, often after a last breast- or bottle-feeding. How does all this fall into place? It isn't only what the parents do. It's the baby herself, gradually lengthening the time between feedings and shortening the sleep periods. Along with her own maturation, she just naturally tends to fit into the family's schedule.

Most babies soon fall into a regular pattern of feeding and sleeping. Some newborns seem to come out of the hospital already set on a two- to four-hour feeding interval. Others seem to fashion a schedule of their own, though it may take a few weeks for them to become consistent about it. Smaller babies tend to eat more frequently than bigger babies. Breast-fed babies on average eat more often than bottle-fed babies because breast milk is digested more quickly than formula. All tend to gradually lengthen the interval between feedings as they grow bigger and older.

The intervals between feedings may vary within each twenty-four-hour period but tend to have some consistency from one day to the next. At some times of the day, babies are apt to want to eat more frequently. They may have a stretch of fretfulness lasting several hours, which usually occurs in the early evening. During these hours, a breast-fed baby may want to nurse almost continually, crying if she is put down. A bottle-fed baby may act hungry but not take much if offered a bottle, though she may suck avidly at the dummy. The evening fussiness gradually improves over the first few months – though it may seem to take forever.

By one, two or three months old, babies come to realize they don't need the middle-of-the-night feeding and will give it up. Somewhere between the fourth and twelfth month, they will be able to sleep through the feeding at the parents' bedtime, too.

Helping your baby get on schedule. Individual babies differ widely in how soon they can comfortably settle down to regular schedules. Here's what you can do to help. If you wake your baby during the day whenever he's still asleep, four hours after the last feeding, you are helping him to establish regular daytime eating habits. If, when he stirs and whimpers a couple of hours after the last feeding, you hold back for a few minutes and give him a chance to go to sleep again or offer a dummy if he really wakens and cries, you are helping his stomach adjust to a longer interval. If, on the other hand, you always pick him up and feed him as soon as he stirs, even though it's shortly after the last feeding, you keep him accustomed to short intervals and small feedings.

Most babies who are good feeders can be eased into a reasonably consistent schedule and will give up the middle-of-the-night feeding a couple of months after birth. On the other hand, if a baby is a listless, sleepy feeder at first, or a restless, fretful waker, or if the breast milk supply is not yet well established, it will be more comfortable for all concerned to go more slowly. But even in these cases, there will be less perplexity on the part of the parents every day about whether to give a feeding right away or to wait, and an earlier settling down on the part of the baby, if the parents are always working gently towards more regular feedings, with an average interval of two to three hours for breast-fed babies and three to four hours for bottle-fed babies.

The easiest way to begin scheduling a baby is to wake her during the day if she is still asleep, four hours after her last feeding. You won't have to urge her to eat; she will probably act starvingly hungry within a few minutes. But suppose she wakes an hour after her last feeding. You don't have to feed her the minute she whimpers. She's not sure herself whether she's hungry. But if instead of settling back to sleep she wakens fully and starts crying hard, it does no good to wait any longer. What if she starts a pattern of waking soon after each feeding? Perhaps she needs more to eat. If she is breast-fed, nursing her more frequently will increase the milk supply in a few days, so she'll be able to take more at each feeding and again lengthen the time between feedings. (It's important for the mother to take care of herself, so she can produce more milk as the baby needs it; see page 291.) If your baby is bottle-fed, increase each feeding by an ounce or more and see if that helps lengthen the intervals.

Just how soon should you give another feeding? If a baby who generally can go three or four hours awakens after two or two and a half hours and seems really hungry, it is all right to feed her then. But suppose she wakes up after only an hour. If she finished her usual bottle at her last feeding, she probably isn't hungry again so soon. It is more likely that she has been awakened by indigestion. You can try burping her again, or see whether she will be comforted by 60 ml (2 fl oz) of water or a dummy. There is no rush to feed her again, though you may decide to try it in a little while if nothing else works.

You can't be sure it's hunger just because a baby tries to eat her hand or starts to take the bottle eagerly. Often a baby who is having colic will do both these things. It seems the baby herself can't distinguish between colic pains and hunger pains. In other words, you don't always have to feed a baby every time she cries. If she is crying at the wrong times, you have to study the situation. She may be wet or too warm or cold; she may need to burp or be comforted; or she may just need to let out a few cries to release tension. If this keeps happening and you can't work it out, discuss the problem with your health visitor. (For more on crying, see page 60.)

Middle-of-the-night feedings. The easiest rule for night feedings is not to wake your baby but to let him wake you. A newborn usually wakes surprisingly close to the hour of 2 am. Then some night, probably when he's between two and six weeks old, he will sleep through until 3 or 3.30 am. Feed him then. The next night he might wake still later. Or he might wake but cry in a drowsy way, and go back to sleep if he is not fed right away.

When babies get ready to give up the middle-of-the-night feeding, somewhere between six and twelve weeks,

they usually do it in a hurry, within two or three nights. In the case of the breast-fed baby, he may nurse longer at his other feedings. In the case of the bottle-fed baby, you can increase the amount in his other bottles to make up for the bottle he's given up, if he wants that extra amount. Night feedings should be given quietly in a darkened room, in contrast to daytime feedings, which can be accompanied by more stimulation.

Giving up the middle-of-the-night feeding. If a baby reaches the age of two or three months and weighs 5.4 kg (12 lb) but still wakes for a middle-of-the-night feeding, it's sensible to try to influence him to give it up. Instead of hurrying to him as soon as he stirs, you can let him fuss for a little while. If he doesn't quiet down but instead is soon crying furiously, apologize to him and feed him promptly. But try again in another week or two. From a nutritional point of view, a 5.4 kg (12 lb) baby who's eating well during the day doesn't really need this feeding.

The feeding at the parents' bedtime is the one that you can probably time to your own convenience. Most babies, by the time they are a few weeks old, are perfectly willing to wait until 11 pm or even midnight for it. If you want to get to bed early, wake your baby at 10 or even a little before. If a later feeding is more convenient, suit yourself, as long as your baby is willing to stay asleep. For those babies who are still waking for middle-of-the-night feedings, it's best not to let them sleep through the 10 or 11 pm feeding, even though they're quite willing to do so. When they're ready to give up one of them, you'll want them to give up the middle-of-the-night feeding first, so that your sleep won't be interrupted.

For those babies who are already off the middle-of-the-night feeding but are still quite irregular about their daytime feeding hours, I'd continue to wake them at 10 or 11 pm, provided they're willing to be fed. This at least ends the day on schedule, helps very much to avoid a feeding between midnight and 4 am, and tends to encourage them to sleep until 5 or 6 am the next morning.

GETTING ENOUGH AND GAINING WEIGHT

Average weight gain. We can talk about average babies if you remember clearly that no baby is average. One baby is meant to be a slow gainer, and another is meant to be a fast gainer. When doctors talk about an average baby, they mean only that they have added together the fast gainers, the slow gainers and the medium gainers.

The average baby's weight is a little over 3.2 kg (7 lb) at birth and 6.35 kg (14 lb) between three and five months. That is to say, the average baby has doubled its birth weight by three to five months. In actual practice, babies who are small at birth are apt to grow faster, as if trying to catch up, and babies who are born big often grow more slowly at first.

The average baby gains close to 900 g (2 lb) a month (170 to 225 g/6 to 8 oz a week) for the first three months. Of course, some healthy ones gain less and others more. Then the baby slows down. By six months, the average gain is down to 450 g (1 lb) a month (115 g/4 oz a week). That's quite a drop in a three-month period. In the last quarter of the first year, the average gain is down to 285 g (10 oz) a month (55 to 85 g/2 to 3 oz each week) and, during the second year, to about 225 g (8 oz) a month (55 g/2 oz a week).

As babies grow older, as you see, they gain more slowly. They also gain more irregularly. Teething or illness may take their appetite away for several weeks and they may hardly gain at all. When they feel better, their appetite revives and their weight catches up with a rush.

You can't decide much from how babies' weights change from week to week. What they weigh each time will depend on how recently they have urinated, how recently they have moved their bowels, how recently they have eaten. If you find, one morning, that your baby boy has gained only 115 g (4 oz) in the past week when before he had always gained 200 g (7 oz), don't jump to the conclusion that he is starving or that something else is wrong. If he seems perfectly happy and satisfied, wait another week to see what happens. He may make an extra large gain to make up for the small one.

For the breast-fed baby, wetting the nappy at least six to eight times a day, being alert and happy when awake, and sleeping well are good indications that he's getting enough to eat. Always remember, though, that the older he gets, the slower he will gain.

How often to weigh. Most parents don't have scales, so most babies get weighed only when they go to their doctor or visit the health visitor's baby clinic. When a baby is happy and doing well, weighing more frequently than once a month serves no purpose but to satisfy curiosity. On the other hand, if your baby is crying a lot, having indigestion or vomiting a great deal, more frequent weighing may help you and your health visitor to decide what the matter is. For instance, excessive crying in a child who is gaining weight rapidly usually points toward colic (see page 104), not hunger.

Slow weight gain. Many healthy babies gain weight slowly, compared to the average. But if babies are gaining slowly, that doesn't mean for sure that they were meant to. If they are hungry all the time, that is a pretty good sign that they are meant to be gaining faster. Once in a while, slow gaining means that a baby is sick. Slow gainers particularly need to be seen regularly by a doctor to make sure that they are healthy.

Occasionally you see exceptionally polite babies who are gaining slowly and who don't seem too hungry. But if you give them more to eat, they take it quite willingly and gain more rapidly. In other words, not all babies yell when they are being fed too little.

Fat babies. It seems hard for some people to change their feeling that fatness in babies is attractive and desirable. Relatives and friends may compliment the parents on it as if it were proof of superior care. Some parents think of baby fat as a reserve – like money in the bank – against some possible future adversity or illness. Of course, this isn't so. Babies who carry around a lot of fat are no happier or healthier than leaner ones, and they tend to develop rashes where their fat folds rub together. Fatness in infancy does not necessarily mean that the baby will be fat for life, but it's not a kindness to babies to get them fattened up.

Refusal to nurse in later months. Once in a while a baby between four and seven months old acts oddly at feeding time. The mother will say that her baby nurses hungrily at the breast or bottle for a few minutes. Then he becomes frantic, lets go of the nipple and cries as if in pain. He still seems very hungry, but each time he goes back to nursing he becomes uncomfortable sooner. He takes his solid food eagerly if he has already been weaned.

It may be that this distress is caused by teething. As the baby nurses, the suction engorges his painful gums and makes them tingle unbearably. You can break each nursing period into several parts and give the solid food in the intervals, since the distress comes on only after a number of minutes of sucking. If he is on a bottle, you can experiment with enlarging the hole in a few nipples so that he finishes the bottle in a shorter time with less strenuous sucking. If your baby's discomfort is excessive and comes on very promptly, you could, for a few days, give up the bottle altogether. Give him his milk from the cup if he is skilful enough, or from a spoon, or mix a large amount of it with his cereal and other foods. Don't worry if he doesn't get his usual amount.

An ear infection, complicating a cold, may cause enough pain in the jaw joint so that babies will refuse to nurse even though they may be able to eat solids pretty well. Occasionally a baby will decline to take the breast during the mother's menstrual periods. Offering the breast more often during those days may help the baby take at least a little. Pumping the breast milk or expressing it manually may help to relieve the fullness and keep the supply going until baby and mother can return to business as usual.

Drinking water for babies. Some babies want water; others don't. It is sometimes recommended that a baby be offered a few ounces of water between meals once or twice a day. It isn't really necessary, because the amount of fluid in breast milk or formula will satisfy the baby's ordinary needs. It is more important to offer water if the baby has a fever, or during excessively hot weather, especially if his urine turns dark yellow or he appears very thirsty. Babies who ordinarily refuse water often take it at these times. Some mothers have found that adding a small amount of apple juice to the water gets the baby more interested. If

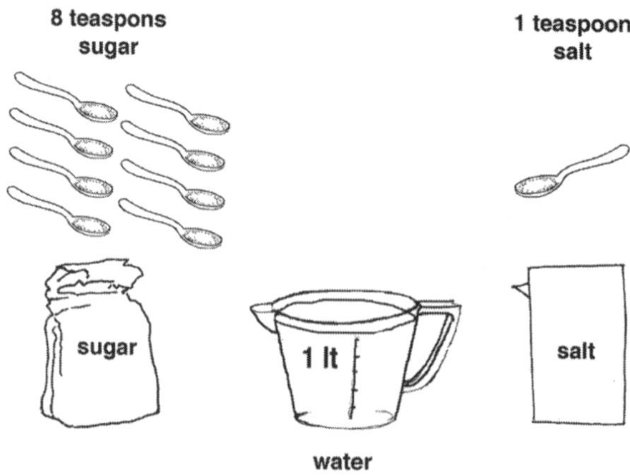

you are giving extra water, it's important to continue giving the regular amount of formula or breast milk as well. Babies given *only* water can become quite ill.

A lot of babies don't want any water from the time they are a week or two old until they are about a year. During this age they fairly worship anything with nourishment in it, but they feel insulted by plain water. If your baby likes it, by all means give it to him once or several times a day when he is awake between meals, but not just before the next meal. You can give him as much as he wants, as long as he is taking his usual amount of formula or breast milk as well. He probably won't want more than 60 ml (2 fl oz). But don't urge him to take water if he doesn't want it. There's no point in getting him angry. He knows what he needs.

You may particularly want your baby to drink water if he is taking little milk because of an illness or if the weather is hot. If he won't take his water plain, you can try giving him sugar water. Add eight level teaspoons of granulated sugar and one level teaspoon of salt to a litre of water, stirring until dissolved. For extra sweetness, add 120 ml (4 fl oz) of orange juice. This solution works well to prevent dehydration in cases of mild diarrhoea.

CHANGES AND CHALLENGES

Slowing down after six months. A baby may take solids eagerly at first, and then rather suddenly lose a lot of his appetite. One reason may be that he is simply not growing as fast – that's normal. Or he may be bothered by teething. One baby wants to leave out a lot of his solid food; another turns against his formula or breast milk. After six months, some babies refuse to be fed. If you let them have finger food while you're offering food on a spoon, it often will solve this problem.

When your baby's appetite falls off after six months, it may be time to go to a three-meals-a-day schedule during the daytime, whether or not he is still on the breast or bottle at bedtime. If a baby's appetite still doesn't revive with these measures, it's important to get him to the doctor to be sure that he's otherwise healthy.

Refusing vegetables. If your one-year-old daughter suddenly rejects the vegetable that she loved last week, let her. If you don't make a fuss today, she will probably come back to it next week or next month. But if you pressure her, you only make her decide that that particular food is her enemy. You turn a temporary dislike into a permanent hate. If she turns down the same vegetable twice in succession, leave it out for at least a couple of weeks.

It is naturally irritating to a parent to buy a food, prepare it, serve it and then have it turned down by an opinionated tyke who loved the same thing a few days ago. It is hard not to be cross and bossy at such a time. But it is worse for the child's feeling about food to try to force her to eat it. If she turns down half her vegetables for a while, as is common in the second year, serve her the ones that she does like. This is the wise and pleasant way to take advantage of the great variety of fresh, frozen and canned vegetables that we have. If she turns against all vegetables for a while but loves her fruit, let her have extra fruit. If she is taking enough fruit, milk (soy or cow's) and good-quality grains, she is not missing any of the nutrients in vegetables.

Eating less and choosier at a year. Somewhere around a year old, babies are apt to change their feelings about food. They become choosier and less hungry. This is not surprising. If they kept on eating and gaining the way they did when they were little babies, they'd turn into mountains. Now they seem to feel that they have time to look the meal over and ask themselves, 'What looks good today and what doesn't?' What a contrast to their behaviour at eight months! In those days they felt starved when mealtime came around. They'd whimper pathetically while their parent tied the bib, and lean forward for every bite. It wouldn't matter much what was served. They were too hungry to care.

There are other reasons, aside from not being so hungry, that make them choosy. They're beginning to realize, 'I'm a separate person with ideas of my own,' so they become definite in their dislike of a food that they were doubtful about before. Their memory is getting better, too. They probably realize, 'The meals here are served up pretty regularly, and they stay around long enough for me to get what I want.' Also, teething often takes away a child's appetite, especially when the first molars are on their way. He may eat only half his usual amount for days, or he may occasionally refuse an entire meal.

Finally, and perhaps most important, there is the fact that appetite naturally varies from day to day and from week to week. We grown-ups know that one day we grab a big glass of tomato juice and another day split pea soup looks better. It is the same way with children and babies. The reason you don't see this variation more often in infants under a year is that most of the time they are too hungry to turn anything down.

Fed up with cereal. Many babies get tired of cereal sometime in the second year, especially for supper. Don't try to push it in. There are many substitutes you can offer, such as breads or pasta (see page 384 for more). Even if they give up all starches for a few weeks, it won't hurt them. Expect your baby's tastes to change from month to month. If you don't make a battle of it, your child will probably eat a reasonably balanced diet from week to week, though it may be somewhat lopsided from meal to meal or from day to day. If it stays unbalanced for weeks, however, you should discuss the problem with your child's doctor.

Fooling around at meals. This may be quite a problem even before a year. It comes about because the baby is less ravenous for food and more interested in all kinds of new activities, like climbing, handling the spoon, messing in the food, tipping the cup upside down and dropping things on the floor.

Fooling around at meals is a sign that children are growing up and that parents are sometimes more keen about children eating than the children are. This behaviour is inconvenient and irritating, and can lead to feeding problems, too. You don't have to put up with it. Children climb and play when they're partly or completely satisfied, not when they're really hungry. So whenever they lose interest in food, you can assume they've had enough; let them down from the chair and take the food away.

It's right to be firm, but you don't need to get angry. If they immediately whimper for the meal, as if to say they didn't mean they weren't hungry, give them one more chance. But if they show no regret, don't try to give them the meal a little later. If they get really hungry between meals, give them a little more than usual for their snack, or give them the next regular meal early. If you always stop the meal casually when they lose interest, they will do their part by paying attention when they are hungry.

This doesn't mean that you should expect perfect table manners from a toddler. Babies around a year old have a powerful urge to dip their fingers into the vegetable, squeeze a little cereal in their hands, and stir a drop of milk around on the tray. This isn't fooling around; they may be opening their mouths eagerly for food at the same time. Babies need to experiment with the feel of food. But if they try to turn the dish over, hold it down firmly. If they insist, keep it out of reach for a while or end the meal.

SELF-FEEDING

Early practice. The age at which babies feed themselves depends largely on the adults' attitude. Some infants are efficiently spoon-feeding themselves before the age of one year. Other parents swear that their two-year-olds can't possibly feed themselves at all. It all depends on when you give them a chance. Most babies show an ambition to manage the spoon by nine to twelve months, and with practice, a lot of them can do a good job without help by fifteen months. Babies get some preparation for spoon-feeding way back at six months when they hold their own bread crusts and other finger foods. Then at around nine months, when they get chopped foods, they want to pick up each piece and put it in their mouths. Babies who have never been allowed to feed themselves with their fingers are apt to be delayed in taking to spoon-feeding.

Around ten to twelve months, most babies try to yank the spoon out of the parent's hand. Don't think this has to be a tug-of-war; give your baby that spoon and get another one to use yourself. Your baby will soon discover that feeding himself is more complicated than just getting possession of the spoon. It may take weeks for him to learn how

to get a speck of food on the spoon, and weeks more to learn not to turn it upside down between the dish and his mouth.

Making messes. When babies become bored with trying to eat and start stirring or slopping the food instead, it's time to move the dish out of reach, perhaps leaving a few crumbs on the tray for them to experiment with. Even when they're trying very hard to feed themselves correctly, they make plenty of accidental messes, and this you've got to put up with. If you're worried about the rug, put a big plastic tablecloth under the high chair. Children's spoons with wide, shallow bowls and short, curved handles work well. Or use a regular teaspoon.

Giving up control. When your one-year-old can feed herself, let her take over completely. It isn't enough to let the baby have a spoon and a chance to use it; you've got to gradually give her more reason to use it. At first she tries because she wants to do things for herself. But after she sees how complicated it is, she's apt to give up the whole business if you keep on rapidly feeding her anyway. When she begins to be able to get a speck to her mouth, let her have a few minutes with the food at the beginning of the meal, when she's hungriest. Then her appetite urges her on. The better she gets at feeding herself, the longer she should have at each meal to do it.

By the time she can polish off her favourite dish in ten minutes, it's time for you to get out of the picture. This is where parents often go wrong. They say, 'She can eat her own cereal and fruit all right now, but I still have to feed her the vegetable and potato.' This attitude is a little risky. If she's able to manage one food, she has skill enough to manage the others. If you go on feeding her the ones she doesn't bother with, you build up a sharper and sharper distinction between the foods she wants and the foods you want her to take. In the long run, this takes away her appetite for your foods. But if you put thought into serving a well-balanced diet from among the foods she is presently enjoying and let her feed herself entirely, the chances are great that she will strike a good balance from week to week, even though she may slight this or that food at certain meals.

Don't worry about table manners. Babies want to eat more expertly, more neatly, all by themselves. They want to graduate from fingers to spoon and from spoon to fork as soon as they feel equal to the challenge, just as they want to try all the other difficult things that they see others doing.

DR SPOCK COMMENTS

I have been making quite a point about letting children learn to feed themselves somewhere between the ages of twelve and fifteen months, because that is the age when they want to try. Suppose a parent keeps a baby from doing it at this age, and then at twenty-one months declares, 'You big lummox, it's time for you to feed yourself.' Then the child is apt to take the attitude, 'Oh, no! It's my custom and my privilege to be fed.' At this more advanced stage, trying to manage a spoon is no longer exciting. In fact, the child's whole sense of what's proper rebels against it, and the parents have lost the golden opportunity. Don't take all this so seriously that you think there is only one right age, don't worry because your baby is not making sufficient progress and don't try to force the issue; that would only create other problems. I'm only making the point that babies want to learn this skill and can do so more easily than many parents realize.

VITAMINS, SUPPLEMENTS AND SPECIAL DIETS

Vitamin D. This vitamin is important for healthy bones and skin, and for the immune system; it also helps prevent cancer. We get vitamin D from food and from sun exposure. Living at higher latitudes (above 40°, where there's less sun exposure), shorter days in winter, cloud cover, cold weather, sunblock and schedules that keep us indoors all lower vitamin D production. Darker skin pigment increases the amount of sun exposure needed, and thus increases the risk of vitamin D deficiency. Mothers with low D throughout pregnancy give birth to babies with low D, and babies born prematurely start life with low stores of D. These babies need extra amounts of vitamin D in their diets to prevent serious problems.

Breast milk, although wonderful in many ways, contains very little vitamin D. Breast-fed babies need an extra 400 IU of vitamin D every day, or more (if a doctor recommends it). Over-the-counter baby vitamin drops contain 400 IU of vitamin D per dose, along with other vitamins. You simply fill the dropper up to the line and squirt the vitamins into your baby's mouth once a day. Bottle-fed babies probably get enough vitamin D from their formula if they're good eaters, but a daily dose of baby vitamins is a safe way to make sure. Talk with your baby's doctor before giving any more than that, though, because too much vitamin D can be harmful.

Vitamin B_{12}. People on plant-based (vegetarian and vegan) diets enjoy many health advantages. Breast-feeding mothers who are vegans should probably take a multivitamin with B_{12}; their infants may get additional B_{12} from the same multivitamin that gives them the vitamin D they need (above). After weaning, children who are being raised on vegan diets also need a vitamin B_{12} supplement. Mothers and children who consume eggs and dairy products daily should get plenty of B_{12} in their diet without needing a supplement.

Other vitamins. Multivitamin drops usually contain vitamins A, D and C, as well as many B vitamins. Cereals and other foods that babies eat usually provide sufficient B vitamins, and fruits and vegetables provide A and C. If you're giving your baby a multivitamin to prevent vitamin D or B_{12} deficiency (see above), you're covered for all the rest. The best source of vitamins – for you and for your child – comes from eating a variety of fresh (or frozen) fruits and vegetables and other wholesome foods.

Iron. Iron-fortified formulas provide enough iron for a young infant's rapid growth. Breast milk has less iron, but it is much more readily absorbed. Store-bought infant cereals are usually iron-fortified. But if you're giving your baby mostly homemade foods and breast milk, you may need to add iron drops. One dropperful a day of a baby's multivitamin with iron usually takes care of any iron needs. Cow's milk provides very little iron, and it can also cause iron to be lost in the stool. For these reasons, babies under a year old should *not* be given cow's milk. After a year, if your toddler drinks a lot of milk, be sure she has good sources of iron in her diet, such as meat. Babies should have their blood tested for iron deficiency around age twelve months and again around twenty-four months.

Fluoride. Fluoride is recommended for infants if the water supply is not fluoridated. Only 10 per cent of the UK (mainly the West Midlands and Northeast) receive fluoridated water. Check www.bfsweb.org for more information. If your child drinks fluoridated water, there is no need for extra fluoride. If your water has less than 0.6 parts per million (ppm) of fluoride, ask your baby's doctor if you should give vitamin drops with extra fluoride. Toothpastes also contain fluoride.

Low-fat diets. A low-fat diet is not wise for infants and children under two years of age. Some fat is needed for proper growth and brain development, and children under two years need the concentrated calories provided by the fats in foods such as soy products, peanut butter, other nut butters and avocados. Children who eat meat and full-fat dairy products usually get plenty of fat, but *essential* fats (see page 364) are found in vegetable oils. The typical UK diet is very high in fat; most children over the age of two (and most of us grown-ups) would be better off taking in far less fat. But babies are different. Low-fat diets for children under age two can cause serious growth problems and possible long-term learning problems. Of course, if your baby has a special medical condition, you should follow the doctor's advice.

BREAST-FEEDING

BENEFITS OF BREAST-FEEDING

Health benefits. When commercial infant formulas were first developed they were advertised as being the scientific way to feed a baby. But science has found just the opposite: with few exceptions, breast milk is more healthy than formula. Breast milk contains antibodies and other substances that help babies fight off infections and reduce the risk of allergies, obesity and other chronic illnesses. A number of studies have even shown that, on the whole, breast-fed babies are a little smarter than formula-fed ones. Breast milk is rich in the essential fatty acids required for brain growth. Formula manufacturers now add these substances to their formulas, but breast milk is so chemically complex that no formula manufacturer can completely reproduce it.

The NHS recommends breast-feeding for at least the first six months of life; the World Health Organization recommends two years. Even a short time is better than none at all.

Practical and personal benefits. From a purely practical point of view, breast-feeding means no formula to buy, carry home and mix, and no bottles to warm and wash. It costs less to breast-feed.

Breast-feeding can help mothers lose weight after pregnancy (it takes a lot of calories to make milk). When the baby nurses, the mother's body releases oxytocin, a hormone that causes feelings of contentment and happiness and helps the uterus to shrink back to its prepregnancy size. Breast-feeding mothers often speak of the satisfaction they experience from knowing that they are providing their babies with something no one else can give them.

DR SPOCK COMMENTS

Parents don't get to feel like parents, come to enjoy being parents, or feel the full parental love for their child just because a baby has been born to them. Particularly with their first infant, they become real parents only when they take care of their child. In this sense, breast-feeding does wonders for a young mother and her relationship with her baby. She and her baby are happy in themselves and feel more loving towards each other.

FEELINGS ABOUT BREAST-FEEDING

Mixed feelings. A few women feel uncomfortable about breast-feeding; it may seem too immodest or too animal-like. They often fear failure, the embarrassment of breast-feeding in public, or that breast-feeding will cause their breasts to lose their shape (see page 293 for more on this). First-time mothers often worry that motherhood will completely change who they are. Rejecting breast-feeding might be a way for them to reassure themselves on that score. All of these feelings are normal and understandable; some mothers work through them, others decide that the prize is not worth the fight. This is not a choice for anyone to make other than the mother herself.

The father (or non-breast-feeding partner) can also have mixed feelings. While many are delighted and amazed by their babies and awestruck by their partner's ability to nourish them, others can't help feeling shut out. Jealousy of the baby is normal in response to breast-feeding and to the intense closeness of the mother-child bond in general. It helps if fathers remember that they have an important supporting role to play. Making milk is tiring, and stress tends to shut down the flow. Everything fathers do to make the mother's life easier – bringing a cushion or a glass of water, looking after the other children, rocking the baby and taking the baby for walks – makes the breast-feeding that much more successful.

Sexual feelings. Most nursing mothers describe a powerful feeling of love and connection while nursing. Some also experience pleasurable sensations in their breasts and in their genital region similar to the sensations they experience during sexual excitement. A woman might feel unsettled by these sensations unless she understands that they are the normal response to oxytocin, a hormone produced in the brain during breast-feeding.

Some mothers and fathers are embarrassed by milk leaking during lovemaking, while others find this arousing. So you can see that it's really important for the parents to try to openly discuss their feelings about nursing. Sometimes having this discussion with the doctor, nurse practitioner or lactation consultant present can help the parents realize that there's nothing wrong with feeling the way they do.

Leaking. Many nursing mothers have the experience of beginning to leak milk from their breasts when another woman's baby cries hungrily nearby. This can be embarrassing to mothers who don't understand that this, too, is entirely normal.

HOW TO GIVE BREAST-FEEDING A FAIR TRIAL

Tips for success. You hear of women who want to nurse their babies but don't succeed. Sometimes medical conditions make breast-feeding difficult or ill-advised. But by far, most women who choose to breast-feed can succeed if they give breast-feeding a fair trial.

Three factors can make a big difference: keeping away from formula, not getting discouraged, and sufficient stimulation of the breasts. It helps greatly to have a supportive coach, either a trained lactation consultant or a woman with a lot of experience breast-feeding. While books can give you encouragement and ideas, there's no substitute for hands-on assistance. Most postnatal nurses, midwives and doctors know who the best breast-feeding coaches are. If you're new at breast-feeding, try to find your coach early so that your breast-feeding can get off to a good start.

First days. Breast-feeding naturally starts right after delivery. A newborn baby who is dried and laid naked on her mother's abdomen will often wriggle up to the breast and begin to nurse even before she is an hour old. Nobody has to direct the baby or make her take the breast in her mouth; she already knows exactly what to do. Until you have seen this happen, you might find it hard to believe that an infant straight from the womb has this inborn ability to seek out sustenance. Hospitals now make it a policy that all healthy mothers and babies have a chance to experience this powerful connection.

Keep your baby with you as much as possible in the first hours and days after birth. Holding your baby to your chest will stimulate milk production and help your baby develop the muscle control to nurse effectively. You won't make much milk for the first few days, but your baby won't need much, either. Let your baby feed as often as she wants at the beginning, until nursing and your milk supply are well established. With practice, babies become more and more skilled at latching on and sucking, and the more your baby nurses, the more milk you'll make.

Avoid early formula. Babies who take formula from a bottle for the first three or four days of life are less likely to breast-feed successfully. The baby who fills up on formula will not try so hard at the breast. Inexperienced mothers then believe the baby prefers the bottle to the breast, but this is not really the case. The best policy is to avoid formula for as long as possible, certainly until breast-feeding is well established. Babies are born with extra fluid in their bodies; they don't need to drink a lot in the first day or two while the milk is coming in.

Listen to your supporters. Seek out and listen to friends and family members who have breast-fed successfully. Don't let others discourage you. A mother who chooses to breast-feed may occasionally be subjected to a surprising amount of scepticism from friends and relatives who are otherwise quite sympathetic. There are remarks like: 'You aren't going to breast-feed, are you? Why in the world are you trying to do that? With breasts like yours, you'll never succeed. Are you trying to starve the child to prove a point?'

The milder remarks can perhaps be blamed on surprise, but the meaner ones strongly suggest envy. Even later on, you might have friends who urge you to stop. It's important to listen to people who support your decision. Your mother or mother-in-law might be a key ally, or you may want to connect with community resources that support breast-feeding (see below).

Milk supply concerns. It is normal for mothers to worry that they aren't making enough milk. Sometimes a mother becomes discouraged just as her milk is coming in, or perhaps a day or two later, because she isn't producing very much. This is no time for her to quit. She hasn't given herself half a chance.

If you find yourself in this position, be sure you are getting enough to eat and drink and as much rest as possible.

Drinking several glasses of water a day is crucial: without plenty of water, the body can't produce much milk. (Juice is fine, too, if you prefer, but stay away from coffee, tea and other caffeine-containing drinks.) Put your baby to the breast often, even if she seems uninterested at first. With increased breast stimulation, milk production goes up.

Middle-of-the-night feedings are especially important at first in giving the breasts regular stimulation. Young babies are often more awake – and therefore more effective nursers – in the middle of the night. So in the early weeks it's fine to give nighttime feedings if that's when your baby wants to feed most; that's the best way for your milk supply and your baby to grow. If your baby sleeps next to you in a cradle or co-sleeper (page 31), you'll be able to get her without having to get up. Plan to sleep more during the day so that you can be up more at night. When breast-feeding a new baby, often you need to get used to working the night shift.

If your baby isn't taking much to begin with, it helps to empty your breasts after each feeding so that milk production continues to increase. Some mothers can express milk by hand (page 311), but others find a high-quality electric breast pump essential (see page 312).

What if your baby seems to be losing weight? Newborns normally lose about one-tenth of their body weight in the first week, but after that they should gain steadily. If you're concerned, make sure you talk with the doctor, midwife or health visitor. That way, you can be sure that your baby is getting what she needs, and that you are doing all you can. If you make it clear that you are determined to breast-feed, the professionals will give you the guidance to make it possible.

One common strategy is to use a supplemental lactation system. This is simply a piece of narrow tubing taped to the breast and attached on the other end to a plastic bottle. When the baby sucks at the nipple, he gets formula through the tubing. After nursing in this way, the mother then has to use an efficient breast pump to empty her breasts as much as possible in order to stimulate her milk production. These systems, used under the guidance of a lactation consultant, give babies the nourishment they need while the mother's breast milk supply increases.

Why some mothers give up. Many mothers start breast-feeding in the hospital and continue for a short time afterwards, but then get discouraged and give up. They say, 'I didn't have enough milk,' or 'My milk didn't seem to agree with the baby.'

DR SPOCK COMMENTS

Why is it that it's only in bottle-feeding countries like ours that the breast milk supply so often seems to fail? The mother here who tries to breast-feed, instead of feeling that she is doing the most natural thing in the world and assuming that she'll succeed like everyone else, feels that she is attempting to do the unusual, the difficult thing . . . Breast-feeding is how we humans have survived for millennia. The way to make breast-feeding a success is to assume that it will be, keep on breast-feeding and keep away from formula, at least until the breast milk supply is well established.

Of course, employment outside of the home can be a major barrier to breast-feeding. Even the knowledge that they *will* have to go back to work is enough to discourage many women from starting, or sticking with, breast-feeding. However, with determination and a good breast pump, it's often possible to continue nursing (see page 302). Many women are able to continue breast-feeding in the evenings and mornings, while the child care provider or father gives bottles during the day. If the mother is able to pump at work, the daytime bottles can be of stored breast milk.

Community resources for nursing mothers. Most hospitals now have midwife lactation consultants who counsel breast-feeding mothers. You can visit their drop-in sessions even after you have been discharged from hospital. The La Leche League is composed of mothers who have succeeded at breast-feeding and who are eager to support inexperienced mothers (www.llli.org.uk). The National Childbirth Trust can provide support and usually refer you to a lactation consultant. These experienced, knowledgeable consultants, certified by the International Board of Lactation Consultant Examiners, have a remarkably high rate of success with mothers who are having breast-feeding problems (a certified lactation consultant can have the initials IBCLC after her name). See www.lcgb.org for more details. Breast-feeding support groups and helplines can be very beneficial. See the Resource Guide, page 1048, for contact details.

HOW THE NURSING PATTERN GETS ESTABLISHED

When the milk comes in. At first the breast doesn't produce milk at all, but rather a liquid called colostrum. Although there's not much of it and it looks thin, colostrum is high in nutrients and infection-fighting substances.

The milk most often starts to come in on the third or fourth day of the baby's life, the same time that many babies become distinctly more wakeful and hungry. This is one of the many examples of how smoothly nature works things out. Milk tends to come in earlier in mothers who have had a child before or who have been able to feed on demand from day one. Sometimes it comes so suddenly that the mother can name the hour; more often the progress is gradual.

Starting on day three or four, most breast-fed babies want to nurse up to ten or twelve times a day. (The stools may become frequent on these days, too.) Frequent nursing doesn't mean that the breast milk supply is inadequate. It's just that the baby is now settling down to the serious business of eating and growing. It is during this latter half of the first week, too, that the breasts receive the strongest stimulation from hormones. It is no wonder that in the first few days they sometimes become too full or that sometimes there isn't enough to satisfy the newly hungry baby. Still, the system works remarkably well.

Hormone production slows down at the end of the first week. After that, it is how much the baby demands that determines how much the breasts produce. In the changeover period (usually the second week) there may not be quite enough milk until the breasts adjust to the demand. The baby's hunger teaches the breast how much to produce, not just in the second or third week, but on through the succeeding months. In other words, the supply may still be increasing when the baby is several months old, if she wants more.

How long to nurse at each feeding. It used to be assumed that it was better to limit the nursing time at first and then gradually increase it, in order to prevent nipple soreness. But experience has shown that it's better to let the babies decide from the beginning. If they are always allowed to nurse promptly when hungry and for as long as they wish, they take their time to latch on properly, thus avoiding nipple soreness. Longer nursing from the start allows the letdown reflex, which is slower to respond at first, to come into play. This means that a new mother who wants to breast-feed needs to prepare herself for doing that, and not very much else. Other adults in the family need to take up the slack, to allow the nursing mother to focus on meeting the needs of the newborn.

How often can you nurse? In one sense the answer is as often as your baby appears hungry and as often as you feel able to accommodate her. Mothers in nonindustrialized societies occasionally nurse again as soon as a half hour after the last feeding, though the baby will probably nurse only briefly at one or the other of these feedings. The mother in our society who has successfully nursed a previous baby and has plenty of self-assurance might not hesitate to nurse occasionally after an hour, if she thought there was a special reason for hunger.

But it wouldn't be helpful to tell you to nurse whenever your baby cries. Babies cry for reasons other than hunger: colic, other forms of indigestion, spells of irritability that we don't understand, fatigue that for some reason doesn't bring sleep (see page 60). An anxious, inexperienced mother can get to a point of frantic fatigue if she's worrying and nursing all day and half the night. This worrying can cut down on the milk supply and interfere with the let-down reflex, too.

It's fine to nurse as often as you wish, but it's also okay to let a baby fuss a bit in the hope that she'll go back to sleep. Sometimes if the father takes the baby and holds her against his bare chest, the warmth and smell, different from the mother's, will be soothing; sometimes swaddling or rocking can help. But if none of these things works, you have to go back to feeding.

A baby who sucks and sucks and never seems content may not be getting much milk. Make sure you hear gulping sounds; check that the baby is having several loose stools a day, and wetting frequently; let the midwife or health visitor check that her weight gain is good. Get a lactation consultant's help early, before the problem becomes severe.

One or both breasts? In many parts of the world, where nursing is the main way babies are fed and where mothers carry their babies around with them in slings while they work, babies wake and are put to the breast frequently. They nurse relatively briefly at one breast, then fall asleep again. In our society, which runs pretty much according to the clock and in which many babies are put in a cot in a quiet room after a feeding, the tendency is towards fewer and larger feedings. If a mother produces ample amounts of milk, her baby may be quite satisfied with one breast at each feeding. Each breast receives the stimulation of very complete nursing, even though this occurs only once every four to eight hours.

In many cases, however, the amount of milk in one breast does not satisfy the baby and both breasts are given at each feeding, the left breast being offered first at one feeding, the right breast first at the next. Some mothers and doctors advocate both breasts anyway. A simple, reliable method is to let the baby finish one breast first, then offer the other. You'll know when the baby is finished when he lets go. He might take a little from the second breast, or a lot; the choice is his. Letting the baby decide guarantees that he ends the feeding full but not too full.

Patterns of early nursing behaviour. A physician with a sense of humour who has studied the behaviour of hundreds of babies when first put to the breast has pointed out the different types. *Eager beavers* avidly draw the breast in and suck vigorously until satisfied. The only problem is that they may be too hard on the nipple if they are allowed to clamp down on it.

Excitable babies may become so agitated and active that they keep losing the breast and then, instead of trying again, they scream. They may have to be picked up and comforted for several minutes before they are calm enough to try again. After a few days they usually settle down.

Procrastinators can't be bothered to nurse the first few days; they are waiting until the milk comes in. Prodding them only makes them balky. They do well when the time comes.

Tasters must, for a little while, mouth the nipple and smack their lips over the drop of milk they taste, before they settle down to business. Efforts to hurry them only make them angry.

Resters want to nurse a few minutes and then rest a few minutes before starting again. They can't be rushed. They usually do a good job in their own way, but it takes them longer.

There are other patterns of behaviour in the early weeks of nursing that make the mother's job much more difficult, and may nearly drive her mad. Fortunately, most babies outgrow these inconvenient patterns in a few weeks.

Short nursers who fall asleep. These babies never seem to nurse very vigorously and fall asleep five minutes or so after starting. You don't know whether they have taken a reasonable amount or not. It wouldn't be so bad if they'd sleep for two or three hours, but they may wake and cry again a few minutes after they're put back to bed. We don't really know what causes this behaviour. One possibility is that the baby's nervous system and digestive system are not yet working well enough together. Perhaps the comfort of their mother's arms and the breast in the mouth is enough to put them back to sleep, but when they're put back into the harder, cooler bed, their hunger wakes them up again. When they're a little older and know what it's all about, their hunger will keep them awake until they're well satisfied. If your baby gets sleepy or restless after a few minutes at one breast, you can try shifting right away to the other breast, to see if the easier flow of milk will help. You'd like her to work at least fifteen minutes on one breast to be sure that it is well stimulated, but if she won't, she won't.

Irritable nursers. Other babies, hungrier or more wide awake or more assertive, react with irritation when they find they can't get enough milk. They jerk their heads away from the breast and yell, try again, then get angry again. The fact that the baby doesn't nurse well only increases the mother's uneasiness, and a vicious cycle sets in. If a mother understands how tension can interfere with milk letdown, she can use all her ingenuity in finding her own best way to relax before and during nursing. It's different for each individual. Music, a magazine, television – whatever works best is what she should adopt.

DR SPOCK COMMENTS

When a baby is refusing to take the breast and carrying on, a mother can't help feeling spurned, frustrated and irritated. She shouldn't let her feelings be hurt by this inexperienced but apparently opinionated newcomer. If she can keep trying for a few more feedings, the chances are that the baby will figure out what it's all about.

IS YOUR BABY GETTING ENOUGH?

Weight gain and satisfaction. If your baby acts contented and looks well, it's very likely that she is getting enough milk. Having a health visitor check your baby's weight gain adds an extra measure of safety. A baby who cries hard every afternoon or evening but is gaining weight at the average rate is probably well nourished but having colic. A baby who gains slowly but is quite contented is, in most cases, a baby who is meant to be a slow gainer. However, there are a few babies who don't protest even when they are not gaining at all.

A baby who is gaining very slowly and acting hungry most of the time is probably not getting enough. He may act either unusually upset or lethargic. He'll have fewer than six wet nappies a day, his urine will look dark or smell strong, and he'll have infrequent bowel movements. Any baby who is not gaining weight well by the end of the second week of life should be awakened every two or three hours and encouraged to feed more frequently. Babies who are sleepy at the breast can be encouraged to feed by being burped and switched to the other breast when they fall asleep. If this routine is repeated four or five times during a feeding, most babies will be gaining weight and nursing more vigorously after five to seven days.

Your community midwife will visit you at home for up to ten days after the birth. She will check on how breast-feeding is going and weigh your baby to make sure she is gaining well. If your baby has regained her birth weight after about ten days, a health visitor will make further home visits and point you in the direction of your local baby clinic, where she can be weighed regularly.

In the long run it's best to assume that your baby is getting enough, unless your baby and the health visitor definitely tell you differently. Certainly at any one feeding you should be satisfied if your baby seems satisfied.

Hard to tell how much. This question of whether the baby's getting enough is likely to baffle the new mother. A good rule of thumb is that by the fifth day of life, babies will usually have six to eight wet nappies and four to ten bowel movements a day, and will be nursing eight to twelve times in each twenty-four-hour period.

You certainly can't tell from the length of time the baby nurses. She goes on nursing after she's already obtained most of the milk – sometimes for ten more minutes, sometimes for thirty – because she's still getting a trickle of milk, or because she enjoys sucking, or because she's still awake and having a good time.

Most mothers with experience have decided that they can't tell from the apparent fullness of the breasts before feeding how much milk is there. In the first week or two, the breasts are noticeably full and firm as a result of hormonal changes, but after a while they normally become softer and less prominent, even though the milk supply is increasing. A baby can get 180 ml (6 fl oz) or more from a breast that to the mother does not seem full at all. You can't tell anything from the colour and appearance of the milk, either. Breast milk always looks thin and bluish compared to cow's milk.

Crying and hunger. Hunger is not the most common reason for crying. Mothers often worry when their babies begin to fret right after feedings or between feedings. Their first thought is that their milk supply is failing. But this assumption is usually not correct. The fact is, almost all babies have fretful spells, usually in the afternoon or evening. Bottle-fed babies fuss as much as breast-fed babies. Babies who are getting all the milk they can possibly hold have crying spells just the same as babies who are receiving less (see pages 60 and 104 for more on crying and colic). If a parent realizes clearly that most of the fussing in the early weeks is not caused by hunger, she won't be so quick to lose confidence in her breast milk supply.

Hunger is much more apt to wake a baby a little earlier for the next feeding than to bother her in the first hour or two after the last feeding. If she is hungry, it may be because her appetite has taken a sudden spurt, or it may possibly mean that her mother's milk has decreased slightly because of fatigue or tension. In either case the answer is the same: take it for granted that she'll wake and want to nurse more frequently for a day or for a few days until the mother's breasts have adjusted to the demand, and then she will probably go back to her previous schedule.

For a fretful baby, the key is to give breast-feeding a good chance to work. Any thought of giving a bottle of formula should be postponed for at least a couple of weeks. The baby should be allowed to nurse as often as she wants, for as long as she wants. If she makes a reasonable weight gain in that week or two, consideration of formula should again be put off for at least two more weeks. Sometimes, though, it can be too stressful to nurse a fussy or colicky baby. If you feel this way, it may be best to give the nursing a break. Try a bottle; let someone else (father, friend, grandparent) take over the comforting. Once you have a chance to relax, you can return to the nursing with renewed energy.

THE NURSING MOTHER'S PHYSICAL CONDITION

General health. Nursing mothers need to take good care of themselves: unplug the phone, nap when the baby naps, let the housework go, forget about outside worries and obligations, keep visitors down to one or two comfortable friends, and eat and drink wisely.

Most women can breast-feed safely and successfully. If you take medication for a chronic medical condition, it's wise to check with your doctor. If you are determined, there are often ways to proceed. Even women who have had mastectomies for breast cancer can still nurse their babies, using special equipment. Lactation consultants are very resourceful people.

Breast size. Some women with small breasts assume that they will be less able to produce milk. There is no basis for this belief. When a woman is not pregnant and not nursing, the milk-producing glands are inactive and make up only a minor part of the breast. The rest is mainly fat. Larger breasts have more fat tissue, smaller breasts have less. As a woman's pregnancy progresses, hormones stimulate the milk glands to develop and enlarge. The arteries and veins that serve the glands enlarge, too, so the veins become prominent on the surface of the breasts. The milk, when it comes in a few days after delivery, causes further enlargement of the breasts. A woman with very large breasts may want to talk with a lactation consultant for advice about special techniques to make breast-feeding easier.

Flat or inverted nipples. The areola is the ring of darker skin surrounding the nipple. Gently compressing the areola between a finger and thumb causes the nipple to stick out more. If your nipples retract or sink back in (inverted nipples), consult a lactation consultant *before the baby is born* so that breast-feeding can get off to a good start.

Exercise. Regular exercise helps to tone the body and lift the spirits; it can also help you lose weight if need be. A thirty-minute walk several times a week, with the baby in a sling, can be very helpful. In addition to aerobic exercise, weight training can build strength and increase your metabolic rate so that you burn calories faster. This doesn't require elaborate equipment. A lot can be accomplished with cheap hand weights, an exercise book from the library, and just a few minutes each day. There is no evidence that it harms the baby if a nursing mother plays sports.

Changes in breast shape. Some mothers shy away from breast-feeding because they are concerned about the effect of nursing on the shape and size of their breasts. The breasts enlarge during pregnancy and even more during the first days after birth, whether or not the baby is nursed. They become much less prominent and firm by the time a baby is a week old, even if the mother continues to nurse successfully, so much so that she may wonder whether her milk has stopped.

Breast shape depends on the character of the supporting tissue of the breasts, which varies from person to person. There are women who never breast-feed but whose breasts flatten after pregnancy; others may breast-feed several babies with no effect on their figures, or may end up liking their bodies more.

The mother should wear a well-fitting bra that supports the breasts, not only when she is nursing but also during the later part of pregnancy, when the breasts are definitely enlarged. This is to prevent stretching of the skin and of the supporting tissues in the breasts during the time the breasts are heavier. It is worthwhile to buy nursing bras, the fronts of which can be opened for nursing (get the kind that you can open easily with one hand).

The mother's diet during nursing. Most nursing mothers can eat what they want. Occasionally a baby reacts every time the mother eats a certain food. For example, if a mother drinks milk, some of the proteins pass into the breast milk and may irritate the baby's stomach (some very sensitive children even develop an allergic rash from this secondhand cow's milk). Caffeine, chocolate and some other foods will occasionally do the same thing. Naturally, if this happens several times in succession, the mother should give up that particular food.

Check with your doctor about which drugs are safe or unsafe to take while breast-feeding. Of course, smoking is unhealthy for mothers and children, both during pregnancy and after. However, it is better for a mother to continue breast-feeding, smoke away from the baby and try to decrease smoking than to quit breast-feeding. (For help quitting, call the NHS helpline on 0800 0224 332.)

A nursing mother who drinks a glass of wine or beer a day is not harming her baby. But the first months of having a new baby are stressful, and a new mother might easily have one drink to relax, then another and another. So if there is alcoholism in your family – as there is in many – or if you think you could possibly develop that problem, you ought to avoid alcoholic beverages while breast-feeding.

A nursing mother needs to take in what she's putting out, plus a bit more. Breast milk contains lots of calcium for the baby's fast-growing bones. If you normally drink little milk or have chosen a nondairy diet, you can get plenty of calcium from calcium-supplemented juices or soy milk, or from calcium supplements in tablet form. High-calcium nondairy foods are listed on page 381. Nursing mothers also need vitamin D, both for themselves and to pass on to their babies in their milk. Sources include milk, some yogurts and vitamin supplements (including antenatal vitamins).

There are two sides to the matter of fluids. There is no good to be gained from drinking more fluid than feels comfortable, because the body promptly gets rid of excess water through the urine. On the other hand, a new, excited, busy mother may forget to drink as much as she needs and go thirsty through absentmindedness. A good time to drink something is whenever you are nursing.

The nursing mother's diet should include the following nutrients: (1) plenty of vegetables, especially green leafy vegetables like broccoli and kale, (2) fresh fruit, (3) beans, peas and lentils, which have vitamins, plenty of calcium and traces of healthy fats, and (4) whole grains. These foods are rich in vitamins and minerals and in fibre, which helps keep the bowels running smoothly.

A benefit of increasing vegetables and reducing meats is that animals concentrate pesticides and other chemicals in their meat and milk. This is especially true of fish. Breast-feeding mothers should probably limit their intake of tuna fish, for example, and avoid entirely other fish that have a high mercury content (see page 20). Traces of toxic chemicals can easily end up in a mother's breast milk if she eats lots of meat products. Plant foods have much less contamination, even if they are not organically grown.

Does nursing tire the mother? You occasionally hear it said that breast-feeding takes a lot out of a woman. Many women do feel fatigued in the early weeks of nursing, but so do many who are feeding by bottle. It's true that the breasts are providing a good number of calories each day for the baby, and so a mother must eat more than usual just to keep her weight up. If a nursing mother is healthy and happy, her appetite will naturally take care of the need for extra calories for the baby's milk. A nursing mother who is not feeling well or is losing weight too quickly should consult her doctor.

A mother who is nursing is forced to spend several hours each day sitting down; sometimes bottle-feeding mothers become more tired out because they feel compelled to do household chores, while a nursing mother has an excellent excuse to let someone else worry about the washing. Nursing certainly is tiring for the mother who has to wake up three times a night. An eager father can't take over that chore entirely, of course, but he can bring the baby to the mother, change the nappy if need be, and return the baby to the cot. Once the nursing is well established, if the father wants to offer a bottle of breast milk during a nighttime feeding, there's no harm in that. If the mother nurses at nine and goes to sleep, the father can give a bottle around midnight, and the mother can be reasonably well rested in time for the 3 am feeding. With luck, both parents can look forward to stopping the nighttime feedings within the first four to six months.

Menstruation and pregnancy. Some women never menstruate so long as they continue to nurse. Others menstruate regularly or irregularly. Once in a while, a nursing baby will be mildly upset during the mother's menstruation or temporarily refuse to nurse.

The likelihood of becoming pregnant does go down while breast-feeding. If the baby is less than six months old, taking only breast milk, and not going more than five hours between feedings, and if the mother is not having periods, there is a very small chance (about 2 per cent) that she will become pregnant, even without using any other contraception. It's important to consult your doctor about when to resume the family planning method of your choice.

BREAST-FEEDING TECHNIQUES

Relaxation and letdown. You'll probably notice that the state of your feelings affects how easily your milk comes. Worries and tension can hold the milk back. So try to get troubles off your mind before beginning. Take some deep breaths and relax your shoulders. If possible, lie down for fifteen minutes before you expect your baby to wake, and do what is most relaxing, whether it's shutting your eyes, reading or perhaps listening to music.

After you have been nursing for a few weeks, you may notice a distinct sensation of letdown, or the milk coming in at nursing time. Milk may start leaking from your breasts when you hear your baby beginning to cry in the next room. Not all mothers experience this feeling of letdown, however.

Positioning. Find a comfortable position and take care that your baby is properly positioned on your breast, so he can latch on effectively. Latching on to the breast occurs when part of the areola (the dark area surrounding the nipple) is inside your baby's mouth. A mother can help her baby to find a comfortable and effective nursing position by controlling the baby's head with one hand and moving the nipple and areola into his mouth with the other.

For women with large breasts, it's very helpful to have a supportive nursing bra to hold the breast up; it's simply too difficult to hold up a heavy breast *and* a heavy baby with one arm.

There are two things to avoid when putting babies to the breast. The first is holding the head with both hands when trying to direct it towards the breast. Babies hate to have their heads held; they fight to get free. The other is squeezing the cheeks to get the mouth open. Babies have an instinct to turn towards anything that touches their cheeks. This reflex helps them find the nipple. When you squeeze both cheeks at the same time, it confuses them.

Sitting position. Some mothers prefer to nurse sitting up. The cradle hold works well in a sitting position. Hold your baby with his head in the crook of your elbow, facing your breast, with his back supported by your forearm. You can hold his bottom or thigh with your hand. His face, chest, stomach and knees should all be facing you. A pillow under him and another under your elbow will provide good support. With your opposite hand, support your breast by placing your four fingers under it and your thumb on top, well behind the areola.

Gently tickle your baby's lower lip with your nipple until he opens his mouth very wide. (Be patient; this sometimes takes a few minutes.) When your baby's mouth is wide open, pull him in close so his mouth is over the nipple and his gums are well behind the nipple, with most or all of the areola in his mouth. His nose will be touching your breast, but there's usually no need to make an airspace, unless you hear him snuffling as he tries to nurse. If his breathing seems at all obstructed, pull his bottom closer to you or lift up your breast gently with your lower fingers. This will make the extra space he needs to nurse without his nose being plugged.

Lying on your side. If you prefer to nurse lying on your side, or if you're more comfortable that way because you've had stitches, have someone help you position pillows behind your back and between your legs. Your baby should lie on his side facing you. You may need to experiment with pillows under your baby and under your head and shoulder to bring the nipple to the right height for your baby. Let's say you're on your left side: curl your left arm around your baby in the cradle hold and then get him latched on as described above.

The football hold. This position works well if you had a caesarean section, or to nurse a small baby, or just for a different position. Sit in a comfortable chair (most prefer a rocking chair) or in bed with lots of pillows keeping you upright. Rest your arm on a pillow and tuck your baby's trunk and legs under your elbow, with his head resting in your hand and his legs pointing straight up the back of the chair or the pillows behind you. Help your baby latch on to the breast as described for the cradle hold.

Latching on and sucking. In order to suck effectively, babies have to latch on by taking the whole nipple and much of the areola into their mouths. The nipple should be pointing towards the roof of the baby's mouth. A baby latching on does the same thing you do when you eat a really fat sandwich. You need to hold the breast a little bit like that overstuffed sandwich, too, squeezed down between your thumb and forefinger.

Babies do not get the milk simply by taking the nipple into their mouths and sucking. The milk is formed in glands throughout the breast. It then passes through small ducts toward the centre of the breast, where it collects in a number of storage spaces located behind the areola. A short duct leads from each space through the nipple, so there are a number of openings in each nipple. When babies are nursing properly, most or all of the areola is in their mouths. Babies use their gums to squeeze the storage spaces behind the areola, forcing the milk through the nipple and into the mouth. The sucking action of the baby's tongue keeps the areola drawn into the mouth and gets the milk from the front of the mouth back into the throat.

If babies take only the nipple into their mouths, they get almost no milk. And if they clamp down on the nipple, they are apt to make it sore. But if they take most or all of the areola into their mouths, their gums squeeze the areola and cannot hurt the nipple. If your baby starts to clamp down on the nipple alone, slip your finger into the corner of his mouth or between the gums if necessary to break the suction. Always break the suction first, before pulling the breast out, otherwise the nipple is apt to become bruised and sore. Then help your baby latch on again, with the areola well into the mouth. If your baby persists in clamping onto the nipple, stop that feeding.

It's common for the breasts to become engorged when the milk first comes in. This may pull the nipple flat, which in combination with a firm breast may make it difficult for a newborn to latch on. Your baby may get frustrated. Warm compresses and expressing some milk for a few minutes before nursing will pull the nipple out enough to help your baby get the areola into her mouth. Some women find that cold compresses work better for them.

Care of the nipples. Some doctors recommend regular massage of the nipples during the last month of pregnancy, to toughen them. But it's not clear that this helps, and a lot of rubbing might actually cause cracking or soreness. Excessive washing with soap can also cause the nipples to become dry and sore. The best rule is, if it hurts, don't do it! Also, if you notice that nipple massage late in your pregnancy causes your uterus to contract, it's wise not to do it.

After the baby is born and begins to nurse, glands in the areola secrete a lubricating substance. No other special care of the nipples, no wiping or ointment, should ordinarily be necessary. A purified lanolin made especially for breast-feeding, such as PureLan or Lansinoh, can be very soothing.

Some experienced mothers are convinced that the most helpful step in keeping nipples healthy is to allow a small amount of breast milk to dry on them after a feeding. Nipples will also be healthier if there is no waterproof lining in the bra, so that the nipple is not constantly damp. Any preparation that causes drying and cracking of the nipples should be avoided, such as harsh soaps or solutions that contain rubbing alcohol.

There's no reason for a nursing mother to develop cracked nipples if the infant is nursing correctly. Cracked, sore nipples are a sign to get assistance with nursing technique. With good technique, nursing should be a comfortable experience, not an ordeal. (For nipple soreness, cracked nipples or inverted nipples, see page 306.)

THE WORKING MOTHER

Nursing and working. Some women hesitate to breastfeed if they know they will have to return to their jobs early. If you are determined, chances are you can make breast-feeding succeed no matter what your schedule or situation is.

Many employers allow nursing mothers breaks during which they can pump, and a place to do it, not just the toilets, although in the UK (unlike the USA) this is not protected by any direct legal rights. An obstetrician colleague of mine, Marjie Greenfield, provides her patients with a letter for their employers explaining the benefits of pumping on the job, including less stressed and more productive workers, healthier babies and fewer work days lost.

Mothers who work outside the home can breast-feed their babies all day long on their days off. This helps to maintain a good milk supply. Even if you decide not to nurse after you return to your job, it is still good for your baby's health to breast-feed while you can.

Breast milk in the bottle. You can give your baby breast milk from a bottle during the workday. Wait until she is three to four weeks old, if possible, to begin introducing the bottle. By this time she should be used to nursing on somewhat of a schedule and your milk flow should be well established.

One fast way to express and store milk is to nurse your baby on one breast and use the breast pump on the other (it may take some practice to do this). This really helps because the letdown reflex from nursing seems to allow the milk to be pumped more easily. Another strategy is to pump one hour after a feeding. Doing this will increase your milk supply, just as if you were feeding another baby.

Breast milk keeps eight days in the refrigerator and four to six months in the freezer. But smell and taste it to be sure it's not sour before giving it to your baby. Once you start a bottle of stored breast milk, discard any unused portion after two hours. Most good breast pumps allow you to pump directly into small bottles with good sealer caps. These can be labelled and stored in the freezer. Or you can buy ice cube trays and freeze the breast milk in individual cubes (wrapped in plastic wrap) for use by your child care provider when a bottle is given. Never add warm milk to a bottle of cold or frozen milk; doing so encourages spoilage.

Begin by giving a bottle of breast milk three times a week. Many babies won't take the bottles from their mothers – they know the difference – so the father, an older brother or sister, or a sitter may need to take over. Warm milk works best since breast-fed babies aren't used to cold temperatures yet. Some babies will have no difficulty accepting a bottle, but with others it's a struggle and requires patience.

If your baby is reluctant to take the bottle, try leaving the room or even the house while someone else feeds her, since some babies will refuse the bottle if they can even hear their mothers talking. You can also try holding your baby in a non-nursing position. For example, she can be lying in your lap with her feet towards you and her head towards your knees while you offer her the bottle. Sometimes babies who really seem to like a sweet taste will at first accept apple juice, diluted half and half with water, from the bottle better than milk. It's best to avoid juice altogether up to three or four months; after that, about 120 ml (4 fl oz) of juice a day is the most a nursing baby should get, since juice has very low nutritional value compared to human milk.

Ideally, before you return to work, your baby should be taking at least one bottle a day well. You can express or pump while you're at work to keep your supply up and prevent engorgement. Try to express your milk every two and a half to three hours while at work, and breast-feed right after you get home.

PROBLEMS DURING BREAST-FEEDING

Biting the nipple. Once the baby gets teeth, you can't blame her for trying a few bites when her gums are tingling during teething or when a couple of teeth have come in. She doesn't realize it hurts her mother. But it's not only painful; it may make the nipples so sore that nursing has to be stopped. Most babies can be taught quickly not to bite. Instantly slip your finger between her gums and gently say no. If she does it again, put your finger in again, say no, and end the feeding. It's usually late in the feeding anyway when a baby starts to bite.

Fussing at the breast. Occasionally a baby who has been nursing well for four or five months will start to cry or fuss a few minutes after starting to nurse. Teething pain might be the cause. For more on this, see page 522.

Pains during nursing. You may be bothered the first week or so by cramps in your lower abdomen as soon as the baby starts nursing. Nursing releases hormones that cause the uterus to contract, returning it to its nonpregnant size. The cramps disappear after a while. During the first few days or weeks, sharp pains in the nipple that last a few seconds after the baby begins to nurse are very common, mean nothing and will soon go away.

Sore or cracked nipples. If soreness starts to develop, the first things to check are the way the baby is latching on and the nursing position. Increase the frequency of nursing to empty the breasts better and prevent your baby from becoming too hungry. Change nursing positions so that the pressure of the baby's gums is distributed over different areas of the areola (the dark area around the nipple). Applications of ice packs can prevent engorgement and make it easier for the baby to latch on to the areola rather than the nipple. The doctor or nurse practitioner may prescribe an ointment or dressing such as hydrogel. Sometimes, when nipples are very sore, the only thing to do is to pump and give the baby a bottle, giving the nipples a rest. This is a situation where help from an experienced lactation consultant can be the key to continued nursing success. Pain that persists throughout the nursing may point to a cracked nipple, and a careful search should be made. (A very few mothers are unusually sensitive and continue to feel pain even though their nipples remain healthy.)

Inverted nipples. If a mother's nipples are flat or retracted (drawn back into the breast by the supporting tissue), it may further complicate the business of getting a baby started at the breast, especially if the baby is the excitable type. If she searches around and can't find the nipple, she may cry angrily and pull her head back. There are several things you can try. If possible, put her to the breast when she first wakes up, before she gets too cross. If she starts crying at the first attempt, stop right away and comfort her before trying again. Take your time. Sometimes a nipple can be made to stand out better if you massage it lightly with the fingers first.

A few women have truly inverted nipples that don't become erect, but this doesn't prevent nursing. They sometimes benefit from the use of breast shells or milk cups. Your doctor, midwife, health visitor or lactation consultant will explain how to use them. An efficient breast pump can also help draw the nipples out. Probably the most valuable procedure is for the mother (or nurse) to squeeze some of the milk from the breast by manual expression (see page 311) so that the areola will be softer and more compressible. Then press the areola into a more protruding shape, between thumb and finger, when putting it into the baby's mouth.

A breast shell or milk cup. Many women have found these valuable in making retracted or inverted nipples stand erect, in lessening engorgement, and in keeping the nipple dry. The shell is worn under the bra except when nursing. An inner dome with a hole in it fits over the nipple. A more prominent dome, attached to it, protects the nipple from the bra and creates a space that will contain any milk that leaks from the nipple. (Milk leaking directly into a bra keeps the nipple wet.) The pressure of the inner dome and of the rim reduces engorgement; also, the pressure makes the nipple protrude, and the protrusion continues for a while after the cup is removed. These cups should be worn in the last weeks of pregnancy if the nipples are flat or inverted.

Breast engorgement. When the breast is overfull with milk, the entire breast becomes firm and uncomfortable. Most cases are mild, but in the rare case that becomes severe, the whole breast is enlarged, surprisingly hard and very painful. Left untreated, engorgement can also result in decreased milk supply. The usual mild case can be relieved promptly by having the baby nurse. It may be necessary to soften the areola first by manual expression if it is too firm for the baby to get it into her mouth.

The severe case may require several different kinds of treatment. Try massaging the entire breast, starting at the outer edges and working towards the areola. Try this in a warm shower; the water is relaxing, and there's no mess when milk squirts all over. You can use an ointment containing purified lanolin or a vegetable oil to avoid irritating the skin, but keep the ointment off the areola, because it makes it too slippery for areolar expression.

Breast massage may be performed once or several times a day, either by the mother or by a helper. Taking a warm shower is soothing generally, and the water makes it easy to massage the breasts. The application of cloths wet with comfortably hot water seems to help prepare the breasts for massage. An electric breast pump can also help relieve the engorgement, in combination with massage or alone (see page 312).

Between nursings or treatments, firm support should be given to the breasts from all sides by a well-fitting, supportive bra. Paracetamol or ibuprofen can help with the pain. You can apply an ice pack or hot-water bottle for short periods, or try cool cabbage leaves. Severe engorgement practically always occurs, if at all, in the latter half of the first week, and usually lasts only a couple of days. It is rare after that.

Feed more frequently before breasts get too engorged for the baby to latch on. Engorgement may also happen if a baby starts sleeping longer at night or if the mother returns to work or is away from the baby and does not express her milk.

Plugged ducts. Sometimes only one part of the breast feels firm, hard or like a lump. When one of the milk ducts is plugged, the milk made behind it cannot drain. Plugged ducts typically occur in the early weeks after the milk has come in. Treatment is similar to that for whole-breast engorgement:

- Hot applications followed by massage of the engorged area
- Support by an efficient nursing bra
- Use of an ice pack or hot-water bottle between treatments

- Increased frequency of nursing
- Nursing with the baby's nose pointing towards the blocked segment, because the suction is strongest right in the middle, under the baby's nose
- Frequent changes of the baby's nursing position
- Adequate rest for the mother
- Massage of the hard area by a helper while breast-feeding (takes three hands)

Breast infection (mastitis). A breast infection often begins as a sore spot inside the breast; the skin may become red over the spot, and fever and chills may develop. Headache, achiness and other flu-like symptoms may be the first signs of breast infection. Take your temperature and call the doctor. If you have mastitis, you'll need antibiotics; while you take them, you should continue to empty your breasts by feeding your baby or by expressing your milk.

When the mother is ill. In ordinary illnesses during which the mother stays at home, it is customary to allow the baby to continue to nurse as usual. To be sure, there is a chance of the baby's catching the ailment, but this would be true even if the infant weren't being nursed. Besides, most infections are contagious before any symptoms are noticed. You can protect your baby by washing your hands more often. Babies on average have milder colds than older members of the family, because they receive antibodies from their mothers before birth and in the breast milk. Some mothers notice a decrease in milk supply when they're sick, but it comes right back with increased nursing.

MANUAL EXPRESSION AND BREAST PUMPS

Nursing mothers need a way to empty their breasts that doesn't rely on baby power. Engorged breasts need emptying but may be too hard for infants to handle. A small number of babies cannot nurse because of prematurity, cleft palate or another medical condition. Mothers employed outside of the home often prefer to collect their own milk to give later by bottle, rather than using formula. Manual expression – using the fingers to squeeze the milk out of the breast – is a handy skill to acquire. But for any kind of regular milk collection, there's no substitute for a high-quality electric breast pump.

Manual expression. The best way to learn manual expression is from an experienced person while you are in the hospital. It's a good idea to get some instruction even if you don't anticipate using it. A visiting midwife, health visitor or lactation consultant can teach you at home later on, if necessary. A mother can learn by herself, but this takes longer. In any case, it seems like an awkward business at first, and several practice sessions will be necessary before you become efficient. Don't be discouraged.

The finger-and-thumb method. Massage the breast to bring the milk towards the areola. Place the tips of your thumb and index finger on opposite sides of the areola, just at the edge of the darker skin. Then press thumb and finger in deeply toward the ribs. In this position, squeeze them rhythmically together, while sliding the fingers forward slightly, to push the milk along. Use one hand to express the breast on the opposite side, and the other hand to hold the cup that catches the milk. The main thing is to press in deeply enough and at the edge of the areola. Don't squeeze the nipple itself. You may be able to get more milk with each squeeze if you not only press thumb and finger towards each other but pull slightly outwards with them (towards the nipple) at the same time to complete the milking motion. After a bit, shift the thumb and finger partway 'around the clock', to be sure that all the milk storage areas are being pressed. If the finger and thumb become tired – and they will at first – you can shift back and forth from side to side.

Breast pumps. Mothers who have to express their milk regularly – especially working mothers who may be doing it for many weeks or months – usually prefer to use a breast pump. It's worth buying or renting a high-quality one. A good pump is likely to cost between £150 and £250. Inexpensive hand-operated ones work so slowly that they aren't really practical. Many companies offer rental of hospital-grade electric pumps. For example, try www.expressyourselfmums.co.uk and the National Childbirth Trust at www.nct.org.uk.

BREAST AND BOTTLE COMBINATIONS

An occasional bottle is all right. Once your milk supply is well established, you can safely offer your baby a bottle now and then without worrying that she will reject the breast. As much as one bottle per day should be fine; more than that and some babies will begin to turn up their noses at the breast, and because they are not suckling enough, the milk supply decreases.

If you plan to wean your baby from breast to bottle some time between two and nine months, it's a good idea to offer a bottle at least once a week, even though you could nurse just as well. The reason is that some babies become so set in their ways during this age period that they will refuse to take a bottle of milk if they are not used to it, and this can cause quite a struggle. A baby rarely gets this opinionated before the age of two months, and after nine months she can be weaned directly to the cup, if you prefer, and she accepts it readily.

WEANING FROM THE BREAST

The meaning of weaning. Weaning is important for both babies and mothers, not just physically but emotionally as well. A mother who has set great store by nursing may feel mildly depressed after she stops, as if she has lost some of her closeness to her baby. It may help to make weaning a gradual process if possible. Weaning doesn't have to be an all-or-nothing phenomenon; a woman can nurse one or two times a day until her baby is two years old.

The ordinary weaning process begins with the introduction of solid foods at around six months and is completed gradually over the next four to eighteen months, depending on the baby and the mother.

Weaning from breast to bottle. How long is it important to nurse? The decision is personal. The physical advantages of breast milk are most valuable to the baby at first, but there is no age at which they suddenly become of no benefit. The emotional advantages of breast-feeding will not cease at any definite point either (see also page 274).

If the breasts have been producing a good amount of milk, start weaning gradually. Begin at least two weeks before you want weaning to be complete. First, omit one breast-feeding a day, the one when your breasts are the least full, and give a bottle instead. Let the baby take as much or as little of this as she wants. Wait two or three days until your breasts become adjusted to the change, then omit another breast-feeding and substitute a second daily bottle. Again, wait two or three days and then omit another breast-feeding. Now the baby is getting the breast at only two feedings and a bottle at each of the other three feedings. You will probably need to wait three or even four days each time before omitting these last two nursings. Any time your breasts become uncomfortable, you can use a breast pump for a few minutes or express some milk in a warm shower, just enough to relieve the pressure.

Just as breast-feeding is a partnership between you and your baby, so is weaning. Both of you need to agree to wean. If the baby is very upset about weaning, maybe this is not a good time to wean, and you need to slow down the weaning process or put it off for a month and try again.

If the baby won't take the bottle. A baby of four months or more who has not regularly had a bottle may balk completely. For one week try offering a bottle once or twice a day, before the breast or solid food. Don't force it; don't get her angry. Take the bottle away if she refuses, and give her the rest of her meal, including the breast. In a few days' time she may change her mind.

If she's still adamant, omit an afternoon breast-feeding altogether and see if this makes her thirsty enough so that she will try the bottle in the early evening. If she still holds out, you will probably have to give her the breast, because you will be uncomfortably full. But continue to omit an afternoon nursing for several days. It may work on a subsequent day even though it didn't on the first.

The next step is to try omitting every other breast-feeding over a twenty-four-hour period and reduce the amount of solid foods so that she's pretty hungry – or omit solids altogether. You can use a breast pump or manual expression (page 311) just enough to relieve the pressure and discomfort.

If you need to wean quickly. The simplest method to wean a baby rapidly is to make up a twenty-four-hour supply of formula and divide it into as many bottles as the baby is presently taking breast-feedings. Give her a bottle at each feeding, after the breast, letting her take as much or as little of it as she wants. Omit first the breast-feeding when your breasts are the least full. Two days later also omit the breast-feeding when your breasts are the least full. Discontinue the remaining breast-feedings, one every two or three days. If your milk is decreasing only gradually and the baby is only slightly dissatisfied, it will work better to introduce the bottles one feeding at a time.

Rarely, a woman has to stop breast-feeding suddenly. Manual expression will relieve the pain, and you can gradually decrease the expression over several days. Avoid pills that promise to dry up the milk: they're expensive, have side effects and often produce a rebound effect that increases the pressure in the breasts.

Weaning from breast to cup. After nine to twelve months it may be easiest to wean from breast to cup, omitting the bottle altogether. Most babies start showing signs that they need to nurse less about that time. They stop nursing several times during a feeding and want to play. They may have to be nudged back onto the breast. With encouragement, they will learn how to take more milk from the cup and will switch over completely in a few weeks without any sign of deprivation or regret. On the other hand, there are many breast-feeding mothers who definitely want to go to at least one year of age or even to two years, and that's fine, too.

It's a good idea to begin offering a sip of formula or other liquid from the cup from the age of six months, so that your baby gets used to it before she is too opinionated. By nine months, encourage her to hold the cup herself. If by nine months she is nursing for shorter periods, she may be ready for gradual weaning. Now offer her the cup at all her meals and increase the amount as she shows her willingness to take more, but continue to breast-feed her at the end of the meal. Next leave out one of her daily breast-feedings, the one that she seems the least interested in, and give her only the cup. This is usually at breakfast or lunch. In a week, omit another breast-feeding, if she seems willing, and in another week, the last one. Her willingness to be weaned may not progress steadily. If she gets into a period when she is miserable from teething or illness, she may want to go back to nursing a little more. This is natural, and there is no danger in accommodating her.

When weaning is carried out this gradually, there is usually no problem with the mother's breasts. If, however, they become uncomfortably full at any time, the mother needs only to use manual expression for fifteen to thirty seconds to relieve the pressure.

Most mothers are surprised to find that they are reluctant to end this emotional tie, and some will put off weaning week after week. Sometimes a mother will be afraid to give up nursing altogether, because the baby is not taking as much from the cup as she used to take from the breast. This may postpone the weaning indefinitely. It's safe to stop the nursing once the baby is taking an average of 120 ml (4 fl oz) from the cup at each meal, or a total of 360 ml (12 fl oz) to 480 ml (16 fl oz) a day. After the nursing is stopped, she will probably increase the amount she takes from the cup up to a total of 480 ml (16 fl oz) or more. This is usually enough with all the other things she is eating.

FORMULA-FEEDING

CHOOSING AND PREPARING FORMULA

Even though mother's milk is better, many babies grow up healthy on formula. The decision to go with formula is usually a personal one; only rarely is there a medical reason for it. Breast-feeding is not recommended for women with HIV/AIDS and certain other chronic conditions, and for those taking certain medications. If you're unsure, ask your doctor. If you've chosen formula, your next decision is, which one?

Standard infant formulas are made from cow's milk. The manufacturers replace the butterfat with vegetable oils, lower the protein content and add carbohydrates, vitamins and minerals. Many formulas now also contain essential fatty acids, substances that play a role in brain development. Of course, breast milk has always provided all of these substances, in exactly the right amounts, plus literally hundreds of others. For example, breast milk contains specific cells and chemicals that give babies ready-made immunity to the germs that are most common in their particular environments. No formula is even close to being able to do this.

Cow's milk and soya: the usual formulas. It's surprising that most infants can digest cow's milk formula, given how different baby cows are from baby humans. Indeed, cow's milk itself – as opposed to cow's milk *formula* – is *not* safe for infants. The protein and sugar mix is wrong, and infants fed straight cow's milk are likely to become seriously ill. In the past, some mothers made up their own 'formulas' using evaporated milk, but these homemade mixtures aren't as safe as commercially manufactured formula. Formulas made from nuts and grains, likewise, aren't nutritionally sound.

Cow's milk formulas are the most common, but infant formulas made from soya beans are also widely available. While they were once reserved for children who couldn't drink cow's milk formulas, most doctors now consider soya formula appropriate for any full-term infant who is not breast-feeding. Premature infants weighing less than about 1.8 kg (4 lb) at birth shouldn't use soya formulas. Soya milk – as opposed to soya-based formula – is *not* safe for babies, because it does not have the right mix of nutrients for rapidly growing infants.

Soya versus cow's milk formulas. Neither cow's-milk-based nor soya-based formula is ideal. Certain proteins in cow's milk formula cause allergic reactions in some children and excessive crying in others. In rare cases, similar proteins may even cause type 1 (early onset) diabetes. Soya formulas don't have these problem proteins, and they are also free of lactose, a sugar that some infants find hard to digest. Although the research does not show that soya formulas cure colic, some infants clearly feel better on them.

On the other hand, soya formulas tend to contain high levels of aluminium. It's clear that aluminium does no good in the body, and in preterm infants (at least) it can cause serious harm. Research has not shown that the aluminium in soya formulas is harmful to full-term infants, but ingested aluminium may be one cause of Alzheimer's disease later in life. Some scientists have also speculated that certain chemicals in soya formulas (phyto-oestrogens) may interfere with sex hormones. Again, scientists are undecided about this point, but there is enough evidence to at least raise the question.

How to choose among these risks? For some babies and parents, one risk or benefit might outweigh the others. For example, if you've decided to raise your child on a low-dairy diet – a reasonable approach that is discussed in detail beginning on page 378 – then it certainly makes sense to choose a soya-based formula. If you have a family history of Alzheimer's, you might choose cow's milk formula.

Cow's milk allergy. Many parents are concerned about allergy to the protein in cow's milk. Severe forms of this allergy are hard to miss. The symptoms include diarrhoea, poor weight gain and a dry, irritated rash. Milder forms of this allergy might be more difficult to detect, because so many babies are fussy or develop a little rash now and then.

A family history of milk allergy can be an important clue. However, most adults who can't digest cow's milk are not actually allergic, but simply make too little of a particular enzyme (lactase) needed to break down the main sugar in milk (lactose). Most infants make enough lactase, even if their parents don't. To further complicate matters, many children who are truly allergic to cow's milk protein are *also* allergic to soya protein. For these children, there are specialized formulas that contain neither cow's milk nor soya protein. It's best to use these formulas under a doctor's guidance.

Liquid, concentrate or powder. Formulas come in three forms: ready-to-drink, concentrated and powder. There isn't any difference nutritionally. Powder costs the least, ready-to-drink costs the most. It's fine to use some of each – powder for everyday feedings, ready-to-drink in single-serving bottles for trips. When you do use powder or concentrate, it's important to follow the mixing instructions carefully (see page 324 for details).

Iron-fortified or low-iron. Iron is important for building red blood cells, and also for brain development. Iron deficiency in infancy can cause learning problems later in childhood. So it's very important that babies have enough iron in their diets. Mothers often believe that the iron in iron-fortified formula causes constipation. Research hasn't found this to be the case. But even if it were, I'd still argue for iron-fortified formula. There are ways to handle constipation (see page 131), but the ill effects of iron deficiency can be permanent.

WASHING AND STERILIZATION

Washing. Careful washing of the bottles, nipples, screw rings, disks and jars is important. Rinse out the bottle, nipple and ring soon after your baby has finished each bottle, before any leftover formula dries. Later, when it's convenient, you can use washing-up liquid and a brush. Or simply rinse the bottles and rings and put them in the dishwasher. (Nipples are apt to deteriorate in the dishwasher, so it's best to wash them by hand.) Clean a milk storage jar and its lid the same way you clean the bottles.

A bottle brush is a must for washing the insides of the bottles. To get the inside of the nipples clean, use a nipple brush, then twist a needle or toothpick in each nipple hole and squirt water through the holes.

Bottles with disposable plastic liners. This kind of bottle appeals to parents who are willing to pay a little more to save time washing or sterilizing. The holder is a cylinder of hard plastic, open at both ends. It has slits on two sides, with quantity markings at the edges, so that you can look through to see how much formula you have put in the inner liner or how much the baby has drunk. You can't use these quantity markings for diluting formula – they're not accurate enough. When you put in a new bag, be sure to remove any small pieces of plastic that could create a choking hazard. You'll still have to sterilize the nipples and caps by your usual method.

Do you need to sterilize your water? Tap water in the UK is reliably clean and safe for mixing formula. If you use well water or for any other reason have any question about your water supply, check with your doctor or water board to see whether or not you have to sterilize.

Equipment for sterilization. You can buy a stovetop sterilizer, which is essentially the same thing as a kettle, or an electric sterilizer that turns itself off at the right time. Sterilizers usually come with all the racks, bottles, lids, nipples and rings that you'll need to get started, along with bottle and nipple brushes and tongs. Or you can get a kettle large enough to hold a day's worth of bottles along with all other parts.

A pair of tongs sterilized with the rest of the equipment will be helpful in lifting the bottles out of the rack if they are still hot. (You can use a pot holder to pick up the handles of the hot tongs.) Handle the nipples by the edges, not by the tip that may touch the formula and that will later go into the baby's mouth.

How to sterilize your bottles. You need to sterilize each bottle shortly before you use it, then make a sterile formula with recently boiled water. Follow the directions that come with your stovetop or electric sterilizer. If you're using a regular kettle, put the bottle in the rack upside down so that the steam can more easily get into it and the water can run out. The same goes for the container holding the nipple and other equipment. Put a few centimetres of hot water in the bottom of the kettle, add the filled racks, put the top on, bring the water to a boil and boil hard for five minutes, using a timer to be sure. Let the kettle cool.

The bottle is now ready for the formula. If you want a sterile place to lay nipple, screw ring and lid while you are bottling the formula, put them on the inverted top of the kettle or sterilizer.

What to sterilize. You don't have to boil dishes and cups and feeding spoons, because germs don't get a chance to grow on clean, dry utensils. When you first buy teething rings, dummies and toys that babies put in their mouths, you can wash them with washing-up liquid. But there is no need to keep on washing them afterward unless they fall on the floor, because the only germs on them will be the babies' own germs, which they're used to.

When to stop sterilizing. When can you stop sterilizing the formula and bottles? Talk to your doctor about when it's safe to stop sterilizing, but the NHS guideline is to carry on for at least the first year.

MIXING THE FORMULA

If you are using powdered formula or concentrate, always follow the mixing instructions on the package. A formula that's too strong or too weak can make a baby sick.

Mixing powdered formula. Powdered formula often comes in 600 g (21 fl oz) cartons or cans, with measuring scoops and reclosable plastic lids or resealable foil packets.

Powder is cheaper than concentrate or ready-to-drink. Powder also works well for breast-fed babies who only need formula once in a while.

The powder and boiled water must be mixed together in the right order to avoid lumps; follow the instructions on the can. Formula can keep for two hours after it's made up; after that, it's safest to throw it away. Once a baby has sucked on the bottle, you can put any leftover formula in the fridge for up to an hour; after that, it's safest to toss it out. (In the USA, the standard advice is to refrigerate formula as soon as it is mixed up, and dispose of any unused formula within twenty-four hours.)

Concentrate. Concentrated liquid formula has to be diluted with an equal amount of water before it can be used. Concentrate is less convenient than the ready-to-drink, but it costs only about two-thirds as much, and the cans are less bulky to store or to travel with.

Before you open the can, wash and rinse the top of the can and also wash the can opener. To measure the correct amount of water, add one can of liquid concentrate to one can of water, or pour 120 ml (4 fl oz) of concentrate into a bottle and add to it 120 ml (4 fl oz) of water.

Ready-to-drink formula. It's already sterilized and no water needs to be added, so it's easy. First, wash the top of the can and your can opener. Pour the formula directly into a clean bottle. You can also buy formula already in bottles, ready to feed. It costs more but saves a little time, and may be easier if you only give a bottle now and then.

How many bottles? During the first week, bottle-fed babies often want to nurse six to ten times in a twenty-four-hour day. Most babies start off slow and then become more wakeful and hungry after three or four days, so don't be surprised. After that, the number of bottles you need will depend on how fast your baby grows, which changes from week to week, and how much other food she eats. Start with 120 ml (4 fl oz) in a bottle. Your baby will let you know when that is no longer enough. In the first month of life, most babies will want between 630 and 720 ml (21–24 fl oz) a day.

FORMULA REFRIGERATION

Saving formula. If you use less than a full can of concentrated liquid formula or ready-to-use formula, you can save what is left for the next day. Leave it in the can, cover the top, and keep it in the refrigerator. Use it all up the next day, or discard what's left. Never keep an opened can longer than the time specified on the label. Never keep powdered formula more than two hours, as specified on the label. Any time a bottle sits at drinking temperature, room temperature or pleasant outdoor temperature, any bacteria that may have got into the formula will multiply rapidly.

If you know that you'll be away from home for more than a couple of hours, you can carry an insulated bag with an ice pack in it, or you can carry powdered formula to mix with boiled water when you need it.

GIVING THE BOTTLE

The first few days. Most babies aren't very hungry for the first few feedings. They might just want 15 ml (½ fl oz). It's often three or four days before they want the amounts you expect them to need, and it may even be a week or more. Don't worry, and don't push; it may be better for their digestion to start gradually. They'll find out what they need when they become more active in a few days.

The right temperature. If they are using liquid or concentrate many parents warm up the bottles because they have always thought of bottles as being warmed and because breast milk is warm. But most babies enjoy formula right out of the refrigerator, and it's just as good for them as formula that's room temperature or warmer. Most babies do insist, though, that the formula come at the same temperature at each feeding.

If you warm the bottle, do it in a saucepan, a bowl of hot water or a washbasin. Body temperature is the right temperature to aim for whether you are cooling down powdered formula or warming up ready-to-drink formula. The best way to test this is to shake a few drops on the inside of your wrist. If it feels hot, it is too hot.

Warning about microwave use. The safest advice is to *never* heat a baby's bottle in a microwave oven. The contents can be hot enough to burn the baby even though the bottle feels cool to your touch. If you do resort to the microwave sometimes (and many parents do, no matter what the experts say), it is *very important* that you *stir the formula well with a spoon*, so that there are no hot spots in the formula. Then feel the temperature of the formula with your finger or drop a few drops onto your wrist before offering it to your baby. If the formula feels hot, it's hot enough to burn your baby's mouth. Only use specially designed microwave sterilizers to sterilize bottle equipment.

Getting into position. Sit in a comfortable chair and cradle your baby in your arm. Most parents like a chair with armrests or a pillow under their elbow. Some find a rocking chair is perfect. Keep the bottle tilted up so that the nipple is always full. Most babies want to work steadily until they have taken all the formula they need.

Angle the bottle so that the air pocket inside the bottle is well above the nipple; this way your baby doesn't swallow a lot of air. If the air bubble in their stomach gets too big, babies feel uncomfortable and might stop nursing. A few babies need to be burped two or even three times in the course of a bottle, others not at all (see page 253). You will soon find out what works for your baby.

BOTTLE-FEEDING PROBLEMS

Bottle propping. Hold your baby during bottle-feedings rather than propping the bottle. That way you and your baby are as close as can be, and can watch each other's faces. You want your baby to connect the joy of eating with your face, your touch and the sound of your voice. Babies who take their bottles lying flat on their backs sometimes develop ear infections when the formula runs down the Eustachian tube into the middle ear.

Overfeeding and spitting up. The most a baby should need in a twenty-four-hour day (with rare exceptions) is about 960 ml (32 fl oz); most babies do well with closer to 720 ml (24 fl oz). A baby who takes much more than 960 ml (32 fl oz) may be using the bottle for comfort more than nutrition. Sucking on a dummy may serve the same need. If you've got into the habit of giving a bottle every time your baby fusses, think about trying other comforting measures first (see page 60). When babies overfeed, they tend to vomit to relieve the uncomfortable stomach pressure. See page 128 for more on spitting up and vomiting.

Nipple holes too small or too large. If the nipple holes are too small, babies have to suck too hard. They may fuss because they are getting too little, or become tired and go to sleep long before finishing the bottle. They also tend to swallow lots of air, causing gassiness. If the holes are too large, babies may choke or get indigestion and, in the long run, may get too little sucking satisfaction and do more thumb-sucking. Gulping formula too quickly also increases swallowed air and gassiness.

For most babies, the right speed is when the bottle takes about twenty minutes of straight sucking time. The holes are generally right for a young baby if, when you turn the bottle upside down, the milk comes out in a fine spray for a second or two and then changes to drops. If it keeps coming in a spray, the holes are probably too large. If it comes in slow drops from the beginning, the holes are probably too small. These days, nipples can be bought in a range of hole sizes.

The holes in some new nipples are too small for a young baby but are right for an older, stronger one. If they are too small for your baby, enlarge them carefully as follows: stick the dull end of a fine (no. 10) needle into a cork. Then, holding the cork, heat the needle point in a flame until it's red-hot. Stick it a short distance into the top of the nipple. You don't have to poke it into the old hole. Don't use too large a needle or poke it in too far, until you can test your results; if you make the holes too large, you'll have to throw the nipple away. You can make one, two or three enlarged holes. If you have no cork, you can wrap a piece of cloth around the dull end of the needle or hold it with a pair of pliers.

Nipple holes clogged with scum. If you have trouble with clogged nipple holes, you can buy nipples that are cross-cut instead of having small holes. This means that a small cross has been cut in the tip of the nipple. The milk does not pour out, as you might expect, because the edges of the cut stay together until the baby sucks. You can make small crosscuts in your regular nipples with a clean razor blade. First pinch the nipple tip to make a narrow ridge, then cut across it. Then pinch again at a right angle to the first pinch and make another cut. Crosscut nipples should not be used for feeding pureed foods from a bottle.

Getting babies to take more. Quite a number of children develop feeding problems. They lose the natural appetite that they were born with and balk at many foods. These problems often develop because parents think they have to get their children to eat more than they want to. When you succeed in getting a baby or child to take a few more mouthfuls than she is eager for, it looks to you as if you have gained something. But this isn't so. She will only cut down at her next feeding. Urging children isn't necessary, and it doesn't get you anywhere. It is harmful because after a while it begins to take away the child's appetite, and makes her want to eat less than her system really needs.

In the long run, urging does more than destroy appetite. It robs children of some of their positive feeling for life. Babies are meant to spend their first year getting hungry, demanding food, enjoying it and reaching satisfaction. This lusty success story nurtures self-confidence, an outgoing nature and trust in their parents. But if mealtime becomes a struggle, if feeding becomes something that is done *to* them, they go on the defensive and build up a balky, suspicious attitude toward meals and towards people.

This doesn't mean that you have to snatch the bottle away for good the first time your baby pauses. Some babies like to rest a bit several times during a feeding. But if she seems indifferent when you put the nipple back in her mouth (and she doesn't need to be burped), then she's satisfied, and you should be, too.

DR SPOCK COMMENTS

The main trouble with bottle-feeding, to my mind, is that the caretaker can see how much formula is left. Some babies always want the same quantity at every feeding of the day, but there are others whose appetites are much more variable. You mustn't get the idea that your baby has to have a certain amount at each feeding. It may help you acquire a more relaxed feeling about this if you realize that breast-fed babies may get as much as 300 ml (10 fl oz) at the morning nursing and as little as 120 ml (4 fl oz) at the evening feeding and be perfectly happy with each. If you can trust breast-fed babies to take what they need, you can trust your bottle-fed baby.

Babies who wake in a few minutes. What about babies who go to sleep after they've taken 120 ml (4 fl oz) of their 150 ml (5 fl oz) and then wake up and cry a few minutes later? Waking like this is more apt to be due to an air bubble or colic than to hunger. Babies won't notice a difference of 30 ml (1 fl oz), especially if they've gone to sleep. In fact, babies will often sleep just as well when they've taken only half their usual amount, though they may wake a little early.

It's perfectly all right occasionally to give the rest of the formula a little later, if you feel sure that your baby's hungry for it. But it's better to assume first that she's not really hungry and give her a good chance to go back to sleep, with or without a dummy. In other words, try to postpone the next feeding for two or three hours, but if your baby is truly hungry, feed her.

The young baby who only half-finishes. A mother may bring her baby home from the hospital and find that he stops taking his bottle and falls asleep when it's still half full. Yet in the hospital he was taking it all. The mother keeps trying to rouse him, to wedge another few sips in, but it's slow, hard, frustrating work. What's the trouble? He may be a baby who hasn't quite 'come to' yet. (An occasional baby stays sluggish like that for the first two or three weeks and then comes to life with a bang.)

The constructive thing to do is to let the baby stop when he wants to, even if he's taken only 30 ml (1 fl oz). Won't he then get hungry long before it's time for the next feeding? He may or he may not. If he does, feed him. 'But,' you say, 'I'll be feeding him all day and all night.' It probably won't be that bad.

The point is that if you let a baby stop feeding when he feels like it and let him come to feel his own hunger, he will gradually become more eager for his feedings and take larger amounts. Then he will be able to sleep for longer periods. You can help him to learn to wait longer and be hungrier by trying to stretch out the interval between feedings to two, then two and a half, then three hours. Don't pick him up as soon as he starts fussing. Wait a while. He may go back to sleep. If he gets to crying hard, though, you'll have to feed him. Sluggishness and refusing to eat can also be signs of illness in a young baby. If you are concerned, have your baby seen by the doctor. It is never wrong to ask for professional advice, especially with a new infant.

Fussing or falling asleep. The baby who fusses soon after starting a bottle or who promptly goes to sleep may be frustrated by a nipple hole that is clogged or too small. See if the milk comes out in a fine spray when the bottle is first inverted. Try enlarging the nipple hole a little anyway as an experiment.

Bottles in bed. Once babies' teeth come in, it's important that they do not fall asleep with a bottle of formula. Formula left on the teeth promotes the growth of bacteria, which cause tooth decay. It's not uncommon to see babies whose top front teeth are completely eaten away – a serious health problem. Falling asleep with milk in the mouth can also lead to ear infections.

After six months, many babies want to sit up, take the bottle away from the parent, and hold it themselves. Practical parents, seeing they're not much use, may put such babies in their cots, where they drink their bottles and put themselves to sleep all in one operation. This may seem like a handy way to put babies to sleep, but in addition to causing tooth and ear problems, it makes it impossible for some of them to go to sleep without a bottle (see page 338). When the parent tries to withhold a bedtime bottle at nine, fifteen or twenty-one months, the baby will cry frantically and be unable to fall asleep for a long time. So if you want to prevent bedtime problems later on, let your baby hold her own bottle, but keep her in your lap (or the high chair, if that's what she'd prefer).

WEANING FROM BOTTLE TO CUP

When to wean. Some parents are eager to get their babies weaned to a lidless cup by a year. Others feel strongly that all babies are entitled to the bottle for two years. The decision depends partly on the parents' wishes and partly on the baby's readiness.

Babies often show less interest in sucking by five or six months. Instead of nursing eagerly for twenty minutes, as they used to, they stop after five minutes to flirt with their parents or play with their bottle or with their own hands. These are the early signs of readiness for weaning. These babies go on being somewhat casual towards the bottle at eight, ten or twelve months, though in most cases they'll take it as long as it's offered. They also like formula from the cup, and they continue to do so once the bottles stop coming.

The main reason for weaning babies from the bottle by one year is that this is the age when they'll accept the change most easily. By this age most babies will be holding their own bottles at feeding time, and it's best to let them take over. You can help them be more grown-up by getting them started with a cup.

Weaning by a year also prevents some problems. Toddlers who sip milk or formula on and off during the day are prone to develop tooth decay, because the sugary fluid coats the teeth, promoting the growth of bacteria. Toddlers who take frequent sips of milk may eat poorly, because the steady trickle of milk takes the edge off their appetite, and their growth may suffer. Or they may put on too much weight.

Sips from a lidless cup by five months. It's a good idea to begin offering babies a sip of formula from a lidless cup each day by the time they're five months old. You aren't going to try to wean them to the cup right away. You only want to accustom them, at an age when they're not too opinionated, to the idea that formula comes in cups, too.

Pour 15 ml (½ fl oz) of formula into a small lidless cup or glass once a day. Your baby won't want more than one sip at a time, and she won't get much at first, but she'll probably think it is fun. Once the baby is comfortable taking formula from the cup, offer her water and diluted juice from the cup, too. This way she'll learn that all liquids can come in a cup.

Helping a baby get used to a lidless cup. Once the cup has been introduced, offer it matter-of-factly once or twice at each solid meal, holding it to your baby's lips. Keep the cup in sight so he can indicate if he'd like more. (If you usually give him a bottle at the end of his meal, keep it out of sight until then.) He'll also be interested in anything you're drinking, and you can hold your glass to his lips and let him have a taste if the contents are suitable.

You can let him try his own skills, too. Suppose he's six months old and wants to grab everything and put it in his mouth. Give him a small, narrow, empty plastic glass or cup that he can hold easily by himself, or a baby's mug with two handles. When he does it fairly well, put a few drops of formula into the cup. Increase the amount as he gains in skill. If he gets balky or loses interest in trying it himself, don't urge him. Drop the matter for a meal or two, then offer the cup again. Remember that in the early months of cup drinking, he'll probably want only one swallow at a time. Many babies don't learn to take several gulps in succession until they are one to one and a half years old. One good place to practise is in the bathtub.

Wean gradually. Take it easy and follow your baby's lead. Perhaps your baby is around nine months old and is becoming a little bored with her bottle and likes formula from the cup. Gradually increase the amount in the cup. Give her the cup at every meal. This leaves less and less in the bottle. Then leave out the bottle that she takes least interest in – probably the lunch or breakfast one. In a week, give up the second bottle and then the third. Most babies love their supper bottle most and are slowest in giving it up. Others feel that way about the breakfast bottle. Willingness to be weaned doesn't always increase steadily. Misery from teething or a cold often makes babies want more of the bottle for the time being. Follow your baby's needs. The trend that made him start to give up the bottle before will set in again when he feels better.

There are special beakers designed for weaning that have a lid with a flat spout. The lid keeps the milk from spilling, and the spout goes into the baby's mouth. Some parents like them because they prevent spilling for the first few months of cup drinking. Other parents object that a baby may first balk at the transition from bottle to beaker and then object again as he changes to cup or glass without a spout. There are beakers with two handles that are easier for a baby to hold, and others with a weighted base.

The reluctant weaner. Babies who are reluctant to give up the bottle at nine to twelve months may take one sip from the cup and push it away impatiently. Or they may pretend they don't know what it's for; they let the formula run out at the sides of their mouths, smiling innocently. They may relent a little at twelve months, but it is more likely that they'll remain suspicious until fifteen months or even later. Put 30 ml (1 fl oz) of formula in a small plastic cup that they can handle and just set it on the tray every day or so, hoping that they'll drink it. If one sip is all they take, don't even try to give them two. Act as if it doesn't make any difference to you.

When a suspicious baby does start to take a little formula from the cup, you must still be patient, because it will probably take several more months before he is ready to give up the bottle altogether. This applies particularly to the supper or bedtime bottle.

Children between one and two who are suspicious of the old cup they have always been offered may be delighted with a new cup of a different shape or colour. Offering them cold milk sometimes changes their minds. Some parents have found that adding a little cereal to the cup of milk makes it different enough to be acceptable for drinking. The cereal can gradually be removed a few weeks later.

Preventing weaning problems. Weaning problems often arise because babies have developed an emotional attachment to their bottles. If babies get into the habit of taking a bottle to bed with them, the bottle becomes a source not just of sustenance but also of emotional comfort. Children who are still taking their bottle in the parent's lap at five, six or seven months don't tend to develop the same attachment to the bottle, because their real parent is right there. So to keep your baby from forming a lasting dependence on the bottle, which may delay final weaning until eighteen to twenty-four months, always give her the bottle while you hold her, and don't let her take the bottle to bed (see page 334).

If your baby already has a bedtime bottle attachment, after about six months (or when the first tooth emerges) it's important to at least change what's in the bottle from formula to water. That way, cavities ('bottle mouth') won't be such a problem. If you make this change gradually, watering down the nighttime bottles bit by bit, you should be able to get your baby to accept straight water at night without too much of a fuss. From there, it may be easier for your baby to give up the nighttime bottle altogether.

Parents' weaning worries. Sometimes it's the parent who is worried about weaning. Sometimes a baby is kept on the bottle because her parents worry that she isn't taking as much from the cup as she used to take from the bottle. Let's say that at nine to twelve months she's drinking about 180 ml (6 fl oz) from the cup at breakfast, at lunch and 120 ml (4 fl oz) at supper and that she's not especially eager for the bottle, but if her mother gives it to her at the end of the meal, she is willing to take 90 ml (3 fl oz) more that way. A baby of nine to twelve months who is taking as much as 480 ml (16 fl oz) a day from the cup and not acting as if she misses the bottle can be taken off the bottle altogether if the parents wish.

Another problem may develop for the parent who uses the bottle as a dummy during the second year. Whenever the child has a crying spell in the daytime or wakes at night, the mother or father kindheartedly makes another bottle. The child may get as many as eight bottles in twenty-four hours – a total of 1900 ml (64 fl oz) of formula. This naturally takes away most of the baby's appetite for meals. It's important from a nutritional point of view that children not take more than 960 ml (32 fl oz) of formula or milk a day.

If you do decide that you need to take the bottle away, because your child has become overly dependent on it or because it's interfering with your baby's health, then just do it. You can expect that your child might be upset, angry or even sad for a bit. But I don't think you have to worry about lasting psychological damage: children are tougher than that!

STARTING SOLID FOODS

HEALTHY FROM THE START

As your baby begins to eat solid food, he or she is passing a milestone towards independence. In the process, you have a once-in-a-lifetime opportunity to introduce eating habits that will promote good health in the years to come. When healthy foods are the order of the day, children follow this pattern as a matter of course.

Food tastes form early in life and then tend to persist. For example, an individual's preference for how much table salt she or he wants is set in infancy and early childhood. High salt consumption can lead to the development of high blood pressure. So when parents add salt to their baby's foods (because the parents like added salt, not because the baby asks for it), they increase the risk of high blood pressure down the road.

Preferences for highly sweetened foods also seem to start early. Children who develop a taste for highly processed, low-fibre, high-sugar foods early on are at risk of a host of problems in later life, including heart attacks, high blood pressure, diabetes and some cancers. When children start out enjoying fruits, vegetables, whole grains and proteins that are low in saturated fats, they reap rewards for the rest of their lives.

WHEN AND HOW TO BEGIN

When to start spoon food. A baby's first solid foods aren't really solid; they're mushy. The main thing is, they arrive on a spoon rather than squirting from a nipple and they require different mouth actions to get down. A hundred years ago, solid food was introduced when a baby was a year old. In other eras, doctors advised giving it as early as one or two months. Nowadays, the NHS advises offering the first spoon food at six months.

Why start then? First, babies take to the idea more easily than when they are older and more opinionated; second, solid foods add various nutrients, particularly iron. There is no advantage to starting much earlier, unless your doctor or health visitor advises it, and there is some concern that it might make children overweight to take solids any earlier than about four months. Breast milk or formula supplies all the calories most babies need for the first six months.

If you have a family history of food allergies, the doctor may advise you to wait past six months or even longer before introducing certain solid foods. The older a baby is when he receives a new food, the less apt he is to develop an allergy to it.

There's no rush. One factor in giving solids earlier has been the eagerness of parents who don't want their baby to be one day later than the baby up the street. But with eating, like many aspects of development, earlier does not mean better. If you pay attention to your baby's signs, you can pick up cues to tell you when starting spoon foods is developmentally right for him. Look to see that he can hold his head up well. He may be interested in table foods and may try to grab your food. See how he responds when you put a small amount of food on his tongue.

Young infants have a reflex that causes them to thrust out their tongue in response to solid (mushy) foods. It's frustrating to try to feed a baby who still has an active tongue thrust reflex. If your baby sticks out his tongue as soon as any little bit of food touches it, don't force the issue. Instead, wait a few days, then try again.

Give your baby time to learn to like each new food. Start with a teaspoonful or less and work up gradually to two or three tablespoonfuls if your baby wants it. Give just a taste for several days, until your baby shows signs of enjoying it.

Solids before or after the milk? Most babies who are not used to solids want their milk first when it's feeding time. They become indignant if offered a spoonful of something mushy instead. So start with formula or breast-feeding. A month or two later, when your baby has learned that solid foods can ward off starvation just as well as milk, you can experiment with moving the solids up to the middle or the beginning of the meal. Eventually almost all babies are happy to take all their solid food first and then top it off with the beverage, the way so many adults do.

What kind of spoon? A teaspoon is pretty wide for a small baby's mouth, and most spoons have a bowl so deep that the baby can't scoop all the contents out. Better is a spoon made especially for babies, or a small demitasse spoon with a shallow bowl. Some parents like to use a flat butter spreader; others prefer a wooden tongue depressor, the kind that doctors use, which can be bought in bulk at the pharmacy. There are spoons with rubber-coated bowls for teething babies who want to bite. For babies who are feeding themselves, wide-bowled, short-handled spoons work well.

How to introduce solid foods. It doesn't matter much at which meals you start the solid foods. The process will be easier when the child is hungry but not ravenous or overtired. It often works well to offer solids an hour or so after a regular breast- or bottle-feeding. The baby should be wide awake, in a good mood and ready for an adventure – and so should you. It helps for the baby to be sitting in a sturdy high chair, wearing a bib.

Begin with only one meal of solids a day until you're both used to it. If you start weaning before six months, it's probably best to limit solid meals to no more than two a day, because the breast milk or formula is so important in the early months.

A baby girl taking her first teaspoonful of solid food is quite funny and a little pathetic. She looks puzzled and disgusted. She wrinkles up her nose and forehead. You can't blame her. After all, the taste is new, the consistency is new, the spoon may be new. When she sucks on a nipple, the milk gets to the right place automatically. She's had no training in catching hold of a lump of food with the front of her tongue and moving it back into her throat. She just clacks her tongue against the roof of her mouth, and most of the cereal gets squeezed back out onto her chin. You will have to scrape it off her chin and scoop it back into her mouth. Again, a lot will ooze out, but don't be discouraged – some goes down inside, too. Be patient until she is more experienced.

Which food first? The exact order isn't important. Parents often give rice cereal first. You can mix it with a familiar beverage, either expressed breast milk or formula, whichever the baby is used to. Some babies prefer starting with a pureed vegetable; that's fine, too. Many babies love pureed fruits but then reject other foods that aren't as sweet, so it's probably better waiting until other foods are well accepted. There is some advantage in getting a baby used to variety, but it's wise to introduce only one new food at a time.

If food allergies run in your family, it's probably a good idea to start cereals at a later age than usual, beginning with rice, oats, corn or barley. Omit wheat for several more months, because wheat causes allergy more often than other cereals. You'll also want to delay the mixed-grain cereals until you know that your baby can take each of the separate kinds without trouble.

Cereals. Most parents begin with one of the precooked cereals made especially for babies. They are ready to eat as soon as they're mixed, which is a great convenience. Most are fortified with iron, which is very important in a baby's diet. You can also give your baby the same cooked cereals you serve the other members of the family. But these grown-up cereals shouldn't be the mainstay of your baby's diet because they do not have enough iron in them to meet a growing baby's needs.

It's a good idea, if you are starting with cereal, to mix it a little thinner than the directions on the box say. Then it will seem more familiar to the baby and be easier to swallow. Also, babies and small children dislike food with a sticky consistency.

You will know within a few days after starting how your baby is going to take to cereal. Some babies seem to decide, 'It's weird, but it's nourishment, so I'll eat it.' As the days go by, they grow more and more enthusiastic. They open their mouths for it like baby birds in the nest.

But there are other babies who decide on the second day of cereal that they don't like it at all. And on the third day they dislike it more than on the second. If your baby feels this way, be careful. Take it easy. If you try to push the cereal into your baby against his will, he will get more and more rebellious. You will get exasperated, too. In a week or two he may become so suspicious that he will balk at the bottle also.

Offer the cereal just once a day. Give only enough to cover the tip of the teaspoon until he is used to it. Add a little fruit to see if he likes it better that way. If in two or three days he is getting more set against it in spite of all these precautions, then stop altogether for a couple of weeks. If he still balks when you try again, report the problem to your health visitor.

It's a great mistake to get into an argument with babies about their first solid food. Sometimes a long-lasting feeding problem starts in this way. Even if it doesn't last, why go through an unnecessary fight?

If your baby is balking at cereal, you can start with pureed vegetables or fruit instead. At first, babies are puzzled by these foods, too. But within a day or two, practically all of them decide they love them. By the end of two weeks they are ready to assume that anything that comes on a spoon is wonderful. Then you can add cereal, too.

Vegetables. A possible advantage of adding vegetables before fruits is that your baby will not be expecting everything to taste sweet. Start with string beans and peas. Butternut squash, carrots, beetroots and sweet potatoes can come next; they're sweet, but not as sweet as most fruits. Give each one for a few days, to be sure that your baby doesn't develop a rash.

There are other vegetables – such as broccoli, cauliflower, cabbage, turnips, kale and onions – that, as usually cooked, are so strong-tasting that some babies don't like them. If your family likes these foods, try straining them and serving them to your baby, perhaps mixed with a little apple juice to counteract their strong taste. Corn is not given initially because the large husks on the kernels can cause choking.

You can serve your baby fresh or frozen vegetables,

cooked and strained or pureed in a food processor, blender or grinder. Shop-bought baby vegetables in jars are fine, too. Buy the straight vegetables rather than mixtures. Work up to several tablespoonfuls or half a baby jar, as desired. The rest, if refrigerated, can be given the next day. But only feed your baby directly out of the jar if you plan to use the whole jar, because saliva can spoil foods. Cooked vegetables spoil fairly rapidly.

Babies are more likely to be choosy about vegetables than about cereals or fruits. You will probably find one or two vegetables that your baby doesn't like. Don't urge them, but try them again every month or so. There's no point in fussing over a few foods when we have so many to choose from.

It's common for undigested vegetables to appear in the bowel movements when the baby first starts those foods. This is not a bad sign so long as there is no looseness or mucus, but increase the amount of each vegetable slowly until the baby's digestion learns to handle it. If a vegetable causes looseness or much mucus, omit it for the time being and try a very small amount after another month.

Beetroot may colour the urine or show up red in the bowel movement. This is nothing to worry about if you remember that it is caused by beetroot and not blood. Green vegetables often turn the bowel movement green. Spinach can cause chapping of the lips and irritation around the anus in some babies. If this occurs, omit spinach for several months and then try again. Babies who eat a lot of orange or yellow vegetables, such as carrots or butternut squash, often develop an orange or yellow tinge to their skin. This condition is not dangerous, and it goes away once the baby cuts back on the yellow and orange vegetables.

Fruits. Fruits are often the second or third solid foods added to the diet, a few weeks after cereal and perhaps vegetables. Apples, peaches, pears, apricots and prunes are usually good first fruits. For the first eight months of a baby's life, the fruit is stewed, except for raw ripe banana.

You can buy jars of ready-made baby food, but it's easy and much cheaper to make your own. Just stew the fruit in a pot until it's soft, then mash it up (or use a blender). Make sure it's smooth, with no lumps to choke on. Bananas that are very ripe don't need cooking; just mash and serve.

If you buy baby food, look at the label to make sure it is all fruit. (Fruits packed in syrup can be useful if your baby's bowel movements are hard, however.)

You can give fruit at any one of the feedings, even twice a day, depending on your baby's appetite and digestion. Increase each fruit gradually as your baby learns to like it. Most babies are satisfied with half a baby jar. You can give the other half the next day. Fruit can be kept three days if it is well refrigerated. But don't feed your baby out of the jar unless you plan to use it up at one meal. Saliva introduced into the container can spoil food rapidly.

Fruit has the general reputation of being a laxative, but most babies don't show any definite looseness or cramps from most fruits except for prunes. Prunes, prune juice and sometimes apricots are mildly laxative for almost all babies. This makes them doubly valuable if your baby tends to have hard stools (on constipation, see page 131). You can give pureed prunes or prune juice at one feeding and some other fruit at another feeding each day.

If your baby's bowels become loose, you will probably want to omit prunes and apricots for a couple of months and give other fruits only once a day.

After a few weeks or so, you can begin adding or substituting other raw fruits besides bananas: grated apple, pear, avocado. One main concern is the risk of choking: it's safest to wait with berries and seedless grapes until your baby is two, and then cut them up or mash them until your child is past age three.

Higher-protein foods. Once your baby is familiar with cereals, vegetables and fruits, you can introduce other foods. Try very well-cooked beans and legumes, like lentils, chickpeas and kidney beans. Start with small amounts of cooked beans. If you notice that your baby develops an irritated bottom and you see bits of undigested bean in his bowel movement, wait a few weeks before reintroducing beans, and make sure they are very well cooked. Tofu is also a good choice. Many babies happily eat it in small cubes or mixed with apple sauce, other pureed fruits or vegetables.

For beans and legumes, it's easy and economical to buy them dried. Simply soak a bowl of them overnight, then boil them until they are as soft as you want. (This takes planning, but it is otherwise rather easy; see page 384.) If you use canned beans, put them in a strainer and rinse them well to remove some of the sodium; still, they'll never be as sodium-free as the beans you boil yourself. (See page 903 on concerns about BPA in cans.)

Some people rely on red meats, poultry and dairy products as protein sources. These products are now seen by many nutritionists in a much less favourable light, however (see page 374 for more on this point). Children who become used to them during their early years may pay a price in adulthood for the saturated fat and animal protein these foods contain. Fish, such as cod or haddock, are a healthier source of meat. Be sure to cook fish well and remove all the bones. Avoid shellfish for the first year or two. Whether or not you decide to bring up your child on an exclusively vegetarian diet, it makes good sense to explore vegetarian foods early, so that your children can enjoy the advantages these foods offer.

There is a special concern about meats for very small children. Poultry, beef, pork and other meats often contain bacteria that are not visible to the eye but can cause serious infections. Such illnesses have become alarmingly common in recent years, and infants are much more sensitive to them than adults. Meats must always be thoroughly cooked so that there is no pinkness at all, and any surfaces or utensils touched by raw meat must be carefully cleaned with soap and water. (See page 590 for more on food poisoning.)

Eggs. Eggs can be a healthy part of a baby's diet, but it's probably best to wait until around a year old. Egg yolks supply healthy fats, calories, vitamins and iron, but the body absorbs iron from egg yolks best if they're eaten along with a source of vitamin C, such as oranges or other citrus fruit, tomatoes, potatoes or cantaloupe melon. It's wise to wait until your baby accepts these foods before adding egg yolks. Egg yolks contain a large amount of cholesterol, but it's not clear that this is a bad thing (see page 387). Egg whites cause allergies in some babies, especially those with a family history of allergies, so again it may make sense to wait to introduce them. (Tofu is quite high in iron, with no cholesterol and probably less chance of triggering an allergy.)

Dinners. There are a variety of 'dinners' in jars for babies. They usually consist of small amounts of meat and vegetable with a larger amount of potato, rice or barley. If you buy vegetables, grains, beans and fruits in separate jars, it's easier to know how much of each food your baby is getting. When there is a tendency to allergy, these ready-made mixtures may be problematic unless the baby has already taken each of the foods included in the mixture without reaction.

MEALS AT SIX TO TWELVE MONTHS

Two or three meals a day. After the first few weeks, your baby may well be eating cereal and a variety of fruits, vegetables and beans. He may be taking one, two or three meals of solids a day. A common arrangement for a moderately hungry baby is cereal for breakfast, vegetable and tofu or well-cooked beans for lunch, and cereal and fruit for supper. But there are no hard-and-fast rules. It all depends on your convenience and your baby's appetite.

For instance, a not very hungry baby could be given fruit at breakfast, a vegetable and tofu or beans at lunch, and cereal alone at supper. A baby who tends to be constipated can be given prunes every night along with the cereal, and another fruit at breakfast or lunch. You may want your baby to have beans and vegetable at supper with the rest of the family, the cereal and fruit at lunch.

Finger foods. By the time babies are six or seven months old, they can use their whole hands to grab food and get it to their mouths. As with most things, once babies *can* do this, they *want* to do it. Hand-to-mouth feeding prepares babies to spoon-feed themselves at about a year. If babies aren't allowed to feed themselves with their fingers, they're less likely to have the ambition to try the spoon.

The traditional first finger food is a crust of stale whole-wheat bread or toast. A dry bagel is also great for sucking or chewing on, especially if babies are teething. As the bread or toast softens gradually with their saliva, some of it rubs or dissolves off into their mouths, enough to make them feel they're getting somewhere. Most of it, of course, ends up on their hands, faces and hair, as well as on the furniture. Teething biscuits often contain extra sugar, which tends to make babies crave sweets. It's better to let your baby get used to enjoying things that aren't so sweet.

By eight or nine months, most babies have developed enough eye-hand coordination to pick up small objects with their fingers. At this point, you can start putting pieces of fruit or cooked vegetable and tofu chunks on your baby's high chair tray for her to pick up. (This is also the age when you have to make sure your floors are free of possible choking hazards. A good rule of thumb is, if it can fit inside a toilet paper tube, it's a choking hazard.)

Babies love being offered pieces of food from their parents' plates. Some babies happily feed themselves but refuse the same food if their parents try to feed it to them. Many babies like to cram everything into their mouths all at once. A good strategy is to offer such a baby only one piece of food at a time in the beginning.

With or without teeth, by their first birthdays almost all babies can handle the same foods as the rest of the family, as long as the pieces are cut up small enough and hard foods that are choking hazards are avoided.

Mashed and lumpy foods. Some time after six months, you'll want your baby to get used to lumpy or chopped foods. If a baby goes much beyond that time eating nothing but pureed things, it will get harder and harder for the baby to accept lumpy textures. People have the idea that babies can't handle lumps until they get a fair set of teeth. This isn't true. They can mush up lumps of cooked vegetables or fruit and pieces of whole-wheat bread or toast with their gums and tongue.

Some babies seem to be born more squeamish about lumps than others. Other babies and older children who gag easily on particles of food have become that way either because the parents introduced chopped foods too abruptly or too late, or because they have been forcing food when the child didn't want it.

There are two important points to remember when shifting to chopped foods. First, make the change a gradual one. When you first serve chopped vegetables, mash them up pretty fine with a fork. Don't put too much in the baby's mouth at a time. When the child is used to this consistency, gradually mash less and less. And second, allow the baby to pick up a cube of cooked carrot, for instance, in his fingers and put it in his mouth himself. Babies can't stand to have a whole spoonful of lumps dumped into their mouths when they're not used to it.

So start the change after first foods have been accepted by offering finger foods. You can mash and chop the cooked vegetables and fresh and stewed fruits that you prepare for the rest of the family for the baby, or you can buy the chopped foods in jars prepared for babies. You don't have to make all the foods lumpy. But it's good for your baby to get used to eating some lumps each day.

If you're giving your baby meats, you should still serve them ground or minced fine. Most small children dislike chunks of meat that they can't chew easily. They often chew on such a piece for a long time without getting anywhere. They don't dare try to swallow too big a piece, as adults do when they are desperate. This may lead to gagging.

Potatoes, pasta and rice are popular with most children and can be introduced along with other table foods. Try to choose whole-grain pasta and brown rice. These contain more fibre and vitamins than more-refined products. Also try other grains, like bulgur and quinoa, for variety.

Making your own baby food. Preparing food for your baby lets you control the ingredients and the preparation method, and it saves money. You can use fresh, organically grown foods. It's easier than you might think.

You can make a large batch of any healthy food you choose, then puree it to a consistency that your baby currently likes. You can add moisture, if you like, with water, expressed breast milk or formula. Freeze serving-size portions in ice cube trays and then store them in plastic freezer bags until they're used. Foods for children under a year should not be seasoned.

You can reheat individual portions in the small compartments of a cheap egg-poaching pan, double boiler or microwave oven. Be sure to stir the food well and test the temperature – especially if it's been heated in a microwave – before feeding it to your baby. Microwaves create hot spots in food, so one spoonful can be cool and the next one scalding.

Once your child begins eating the same food as the rest of the family, you may want to cut down on the salt or sugar. The earliest experiences with food set a child's idea of what tastes good, so it's important to get your child started on healthy foods. (This is another reason for avoiding processed foods, which are often very high in salt.) A small, handheld food grinder will come in handy for sharing grown-up food with your baby.

Commercial baby foods. When baby foods in jars were first produced, they consisted of single vegetables, single fruits and single meats. Since then, the companies have tended toward mixtures of vegetables and starches, fruits and starches, and 'dinners' consisting of starches, vegetables and meats. Most often, the starches are refined rice, refined corn and refined wheat. And the refining of any grain reduces its vitamins, proteins and roughage.

In order to make their foods appealing to babies and their parents, baby food companies added sugar and salt for many years. But because of the complaints of doctors, nutritionists and parents, this practice has been largely discontinued.

When you buy baby food in jars, read the fine print on the label. When the large print says 'creamed beans', the fine print may say 'beans with cornstarch'. Choose plain fruits or plain vegetables to be sure that your baby is getting enough of these valuable foods and is not being overloaded with refined starches. Avoid jars that contain added sugar or salt.

Don't get started on cornstarch puddings and gelatin desserts. They don't have the right food values, and they contain a lot of sugar. Instead, give your baby plain strained fruits. A baby who has never been exposed to refined sugar will find plain fruit to be delightfully sweet.

Choking on solid foods. All babies choke a little as they get used to eating lumpy foods, just as they fall when they're learning to walk. The ten most common foods associated with dangerous choking in children under the age of five are:

- Hot dogs
- Round sweets

- Peanuts
- Grapes
- Biscuits
- Meat chunks or slices
- Raw carrot slices
- Peanut butter
- Apple chunks
- Popcorn

You can make some of these foods safer by cutting them small enough (grapes, apples, meat) or breaking them up. Peanut butter is safer spread on bread than eaten off a spoon or finger. Some of these foods are best avoided altogether (hot dogs, hard round sweets) because there's no way to make them safe and they're not good for children anyhow.

Nine times out of ten, babies who are choking easily bring the food up or down themselves and don't need any help. If they can't get it up or down right away, pull the food out with your fingers if you can see it. If you can't see it, put the baby over your lap with her head down and her bottom up. Hit her firmly between the shoulder blades a couple of times with the palm of your hand. This virtually always solves the problem, and she's ready to go back to her meal. See page 512 for emergency treatment of choking.

Some parents worry so much about what to do if their baby chokes that they delay giving finger foods and lumpy foods until way after the baby is old enough for them. The problem is not caused by young children's inability to chew and swallow. It's the result of the sudden deep inhalation that a child takes when he laughs, giggles, cries or is surprised. The inhalation can send food from the mouth directly into a lung, blocking off the lung or causing it to collapse.

For safety, and because eating should be a social activity, children should eat sitting at a table together with a parent or responsible adult. Make mealtime relaxed and pleasant. Show your child how to chew well. And cut burgers, veggie hot dogs, grapes and similar foods into smaller pieces.

NUTRITION AND HEALTH

WHAT IS GOOD NUTRITION?

It's natural for parents to give their children the foods they remember from their own childhoods. Food traditions are as much a part of culture as language; they bind families together and link the present to the past. On the other hand, we've learned that some diets are healthier than others. For many of us, the more we know about nutrition and health, the more determined we are to change our own diets and what we give our children.

Awareness of the role of nutrition in health has never been higher. In fact, there is so much information coming out all the time that it's easy to become confused. If you were actually to follow each new recommendation, you'd never know what was going to show up on your plate.

There are some basic concepts, though, that almost everyone agrees on. Healthy diets contain less saturated fat and refined sugar and more complex carbohydrate, lean protein and unsaturated fat. Simple foods – whole grains, fruits and vegetables – provide a complex mix of nutrients that support health during childhood and throughout life. If you offer healthy foods in a predictable and pleasant setting, you can count on your children to eat enough to meet their needs. The sections that follow should help you to work out how to make these principles work for you and your children.

Food preferences are learned early. Children who are cheerfully and regularly offered a variety of healthy foods learn to prefer these foods. The trick is to make them a regular part of the family diet without putting too much emphasis on the fact that they are 'good for you' (with the clear implication that 'nobody really likes to eat this stuff'). Telling a child, 'If you eat your broccoli, I'll give you some dessert' just makes him hate broccoli. If healthy foods are part of the family routine, children accept most of them naturally.

AS A SOCIETY, WE NEED TO CHANGE

The evidence couldn't be more compelling: the large amounts of animal fat and calories in the typical British diet contribute to a host of illnesses in adults, including heart disease, strokes, high blood pressure, diabetes, cancer and of course obesity. What's more, many of these diseases have their roots in childhood. American studies have shown that, as early as age three, some children already have fatty deposits in their arteries – the first steps on the road to heart attacks and strokes. By age twelve, 70 per cent of children have these early signs of blood vessel disease, and by age twenty-one, virtually all young adults have them. It's unlikely that things are very much better in the UK. Before long, high blood pressure and other problems start taking their toll. An epidemic of obesity is spreading among Western children, causing both physical and psychological pain. Severely overweight children are much more likely to develop diabetes and joint problems, for example. They often suffer socially as well.

Guiding our children towards healthy eating habits isn't easy. Children are not particularly concerned about the problems that come from unhealthy diets. The foods served at school may not be what you would offer at home. Ads for junk food are now banned during children's TV programmes, but many unhealthy foods are still marketed squarely at children – just take a look at the packaging of sugar-coated cereals and fast foods. It's no wonder that some children grow up with the message firmly implanted that junk foods are what they want.

The link between TV viewing and obesity is very strong: the more TV a child watches, the more likely he is to become obese. Better nutrition is just one of the many good reasons to limit TV viewing (see page 723 for more on TV). Of course, what we feed our children is only part of the equation; we also have to work out better ways to build exercise into our lives and our children's. As a general rule, children pay more attention to what their parents do than to what they say. So if we want our children to get a healthy start in life and to maintain it by continuing to eat well and stay fit, we have to lead by example.

BUILDING BLOCKS OF NUTRITION

As you think about what to feed your children, it helps to consider the more important chemical substances in foods and what the body uses them for.

Calories. Calories aren't actually nutrients themselves. They're a measure of the energy content of proteins, carbohydrates and fats. Proteins and carbohydrates contain about 4 calories per gramme (113 calories per ounce); fats and oils contain 9 calories per gramme (255 calories per ounce), more than twice as much as either proteins or carbohydrates. A small amount of fat goes a long way.

Children need calories to grow and to fuel their bodies. How many? It varies. Young children (age one to three) need as few as 900; a moderately active young man may need 3,900, more if he's an athlete. Women and children at different ages fall in between. When children take in the right number of calories, they grow normally (see page 394) and have plenty of energy to work and play. Counting calories is usually a waste of time; generally, the body does a good job of working out when it needs more energy and when it's had enough.

In addition to the total number, where the calories come from is also important. Standard recommendations are that children should get about 50 per cent of their calories from carbohydrates, about 30 per cent from fats, and about 20 per cent from proteins. All of these are pretty rough averages, with lots of room for individual differences. Diets that provide these nutrients in roughly these amounts give most children what they need to thrive.

Complex and simple carbohydrates. These are the starches and sugars that supply much of your child's energy requirements. Complex carbohydrates release their energy slowly because they have to be broken down before they can be absorbed and used as fuel. Simple carbohydrates, such as sugar and honey, come in a form that is ready for the body to use. They provide quick energy, but they don't stave off hunger for very long. Simple carbohydrates are absorbed fast, causing blood sugar to rise quickly. The body responds by releasing insulin, which drives the blood sugar level back down. Foods that evoke this response are said to have a high *glycaemic index*. The rapid rise and fall of blood sugar makes some children irritable and may increase cravings for sweets.

Vegetables, whole fruits (not juice), grains and legumes are good sources of complex carbohydrates. Sugary and highly processed foods like sweets, doughnuts and white bread provide 'empty calories' – that is, calories with few or no other nutrients. They satisfy short-term cravings but leave the body's needs for nutrients unmet. The result is that children quickly feel hungry again. Simple sugars also provide fuel for the bacteria that cause tooth decay.

Fats, fatty acids and cholesterol. Fats and oils (liquid fat) supply both energy and building materials. Gramme for gramme, fats contain twice as many calories as either carbohydrates or proteins. There are two main kinds of fats that appear naturally in foods. *Saturated* fats are the more solid fats found mainly in meat and dairy products. *Unsaturated* fats (either *monounsaturated* or *polyunsaturated*) are the more liquid fats found primarily in plant-based foods, especially nuts, seeds and oils, and also in fish.

A third type of fat is wholly artificial: *trans* fats are manufactured by heating vegetable oil in the presence of hydrogen gas. Another term is 'hydrogenated vegetable oil'. These fats show up in margarines and most commercial baked goods.

A healthy diet provides about 30 per cent of its calories as fat, with twice as much unsaturated fat (20 per cent) as saturated fat (10 per cent), and no trans fat at all. Diets with even less saturated fat are probably even better, since saturated and trans fats – both fats that are solid at room temperature – contribute to hardening of the arteries, while unsaturated fats have the opposite effect.

As with proteins, the body takes in fats from the diet, breaks them down into their components (in this case, fatty acids), then uses them for its own purposes. Fats make up the walls of cells and a large part of the brain. A few varieties of fat are *essential*, meaning that they have to be part of the diet, because the body can't make them itself. The two main essential fatty acids are linoleic acid (LA) and alpha-linoleic acid (ALA), also referred to as omega-6 (LA) and omega-3 (ALA) fatty acids. The body uses these to make a long list of chemicals, including DHA and EPA, which are important in the brain and elsewhere.

Good sources of essential fatty acids include fish oils, soya products (tofu and soya milk, for example), nuts and seeds, and many green leafy vegetables. ALA is particularly high in fish and also in flaxseed, walnuts and soya. (You can find ground flaxseed in most natural food stores; it tastes especially good in smoothies, salads and breakfast cereals.)

Finally, there is cholesterol. Cholesterol is an important part of cells and hormones, but excess cholesterol tends to build up in the walls of arteries, leading to high blood pressure, stroke and heart attacks. Cholesterol binds to certain proteins to make lipoproteins. One kind (LDL) carries cholesterol to blood vessel walls, where it builds up; hence LDL is called 'bad cholesterol'. Another kind (HDL) carries the cholesterol away from the blood vessels back to the liver, where it gets broken down; hence HDL is 'good cholesterol'.

Most of the cholesterol in the body is made in the body itself, but diet is also important. Diets that are very high in cholesterol tend to promote high levels of LDL and thus high rates of heart disease. It's easy to lower cholesterol in your diet: eat less meat. Animal products are the only foods that contain cholesterol. Plants don't make cholesterol at all. Any food that is entirely made from plants contains zero cholesterol. It's that simple.

Proteins. These are the body's main building material, as well as a source of energy. The muscles, heart and kidneys, for instance, are largely made of protein and water. Bones consist of a protein matrix filled in with minerals. The enzymes that make the body's chemistry possible are proteins. Proteins, in turn, are made up of chemicals called amino acids. When protein-containing foods are eaten, the body first breaks them down into their amino acids, then uses those to make its own proteins.

In order to build proteins, the body needs to start with a complete set of amino acids. If certain amino acids are in short supply, the process of protein making slows down and left-over amino acids are burned for fuel, stored as fat, or wasted in the urine. That's why, in a growing child, each day's intake needs to provide all the necessary amino acids. Complete or high-quality proteins include all of the required amino acids. Meats and soya foods are complete proteins, as are combinations of a grain and a legume (peanut butter on whole-wheat bread, for example). An advantage of nonmeat protein is that it comes with less saturated fat and no cholesterol, both substances that meats have in abundance.

How much protein do children need? It depends on their size, sex and stage of maturation. They need more when they are growing rapidly. The quality of the protein also matters: some protein foods are more completely digested than others. A ballpark figure is about one gramme of protein per kilogramme of body weight per day. Of course, no sane parent would try to go by the numbers. On the plate, an average adult serving of meat – the amount needed in a meal – is only the size of a deck of cards or what fits in the palm of one hand. Children, being smaller, need less. If you offer a reasonably small amount of a high-quality protein food, you can trust your child to eat what he needs.

Fibre or roughage. Vegetables, fruits, whole grains and legumes contain a lot of fibre, material that our bodies can't digest. Fibre plays a key role in promoting normal bowel movements. A person on a low-fibre diet – let's say milk, meat and eggs – is apt to become constipated because after the food is digested there is too little substance left in the lower intestines to form healthy bowel movements. Fibre of the sort found in beans and oats (soluble fibre) also helps lower cholesterol levels. Granulated sugar and refined grains such as white flour contain little if any fibre; meat, dairy products, fish and poultry contain no fibre at all.

Minerals. Many different minerals play vital roles in the structure and functioning of the body, including calcium, iron, zinc, copper, magnesium and phosphorous. All natural, unrefined foods contain a variety of valuable minerals, but the refining of grains removes some of the mineral content. Nearly all foods are rich in phosphorous and magnesium. Calcium, iron and zinc, however, require special attention.

Calcium. Bones and teeth are mostly made up of calcium and phosphorus. Over the years, doctors have counselled children and teens to consume plenty of calcium in order to prevent weakening of the bones in old age (osteoporosis). They have told us that from age one to three, children need 500 milligrammes of calcium a day; from age four to eight, 800 milligrammes, and from age nine to eighteen, 1,300 milligrammes per day. A convenient way to take in this much calcium is through dairy products such as milk.

Recently, however, experts have begun to question whether children and adolescents really need this much calcium. In one study of girls age twelve to twenty, for example, extra calcium above 500 milligrammes (just over half of the standard recommend amount) did not seem to increase bone density. What *did* matter was a girl's level of physical activity: girls who were more active had higher bone densities.

Other research suggests that dairy products also tend to increase the amount of calcium that is lost each day in the urine. The point of taking in lots of calcium is to keep it in the bones, so calcium that is excreted in the urine might as well not have been taken in at all. The health benefits of getting calcium from nondairy sources are discussed in detail below (page 381).

Iron. Iron is a key crucial ingredient of haemoglobin, the substance in red blood cells that carries oxygen, and iron plays a role in the development and functioning of the brain. Even mild iron deficiency in early childhood can cause long-term learning problems. Breast milk contains a highly absorbable form of iron, so exclusively breast-fed babies get enough iron for healthy brain development; infant formulas have extra iron added for the same reason. (Regular cow's milk is not safe for infants because it contains too little iron and also can block the absorption of iron from the intestines.) Iron-fortified cereals and other iron-rich foods become important after about six months old. Meats contain iron, but children can also get their iron needs met by eating iron-rich vegetables and iron-fortified foods, without the saturated fat and cholesterol found in meat (see page 378). Most children's multivitamins contain iron as well.

Zinc. Cell growth depends on zinc, and rapidly growing cells are especially vulnerable to zinc deficiency. These include the cells that line the intestines, cells in wounds that are healing, and the immune cells that fight off infection. Breast milk contains a form of zinc that is well absorbed by babies. Zinc can come from meat, fish and cheese as well as whole-grain cereals, peas, beans and nuts. While zinc from plant sources comes unaccompanied by cholesterol and animal fat, it tends to be less easily absorbed than zinc from animal sources. Young children on vegan diets (see page 376) need to eat plenty of zinc-rich foods, and perhaps take a daily multivitamin with zinc for extra insurance.

Iodine is necessary for functioning of the thyroid gland and the brain. Iodine deficiency is on the increase in the UK. Around the world, iodine deficiency has been one of the major causes of cognitive disability in children. Children who do not drink enough milk or eat enough oily fish might need an iodine supplement. Recent research also suggests that organic milk contains lower levels of iodine than non-organic milk.

Sodium is one of the main blood chemicals, and the kidneys keep sodium levels under tight control. Table salt contains sodium, and many processed foods are extremely high in it. The main concern with sodium is that excess intake can lead to high blood pressure. But even if that doesn't occur, a high sodium load may not be good for children. For example, if your child lunches on canned soup, which most likely contains a great deal of sodium (check the label), his kidneys will have to work to get rid of all the extra sodium. In the process, some other minerals, including calcium, will also be lost in the urine. In fact, high sodium intake appears to contribute to calcium loss, causing bone weakness (osteoporosis) in later life.

Vitamins. These are special substances that the body needs in small amounts. All vitamins can be obtained from a diet of lean meat, low-fat dairy, vegetables, whole grains, fruits, beans and peas, and nuts and seeds. Diets that avoid meats, eggs and dairy products can also provide all of the necessary vitamins and may actually be richer in certain vitamins, such as folic acid and vitamin C. One important exception is vitamin B_{12}, which is found only in animal sources, supplemented cereals, and a few other fortified products. Therefore, a child who consumes no meat, eggs or dairy products should probably take a multivitamin supplement. Supplements also make sense for children whose intake is low because of food refusal (especially vegetables and fruits). Children who don't get at least an hour a day out in the sun should probably take extra vitamin D (see below).

Vitamin A. The body manufactures vitamin A from beta-carotene, the chemical that makes carrots and butternut squash orange. Body systems that rely on vitamin A include the lungs, the intestines, the urinary system and especially the eyes. Vegetables and fruit, particularly yellow and orange ones, supply all of the vitamin A children need. Few children have vitamin A deficiency. Excess vitamin A from supplements is dangerous, but this won't happen from eating a lot of vegetables.

B vitamins. The most important B vitamins are thiamine (B_1), riboflavin (B_2), niacin (B_3) and pyridoxine (B_6). Every tissue in the body needs these four vitamins. They're quite common in many meats and vegetables and are added to many breakfast cereals and breads; deficiencies are rare unless children are eating mainly refined starches and sugar. Cobalamin (B_{12}) is plentiful in meats and dairy foods but absent from most nonmeat foods. Vegans need to take a multivitamin to be sure they get the B_{12} they need.

Folic acid. It's hard to overestimate the role of folic acid (vitamin B_9) in preventing serious birth defects involving the development of the spinal cord (spina bifida). This isn't an issue for children, but as soon as a young woman enters the age when she *might* become pregnant, she ought to take a daily folic acid supplement, to ensure that there's plenty of this key vitamin on hand. Folic acid also plays a role in making DNA and red blood cells. Spinach, broccoli, turnip greens, whole grains and fruits such as cantaloupe melon and strawberries are good sources.

Vitamin C (ascorbic acid). The development of bones, teeth, blood vessels and other tissues depends on vitamin C, as do many other body functions. Vitamin C deficiency is rare in the United Kingdom; the main symptoms are bruising, rash, painful bleeding of the gums and joint pain. Good sources include oranges, lemons, grapefruit, raw and properly canned tomatoes and tomato juice, raw cabbage, and other fruits and vegetables. Vitamin C is easily destroyed in cooking, however. People whose diets contain lots of vegetables and fruits rich in vitamin C tend to have lower cancer rates, although some of the credit for this may go to other nutrients in these foods. Megadoses of vitamin C do not prevent or cure the common cold.

Vitamin D. This vitamin increases absorption of calcium and phosphorous from the intestine, and aids their incorporation into bones. Unlike other vitamins, vitamin D is one that the body can make for itself. Sunlight stimulates the manufacture of vitamin D in the skin, so people naturally get this vitamin when they spend time outdoors on a regular basis. People living in cold and cloudy climates, such as in Scotland, for example, need to take extra vitamin D, as do people with darker skin tones because the pigment in their skin blocks some of the rays. More and more, we are finding vitamin D deficiency among school-age children and teens who spend much of their day indoors. Low vitamin D may predispose children to sleep problems, moodiness and perhaps obesity. Mothers need extra vitamin D during pregnancy and breastfeeding. Many experts now recommend a daily vitamin D supplement of 400 IU for *every* breast-fed child, starting at two months (see page 269).

Vitamin E. This vitamin is found in nuts, seeds, wholegrain cereals, many vegetable oils and other vegetables such as corn, spinach, broccoli and cucumbers. One of the roles of vitamin E may be to help the body deal with harmful chemicals that may contribute to ageing or cancer. A vegetarian diet is bound to be naturally rich in vitamin E. It's not clear that taking a lot of additional vitamin E does any good, and it *is* possible to overdose. On the other hand, a child whose diet is very poor in vegetables might benefit from a daily multivitamin that contains E.

Vitamin toxicity. Very high doses of vitamins (megadoses) are sometimes suggested for treating or preventing certain conditions; more often, though, these high doses don't do any good or actually cause harm. Vitamins A,

D and K are the ones most likely to cause serious problems with toxicity, but other vitamins such as pyridoxine (B_6) and niacin (B_3) can also cause severe negative effects. Before you give your child vitamins in higher-than-usual doses, be sure to check with your doctor.

Phytochemicals. This refers to a large number of chemicals that are made by plants and which have been found to have beneficial effects in the human body. These effects include protecting against oxidation (destruction) of proteins; reducing inflammation and the tendency of blood clots to clog arteries; preventing bone loss; and fighting off certain cancers. Plants that are grown in healthy soils, without pesticides, may make more of these beneficial chemicals; cooking may reduce them. Food manufacturers sometimes claim that their products contain added antioxidants, flavonoids or carotenoids. However, the best sources seem to be the fruits and vegetables themselves.

A HEALTHIER DIET

There's no question that the typical UK diet is too rich in fat, sugar and salt. Pretty much everybody agrees that children should eat more vegetables and whole grains and fewer meats, cheeses and sweets. Dr Spock's nutritional philosophy went several steps further. He believed that the healthiest diet was plant-based, without any meat, eggs or dairy products at all. This approach is not as far out as it may seem, and in fact his conclusions were based on solid research studies. Even though the official government health agencies and large expert groups support milk and moderate amounts of meat for children, many respected scientists now side with Dr Spock.

In a 2009 position paper, the American Dietetic Association concluded that 'appropriately planned vegetarian diets, including total vegetarian or vegan diets, are healthful, nutritionally adequate and may provide health benefits in the prevention and treatment of certain diseases.' Which diseases? Heart attacks, high blood pressure, diabetes, obesity, cancer, osteoporosis, dementia, diverticulitis and gallstones. Imagine being able to protect your child from these plagues.

DR SPOCK COMMENTS

I have personally been on a nondairy, low-fat meatless diet since 1991, when I was eighty-eight years old. Within two weeks of beginning this diet, my chronic bronchitis went away after years of unsuccessful antibiotic treatments. I have several middle-aged and older friends who have halted heart disease by eliminating dairy products, meats and other high-saturated-fat foods from their diet. To achieve this kind of success, it's important to substitute whole grains and a variety of vegetables and fruits and to become more active. . . I no longer recommend dairy products after the age of two years. Of course, there was a time when cow's milk was considered very desirable. But research, along with clinical experience, has forced doctors and nutritionists to rethink this recommendation.

Where does that leave you as a parent? In the area of nutrition, like a lot of other aspects of child rearing, there is no one 'right' answer that's best for everyone. A diet based on the NHS's recommendations, including small portions of meat, low-fat milk, eggs and a variety of plant-based foods, is a common choice for many children. On the other hand, a diet that's mostly or completely free of milk, eggs and meat, while it requires some thought to set up, can be equally delicious and may offer even more long-term health benefits to you and your children.

Are vegetarian diets safe? A vegetarian diet excludes red meat, poultry, fish and other animal foods (oysters and lobsters, for example). Lacto-ovo vegetarians eat dairy products and eggs; vegans don't. Lots of people consider themselves vegetarians but eat some meat now and then. There's no point in being too picky about the terminology.

According to the NHS, children who eat a variety of whole grains, fruits and vegetables, legumes, nuts and seeds, dairy products and eggs don't need any special diet planning or supplements to be healthy. They should avoid highly sweetened foods and trans fats, like everybody else. Children who don't eat dairy and eggs should make sure they have a regular source of vitamin B_{12} and vitamin D. A daily multivitamin and time in the sun will do the trick.

Vegetarian diets tend to be lower in calories than diets that include fatty meats. That may be a challenge for young children, who need lots of calories for growth. Nuts and nut butters, seeds, avocado and different oils are among the foods that pack a lot of energy into a small volume. If vegetarian eating is new to you, you may need guidance from a good cookbook or (better yet) from friends who can show you what to do. Your child's health visitor will follow weights and heights to monitor for any growth problems. But you shouldn't expect any. You may also want to consult a professional nutritionist.

Getting started eating better. Most families have become more conscious about the fat content of meats, and many are choosing the lower-fat cuts. There is no question that it's better to eat smaller portions of meats than larger ones. Unfortunately, switching from red meat to chicken does not help very much. Chicken actually has just as much cholesterol as beef (about 100 mg of cholesterol in a 100 g/4 oz serving) and almost as much fat. Researchers have also learned that the cancer-causing chemicals that form in beef when it is grilled also tend to form in grilled chicken.

You can take the first step towards a healthier diet by finding one or two meatless recipes that you like. Make these a part of your weekly menu, and add a new meatless dish every month or so. Explore different products that take the place of meats. Some of these, such as meatless burgers and meatless sausages, are in the freezer case of your supermarket or health food store. Tofu is a versatile, inexpensive, cholesterol-free protein source. If you can't imagine any way to make it appealing, go out to some vegetarian or Asian restaurants for inspiration, or let a friend who has already taken the plunge show you the way.

Iron without meat. Iron is important for growing children, and red meat is a good source of it. A typical serving of beef, 85 g (3 oz), provides 2.5 mg of iron, about the same as 85 g (3 oz) of canned sardines, although less than 85 g (3 oz) of canned clams (which has a whopping 23.8 mg). By comparison, chicken and pork only yield about 0.9 mg for the same size serving. Vegetarian foods can be rich in iron as well. The iron from nonmeat sources is less well absorbed, so children may need to take in more. But more is what they get: 7 mg in 50 g (1½ oz) of cooked fortified oatmeal, 16.7 mg in 50 g (1½ oz) of tofu, 4.1 mg in 50 g (1½ oz) of cooked lentils. Other good sources include whole-wheat bread, hard-boiled eggs, kidney beans, prunes and raisins, all of which are up there with chicken and pork. Iron deficiency is no more common among vegetarian children than it is among meat-eaters.

Concerns about cow's milk. Milk and other dairy foods are the main sources of calcium and vitamin D in the British diet, and they provide much of the protein and fat as well. Most of us grew up being told that milk was good for you, so it's hard for us to imagine that milk might actually pose health risks or that alternative sources of nutrition might be better. While some of the concerns about dairy products are widely agreed on, others are more controversial.

Dairy foods are rich in the saturated fats that block arteries and cause heart attacks. In fact, milk is the number one source of fat in children's diets – higher than burgers, crisps and chips. (A cup of whole milk has 4.6 g of saturated fat, more than four slices of bacon; a tablespoon of butter has 7.3 g.) Doctors recommend whole milk for toddlers from age one to two, because the brain is growing rapidly then. But the omega-3 fatty acids that are also essential for brain development are found in vegetable oils; cow's milk is very low in these healthy fats.

There are other concerns about dairy products, too – even the low-fat ones. Dairy foods can impair a child's ability to absorb iron, and can cause blood loss from the intestines in small children and in children who are allergic to cow's milk. These problems, combined with the fact that cow's milk has little iron of its own, can lead to iron deficiency (see page 321 for the connection between iron and brain development).

Allergic reactions to the proteins in cow's milk are common. If asthma or eczema runs in the family, there's a good chance that milk might be a contributing cause. Removing dairy products from the diet sometimes eliminates these problems. A sensitivity to cow's milk sometimes triggers constipation, ear infections and even (in rare cases) type 1 diabetes.

Finally, as children grow up, many will develop stomachaches, bloating, diarrhoea and gas caused by undigested lactose (milk sugar). The ability to digest milk sugar disappears for many people in late childhood. In nature, animals do not drink milk after infancy, and that is probably the normal pattern for humans, too.

There is controversy about the possible role of cow's milk in a variety of adult diseases, including cancers of the prostate, ovary and breast. Some studies have found a connection; others have not. Concern focuses on the hormones in milk, which are dissolved in the milk fat. Choosing skimmed milk and fat-free milk products should, in theory, lower or eliminate the risk.

Cow's milk, calcium and bones. Childhood and adolescence are key times for building bone. The standard dietary advice is that children need approximately 900 mg of calcium per day – the equivalent of three 240 ml (8 fl oz) glasses of milk.

Thanks in part to clever and persuasive advertising, everyone knows that milk is an important source of calcium. But among themselves, scientists debate the pluses and minuses of cow's milk when it comes to bone health. For example, several well-done studies found *no* connection between the amount of cow's milk children drink and the amount of calcium they store in their bones. That really is a remarkable finding. If drinking cow's milk is important for bone growth, then you'd expect that people who drink more milk would have stronger bones. But they don't. In fact, the United Kingdom has very high per capita milk consumption and also very high rates of osteoporosis.

Calcium intake is just one of many factors that influence bone density. Researchers have found, for example, that exercise is a more important factor when it comes to building bones during adolescence. It's also important to consider not just how much calcium gets taken in but also how much leaves the body. Diets that are high in dairy are often also high in sodium. In some people, high sodium intake results in loss of calcium in the urine. The proteins in milk and meat also tend to be high in certain amino acids that cause the kidneys to lose calcium. So, as far as building bones is concerned, it may be just as good, if not better, to take in less calcium along with less sodium and animal protein.

Healthy, calcium-rich foods. Other calcium sources offer many advantages that dairy products do not have. Most green leafy vegetables and beans have a form of calcium that is absorbed as well as or even a bit better than that in milk. Along with this calcium come vitamins, iron, complex carbohydrates and fibre. Calcium-enriched soya or rice drinks are just as tasty on cereal as cow's milk (once you get used to them), and they are free of animal proteins and cholesterol. These beverages, as well as calcium-enriched orange and other juices, provide as much calcium, gramme per gramme, as cow's milk. Vegetables and legumes can provide a healthy source of calcium, along with many other nutritional advantages. Here is a list of calcium-rich foods:

CALCIUM SOURCES

(approximate number of milligrammes per serving)

100 mg

225 g (8 oz) cooked kale

85 g (3 oz) baked, refried or navy beans

100 g (3½ oz) tofu

225 g (8 oz) cottage cheese
1 tablespoon blackstrap molasses
1 English muffin
300 g (10½ oz) boiled sweet potato

150 mg
170 g (6 oz) cooked broccoli
30 g (1 oz) mozzarella or feta cheese
5 medium figs, dried

200 mg
225 g (8 oz) beetroot or turnip greens
30 g (1 oz) cheddar
85 g (3 oz) canned sardines or salmon with bones

250 mg
30 g (1 oz) Swiss cheese
110 g (4 oz) raw firm tofu
110 g (4 oz) rhubarb

300 mg
240 ml (8 fl oz) cow's milk
240 ml (8 fl oz) yogurt
110 g (4 oz) ricotta cheese
240 ml (8 fl oz) enriched soya or rice milk (but check the label; some brands may vary)
240 ml (8 fl oz) calcium-fortified orange or apple juice

Sources: Jean A. T. Pennington and Judith Spungen, *Bowes and Church's Food Values of Portions Commonly Used* (New York: Harper & Row, 1989).

WHAT TO COOK

We used to think of vegetables, grains and beans as side dishes. Now we know better. These foods take centre stage in a healthy diet. If you are a recipe follower, you can find an infinite number of recipes online and in books. Otherwise, you may be happier improvising. Children can certainly thrive on simple foods, cooked simply. Here are some ideas.

Green leafy vegetables. Broccoli, kale, watercress, Swiss chard, Chinese leaf, pak choy, spinach and other green vegetables are loaded with absorbable calcium, iron and vitamins; the darker the colour, the richer the nutritional value. Leafy greens should be steamed or stir-fried quickly, some just one or two minutes, so that they come out bright green. They can be seasoned with a little salt and pepper when your child is older, but it's best to avoid added salt for younger children so that they don't develop a taste for very salty foods.

Other vegetables. Squashes of all sorts, including pumpkins, are good baked or used in soups and stews, along with carrots, swedes, potatoes and other roots. Baked sweet potatoes (yams are the same thing) and beetroots are naturally sweet. Peppers of all varieties are vitamin-rich. Green beans provide vitamins and fibre.

Beans and legumes. Red beans, black beans, black-eyed peas, chickpeas and lentils are rich in protein, calcium, fibre and many other nutrients. They are also a good source of calories. Tofu and tempeh, both made from soyabeans, work well in salads, stews, stir-fries and soups. A meal that includes beans and brown rice – or any bean and grain combination – delivers a complete protein with no cholesterol and little saturated fat.

Whole grains. A generous part of a child's diet should be composed of whole grains. Brown rice, barley, oats, millet, whole-wheat noodles and pasta, and whole-grain bread provide complex carbohydrates for sustained energy as well as protein, fibre and vitamins. The process of refining removes most of the fibre and much of the protein. What's left is mainly starch, which is quickly broken down into simple sugars. White bread and white rice provide mainly energy with some vitamins added, but little else.

Meats. Quality matters here: animals that are allowed to graze on grass produce meat that is lower in saturated fat and these animals usually are given fewer hormones and antibiotics than conventionally raised meat. High-quality meat costs more, but if you use less of it, you can save money in the long run. Remember, an adult serving is only 85 g (3 oz); a child-size portion is smaller yet. Ground beef is a special concern because modern production methods mix beef from many animals in a single package, increasing the risk of bacterial contamination. To be safe, it has to be cooked so that no pink remains; rare burgers shouldn't be on the menu any more.

Fish. Fish is a good source of unsaturated fats, including omega-3 fatty acids (see page 365). Many experts suggest two or three servings of fish a week, but it's possible to get plenty of omega-3 fatty acids from vegetarian sources. Contamination of fish with mercury and other heavy metals is a concern, as is overfishing. Pregnant women should limit their intake of high-mercury fish (page 486) or avoid those fish altogether.

Fish farming, especially for salmon, has expanded rapidly. But farm-raised fish may not be the same, nutritionally, as their wild-caught cousins; it depends on what they have been fed. Wild-caught fish can be hard to find and expensive; buying it frozen lowers the cost but not the nutritional value. Small, short-lived fish such as sardines provide healthy fats with low risk of heavy metal contamination, and the fisheries are not endangered. A taste for sardines is worth acquiring.

Fats and oils. The healthiest oils contain the lowest percentage of saturated fat. Canola oil is very low in saturated fat (7 per cent), followed by sunflower (10 per cent) and corn, peanut and olive oils (all about 14 per cent). All of these are markedly better than butter (50 per cent saturated fat) or lard (39 per cent). Any of the healthy oils work well as the base for a salad dressing or brushed on the bottom of a skillet for stir-frying. Tofu or sweet potato slices sprayed lightly with oil, then baked in a hot oven, come out with a crispy top. Instead of using margarine or butter on a baked potato, try Dijon mustard, salsa or steamed vegetables. Jam and cinnamon work well on toast without the layer of butter in between, and whole-grain bread can be delicious with no topping at all.

Fruits, seeds and nuts. These foods make delicious treats. Locally grown fruits in season are fresher and often cheaper. Baking or stewing makes fruits sweeter and easier to digest. Drying makes them easy to pack as snacks. Seeds and nuts can be roasted and eaten alone or in salads. Almond butter and organic peanut butter are a healthy substitute for sweets or ice cream.

Dairy. If you do choose to include dairy in your child's diet, pay attention to the fat content. Whole milk is best from twelve to twenty-four months. Change to semi-skimmed milk (1.7 per cent fat) at age two, and 1 per cent fat milk (if it is available) at age five. Skimmed milk (0–0.5 per cent fat), which is not recommended for under-fives, is free of saturated fat and cholesterol, and it provides protein, calcium and vitamin D. Concerns about milk proteins are discussed on page 378. These concerns are controversial, but there is no disagreement about the value of milkfat in the diet after age five: less is best. Nondairy milks (soya, rice, almond) are readily available.

Eggs. Egg whites are high on the list of allergy-causing foods, so they are best avoided until after one year of age. They are a great source of protein, fat-free and low in calories (about 16 in the white of one large egg). Egg yolks are good sources of vitamin B_{12} and other vitamins, minerals (iron, calcium) and protein. They are high in cholesterol but quite low in saturated fat, about the same as a tablespoon of olive oil. An egg yolk whipped with sunflower oil and a bit of lemon juice makes mayonnaise.

Sugar. Refined sugar, a simple carbohydrate, is full of calories but not much else. Brown sugar and raw sugar are nutritionally about the same as white sugar. When children eat sugar-sweetened foods all day, other foods taste bland by comparison. When you use sweet vegetables such as pumpkin, corn, butternut squash and carrots, you don't need to add sugar. At first these foods don't taste sweet, in the sense that they don't taste like sugar. But after you take sugar out of your cooking, you begin to notice the real taste of sweet vegetables and fruits. For a sweet treat, the healthiest choices are fresh fruits and fruit juices.

Salt. Most processed foods are very salty, which makes food with a normal amount of salt taste bland. It's better to cook food yourself and use salt sparingly.

Beverages. The beverages most actively marketed to children range from 100 per cent fruit juice to drinks that are essentially sugar water with flavouring; some have added vitamins. These drinks all deliver a large dose of simple carbohydrates (sugar), which outweighs the benefits of the added vitamins. They are a major cause of obesity. Sugar-free, artificially sweetened drinks don't add calories themselves, but are so sweet that they make naturally sweet things (fruit, for example) taste bland by comparison.

The beverage children really need is pure, clean water. For variety, they can have teas made from grains, herbs or fruit juices, and they can also enjoy sweet vegetable drinks made from carrots, winter squash, even onion. Be aware of caffeine in coffee, of course, but also in black and green teas, and in many popular soft drinks marketed to children. (Chocolate also contains a fair amount of caffeine.)

Sweets. Biscuits, cakes and pastries satisfy a child's appetite for a short time, but they provide little other nutrition and are the greatest source of invisible fat in the diet. Empty calories cheat children by making them feel well fed when they are being partly starved, and by spoiling their appetite for better foods.

You don't have to be so worried about rich, refined foods that you stop your children from eating cake at a birthday party or on other special occasions. It's a steady diet of such foods that deprives them of nutrition. There is no reason to train your child to expect a rich dessert after every dinner. You don't need to keep your home stocked with shop-bought biscuits or ice cream. Instead, make a batch of biscuits with your child, enjoy the process and the product, and when the biscuits are gone, enjoy other sweet things (fruit, for example). When sweets take their rightful place as special treats, children appreciate them more and are able to enjoy healthier foods every day.

SIMPLE MEALS

The whole business of diet sounds complicated, but it needn't be. The ideal diet is based on fruits, vegetables, whole grains, beans and the like. Meat, poultry and fish can be offered in small portions or eliminated entirely. If you exclude all animal-based foods, including eggs and dairy, be sure to include a daily multivitamin (see page 371). Roughly speaking, the following foods are required every day:

- Vegetables, green or yellow, three to five servings. Ideally some of these are raw.
- Fruit, two or three servings, at least half of them raw. Fruit and vegetables may be interchanged.
- Legumes (beans, peas and lentils), two to three servings.
- Whole-grain bread, crackers, cereals or pasta, two or more servings.

Suggested meals. If some of these suggestions seem odd or unusual, that's the point. If you want to change what you and your children eat, you need to be willing to try different things. Keep an open mind and see what works for you.

Breakfast

- Fruit or fruit juice or green leafy vegetables
- Whole-grain cereal, bread, toast or pancakes
- Scrambled tofu with greens
- Soya milk
- Vegetable soup

Lunch

- A filling dish such as baked beans; whole-wheat or oat cereal, millet or barley soup with vegetables; whole-grain bread or sandwiches with tofu spread or nut butter; potato; soup with crackers, toast, barley or a milk pudding; steamed, boiled or stir-fried leafy greens
- Vegetable or fruit, raw or cooked
- Dry-roasted sunflower seeds
- Soya milk, caffeine-free tea or apple juice

Dinner

- Green leafy vegetables, briefly cooked with a little water
- Beans or bean products such as tofu or tempeh
- Whole-grain rice, whole-wheat bread or pasta, or other whole grain
- Raw fruit or apple sauce
- Juice or water

Variations. Many parents complain that they don't know how to vary lunch. A good rough rule is to serve three items.

1. A filling dish with plenty of calories
2. A fruit or a vegetable
3. A green leafy vegetable (kale, broccoli, spring onions) cooked in a variety of ways

Breads and sandwiches of several kinds can be the filling dish as children approach the age of two. Use whole-wheat bread to start with. In general, avoid butter and margarine, which are often high in saturated or trans fat. Nut butters are better. Mustard is a fat-free, well-accepted spread for sandwiches and potatoes. While ketchup is loaded with sugar, salsa can be equally delicious and is much healthier. Sandwiches can be made with a wide variety of other foods, plain or in combination: raw vegetables (lettuce, tomato, grated carrot, cabbage), stewed fruit, chopped dried fruit, peanut butter or tofu.

A fairly substantial dish is a broth or soup containing lots of barley or brown rice; or a vegetable soup, plain or creamed, with a couple of handfuls of whole-wheat toast cut into small cubes to toss in. Lentil, split pea and bean soups are a good balance with a grain dish and a green vegetable.

Simple unsalted whole-grain crackers can be served plain or with one of the spreads mentioned above. Potato is a good, filling, low-fat dish. A baked potato can be topped with vegetables, baked beans, mustard, black pepper or salsa. A small amount of salsa (or ketchup) entices many a child to eat a greater variety of vegetables.

Cooked, precooked or dry cereal can be made more exciting by adding sliced raw fruit, stewed fruit or chopped dried fruit. Instead of a filling first course followed by stewed or raw fruit, you can serve first a cooked green or yellow vegetable, or a vegetable or fruit salad. A banana makes an excellent and filling dessert.

Pasta, hot or cold, is a good source of complex carbohydrates and fibre. It may be mixed with steamed vegetables and tomato sauce. Some children don't seem to like grains and pasta. They will do just fine nutritionally on a variety of fruits, vegetables and beans. Their taste for grains will develop later if it's not forced on them early on. Pastas made without eggs are available in many supermarkets. Noodles made with whole grains are best. You can add noodles to a stir-fry or have noodles in a broth with greens added.

A world of vegetables. Vegetables are so important that they deserve featured status on a child's plate. During the first year, a baby has probably had most of the following cooked vegetables: spinach, peas, onions, carrots, asparagus, chard, butternut squash, tomatoes, beetroots, celery and potatoes. After the first few weeks, most table vegetables eaten by the rest of the family can be fed to your infant after placing them in the blender and serving them in pureed form. These same vegetables can be bought in a jar of baby food. Be sure to read the nutritional information on the label and choose ones that only contain the vegetable, without added tapioca or other starch.

By the end of the first year the vegetables can be offered in a more coarsely mashed consistency. Peas should be mashed slightly to avoid their being swallowed whole. Steamed vegetables such as carrots, potatoes and green beans, cut into pieces, make good finger foods.

Try sweet potatoes instead of white potatoes. If you have been sticking to the easily digested vegetables up to the age of a year, you can try gradually the less popular and sometimes less digestible ones such as butter beans (mashed), broccoli, cabbage, cauliflower, turnips and parsnips. If you persist in offering them without trying to force it, over time your child will develop a taste for them.

Wait until two years to serve kernel corn. Young children don't chew it; it passes through them unchanged. Use only tender corn. When cutting it off the cob, don't cut too close; then each kernel will be cut open. When your child is three or four and you start to offer corn on the cob, slice down the centre of each row of kernels so that they are all split. Corn off the cob can be served either warm or frozen, right from the bag; children often enjoy picking up the crunchy kernels one at a time.

The more easily digested raw vegetables are usually started between one and two years. The best are peeled tomatoes, sliced string beans, shredded carrots and grated or chopped celery. They should be well washed. Go slowly at first and see how they are digested. You can use orange juice or sweetened lemon juice as a dressing.

Vegetable and fruit juices can be started at the same time. These are not as healthy as the whole food because the juice lacks the fibre contained in the fruit or vegetable. One advantage of juice over cooked vegetables is that no vitamins are destroyed in cooking. If a child has temporarily turned against plain vegetables, try soups made with one or several vegetables: pea, tomato, celery, onion, spinach, beetroot, corn. Some commercially prepared vegetable soups are very high in salt (sodium), so you need to read the label carefully. Some commercially prepared soups need to be diluted with equal amounts of water. If they're given to children in the undiluted form right out of the can, they can be harmful because the salt is too highly concentrated.

TIPS FOR HAPPY EATING

Have fun with foods. Give your child a wide variety of foods with different colours, textures and taste. Try to create balance, not only in the different flavours, textures and nutrients, but also among the colours on the plate. Whenever you can, let your children help you choose and prepare the food, set the table and clean up. All of these activities can be joyful.

Keep mealtime free of the distractions of television and the telephone. Some families say grace or meditate for a few minutes, which can establish a spirit of thankfulness and togetherness for the meal. Scoldings should not be part of the dining experience, despite the inevitable spills and lapses of manners.

Keep a balanced attitude about food. Don't judge foods on calories, vitamins or minerals alone. Other important considerations are fat, protein, carbohydrates, fibre, sugar and sodium. You don't need to calculate grammes and percentages: just offer well-balanced meals. Remember that not all essential foods need to be eaten at every meal. What's important is what is taken in over the course of a day or two.

In the long run, everybody needs a balance of low- and

high-calorie foods, as well as a balance of other nutrients. If a person takes one aspect of diet too seriously and forgets the others, it's apt to lead to trouble. An adolescent girl, for example, acquires a fanatical zeal to lose weight. She leaves out all the foods in which she has heard there are more than a few calories, and she tries to live on salad, juice, fruit and coffee. She is bound to be sick if she keeps on.

Serious-minded parents who have the mistaken idea that vitamins are the whole show and that starches are inferior may serve their child carrot salad and grapefruit for supper. The poor child can't get enough calories out of that to satisfy a rabbit. A plump mother from a plump family, ashamed of her son's scrawniness, may serve him only rich foods, crowding out vegetables, beans and grains. In the process, he is apt to be deprived of minerals and vitamins.

Temporary substitutes for vegetables. Suppose a child has refused vegetables in any form for weeks. Will her nutrition suffer? Vegetables are particularly valuable for various minerals, vitamins and fibre. But fruits also supply many of the same minerals, vitamins and fibre. Whole grains also offer some protein and many of the vitamins and minerals found in vegetables. So if your child refuses to eat vegetables for a period of time, don't make a big issue out of it. Continue to keep mealtime relaxed and fun. If you are really concerned, give your child a daily multivitamin. Her taste for vegetables will return – unless you turn eating them into a power struggle, in which case she may refuse to eat them just to show you who's boss.

Taming a sweet tooth. The craving for sweets and fatty foods often starts at home. Children learn these tastes when there is a rich dessert with every meal, when sweets are always offered between meals, and when the highest reward is considered to be a junk food splurge. When parents say, 'You can't have your ice cream until you finish your vegetables,' they are giving the wrong message and basically using junk food as a bribe. Teach your young child, instead, that a banana or a peach is the greatest treat of all.

Children tend to eat whatever their parents eat. If you drink a lot of fizzy drinks, eat a lot of ice cream or chocolate, or have crisps around all the time, your children will want these things too. Sweets brought by a grandparent who visits occasionally can be regarded as a special treat; if grandparents bring sweets every day, they need to find other ways to show love to their grandchildren, such as games, walks or stories.

Feeding between meals. Use common sense between meals. Many young children and some older ones want a snack between meals, but others never snack. If it's the right kind of food, given at a sensible hour and presented in the right way, a snack shouldn't interfere with meals or lead to dietary problems. When the regular meals contain plenty of carbohydrates in the form of grains and vegetables, children are much less likely to feel ravenous between meals.

Milk isn't a good snack food since it is more likely to take away the child's appetite for the next meal. A snack shouldn't contain too much fat or protein. Fruits or vegetables are the best bet. Occasionally, though, you see children who never can eat very much at one meal and get excessively hungry and tired before the next; they may thrive when given richer, more caloric snacks between meals. They have a better appetite for the next meal because they're not exhausted. Cakes, biscuits, pastries and salty and fried snack foods are rich in calories and fat, but poor in other food values.

For most children the snack is best given midway between meals, no closer than an hour and a half before the next one. Even here there are exceptions. There are children who have a snack in the middle of the morning but still get so hungry and cranky before lunch is ready that they pick fights and refuse to eat. Getting a glass of orange or tomato juice the minute they get home, even though it is twenty minutes before lunch, may improve their disposition and their appetite. What and when to feed a child between meals is a matter of common sense and doing what suits the individual child.

Parents may complain that their child eats badly at meals but is always begging for food between meals. This problem doesn't arise because the parents have been lenient about offering snacks between meals. Quite the contrary. More often, the parents have been urging or forcing the child to eat at mealtimes and holding back on food at other times. It's the pushing that takes away the appetite at meals. After months of it, the very sight of the dining room is enough to make the child's stomach revolt. But when the meal is safely over (though little has been eaten), the stomach feels natural again. Soon it's acting the way a healthy empty stomach is meant to act – it's asking for food. The treatment, then, is not to deny children food between meals, but to let mealtime be so enjoyable that their mouths water then, too. After all, what is a meal? It's food specially prepared to be appetizing. When a child finds it less appealing than snacks, something has gone wrong.

SECTION III

Health and Safety

GENERAL MEDICAL ISSUES

YOUR CHILD'S DOCTOR

Children get health care from paediatricians, family doctors (GPs) and nurse practitioners. To keep things short, I'll refer to all of these professionals simply as doctors.

You are partners. The doctor is the medical expert, but you know your child best. The doctor's advice depends on the information you supply and the questions you ask. Communication is a two-way street. Remember, you and the doctor have the same goal: to help your child to grow up healthy and happy.

Asking questions. Most new parents hesitate to ask questions that they think might be too simple or silly. But if there's any kind of question on your mind, you're entitled to an answer. Most doctors are happy to answer any questions they can, the easier the better. If you write down your questions before each doctor's visit, you won't worry about forgetting any of them.

It often happens that a parent asks about a problem and the doctor explains part of it, but gets sidetracked before having answered the most important part. It's best to be bold and make clear exactly what you want to know. Often, on getting home from a surgery visit, parents find that they forgot to bring up their most important questions and are embarrassed to call back so soon. Doctors are not bothered by this; they are quite used to it.

If you are worried about anything you should always call the doctor, even if you are pretty sure that the problem is trivial. It's much better to ask and be reassured than to sit and worry.

Disagreements with the doctor. In most cases parents and doctors soon come to know and trust each other. But occasionally, since they are all human beings, there are misunderstandings and tensions. Most of these are avoidable or easily cleared up with frankness on both sides. It's best to lay your feelings on the table. If you are unsatisfied with your doctor's advice or care, you should bring the problem out into the open right away in the most matter-of-fact manner you can muster. Some parents are too intimidated to express their misgivings about a diagnosis or the way the doctor handles their child during a physical examination. If these feelings are out in the open, they can be addressed. An early meeting of minds is easier for both of you than allowing your tension and irritation to accumulate.

Asking for a second opinion. If your child has some illness or condition that worries you intensely, it is always your right to ask for a second opinion. Many parents are hesitant about doing so, fearing that this would express lack of confidence in their doctor. But it is a regular procedure in the practice of medicine, and the doctor should take it in his or her stride. Doctors, like any other human beings, sense uneasiness in the people they deal with even when it is unspoken, and it makes their job harder. A second opinion usually clears the air for them as well as for the family.

DR SPOCK COMMENTS

Sometimes a parent and doctor find that they can't get along, no matter how frank and cooperative they try to be. In this case it's better all around to admit it openly and find a new doctor. All health professionals, including the most successful, have learned that they don't suit everybody, and they accept this fact philosophically.

REGULAR CHECKUPS

The best way to be sure that your baby is doing well is to have her regularly checked by a doctor. The check-up schedule varies but most practices suggest a visit in the first twenty-four hours after birth, then at six weeks and again at eighteen months and three years. If you'd like additional visits, ask for them.

During a regular checkup, the doctor will ask you how your baby is doing. Your baby will be weighed and measured to see how she's growing. She'll be given a full physical examination to make sure she's healthy. Even if your baby is perfectly healthy, these visits allow you to develop a relationship of trust and familiarity with the doctor, ask any questions you have and hear any words of wisdom the doctor has to offer. Doctors generally address feeding and nutrition, behaviour, sleep and safety – all topics in this book.

Remember to keep your baby up to date with her immunizations (see page 434), which will usually be carried out by a nurse.

TELEPHONE CALLS TO YOUR DOCTOR

Phone policies. Find out the policy of your doctor's practice for taking calls about ill children. Most practices have a nurse during the workday who answers questions and decides if the child needs to see a doctor. Ask about the best time to phone during the day, particularly about a new illness that may require a visit to the surgery. Sick children often show their first definite symptoms during the afternoon, and most doctors would like to know about them as early in the afternoon as possible so that they can plan accordingly.

At night or at weekends, all practices have a number to call if you are worried about your child. Usually you will reach an answering service, which will notify the doctor who is on call that night.

When to call, in general. After you've brought up a couple of babies, you'll have a good idea which symptoms or questions require prompt contact with the doctor and which can wait until the next morning or the next week.

New parents often feel more comfortable with a list of

symptoms that require a call to the doctor. No list, however, can be anywhere near complete. After all, there are thousands of different diseases and injuries. You always have to use your own common sense. A good general rule is that if you're concerned, you should call, even if you think the call might be unnecessary. It's better to call too much, especially in the beginning, than to not call when you should have.

By far, the most important rule is to consult the doctor promptly, at least by telephone, *if a baby or child looks or acts sick*. Pay attention to signs such as unusual tiredness, drowsiness or lack of interest; unusual irritability, anxiousness or restlessness; or unusual paleness. These general signs of illness are particularly important in the first two or three months of life, when a baby can be seriously ill without fever or other specific symptoms and signs of illness.

Specific symptoms to call about. If your child looks sick, you should contact your doctor whether or not there are specific symptoms. The flip side is also usually true: if your child looks well and is playful, active, alert and bright-eyed, then serious illness is unlikely. However, there are a few symptoms that should trigger a call to the doctor, no matter what else is going on.

Fever. If your baby is less than three months old, call right away for any temperature of 38°C (100.4°F) or more (taken rectally – see page 414). Young infants can become quite ill quite fast, with only a low fever or no fever at all. From three months to about three years, most serious infections will cause a fever, but call right away if your baby looks truly sick, even if the temperature is normal. You should consult the doctor if your baby over three months has a temperature of 38.3°C (101°F) or more, but you don't have to call in the middle of the night if your baby has a 38.3°C (101°F) fever but otherwise seems happy. After the age of three or four years, a high fever (up to 38.8°C/102°F or even 39.4°C/103°F) can accompany a mild infection, so you have to rely on your judgment.

Rapid breathing (tachypnea). Children breathe faster than adults. Healthy infants breathe up to forty times a minute, young children up to thirty, and children ten years and above up to twenty. Count the number of breaths in sixty seconds, with each in-out being one breath. Once in a while, pay attention to your child's breathing so you'll know if there's a real change from normal. Fever and pain drive up the respiratory rate, as do illnesses such as pneumonia and asthma. Rapid breathing that doesn't slow down after a few minutes is usually a sign that there's something seriously wrong.

Retractions. Difficulty in moving air in and out of the lungs will cause a child to pull with the muscles in the stomach, chest and neck. You can see the skin suck in (retract) over the collarbones and between and under the ribs. Other signs of difficulty in breathing are flaring of the nostrils or grunting sounds with each breath. Often the culprit is simply mucus blocking up the nose, but signs of difficulty in breathing should probably trigger a doctor visit to make sure it's nothing more serious.

Noisy breathing. Children with chest infections or

asthma often have noisier breathing than usual. It may be hard for you to tell exactly where the noise is coming from. Sometimes it's just from mucus in the nose, not a lung problem at all. Other times it may come from the windpipe (in which case the noise is called *stridor*) and will be loudest when the child is breathing in. Sometimes the noise comes from farther down in the lungs. If these are high-pitched, almost musical noises, usually louder when breathing out, they may be wheezes, as children with asthma are prone to.

Noisy breathing means that at least some air is moving in and out. If a child has retractions and tachypnea *without* noisy breathing, this is a true medical emergency. Hoarseness of voice accompanied by difficulty in breathing should always be reported immediately, especially if there is associated drooling.

Pain. Pain is the body's internal alarm that something is wrong. If the pain is not severe and there are no other symptoms (such as fever), you can probably safely wait and watch. If the pain seems severe, if the child cannot be consoled or if he seems quite ill, then by all means call the doctor. When in doubt, call.

Vomiting of any unusual type should be reported promptly, especially if the child looks sick or different in any other way. This does not apply to the spitting up after meals that is so common in young infants. Bright yellow vomit is sometimes a sign of blocked intestines; this needs medical attention right away.

Diarrhoea of the more serious sort, such as bloody diarrhoea and unusual quantities of loose or watery stools in infants, should be reported to the doctor immediately. The milder kinds can wait. Look for signs of dehydration (tiredness, decreased urine output, dry mouth and decreased tears) and report them to your doctor. Call right away for blood in the bowel movements or urine, or bloody vomit.

Injury to the head should be reported if your child loses consciousness. Other concerning signs: your child isn't happy and healthy-looking within fifteen minutes, begins to look more lethargic and dazed as time goes by, or begins to vomit. Any of these changes after a head injury merits a call to the doctor.

Ingestion of poisons. If your child has eaten anything that might possibly be dangerous, call an ambulance immediately (see page 480).

Rashes. If a child seems sick and has a rash, or if a rash is extensive, you should call the doctor right away. Any rash that could be from bleeding into the skin – either large purplish blotches or small red spots that don't go away when you stretch the skin over them – should be looked at right away.

Remember, this is only a partial list of situations when you should call your doctor. When in doubt, call!

Before you call. It's sometimes hard for the doctor or nurse to tell if your child is really sick and should be seen right away or if the problem can wait until the next day. Before calling, make sure you have the following information handy (write it down if you need to):

1. What are the troubling symptoms? When did they start? How often are they occurring?
2. What are your child's temperature and breathing rate? How is her skin colour – pale or flushed? (For more on temperatures, see page 412.)
3. How sick does your child appear to be? Is she alert or lethargic? Bright-eyed or dazed? Happy and playful, or miserable and crying?
4. Does your child have any past medical problems that could relate to your current concern?
5. Is your child on any medication? If so, what are they? What have you tried so far? Has it worked?
6. How worried are you about the situation?

The quality of the phone diagnosis depends on the quality of the information you give. Doctors and nurses, being human, sometimes forget to ask all of these important questions. It's up to you to make sure that all important information is relayed on the phone so an appropriate decision can be made. If you remain deeply concerned after an over-the-phone diagnosis, insist that your child is seen by a doctor, either at A&E or the surgery.

CARING FOR A SICK CHILD

Special care without spoiling. When children are ill, it's natural to give them special care and consideration. You don't mind preparing drinks and foods for them at frequent intervals, or even putting aside a drink they refuse and making another kind right away. You are glad to get them new playthings to keep them happy and quiet.

A child can easily get used to this arrangement, and may start bossing his parents around and expecting instant service. Fortunately, most children are on their way to recovery within a few days. As soon as the parents stop worrying, they stop putting up with the child's unreasonable demands. After a couple of days, things are back to normal.

With longer illnesses, the persistent high level of concern and special treatment may have a bad effect on a child's spirits. He's apt to become demanding. If he's too polite for that, he may just become excitable and temperamental. It's easy for him to learn to enjoy being sick and receiving sympathy. His ability to make his own way agreeably may grow weaker, like a muscle that isn't being used.

Getting back to normal. It's wise for parents to get back into normal balance with the sick child as soon as possible. This means such little things as having a friendly, matter-of-fact expression when entering the room, rather than a worried one. Ask him how he feels today in a tone of voice that expects good news rather than bad, and perhaps ask only once a day. When you find out by experience what he wants to drink and eat, serve it up casually. Don't ask timidly if he likes it, or act as if he is wonderful to take a little. Keep strictly away from urging unless the doctor feels it is necessary. A sick child's appetite is more quickly ruined by pushing and forcing.

If you are buying new playthings, look particularly for the types that encourage children to take an active role and use their imaginations: blocks and building sets; sewing, weaving and bead-stringing kits; painting, modelling and stamp-collecting supplies. Deal out one new plaything at a time. There are lots of homemade occupations, like cutting pictures out of old magazines, making a scrapbook, sewing, or building a farm or town or dollhouse of cardboard and masking tape. A little extra TV and video game playing is fine; too much is bound to make your child feel listless, or encourage him to stay sick longer in order to continue indulging his obsession.

If a child is going to be laid up for a long time but is well enough to study, start him on his schoolwork again for a regular period each day as soon as possible. It's fine to spend time each day keeping your sick child company, but you don't need to be there every minute. It's healthy for a child to know that there are times when his parents will be busy elsewhere, as long as they are available for any emergency. If the child has a disease that isn't catching and the doctor lets him have company, invite other children in regularly to play and to stay for meals.

The hardest part can be when the child is over his illness but not yet fully back to his old self. You have to use your best judgment about how much special consideration he still needs. The best policy is to let your child lead as normal a life as possible under the circumstances. You should expect reasonable behaviour towards you and the rest of the family, and avoid worried talk, looks and thoughts.

FEVERS

What's fever and what isn't? The first thing to realize is that a healthy child's body temperature doesn't stay fixed at the 'normal' temperature of 37°C (98.6°F). It is always going up and down a little, depending on the time of day and what the child is doing. It's usually lowest in the early morning and highest in the late afternoon. This change during the day is only a slight one, however. The change between rest and activity is greater. The temperature of perfectly healthy small children may be 37.6°C (99.6°F) or even 37.8°C (100°F) right after they have been running around.

From birth up to three months of age, any temperature of 38°C (100.4°F) or more could be a sign of serious illness and should be reported to the doctor. This is one of the few facts that you really must remember to keep your baby safe. A serious infection could include bacteria in the blood, bones, kidneys, brain or elsewhere; these infections need to be taken very seriously. There is one exception: if your baby has been wrapped up overly snugly, unwrap her a bit and take the temperature again in a few minutes. If it's normal and stays normal, and if your baby acts healthy, she was probably just overheated.

In an older child, a temperature of 38.3°C (101°F) or higher probably means illness. In general, the higher the fever, the more likely the illness is a serious infection, as opposed to a mild cold or viral infection. But some children with mild infections run high temperatures, and some children with serious infections run lower ones. Fever itself only becomes harmful to a child at temperatures of 41.1°C (106°F) or more – higher than most children ever go.

In most feverish illnesses, the temperature is apt to be highest in the late afternoon and lowest in the morning – but don't be surprised if a fever is high in the morning and low in the afternoon. There are a few diseases in which the fever, instead of climbing and falling, stays high steadily. The most common of these are pneumonia and roseola. An infant who is very sick may also have a below-normal temperature. Slightly low temperatures (as low as 36.1°C/97°F) sometimes occur at the end of an illness, and also in healthy babies and small children in the morning. This is no cause for concern as long as the child is feeling well.

What causes fever with illness? Normally, body temperature is controlled by a part of the brain called the hypothalamus. When the body becomes too warm, the hypothalamus calls for sweating to cool it down; when the body becomes too cold, it calls for shivering, which generates heat through muscle activity. The system works like the thermostat for the boiler in a house. In response to an infection, the immune system releases chemicals that turn up the thermostat in the brain. So even though body temperature may be 37.8°C (100°F), if the new thermostat setting is 38.8°C (102°F), the child will feel chilled and may even shiver (shaking chills). Medicines like paracetamol (Calpol) work by blocking the production of these fever-inducing chemicals, allowing the body's thermostat to return to normal. As the fever breaks, the child may sweat, a sign that the brain now recognizes that the body is overheated.

Fever is not a disease. Many parents assume that fever itself is dangerous. But the fever is not the disease. In fact, fever actually helps the body fight off many infections. (Other animals, not just humans, also run fevers as a way of killing germs.) Monitoring a child's fever also helps keep track of how the illness is progressing. It's sometimes helpful to bring a fever down because it is interfering with the child's sleep or exhausting him. In other cases, the best thing may be to leave the fever alone and concentrate on curing the infection.

Taking the temperature. Experienced parents often feel that they can tell a child's temperature using the back of their hand or by touching their lips to the child's forehead. The problem, of course, is that it's impossible to communicate to a doctor (or anyone else) just how warm the child feels.

I like digital electronic thermometers. They are faster, more accurate and easier to read than traditional – and dangerous – mercury-filled glass thermometers. If you own a glass thermometer, you should get rid of it. But don't simply throw it in the bin. Mercury is a poison that should never go into landfills. Instead, take it to your council refuse site, following the procedure for toxic waste. High-tech electronic thermometers that read the temperature through the ear are expensive and don't offer any real advantage, except for the rare child who simply will not hold still. Thermometers that read temperature by scanning the skin may not be particularly accurate.

With a digital thermometer, all you do is wipe it off, turn it on and pop it in. A friendly beep lets you know when it's time to read the temperature. For infants, it's most accurate

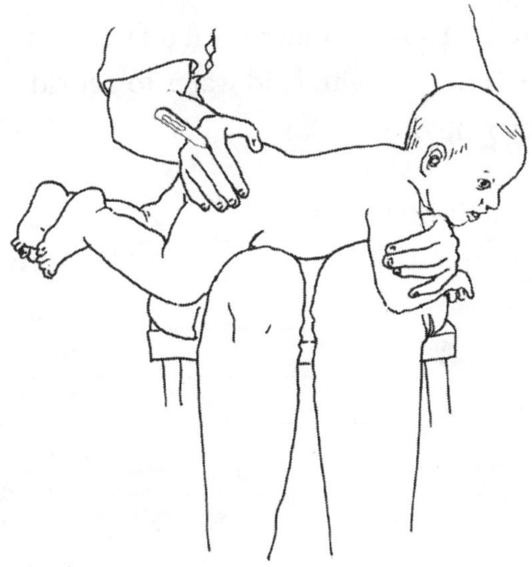

to take a rectal temperature. Use a little Vaseline or other mild lubricant, lay your baby over your knee or hold your baby's legs up with one hand, and slide the thermometer tip in about 1 cm (½ in). After age five or six, most children can cooperate with holding the thermometer under their tongue with their lips closed for a minute or so.

You can also take the temperature under your child's armpit (an axillary temperature), but this is not as accurate as either rectal or oral. In one child, the blood vessels lie close to the skin and the axillary temperature reads higher; in another child, they lie farther from the skin and the temperature reads lower. When accuracy matters, either rectal or oral is the way to go. When reporting the temperature to your child's doctor, pay attention to the decimal point. Sometimes parents say 'one hundred and three' (103°F) when they mean 'one hundred *point* three' (100.3°F). The more precise you are, the better advice you'll get.

Clean a thermometer by washing it with lukewarm water and soap. You can then wipe it off with surgical spirit, but be sure to rinse it with cold water to get rid of the taste before using it again.

Temperature Equivalents

Centigrade (Celsius)	Fahrenheit
37°	98.6°
38°	100.4°
39°	102.2°
40°	104°

How long to keep taking the temperature. Here is what happens occasionally. A child has a bad cold with a fever. The doctor sees the child and has the parents take the child's temperature twice a day. Finally the fever is gone and the child is convalescing well, with only a mild cough and running nose. The doctor tells the parents to let the child go outdoors as soon as the cold is gone completely. Two weeks later, the parents telephone to say that they and the child are getting desperate staying indoors, that the running nose and cough have been completely gone for ten days, that the child looks wonderful and eats well, but that the fever is still going to 37.6°C (99.6°F) each afternoon. As I explained earlier, this is not necessarily a fever in an active child. The ten days of staying indoors and worrying over the temperature have been a waste.

Under most circumstances, when the temperature has stayed under 38.3°C (101°F) for a couple of days, it's a good general rule to forget about the thermometer unless the doctor asks you to continue or unless the child seems sicker in any way. Children should be kept home from school until the temperature has been normal for twenty-fours hours and they are definitely feeling better; all the cold symptoms don't have to be gone. Don't get into the habit of taking your child's temperature when she is well.

Treating a fever (until you reach the doctor). Between the ages of one and five years, children may develop a fever as high as 40°C (104°F), sometimes even higher, with the onset of a mild infection such as a cold, a sore throat or the flu, just as they would with a serious infection. On the other hand, a dangerous illness may never bring a temperature higher than 38.3°C (101°F). So don't be influenced too much one way or the other by the height of the fever. Get in touch with the doctor when your child looks sick or different, whatever the temperature.

Sometimes a child feels especially uncomfortable with a high fever. If on the first day of an illness a child's temperature is 40°C (104°F) or higher, you can bring the fever down a little with an antifever medication such as paracetamol (Calpol) or ibuprofen (Calprofen). Follow the directions on the package for the correct dose. Remember that doses change based on age and weight.

The medicine to bring the fever down should be given one time only, unless you still haven't reached the doctor after three to four hours, in which case you can give a second dose. (Be sure to keep these medications out of your child's reach and in a childproof container. Even though they are sold without prescription, they are not harmless: a large overdose of either paracetamol or ibuprofen can be quite dangerous.)

You may want to give your child a tepid bath or wipe his skin with a damp cloth or sponge. The purpose is to bring the blood to the surface by rubbing and to cool it by the evaporation of the water off the skin. Alcohol has traditionally been used in a wet rub, but if it is applied very freely in a small room, too much may be inhaled. Water works just as well and is free and safe. These methods provide only temporary relief, however, because the body's thermostat remains set at a higher temperature and will quickly cause the fever to return.

When a child's fever is very high and he is flushed, use only light covers at ordinary room temperature, perhaps as little as a sheet. Your child will be more comfortable that way, and it may help his temperature come down.

Fevers and seizures. Parents often worry that prolonged high fever can cause a convulsion or seizure. Actually, it's the quick rise in temperature at the onset of an illness that occasionally causes a convulsion in small children (see page 511). The reason for trying to bring a high fever down is to help the child feel less miserable, not to prevent a convulsion.

WARNING

Never give aspirin to a child or teenager for fever or for cold or flu symptoms unless the doctor prescribes it. Only paracetamol, ibuprofen and other nonaspirin products should be used for these symptoms in children and teenagers. If it turns out to be a viral illness, especially influenza or chicken pox, aspirin can make the child more susceptible to Reye's syndrome, an uncommon but very dangerous condition (see page 613).

DIET DURING ILLNESS

Your doctor will tell you what diet to use in each of your child's illnesses, taking into account the nature of the disease and the child's taste. What follows are some general principles to guide you until you are able to get medical help.

Colds without fever. Children may lose some of their appetite with even a mild cold because they're indoors, they're not moving around as much, they're a little uncomfortable or they're swallowing mucus. Don't urge them to take more food than they want. If they're eating less than usual, offer them extra fluids between meals. There is no harm in letting children drink all that they feel like drinking, but excessive amounts of fluid don't do any more good than reasonable amounts. There's scientific evidence that chicken soup – a traditional remedy in many cultures – actually helps. Small amounts, sipped frequently during the day, seem to work best.

Fever. When children have fever above 38.8°C (102°F) with a cold, flu, sore throat or another contagious disease, they usually lose their appetite in the beginning, especially for solids. In the first day or two of such a fever, don't offer them solid food at all if they don't seem hungry, but do offer fluids frequently when they're awake. Orange juice, pineapple juice and water are the most popular fluids. Water has no nourishment, but it's for this very reason that it often appeals to the sick child most. Other fluids depend on the child's taste and the illness.

Some children love grapefruit juice, lemonade, pear juice, grape juice or weak tea. Ice lollies are also a good source of fluid. Older children like carbonated drinks such as ginger ale and fruit-flavoured sodas. If a child has an infection that causes sores in his mouth, he may not want citrus drinks, which are acidic and may make the sores sting. Cola drinks often contain caffeine, so it's preferable to avoid them. Dairy products may cause more mucus complications and more discomfort with upper respiratory infections, but if all your child wants is milk, go ahead and give that.

The most important rule is, do not press a sick child to eat anything that she doesn't want unless the doctor has a special reason for urging it. It's only too likely to be vomited, to cause intestinal upset or to start a feeding problem.

Vomiting. Vomiting occurs in many different diseases. The diet depends on many factors and should be prescribed by the doctor. However, if you cannot reach the doctor immediately, you can follow these suggestions: start with small sips of water or Dioralyte (oral rehydration solution), which is water with the right amount of salt and sugar to be absorbed best (see page 260). You can also give a homemade oral rehydration solution made by mixing one level teaspoon of salt and eight level teaspoons of sugar in a litre of water.

At first, give only 15 ml (½ fl oz) every fifteen to twenty minutes. Gradually increase the amount, as the child tolerates it, up to 120 ml (4 fl oz; half a glass) every half hour or so. If she has gone this far without vomiting, you can try a little diluted apple juice or herb tea (peppermint or chamomile often stay down well). Many children tolerate ice lollies well.

It's okay to offer solid foods, too. Start simple, with a

cracker or a piece of toast, a little banana or a tablespoon of pureed apple. Take care with milk and milk products, which may be harder to digest. Any food that your child wants is fine, but start with small amounts, giving time for the digestion to work.

Diarrhoea. The key feature is to make sure your child takes in sufficient fluids so as not to become dehydrated. Dehydration occurs when the amount the child takes in through drinking is less than what goes out in diarrhoea and vomiting. The first sign is listlessness; dry mouth, sunken eyes, and skin that feels doughy are signs of worsening dehydration.

By the time a child is two or older, there is much less chance of severe or prolonged diarrhoea. Until the doctor can be reached, the best treatment is as much of his normal diet as he seems hungry for. Research has shown that the traditional 'diarrhoea diet' of sugary fluids such as fruity drinks or apple juice actually increases and prolongs diarrhoea, so this approach is no longer recommended. With significant diarrhoea, consider using Dioralyte or the homemade oral rehydration solution described above (in the section on vomiting, see page 421). It's best, though, to talk with the doctor first. A child who is ill enough to need Dioralyte may need to be evaluated medically. A child who can't hold down even small sips may need fluid through an IV in the hospital.

Children with chronic illnesses. Nutrition can be a critical issue for children with chronic illnesses such as diabetes, coeliac disease or cystic fibrosis, particularly when they have an infection on top of their underlying condition. It's best in these situations to work closely with a doctor, and often with an experienced nutritionist or dietician as well.

Feeding problems at the end of illness. If a child has a fever for several days and wants little to eat, he naturally loses weight. This worries parents the first time or two that it happens. When the fever is finally gone and the doctor says it's all right to begin working back to a regular diet, they are impatient to feed the child again. But it often happens that the child turns away from the foods that are first offered. If the parents urge him to eat, meal after meal and day after day, his appetite may never pick up.

Such a child has not forgotten how to eat, nor has he become too weak to eat. At the time the temperature went back to normal, there was still enough infection in his body to affect his stomach and intestines. As soon as he saw those first foods, his digestive system warned him that it was not ready for them yet. When food is pushed or forced onto a child who already feels nauseated because of illness, his disgust builds up more easily and rapidly than if he had a normal appetite. He can acquire a long-lasting feeding problem in a few days' time.

As soon as the stomach and intestines recover from the effects of the illness and are able to digest food again, children's hunger comes back with a bang – and not just to what it used to be. Children are usually ravenous for a week or two in order to make up for losses. You sometimes see such children whimpering for more food just two hours after a large meal. By age three, they may demand the specific foods that their starved system craves most.

The best thing to do at the end of illness is to offer your child only the drinks and solids she wants, without any urging, and to wait patiently but confidently for signals that she is ready for more. If her appetite has not recovered in a week, talk with the doctor again.

GIVING MEDICINE

Check with the doctor. It's always safest to check with a doctor before giving any medication, and before continuing to give a medicine for longer than the original prescription. Here are some examples of why: a child has a cough with a cold and the doctor suggests a certain cough medicine. Two months later the child develops a new cough, and the parents buy it again without consulting the doctor. It seems to help for a week, but then the cough becomes so bad they have to call the doctor anyway. The doctor realizes right away that the disease this time is not a cold but pneumonia; he would have suspected it a week earlier if the parents had called.

Parents who have treated colds, headaches or stomachaches a few times in the same way come to feel like experts – which they are, in a limited way. But they're not trained, as a doctor is, to first consider carefully what the diagnosis is. To them, two different headaches (or two stomachaches) seem about the same. To the doctor, one may have an entirely different meaning from the other and may call for different treatment.

People whose children have been treated by a doctor with an antibiotic (such as penicillin) are sometimes tempted to use it again for similar symptoms. They decide that they have some left over, it produces wonderful results, it's easy to take and they know the dosage from the last time, so why not? First, the medicine may not be effective any longer, or the child may need a different dosage or a completely different medication. Second, the antibiotic may interfere with diagnosis when the doctor is finally consulted. If you do have medication left over after a course of treatment, the best thing to do is throw it out.

Finally, children occasionally develop serious reactions to the use of these drugs – fevers, rashes, anaemia. Fortunately, these complications are rare, but they are more likely to occur if the drugs are used often, especially if they are used improperly. That is why they should be given only when a doctor has decided that the danger from the disease and the likelihood of benefit from the medicine outweigh the risks of treatment. Even the continued use of as common a drug as paracetamol can occasionally cause serious trouble. For the same reasons, you should never give a neighbour's, friend's, or relative's medicine to a child. Overuse of antibiotics leads to resistance in the bacteria, so that higher doses or completely new antibiotics become necessary.

DR SPOCK COMMENTS

'Antibiotic' really means 'anti-life'. I would prefer to see terms like 'antibacterial', 'antifungal', or 'antiviral' used, which would be more accurate and be specifically for what they are treating.

Getting the medicine in. It's sometimes quite a trick getting a child to take medicine. The first rule is to slip it into her in a matter-of-fact way, as if it has never occurred to you that she won't take it. If you go at it apologetically, with a lot of explanation, you convince her that she's expected to dislike it. Talk about something else when you put the spoon into her mouth. Most young children open their mouths automatically, like baby birds in their nest. With babies, it often works to draw up the medicine in an oral syringe (available from pharmacies) and gently squirt it into the mouth along the side of the cheek, towards the back.

Tablets that don't dissolve can be crushed to a fine powder and mixed with a good-tasting food like apple puree. Mix the medicine with only one teaspoon of the apple puree, in case she decides she doesn't want very much. Bitter pills can be mixed in a teaspoon of apple puree, rice syrup or rice milk. (Some foods interfere with the absorption of certain medicines; check with a pharmacist before you give your creativity free rein.)

When giving medicine in a drink, it's safer to choose an unusual fluid that the child does not take regularly, such as grape juice or prune juice. If you give a strange taste to orange juice, you may make the child suspicious of it for months.

Pill-taking fears. Children who gag at the very thought of swallowing a pill can sometimes overcome their fears by practising with small sweets or mints. (Children under about four or five shouldn't try this, because of the risk of choking.) You can also try special plastic cups that have a spout that holds the pill. When your child takes a drink from the cup, the pill gets washed down. Bribes sometimes work, too. But it's best not to get into a fight with a fearful child about taking pills if there is any other way to get the medicine in.

Over-the-counter medicines. Just because a medicine is sold without a prescription does not mean that it is safe. Cough medicines and other cold medicines, in particular, have caused many serious reactions and are never to be given to children under six.

Eye ointments and drops. These can sometimes be applied during sleep. For a child who is not sleeping and not cooperating, try placing him on your lap with his legs around your waist and out of kicking range. Place his head gently but firmly between your knees and hold it with one hand while applying the medicine with your other hand. (This position is also good for suctioning the nose or inserting nose drops.)

ISOLATION FOR CONTAGIOUS DISEASES

It's a good idea to keep a sick child in the house until he no longer has a fever and the doctor says that he no longer is contagious. It's sensible to keep the amount of intimate contact (kissing, hugging and cuddling) to a minimum, except for people who are taking care of the sick child. This precaution helps to prevent others from catching the disease unnecessarily. Another reason for keeping sick children isolated is so that they will not pick up new germs from others to complicate their illness.

Grown-ups in the family are generally not restricted from leaving the home or going to their jobs when a member of the household has a contagious disease. You have to use your own good sense, though, about visiting others' homes. The chances of your carrying your child's germs to other children are practically zero so long as you keep away from them. Just the same, you may be blamed if anyone in their family catches your child's disease any time in the near future.

Hand-washing. The best way to limit the spread of disease is through frequent, thorough hand-washing. Teach children to wash up to their wrists and between each finger, scrubbing for 20 seconds or more – long enough to sing Happy Birthday twice or the ABC song once. A stepstool makes it easier for a child to reach the sink comfortably; small bars of soap, like the bars in hotel bathrooms, make it easy for small hands. Put boxes of tissues around the house to inspire frequent nose-blowing, and offer paper rubbish bags so that used tissues don't end up on the floor. Many soaps are now advertised as 'antibacterial', but it's not clear that these work any better than normal soaps, and the disinfectant in these soaps may pose health risks of its own. Between trips to the sink, alcohol-based hand sanitizers help to limit the spread of germs. You need to use a good amount with each application, work it into all the crevices and rub it around for about ten seconds or longer.

GOING TO THE HOSPITAL

A child who ends up in the hospital after a sudden illness or trauma is bound to be disoriented and scared. Having a parent or other close family member nearby at all times makes a huge difference psychologically. Children who go to the hospital for planned procedures, such as surgery to remove enlarged tonsils and adenoids, can become terribly anxious in anticipation of what will be done to them. A chance to voice their fears and receive reassurance can help tremendously. Children with chronic illnesses and special health care needs may be hospitalized frequently. For all of these children and families, the expertise of child life specialists – professionals who are trained to help children adapt to hospitals and medical procedures – can be invaluable.

Why the hospital is upsetting. Between the ages of one and five years, the child is most worried about being separated from the parents. As long as at least one parent is present full time, most young children can handle being in the hospital. The illness itself will be upsetting, as will the needles and any other painful procedures, but having a trusted parent right there is tremendously comforting.

After the age of five the child is apt to be more fearful about what's going to be done to him – the injury to his body, and the pain. It won't do for the parents to promise that the hospital will be a bed of roses. If unpleasant things happen, as they surely will, the child will lose confidence in his parents. On the other hand, if he is told everything bad that might happen, he is apt to suffer more in anticipation than he will when he is there.

The most important thing is for the parents to show all the calm, matter-of-fact confidence they are capable of, without forcing it so much that it sounds false. Unless the child has been a hospital patient before, he is bound to imagine what it will be like, perhaps fearing the worst. The parents can set his mind at rest better by describing hospital life in general, rather than by arguing with him about whether it's going to hurt a lot or a little.

It also helps for parents to mention some of the fun things about the hospital – the books and toys brought from home, the TV right over the bed, and button that calls the nurse. Many children's units also have playrooms stocked with all sorts of games and toys. It's fair to dwell on these more pleasant everyday aspects of hospital life because, even at the worst, the child will spend most of his time amusing himself. You don't have to avoid discussing the medical programme altogether, but let the child see that it's a small part of hospital life.

Some hospitals arrange visits for children and their families before a child is admitted for a planned treatment or operation. They come to the hospital a few days before the actual admission and see various parts of the hospital and have their questions answered.

Let them tell you their worries. Most important of all is giving your child the opportunity to ask questions and tell you what he imagines. Young children view these things in ways that would never occur to adults. In the first place, they often think they have to be operated on or taken to the hospital because they have been bad – because they haven't worn their boots, haven't stayed in bed when sick, or have been angry with other members of the family. A child may imagine that his neck has to be cut open to remove his tonsils, or his nose removed to get to the adenoids. So make it easy for your child to raise questions. Be ready to hear about strange fears, and try to reassure him.

When to tell your child. If there is no chance of his finding out, I think it is kinder to wait to tell a small child until a few days before it's time to leave. It won't do him any good to worry for weeks. It may be fairer to tell a seven-year-old some weeks ahead if he's the kind who can face things reasonably, especially if he has some suspicions. It's always wise to give a child basic information and then answer the child's questions; well-meaning parents often make the mistake of saying too much. Instead, try to follow your child's lead. Certainly don't lie to a child of any age if he asks questions, and never lure a child to a hospital pretending it's something else.

Anaesthesia. If your child is going to have an operation and you have a choice in the arrangements, you can discuss the matter of anaesthetists and anaesthesia with the doctor. How a child accepts the anaesthesia is apt to make the biggest difference in whether he becomes emotionally upset by an operation or goes through it with flying colours. Often in a hospital there is one or another anaesthetist who is particularly good at inspiring confidence in children.

It is worth a great deal to obtain the services of such an anaesthetist if you have a choice. In some cases, there is also a choice as to the kind of anaesthetic that the doctor is considering, and this also makes a difference to the child psychologically. Generally speaking, it is less frightening to the child to start with gas instead of an intravenous line. Naturally, the doctor is the one who knows the facts and has to make the decision, but when the doctor feels that there is an equal choice medically, the psychological factor should be considered carefully.

You shouldn't use the expression 'put to sleep' when you explain the anaesthesia to a child. That expression can make children think of a dog or cat who was sick and was euthanized; it can also lead to a child's developing sleep problems after surgery. Instead, explain that the anaesthesia causes a special kind of sleep, from which the anaesthetist will awaken the child as soon as the operation is over. Let your child know that he won't feel or remember anything that happens during the operation. Try to stay with your child until he is under. It's been shown that having a parent present when the anaesthesia is given makes a child much less frightened and nervous about the surgery and cuts down on the need for drugs to calm the child.

Visiting. A parent should stay in the hospital with a child between the ages of one and five years if at all possible, especially in the daytime. At the very least, a parent should visit daily. Most hospitals now have rooming-in facilities so that a parent or other adult well known to a child can stay overnight in the child's room.

If the parents are able to visit only intermittently, the visits can create temporary difficulties for the small child. The sight of the parents reminds him how much he has missed them and how much he has lost. He may cry heartbreakingly when they leave or even cry through the entire visiting period. The parents are apt to get the impression that he is miserable all the time. Actually, young children often seem to calm down when their parents are out of sight, even though they are feeling sick or having uncomfortable treatments. In fact, they may feel too scared to show any emotion, but when the parents return their real feelings come out.

None of this, however, should be taken to mean that the parents should stay away. The child gets security from realizing that his parents always come back when they leave. If you have to go, it's best to act as cheerful and unworried as possible. If the parents have an anguished expression, it makes the child more anxious.

Late reactions to hospitalization. A young child may seem to pull through a hospitalization all right, only to show disturbing behaviours once back at home – either clinging and being excessively fearful or acting out in aggressive ways. These are normal, if unpleasant, responses. Patience, reassurance and calm insistence that the child will feel more comfortable soon is usually all a child needs to begin to put the hospitalization in the past and move on with the business of being a child.

IMMUNIZATIONS

DR SPOCK COMMENTS

I grew up in a time when every parent was worried sick about their child contracting polio, a paralytic virus. This illness killed about twenty-five thousand people, mostly children, each year. We were warned not to drink from drinking fountains, to avoid crowds in the summer, and to fret about every viral infection. But no more. There has not been a naturally occurring case of polio in the United States since 1979 [or in the UK since 1984]. The rest of the world is a little behind us, but on the same track. Smallpox has been totally eradicated from our planet. The elimination of these illnesses is nothing less than a medical miracle, one of mankind's proudest achievements, and it came to pass because of vaccines.

HOW VACCINES WORK

When a person fights off an infection, the immune system remembers and fights off the same infection more easily in the future. Vaccines create the same immune memory without the illness. The body responds to vaccines by producing antibodies – proteins that recognize and target particular

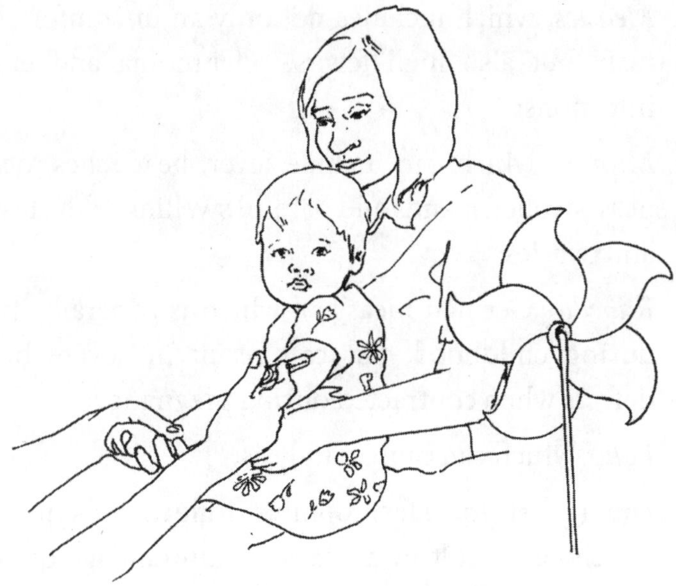

disease-causing bacteria and viruses and help eliminate them from the body before they actually cause disease.

Infections prevented by vaccines. Currently, most preschool children in Britain are vaccinated against ten different diseases, listed here along with some of their more serious complications:

- *Diphtheria*, in which a thick covering forms in the throat, leading to severe breathing problems;
- *Pertussis* (whooping cough), which often includes coughing spells so bad that a child can't eat, sleep or breathe well for weeks;
- *Tetanus* (lockjaw), in which muscles involuntarily tighten, so that breathing becomes difficult or impossible;

- *Measles*, which includes not only an uncomfortable rash, but also high fevers, pneumonia and brain infections;
- *Mumps*, which can include fever, headaches, deafness, swollen glands and painful swelling of the testes and ovaries;
- *Rubella* (German measles), which is generally mild during childhood, but can result in severe birth defects when contracted during pregnancy;
- *Polio*, which can cause paralysis;
- *Hib* (short for Haemophilus influenzae type B), which can result in deafness, brain damage or suffocation caused by blockage of the windpipe;
- *Pneumococcal* infections of the lungs (pneumonia) or brain (meningitis);
- *Meningitis C*, an infection with a particular bacteria (meningococcus, type C) that can infect the lining of the brain, and many other places throughout the body, with very dire consequences. Immunization in infancy also protects children through their young adult years, a time when the risk of the disease goes up.

Some babies will also need Hepatitis B and/or BCG (for tuberculosis) vaccines:

- *Hepatitis B* can result in liver failure or a high risk of liver cancer. Pregnant women are screened for hepatitis B and, if infected, their baby can be vaccinated shortly after birth to prevent infection.

- *Tuberculosis (TB)* is a bacterial infection which most commonly affects the lungs, but it can affect other parts of the body such as lymph nodes, bones, joints and kidneys, or the covering of the brain (meningitis). With effective treatment, it is possible to make a full recovery from tuberculosis. The vaccination is called the BCG and is recommended for all babies who live in an area where the rates of TB are high.

Along with protection for the vaccinated child, vaccines reduce the danger that other people will get the illness, by cutting down on the number of susceptible individuals who can spread the disease through the community. On the flip side, if enough people refuse vaccines, this 'herd immunity' begins to break down, allowing more and more people to become infected.

Other vaccines. There are many other immunizations not listed above. For example, children living in some areas benefit from vaccination against Hepatitis A, a virus that infects the liver. It is also possible to receive immunization against varicella (chicken pox). Children who travel to countries in Africa, Asia and South and Central America often need additional immunizations. Your child's doctor can tell you if your child has special immunization needs.

HPV vaccine. The vaccine for human papillomavirus (HPV) is relatively new. It was developed following the discovery that cervical cancer and genital warts can be triggered by infection with this sexually transmitted virus. The same virus may also cause a very dangerous cancer of the throat. The vaccine prevents infection by most of the cancer-causing strains of the virus, although not all of them. Cervical cancer kills thousands in the United Kingdom, and millions worldwide. The vaccine greatly reduces the risk of a woman developing cervical cancer, but only if it is given before the woman is exposed. The vaccine is recommended for girls aged twelve to thirteen and will usually be given at secondary school. While it's hard for many parents to think about their twelve-year-old ever having sex, we know that many teenagers will engage in sexual activity. There is no reason to think that getting the vaccine encourages teens to have sex, or that not getting it deters them. Full protection requires three doses spread out over six months or more.

Flu vaccine. Several different strains of influenza circulate around the world all the time, and in any given flu season a certain strain spreads quickly, creating an epidemic. If the epidemic strain happens to be very virulent, illness and death can be widespread. Scientists try to predict which strains are most likely to trigger an epidemic, and create a vaccine against these strains. In 2009, the H1N1 strain showed up only *after* the flu vaccine for that year had been engineered. As a result, people needed to receive both the usual seasonal vaccine and the 2009 H1N1 vaccine – a logistical nightmare. The following year, this strain was included in the usual vaccine. The NHS recommends that children aged over six months who suffer from certain chronic illnesses, such as asthma or diabetes, should receive the flu vaccine every year.

RISKS OF IMMUNIZATION

Weigh risks and benefits. A lot of information is available about the risks of immunization. Unfortunately, there is a lot of misinformation out there, too. Many parents are concerned; some are frightened. The bottom line, however, is that the benefits of preventing these diseases far, far outweigh any risks of the vaccines themselves. Every expert panel and every responsible physician stands behind this conclusion.

Take Hib (*Haemophilus influenzae* type B), for example. Before this vaccine was introduced in the UK in 1992, Hib struck roughly one child in 600 before their fifth birthday. About one child in twenty who develops Hib meningitis dies. One of the first children I met in medical school was a baby who had lost her hearing after a Hib infection. For the past twenty years, Hib disease has been rare in the United Kingdom thanks to the vaccine. But recently, during a temporary shortage of vaccine, five children in Minnesota, USA, got the disease, and one died.

The risks of vaccines are usually very mild. Injections hurt more than a pinch but less than a stubbed toe. Some children develop soreness at the injection site, and occasionally a firm swelling that can take weeks to go away.

Rarely, a high fever develops. In very rare cases (about one in a hundred thousand) children show worrisome behaviour, crying for hour after hour, not responding normally or having an actual seizure. These reactions are frightening, and in very rare cases do lead to serious long-term problems. But – and I can't say this too many times – without the immunizations, the diseases being prevented would be *much* more common, and much worse.

How vaccines are made. Most vaccines are made from viruses or bacteria that have been killed and either left whole or chopped up. Some vaccines are made against the poisons produced by bacteria, and a few vaccines are made from live viruses that have been changed so that they cannot cause disease in healthy children, or cause only a very mild disease. Live virus vaccines are not safe for children who have seriously weakened immune systems (such as children receiving some cancer treatments) or children who live with people who have weakened immune systems.

Vaccines are getting safer. Pertussis vaccine used to be notorious for causing pain, swelling, redness and fever. The new version of the vaccine, *acellular* pertussis (aP) vaccine, is much gentler. In the past, several vaccines contained a preservative called thimerosal, which is made with mercury. The thimerosal in vaccines was never proven to be harmful. Still, just to be safe, all vaccines commonly used for children are now thimerosal-free. Vaccine reactions are tracked nationally so that even very rare dangers can be flagged and avoided.

Vaccines and autism. The number of children with autism appears to be rising fast, and no one knows exactly why. Many theories and rumours have focused on the measles, mumps and rubella vaccine (MMR). However, carefully done studies have failed to find any connection between MMR and autism. There is no difference in the rate of autism in children who have received MMR compared to those who have not.

In 2001, an expert panel of the American Institute of Medicine concluded that MMR *cannot* be responsible for the vast majority of cases of autism, although the research leaves open the possibility that MMR causes some rare cases. The panel recommended that children continue to get this vaccine. Expert committees of the American Academy of Pediatrics and the US Centers for Disease Control (CDC) agree. Recently, the original studies that purported to show a link between autism and MMR were withdrawn by the journal in which they were published because the researcher was found to have lied about the science. By now, however, the fear of vaccines has itself spread like a virus, and many parents are unwilling to listen to assurances from the government and respected scientists. In communities where the fear has taken hold, immunization rates have fallen, and epidemics of measles have broken out. For more on autism and its causes and treatment, see page 930.

Vaccines have also been blamed for other diseases,

including a serious condition called inflammatory bowel disease. Again, a lot of careful study has shown no connection at all between vaccines and this condition.

Where to learn more. Every doctor or nurse who gives vaccines will have a fact sheet about them. You can ask for these handouts ahead of time so that you can read about upcoming immunizations.

THE IMMUNIZATION SCHEDULE

So young, so many injections. To most of the illnesses prevented by vaccines, little babies are the most vulnerable. So it makes sense to start immunizing as soon as possible. But with many vaccines, children require more than one exposure to develop a full-strength immune response. That's why many of them are given several times in the first year to get the maximum protection as early as possible.

Alphabet soup. Many of the shots are referred to by their initials. The following glossary should help (see page 535 for more about the diseases themselves):

- *BCG* (tuberculosis vaccine)
- *DTaP* (diphtheria, tetanus and acellular pertussis, a three-in-one multiple vaccine combination); *Td* (tetanus, with diphtheria at a lower dose)
- *Hib* (*Haemophilus influenzae* type B)
- *HPV* (human papillomavirus)

- *IPV* (inactivated polio vaccine)
- *MenC* (meningococcus type C vaccine)
- *MMR* (measles, mumps and rubella, another three-in-one combination)
- *PCV* (pneumococcus vaccine)

The immunization schedule. To get the maximum protection, children need to get their immunizations on time. But the schedule allows some flexibility. Doctors and parents can choose to delay some of the immunizations by up to several months, either to spread out the needles or because a child is ill when a particular immunization is due. If children fall far behind in their immunizations, doctors can help to catch them up quickly. The goal is to have the primary series completed by the time your child starts school.

Age	Vaccines	Needles
Birth, depending on area	BCG	1
8 weeks	DTaP/IPV/Hib, PCV	2
12 weeks	DTaP/IPV/Hib, Men C	2
16 weeks	DTaP/IPV/Hib, Men C, PCV	3
12–13 months	Hib/Men C, MMR, PCV	3
3 years and 4 months	DTaP/IPV, MMR	2
12–13 years, for girls	HPV	3
13–18 years	Td/IPV	1

The immunization schedule is sure to change as new vaccines are developed and approved. By the time you read this, more of the vaccines may be available in multivaccine formulas that lower the number of needles. Eventually vaccines may be given in edible form, with no pain at all. In the meantime, there are many things you can do to help your children cope.

COPING WITH INJECTIONS

Medication. Talk with your doctor about medication that might lessen the pain of immunizations. Numbing with a cold spray can help; paracetamol taken before and after immunizations can lessen the ache (although some experts think it may also lessen the effectiveness of the immunization).

Body comfort. Babies feel safe in their parents' arms. Newborn infants getting their heel stuck for blood cry less and show fewer physical signs of stress if their mothers hold them close during the stick. For immunizations, a good position is with your child facing you, chest to chest, arms and legs wrapped around your body. This position works for children up through five or six years old. Sucking on a dummy, rocking and stroking are all effective comfort measures for babies.

Use your voice. For infants, it doesn't matter what you say. The tone of your voice will make them feel safe. For toddlers and preschool children, the fear of the jab is often worse than the actual feeling. To lower fear, tell your child what is going to happen just before it happens. For example, 'Now you'll feel the alcohol wipe – does it feel chilly?'

You might want to use words other than 'jab', such as 'vaccine' or 'medicine'. When children are scared, they often ignore negative phrases. That is, if parents say 'Don't scream', they hear 'scream'. If parents say 'Stop crying', they hear 'crying'. It's better to use only positive words: 'You're okay; there, there; it'll be over soon.'

Give your child choices. Some children want to see what the nurse or doctor is doing, while others don't. A child who has a choice feels more in control. Also, you can give your child permission to holler if that helps. 'It's okay to yell, if you want to, but you need to hold still. Why not wait till you feel the pinch?'

Distraction. A very effective technique for toddlers and preschoolers is to tell a story, sing a favourite song or look at a picture book. Children have strong imaginations. A child who is imagining herself doing a favourite activity – running, riding a bike fast or jumping on a bed – will actually feel less pain. Two powerful distraction techniques, great for four- and five-year-olds, are blowing at a pinwheel and blowing bubbles. If your child loves bubbles, bring a bottle of bubble soap and a plastic wand to the surgery.

Helping a fearful child. If your child is especially fearful of jabs, ask him to draw a picture of what he thinks is going to happen. Don't be surprised if the picture shows a very small person next to a huge, terrifying needle! Help your child to see that the needle is really very, very small.

Children often cope with scary things through play. Give your child a toy syringe and stethoscope, and let him practise being the doctor to a doll who needs 'medicine'. By giving pretend jabs, your child may come to feel more control and therefore less fear.

If severe fears persist, talk with your child's doctor or nurse. There are professionals called child life specialists in most children's hospitals who are experts at helping children cope with medical procedures. It's worth a visit with one to have your child feel more comfortable. Getting a jab and coming away feeling all right helps a young child realize that he can handle things that make him afraid; this is a great lesson at any age.

DR SPOCK COMMENTS

The best way to get your child ready for each immunization is to be as honest and simple in your explanations as possible, considering his age and understanding. Tell him that the shot will hurt a little ('like a hard pinch'), but that it will protect him from sickness that would hurt much more than the shot.

YOUR RECORD

Keep your record safe. The doctor or nurse will always make a note of the immunizations in your child's 'Personal Child Health Record' ('Red Book'). Carry it with you when the family goes on trips or changes doctors. The commonest emergency occurs when a child away from home receives a wound that calls for extra protection against tetanus. Then it is very important for the attending doctor to know for certain whether the child has received tetanus immunizations. If a child has been fully immunized, very few wounds will require extra protection against tetanus.

PREVENTING INJURIES

KEEPING CHILDREN SAFE

Safety is every parent's first and most important job. The rest of parenting – love, limits, values, fun and learning – means nothing without safety. We promise our children that we will keep them safe, and our children expect this of us. The beginning of psychological health is the deep-down belief that there is a big person out there providing security.

Our most basic instincts centre on safety: infants cry and parents have the urge to pick them up. It's easy to imagine how these protective responses helped our prehistoric ancestors survive. But even in our modern world, dangers abound. In the United Kingdom, unintentional injuries send two million children to A&E each year, and are a leading cause of death in children over age one. Up to one out of six children hospitalized because of injury comes away with a permanent disability. More than 200 die each year.

The point of telling you this is not to frighten you but to help you take reasonable precautions. You need to be aware of the dangers out there – and those in your own home – but you don't need to be afraid. Children need to know that their parents are looking out for them, but they also need to be able to explore, make choices and even take some risks. Children learn to balance caution and boldness by watching their parents do it.

Why not just call them 'accidents'? For many people, the word 'accident' implies something that is unavoidable, as in 'I couldn't help it, it was an accident.' The truth is, many childhood injuries that might be called accidental really can be avoided. They don't just happen; they happen because adults tolerate the conditions that make them possible. Consider, for example, a car with seat belts that are not made to fit small bodies – that is, *any* car without a car seat. If a child riding in such a car is killed in a crash, the death of the child is not truly accidental. It was predictable and most likely could have been prevented.

Who is injured, and how. In terms of sheer numbers, injuries to children riding in cars top the list. Injuries to pedestrians and bicyclists are also common, along with burns, suffocation, poisoning, choking and falls. A child's age determines which form of unintentional injury is most likely to be deadly. Under age one, suffocation and choking are the most common. From one to four, drowning kills more children. After five, it is children riding in cars who are most likely to die from unintentional injuries.

Other unintentional events cause injuries but not death. Falls from heights, for example, or collisions with coffee tables commonly result in cuts, bruises and broken bones. Falls from bicycles often result in serious brain injury unless the child is wearing a helmet. Lead poisoning, another very common form of unintentional injury, rarely kills but regularly causes learning problems that can limit a child's life success.

Principles of prevention. It may not be possible to prevent every single injury, but we know enough now to bring the risks way down for most children. It's a natural human tendency to go through life with an attitude of 'It can't happen to me'. So the first step is to stop denying the possibility of an injury. Then practise these three basic principles:

- *Childproof your child's environment.* Certain dangerous items simply don't belong in a house with young children, such as coffee tables with sharp corners, unguarded stairs and furniture and beds next to open windows. Use a checklist (see page 492) to systematically identify hazards and remove them.
- *Supervise your child closely.* Even in a childproofed environment, children require close supervision. Toddlers, especially, take chances, lack judgment and need the protection of an adult. Of course you can't spend every waking minute keeping track of your child, but some environments are inherently more dangerous than others. If a playroom has been well childproofed, you can relax a little. But out in the big world – and in the bathroom and kitchen – you must be more vigilant.
- *Be particularly careful during stressful times.* Injuries happen when routines change and parents' attention

is diverted. When the in-laws come for a surprise visit and you've got a critical deadline at work, that's when you need to make yourself think about where you left the scissors, whether or not your father-in-law put away his bottle of heart pills, and if the cup of hot coffee you desperately need is sitting too near the table edge.

Safe outside and in. In planning for your child's safety, it may help to think about safety issues in two settings: outside the home and inside the home. The topics that follow are organized into two parts that correspond roughly to those two settings. Of course, no list of safety topics can be absolutely complete, because dangers pop up in so many different ways. So please consider the advice below, and use your own good sense, too. Also, please refer to the chapters in section I of this book, 'Your Child Age by Age', which describe safety precautions that apply to children at specific ages.

Part 1: Safety Outside the Home

RIDING IN CARS

Injuries to passengers. More children die in car crashes than by any other unintentional injury. It's hard to overestimate the importance of seat belts with shoulder harnesses for adults and older children, and properly installed child safety seats for infants and young children. It is the law for all children travelling in cars to use the correct child restraint until they are either 135 cm (53 in) or twelve years old. After that they must wear an adult seat belt. Some parents claim that their children refuse to be belted in. These parents need to stop making excuses and take charge. No sane parent gives a two-year-old a sharp knife to play with, and no responsible parent operates a vehicle until every passenger is secured in a car seat or seat belt.

There's an added benefit to keeping children in car seats or seat belts: they behave better when they're secured than when they're not!

Car seat choice and installation. If you can afford it, buy a new car seat. If you do use a secondhand seat, be certain that it has never been in a crash and is not more than a few years old. A seat that has been through a crash can look fine but fall apart at the next impact, and plastic weakens over time. Newer cars use a system called Isofix which makes the seat much easier to install.

Read all the instructions that come with the seat and do your best putting it in, but then, if at all possible, go to an official child safety seat inspection station and get a free inspection done by a member of the Fit Safe Sit Safe scheme. To find the inspection station nearest you, have a look at www.childcarseats.org.uk. Inspectors find problems with three out of four seat installations. So when you show up for a free car seat check, chances are that your children will be safer when you leave than when you came.

Infant seats. Your baby's first ride after birth and every ride thereafter should be in a safety seat that meets the United Nations standard Regulation 44.03 or 44.04 – look for the

'E' mark. Car seats are required by law and also by common sense. While it might seem that you can hold a baby safely in your lap, you simply can't. In a sudden stop from 40 mph, a 10 lb (4.5 kg) baby can pull away with a force of 200 lb (90 kg) or more. Placing a baby under your own seat belt is even more dangerous, because if the car stops suddenly, your body will crush the baby against the belt.

For babies who are less than twelve months old, or those who weigh less than 9 kg (20 lb) regardless of their age, the only safe way to ride is in a rear-facing infant seat secured in the backseat of the car. (For safety, the rear centre is the best seat for people of all ages.) A ten-month-old who weighs 12 kg (26 lb) should still be facing backward, as should a fourteen-month-old who weighs 8 kg (18 lb), because both are at risk for serious spine and neck injuries

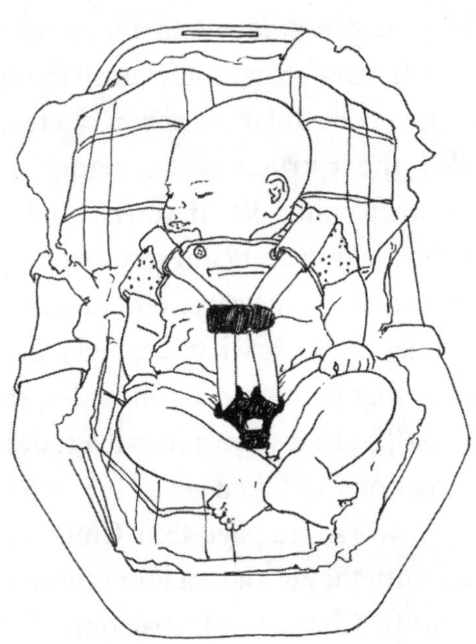

if they sit facing forward. Keep your child in a rear-facing seat for as long as possible, preferably until the age of two. But once your child is above the maximum weight for a rear-facing seat, or their head is above the top of the seat, they should be moved into a forward-facing seat. It is not important if their knees are bent in the seat. You can choose a rear-facing-only seat, which might do double duty as an infant carrier, or a convertible seat that can be turned to face forward once your baby is old enough and big enough.

It's critically important that infants and children twelve years and under never ride in the front passenger seat of a car that is equipped with airbags (most cars now on the road). Airbags save adult lives, but they inflate outward with a force that can kill or severely injure a child.

Toddler seats. Once a baby is twelve months old and at least 9 kg (20 lb), he can graduate to a forward-facing toddler seat, although rear-facing is safer until the age of two. If you bought a convertible infant seat, you can turn it around. Be sure to follow the instructions for changing around the straps and anchoring the seat. If you're buying a toddler seat, you can choose one that converts to a booster seat so that you save having to make yet another purchase later on.

The best toddler seats use what is called a five-point harness, with straps that go over each shoulder, each hip and between the legs. The best way to install a toddler seat is to follow the instructions and then get a Fit Safe Sit Safe member to check your work (see page 452). Children should use the toddler seat until they are about four years old and weigh about 18 kg (40 lb). Check the instructions for the upper weight limit of your particular seat. Only move your child to a booster seat once they have outgrown the maximum weight limit or their head is higher than the top of the seat.

Booster seats. Booster seats are for children after they have outgrown their toddler seats. Children should use booster seats until they weigh 36 kg (79 lb). Here's why: without a booster seat, the lap belt tends to run across the child's abdomen, and in a crash, the belt can injure the child's internal organs or spine. With a booster seat, the belt runs across the child's pelvic bones; in a crash, these strong bones take the pressure rather than the soft internal organs. A booster seat also makes the shoulder strap fit comfortably over the shoulder rather than against the neck, so the child is more likely to keep the shoulder belt on. In fact, booster seats *have* to be used with lap-shoulder belts. With a lap belt alone, they don't do a good job of holding the child in place during a crash. Some parents might want to skip the booster seat because they don't want to buy another restraint system. But booster seats are the cheapest type of car seat by far, and they make a huge difference in a child's safety and comfort.

Car Safety Key Points

- Never place a child twelve years of age or under in front of a working airbag.
- The safest place at any age is the centre of the backseat.
- A good rule is that the car doesn't move unless everyone is buckled up.

- It isn't safe (or legal) to hold a child on your lap once the car starts moving, or to put your own seat belt around the child.
- Even when you think you've got the car seat installed correctly, chances are you don't: it's a lot harder than it looks. Let a Fit Safe Sit Safe member do a free check to be sure.

On aeroplanes. The recommendations for safe travel and the use of child safety seats on aeroplanes are confusing. On British-registered planes babies under six months must sit on your lap with the seat belt in place. Children under age two can fly for free, but if they do not have their own ticket, they are not given a seat. As a result, you may not be able to use a child safety seat unless there is a vacant seat next to you. Of course, holding a child in your arms on an aeroplane is not as safe as securing a child into a safety seat (but not as dangerous as doing the same thing in a car, because planes don't usually make sudden stops). If you don't want to pay for an extra seat for your baby on the plane, it's still safer to fly than to drive to your destination. Take your car safety seat along, whether or not you use it on the plane, so you'll have it for travel when you reach your destination, as long as it is compatible with the car you hire.

Beds are available for use on aeroplanes by infants under two, but they can be used in the bulkhead seats only. For children over age two a ticket is required, and it is recommended that you bring a toddler seat on board for your child under 18 kg (40 lb). Harnesses and inflatable seat vests are not recommended by the FAA.

STREETS AND DRIVEWAYS

Injuries to pedestrians. Children between the ages of five and nine are at great danger of being hit and killed by cars. They think they can keep themselves safe on the street, but they really can't. Their peripheral vision isn't fully developed. They can't accurately evaluate the speed and distance of oncoming cars. Many don't have the judgment to know when it's safe to cross.

Adults generally give their children credit for more street smarts than they actually have. The hardest job for parents is to teach children that drivers regularly ignore red lights and that zebra crossings are not automatic safety zones. More than 100 people die on pedestrian crossings in the UK every year. Car parks are another high-risk zone, as drivers backing out of spaces may not be able to see children behind their cars.

Guidelines for Pedestrian Safety

- From the time your child begins to walk on the pavement, teach him that he can step off the kerb only when you are holding his hand.
- Always supervise the outdoor play of preschoolers, and make sure they never play in driveways or streets.

- Explain to five- to nine-year-olds over and over again the rules about crossing residential streets. Model safe pedestrian behaviour yourself when you walk with them. Point out how traffic lights and cross-walks work and why they need to look left, right and left again, even when they have the traffic light in their favour and even when they are in a crossing.
- Remember that children aren't developmentally ready to cross a heavily travelled street without adult supervision until they're at least nine or ten years old.
- Together with your child, find the safe places to play in your neighbourhood. Explain repeatedly that he must never run into the street when playing, no matter how important the game may seem.
- Think about where your child walks, especially on the way to school, to playgrounds and to playmates' houses. Explore the neighbourhood with him to find the safest route with the easiest street crossings. Then teach him that the safest route is the *only* route he should use.
- Try to find the time to get involved in community safety. Find out if there are enough traffic signals and lollipop people on the way to your child's school. If a new school is being built, look into the traffic pattern in that area. Will there be enough pavements, lights and lollipop people?
- Be particularly cautious with toddlers in car parks and insist that they hold your hand. Keep toddlers in shopping trolleys or put them in the car while loading bags.

Driveways. Driveways are a natural place for children to play, but they can be very dangerous. Children need to be taught that as soon as they see a car pulling in or pulling out, they must get off the driveway immediately. Drivers need to *always* walk once around their cars before backing out, to make sure there are no small children playing behind the car. Just glancing back isn't good enough, because a child can be easily overlooked.

BICYCLE INJURIES

Cycling hazards. In children aged eight to eleven in the United Kingdom, bicycle injuries cause more than 200 deaths each year. These injuries are especially common in the after-school hours before darkness. Following basic safety rules can prevent the majority of serious injuries. Sixty per cent of all serious bike injuries are head injuries, and a head injury means a potential brain injury, which always carries the possibility of permanent brain damage. Proper use of bicycle helmets can reduce the incidence of head injuries by 85 per cent.

Choosing helmets. A helmet should have a solid, hard outer shell and a firm polystyrene liner. The chin strap should be attached to the helmet at three points: beneath each ear and at the back of the neck. Check that the helmet meets safety standards (BST or Snell).

The helmet must fit properly. It should sit on top of the child's head in a level position and should not rock back and forth or from side to side. Measure your child's head with a tape measure and select the appropriate size according to the information on the box. Be sure the box tells you the head size in centimetres or inches to ensure proper fit – do not rely entirely on the age recommendations. A general guideline to follow is that infant-size helmets are recommended for children age one and two years, a child's size will fit a child between three and six, a youth helmet can be used from age seven to eleven, and then an adult size will be required. Adult helmets come in small, medium, large and extralarge sizes.

Replace the helmet if it is involved in any crash or serious head thump. Most companies will replace the impact-absorbing liner free if you send them the helmet. You should be able to get a safe helmet for £20 or less.

Bike safety tips and rules. The most important rule is, 'No riding without a helmet – ever.' When parents ride, they must wear helmets, too. You can't expect your children to follow this rule if you don't set an example. Children should ride only on pavements until age nine or ten, when judgment matures enough to handle traffic while riding in the street. Then teach them the basic rules of the road so they can obey all the same traffic rules that car drivers follow.

It's safest to get your child a tricycle or bicycle that fits her, not one that she will have to grow into. Children generally aren't ready for a two-wheeler until they're five to seven years old. Choose bikes with coaster brakes for children up to age nine or ten, when they will have developed the strength and coordination to manage hand brakes. Put reflective materials on the bike, the helmet and the child for better visibility. This is especially important for children who ride at dawn or dusk. Headlamps are required for any night riding, but night riding is not recommended for children.

Bicycle carrier seats. Parents bicycling with a child in a carrier should follow several additional rules. Select a child carrier with headrest protection, spoke guards and shoulder straps. Never use a backpack to carry your child on a bike. Before biking with your child, practise riding your bike with a weighted carrier in an open area, free of traffic and other cyclists, to get used to the extra weight and to gain confidence with balancing a child in a carrier. Never carry a child who's less than one year old or who weighs over 18 kg (40 lb).

A child should wear a helmet at all times while strapped in the carrier seat. Never leave your child unattended in the carrier. Bikes are not made to stand with loaded carriers, and many injuries are caused by falls from a standing bike. Ride on safe, uncongested bike paths, not in the street. Don't ride after dark. Be sure to wear a helmet yourself.

PLAYGROUND INJURIES

Many hundreds of children end up in A&E each year as a result of playground injuries. Many of these injuries are severe – broken and dislocated bones, concussions and injuries to internal organs. A small number result in death, often by strangulation: a loose drawstring or hood becomes caught on the climbing structure during a fall, and chokes the child. Children age five to nine are most at risk.

Making playgrounds safer. Check the parks and schools in your neighbourhood. Make sure the playground equipment is well maintained and that there are impact-absorbing surfaces such as rubber mats, sand, pea gravel or wood chips under the climbing structures and swings. Check that the surfaces have not become packed down or dispersed with use. If the playground needs improvement, talk with the local parks department or education authority. If necessary, consider joining or organizing a group of citizens to tackle the problem. It's remarkable what people can do together.

At home, be sure any playground equipment is sturdy and well maintained. Make sure that children take off all loose clothing before going to play, including drawstrings on hoods of jackets and sweatshirts. Several clothing manufacturers have voluntarily discontinued using drawstrings in children's garments because of such concerns.

Toddlers are all about testing their limits and learning new skills, but they don't have the balance and coordination they need to keep from getting hurt. They need sharp-eyed adult supervision at the playground.

SPORTS SAFETY

Millions of children play organized sports, both on school teams and in competitive leagues. Participation in sports improves physical fitness, coordination, self-discipline and teamwork. But injuries take a heavy toll in pain, lost practices and play, and sometimes long-term disability or worse.

Who is most at risk? Young children are especially susceptible to injury while training and competing, because their bodies are still growing. Before puberty the risk of sport-related injury is the same between boys and girls, but after puberty, as boys grow in strength and size, they are more frequently and severely injured than girls. Overall, boys incur 75 per cent of all sports injuries.

Collision and contact sports, as well as all forms of skating, have the highest rate of injury, with football, rugby, skateboarding and basketball topping the list for boys and football, horseriding, netball and roller and ice skating topping the list for girls. Overuse injuries from playing while injured or tired may cause chronic conditions like tendonitis and arthritis. Head injuries, though less frequent, can result in more serious problems.

Protective gear. Equipment to protect the eyes, head, face and mouth is a must for many sports. Mouth guards help to prevent dental injuries, which are the most common type of sports-related facial injury. Mouth guards also cushion blows that could cause a concussion or a jaw fracture. Eye protection makes sense for ball sports, including basketball.

Specific sports. *Football.* Heading the ball is not recommended for young children just learning to play the game; it's probably not good for anyone to clobber the head over and over, which is what heading is. Goals need to be anchored to the ground so that they cannot tip over on players, and children should not be allowed to climb on movable goals. Competitive football players often sustain knee injuries, as do athletes in other sports that require rapid changes in direction (basketball and lacrosse, for example). Girls, in particular, are at risk for rupture of their anterior cruciate ligament (ACL), a key structure that stabilizes the knee. ACL ruptures are devastating. They require surgery and long periods of rehabilitation, and the ligament often quickly becomes re-injured. Such an injury can leave an athlete walking in pain for life. Training programmes have been designed specifically to prevent ACL injuries, and all competitive football teams – especially girls' teams – should use them.

Rollerskating and skateboarding. These sports result in hundreds of injuries each year, mostly sprained and broken wrists, elbows, ankles and knees. These can be minimized by wearing knee pads, elbow pads, and wrist guards. Head injuries, which tend to be more serious, can be reduced by wearing a helmet. Best are multisport helmets that provide extra protection to the back of the head. If your child does not own a multisport helmet, a bicycle helmet is better than nothing. Be sure your child always skates on smooth, paved surfaces without any traffic; warn her to avoid streets and driveways. Make sure she learns to stop safely using the brake pads on the heels of most rollerskates.

Sledding. Wintertime fun includes sledding down snowy hills. It is a surprisingly hazardous pastime. Before you begin, review these safety tips:

- Survey sledding areas before letting children use them. Look for hazards such as trees, benches, ponds, rivers, rocks and excessive elevation.
- The bottom of the hill should be far from traffic or bodies of water.
- Inflatable snow tubes are fast and unsteerable; use extra caution when children are using them. Sleds with steering mechanisms are safer.
- Never allow a child under four years to sled unsupervised. The steepness of the hill should be your guide as to whether older children should be allowed to sled alone.
- Avoid crowded hills, and don't overload a sled with children.
- Do not sled alone or after dusk without adequate light.
- Consider having your child wear a helmet for head protection, but warn him not to let it be an excuse for recklessness.

COLD- AND HOT-WEATHER INJURIES

Cold weather. When the weather turns cold, children should dress warmly and stay dry, preferably in multiple layers with special attention to hands and feet. Below 4°C (40°F), infants should stay outdoors only for short periods of time. Pay attention to shivering. Persistent shivering is a sign to head indoors. Serious health risks from cold weather include hypothermia and frostbite.

Hypothermia is a result of loss of body heat due to

prolonged exposure to cold temperatures. Warning signs in infants include red, cold skin and very low energy. Shivering, drowsiness and confusion or slurred speech are danger signs in older children. If a child's temperature falls below 35°C (95°F), seek medical attention immediately and begin warming the child.

Frostbite most often affects the nose, ears, cheeks, chin, fingers or toes. Signs of frostbite are a loss of feeling and colour or the appearance of a white or greyish yellow patch. Frostbite can permanently damage the body. To treat frostbite, immerse the affected area in warm – not hot – water, or warm the affected area with your body heat. Skin damaged by frostbite is very delicate. Massaging, rubbing or walking on it can cause further injury; heating it with a stove, fireplace, radiator or heating pad can cause burns on top of the frostbite. The best treatment is prevention. Wet gloves or socks raise the risk of frostbite, so staying both dry and warm is important.

Hot weather. Infants and children up to the age of four are sensitive to high temperatures. They should drink liquids frequently through the day, wear sun hats, avoid overexertion and stay indoors during the hottest part of the day – 10 am to 2 pm – if possible. All children should wear sunscreen, no matter what the colour of their skin, to protect them from the harmful rays of the sun (see below). Besides sunburn, heat rash is the most common heat-related illness for young children; heat exhaustion and heat stroke are the most serious.

Heat rash is an irritation caused by excessive sweating

during hot, humid weather. It looks like a cluster of red spots or blisters. The best treatment is to keep the area dry and avoid creams – they keep the skin moist and make the condition worse.

Heat cramps, heat exhaustion and heat stroke are most likely to affect children under five as well as elderly people. But even healthy teens are vulnerable if they exercise in the heat for long periods of time with limited access to water. Signs of heat exhaustion include heavy sweating, paleness, muscle cramps, tiredness or weakness, dizziness or headache, nausea or vomiting, and faintness. Heatstroke, an even more serious condition, appears as red, hot and dry or sweaty skin along with a strong, rapid pulse, throbbing headache or dizziness, confusion and unconsciousness.

Prevention is the key. Make sure children take frequent breaks for shade, rest and fluids. Stop them altogether at the first signs of weakness, nausea or excessive sweating. Be especially careful when children are dressed heavily, or when humidity is high – two factors that increase overheating.

Never leave an infant or toddler alone in a car. Even on a cloudy day, the inside temperature can rise to dangerous levels in less than the time it takes to buy a tube of sunblock.

SUN SAFETY

It can feel great to be out in the sun, but the cost can be steep. The same ultraviolet rays that tan can also burn, and sunburns early in life increase the risk of skin cancer later. Even minor UV exposure adds up over time, causing wrinkles and spots on exposed skin surfaces, and cataracts in the eyes. If you grew up loving the sun, you may need to think about it differently now as a parent.

Who is at risk? The fairer the skin, the greater the danger. Melanin, the pigment that makes dark skin dark, protects against UV light. But even dark-skinned people need to exercise caution. Infants are especially at risk, because their skin is thin and tends to have less pigment. Activities near water – at a pool, on the beach, on a boat – double the risk of sunburn, because UV rays both stream down from above and reflect up off the water. Snow and light-coloured sand have a similar amplifying effect. What's more, you can't trust your body (or your child's) to tell you when you've had too much sun. By the time the skin begins to feel warm and red, it's too late to prevent the sunburn. You have to think ahead and limit sun exposure before any symptoms appear.

Made in the shade. First, protect your child's skin from direct exposure to sunlight, especially between 10 am and 2 pm, when sunlight is the strongest and most harmful. A good rule is that if your shadow is shorter than you are, the sun is strong enough to burn you. Remember that ultra-violet rays can damage the skin and eyes even on hazy or cloudy days. Use umbrellas at the beach. Look for a shady tree at a barbecue. Children should wear long-sleeved shirts and trousers and broad-brimmed hats. But not all clothing blocks the sun well; it is quite possible to get a sun-burn through a shirt. Water does not block UV rays, so be especially cautious during swimming.

Sunscreen is a must. Sunscreens can irritate the skin of babies less than six months; it's best to keep them out of the sun. After six months, use a sunscreen with a sun protection factor (SPF) of 15 or more. This means that only one-fifteenth of the harmful rays get through, so that fifteen minutes of sun exposure with sunscreen is like one minute in the sun without sunscreen. The most effective sunscreens are thick white pastes that contain chemicals such as zinc oxide and titanium dioxide. These are very effective and safe, but only practical for small areas of the body – the tips of noses and ears, for example.

For the rest of the body use waterproof sunscreen, slather it on liberally at least a half hour before sun exposure, and be sure not to miss any spots. Avoid the eyes, however; sunscreen stings. Reapply it frequently, every half hour or so. For a fair-skinned child during the summer, putting on sunblock cream or lotion should be

part of the morning routine, with a second application in the afternoon.

Sunglasses. Everybody should use sunglasses, even infants. You don't need to buy expensive sunglasses; just check that the label states that they block UV rays. The darkness of the lens has nothing to do with UV protection; the lenses must be coated with a special compound that specifically blocks out UV light. Sunglasses are well tolerated by most infants, and they get the child used to wearing them.

INSECT BITES

Bug bites and stings are always unpleasant and sometimes dangerous. Simple precautions can lower the risk and allow your child to enjoy the outdoors without worry.

What you can do. Protect your child against all insect bites and stings by making sure his clothing covers as much skin as possible when the insects are out in full force. Light-coloured clothing is less attractive to insects. Avoid heavily scented detergents and shampoos. Use insect repellents designed for children. If the product contains DEET, the concentration should not exceed 10 per cent. Try to keep the child's hands free of repellent so it doesn't get in his eyes or mouth. DEET may be harmful if ingested. Wash all repellent off once the child is back indoors.

Mosquitoes. Drain any still water on your property to cut down on mosquitoes. Keep toddlers indoors at dusk when mosquitoes arrive in full force.

Bees and wasps. When bees are about, avoid snacking outdoors. Wash your children's hands after eating to avoid attracting bees. It's safest to have nests removed professionally. Children are often stung on their feet when they step on a bee; wearing shoes solves this problem.

Ticks. Deer ticks, the carriers of Lyme disease, are very tiny creatures – the size of a pinhead. (Wood ticks or dog ticks, about the size of a nailhead, are more common.) If you're not sure whether there is Lyme disease in your area, check with your doctor. You can also find information on Lyme disease at www.nhs.uk/conditions/lyme-disease.

Protective clothing and DEET-containing repellents help, but you'll still need to check carefully for ticks after your child has been playing outside, especially in tall grass or near wooded areas. If you find a tick that hasn't been attached very long, chances are good that it has not had a chance to transmit disease. The best method for removing ticks is to use tweezers to grab the tick as close to the skin as possible, then pull straight out. Don't use petroleum jelly, nail polish or a hot match to force it to back out. Wash the skin with an antiseptic, and ask your child's doctor whether your child needs to take antibiotics.

PREVENTING DOG BITES

Children need to learn to leave strange dogs alone. Small children may be more likely to startle or hurt the animal, and so are more likely to be bitten. Most of the people injured by dog bites are ten years old and younger. Before you choose a family dog, read about the various breeds and steer clear of aggressive and high-strung breeds, especially pit bulls, Rottweilers and German shepherds. Be wary of dogs that may have been raised badly or subjected to cruelty. Spay or neuter your dog to reduce aggressive tendencies related to territorialism. Never leave an infant or young child alone with any dog. (There is a series of wonderful wordless picture books about a dog named Carl who proves to be an excellent babysitter. Enjoy the books, but don't try it at home.)

Dog rules for children. A sensitive, anxious child may need lots of reassurance before he goes anywhere near a dog. A bold, fearless child may need to be taught specific rules for dealing with dogs. Here are some commonsense ones:

- Keep away from dogs you don't know, even if they're tied up.
- Always ask the owner before petting or playing with a dog.
- Never tease a dog or stare directly into the eyes of a dog you don't know. Many dogs take staring as a threat or a challenge.
- Don't disturb a dog who is sleeping, eating or caring for puppies.
- If a dog comes near you, don't run away; he probably just wants to sniff you.
- If a dog knocks you over, just curl up in a ball and stay still.
- Beware of dogs while biking or skating.

FIREWORKS AND TRICK-OR-TREAT

Bonfire Night. Bonfire Night fireworks injure around 500 children each year. These injuries usually involve the hands, fingers, eyes or head, and sometimes result in loss of a finger or limb or in blindness. Fireworks for personal use are dangerous. Even sparklers, which seem so harmless, are a tragedy waiting to happen. Parents who insist that sparklers are an inalienable right of childhood need to supervise very closely, to ensure that no one gets hurt. Professional fireworks look as nice from a distance as up close, and the loud explosions won't scare your small child or hurt her ears.

Halloween. Trick-or-treating is increasingly popular in the UK. Injuries on October 31 are often caused by falls, pedestrian mishaps and burns. Most important, make sure that costumes and masks don't obstruct your child's vision. Face paint or makeup is safer than a mask. Trick-or-treaters should carry torches and stick to pavements. Shoes and costumes should fit to prevent tripping. Swords, knives and similar implements should be made of flexible material that cannot cause injury. To prevent burns, make sure costumes, masks, beards and wigs are made of flame-resistant materials. Clothing that is very loose is more likely to come into contact with any candles (in a pumpkin, for example). Put reflective tape on bags and costumes so that drivers can see trick-or-treaters, and remind children to obey all traffic rules and not to dart out from between parked cars. Children under age eight should not trick-or-treat without the supervision of an adult or older sibling. It is a good option to allow children only to call upon pre-agreed friends and neighbours.

Part 2: Safety at Home
DANGERS AT HOME

Home can be a dangerous place for children. Drowning, one of the most common causes of injury-related death after car crashes, often occurs in bathtubs and garden pools. Burns, poisons, medication, choking, falls – it's enough to scare anyone. But there's no point being scared; instead, be prepared! By childproofing your home, you can reduce your child's chance of injury and lower your own level of anxiety. Close supervision is a must, and planning ahead is also critical. (Please refer, too, to 'The First Year' and 'Your Toddler' in Section I for more safety strategies for infants and toddlers.)

DROWNING AND WATER SAFETY

Drowning takes the lives of more than 350 children each year in the United Kingdom. For every child who drowns, four more are hospitalized after nearly drowning, and many have permanent brain damage. Children under age four have a two to three times greater drowning rate than other age groups.

Preschoolers are most likely to drown in the bathtub. Children have been known to crawl into a dry bathtub, turn the tap on, and drown. They can fall into a toilet or a bucket of water headfirst and drown in just a few centimetres of water. Empty dustbins left outside can collect rainwater and a child can drown if he falls in. Keep toilet seats down; plastic latches also help keep out curious hands and heads.

Water safety. Prevention of drowning requires constant parental awareness and supervision. Emphasize these points with any babysitter as well:

- Never leave a child age five or younger alone in the bathtub, even for an instant. A child can drown in as little as 2 cm (1 in) of water. Do not leave her in the tub in the care of another child under age twelve. If you absolutely must answer the phone or the doorbell, wrap up the soapy child in a towel and take her with you.
- Keep your eyes on your child when he is near the water, even when a lifeguard is present. When your child is an accomplished swimmer with enough skill and judgment to stay out of trouble, at age ten to twelve, she can swim without adult supervision as long as she always swims with a buddy. Do not permit her to dive unless the water is at least 1.5 m (5 ft) deep and an adult is present.
- If you have a paddling pool, be sure to empty it and turn it upside down after use to prevent small children from drowning.
- If you have a swimming pool, it should be fenced on all sides. The fence should be at least 1.5 m (5 ft) high, with slats no more than 10 cm (4 in) apart and a lock

on the gate. The gate should be self-closing and self-latching. Don't consider the house as one side of the fence; it's too easy for a child to slip out through a door or window.

- Do not rely on pool alarms to warn you; they don't go off until the child is in the water, which may be too late. A better warning system would be an alarm on the pool gate.
- Keep everyone away from pools or other bodies of water during thunderstorms.
- Stay away from frozen ponds and lakes.
- Do not allow children to sled near water. Golf courses, a popular spot for sledding, often have bodies of water that are potentially dangerous.
- Wells and cisterns should be securely protected.

Swimming lessons. You might think that swimming lessons would protect infants, toddlers and preschoolers against drowning, but there is no evidence that they do. Even with lessons, children up to age five just don't have enough strength and coordination to float or swim out of danger. Early lessons may even increase the risk of drowning by giving parents and children a false sense of security.

FIRE, SMOKE AND BURNS

Fire is one of the most common causes of death from injury in childhood. Children under five are at the greatest risk.

Approximately 80 per cent of all fire-related deaths occur in house fires. Half of all house fires are due to cigarettes – another good reason not to smoke. Fire can spread rapidly, so *never* leave young children alone in a house; take them with you if you have to go out. Most fire-related deaths are actually due to smoke inhalation, not burns.

The most common nonfatal burn injuries result from scalding. About 20 per cent of these cases result from tap water; 80 per cent are from spilled foods and liquids. Half of all scald burns are serious enough to require skin grafting.

What you can do. Take these simple steps to ensure long-term protection:

1. Install smoke detectors on each floor of your home. Place them in the hallways just outside sleeping areas and outside the kitchen. Change the batteries when you reset your clocks for Daylight Saving Time.
2. Keep a dry chemical fire extinguisher in the kitchen.
3. Turn the temperature of your water heater down to 49°C (120°F). Most manufacturers preset their water heaters at 65–70°C (150°–160°C). At this setting, a small child will receive full-thickness burns in less than two seconds. At 49°C (120°F), it takes five minutes to produce a scald burn. If you live in a flat, ask your landlord or residents' association to turn the water heater down. You can still get your dishes clean in water temperature less than 49°C (120°F), and your energy bill will go down. Antiscald devices can

be installed in your shower, bathtub and sink fixtures to stop the flow of water when the temperature exceeds 49°C (120°F).

4. Space heaters, woodstoves, fireplaces, poorly insulated ovens and easily opened broilers are dangerous. Place grilles or guards around woodstoves, fireplaces and wall heaters. Install radiator covers to prevent burns.
5. Put socket covers on all electric sockets to protect children from shocks. Don't overload sockets.
6. Replace worn electric cords. Tightly tape the connections between cords and extension cords. Don't run cords under rugs or across walkways.

You can also lower the risk of fire and scald burns by these prudent habits:

1. Always feel the temperature of bathwater right before you put your child in, even if you remember doing it earlier. Also, feel the taps to make sure they're not hot enough to burn.
2. Never drink hot coffee or tea with a small child in your lap. Be sure that hot beverages aren't near the edge of the table, where a small child can reach up to pull them off. Avoid using tablecloths or placemats, which a small child can pull off the table.
3. Always turn pot handles towards the rear of the stove. Using the back burners is preferable.
4. Keep matches in high places that are impossible for even a determined three- or four-year-old to

reach. Starting at this age, many children go through a phase of being fascinated by fire, and it's very hard for them to resist the temptation to play with matches.

5. If you use space heaters, check to make sure that they aren't in contact with curtains, bedclothes or towels.
6. Children's sleepwear is required by law to be flame-retardant. It is important to choose this sleepwear and not all-cotton underwear for sleeping. Fire-retardant sleepwear must be washed with detergent; repeated washing with soap or chlorine bleach may reduce the flame-retardant properties.

Finally, keep your children safe by teaching them what to do to prevent fires, and how to respond if one occurs.

1. Talk to toddlers about what is hot, and warn them not to touch these things.
2. Discuss fire safety with young children. Include instructions to 'stop, drop and roll' and 'crawl low under the smoke'.
3. Teach your children that if they smell smoke and suspect a fire, the first thing they should do is get out of the house. They can call the fire brigade from a neighbour's phone.
4. Make an emergency plan with two escape routes from each bedroom, and choose a designated meeting place outdoors. Have the whole family practise the plan.

POISONS

Young children put everything in their mouths. Common childhood poisons include aspirin and other medicines, insect and rat poisons, kerosene, petrol, benzene, cleaning fluids, liquid furniture polish, car polish, lye, drain and toilet cleaners, oven cleaners, oil of wintergreen and plant sprays. Potential bathroom poisons include perfume, shampoos, hair tonics, home permanents and beauty preparations.

Every medicine, prescription item, vitamin and household product should be considered poisonous to your child. Even medicines that your child may take on a regular basis can be dangerous if taken in large enough quantities. Substances that may seem safe but which are actually dangerous include tobacco (a single ingested cigarette is dangerous for a one-year-old), aspirin, vitamin pills containing iron, nail polish remover, perfume and dishwasher detergent.

Children between about twelve months and five years are at greatest risk. More poisonings happen in the home than anywhere else. A child who is active, bold and persistent is more likely to get hold of a poison, but even quiet toddlers who seem to prefer to stay in one place can find opportunities – an open bottle of pills or an irresistible house plant – to swallow something they shouldn't.

Childproofing your home. The first step is to inspect your house with an eagle eye – or, rather, a child's eye.

Then follow these steps to childproof your home against poisoning.

1. If you think your child has swallowed anything poisonous, act quickly to get them to hospital. Call 999. If you can, write down the name of what you think your child has swallowed.
2. Store potentially hazardous household cleaners and medications in the bathroom and kitchen out of reach, or in cabinets with childproof locks or latches. Simple hook-and-eye latches can be installed high up on bathroom doors to prevent a child from exposure to all of the hazards associated with the bathroom, from poisoning to drowning to scalding.
3. Find safe places in the kitchen and utility room to store detergents; drain, toilet bowl and oven cleaners; ammonia; bleach; wax remover; metal polish; other cleaning fluids and powders; borax; mothballs; lighter fluid; shoe polish; and other dangerous substances. A safe place is a cabinet that locks, or one that is high up, with nothing under it that a child can climb on. Get rid of rat poisons and insect pastes and poisons. They are just too dangerous.
4. In the basement or garage find truly safe places (ideally, locked) for turpentine, paint thinners, kerosene, petrol, benzene, insecticides, plant sprays, weed killers, antifreeze and car cleaners and polishes. Before you discard containers, check with your council

refuse department for instructions on disposing of hazardous waste.

Helpful habits. Effective poisoning prevention depends on what you do every day. Here are some things to think about:

- Put all medicine safely out of reach immediately after each use. A cabinet or drawer with a childproof latch is best.
- Put bold, clear labels on all medicines so that you won't give your child the wrong one. Flush medicine down the toilet after an illness is over. It's unlikely you'll use it again, and it may deteriorate anyway. It's confusing to have old medicines mixed in with others still in use.
- More than one-third of medicine poisonings are due to children taking their grandparents' prescription drugs. Before a visit, check to be sure that the grandparents' medicines are locked away or completely out of reach.
- All medicines dispensed by a pharmacist come in childproof containers. Don't put medicine in another container. Don't assume that a childproof container is truly childproof.
- Keep cleaning supplies and other chemicals in their original containers. Don't put plant spray in a soft drink bottle, for example, or oven cleaner in a cup; this is a frequent cause of serious injuries.

Plant poisons. We think of plants and flowers as beautiful. Crawling babies and small children think of them as possibly tasty. Taken together, these attitudes spell trouble. Many plants and flowers – over seven hundred of them in all – can cause illness or death. It's safest to keep plants or flowers outdoors until children are past the 'eat everything' stage. At least, place plants high out of reach. Watch small children when they are around plants and flowers in the garden or away from home.

Here is a partial list of potentially fatal plants: caladium, dieffenbachia, philodendron, elephant's ear, English ivy, hyacinth, daffodil, narcissus, mistletoe, oleander, poinsettia, rosary pea, castor bean, delphinium, larkspur, belladonna, foxglove, lily of the valley, azalea, laurel, rhododendron, daphne berries, golden chain (laburnum), hydrangea, jessamine (cestrum) berries, privet (hedges), yew, jimsonweed (thorn apple), morning glory seeds, mushrooms, nightshade, holly berries. Some plants are toxic but not fatal; they will cause skin irritation if touched or swelling of lips and tongue if ingested.

LEAD AND MERCURY

The danger of lead. Lead is everywhere in our industrial world. It is only in recent decades that lead has been removed from house paint, petrol and food cans in the United Kingdom. At very high levels, lead causes obvious brain damage and other severe illness. But even at very low levels, it's likely that lead has negative effects *on average* on children's learning.

I stress the words 'on average' because the effects of low levels of lead are hard to see in any individual child. It's only when scientists study hundreds or thousands of children together that it becomes clear that lead lowers children's IQs. In other words, if a child has a slightly elevated lead level – in the range of 10 to 15 microgrammes per decilitre – no one can say for sure whether that lead level is harmful to that particular child. (It certainly is not doing any good.) That doesn't mean we can forget about lead, but it does mean that you don't need to panic if your child's lead level comes back in the slightly high zone.

Who gets it, and how. Lead poisoning is mostly a problem for young children who crawl around the floor and often put things other than food into their mouths. Children who are hungry or low on iron absorb more lead. Good general nutrition is important to prevent lead poisoning.

The source of lead is often old paint around windows or on outside walls. As the paint deteriorates, children may ingest flakes or pick up lead-contaminated dust on their hands. Other sources include pottery with lead glazes (modern machine-made pottery does not contain lead), lead in the water pipes leading to older buildings, and some traditional medicines.

What to do. If you live in housing built before 1970, which may have old lead pipes or paint, your children should have their blood lead levels checked regularly in their early years. With high levels, doctors prescribe medicine to remove the lead from the body; with lower levels, the main treatment is to remove the lead from the environment, make sure the child has plenty of iron, and allow the child's body to get rid of the lead on its own. Some tips for dealing with lead include:

- Check for peeling and cracking paint, especially around windows and doors. Remove whatever comes off easily, then cover the rest with new paint.
- Don't try to remove lead paint by stripping, sanding or using a heat gun; these methods dramatically *increase* lead exposure. If you have to remove lead-containing paint, have a professional do it while you and your child are out of the house.
- Mop floors regularly with a lead-specific cleaning solution to pick up lead dust.
- Pay attention to all the places your child spends time: your home, outside, the sitter's house, the nursery and so on.
- If you have older plumbing (in a home built before 1970), let the cold water run for a few minutes before using it for drinking or cooking. That way you don't use water that has been sitting for a long time in the pipes, collecting lead. (Boiling water doesn't remove lead – it makes the problem worse.) If you live in a hard water area, lead in the pipes is less of a concern.
- Avoid glazed pottery unless you are sure it is lead free.

- Be careful about using folk medicines made from old recipes (perhaps these are medicines your grandmother swears by, for example), because some of them contain lead.

Learn more! If you have lead in your environment, you need to know much more than there is space for here. Talk with your child's doctor. Have a look at the Chartered Institute of Plumbing and Heating Engineering's website at www.ciphe.org.uk and the Lead Paint Safety Organisation at www.lipsa.org.uk.

Mercury. Mercury is like lead in many ways: both are metals, both are common in our industrial world, and both cause brain damage at high levels and abnormal brain development even at low levels. Mercury from factories and mines makes its way into lakes and oceans. From there, it is picked up by microscopic organisms, little fish, bigger fish and the final consumers – us. For this reason, it's a good idea to avoid eating a lot of fish during pregnancy and early childhood. Fish caught in highly polluted waters and large predator fish such as swordfish that collect mercury over their relatively long lifetimes are probably best avoided altogether.

Another source of mercury is the everyday mercury thermometer. When thermometers break, the beads of liquid mercury give off a vapour that is odourless but poisonous. It's best to treat your glass thermometer like the toxic waste it is: ask your council how best to dispose of it. Then buy a cheap, accurate, safe digital thermometer (see page 415).

CHOKING

Choking is the fourth leading cause of death in young children. Small children who put things in their mouths should not have little objects (like buttons, beans or beads) within reach. These are easily breathed into the windpipe.

Dangerous toys. Children under age five are most at risk of choking on toys or parts of toys. A good test uses a standard toilet paper tube – if a toy is small enough to fit inside the tube, it's small enough to be a choking hazard. The British Standards test uses a similar device called a choke test cylinder that is a bit smaller than a toilet paper tube.

Look also for any small parts that might break off a toy with rough play. Try pulling off the parts yourself. Small balls or dice from children's toys and games are other common items that children under the age of three choke on. Keeping an older child's toys away from a younger sibling or a young visitor to your home is always a challenge.

Children often choke on balloons that have burst, sometimes while they are blowing them up. For this reason, it's best to keep balloons away from small children.

Choking on foods. By age four or five, most children are able to handle the same foods that adults can. Before that, you have to be very careful with certain foods. Round, hard foods such as nuts, hard sweets, carrots, popcorn and grapes are especially dangerous to young children. Hot dogs can plug up the windpipe like a stopper in a bottle.

One of the most dangerous foods is peanut butter eaten directly off a spoon or knife; if it is aspirated, nothing can remove the peanut butter from the lungs. It should always be spread thin on bread.

An excellent way to prevent choking on large pieces of food is to chew well. Children can be taught to chew properly, and if you set an example, they will most likely follow, especially if they are not rushed. Take away lollipops and ice lollies if small children keep them in their mouths while running. Don't let your child lie down while eating, and never leave a baby alone with a propped-up bottle. See page 487 for first aid for choking.

SUFFOCATION AND STRANGULATION

In children under age one, suffocation is the leading cause of death from unintentional injury. An infant spends most of his time in his cot, so steps should be taken to make sure this is a safe environment. See page 59 for guidelines for preventing suffocation in infants.

Toddlers can strangle themselves in cords hanging down from curtains, blinds or appliances. Tie cords up, wrap them around cleats mounted on the wall, hide them behind heavy furniture, or use cord shorteners (little plastic devices that cords wrap tightly around).

For older children, be aware of the risk of plastic bags. For some reason, many children have the urge to play with plastic bags by putting them over their heads, occasionally with tragic results. Keep all plastic bags stored where you have your other hazardous household materials, in a locked or inaccessible cabinet or drawer. If you have an unused refrigerator or freezer or other large appliance or are in the process of discarding one, be sure to take the doors off.

FALLS

Falls are the leading cause of nonfatal injuries to children in the UK. The highest death rate due to falls is during the first year of life. Around ten children in the UK die from falls each year.

Falls occur from as many places as you can imagine: beds, changing tables, windows, trees, bicycles, playground equipment, ice and stairs. Toddlers often fall from windows and down stairs; older children fall from rooftops and recreational equipment. Most falls in the home occur with children age four and under. The peak hours for falls in the home are around mealtimes, when parents are busy doing many things at once.

Stairs. Install gates at the top and bottom of stairs, until your children can go up and down steadily. Teach your children to use handrails, and let them see you taking the same precaution.

Falls from windows. If your child's room is on the first floor or above, you need a plan to keep him from falling out of the window. You can keep windows locked, of course, but that's not always feasible in summer. You can move all toys and furniture away from windows, but your child will soon be able to slide a chair over. You may be able to open windows from the top.

If you're good with tools, you can screw metal stopper devices or blocks of wood into the window frame to keep the window from opening more than 10 cm (4 in). Window guards are sturdy metal gates that have a maximum of 10 cm (4 in) between the bars. You can place guards on all the windows in a room. But at least one window must have a guard that can be opened or removed without the use of a special key or tool, in case of fire.

Baby walkers. Once considered a necessary piece of infant equipment, the walker, especially those with built-in seats, is now seen as a menace. Walkers give a great deal of mobility to infants who have no sense of the risks. They can easily walk right off the stairs and have no way to break their fall. All it takes is for a parent to turn his back for an instant. Many thousands of babies are hurt this way each year around the world.

Walkers don't teach babies to walk. In fact, babies who rely on walkers to get around are often slow to develop the strength and coordination needed to walk on their own. Stand-up activity centres or a walker with the wheels removed can give a child a sense of independence without the risk of falls. Make sure there are no exposed springs to pinch your baby's fingers.

TOY SAFETY

Every year, thousands of children are injured by their toys, and hundreds of toys are recalled because they prove dangerous. Pay attention to the age recommendations when buying toys, and use your own judgment. Toys such as marbles, balloons and small blocks present a choking hazard for a child three and under, or one of any age who puts objects in his mouth. Look out for sharp points or edges, and for projectiles that can injure eyes. Electric toys should only be used by children eight or older. Certain toys made out of soft plastic contain chemicals called phthalates, which can cause kidney damage and other health problems. If you're unsure about whether a product contains phthalates, you can call the manufacturer.

Even your child's toy chest can be a hazard. Make sure yours has a lid support, so the top can't come down fast on your child's head. You can learn much more about toy safety at www.toysadvice.co.uk.

HOME SAFETY EQUIPMENT

What to buy? Gizmo makers love to sell safety equipment to nervous parents. My favourite would have to be the rubber bathtub spout cover in the shape of an elephant's trunk; this item scores high for cuteness, even if it doesn't add much security. There are really only a few things that are absolutely necessary for home safety. These include working smoke detectors with fresh batteries, a fire extinguisher in the kitchen, and locked cabinets for medications and other dangerous chemicals. If you have stairs in your home, gates at the top and bottom can prevent tumbles. If your home is on the first floor or above, you may need window guards.

The list below contains several other items that you

might find useful and that aren't too costly. Most are mentioned in the sections above. But remember, no item is a substitute for close adult supervision.

- ✓ Childproof cabinet and drawer latches in the kitchen and bathroom.
- ✓ Hook-and-eye door latches, mounted high on the door, to keep young children away from bathrooms, stairs or areas where dangerous cleaners or tools are stored.
- ✓ Velcro latches to keep toddlers out of hard-to-lock objects such as refrigerators, toilets or sliding cabinets.
- ✓ Cord shorteners to prevent children from putting long cords around their necks.
- ✓ A water temperature gauge to ensure that your hot water is no hotter than 49°C (120°F).
- ✓ Socket covers to prevent shocks. (Spring-loaded covers that mount permanently to the wall are better than the little plastic plugs; they don't get lost and they automatically block off the outlet when you take out the plug.)
- ✓ Corner and edge cushions to soften the blow from coffee tables.
- ✓ Plastic covers to cushion any impact with the bathtub spout. (But any child who is young enough to possibly bonk her head on the spout needs to have an adult right there during the bath, anyhow.)

FIRST AID AND EMERGENCIES

CUTS AND SCRATCHES

The best treatment for scratches and small cuts is to wash them with soap and warm water. Careful washing is the key to preventing infection. After drying the cut with a clean towel, cover it with a bandage to allow it to remain clean until it is healed. Wash the cut once a day until it has completely healed.

For large cuts that spread open, you should consult your doctor. Many of these larger cuts will require stitches to close the wound and lessen the chance of a disfiguring scar. It is important to keep the stitches clean and dry until they are removed. Inspect the wound each day for signs of infection, such as increased pain, swelling, redness or drainage from the wound. Many cuts are now closed using tissue adhesives that are faster than sutures and just as effective.

Wounds that might be contaminated by dirt or soil, or those caused by dirty objects such as knives, should be reported to your doctor. The doctor may recommend a tetanus booster, especially for deep cuts or puncture wounds. If your child has completed the initial series of four DTaP immunizations and it hasn't been more than five years since the last booster, he may not need a tetanus booster.

It is always best to check with your physician if you are uncertain.

Occasionally a bit of glass, wood or gravel may remain in a wound. Unless you can easily remove the fragments, it's best to have a doctor evaluate these cuts. An X-ray may be needed to show the foreign object. Any cut that does not heal properly or that becomes infected (with redness, pain or drainage) may have a retained foreign object.

SPLINTERS

Next to small cuts and bruises, splinters are probably the most common minor injury during childhood. Try the soak-and-poke approach: wash the area with soap and water, then soak it in fairly hot water for at least ten minutes. Use a hot compress if you can't cover the area with water. (You'll have to reheat your water or compress every couple of minutes.) If one end of the splinter is sticking out of the skin, you can now grasp it with a good pair of tweezers and gently pull it out. If the splinter is entirely under the skin, you'll need a sewing needle that's been wiped with surgical spirit. The soaking softens the skin so that you can gently prick it open with the tip of the needle, making a big enough opening for you to grasp the splinter with tweezers. After the splinter is out, wash the area with soap and water and then cover the area with a clean bandage.

Don't poke at the skin too much. If you can't get the splinter out after the first soak, give it another ten minutes of hot soaking and then try again. If you still can't get it, let a doctor take over.

BITES

Animal (or human) bites. The mouths of all animals, including humans, contain many bacteria that can cause infection. A bite injury usually results in a deep puncture wound, which may be more difficult to clean than a simple cut. Wash the wound with lots of running water and plenty of soap for several minutes. Call the doctor for any bite that breaks the skin. To prevent an infection from developing, the doctor may prescribe an antibiotic. Even if your child is receiving antibiotics, be sure to notify the doctor if you see signs of infection, such as redness, swelling, tenderness or drainage.

Rabies has been eradicated in the UK, but if you are abroad, think about rabies with any animal bite. Rabies can be fatal, and there is no cure once the infection has set in, but a special vaccine given as soon as possible after the bite can prevent the most serious illness. Wild animals, especially foxes, raccoons and bats, often carry rabies. Pets, including dogs and cats, can also transmit the virus; you probably don't need to worry about gerbils, hamsters or guinea pigs.

Insect bites. Most don't need any treatment, but watch for signs of infection (see page 493), which can follow as a result of scratching. For bee stings, check to see if the stinger is still in the skin; if it is, gently scrape the area with a credit card or other small piece of plastic. Don't use tweezers, because you might squeeze more venom into the skin. Gently clean the area, and apply ice to help with swelling.

For an insect bite that is itching (a mosquito bite, for instance) you can apply a paste made by running a few drops of water into a teaspoonful of baking soda (bicarbonate of soda). The oral antihistamine diphenhydramine (Benadryl) can help reduce itching; however, antihistamines make some children tired, while others become hyper and yet others are unaffected. The best strategy, clearly, is prevention (see page 470).

BLEEDING

Minor wounds. A little bleeding for a few minutes helps clean the wound. Only profuse or persistent bleeding requires special treatment. To stop the bleeding, apply direct pressure while elevating the wound. Have the child lie down and put a pillow or two under the limb. Press on the wound with a sterile gauze square or any clean cloth until the bleeding stops. Clean and bandage the wound while the limb is still elevated.

When bandaging a cut that has bled a lot or is still bleeding, use a number of gauze squares (or folded pieces of clean cloth) on top of each other so that you have a thick pad over the cut. Then, when you snugly apply the adhesive or gauze roll bandage, it will exert more pressure on the cut and make it less likely to bleed again.

Severe bleeding. If a wound is bleeding at an alarming rate, you must stop the bleeding immediately. Apply direct pressure to the wound and elevate the limb if possible. Make a pad of the cleanest material you have handy, whether it's a gauze square, a clean handkerchief or the cleanest piece of clothing on the child or yourself. Press the pad against the wound and keep pressing until help arrives or until the bleeding stops. Don't remove your original pad. As it becomes soaked through, add new material on top. If the bleeding is easing up and you have suitable material, apply a thick pad over the wound so that when it is bandaged, the pad presses on the wound. If that doesn't control the bleeding, continue hand pressure directly over the wound. If you have no cloth or material of any kind to press against a profusely bleeding wound, press your hands on the edges of the wound or even in the wound.

Most bleeding can be stopped by simple direct pressure. If you are dealing with one that doesn't stop, continue to apply direct pressure and have someone call an ambulance. While awaiting the ambulance, have the patient lie down, keep her warm and elevate her legs and the injured body part.

A minor cut to the scalp can cause a lot of bleeding. Pressure on the wound should stop it quickly.

Nosebleeds. Almost every child has nosebleeds, and they are almost never dangerous. A little blood can look like a lot when it comes out of the nose. Most nosebleeds stop on their own if the child just sits still for a few minutes. For more severe nosebleeds, gently pinch the whole lower part of the nose for five minutes. (Look at your watch; five minutes seems like an eternity in these circumstances.) Let go slowly and gently. If the nosebleed continues for ten minutes in spite of these measures, get in touch with the doctor.

Common causes of nosebleeds include dry air, nose picking, allergies and colds. After the bleeding stops, a scab forms in the nose; a day later the scab falls off (or the child picks it off) and the nose bleeds again. A little Vaseline to the inside of the nose can sometimes keep the scab from drying up too quickly.

If a child has repeated nosebleeds, the doctor may offer to cauterize an exposed blood vessel or run a test to make sure the blood can clot normally. Almost always, though, the treatment of choice is patience.

Nosebleeds in infants are not common and sometimes spell trouble. They should be reported to the doctor.

BURNS

Burn severity. Burns are categorized into one of three types. Burns involving only the topmost layer of the skin usually produce only redness; these are often called superficial or first-degree burns. Partial-thickness burns (what used to be called second-degree burns) have injured the deeper layers of the skin and usually result in the formation of blisters. Full-thickness burns (formerly called third-degree burns) involve the deepest layers of the skin, often damaging the nerves and blood vessels beneath the skin. Full-thickness burns are serious injuries and often require a skin graft. The size of the burn is also important. A superficial burn over much of the body (as with a sunburn) is often enough to make a child feel quite ill.

Minor burns. For minor burns, hold the burned area under cold running water for several minutes, until the area feels numbed. Don't use ice; freezing can worsen the injury. Never apply any ointment, grease, butter, cream or petroleum product, because these can hold heat in at the site of the burn. After rinsing the burn with cold water, cover the area with a bulky sterile dressing to decrease the pain.

If blisters form, leave them intact. As long as the blister is unbroken, the fluid inside is sterile; once opened, germs get in. If a blister does break, it is better to remove all the loose skin with a pair of nail scissors or a pair of tweezers that have been boiled for five minutes. Then cover with a sterile bandage. A prescription ointment may prevent infection. If you see signs of infection – like pus in the blister and redness around the edge – you should certainly consult a doctor. Never put iodine or any similar antiseptic on a burn unless directed by a doctor.

It's especially important for a physician or nurse practitioner to see all burns on the face, hands, feet and genital area, as delays in treatment can lead to scars or functional impairments. Mild sunburns are the exception.

Sunburn. The best treatment for sunburn is not to get it in the first place (see page 467). Severe sunburn is painful, dangerous and unnecessary. A half hour of direct sunshine at a beach in summer is enough to cause a burn on a fair-skinned person who is not prepared for the sun.

For relief of sunburn, you can apply a cool compress

and give a mild nonaspirin pain reliever such as ibuprofen or paracetamol. If blisters develop, they should be treated as described in the previous section. If a person with a sunburn develops chills and fever and feels ill, call a doctor. Sunburn can be just as serious as a heat burn. Keep sunburned areas completely protected from sunshine until the redness is gone.

Electrical injuries. Most electrical injuries in children occur at home. The degree of injury is directly proportional to the amount of current that passes through the child. Water or moisture of any kind increases the risk. For this reason, no electrical device should ever be operated in a bathroom where a child is washing or bathing.

Most often, contact with an electrical current causes a shock and the child pulls his hand away before any damage is done. If there is a small blister or area of redness, or a small patch of charred tissue, you can treat the injury like a burn caused by heat (see page 498). An electrical current can travel through nerves and blood vessels. If your child has entrance and exit wounds, the current may have damaged nerves and blood vessels along the way. If your child has any neurologic symptoms such as numbness or tingling, or if she complains of pain anywhere other than right at the site of the electrical contact, she should be examined by a doctor.

Occasionally children will develop an electrical burn after they bite into an electrical cord, perhaps a small burn near the corner of the mouth. All children with this type of burn need to be evaluated by a doctor. Since all burns can leave scars, your child may need special care to avoid developing a scar that could interfere with his ability to smile and chew.

SKIN INFECTIONS

Minor skin infections. Look for redness, swelling, warmth, pain or pus. If a child has a boil, an infection at the end of his finger, or an infected cut of any type, it should be examined by a doctor. The best first-aid treatment is to soak the infected area in warm water or apply warm wet dressings; this softens the skin and hastens the time when it will break open and allow the pus to escape, and then it will keep the opening from closing over again too soon. Place a fairly thick bandage over the infection and pour enough warm water onto the bandage to make all of it thoroughly wet. Let it soak for twenty minutes, and then replace the wet bandage with a clean, dry one. Repeat this wet soak three or four times a day until you can see the doctor. If you have an antibiotic ointment you can apply it over the affected area, although this should not replace the visit to the doctor.

More serious skin infections. Signs that a skin infection is more serious include fever, a rapidly enlarging red area, red streaks starting from the site of infection and tender lymph glands in his armpit or groin. These infections are medical emergencies. Get the child to a doctor or hospital A&E department at once.

OBJECTS IN NOSE AND EARS

Small children often stuff things – beads, small pieces from toys or games, or wads of paper – into their noses or ears. Using a pair of tweezers, you may be able to grasp a soft object that isn't too far in. Don't try to go after a smooth, hard object; you are almost certain to push it in farther. If your child won't sit still, be careful with the tweezers so that you don't cause more damage than the foreign object itself. Even if you can't see the object, it may still be there.

Sometimes an older child may be able to expel an object in her nose by blowing her nose, but don't try this if she's so young that she sniffs when told to blow. Other children sneeze the object out in a little while. Try squirting a little saline solution into the nose to loosen things up. If that fails, let your doctor take a look. Objects that remain in the nose for several days usually cause a bad-smelling discharge tinged with blood. A discharge of this kind from one nostril should always make you think of this possibility.

OBJECTS IN THE EYE

To remove specks of dirt or grit, try having your child blink several times while holding his eye in a sinkful of water, or while you pour water gently over it. If the feeling of grittiness persists for more than about thirty minutes, talk with the doctor. If the eye was hit forcefully or by a sharp object, or if it hurts, cover the eye with a damp cloth and go for help. Blood in the eye, significant lid swelling, purple discolouration around the eye, or sudden blurring of vision are all reasons for prompt medical attention.

SPRAINS AND STRAINS

Tendons connect muscles to bones; ligaments hold joints together. When muscles, tendons or ligaments are overstretched or torn, that's a strain or a sprain. These injuries can hurt so much that you might wonder if a bone is broken, too. But in either case the first aid is the same: elevation, ice and immobilization.

Have your child lie down for a half hour and elevate the sprained limb on a pillow. Put an ice pack over the injured area. Applying cold immediately helps to prevent swelling and decrease the pain. Use an elastic bandage to wrap an ankle, knee or wrist in order to immobilize it. Give a non-aspirin pain reliever such as ibuprofen (Calprofen). If the pain isn't too severe, you can watch it for a few hours or a day. If your child can resume normal movement without pain, there is no need to see a doctor.

If the area stays painful and swollen, have your child seen by a doctor. Even if there isn't a broken bone, your child may require a cast or a splint to allow the ligaments and tendons to heal properly. Some sprains and strains take a long time to heal. If a child goes back to vigorous activity too soon, there's a risk of reinjuring the joint. It's best to follow the doctor's instructions; a physiotherapist can often help with specific exercises.

Elbow injury in toddlers. Sometimes a toddler suddenly refuses to use his arm and lets it hang limply at his side. This often begins right after the arm has been pulled sharply, as when the parent catches the child by the hand to prevent a fall. What has happened is that one of the bones at the elbow has been pulled out of position. A doctor who recognizes 'toddler's elbow' can usually pop the joint back into place painlessly.

FRACTURES

Children's bones are different. A fracture is a broken or splintered bone. Unlike adults, children often fracture the growth plate, where the bone is actively growing. This kind of fracture can interfere with future growth, causing one limb to be short or bent. Children's bones are flexible, so sometimes only one side of a bone breaks (a greenstick fracture). They can also have the typical adult pattern, which is a crack all the way through a bone.

It can be hard to tell the difference between a sprain and a fracture. If there is an obvious deformity – an arm bent at an odd angle – then there's little doubt that the bone is broken. Often, however, the only signs are mild swelling or tenderness. Bruising at the site of injury or pain that persists for days suggests a fracture. Often the only way to be sure is to take X-rays.

If you suspect a fracture, avoid further injury by preventing movement to that area. A nonaspirin pain reliever can reduce pain. If you can, apply a splint and ice, and then take your child to the doctor.

Broken wrists. A child who falls from a climbing frame or slips on the ice and catches himself with his arm outstretched is apt to break his wrist. The wrist hurts right away, but the pain might not be severe, so days may go by before the child gets taken to the doctor. One clue to this very common type of fracture is sharp pain at a particular spot just below the base of the thumb. An X-ray confirms the diagnosis, and a cast takes care of the problem.

Splinting. Most broken bones should be seen at A&E as soon as possible. For any serious break, call an ambulance; don't try to move the child yourself unless you have to. If for some reason you can't get your child to medical attention right away, you may need to apply a splint. Splinting reduces pain and prevents further damage that could be caused by movement of the broken bones. The splint should hold the limb motionless above and below the injury. An ankle splint should reach to the knee; for a broken wrist, the splint should go from the fingertips to the elbow.

You need a board to make a long splint. You can make a short splint for a small child by folding a piece of cardboard. Move the limb with extreme gentleness when you apply the splint and avoid any movement near the area of the injury. Tie the limb to the splint snugly in four to six places using handkerchiefs, strips of clothing or bandages. Be sure you don't cut off the circulation. Two of the ties should be close to the break, on either side of it, and there should be one at each end of the splint.

After you apply the splint, place an ice pack over the

area of the injury. Never apply ice directly to the skin without a bag or cloth in between, and as a general rule, apply ice for no more than twenty minutes at any one time. For a broken collarbone, make a sling out of a large triangle of cloth and tie it behind the child's neck so that it supports the lower arm across the chest.

NECK AND BACK INJURIES

The spinal cord is a thick bundle of nerves that connects the brain to the rest of the body. Damage to the cord can result in paralysis, loss of control over bladder and bowel functions, loss of sensation and ongoing pain. The spinal cord runs inside the vertebral column, a protective cylinder formed from the bones of the neck and back.

If the vertebral column has been damaged in a fall or other impact, the nerves of the cord are also in danger, both from the original trauma and from attempts to move the child afterward. Therefore, *never* try to move a person after an injury that may have damaged the neck or back. This includes any trauma in which the child has lost consciousness, and any serious high-impact injury. Instead, make the child comfortable and try to keep her quiet until an ambulance arrives. Only a specially trained health care professional should move a child suspected of having a neck or back injury.

If the child *must* be moved and professional help has not arrived, one person should be assigned to hold the child's head and neck steady. When moving the child, keep her head and neck in the same position at all times. Never turn the body separately from the head. This decreases the chance of further injury to the spinal cord.

HEAD INJURIES

Even before a baby has begun to walk, she may suffer a head injury by rolling off a bed or a changing table. If she cries immediately and then stops crying within fifteen minutes, keeps a good colour, doesn't vomit, acts as if nothing has happened and doesn't develop significant swelling on her head, there is little chance that she has suffered an injury to her brain. A swelling that puffs out quickly on a child's forehead after a fall doesn't mean anything serious in itself, as long as there are no other symptoms. It is caused by a broken blood vessel just under the skin. Swellings on other parts of the skull could be a sign of broken bones.

When a head injury is more severe, the child is apt to vomit, lose her appetite, be pale for a number of hours, show signs of headache and dizziness, alternate between agitation and lethargy, and seem sleepier than usual. If a child has *any* of these symptoms, call the doctor. Any child who has lost consciousness after a fall should be seen by a doctor immediately, even if there are no other symptoms.

After any head injury, a child should be observed closely for the next twenty-four to forty-eight hours. Bleeding under the bones of the scalp can put pressure on the brain, causing symptoms that are not obvious at first but which develop over a day or two. Any change in behaviour, especially increased sleepiness, agitation or dizziness, is a red flag.

Finally, keep an eye on your child's performance in school after a head injury. Children who have a concussion – that is, a head injury with loss of consciousness or memory loss for the incident – may develop difficulty with concentration or memory loss. Also, look closely for any injury to the teeth, see page 531.

SWALLOWED OBJECTS

Objects that aren't food usually pass through a child's stomach and intestines without difficulty. They might not even be noticed. If they get stuck in the oesophagus (the tube between the throat and stomach) or further down the digestive tract, they can cause coughing or choking, the sensation of having something caught in the throat, pain or difficulty with swallowing, refusal to eat, drooling or persistent vomiting.

Certain objects – including needles, pins and coins – are likely to cause problems. Button batteries are particularly dangerous because they can leak acid, causing internal burns. Small, smooth objects, like prune stones or small buttons, usually pass within a day or so. If your child feels completely well, you can check your child's bowel movements. Once the object has passed, there's nothing more to do. If your child develops any of the symptoms listed above or has swallowed a sharp or irregularly shaped object or *any* battery, then you need to call the doctor right away.

You might think that making your child vomit or giving a strong laxative (or cathartic) would help flush out a swallowed object. Usually these measures don't work, and sometimes they make the situation much worse. It's better to let the doctor remove the object safely. For objects lodged in the windpipe or bronchial tubes, see 'Choking and Rescue Breathing' on page 512.

POISONS

First aid for suspected poisoning is simple: if your child appears ill, call 999 for an ambulance. If your child appears well, call NHS Direct (0845 4647 in England and Wales; 08454 242424 in Scotland) first. Other tips:

1. Stay with your child and make sure she is breathing and alert. If not, call 999 for immediate help.
2. Remove any remaining substances or solutions to prevent her from ingesting any more.
3. Do not delay seeking help because your child seems well. The effects of many drugs and poisons – aspirin, for instance – may take hours to show. Early treatment can prevent serious harm.
4. Call 999 or NHS Direct (see above). Tell them the name of the medication or product your child swallowed, as well as the amount of the substance, if known.

Poisons on the skin. Medications and poisons can be absorbed through the skin, sometimes reaching toxic levels within the body. If your child's clothes or skin come in contact with a potential poison, remove the contaminated clothing and steadily flush the skin with plenty of plain water for fifteen minutes. Then gently wash the area with soap and water and rinse well. Place the contaminated clothing in a plastic bag, keeping it away from other children. Call NHS Direct or your doctor. If they refer you to a hospital, take the contaminated clothes with you in case they wish to test the clothes to identify the poison.

Harmful fluids in the eye. If a child is accidentally squirted or splashed in the eye with a possibly harmful fluid, promptly flush the eye. Try to keep the child from rubbing his eyes. Have him lie on his back and blink as much as possible while you flood the eye with lukewarm (not hot) water poured from a large glass held 5–8 cm (2–3 in) above the face. Don't force the eyelid open. Keep this up for fifteen minutes; meanwhile, have someone call the doctor. If you're alone, flush the eye first, then call. Some liquids can cause serious damage to the eye. Caustics, such as drain cleaners, are especially dangerous and require emergency medical care.

ALLERGIC REACTIONS

Children can have an allergic reaction to a food, a pet, a medication, an insect bite or almost anything else. The symptoms can be mild, moderate or severe.

Mild. Children who have mild allergies may complain of watery, itchy eyes. Often there is associated sneezing or a stuffy nose. On occasion they may develop hives, a localized swelling of the skin that looks like a large mosquito bite and itches badly. Other rashes, with small, itchy bumps, can also be caused by allergies. Mild allergic symptoms are usually treated with over-the-counter diphenhydramine or another antihistamine.

Moderate. Moderate allergic symptoms occur when, in addition to hives, the child develops respiratory symptoms such as wheezing and coughing. Children with these symptoms need to be evaluated by a doctor promptly.

Severe. Symptoms of severe allergic reactions, also called anaphylaxis, include swelling in the mouth or throat, difficulty breathing due to blockage of the airway, and low blood pressure. Anaphylaxis can be fatal. Emergency treatment for anaphylaxis is adrenaline (also called epinephrine) injected under the skin, followed by immediate transfer to a hospital A&E department.

A child who has had one anaphylactic reaction could have another. To prevent a serious episode, doctors prescribe a preloaded syringe of epinephrine (EpiPen, Anapen or other brand), to be carried by parents and teachers or by an older child. Any time a child gets adrenaline, he needs to go to the hospital right away, even if he feels better.

An allergist can help you decide whether or not allergy desensitization shots make sense for your child.

CONVULSIONS OR SEIZURES

A generalized seizure or convulsion is frightening to witness. It's important to remain calm and realize that in most cases the child is not actually in danger. Place the child in a position where she can't hurt herself, for example, on a rug some distance from any furniture. Lay her on her side so that any saliva will run out of her mouth and her tongue does not block her airway. Don't reach down her throat. Call 999. See page 593 for more on convulsions.

CHOKING AND RESCUE BREATHING

Most children have a healthy heart. When their heart stops beating, it is usually because they have stopped breathing, cutting off the oxygen supply to the heart. Reasons children may suddenly stop breathing include suffocation, drowning and choking on objects or food. (Severe pneumonia, asthma or other diseases can rarely cause a child to stop breathing, but this doesn't happen suddenly, so it shouldn't be the sort of thing a parent ever has to face alone.) A parent who knows how to unblock a blocked airway and how to give rescue breaths for a child who is not breathing is prepared to deal with most life-threatening emergencies.

CPR. Every adult should be trained in life-saving techniques and cardiopulmonary resuscitation (CPR). Courses are offered by St John's Ambulance, the Red Cross and many hospitals and clinics. These courses will teach you how to assess a seriously ill child and get help, how to administer rescue breathing, and how to try to start the heart beating if it has stopped. The instructions below are not a substitute for taking the course; they are only meant to give you an idea of what to do. To really learn CPR you have to take a course.

Choking and coughing. When a child has swallowed something and is coughing hard, give her a chance to cough it out. Coughing is the best way to clear an object from the air passages. If the person is able to breathe, speak or cry, stay close by and ask someone to call for help. Do not make any attempt to remove the object. Do not slap her on the back, turn her upside down or reach into her mouth and try to pull the object out; each of those actions can drive the object tighter into the airway and is appropriate only if the airway is already completely blocked.

Unable to cough or breathe. When a child is choking and unable to breathe, cry or speak, the object is completely blocking the airway, and air is not entering the lungs. In this situation – but *only* if the airway is completely blocked – follow the emergency steps outlined below.

Up to One Year Old, Unable to Cough or Breathe (Completely Blocked Airway)

1. If the baby is conscious, slide one hand under her back to support her head and neck. With your other hand, hold her jaw between your thumb and fingers, and let your forearm lie along her abdomen.
2. Turn the child over so she is lying face down with her head lower than her trunk. Support her abdomen with your forearm that is resting on your thigh.
3. With the heel of one hand, give the baby up to five rapid blows in the middle of the back, high between the shoulder blades.

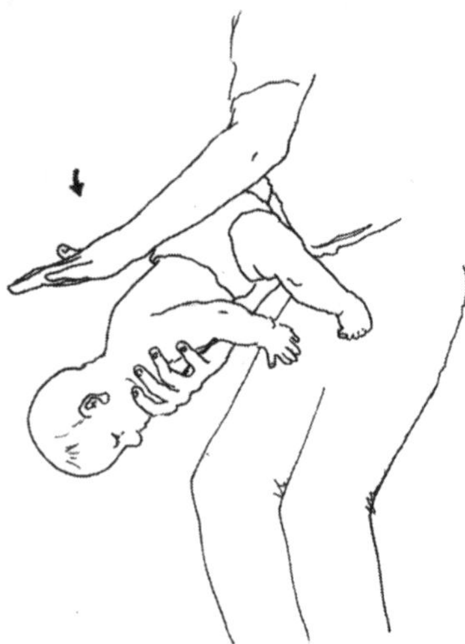

4. If the object was not dislodged by the back blows, turn the infant face up while supporting her back with your forearm. Remember that the child's head should be lower than her feet. Place your middle and index fingers on her breastbone, in the centre of her chest just below the level of her nipples. Give up to five quick downward chest thrusts, trying to create an artificial cough.
5. If the baby doesn't start to breathe or has become unconscious, have someone call for help while you attempt to begin rescue breathing. First, look for the object in the back of the baby's throat by grabbing the tongue and the lower jaw between your thumb and fingers and lifting upward. If you see something, slide your little finger down along the inside of her cheek to the base of her tongue and use a hooking

motion to sweep the object out. (Don't poke your finger in her mouth if you can't see anything; this could make the blockage worse.)

6. Next, reposition the baby to begin rescue breathing. Open her mouth by lifting her chin as you press back on her forehead.
7. If the baby still hasn't started to breathe, tilt her head back, lift up her chin, and completely cover both her mouth and nose with your lips. Breathe into her two times, each time for about one and a half seconds and with just enough pressure to make her chest rise.
8. If the air does not enter the baby's lungs, her air passage is still blocked. Start with the back blows again, and repeat steps 3 to 7. Continue repeating the sequence until the baby starts to cough, breathe or cry, or until help arrives.

Over One Year Old, Unable to Cough or Breathe (Completely Blocked Airway)

1. Remember, if the child is coughing, speaking or crying, watch but don't intervene. If the child is conscious but not able to get any air in or out, start with the Heimlich manoeuvre. Kneel or stand behind the child and wrap your arms around his waist. Make a fist with one hand and put the thumb of your fist just above the child's navel, staying well below his breastbone.

2. Cover your fist with your other hand and press your fist into the child's abdomen with up to five quick upward thrusts. Be gentle with younger or smaller children. Repeat the Heimlich manoeuvre until the object is expelled. This should get the child to breathe or cough. (If this treatment stops the choking episode, call the doctor even if the child seems fully recovered.)
3. If the child still isn't breathing after a Heimlich manoeuvre, open his mouth by grasping both the tongue and the lower jaw between your thumb and fingers, and lift the jaw. Look in his throat for the object. If you see something, slide your little finger along the inside of his cheek to the base of his tongue, and use a hooking motion to sweep the object out. (Don't poke your finger around in his mouth if you

can't see anything, or can't hook the object; this could make the blockage worse.) Repeat the Heimlich manoeuvre until the foreign body is removed or the patient becomes unconscious.

4. If the child becomes unconscious, have someone call 999. Try the Heimlich manoeuvre with the child lying on his back. Kneel at his feet (or straddle the legs of an older or bigger child). Put the heel of one hand above his navel, staying well below his breastbone. Put your other hand over your fist with the fingers of both hands pointing toward his head. Press into his abdomen with a quick upward thrust. Be gentle with smaller or younger children. Repeat until the object is expelled.
5. The next step, if the child remains unconscious and obstructed, is rescue breathing. With the child on his back, open his air passage by tilting his head back and lifting his chin with your fingers. Pinch his nose, cover his mouth completely with yours, and breathe into him two times. Use just enough breath to make his chest rise. If you can't make his chest move, reposition the airway and attempt to give him two more breaths.
6. If the air does not enter the child's lungs, repeat steps 4 and 5. Continue to alternate rescue breathing and the Heimlich manoeuvre until the child resumes breathing or until help arrives.

How to give rescue breathing. Never give rescue breathing to a person who is breathing. With an adult, breathe at your natural speed. With a child, use slightly quicker, shorter breaths. Each of your breaths goes into the victim.

First open the air passages by properly positioning the child's head. Do this by tilting the forehead back while lifting up on the chin with your fingers. Maintain this position every time you provide a rescue breath.

With a child's small face, you can breathe into the nose and mouth together. (With an adult, breathe into the mouth while pinching the nose shut.)

Breathe into the victim, using only minimal force. (A small child's lungs cannot contain your entire exhalation.) Remove your lips, allowing the child's chest to contract while you take in your next breath. Breathe into the child again.

HOME FIRST-AID KIT

When an emergency situation develops, it is human nature to become upset and anxious. This is not the time to locate bandages, phone numbers and other first-aid equipment that may be scattered in various wardrobes throughout the house. It makes sense to keep a small first-aid kit in your house to be used in an emergency. A small box that you can purchase at your local hardware shop would suffice. If you have young children, you'll need to store it in a place they cannot reach. The following items should be included in the kit.

List of Emergency Telephone Numbers

- Obviously, you don't need to write down 999 – you'll remember that even in the worst emergency
- Your child's doctor
- A neighbour to call should you need an adult to assist you

First-Aid Equipment

- Small sterile bandages
- Larger sterile bandages or gauze pads
- An elastic bandage
- Eye patch
- Adhesive tape
- Ice pack
- Any emergency medication your child may require
- A thermometer
- Vaseline
- Small scissors
- Tweezers
- Antiseptic solution
- Antibiotic ointment
- Antifever medication (nonaspirin; either paracetamol or ibuprofen)
- A bulb syringe
- A tube of 1 per cent hydrocortisone cream

DENTAL DEVELOPMENT AND ORAL HEALTH

DR SPOCK COMMENTS

When I was a young man, I asked a wise old gentleman what the secret to a happy life was. 'Take care of your teeth!' was his reply. It was as good advice as I ever got.

As a parent, you can follow that same advice for your children and ensure that their teeth are healthy and a joy to behold. Increasingly, research is showing that oral health is closely linked to general health. We've stopped thinking of cavities as just a nuisance and now see them for what they are: chronic infections with serious health consequences. For example, children who suffer with tooth decay often have a harder time concentrating in school and may sleep poorly. Later in life, tooth decay increases the risk of delivering a baby prematurely and the risk of having a heart attack. Prevention is the key, and it starts even before your baby has teeth.

TOOTH DEVELOPMENT

Baby teeth. How and when will your baby's teeth come through? One baby may get her first tooth at three months, another not until eighteen months. Both are perfectly healthy, normal infants. The age of teething depends on a child's individual pattern of development; only very rarely does disease cause late tooth eruption.

The first two teeth to appear are usually the lower central incisors. The incisors are the front teeth with sharp cutting edges. The four upper incisors come in a few months later. At about one year, most babies have these six teeth, four on the top and two below. After this, there's usually a lull of several months before the next onslaught. Then six more teeth quickly appear: the two last lower incisors and all four first primary (baby) molars. The molars don't come in next to the incisor teeth but farther back, leaving space for the canine teeth.

After the first molars appear, there is a pause of several months. Then, usually between eighteen and twenty-four months, the canines fill in the spaces between the incisors and the molars. Canines are the pointed 'dog' teeth or 'eye' teeth. The last four baby teeth are the second primary molars, which come in right behind the first primary molars, usually in the third year. Remember, it's normal for babies to get their teeth either earlier or later than these average ages.

Permanent teeth. Between about age six and age fourteen is when a child's permanent teeth make their appearance. The six-year molars come through behind the baby molars. The baby teeth are lost in roughly the same order in which they came in. The baby teeth to be lost first are usually the lower central incisors. The permanent incisors, pushing up underneath, come into position where the baby tooth roots have been dissolved away. Eventually all the primary teeth become loose and fall out.

The permanent teeth that take the place of the baby molars are called bicuspids or premolars. The twelve-year molars (second permanent molars) come in behind the six-year molars. The third molars (eighteen-year molars, or wisdom teeth) may be impacted in the jaw and may need to be removed so they won't do any damage to neighbouring teeth or the bone of the jaws. Permanent teeth often appear with jagged edges (called mammelons). Either they wear down or the dentist can trim them. Also, permanent teeth are more yellow than primary teeth.

Permanent teeth sometimes come in crooked or out of place, but they may eventually be straightened out by the muscular action of the tongue, lips and cheeks. If teeth don't straighten out, if they are crowded or crooked, or if the jaw alignment is abnormal, then orthodontic treatment (braces) may be required for bite improvement.

TEETHING

Symptoms of teething. Teething has different effects on different babies. One chews things, frets, drools, has a hard time getting to sleep and generally makes life miserable for the family for a month or two as each tooth comes through. Another baby acquires teeth with no fuss at all. Teeth or no teeth, most babies start to drool at around three to four months as their salivary glands become more active. Don't be fooled into thinking that drooling always means that teething has started.

Since babies get twenty teeth in their first three years, it's easy to understand why they always seem to be cutting teeth, and why it's so easy to blame every ailment on teething. Before viruses and bacteria were discovered, people thought that teething caused colds, diarrhoea and fevers. In fact, some babies have facial flushing, drooling, irritability, ear rubbing and mildly raised temperatures (less than 38°C/100.4°F) during teething. Cough, congestion, vomiting and diarrhoea are not teething symptoms. Mainly, teething causes teeth! If your baby is sick, talk with the doctor; don't simply assume that teething is the cause.

Help for teething. Any teeth may distress a baby, but the first four molar teeth, which erupt around twelve to eighteen months, are more likely to cause trouble than the others. What to do? First, let her chew! Provide chewable objects that are dull and soft enough so that when she falls with them in her mouth, they won't do any damage. Rubber teething rings of various shapes are good. Avoid toys made from thin, brittle plastic, which could break and cause choking, and objects that might be coated with lead paint (that is, anything painted before about 1980, and possibly items imported from overseas). Board books are safe for babies to chew on; they're lead-free, and they get soggy but don't break into pieces a baby could choke on.

Cold things usually help. You can try tying an ice cube or a piece of apple in a square of cloth, or try the cool, damp cloth alone. Some parents swear by frozen bagels or frozen slices of banana. Be creative! Many babies love to have their gums firmly rubbed. And don't fret about germs on the teething ring or piece of cloth. Your baby is putting all sorts of things in her mouth anyway, none of which are germ-free. Of course, it's a good idea to wash the teething ring after it has fallen on the floor or after the dog has slobbered over it.

Ask your child's doctor before giving any medication for teething. There are lots of teething gels on the market that may offer some relief, but some contain potentially dangerous medications. A dose of paracetamol (Calpol) can help with teething discomfort now and then, but even this safe medicine can be harmful if you give too much or for too many days.

WHAT MAKES GOOD TEETH?

Nutrition for strong teeth. Growing teeth need proper nutrition, including calcium and phosphorus, vitamin D and vitamin C. Tooth development actually begins before birth, so pregnant women need to make sure they are getting all of these nutrients. Good sources for calcium and phosphorus include vegetables, cereals, calcium-supplemented juices and milk (see pages 374 and 378 for the advantages of nondairy diets.) Sources for vitamin D include fortified milk, vitamin drops and sunshine (see page 372). Good sources of vitamin C include most fruits (especially citrus), vitamin drops, raw tomatoes, cabbage and breast milk.

Timing is also important. Frequent snacking throughout

the day encourages cavities. The mouth needs time to clean itself between meals. Young children need three meals and three snacks; older children should snack once or not at all. Sugary foods that stick to the teeth feed the bacteria that cause cavities.

Fluoride. It only takes a little fluoride in a mother's diet during pregnancy and in the growing child's diet to make teeth decay-resistant. Fluoride is a naturally occurring mineral; we all have it in our teeth and bones. Fluoride makes the tooth enamel resistant to the action of acid.

In regions with high levels of natural fluoride in the water, tooth decay is rare. The fluoride added to the water in some parts of the UK does the same thing. Adequate fluoridation is 0.7 to 1.0 parts per million. To find out if your water has enough fluoride, you can call the information number on your water bill and request that information.

If your water is low on fluoride, if your family mostly drinks bottled water, or if you use a home purification system that takes out all the fluoride and other minerals, then ask your doctor before taking a fluoride supplement. Most toothpastes also contain fluoride in the UK.

Fluoride for babies and children. If you're breast-feeding and you are drinking fluoridated water, you don't need to give your baby extra fluoride. If your water is not fluoridated, ask your doctor or dentist about giving your baby an infant vitamin with fluoride. Baby formulas do not contain much fluoride, but if you are mixing the formula with fluoridated water, your child is getting plenty of fluoride. If not, consider adding fluoride drops.

If you're giving fluoride drops, it's important to use the right amount. Too much fluoride can cause unattractive white and brown specks on the teeth. Your child's doctor or dentist can tell you how much to give. Fluoridated toothpastes strengthen tooth enamel, but too much fluoride can cause chalky or brown discolouration of the teeth. Children who eat toothpaste (that is, *most* young children) may get too much fluoride, so make sure you use the correct toothpaste for your child's age. For babies use a smear of toothpaste and for older children put a pea-size amount on the brush. It's best to keep toothpaste away from a young child who might decide that it's really delicious.

EARLY DENTIST VISITS

It's a good idea to take your child to the dentist as soon as the first tooth erupts. Early preventive visits allow the dentist to detect problems when they can be solved more easily and painlessly. A child who has positive early experiences in the dentist's chair comes to look forward to dentist appointments, not dread them. Most future visits will be preventive in nature, rather than the traditional 'drill and fill' sessions that haunt the childhood memories of so many adults.

Early care is especially important if you yourself have had bad dental experiences. Tooth decay and gum disease are often passed from parent to child. Early care can help your child take a different path. If your child does have dental problems, then it is especially important that you develop a relationship with a dentist you can trust. More and more dentists see it as their job to create a 'dental home' for each child, just as paediatricians try to create a 'medical home'. Certainly, if dental troubles run in your family, then a dental home is what your child should have.

TOOTH DECAY

Bacteria and plaque. How does tooth decay happen? Bacteria living in the mouth combine with food debris to form a material called dental plaque that sticks to the teeth. The bacteria make acid. The acid dissolves the minerals that make up the teeth, eventually destroying them. The more hours of the day that plaque remains on the teeth, the greater the number of bacteria and the more acid they make.

The bacteria thrive on sugar and starch. Anything that keeps sugars sitting in the mouth is good for the bacteria and bad for the teeth. That's why frequent between-meal snacking promotes tooth decay. Especially harmful are lollipops, sticky sweets and dried fruit, sugary drinks (fizzy drinks and juice) and biscuits, which cling to the teeth.

Saliva contains substances that help teeth resist attack by bacteria. Since the body makes less saliva during sleep, nighttime is when cavities are most likely to form. When children go to bed with food and plaque stuck to their teeth, the bacteria have all night long to do their dirty work. That is why it is so important to clean the teeth before bed and avoid sugary bedtime snacks.

Chewing gum. Regular chewing gum is terrible for teeth, because it keeps sugar in the mouth for long periods of time, feeding the harmful bacteria. Sugar-free chewing gum is a different story altogether. The main sweeteners in sugar-free gum, xylitol and sorbitol, are poisonous to cavity-causing bacteria. Chewing four or more times a day actually prevents cavities. If your child likes to chew, the choice is clear.

Parents who have bad teeth. If you have lots of cavities yourself, you need to take special care to protect your children from the bacteria that are destroying your teeth. See a dentist if you can. Rinse with an antiseptic mouthwash two or three times a day to kill the germs. Chew sugar-free gum, especially gum with xylitol (see above). Don't share spoons or cups with your child, and don't share your child's food; don't clean off your baby's dummy in your mouth, or put your baby's fingers in your mouth. Give your baby his own toothbrush.

Early childhood cavities (bottle mouth decay). When formula or breast milk sits on a baby's teeth, the sugars in it promote the growth of cavity-forming bacteria. Normally, there is enough time between feedings for the flow of saliva to clean off the teeth. But when babies keep a nipple in their mouths much of the time, this normal cleaning may not have a chance to occur. Similarly, putting honey on a baby's dummy – a common practice in some communities – puts the baby at risk for severe tooth decay.

The upper front teeth are most at risk, because the

tongue covers the lower teeth during nursing and sucking. The worst bottle mouth decay happens when babies fall asleep with the bottle or a beaker in their mouths. As they sleep the formula just sits on their teeth, while the bacteria multiply away.

Bottle mouth decay can start even before the first birthday. Sometimes nursing cavities are so severe that the infected teeth have to be removed. For this reason, babies should not be put to bed with a bottle or cup of milk, juice or any sweetened fluid. The only safe fluid for a bedtime bottle is water. Even diluted sweet fluids can promote decay. For nursing babies, it's best to brush their gums and teeth after they nurse and before they fall asleep.

BRUSHING AND FLOSSING

Effective brushing. To keep your child's teeth healthy, get rid of dental plaque before it can do its nasty work. For cleaning your baby's teeth, use a soft-bristled (not medium or firm) toothbrush. There is a myth that one should use a gauze pad or a cloth to wipe a baby's teeth and gums so as not to damage the delicate gum tissue. But those delicate gum tissues chew on table legs, cots, coffee tables, siblings and anything else in their way. Brush, don't wipe. Babies love it.

A child's teeth should be brushed after breakfast and before bedtime, with flossing between adjoining teeth before the evening brushing. If possible, an after-lunch brushing is helpful, too, to remove food residue. Start before one year old so your baby accepts brushing as a normal part of the day. (If your child doesn't have teeth yet, start by wiping the gums.) If your child resists, insist. Brushing should be like seat belts: not optional.

Starting at about two, your child may insist on doing everything herself, but few children have the manual dexterity required for proper brushing and flossing until they are older. You can let your child begin the brushing by herself from the earliest ages, but you will probably need to finish up to ensure that all dental plaque has been eliminated. You can gradually let your child take over as she proves capable, usually between six and ten years.

Flossing. Some parents question the need to floss a child's teeth, but in most cases teeth in the back of a child's mouth contact each other on the sides. Even some front teeth may tightly contact neighbouring teeth. When teeth are so close together, food and dental plaque accumulate between them. No matter how vigorously or carefully those areas are brushed, the toothbrush bristles cannot penetrate and clear out the food and plaque. Dental floss dislodges all that debris so the toothbrush can sweep it away.

It's worthwhile getting your child used to gentle flossing as soon as you notice the teeth touching. Your child's dentist or dental hygienist can demonstrate all the methods used to hold a child for perfect brushing and flossing. When your child is able to brush and floss effectively without your help, she will already be accustomed to the daily habit.

DENTAL VARNISH AND SEALANTS

You can ask your dentist about applying fluoride varnish to your child's teeth. This is a quick, safe, and painless process that can make a big difference.

Older children often benefit from sealants. Many teeth have small grooves or pitted areas in the enamel, where food and plaque can build up and cause pit-and-fissure caries. Dental sealants are liquid resins that flow across the tooth surface and fill the grooves and pits so that food can't get in. Sealants don't bond to primary teeth as well as to permanent teeth. Sometimes dentists seal primary molars, but most sealants are used on permanent teeth. Sealants last for many years, but depending on a child's diet and oral habits, they eventually need to be repaired or replaced.

DENTAL INJURIES

Dental injuries can occur in all teeth, although the teeth in the front of the mouth are most commonly traumatized. Teeth can be cracked, displaced from their sockets or completely knocked out. Dentists are concerned about trauma to primary teeth as well as to permanent teeth. Parents should always consult their child's dentist after tooth trauma. Some injuries are not easily seen; dentists are trained to make a complete diagnosis and perform the proper treatment.

Cracked teeth. A tooth is composed of three layers: the outer protective enamel, the internal supportive structure (dentin) and the soft tissue centre of the tooth (dental pulp), which contains the nerves. A crack (fracture) in a tooth can affect any or all of these layers. A small fracture may require only smoothing by the dentist, using a sandpaper-type of instrument. A more extensive crack may require a dental restoration to reestablish the form, function and appearance of the tooth. If a cracked tooth bleeds, it may be that the sensitive pulp is exposed. A dentist needs to see the child as soon as possible to repair the damage and prevent loss of the pulp.

Loosened teeth. Most slightly loosened teeth will reattach themselves and become stable after a few days' rest, without any special treatment. Sometimes, however, teeth are so loose that the dentist needs to splint them together to stabilize them while healing occurs. Antibiotics may be needed to prevent infection of the dental pulp and attachment tissues. A soft diet for a period of time helps the healing process.

Avulsed teeth. If a tooth is completely knocked out of the mouth, dentists say it is *avulsed.* If a baby tooth is avulsed, it's usually best to leave it out. A permanent tooth should be reimplanted as quickly as possible, usually within thirty minutes, to maximize the chance of keeping the pulp alive. First, make sure that the tooth is indeed permanent and that it is intact. Gently hold the tooth by the crown (the part that shows in the mouth), not by the pointed roots.

Rinse the tooth very gently under tap water. Do not scrub or rub the root in any way; that will damage the attached tissue, which is required for reattachment. Insert the tooth back into its normal position. If you cannot reimplant the tooth, place it in a glass of milk or in a commercially available 'tooth rescue' container. Then take the child to the nearest dentist or seek dental emergency service by calling NHS Direct (0845 46 47 in England and Wales; 08454 24 24 24 in Scotland). Time is important with permanent tooth avulsions. After a tooth has been out of the mouth for thirty minutes, the chances for successful reimplantation drop fast.

PREVENTING MOUTH INJURIES

Young children fall a lot, and their teeth are located at a perfect height to crash into coffee tables and similar objects. As much as possible, try to crashproof your toddler's cruising area by moving these things away. Take extraordinary care to make sure your toddler doesn't have the opportunity to bite any electrical wires. Don't let your child parade around the house with a toothbrush in her mouth. The brush can do serious damage if she falls.

The risk of dental injuries rises once children begin to play sports. A rounders player can be struck by a ball or bat, by a team member going after the same ball, or by an opposing player running around the bases. Similar catastrophes happen in nearly every sport. Children in organized sports generally need to wear a comfortable protective mouth guard – sort of a crash helmet for the teeth.

Mouth guards are sold at sporting goods stores or pharmacies, or your child's dentist can make a custom-fitted mouth guard. Rough individual activities such as roller skating, skateboarding and martial arts also call for mouth guards.

COMMON CHILDHOOD ILLNESSES

Every parent has to deal with colds and coughs, and it's the rare child who doesn't develop diarrhoea at least once. Thanks to vaccines, many serious infections that used to be common are now rare. I'm pretty sure I've never seen an actual child with measles, although I've read about the disease. But new threats emerge each year or two, and chronic conditions such as asthma and eczema are on the rise. Knowing something about the common illnesses of childhood, and some of the uncommon ones, can help you feel more confident to handle problems as they arise. The information that follows, however, isn't meant to be a substitute for a doctor's judgment.

I've organized the sections following roughly by the part of the body most affected: diseases that affect the airways, from the nose and ears to the lungs; those that affect the digestive system, from the oesophagus down to the rectum; those that affect the skin; and so on. Other conditions have ended up in sections on emergencies or prevention (see pages 448–534). If you don't find what you need below, please check the index.

COLDS

What common colds look like. If your baby has a cold during the first six months or so, the chances are that it will be mild. He may sneeze in the beginning; his nose will be runny or bubbly or stuffy. He may cough a little. He is not likely to have any fever. When his nose is bubbly, you might wish you could blow it for him, but it doesn't seem to bother him. On the other hand, if his nose is obstructed with thick mucus, it may make him frantic. He keeps trying to close his mouth and is angry when he can't breathe. The stuffiness may bother him most when he tries to nurse at the breast or bottle, so much so that he refuses altogether at times. But after a few days he starts to get better, and within a couple of weeks he's back to normal.

Older children may have the same mild colds or they can be more dramatic. Here is a common story. A little girl of two is well during the morning. At lunchtime she seems a little tired and has less appetite than usual. When she wakes up from her nap, she is cranky and her parents notice that she is hot. They take her temperature, and it's 38.8°C (102°F). By dinnertime, the temperature is 40°C (104°F). Her cheeks are flushed and her eyes are dull, but otherwise she doesn't seem particularly sick. She may want no supper at all, or she may want a fair amount. She has no cold symptoms, except that her throat is perhaps a little red. The next day she may have a little fever, but now her nose may begin to run. Perhaps she coughs occasionally. After three or four days, the mucus from her nose may change from clear to yellow or green. Maybe she vomits once or twice. But from this point on, it's just a regular mild cold that runs its course in a week or two.

What's happening during a cold? Colds are caused by any one of about a hundred different viruses or other germs. The most common culprits are picornaviruses (translation: little RNA viruses) including the appropriately named rhinovirus (that is, 'nose virus'). These viruses don't do much damage themselves, it's the child's immune system that causes the cold symptoms.

Cold viruses usually enter the body through the nose or eyes, most often carried there on a child's own hands; less often, they fly in, propelled by a sneeze. Once inside, they get into the cells that make up the lining of the nose or throat, and start reproducing the way viruses do. The body responds by releasing chemicals that cause blood vessels to leak fluid into the tissues, resulting in swelling. Other immune signals trigger mucus production and fever. White blood cells rush to the scene, and the battle is on.

It's not always this exciting, however. Children and adults often acquire a cold virus but don't develop any symptoms worth noticing. But they can still pass the virus on, and the next victim might experience all the usual miseries.

When things get complicated. Colds aren't dangerous themselves, but sometimes they lead to worse infections. Cold viruses can lower the resistance to more troublesome bacteria, such as streptococci and pneumococci. These germs often live in healthy people's noses and throats during the winter and spring months but do no harm because they are held at bay by the immune system. It's only after the cold virus has taken hold that these other germs get their chance to multiply and spread. They can then cause infections in the middle ear (otitis media), nasal sinuses (sinusitis) or lungs (pneumonia).

You can tell when these secondary infections arise because the child gets sicker. Her appetite and energy may fall off. She may start running fevers. A fever on the first day of a cold isn't particularly concerning, but a new fever that begins after a cold is well under way often signals the start of a worse infection. Other red flags are ear pain, face pain, a worsening cough or rapid breathing. Any of these changes should trigger a call to the doctor.

Many doctors believe that any runny nose that persists beyond fourteen days should be treated as a bacterial sinus infection, with antibiotics. However, colds sometimes last longer than two weeks, as do allergies (see below). Mucus that turns from clear to green isn't a reliable sign of sinusitis, either; it's simply a sign that the immune system is working. As concerns about antibiotic overuse grow, doctors are becoming more careful about prescribing these drugs only when they are truly needed.

Things that look like colds but aren't. Most colds run their course in one or two weeks; sometimes it takes three. A runny nose that hangs on week after week may not be a cold at all but rather a nasal allergy. Itchy or runny eyes and thin, clear mucus are tips to look for. See page 567 for more on allergies.

When coughing is especially severe, consider the possibility of whooping cough (pertussis infection; see page 435). Don't be fooled: not all people with pertussis make the classic whooping noise, especially if the person with the infection is an older child or adult. When there is persistent dry coughing or wheezing along with the runny nose, the problem might be asthma. Cold viruses are a potent asthma trigger. It's important to consider this possibility, since there is effective medication specifically for asthma. Coughing and wheezing, when severe, can also be due to other infections, such as mycoplasma, which call for specific treatment. A doctor may need to listen to your child's chest or look at an X-ray to make these diagnoses.

An illness may start with a runny nose, cough and fever, but then the symptoms move down into the intestines, with vomiting and diarrhoea for several days. These infections are often caused by different viruses (often adenoviruses), and they may be a bit more severe, because more of the body is affected. See page 588 for more on vomiting and diarrhoea. If headaches, muscle aches and a general loss of energy are the main symptoms, along with fever, the diagnosis may be influenza (see page 562).

Treating a cold. We don't know how to kill cold viruses within the body; luckily, we don't have to. Colds get better on their own. The main point of treatment is to limit the discomfort while your child's immune system takes care of business.

Nasal syringe. For babies and young children, the first step is to unplug their noses. You can use a nasal syringe to suck the mucus out. Compress the bulb, insert the tip into the nose and release the bulb. Remember that the inside of the baby's nose is very sensitive, so don't push too hard. Better yet, buy a nasal syringe with a wide plastic tip that butts up against the nostril but doesn't actually fit inside the nose. This type works best because the tight seal between the nostrils and the tip allows the bulb to suck in air all the way from the back of the nose. With the right bulb, you don't have to worry about irritating the nose while you're cleaning it out.

Nose drops. For thick mucus, put a drop or two of saline solution into each nostril and let it sit there for about five minutes to soften the mucus before sucking it out. Babies hate this process but feel much better afterward. You can mix up a saline solution yourself (dissolve ¼ teaspoon of salt in 240 ml/8 fl oz of water) or buy saline nose drops over the counter. They're cheap and come with a handy dropper.

Avoid medicated nose drops. They work by shrinking blood vessels in the nose, decreasing secretions. But they don't work for long, and after a few treatments they work less and less. After that, the nose often becomes dependent on the drops so that the secretions increase as soon as you stop using the drops. The cure is worse than the disease. Also, some children have serious side effects to these medicines.

Vaporizers and humidifiers. Extra moisture in the room

can make secretions thinner or at least keep them from drying out so fast. How you add that moisture isn't important. In winter, the warmer you keep your home, the dryer the air becomes. A child with a cold might be more comfortable at 20°C (68°F) than at 23°C (74°F). An ultrasonic humidifier can cost as little as £20 or as much as £300. A regular cool-mist humidifier costing £20 or less does an adequate job. With either type be sure to clean the water reservoir at least once a week to prevent the growth of moulds and bacteria; use 240 ml (8 fl oz) of chlorine bleach mixed in 3.8 litres (7 pints) of water.

An electric steam vaporizer uses an electric heating element to boil water. But steam isn't any better than cool mist when it comes to adding moisture to the air. And with steam, there is a danger of scalding if a child puts his hand or face in the steam or knocks the vaporizer over. If you buy one of these steam vaporizers, get a large size that holds a litre (2 pints) or more and turns itself off when the water boils away. Pans of water on the radiator tend to spill, and don't actually add that much moisture.

Antibiotics. The usual antibiotics (amoxicillin, for instance) kill bacteria, but they don't do anything to the viruses that cause colds. Taking antibiotics for a cold may not cause your child any harm right then and there, unless he has an allergic reaction or develops diarrhoea. But over time, and for the population as a whole, the harm is serious. The overuse of antibiotics breeds strains of bacteria that are resistant to antibiotics. This means that the next time your child (or someone else) is truly ill, it's more likely that the usual antibiotics won't work (see page 1032).

Cough and cold medicines. There never was good evidence that over-the-counter cough and cold medicines actually work; now we know that they can be dangerous, especially for infants and young children. None of them should be given to children aged under six.

For older children, short-term (two or three days) treatment with a decongestant such as pseudoephedrine can sometimes relieve the pressure in blocked sinuses. But breathing in the vapour from a sinkful of hot water often works as well. Antihistamines work for allergies but don't do much for colds, and they can make children drowsy and sometimes irritable and overactive. Cough medicines containing dextromethorphan (often with 'DM' in the name) aren't effective. What's more, they can cause dangerous side effects and are sometimes abused by teens trying to get high. Honey is probably a better cough suppressant (see opposite).

Vitamins, supplements and herbs. There is no proof that larger-than-normal doses of vitamin C can prevent colds or make them go away sooner. For a while zinc looked like a possible cure, but more research showed that it didn't work for otherwise healthy children. People who have low zinc levels probably do benefit from taking zinc supplements, however. Echinacea is a herb that may help with colds in adults, but there isn't any proof that it helps for children. There are many different kinds of echinacea, and products made from them aren't tightly regulated, so it's hard to know what you're getting. Just because it's natural doesn't mean that it's safe.

Other nondrug treatments. Chicken soup might actually contain a substance that reduces cold symptoms. Even if it doesn't, the warmth is comforting, the liquid helps keep children well hydrated, the salt may help with electrolyte balance, and the protein and fat are nourishing. Truly, it couldn't hurt. Warm liquids of any kind are helpful. Massaging the back and chest is soothing, but menthol rubs probably don't help and may even make things worse. Gently massaging the forehead and under the eyes (moving your hands down and towards the nose) may help with sinus congestion. There isn't good evidence that milk thickens secretions, but there's no harm in avoiding it for a few days (unless it's all your child wants to drink). A drink of honey and lemon in warm water, with or without tea, may well be a more effective cough suppressant than any over-the-counter medicine. Children under one year shouldn't eat honey, though, because of the risk of botulism.

Preventing colds. A typical child aged under five will get six to eight colds a year; children who go to nursery or preschool get even more. With each cold the child gains immunity to the particular virus that caused it, but that still leaves dozens of cold viruses that the child hasn't yet been exposed to. Over time, as a child's immune system gains more 'experience', the number of colds decreases and their severity slacks off. A final bit of comfort: children who get a lot of colds early in life usually don't get as many later on.

The best things you can do to prevent colds is to avoid close physical contact with anyone who has one, but this is easier said than done if your child goes to nursery or school. Good hand-washing (see page 428) helps. Alcohol-based hand sanitizers may kill cold viruses even better than soap and water. Children should also be taught to cough into their sleeve (not their hand) and to blow their nose into tissues that then go into the bin.

Staying inside when the weather is cold doesn't prevent colds. Just the opposite: it's because children stay cooped up inside during the winter with the windows closed that cold viruses spread so easily. Cold air does make noses run, but only viruses cause colds.

You can increase your child's ability to fight off colds by helping her to eat and sleep well and by keeping your home free of cigarette smoke. Secondhand smoke interferes with the cells in the nose and throat that are responsible for expelling mucus-coated viruses. Children exposed to secondhand smoke may not contract more viruses, but they get sicker and stay sicker longer. If you smoke, this is a good reason to stop.

You can also work on keeping your home as stress-free as possible (for example, keeping shouting to a minimum). Chronic stress increases the level of cortisol, a hormone that reduces immune system function. About one child out of seven inherits genes that make him especially vulnerable to the negative effects of stress (see page 764). But vulnerability or no vulnerability, a peaceful home is healthier for everyone.

EAR INFECTIONS

What is in an ear? To understand ear infections, you have to understand ears. The part of the ear that you can see (the pinna) collects sound waves and funnels them down the ear canal. At the end of the canal, the waves bump into the eardrum, causing it to vibrate. The eardrum can vibrate because it has air on two sides – the air in the ear canal, and the air in the middle ear space. Tiny bones connected to the eardrum pick up the vibrations and transfer them through the middle ear to the inner ear, where an amazing little organ called the cochlea turns them into nerve signals and sends them to the brain.

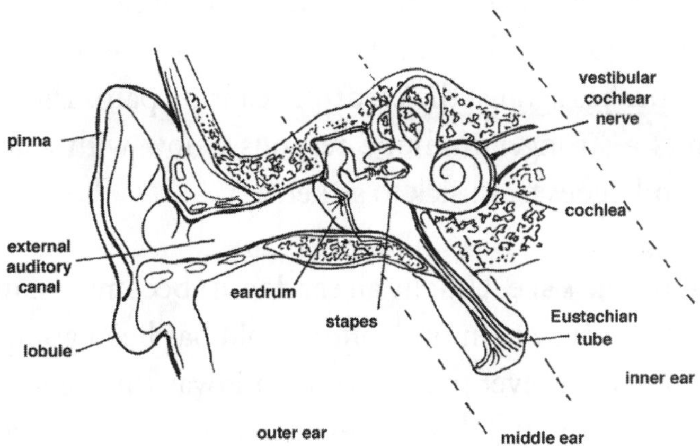

How ears get infected. The air in the middle ear is the key to understanding ear infections. The air gets there through the Eustachian tubes, which connect the middle ear to the back of the throat. These tubes, alas, can let in more than air. When germs from the nose and throat get through the Eustachian tubes, they can fill the middle ear with infected pus. The medical term for this process is *otitis media*, which means inflammation of the middle ear.

Otitis usually begins with a cold. As the body fights off the virus, tissues in the nose and throat swell up, causing stuffiness and affecting the Eustachian tubes. As a result, the tubes are less able to block germs from getting into the middle ear, and less able to expel any germs that do get in.

The first germs to get in are usually the same virus that caused the cold. These viral ear infections are really just part of the cold and, like the cold, are pretty easily defeated by the immune system. Sometimes, though, the virus is followed by a second wave of attack. Bacteria that had been living peacefully in the nose take advantage of the lowered defences to get into the middle ear and set up another, worse infection. The middle ear fills with pus, which pushes against the eardrum, causing pain. The body mounts a stronger immune response, now with a fever. Your child goes from sick to sicker.

What parents see. Usually an ear doesn't become inflamed enough to cause pain until after a cold has been going for several days. A fever that shows up midway through a cold together with irritability makes otitis media pretty likely. A child over two can often tell you what the matter is. His ear hurts, and he may not hear well because the pus in the middle ear is keeping the eardrum from vibrating normally. A baby may keep rubbing his ear or may just cry piercingly for several hours. He seems a little better when you pick him up, because the upright position lowers the pressure in his ear. Sometimes he vomits.

If there's enough pressure in the middle ear, a hole may open in the eardrum, letting the pus out. You might find dried pus and blood on your child's pillow. It sounds awful, but a ruptured eardrum often comes as a great relief to the child and speeds the healing of the infection. You can put a cotton ball loosely in the ear to soak up the pus. It is not safe to introduce a cotton swab into the ear canal to clean the pus since you may accidentally bump the inflamed eardrum, further hurting and damaging it. Medicated ear drops may also be helpful (see below).

Helping the pain. Ear infections can be painful. Keeping your child's head propped up reduces the pressure against the eardrum. A hot-water bottle or an electric heating pad may help, but small children are often impatient with them. (Don't let a child fall asleep on a heating pad; this could result in a burn.) Paracetamol or ibuprofen in the usual doses can provide some relief. Antipyrine and benzocaine ear drops, a prescription medication, can deaden the ache. For severe pain, a doctor can prescribe paracetamol with codeine, although this is rarely necessary. Antibiotics take about seventy-two hours to kick in; therefore, it's a good idea to keep the child on some pain relief medication, such as ibuprofen, round the clock for the first three days.

Over-the-counter cough and cold medicines including decongestants and antihistamines have not been shown to help ear infections, nor have any herbal or homeopathic preparations. But sugar-free gum made with xylitol may actually reduce symptoms of ear infections, because xylitol kills the bacteria that cause most ear infections. Vigorous chewing can sometimes help open up a blocked Eustachian tube, as can blowing up balloons. Tender, loving care (TLC) and quiet reassurance always help, of course.

Antibiotics, or not. It used to be that every ear infection got antibiotics. That has changed. Now we know that the body can fight off most ear infections on its own. Only very rarely does an ear infection spread to nearby tissues, and close observation almost always lets us catch these infections early enough to treat them effectively.

The main reason to hold off on antibiotics is that overuse of antibiotics encourages the development of resistant bacteria. When resistant bacteria emerge – and it has been happening for many years now – doctors have to use ever more exotic, expensive and potentially harmful antibiotics, and they worry more about 'supergerms' that are almost impossible to treat. The more often your child gets a course of antibiotics, the more likely she is to get sick with bacteria that those antibiotics can't kill. The solution to this problem is to use antibiotics only when they are truly necessary. Doctors and parents have to do this together.

Often, a doctor looking at a child's eardrum can't be certain whether there is truly infected pus behind it. Perhaps it's an ear infection in the early (viral) stage, which is very likely to get better on its own. In these cases, it's wise to hold off on the antibiotics, treat the pain and look again in forty-eight to seventy-two hours. By then a lot of the children are better; if not, then it may be time to start antibiotics. Antibiotics make sense for young children who have clear-cut ear infections with fever and other signs of severe illness, and for children who have underlying problems with their immune systems or anatomical problems such as cleft palates.

If the doctor does prescribe antibiotics, be sure to give every dose for the full course of treatment. Stopping early when a child improves is another good way to breed resistant bacteria. If your child throws up a dose right after swallowing it, give the dose again. If your child throws up several doses or develops a rash or diarrhoea, or if she is still miserable and running a fever in forty-eight hours, call the doctor. Sometimes a different antibiotic will be necessary.

Preventing ear infections. There are many things you can do to prevent ear infections. Breast-feeding boosts the child's immune system and exercises the muscles attached to the Eustachian tubes. Bottle-fed babies should take their bottles sitting in a parent's arms rather than lying flat, because lying flat allows milk to pool in the Eustachian tubes, encouraging bacteria to enter. Young children in child care settings where there are fewer than ten children have fewer colds and fewer ear infections; those who stay at home have fewer yet. Secondhand smoke blocks key Eustachian tube defences. Children who are protected from cigarette smoke have far fewer ear infections. Chronic allergies can set a child up for ear infections, so these are worth considering (see page 567). Rarely, repeated ear infections are due to an underlying immune system problem; talk with your child's doctor if you think this might be so.

Chronic ear infections (otitis media with effusion). After the bacteria have been killed off, it's common for some fluid (effusion) to remain in the middle ear. The way a child with an ear effusion hears is the way you would hear if you plug your ears with your finger. This is one reason why a child may tug on his ear even after an ear infection has been cured; thus, persistent ear tugging is *not* a reason for another course of antibiotics. This fluid generally gets absorbed in three months. Meanwhile, language development or a child's ability to pay attention may suffer. This doesn't always happen, but if a child has other reasons for language or attention problems, repeated ear infections or persistent fluid in the middle ear probably make the situation worse. You should think about this possibility if your child has more than three ear infections in a year, or if you think your child may not be hearing, paying attention or speaking normally.

The first step is a hearing test. No child is too young to have one. If your child's hearing is decreased and doesn't return to normal in two or three months, then consultation with an ear, nose and throat specialist is in order. We don't have good medicines to treat otitis media with effusion, but surgery to drain the middle ear may help. The usual operation involves putting little plastic tubes or grommets through the eardrums. This is one of the most common operations done on young children. Unfortunately, there's debate about whether this operation improves language development or attention.

Swimmer's ear (otitis externa). So far I've been talking about infections in the middle ear. The skin lining the external ear canal can also become infected, a condition called *otitis externa*. These infections start with a breakdown of the skin's normal defences, usually because of a small scratch or persistent dampness in the ear canal, or following a draining middle ear infection. The main symptom is pain that becomes worse with tugging on the ear. Sometimes there is pus or an odour. (A very bad odour should make you think about something stuck in the ear; see page 502.) Paracetamol or ibuprofen can help with the pain. Prescription ear drops with antibiotic and anti-inflammatory properties are the main treatment.

To prevent otitis externa, teach your child to use a hair dryer to dry out her ears after swimming (caution: set the heat to low to avoid burns). You can also use a couple of drops of water mixed with an equal amount of white vinegar. This will increase the acidity of the ear canal enough to discourage most bacteria from growing. Finally, don't work too hard to get all the ear wax out of your child's ears. Ear wax (like car wax) serves a protective function. If you clean it all out, you remove that protection and may scratch the canal in the process.

SORE THROATS AND STREP THROATS

Most sore throats are caused by the same viruses that cause colds. These infections are usually mild and get better on their own. Sore throats caused by streptococcus bacteria – that is, strep throat – are more serious. Strep throat also usually gets better on its own, but rarely the infection spreads into the tissues of the neck, a very dangerous complication. The main concern about strep throat, though, is that it can cause rheumatic fever. This is a chronic, difficult-to-treat condition that can include joint pain, serious heart disease and other ailments. It's not something to fool around with. The good news is that treating strep throat with common antibiotics can pretty much entirely erase the threat of rheumatic fever. The bad news is you have to diagnose strep before you can treat it.

Strep, or just a sore throat? A classic case of strep throat is easy to spot. The child usually has a high fever for a number of days and throat pain so severe he can hardly swallow. He's miserable. The tonsils become fiery red and swollen, and after a day or two white spots or patches appear on them. The glands (lymph nodes) in the neck are also swollen and tender. The child has a headache and stomachache, and generally lacks energy. His breath has a musty, unpleasant odour. A runny nose and cough are more often caused by viruses rather than strep; when they're present, strep is less likely.

The problem with this description is, it's not always so. Any of the classic symptoms may be absent. A child with a low fever, mild sore throat and pink tonsils *could* have strep (although he probably just has a throat virus). Young children may be bothered surprisingly little by the sore throat; strep throat is rare under age two. A child who has had his tonsils removed can still have strep. Because it's hard to be certain that a sore throat isn't strep, it's probably wise to have a doctor evaluate any sore throat that accompanies fever of 38.6°C (101.4°F) or more.

Rather than guess, we swab the tonsils and order a lab test. If a rapid test is available, the answer usually comes back in an hour or two; if we have to rely on a culture, it can take a couple of days. Delaying treatment for two days doesn't matter with respect to preventing rheumatic fever; the antibiotics still work very well for that. A common treatment is ten days of bubble-gum-flavoured antibiotics, morning, afternoon and night.

If the tests come back negative for strep, your child probably just has a virus. Rest, paracetamol or ibuprofen, and plenty of fluids help. Warm salt water gargles and throat lozenges for children old enough not to choke (after age four or five) are also good comfort measures.

Sometimes your doctor may discourage you from getting a strep test if there are features of a viral illness, such as a runny nose. Some people harbour strep in their throats. A strep test done on such a person will give a false positive result: the strep is there, but it's not the cause of the problem. If we treat anyway, we haven't helped anything but have merely increased the risk of drug resistance. Even experienced doctors have a hard time pinpointing strep accurately.

Scarlet fever. Although people often regard scarlet fever with dread – remember poor Beth March in *Little Women* – it's usually nothing more than a strep throat with a characteristic rash. The rash typically appears a day or two after the child gets sick. It begins on the warm, moist parts of the body, such as the sides of the chest, the groin and the back. From a distance it looks like a uniform red flush, but if you look at it closely, you can see that it is made up of tiny red spots on a reddish background. If you run your hand over this rash, it feels like fine sandpaper. It may spread over the whole body and the sides of the face, but the region around the mouth stays pale. The tongue may look like a strawberry, red with white dots. When scarlet fever accompanies a sore throat, the treatment is the same as for a regular case of strep. Occasionally a different germ causes scarlet fever and requires different treatment. Once the child recovers from scarlet fever or even a simple strep throat, you may notice some peeling of skin. This problem goes away without any special treatment.

Tonsillectomy. Up until recently, it was common practice for children who had frequent sore throats to have their tonsils taken out. The operation was so common that it seemed almost a normal part of childhood. That practice began to change after research showed that only children with very frequent sore throats – one criterion was seven or more episodes in the preceding year – actually benefited from the operation. And even in these unusual cases, the pain and risks from the surgery have to be weighed against the benefits of two or perhaps three fewer sore throats. Tonsillectomy is becoming much less common, but it still has a role, mainly for children with sleep apnea (page 566).

Other kinds of sore throat. There are all kinds and degrees of throat infections caused by a variety of germs, mainly viruses. Many people feel a slight sore throat at the beginning of every cold. Often the doctor, in examining a child with a fever, finds a mildly red throat as the only sign of disease. The child may or may not notice any soreness. Some children awaken many winter mornings with sore throats. They're otherwise well, and the sore throat goes away shortly. The problem is due to dry winter air, not illness. Runny, stuffy noses can also cause sore throats, especially in the early morning, because mucus runs down the back of the throat during the night, causing irritation.

Mononucleosis. A severe sore throat, often with fever, malaise and swollen glands, may be infectious mononucleosis (glandular fever), usually caused by the Epstein-Barr virus. This can be a mild infection or quite severe; it usually lasts for a week or two but it can drag on. The disease is more common in teenagers; the virus spreads via saliva, giving rise to the nickname 'kissing disease'. There is no specific treatment for glandular fever, but a doctor should test to make sure the diagnosis isn't strep and do a careful examination looking for an enlarged liver or spleen, which require special care.

Diphtheria. In its heyday, this bacterial infection killed thousands each year. Now, it's very rare, thanks to immunization (diphtheria is the 'D' in DTaP vaccinations). The bacteria are still around, though, and threaten to come back if immunization levels drop. The signature feature of this infection is a greyish membrane covering the tonsils, with lots of swelling but not much fever. Death is through suffocation.

Swollen glands. The lymph nodes, or glands, that are scattered up and down the sides of the neck can become sore and swollen as a result of any infection in the throat, mouth or ears. The swelling is normal, part of the body's healthy immune response. Lymph nodes can remain large for weeks or months. Occasionally the glands themselves become infected. In these cases, they are often very swollen, warm or tender. A doctor needs to evaluate all such large neck swellings. Treatment is with antibiotics. It's natural, with any swelling on the body, for parents to worry about cancer. Cancers with neck swelling are rare in children, but of course you should talk with the doctor if you have any concerns.

CROUP AND EPIGLOTTITIS

What croup looks like. A two-year-old boy develops what seems to be a common cold, with a runny nose and an unimpressive fever of 38°C (100.4°F). Two days later, around 9 pm, he starts coughing, making a loud, harsh barking noise. When he breathes in between coughs he makes a different, almost musical sound. The skin sucks in over his collarbones and between his ribs, showing that he is working hard to breathe. Worried, his parents bundle him into the car and drive twenty minutes to the hospital. By the time they get there, he looks much better.

This is a typical picture of croup. For some reason, boys are affected about twice as often as girls. The illness hits infants and toddlers, from about six months to three years, usually in late autumn or early winter. It begins with a cold. In croup, however, the infection moves from the nose down into the larynx, near the vocal cords. The windpipe is normally narrow there, and the swelling caused by the virus narrows it even further. When the child breathes out forcefully past this obstruction, the thickened vocal cords make a barking noise. When he breathes in, the swollen walls of the windpipe collapse towards each other, further blocking the airway and causing a loud noise called stridor. The cough and stridor are almost always worse at night. They can come on suddenly but also can improve almost as quickly, often after the child has been exposed to cool night air.

Croup is scary when you see it for the first time, but it's rarely as serious as it looks. It often sends children to A&E but seldom results in permanent harm. Some unlucky children have several bouts during their early years. In these children, the trigger may be an allergic reaction rather than a virus, a variation called *spasmodic croup*. In the last few years, we've learned effective treatments that make the disease even less dangerous.

Emergency treatment. Stridor, the loud noise on inhalation, always requires a prompt call to the doctor, if not an emergency hospital visit. Even though croup is rarely dangerous, there are other causes of stridor that can be quite threatening. For instance, the child may have an object lodged in his throat, or he may have *epiglottitis* (see below) or a rare but serious bacterial infection of the windpipe called *tracheitis.*

Don't panic, but do act quickly. If you cannot be seen by your doctor right away, take your child to a hospital. Medicines are available that can open up the airway in croup, but these can only be given in a hospital. Any child who is struggling to breathe should have doctors and nurses nearby, just in case.

Home treatment. If the stridor isn't too severe and your child is comfortable and able to drink normally, the doctor may advise you to stay home. Traditionally, we've urged parents to fill the bathroom with warm mist from the shower and sit in there with their croupy child. Recent research shows that humid air may be less effective in reducing croup symptoms than cool air. If the air in your home is very dry, then it does make sense to add some humidity. Perhaps most important, try to keep your child calm. An upset, scared child breathes harder and faster, making croup much worse. Probably the best way to calm your child is to stay calm yourself. A story from a book, or one you make up, can make the time pass more pleasantly.

If your child calms down promptly, she can go back into her cot or bed. You or another adult should stay awake as long as there are any symptoms of croup, and wake up two or three hours after the croup is over to make sure the child is breathing comfortably. Croup symptoms often fade away by morning, only to return the next night, and sometimes for two or three more nights after that.

Epiglottitis. This infection is now quite rare, thanks to the Hib (*Haemophilus influenza* type B) immunization. Epiglottitis looks like severe croup with a high fever. The epiglottis is a small bit of tissue that forms the trap door at the top of the windpipe, to keep food out. If it becomes infected and swollen, it can block off the windpipe altogether.

A child with epiglottitis becomes ill very quickly. He leans forward, drools, refuses to take any food or liquids, and will usually make no sounds at all. He may be unwilling to turn his head in any direction, because he's keeping his neck in the position that gives him the most room for air to pass between the swollen epiglottis and the windpipe. Epiglottitis is a true medical emergency, and everything must be done to get the child to a hospital right away, while keeping him as calm as possible.

BRONCHITIS, BRONCHIOLITIS AND PNEUMONIA

Bronchitis. The largest tubes in the lung are called *bronchi.* When they're inflamed, almost always because of infection with a virus, it's called *bronchitis.* There is usually plenty of coughing and sometimes a low fever. Parents worry when they think they hear mucus vibrating in the chest. Actually, the rattling usually starts higher up in the throat, although the noise is transmitted to the chest. This sort of noisy breathing usually isn't a sign of serious illness.

A mild case of bronchitis, with no fever or loss of appetite, is only a little worse than a cold in the nose. The treatment is the same as for a bad cold: rest, fluids in moderation, honey in milk or water to soothe the cough (for children over twelve months) and tender loving care. Antibiotics don't kill viruses and don't help at all with bronchitis. Over-the-counter cough suppressants aren't effective for children and can be dangerous; – avoid them altogether.

Call the doctor if your child acts sick (no energy, exhausted, dull or limp), becomes short of breath, breathes rapidly when at rest, or has a fever of more than 38.3°C (101°F). Bronchitis can mimic other, more serious infections that may require treatment with antibiotics or even hospitalization, especially in children under six months of age.

Bronchiolitis (RSV). In bronchiolitis, the infection has moved from the larger breathing tubes (bronchi) down to smaller air passages in the lungs (bronchioles). The '-itis' at the end of the word means inflammation, a combination of swelling, mucus and white blood cells that narrows and partly blocks the air tubes. Of the several different viruses that cause bronchiolitis, the most common is RSV (respiratory syncytial virus). RSV infections spread easily through physical contact, most often in the winter months,

Bronchiolitis typically hits children between two and twenty-four months. It starts with a cold, often with fever, followed by cough, wheezing and difficulty breathing.

When the child breathes in, his nostrils flare out, while the skin around his ribs and above his collarbone sucks inward. Doctors learn to look for these signs – flaring and retractions – as well as breathing rate as markers of severe illness. Rapid breathing is an important sign: any child who is consistently taking more than forty breaths per minute should be assessed; faster than sixty breaths a minute (one per second) requires immediate medical attention.

For mild cases, the best treatment is the same as for colds: rest, fluids (offer, but don't force), paracetamol or ibuprofen for fever, gentle suction to clear the nose. Comfortably humid air helps, but very high humidity (a steam bath or rain forest ambiance) will only make your child damp and miserable. A child who has had wheezing problems before might respond to the usual asthma medicine (mainly albuterol, page 1032), but children with bronchiolitis who are wheezing for the first time rarely do.

For severe bronchiolitis, children need to be in the hospital, where they can get extra oxygen if they need it. Extremely ill babies and children sometimes need intensive care. Premature infants and young children who have certain chronic conditions – especially heart or lung disease – should receive special injections during the winter to prevent severe RSV illness.

Pneumonia. In pneumonia, the infection has moved from the bronchi or bronchioles out to the substance of the lungs themselves. Unlike bronchitis and bronchiolitis, pneumonia is often caused by bacteria rather than viruses. Bacterial infections tend to be more serious, but unlike viral infections, they respond to antibiotics, either by mouth or injected. Pneumonias caused by viruses tend to get better on their own over two to four weeks. An X-ray can sometimes help sort out the different types of pneumonia.

Pneumonia usually sets in several days into a cold; sometimes, however, it starts without warning. Look for a fever over 38.8°C (102°F), rapid breathing (over forty breaths per minute) and frequent cough. A child with pneumonia will sometimes make a grunting noise. Children rarely bring up mucus, so don't let the absence of phlegm fool you. Not every child with pneumonia needs to be treated in the hospital, but every child who has a fever and frequent cough needs a medical evaluation.

INFLUENZA (THE FLU)

What to expect with the flu. Influenza is tricky, because the virus changes from year to year. In a usual year, it's miserable but not really dangerous. Sudden-onset fever, headaches and muscle aches are the hallmarks, often with a runny nose, sore throat, cough, vomiting and diarrhoea; it can last a week or two. A few children are sick enough to need hospitalization.

In an unusual year, things can be much worse. If the virus strain is especially contagious, the disease can spread fast, infecting almost everyone in its path. This was the case with the notorious H1N1 'swine flu' pandemic of 2009. (An epidemic affects a community or a country; a pandemic is a worldwide plague.)

Preventing the flu. People typically come down with the flu a few days after being exposed to the virus. But they can pass the disease on even before they feel sick, and they stay contagious for a couple of days after fever is gone. This is one reason the disease spreads so rapidly.

Good hand-washing and sneezing into one's sleeve help, but the only prevention is vaccination. In the UK, only children with certain chronic conditions are currently vaccinated on the NHS. Each year there is a new vaccine, made to protect against the strains of flu that are going around that year.

Treating the flu. Doctors may diagnose flu on the basis of symptoms and physical exam, and lab tests can identify the specific virus. The usual treatments help: rest, quiet, plenty to drink (offer but don't force) and either paracetamol or ibuprofen for the fever and aches. Don't give aspirin to children or teenagers with the flu; it increases the risk of Reye's syndrome (see page 613).

Antiviral medications help, too, especially if they are given early in the illness. Children who get sicker midway though a bout of the flu need to be checked again to make sure they don't have ear infections, pneumonia or other complications.

ASTHMA

When is it asthma? A child who has wheezing spells several times a year probably has asthma. Asthma is a narrowing of the airways in the lungs, usually in response to an allergen (pollen, for example), a virus, cold air, smoke or other fumes, or emotional upset. The wheezing happens as air whistles through the narrowed tubes. With mild narrowing, children wheeze when they breathe out; with moderate narrowing, they wheeze breathing in and out; and with severe narrowing, the wheezing stops because there isn't enough air going in or out to make a sound. Sometimes a child coughs instead of wheezing, usually at night or after exercise.

A single episode of wheezing might be the beginning of asthma, or it could be something else. For example, the child might have swallowed or inhaled a plastic toy or might be having a severe allergic reaction (see anaphylaxis, page 574). Until you know that your child has asthma, and is having a typical asthma attack, you should call the doctor for any new wheezing.

Causes of asthma. Children inherit a vulnerability to developing asthma. Lung irritation then brings on the disease. Certain viral infections, such as RSV, may play a role (page 560). Secondhand cigarette smoke surely does. Allergies to cockroaches and dust mites are common culprits. The shells and droppings of these insects get crushed up into a fine dust that drifts in the air and into children's lungs. Other asthma triggers include cat and dog dander, moulds and various foods.

Young children who wheeze with every viral cold but not at other times may be said to have reactive airways disease. Basically, this is mild asthma. Often it goes away; sometimes it goes on to become full asthma.

Treatment. Treatment starts with removing as many triggers as possible. Dust mites and cigarette smoke are prime targets. Physical conditioning is very important for children with asthma who are overweight or out of shape. Good nutrition, healthy sleep and a low-stress home all matter.

The first-line medications are bronchodilators. These medications open up (dilate) the bronchial tubes by causing the tiny muscles that surround the tubes to relax. We think of these drugs as 'rescue medicines', because they work on tubes that have already squeezed tight. If a child only wheezes every once in a while, a rescue med may be all he needs. Albuterol is the most common of these meds. For athletes, a puff or two of albuterol before a workout can often prevent tight breathing.

A child who wheezes more than once or twice a week may need a stronger controller drug, rather than relying on rescue meds again and again. Controller meds prevent narrowing of the tubes by dialling down the lung's response to asthma triggers. These meds work by blocking inflammation, a main part of the asthma response.

Many children with asthma grow out of the condition, but others carry it with them into adulthood. Prediction is difficult. Early, effective treatment will improve the child's physical activity, decrease the need for A&E visits, and reduce the risk of chronic lung disease later in life.

Asthma care and planning. Every child – and especially every child with a chronic illness such as asthma – deserves a medical home (see page 527). Parents need a steady source of information and support in order to asthma-proof their homes and make sure that their child's other environments (schools, friends' houses, clubs) are as asthma-safe as possible. Successful treatment depends on the details: knowing how to give the medications, when to step up the intensity of treatment, and what to do if a flare-up gets worse. Each child should have an asthma plan that the child, parents and school understand and can put into action.

Poorly treated, asthma carries a high cost in limited activities, missed school, hours in A&E and days in the hospital. With planning and steady care, however, children with asthma can live full, symptom-free lives.

SNORING

Snoring is usually just a nuisance, but sometimes it's a sign of obstructive sleep apnea (OSA), a serious problem. When a person falls deeply asleep, the muscles that hold the throat open relax, and the airway narrows. Large tonsils and adenoids can add to the problem. Air passing through the narrowed airway causes the snoring sound. The snoring stops when the airway closes completely, because air is no longer flowing. The child's blood oxygen begins to fall, and he wakes up gasping for air.

This cycle may repeat many times during the night, and by morning the child feels as though he has barely slept, and he may have a headache. During school he's apt to be either sleepy or wound up (as some children become when overtired) and his grades are likely to drop. Over time, the low blood oxygen can damage the heart. Sleep apnea often runs in families; one or both parents might have snoring problems with chronic overtiredness.

Sometimes a child with OSA will sleep with his head up on several pillows or hanging over the edge of the bed in an effort to keep the airway open. Sometimes, though, the only symptom is snoring. Doctors test for OSA using a sleep study, or polysomnogram, which requires an overnight stay in the hospital. If the tonsils and adenoids are large, they may need to be removed. If the child is obese, weight loss is often the main treatment. Some children need to sleep wearing a mask that blows compressed air into the nose, a device called continuous positive airway pressure (CPAP). The mask takes some getting used to, but the relief can be immediate.

NASAL ALLERGIES

Seasonal allergies (hay fever). You probably know some people who have hay fever. When pollen gets in the wind, they start to sneeze and their noses itch and run. In spring, the usual culprit is tree pollen; in summer, it's grass pollen. (Flowers rarely cause hay fever because their pollen is too big to blow around much; it's designed to be carried from place to place by insects and other creatures.)

Hay fever usually comes on after age three or four. It often runs in families. Persistently watery, itchy eyes are also likely to be an allergic symptom. A doctor can confirm the diagnosis based on the symptoms, the physical exam and knowledge of which pollens are most common in your area at different times of year.

Year-round nasal allergies. Many children are allergic to dust mites or moulds (the most common culprits), pet hair and dander, goose feathers or any number of other substances. Such year-round allergies cause stuffy or runny noses that last week after week, chronic mouth breathing and often fluid in the ears (see page 550) or repeated sinus infections (page 538).

The symptoms may be worse in winter, because closed windows and doors keep allergens in and fresh air out. Physical signs include dark circles and creases under the eyes and a crease across the bridge of the nose. Children with chronic allergies often have difficulty paying attention in school because they're overtired, not hearing clearly or simply feeling bad.

Treating nasal allergies. For hay fever, simple steps are sometimes enough: drive and sleep with the windows up, use an air conditioner if possible, and stay inside when pollen counts are highest. For year-round allergies, blood tests can often pinpoint the causes; sometimes an allergist has to do skin prick testing.

If the cause is goose feathers, you can change the pillow. If the cause is the family dog, you may have to find a different pet. For dust mites, some parents vacuum two or three times a week using a machine with HEPA (high-efficiency) bags; others go as far as to pull up the carpeting and take down the curtains, particularly in their child's bedroom. You can remove stuffed animals (where dust mites often live), or wash them in hot water every week or two. You can encase your child's mattress and pillows in plastic covers that zip shut; duct tape over the zippers seals allergens in. Keeping room humidity at less than 50 per cent cuts down on dust mites and mould. An electrostatic air cleaner can also help.

If avoiding the triggers doesn't work, there are medications of various sorts to try. Antihistamines (Benadryl is one brand) block a key step in the allergic reaction. These medications have been around for ages; they're cheap and safe, but they often make children drowsy and may interfere with school. Newer antihistamines (Clarityn, Piriteze and many others) cost more, don't work any better, but sometimes have fewer side effects. It's worth trying the old-fashioned antihistamines first. Antihistamines come in liquid, pill and spray form.

Other anti-allergy medications block different steps in the allergy response or soften the immune response generally. Medications such as montelukast (Singulair and others) or fluticasone (Flonase, for example) can be helpful, although they require close medical supervision to monitor for side effects. For severe allergies that don't respond to medication, immunotherapy (allergy shots) often can help. You need to weigh the benefits against the cost and discomfort before going this route.

Preventing allergies. Allergies are much more common in wealthy nations than in less developed ones. One reason may have to do with intestinal parasites. Allergies are caused by overactivity of the same part of the immune system that fights off parasites. In places where modern sanitation has banished parasites, the immune system may turn to less serious threats such as pollen or cat dander, threats that were better ignored. We don't know if this theory – called the hygiene hypothesis – is true, although it makes sense. It may be that a certain amount of exposure to dirt and the things that crawl in it is actually good for children. If so, then preventing allergies will turn out to be another good reason for sending your children outside to play.

ECZEMA

What to look for. Eczema is a patchy, rough, itchy rash associated with very dry skin. It usually begins in a young baby on the cheeks or the forehead. From there it may spread back to the ears and neck. Near one year of age, eczema may start almost anywhere – the shoulders, the arms, the chest. Between one and three years, the most typical spots are the creases in the elbows and behind the knees.

When eczema is mild or just starting, the colour is apt to be a light red or tannish pink; when the condition becomes severe the skin turns a deeper red. Constant scratching and rubbing cause scratch marks and weeping or oozing, which dries to form crusts. Scratched areas often become infected with bacteria (usually staphylococcus), making the oozing and crusting worse. When a patch of eczema is healing even after the redness has all faded away, you can still feel the roughness and thickness of the skin. In darker-skinned children, healed areas may look lighter or darker than the rest of the skin for weeks or months. Not all scaly, itchy rashes are eczema. A new rash, especially in a baby, needs to be looked at by a doctor.

The allergy connection. Eczema tends to run in families, along with food allergies and nasal allergies. Together, this unpleasant threesome is known as *atopy*; another term for eczema is *atopic dermatitis*. In eczema, the allergic reaction may be to different foods or to materials like wool or silk that come in contact with the skin. In many cases, both food sensitivity and irritation of the skin from the outside play a role. In general, winter is worst for eczema, because it dries out skin that is already overly dry. Other children develop worse eczema in hot weather because their perspiration irritates their skin. Itching leads to scratching, which further irritates the skin, leading to more itching.

Particularly in severe cases, it's important to try to find out what food may be triggering an allergic reaction (see page 345). Cow's milk, soya, eggs, wheat, nuts (including peanuts), fish and shellfish are the top suspects. A few babies can be cured only by giving up cow's milk altogether. It's best to undertake the search for food allergies under the direction of an experienced doctor; trying to do it yourself often results in confusion.

Treatment. Moisture is the key. A daily bath in warm water (not hot) for about five minutes allows water to soak into the skin. Don't use much soap; 'pure' soap is very harsh and drying. When you have to, use a soap that has lots of moisturizers in it. Stay away from deodorant soaps and bubble baths. Add bath oil near the end of the bath, so that it seals the moisture in. Pat your child dry with a soft towel; don't rub. Then use lots of moisturizing cream. If the skin is very dry, you can use Vaseline to seal the moisture in. Apply moisturizing cream two or three more times during the day. In the winter, run a vaporizer to keep the air in your home comfortably humid.

In order to limit skin irritation, get rid of any wool in clothing or bedding. If cold, windy weather brings out the eczema, so find a sheltered place for outings. It's important to keep the baby's fingernails clipped short. The less the baby can scratch her skin, the less the skin will itch, and the less the chance of an infection getting started. For babies who will tolerate it, using a pair of white cotton mittens to cover the hands at night is helpful, since a lot of scratching can go on while the baby is asleep. Medication to reduce itching can also help.

Along with moisturizers, doctors often prescribe hydrocortisone cream. Hydrocortisone is a corticosteroid. These steroids are very different from the anabolic steroids used by some athletes – and teens who want to look like athletes. Hydrocortisone comes in different strengths, and there are related creams and ointments (for example, triamcinolone) that are stronger yet. Antihistamines can help reduce itching. It's fine to use a moisturizer, 1 per cent hydrocortisone, and an antihistamine on your own to treat mild eczema. But for more severe eczema, it's best to work closely with your child's doctor or a dermatologist. If a bad patch of eczema becomes infected with bacteria, antibiotics can help; usually they have to be taken by mouth.

Eczema can be hard to treat. Often the best we can do is to keep the rash under control. Eczema that starts early in infancy often clears up completely or at least becomes much milder in the following year or two. Among school-age children with eczema, about half are free of it by their teen years.

OTHER RASHES AND WARTS

If your child has a new rash, it's best to let a doctor see it. Rashes are hard to put into words, and it's easy to be confused by them. The purpose of this section isn't to make you an expert, but only to tell you about some of the everyday rashes you can expect to see. For rashes in babies, including nappy rashes, see page 132.

Dangerous rashes. Rashes are irritating but rarely dangerous. A child with a minor viral infection will often develop red blotches, lacy areas or little bumps covering the face, arms or trunk. Recovery follows soon. What's important is that these rashes *blanch.* That is, if you use your fingers to stretch the skin where the rash is, the redness fades out. This is a good sign.

If you can't get the redness to fade by stretching the skin, beware: it may be blood that has leaked into the skin. Tiny blood vessels that break make pinpoint red dots; larger vessels that break or leak create irregular red or purple blotches. The situation isn't always dire. Hard coughing can sometimes cause small blood vessels to burst in the face, for example. But bleeding into the skin *can* be the first sign of a life-threatening infection or a serious blood problem. If you see red spots that don't blanch, even if your child doesn't seem very ill, call the doctor right away.

Hives (urticaria). This is an allergic reaction that causes raised red welts or blotches, often with a pale spot in the middle. Hives itch, sometimes unbearably. Unlike most other rashes, hives move around. They show up for a few hours, then fade, only to show up somewhere else. Hives blanch (see above).

The trigger for this allergic reaction may be clear: your child recently tried a new food or took a new medicine. (Hives, like other allergies, sometimes show up on the second or third exposure; don't be fooled.) Other triggers include heat, cold, plants, soaps or detergents, viral infections (including colds) and even strong emotions. Often, though, it's impossible to tell what set the hives off. A few children get hives repeatedly, but many have them only once or twice for no apparent reason. The usual treatment is an over-the-counter antihistamine. Stronger medicines are available by prescription.

On very rare occasions, hives occur along with swelling of the inside of the mouth and throat and difficulty breathing (anaphylaxis). If this happens, it's a medical emergency; call an ambulance right away. Children who have had even one episode of anaphylaxis should carry a preloaded epinephrine syringe, an EpiPen or Anapen (see page 511).

Impetigo. This often starts as a pimple with a yellowish or milky blister on top, often near the nose, but it could be anywhere. The blister breaks and a brown or honey-coloured scab or crust takes its place. Any scab on the face should call impetigo to mind. The rash spreads easily, carried on the hands to other parts of the body, and to other children.

Impetigo is an infection of the skin caused by staphylococcus or streptococcus bacteria (staph or strep, for short). Prescription antibiotics cure it. Until you can get to the doctor, try to keep your child from rubbing or picking and from sharing towels or bedding; enforce good hand-washing. Untreated impetigo can lead to kidney damage, so you need to take it seriously.

Boils. A red, raised area that is painful may be a boil, an infection in the skin that forms a pus pocket. Increasingly, the cause is a form of staphylococcus called MRSA. These infections can be serious, and they need to be treated right away. A medication by mouth may suffice, or the pus pocket may need to be drained and antibiotics begun in the hospital.

Scabies. An itchy, bumpy rash, scabies is an allergic reaction to a mite, a tiny creature that burrows into the skin. Scabies looks like groups or lines of spots topped with scabs, surrounded by a lot of scratch marks. It itches horribly. Scabies usually shows up in areas that are frequently touched: backs of hands, wrists, pubic area and abdomen (but not on the back). Although scabies is not dangerous, it is highly contagious. Prescription lotion kills the mites, but the itching can continue for weeks.

Ringworm. This skin condition is caused not by a worm but by a fungus (related to athlete's foot) that infects the top layers of the skin. Look for one or more oval patches roughly the size of a pound coin with heaped-up, slightly reddened borders. The outer rim is made up of little bumps or silver scales. The rash enlarges slowly over time, with clearing in the centre, forming a ring. It itches a little, and it's mildly contagious. A prescription cream works well.

Ringworm on the scalp causes flaking and hair loss. Sometimes there is a large oozy swelling, as well as swollen lymph nodes at the back of the head and in the neck. Antifungal creams don't work in hairy areas; for these, treatment requires several weeks of daily medication by mouth.

Warts. Warts can be flat, mounded up or tall and thin. One common type is a hard, rough mound of skin about the size of this capital O. Warts are usually painless, but on the soles of the feet they can hurt. One variety, known by the poetic name of molluscum contagiosum, causes round, white or pink bumps the size of a pinhead, with a small dimple in the centre. They may multiply and enlarge, or just sit there. Warts are caused by viruses. Often, the body eventually fights them off. Over-the-counter wart medicine can speed the process; so can (believe it or not) a daily application of duct tape. If these remedies fail, a chiropodist can freeze or cut them away.

HEAD LICE

Head lice aren't really an infection: they're an infestation. The lice don't enter the body but just set up house, feeding on human blood. The real problem is the itching, which can be intense, and the yuck factor.

Lice pass easily from person to person, either by direct head contact (napping next to each other) or on combs, brushes or hats. They can live for about three days away from a human body, but their eggs survive longer. Poor hygiene is not the problem.

They hide well, so look for the eggs (also called nits): tiny, pearly white, smaller than a sesame seed, cemented to the hair often close to the scalp. There may be itchy red spots where the hair meets the back of the neck, especially behind the ears.

Try over-the-counter lice treatments first, but don't be surprised if the lice survive: resistance to these chemicals is now common. Prescription insecticides usually work well. Treatments that don't work: covering the head in Vaseline or mayonnaise. One foolproof cure is to pick every single last nit off the child's head, and examine the head every few days for any new ones. Wetting the hair and using conditioner make it easier to comb and it becomes harder for the lice to scurry away.

STOMACHACHES

Most stomachaches are brief and mild; simple reassurance often does the trick. Fifteen minutes later, you'll probably notice your child playing normally. For any stomachache that lasts an hour or more, it's reasonable to call the doctor for advice. For very severe stomachaches, don't wait even that long. There are dozens of causes of stomachaches and upsets. A few of them are serious; most are not. People are apt to jump to the conclusion that a stomachache is due either to appendicitis or to something that the child ate. Actually, neither of these causes is common. Children can usually eat strange foods or an unusual amount of a regular food without any indigestion.

Before you call the doctor, take the child's temperature (page 414) so that you can report what it is. The treatment, until you reach the doctor, should consist of putting the child to bed and giving him nothing to eat. If the child is thirsty, small sips of water are fine. For stomachaches that accompany vomiting and diarrhoea, see below and page 590.

Common causes of stomachache. Young infants often have colic (pages 60 and 104), which can look like stomach or abdominal pain. If your baby has abdominal pain and is irritable or vomiting, it's wise to call the doctor immediately.

After the age of one year, one of the commonest causes of stomachache is the onset of a simple cold, sore throat or flu, especially when there is fever. The stomachache is a sign that the infection is disturbing the intestines as well as other parts of the body. In a young child, almost any infection may cause stomachache or abdominal pain. A small child is apt to complain that her tummy hurts when she really means that she feels nauseated. She often vomits soon after this complaint.

The most common reason for repeated stomachaches is constipation (see page 583). The pain may be dull and nagging or sudden and very painful (though it may go away just as quickly). It's often worse after a meal. The source of the pain appears to be cramping of the intestines as they fight to squeeze out the hard, dry bowel movements.

Stomachaches and stress. All kinds of emotions, from fear to pleasant excitement, can affect the stomach and intestines. They can cause not only pains and lack of appetite but also vomiting and diarrhoea or constipation. Pain in such cases tends to be in the centre of the abdomen. Since there's no infection, the child won't have fever.

A child who is under pressure to eat more or to eat different foods (vegetables, for instance) will often complain of stomachaches when he sits down to a meal or after a few bites. The parents are apt to think the child has made up the stomachache as an excuse not to eat. But it's more likely that the pain comes from the child's tense feeling at mealtimes, and that the stomachache is real. The treatment here is for the parents to handle mealtimes in such a way that the child enjoys the food. (See pages 886–911.)

A child who has other worries can have stomachaches, too, especially around mealtime. Think of the child who is nervous about starting school in September and has a stomachache instead of an appetite for breakfast, or the child who feels guilty about something that hasn't been found out yet. Strife between parents, both verbal and physical, frequently causes stomach pain in children.

Stress-related stomachache is common among children

and teenagers, often recurring two or more times a week. The pain is almost always in the midline, either around or just above the belly button. It is often hard for the child to describe.

The treatment is to identify the stresses at home, at school, in sports and in the child's social life, and do whatever is necessary to reduce them. Doctors have studied this condition, which they call recurrent abdominal pain syndrome. It's very important to realize that the pain experienced by these children is real, not all in the child's head or designed just to get attention.

Appendicitis. Let me first contradict some common notions about appendicitis. There isn't necessarily any fever. The pain isn't necessarily severe. The pain doesn't usually settle in the lower right side of the abdomen until the attack has been going on for some time. Vomiting doesn't always occur, though loss of appetite is quite characteristic. A blood count doesn't prove that a stomachache is or isn't due to appendicitis.

The appendix is a little offshoot from the large intestine, about the size of a short earthworm. It usually lies in the central part of the right lower quarter of the abdomen. But it can be lower down, over towards the middle of the abdomen, or as far up as the ribs. When it becomes inflamed it's a gradual process, like the formation of a boil. That's how you know that a sudden severe pain in the abdomen that lasts a few minutes and then goes away for good isn't appendicitis. The worst danger is that the inflamed appendix will burst, very much as a boil bursts, and spread the infection all through the abdomen. The condition that ensues is called *peritonitis.* Appendicitis that is developing very rapidly can reach the point of bursting in less than twenty-four hours. That's why any stomachache that persists for as long as an hour should be discussed with the doctor, even though nine out of ten cases will prove to be something else.

In the most typical cases of appendicitis, there is pain around the navel for several hours. Only later does it shift to the lower right side. There is apt to be vomiting once or twice, but it doesn't always occur. The appetite is usually diminished, but not always. The bowels may be normal or constipated, rarely loose. After this has gone on for a few hours, the child's temperature is apt to be mildly elevated, but it's possible to have appendicitis without any fever at all. The child may feel pain when he pulls his right knee up, when he stretches it way back or when he walks around.

You can see that the symptoms of appendicitis vary a lot, and that you need a doctor to make the diagnosis. When doctors find a tender spot in the right side of the abdomen, they are suspicious of appendicitis, but sometimes they need a blood count, X-ray or ultrasound to help them decide.

It's sometimes impossible for even the most expert doctors to be absolutely certain that a child has appendicitis. When there is enough suspicion, however, an operation is usually performed. That is because if it is appendicitis, it is dangerous to delay surgery. The appendix could burst and cause an infection in the abdomen.

Intestinal obstruction. A fairly common cause of intestinal blockage in a young child is called *intussusception.* This occurs when a bit of the intestine gets pulled into the segment just below it, like a telescope folding up. In a typical case, the baby suddenly looks ill, vomits and draws her legs up to her belly in pain. Sometimes the vomiting is more prominent; sometimes the pain is. The cramps come minutes apart; between them the baby may be fairly comfortable or sleepy. After a number of hours the baby may pass a bowel movement containing mucus and blood – the classic 'currant jelly' stool. This is a sign of injury to the intestines; it's best to treat the problem before this happens.

Children as young as four months to about six years are prone to intussusceptions. The key is to suspect it and go for help. If it's caught early, the problem can often be fixed easily; if the bowel has been injured, however, surgery may be necessary.

Intestinal parasites (worms). In many parts of the world, most children have intestinal parasites. Where sanitation is better, worms are less common, and only a few children have enough of them to cause abdominal pain.

Pinworms, or threadworms, are an exception; they are common everywhere. The adult worms look like white threads about 1 cm (⅓ in) long. They live in the intestine, coming out at night to lay their eggs on the skin around the anus. The eggs may cause itching, disturbing the child's sleep or leading to vaginal irritation, or they may not be noticed at all. (In earlier times worms were thought to be the chief cause of children's grinding their teeth at night, but this is not so.)

Pinworms aren't dangerous, but they can be irritating and hard to get rid of. A single dose of medication kills the adult worms, but the eggs can last for days or weeks outside the body. Children unknowingly pick up the eggs on their fingers and bring them back to their mouths or their parents' mouths. Pinworms spread around families and nurseries, and children are often infested several times. Breaking the cycle requires careful hand-washing (especially under the nails); washing of clothing, sheets, blankets and floors; and sometimes repeated courses of medication.

Roundworms look very much like earthworms. The first suspicion comes when one is discovered in the bowel movement. They usually don't cause symptoms unless the child has a great number of them.

Children born in less-developed countries and those who have lived for a time in a group home or shelter for the homeless may carry intestinal parasites without having any symptoms. Discovering the problem is a simple matter of sending samples of stool to a laboratory for microscopic examination. These problems are fairly easy to treat with prescribed medications.

CONSTIPATION

Constipation is common in children, and commonly misunderstood. A child who passes hard bowel movements or large painful ones is constipated, even if he uses the toilet every day. A child who passes soft BMs isn't constipated, even if he only goes every two or three days. Constipation is a symptom of many diseases – hypothyroidism, for example, or lead poisoning – but most constipated children don't have one of these conditions. Constipation itself frequently causes other problems, however, both physical and psychological.

How constipation develops. Constipation often begins with a mild flu. Any disease that makes a person feel sick all over is apt to take away the appetite and slow down the bowels. Fever and vomiting increase water loss. In response, the colon absorbs more water from the stool, leaving it drier and harder. Passing this hard stool hurts, so the child holds it in. This gives the stool even more time to dry out. When a large stool finally passes, the pain teaches the child to hold it in even harder next time.

Over time, the buildup of hard stool stretches out the colon, weakening the muscles that normally propel the stool along. The result is even slower passage of stool through the colon, with even more drying, hardening and discomfort. In this way, what began as part of a minor illness develops into a chronic problem. Other factors, including genetics, food sensitivities, exercise and diet, also play a role.

Lifestyle and constipation. Diets rich in meats and processed grains often provide too little fibre for regular, soft bowel movements. Children who eat a lot of whole grains, vegetables and fruits are less likely to develop constipation.

In some children, milk proteins inhibit colonic contractions, setting them up for constipation. This tendency often runs in families. Cutting down on dairy products or cutting them out altogether often helps. If you do this, be sure to add other sources of calcium and vitamin D (see page 524).

Constipation is common among overweight and obese children, who often have both low-fibre diets and low levels of physical activity.

Problems caused by constipation. For constipation as a cause of toilet training refusal, see page 869. Constipation often leads to bed-wetting and frequent daytime urination (see page 877). As stool builds up in the rectum, it pushes against the lower part of the bladder, partly blocking the flow of urine. The bladder has to work harder to push the urine past the obstruction; as a result, it loses the ability to relax as it fills with urine, and even a relatively small amount of urine triggers bladder contractions and the urgent need to go.

Stool leakage is a terrible problem for many children. With long-standing constipation, large chunks of hardened stool sit in the colon like rocks in a pipe. Liquid stool passes between the rocks and leaks out of the anus. This condition, called *encopresis*, needs to be treated promptly to avoid serious psychological harm (see page 875).

One of the worst things about constipation is that it draws parents too deeply into what should be, for most school-age children, their own private business. It takes a very sensitive parent to remain involved but not overinvolved. When constipation has set up a power struggle between parent and child or has raised tensions in a family, it makes sense to seek guidance from a psychologist, counsellor or other professional.

Lifestyle treatments for constipation. This is the best place to start. The solution might be as easy as substituting whole-wheat for white bread, and fresh oranges or apples for biscuits or cake. Remember the 'P fruits that make you poo': prunes, plums, peaches and pears. Apricots, too. Try adding unprocessed wheat bran (available in most health food stores) or bran cereal to muffins, apple puree or peanut butter sandwiches. If you add bran or other dried fibre, be sure to also give your child extra water. A slurry of apple puree, bran and prune juice is sweet and crunchy, and it often works well.

It's important to make sure your child has vigorous exercise daily. Abdominal strengthening exercises (crunches, for example) help children push more effectively and gain a sense of control. Children also need time set aside each day to sit quietly on the toilet. The best time is often about fifteen minutes after dinner, because eating naturally activates the colon. A selection of books in the toilet can help a child sit for the fifteen or twenty minutes it takes to let things happen.

Medication for constipation. Painfully hard bowel movements should be treated promptly to avoid the vicious circle of withholding and further constipation, particularly in a younger child. Your doctor can recommend one of several preparations that will keep the movements soft. Treatment usually lasts for at least a month, to allow the child to become confident that the painful hardness will not recur. When constipation has been long-standing, it may take more than lifestyle changes to reverse the process.

There are many medications for constipation, but I would recommend you use them only under a doctor's guidance. Children who use laxatives can sometimes become dependent on them. An experienced doctor should help you avoid such pitfalls.

Whatever medicines are chosen, there are always two phases to the treatment: cleaning out and keeping going. The cleanout is unpleasant, but it's crucial. No medication can succeed if the colon stays plugged by rock-hard stool. Oral solutions containing polyethylene glycol (Miralax and other brands) work by flushing through the intestines. Some children do better with sodium phosphate enemas; the end result is the same.

The next phase is keeping going (maintenance). This requires lifestyle changes along with medication adjusted to produce a soft, formed stool every day. The point is to not allow the stool to build up again, restarting the vicious cycle. This treatment needs to continue for six months or more, until the colon has recovered enough strength to do the job on its own. Children and parents have a hard time keeping up with treatment for that long, and it sometimes takes several attempts before the problem is fully controlled.

When medication fails, further assessments and treatment by a paediatric gastroenterologist may be needed.

VOMITING AND DIARRHOEA

Infections (gastroenteritis). Most diarrhoea in children is caused by viruses. These infections get called different things: stomach flu, intestinal flu, a 'bug' or gastroenteritis. There may be fever, vomiting and stomachache (usually mild). The child normally recovers in a few days, but family members or classmates often fall ill with the same bug.

There is no specific cure. Give frequent small amounts of fluid to prevent dehydration. Store-bought oral rehydration solution is fine, or you can mix your own using salt and sugar (see page 260). Let your child eat what he wants. You don't have to restrict milk or dairy products, but don't push them, either.

If your child seems quite ill, with high fever or severe cramping, or if the diarrhoea contains blood or mucus, the problem could be a bacterial infection. Salmonella is one of the more common culprits, along with *E. coli*, shigella, campylobacter and a few others. Some of these require antibiotics, so bring the doctor a stool sample to send to the lab.

Salmonella, *E. coli* and other potentially dangerous bacteria are routinely found in meat and even vegetables in supermarkets. To protect your children and yourself, follow approved practices for safely preparing, cooking, serving and storing food.

Vomiting without diarrhoea. Vomiting that occurs together with diarrhoea is often due to an infection or perhaps food poisoning. Vomiting in the absence of diarrhoea is more concerning. It can be caused by a blockage of the intestines (especially if what comes up is yellow), a swallowed poison or medication, a serious infection almost anywhere in the body or pressure on the brain. In short, it needs to be evaluated promptly by a doctor.

In an infant the cause of persistent vomiting, sometimes with fussiness, arching of the back and weight loss, may be gastro-oesophageal reflux disease (GORD). Between the oesophagus and the stomach, there is a muscle that works like a valve. It opens to let food into the stomach, then closes to keep the food from squirting back up into the mouth. In babies, the nerves that control this valve are slow and the signals are apt to get crossed. So the valve often opens at the wrong time and stomach contents – food mixed with acid – move in the wrong direction. Over time, the acid can irritate the oesophagus, causing heartburn. The irritation in turn makes the valve even less effective.

Once you know the problem is GORD, the solution may be as simple as giving smaller, more frequent feedings. As a result, the stomach never gets overfilled, pressure in the stomach stays low, and food stays put. You can also thicken a baby's formula with about one tablespoon of rice cereal per 240 ml (8 fl oz) bottle. Try laying your baby on her stomach with her head a few inches higher than her stomach, to let gravity lend a hand. (Be careful to watch your baby, and move her to her back if she falls asleep; SIDS is much less common in babies who sleep on their backs.) When GORD is not responding to these measures, medication can help lower the acid and sometimes strengthen the muscle of the valve.

Food poisoning. This is caused by toxins made by certain bacteria. The food may or may not taste unusual. Beware especially of pastries filled with custard or whipped cream, creamy salads and poultry stuffing. Bacteria multiply readily in these substances if they warm up to room temperature. Another cause is improperly home-canned foods.

Symptoms of food poisoning include vomiting, diarrhoea and stomachache. Sometimes there are chills and fever. Everyone who eats the contaminated food is apt to be affected by it to some degree at about the same time, in contrast to an intestinal flu, which usually spreads through a family over a number of days. The doctor should always be called when you suspect food poisoning.

Dehydration. A major concern with diarrhoea and vomiting is that a child can lose an excessive amount of body water. Babies and young children are more at risk because they don't have as much reserve body water, and they lose water more rapidly through their skin. Certain infections are notorious for creating dehydration. The most famous is cholera, rare in developed countries, but common (and greatly feared) when sanitation is lacking, as in natural and man-made disasters. In young children, dehydration can be dangerous.

The first sign of dehydration is that the child makes less urine than usual; this can be hard to judge, however, if the child is in nappies and the nappy is filled with liquid stool. As dehydration worsens, the child becomes listless or lethargic; his eyes look dry, and there may be no tears when he cries; his lips and mouth look parched and dry; and in a baby, the soft spot on the top of the head appears sunken. If your child begins to show any signs of dehydration, get him to a doctor or to a hospital as soon as possible. (For more on diet for vomiting and diarrhoea, see page 588.)

Persistent diarrhoea. This often occurs in a young child who is obviously thriving and not complaining of feeling sick. It may begin out of the blue or with a bout of stomach flu. The child may begin the day with a normal bowel movement, then pass three to five soft or runny and smelly bowel movements, which may contain mucus or undigested food. His appetite remains good and he is playful and active. He continues to gain weight normally and laboratory tests of the bowel movement reveal nothing abnormal.

Usually the condition gradually gets better by itself. Often the diarrhoea can be much improved by cutting down on juice in the child's diet. The single most likely culprit is apple juice. That's why this condition is sometimes called apple juice diarrhoea or toddler diarrhoea. In general, juice should be limited to 240–300 ml (8–10 fl oz) ounces a day.

When to worry. There are several uncommon but more serious diseases that cause chronic diarrhoea. Poor weight gain is an especially concerning sign. If diarrhoea persists for more than a week, or if the bowel movement is bloody or either unusually dark or very pale in colour, it's a good idea to have the problem evaluated medically.

HEADACHES

Headaches are common among children and teenagers. Though a headache can be an early sign of many different illnesses ranging from the common cold to more serious infections, the most frequent cause by far is stress. Think of the child who's been memorizing for days a part for the school play, or the child who's been practising extra hours after school for the gymnastics team. Often fatigue, tension and anticipation combine to produce changes in the blood flow to the muscles of the head and neck, causing a headache.

When a young child complains of a headache, it's best to call the doctor promptly, because it's more likely at this age that the headache is an early symptom of an oncoming illness. An older child who has a headache can be given the appropriate dose of paracetamol or ibuprofen, followed by a rest period – lying down, playing quietly or engaging in another restful activity – until the medicine starts to work. Sometimes an ice pack helps.

If a headache lasts as long as four hours after the child has taken a medication, or if other symptoms of illness (such as fever) develop, the doctor should be called. If a headache comes on after a fall or a blow to the head, get in touch with the doctor promptly. Headaches in the morning or on rising, or that awaken a child at night, are often signs of serious illness. Discuss with your child's doctor any recurrent early morning headaches and any headaches associated with dizziness, blurred or double vision, nausea and vomiting.

A child who has frequent headaches should have a thorough medical evaluation, including a check of his vision, a dental exam, a neurological evaluation and a careful review of his eating and sleeping patterns. It's also worth considering whether something in the child's home life, school, or social activities may be causing undue stress.

Children do get migraine headaches, although they are less likely to have characteristic symptoms such as an aura of flashing lights or other visual changes, or weakness in one extremity. A pattern of severe headaches in a child ought to raise the question of migraines, particularly (but not only) if migraines run in the family.

SEIZURES

Obvious or not. Sometimes it's obvious that a child is having a seizure. He loses consciousness and falls down; his eyes roll up; his whole body stiffens, then shakes violently. He may froth at the mouth, make grunting noises, become incontinent or bite his tongue. After several minutes his body relaxes, but he remains sleepy or confused for several minutes or even hours before returning to normal. These dramatic seizures are described as *generalized* because large areas of the brain are involved, and *tonic-clonic* because the body first stiffens, then shakes. The old term 'grand mal seizures' is still used.

Other seizure types are less obvious. An infant may suddenly stare off to one side or make lip-smacking or bicyleriding movements. This kind of seizure often follows injury to the brain. A boy between ages five and eight may wake from sleep with twitching on one side of his face or body; a couple of minutes later he is okay. This kind of seizure typically goes away before the child starts Year 9, and does not come back.

Here is another common type of seizure: a child over the age of two, often a girl, suddenly stares blankly ahead and does not respond to her name or being touched. After five to ten seconds she picks up again with whatever she was doing, without ever noticing the interruption. These seizures can occur repeatedly during the day, interfering with the child's learning. Perhaps because the child seems to go away momentarily, these events are called *absence seizures.* They respond well to medication. Yet another child carries out a complicated set of movements over and over – walking around or moving his hands in a particular way – and is unaware of his actions. This could also be a seizure.

In general, any sudden change in a child's behaviour or consciousness *could* be a seizure. When in doubt, get a medical assessment.

When is it epilepsy? *Epilepsy* is the term for seizures that occur repeatedly, in the absence of fever or other obvious cause. Depending on the type of seizures, the age of the child, the findings on physical and neurological examination and various tests, a neurologist may diagnose a particular epilepsy syndrome. The diagnosis will guide the treatment and give some information about what is likely to happen going forward.

Epilepsy is upsetting for children and parents, even more than many other chronic diseases. Ignorance and fear are major hurdles. Through education, children and parents can gain control and comfort. People with epilepsy can and do lead full and rich lives.

Causes of seizures. Nerve cells are constantly firing off tiny jolts of electricity. When thousands or millions fire more or less at once, a large wave of electricity can flow through the brain, resulting in changes in behaviour and consciousness – that is, a seizure. What happens during the seizure depends on which areas in the brain are affected by the abnormal electrical discharge. Sometimes we can discover the underlying cause of the electrical activity – for example, an area of scarring on the brain or a particular gene. Often, though, we cannot pinpoint the cause.

Seizures with fever. By far the most common cause of seizures in young children is fever. One child in twenty-five between the ages of three months and five years will have a brief tonic-clonic seizure during a fever. Most of these children are entirely normal and healthy (except for the infection that is causing the fever); the seizure seems to have no long-term effect, and they never have another. About one-third of the children will go on to have a second seizure with fever, but again, most of them turn out to be completely healthy in the long run. Perhaps one in twenty who has a first seizure with fever will later prove to have epilepsy (see pages 594–5).

Febrile seizures often occur at the beginning of an illness such as a cold, a sore throat or the flu. A sudden rise in temperature seems to set off abnormal brain activity, and some children will have confusion or even hallucinate. Children who have a history of these seizures can sometimes take antiseizure medication right at the beginning of an illness, but because the seizures often come on unexpectedly, it's hard for parents to prevent them.

If your child does have a seizure with fever, follow the instructions below. Chances are good that your child will be fine. Of course, you will have been scared senseless for a bit, because the normal reaction to your child having a seizure is to imagine the worst. Your child will almost certainly get over the episode long before you do.

What to do during a generalized tonic-clonic (grand mal) seizure. Call a doctor right away. If you cannot reach one immediately, don't worry. The convulsion will usually be over anyway and the child will be asleep by the time you talk to the doctor. There is very little you need to do for a child during a convulsion except keep her from hurting herself. Move her to the floor or some other place where she can't fall. Turn her on her side to allow saliva to run out of the corner of her mouth and to prevent her tongue from blocking her airway. Make sure that her flailing arms and legs do not strike something sharp. Don't try to put anything into her mouth. If the seizure lasts more than five minutes, call 999.

EYE PROBLEMS

Reasons for seeing the eye doctor. Children need to go to an eye doctor (opthalmologist) or optometrist if their eyes turn in (crosseyes) or out (walleyes) at any age; if they are having any trouble with schoolwork; if they complain of aching, smarting or tired eyes; if their eyes are inflamed; if they are having headaches; if they hold their books too close when they read; if they cock their head to one side when looking at something carefully; or if their vision is found to be defective by the chart test. Chart testing should be performed between three and four years of age, and regularly thereafter. However, just because your child can read the chart does not guarantee that her eyes are all right. If she is having symptoms of eyestrain, she should be examined anyway. (See page 137 for blocked tear ducts and other common eye problems in babies.)

Nearsightedness (myopia). This means that close objects appear sharp, but distant objects are blurred. This is the most common eye trouble that interferes with schoolwork. Nearsightedness develops most frequently between six and ten years. It can come on quite rapidly, so don't ignore the signs of it (holding the book closer, having trouble seeing the blackboard at school) just because the child's vision was all right a few months before.

Inflammation of the eye (conjunctivitis, pinkeye). Conjunctivitis can be caused by many different viruses, bacteria or allergens. Most of the mild cases, where the eye is only slightly pink and the discharge from the eye is scant and clear, are caused by the same viruses that cause ordinary colds. In a child who doesn't have any other sign of having a cold, pinkeye is more likely to be due to a bacterial infection. Thick yellow discharge, pain or redness of the eyeball also suggest bacteria. The treatment is with antibiotic ointments or drops as prescribed by your doctor. Conjunctivitis is contagious. Its spread can be decreased significantly by frequent hand-washing, especially after any contact with the infected eye or with the discharge.

If the conjunctivitis does not clear up after a few days of medication, there may be a speck of dirt or other foreign material stuck in the eye, visible only through an ophthalmoscope. Persistent tearing of an eye, lid swelling or one eye that seems larger than the other all need prompt medical attention.

Styes. A stye is an infection around the root of an eyelash, caused by ordinary bacteria that live on the skin, usually staphylococcus (staph). The stye usually comes to a head and breaks, then heals. Warm compresses speed this process and reduce discomfort. (Eyelids are very temperature sensitive, so only use warm, not hot, water.) A prescription antibiotic ointment also helps to promote healing. Try to keep your child from rubbing the stye, as this can spread the infection to other hair roots. (Just as with conjunctivitis, an adult with a stye should wash his hands thoroughly before caring for a baby or small child, to limit contagion.)

Things that don't harm children's eyes. Watching television, sitting too close to the set, and reading an excessive amount probably have no effect on the eyes. Habitually reading in poor light may make nearsightedness somewhat worse, however.

JOINTS AND BONES

Growing pains. Children often complain of vague pains in their legs and arms. A child between the ages of two and five may wake up crying, complaining of pain around his thigh, knee or calf. This happens only during the evening but may recur each night for weeks on end. Some people believe this pain is caused by cramps in the muscles or by the aching of the rapidly growing bones.

Generally, if the pains move from place to place, if there is no swelling, redness, local tenderness or limp, and if the child is entirely well otherwise, it is unlikely that a serious cause will be found. If the pain is always in the same spot on the same limb, or if other symptoms are present – especially fever or rash – the problem should definitely be brought to medical attention.

Hips, knees, ankles and feet. Hip pain always needs to be assessed medically, since the hip joint is vulnerable to injury. Pain from the hip joint is felt in the groin or along the inside of the thigh, not the area normally thought of as the hips. Limping is always concerning, with or without hip pain, unless there is an obvious reason such as a hurt foot. Overweight children are prone to hip problems, as well as problems in the knees, ankles and feet.

Pain just below the kneecap, particularly in a growing adolescent, is often caused by strain on the ligament where it connects to the top of the shin bone. The pain is usually worse after sports that involve jumping. This is an overuse injury, similar to tennis elbow; healing requires rest and medication to reduce inflammation (ibuprofen, for example). Pain alongside or underneath the kneecap is also common and responds to rest and medication, as well as exercises to strengthen the muscles that hold the kneecap in place.

Twisted and sprained ankles are common. Ice, elevation and rest are helpful. Exercises prescribed by a physiotherapist can speed recovery. Flat feet that don't hurt are not really a problem; painful flat feet should be evaluated, because surgery is sometimes required. Feet that turn in or turn out are dealt with on page 119.

Spine. Scoliosis is a curvature of the spine that usually appears between the ages of ten and fifteen, more often in girls; it tends to run in families. The cause is unknown. Any curvature warrants an evaluation by a doctor, but most cases are mild and only require monitoring. Low back pain in a child always needs evaluation, to rule out rare but serious causes. Children should avoid power lifting until their adolescent growth spurt is over, when their spines are fully matured and less vulnerable to injury.

When to worry. Any joint pain with fever could signal an infection in the joint, which is an emergency. Limping that is not explained by a recent injury also needs to be seen promptly, since it can sometimes be a sign of serious illness. Persistent aching or swelling in one or more joints may be due to arthritis; there are several different forms, some more serious than others. All need medical attention. Fractures and dislocations are discussed on page 504.

HEART PROBLEMS

Murmurs. A heart murmur is simply a sound made by blood flowing through the heart. Most murmurs are *innocent* or *functional*, which means that the heart is perfectly normal. It's good to know if your child has an innocent murmur, because then you don't have to worry if a new doctor discovers the murmur. A truly new murmur needs to be evaluated. The most common cause is anaemia due to low iron intake.

When a murmur is due to a heart abnormality, the most likely cause is an opening between two of the chambers of the heart. When these openings are small, as they usually are, doctors just wait for them to close on their own. Larger openings sometimes require a procedure, often without surgery. In the meantime, most children with these problems need to take antibiotics before getting their teeth professionally cleaned, but otherwise are just fine. Doctors can usually tell whether or not a murmur is innocent simply by listening. If necessary, an ultrasound can reveal the nature of any abnormalities.

Chest pain. Pain in the chest area is common in children, but heart attacks are very rare. Most chest pain is due to acid reflux (see GORD, page 589). Teenagers are prone to inflammation of the cartilage that attaches the ribs to the breastbone. In these cases, pressing firmly on the chest brings on the pain. Ibuprofen and reassurance usually help. Emotional upset or anxiety can cause chest pain. Very rarely, lung or heart problems are at fault; so, if you're not certain, be sure to ask the doctor.

Fainting. A child who stands up suddenly from a lying position, or who suffers a sudden pain or stress, may feel lightheaded. If she blacks out, it's probably a good idea to have a doctor evaluate her. Most fainting spells are normal and not serious, but rarely, fainting is due to an abnormal heart rhythm. A simple EKG can often give reassurance or point to the need for more assessment. Certainly, if there is a history of passing out or sudden death in your family, let the doctor know.

GENITAL AND URINARY DISTURBANCES

Frequent urination. If a child suddenly begins to urinate frequently, it raises the possibility of a bladder infection, diabetes or another disease. A doctor needs to see the child and test the urine. Sometimes the problem is constipation (see page 583).

A few individuals, even calm ones, seem to have bladders that never hold as much as the average, and this may be the way they were made. But some of the children (and adults, too) who regularly have to urinate frequently are somewhat high-strung or worried. In one case it's a chronic tendency;

in another, the need to urinate often is due to a temporary stressor. A healthy athlete is apt to have to go to the toilet every fifteen minutes just before a race, for example.

The parents' job, then, is to find out what, if anything, is making the child tense. In one case it's the handling at home, in another it's relations with other children, in yet another it's the child's school situation. Most often it's a combination of these.

A common story involves the timid child and the teacher who seems severe. To begin with, the child's apprehensiveness keeps his bladder from relaxing sufficiently to hold much urine. Then he worries about asking permission to be excused. If the teacher makes a fuss about his leaving the room, it's worse still. It's wise to get a note from the doctor not simply requesting that the child be excused but also explaining the child's nature and why his bladder works that way. If the teacher is approachable and the parent is tactful, a personal visit will help, too.

Painful urination. Irritation of the area around the urinary opening can cause painful urination in girls. Common causes are bits of bowel movement wiped the wrong way or chemicals in bubble bath. Mix 120 ml (4 fl oz) of bicarbonate of soda in a shallow, warm bath and have your child sit in it several times a day. After the bath, gently blot dry the urinary region. Get rid of bubble baths, fabric softeners including dryer sheets, and perfumed toilet paper, and use only cotton, not nylon, knickers. If these steps don't take care of the problem, talk with the doctor; it could be a bladder infection.

Infrequent urination. Occasionally in hot weather, when a child is perspiring a great deal and not drinking enough, he may not urinate for eight hours or more. What does come is scanty and dark. The same thing may happen during a fever. When water is in short supply, the kidneys hold on to every drop. In these situations, be sure to give your child plenty of chances and occasional reminders to drink between meals, especially when he is too small to tell you what he wants.

Sore on the end of the penis. Sometimes a small raw area appears around the opening of the penis. There may be enough swelling that it's difficult for the boy to pass his urine. This little sore is a localized nappy rash. The best treatment is to expose the sore to the air as much as is practical. Bathing daily with a mild soap will encourage healing. If the child is in pain from being unable to urinate for many hours, he can sit in a warm bath for half an hour and be encouraged to urinate while in the tub. If this doesn't make him urinate, the doctor should be called.

Infections of the bladder and kidneys. Adults with bladder infections often complain of frequent, burning urination. Children sometimes have the same symptoms, but often they don't. A young child may only have belly pain or fever, or no symptoms at all; the infection is only discovered by testing the urine. If there is a lot of pus, the urine may appear hazy or cloudy, but normal urine can look the same due to ordinary minerals in it. Infected urine may smell somewhat like a bowel movement. If the infection moves into the kidneys, there is often high fever and aching or pain in the back. Children with these symptoms need prompt medical care.

After the first few weeks of life, urinary tract infections are more common among girls than boys. Wiping from back to front is a frequent cause of bladder infections in girls. Boys who have not been circumcised are somewhat more prone to urinary tract infections. It's worth keeping this in mind if your child has a fever and belly pain, or any discomfort with urination.

It's important to treat urine infections to prevent long-term kidney damage. Sometimes an underlying abnormality in the kidneys or the tubes leading from them sets a child up for repeated urinary infections. Testing for these abnormalities is important, because surgery may be needed.

Vaginal discharge. A thin discharge that goes away on its own in a couple of days is not concerning. Try having the child sit in a shallow warm bath to which 120 ml (4 fl oz) of bicarbonate of soda has been added. Wearing white cotton panties, using unperfumed white toilet paper, and wearing clothes that provide adequate air ventilation to the vaginal area may help relieve and prevent further irritation. Proper wiping (from front to back) and avoiding bubble baths may also help.

A thick, profuse discharge that is irritating, or a discharge that lasts for several days, may be caused by a more serious infection. Rarely, it's a sign of sexual abuse. Doctors are trained to ask about abuse, and to examine the genitals for other signs.

A discharge that is partly pus and partly blood is sometimes caused by a small girl having pushed some object into her vagina. If the object remains there, it can cause irritation and infection. If this is found to be the case, it is natural and sensible for her parents to ask her to please not do this again, but it's better not to make the girl feel really guilty or to imply that she might have hurt herself seriously. The exploring and experimenting she has done are not too different from what most young children do.

HERNIAS AND TESTICLE PROBLEMS

Hernias. A swelling that comes and goes in a baby's groin or scrotum could be a hernia. The swelling is caused by a loop of intestine that has slipped down through a small passageway that is normally closed. Straining or coughing pushes the intestine into this area; when the child relaxes or lies down, the bowel moves back to where it belongs.

If the bit of intestine gets stuck, the swelling becomes fixed and painful; this needs immediate medical attention. While waiting to see the doctor, try raising the baby's hips on a pillow and apply an ice bag (or crushed ice in a plastic bag in a sock). These actions may make the intestine slip back into the abdomen. Don't try to push the lump down with your fingers. Don't feed the baby by breast or bottle until you have talked with the doctor. If your baby needs an operation, it's better to go with an empty stomach. For belly button (umbilical) hernias, see page 91.

Hydroceles. Like hernias, hydroceles cause swelling in the scrotum. Each testicle is surrounded by a delicate sac that contains a few drops of fluid; this helps it slide around. In a newborn there is often extra fluid in the sac, making the testicle appear several times its normal size. Sometimes this swelling appears later in infancy. Hydroceles usually get better on their own. Occasionally an older boy has a large hydrocele that may need to be operated on. Hernias and hydroceles may exist together; it can be confusing. Let your child's doctor help work out what's going on.

Undescended testicles. See page 92.

Testicular torsion. Each testicle hangs in the scrotum on a stalk of blood vessels, nerves and tubes. Sometimes the testicle twists around, squeezing the structures in the stalk and cutting off the blood flow. This condition, called testicular torsion, is very painful. The scrotum may be swollen, tender, red or purple. This is an emergency. Prompt medical attention is needed to save the testicle.

Testicular cancer. The risk of testicular cancer rises in the teen years; teenage boys should be taught to examine their testicles once a month, feeling each one carefully to detect any unusual lumps or areas of tenderness. Any suspicious changes need to be checked out promptly. With early treatment, the prognosis is good.

SUDDEN INFANT DEATH SYNDROME (SIDS)

About one in every 1,500 babies born in the United Kingdom dies of sudden infant death syndrome (cot death). Most commonly, it is a baby between three weeks and seven months of age. By definition, no explanation such as an infection is found, even when a postmortem examination is done.

All infants should fall asleep lying on their backs, unless a doctor instructs otherwise. Having infants sleep faceup cuts the risk of SIDS in half. Avoiding secondhand cigarette smoke and overheating are also important (see page 59 for more). However, even with the best precautions, it is not possible to prevent all cases of SIDS.

Responses to SIDS. The parents are shocked – a sudden death is much more shattering than one that follows a worsening illness. They are overwhelmed by guilt, assuming that they should have paid more attention to the cold if the baby had one, that they should have noticed something, or that they should have gone in to check on the child, even though there was no reason to do so. But no sensible parent would call a doctor for every slight cold, and the doctor would not have prescribed any treatment because there would not have been any reason to do so. No one could have anticipated the tragedy.

The parents will usually be depressed for many weeks

or months, with ups and downs. They may experience difficulty concentrating and sleeping, poor appetite and heart or stomach symptoms. They may feel a strong urge to get away or a dread of being alone. If there are other children, the parents may be afraid to let them out of their sight, want to shun responsibility for caring for them, or treat them irritably. Some parents want to talk; others bottle up their feelings.

Other children in the family are sure to be upset, whether they show ordinary grief or not. Small children may cling or behave badly. Older children may appear unconcerned, but experience tells us that they are trying to protect themselves from the full force of grief and guilt. It is hard for adults to see why a child should feel guilty, but all children have resentful feelings at times towards their brothers and sisters, and their immature thinking may tell them that their hostile feelings brought about the death.

If the parents avoid talking about the dead baby, their silence may add to the other children's guilt. So it is good for the parents to talk about the baby, to explain that a special sickness of babies caused the death and that it was not the fault of anyone. Euphemisms like 'The baby went away' or 'She never woke up' simply add new mysteries and anxieties. It's particularly helpful if the parents try to respond in a gentle way to every one of the children's questions and comments, so that they will feel that it is all right to bring up their deeper worries. The parents should seek counselling from a guidance clinic, a psychiatrist, a psychologist or a clergy member so that they can express and come to understand their overwhelming feelings. Call the FSID

(Foundation for the Study of Infant Deaths) helpline on 0808 802 6868 or look at fsid.org.uk – they can put families in touch with a trained 'befriender' straight away.

ACQUIRED IMMUNE DEFICIENCY SYNDROME (AIDS)

AIDS (acquired immune deficiency syndrome) is caused by the human immunodeficiency virus (HIV). Once HIV gets into the bloodstream, it impairs the body's ability to develop immunity to other infections. So a person with AIDS can die of an infection that, in a normal person, would soon be cured by the body's own protective mechanisms. It has been estimated that in 2010, 31 to 35 million people in the world were infected by HIV, although not all have AIDS.

HIV is most commonly transmitted through bodily fluids such as semen and vaginal secretions during sexual intercourse. It is also transmitted from blood to blood in drug users who share needles. The transmission of HIV is higher in people who practise anal intercourse, because the lining of the rectum is more easily injured than the lining of the vagina. HIV may be transmitted by infected men and women even when there are no symptoms. All blood transfusions and other blood products are screened to prevent HIV transmission.

AIDS in children is almost always caused when mothers transmit HIV during pregnancy or at the time of birth. Not all pregnant women with HIV or AIDS transfer the infection to their children. Medications given during pregnancy can greatly reduce the chance that the baby will become infected. With proper treatment, babies who are infected are surviving for longer and longer periods of time. For many people, using a combination of medications has changed AIDS into a manageable disease with a long life expectancy, but there is still no real cure.

HIV is not spread by touching, kissing, living in the same home, sitting in the same classroom, swimming in the same pool, eating or drinking from the same utensils, or sitting on the same toilet as someone with AIDS. Although AIDS is highly lethal and has spread throughout the world, it is not a highly contagious disease.

How (and why) to talk to children and teens about AIDS. By mentioning the subject even in a casual way, you make it possible for your child to ask questions and get your reassurance and support. Most likely your child will hear about AIDS from TV, videos or films, or at school.

DR SPOCK COMMENTS

The two greatest protections against contracting HIV, I feel, are education about safe sex techniques and a belief that the spiritual aspects of sexual love, including the desire of many adolescents raised with high ideals to postpone intercourse until there is a deep commitment, are as important and as worthy of respect as the purely physical.

Adolescents need to know that the greatest risk of becoming infected with HIV comes from unprotected sex with multiple partners. The greater the number of sexual partners, the greater the chance that one of them has AIDS or is carrying HIV without having developed the symptoms of AIDS. The surest way, of course, is to delay intercourse until marriage; but simply telling a teen to do this hasn't been shown to be a reliable strategy (see page 709). Teens should also know that condoms – latex, not lambskin – offer much, though not total, protection during intercourse. The diaphragm and the pill do not protect against AIDS.

Preteens and teenagers should also understand the risks drug addicts take when sharing drug equipment with each other. The fact is that children are hearing about intravenous drug use and anal intercourse in relation to AIDS on television and in the media. That makes open communication and information sharing with parents all the more important. Talking with children about sex and drugs does not make them more likely to indulge in those dangerous activities; in fact, it's just the opposite.

TUBERCULOSIS

Tuberculosis (TB). This disease is fairly uncommon in the United Kingdom but on the increase in urban areas. The children most at risk are those who were born overseas (for example, in South Asia, Southeast Asia or Central and South America), whose family members were born overseas, who live in lower-income communities, or who are exposed to anyone with a chronic cough that could be TB. The BCG vaccination against TB is given soon after birth to babies born in areas with higher rates of TB, such as many parts of London.

Most people think of TB as it occurs typically in adults. A spot or cavity develops in the lung; cough, sputum, fever, fatigue and weight loss follow. However, TB in childhood usually takes other forms. Very young children have little resistance, and the infection often spreads throughout the body. In later childhood, TB may not cause any symptoms; it waits in the body, then emerges when resistance is low. Symptoms of TB, when they do arise, are often not very specific. Therefore, it's important to keep TB in mind when a child has vague symptoms such as unusual tiredness or poor appetite.

Testing for latent TB is with the tuberculin skin test (TST, PPD or Mantoux test) followed by a chest X-ray if necessary. New tests are being developed as well. Anyone with suspected TB exposure should be tested. It's also wise to have a new housekeeper, nanny or any other new member of the household tuberculin-tested. (Everyone who works in a hospital should be tested each year.)

What if your child tests positive? There's no need to be alarmed, since a great majority of the cases discovered throughout middle childhood have either healed already or will heal gradually with care. Typically, treatment with medication for about one year prevents the actual disease from developing later.

REYE'S SYNDROME

This rare but serious condition can cause permanent damage to the brain and other organs. It can also be fatal. Its cause is not completely understood, but it usually occurs during a viral illness. It is now known that children and adolescents who receive aspirin when they have a viral illness, especially influenza or chicken pox, are much more likely to get Reye's syndrome than those who are given paracetamol or another nonaspirin product.

SECTION IV

Raising Mentally Healthy Children

WHAT CHILDREN NEED

LOVE AND LIMITS

The surest way to raise mentally healthy children is to cultivate loving, nurturing and mutually respectful relationships with them. Loving means, first of all, accepting your child as a person. Every child has strengths and weaknesses, gifts and challenges. Loving means adjusting your expectations to fit your child, not trying to adjust your child to fit your expectations.

Another part of loving is finding ways to be happy together. That might mean playing a tickling game, looking at picture books, going for a walk in the park, or just talking about different things. Children don't need such experiences all day long. But they do need at least some shared happiness every day.

DR SPOCK COMMENTS

Love and enjoy your children for what they are, for what they look like, for what they do, and forget about the qualities that they don't have. I don't give you this advice just for sentimental reasons. There's a very important practical point here. The children who are appreciated for what they are, even if they are homely,

> or clumsy or slow, will grow up with confidence in themselves and happy. They will have a spirit that will make the best of all the capacities that they do have, and of all the opportunities that come their way.

Of course, children have other needs, too. Understanding those needs and making the commitment to meet them is what nurturing is all about. Newborn babies need *everything*: feeding, changing, bathing, holding and talking to. Over the first year of life, the experience of being nurtured creates a sense of basic trust in other people and optimism towards the world in general.

As their abilities grow, children need more and more chances to do things for themselves. They need challenges that stretch their skills without overwhelming them. They need to be able to take risks without getting hurt. Babies can't learn to feed themselves if they aren't first allowed to make a mess. Children learning to tie their own shoes have to try and fail, try and fail and try again. A parent's job is to set the limits within which safe risk taking can happen.

Children want what they want when they want it. They need to learn the difference between wanting and needing. Secure children know that they always get what they need but not always what they want. They also understand that other people have needs and wants, too. Children learn these lessons when parents treat them with kindness and respect and require respect, cooperation and politeness in return. When it comes to bringing up children, love is not enough. Children need love *and* limits.

EARLY RELATIONSHIPS

Relationships and the wider world. What stimulates normal, well-rounded development – emotional, social and intellectual? Babies and children, by their nature, keep reaching out to people and to things. Loving parents, watching and coaxing, respond enthusiastically to their baby's first smiles with smiles of their own; similar interactions are repeated every waking hour for months. Parents give food at times of hunger, comfort during times of misery. All of these things reinforce the child's feelings of being well cared for and connected to others.

These first feelings create a sense of basic trust that will colour the child's future relationships. Even her interest in things and her later capacity to deal with ideas and concepts in school and at work rest on this foundation of love and trust.

A child needs to know that there is at least one loving, reliable adult to whom she belongs. Starting from such a secure base, the child can more readily face the challenges of growing up – going off to school, trying difficult things – and coping with obstacles and disappointments. Positive traits in children emerge naturally when they are given love and nurturing. Then when they are exposed to a variety of experiences, they have the confidence and motivation to attempt to master the skills that match their inborn talents.

As children grow, they reach out to embrace the world. Through the ages, the natural interplay between this outward reaching and the parents' sensitive loving responses has been sufficient to produce bright, capable, sociable, loving young people.

EMOTIONAL NEEDS

Early care. A child's experiences in the first two or three years of life have a profound effect on her personality. Babies and toddlers who are cared for by loving, enthusiastic parents, perhaps with the help of others, develop inner resources for coping with the inevitable challenges of growing up. By contrast, babies whose caregivers are distracted, distant or unpredictable begin life with deficits that are hard to make up. They may find it hard to keep fear and anger in check and to respond with openness and generosity. They may find learning difficult, because they can't tolerate the feeling of not knowing something yet. Their first instinct may be to suspect that others are trying to take advantage of them, and so they try to be the ones who take advantage.

We've learned about the effects of extreme emotional neglect by studying babies and young children in orphanages where they are fed and changed or taken to the bathroom, but otherwise left alone in their cots most of the time. (These places used to be common in the United Kingdom; now, sadly, they are still found elsewhere.) These children wither physically and emotionally, and few fully recover. The destructive effects of such empty childhoods start showing up after about six months of age, and by twelve months they become hard to reverse. Most children who spend two or three years in an orphanage carry scars for life.

A few emerge undamaged, however. They are the ones who manage, even in the face of institutionalization, to develop a warm, loving relationship with one stable caregiver.

Why is a loving caregiver – whether mother, father, grandparent or child care professional – so important to a young child's development? In the first year, a baby has to depend mainly on the attentiveness, intuition and helpfulness of adults to get her the things that she needs and craves. If the adults are too insensitive or indifferent to her, she may become somewhat apathetic or depressed.

Children develop all of their core attitudes and skills through relationships. When they are treated with consistent kindness, they come to see others as loving, and themselves as worthy of being loved. Language skills, so central to a child's eventual ability to cope with emotions and the world, begin with the exciting back-and-forth exchanges between a baby and an attentive and responsive caregiver.

Parents give their children their pride and joy in their tiny accomplishments, thoughtful playthings, answers to their questions, and a willingness to let them play freely as long as they do no damage. Parents read to their children and show them the pictures, conveying a love of stories and art. These are the attitudes and activities that foster emotional depth and keen intelligence.

Whether children will grow up to be lifelong optimists or pessimists, warmly loving or distant, trustful or suspicious, depends largely, although not entirely, on the attitudes of the individuals who care for them in their first two years. Therefore, the personalities of parents and caregivers are of great importance.

One person acts towards children as if they are basically bad, always doubting and scolding them. Children raised in this way may grow up doubting themselves, full of guilt. A person with more than average hostility finds a dozen excuses every hour for venting it on a child, and the child acquires a corresponding hostility. Other people have the itch to dominate children, and unfortunately they can succeed. These children often grow up to dominate their own children or to have such difficulty exerting authority that they can't set appropriate limits. (Remarkably, this isn't always the case: some people who had awful childhoods become excellent parents by force of will. They are truly heroes.)

Continuity of caregiving. A very particular need of young children is continuity in their caregivers. From the age of a few months, babies come to love, count on and derive their security from the one person, or at most a very few people, who provide most of their care. Even at six months, babies become seriously depressed, losing their smile, their appetite and their interest in things and people, if the parent who has cared for them disappears for more than a brief time. There will be depression, lesser in degree, if a person who assists the parent on a regular basis leaves.

For this reason, it's important that caregivers don't change suddenly during the first two or three years. If the main caregiver has to leave, it should be only after a substitute has very gradually taken over. The substitute, in turn, needs to be committed to sticking with the job. In the group care of young children, if there are two or more staff people assigned to one group of children, each child should be paired up with one particular nanny, or perhaps two, so that there will be a relationship more like that of child and parent.

Emotional needs after three years. Children know that they are inexperienced and dependent. They count on their parents for leadership, love and security. They instinctively watch their parents and pattern themselves after them. This is how they get their own personalities, their strength of character, their assurance, their ability to cope. They are learning, in childhood, how to be adult citizens, workers, spouses and parents by identifying with their parents.

The greatest gift from parents is love, which they express in countless ways: a fond facial expression, spontaneous demonstrations of physical affection, pleasure in their children's accomplishments, comforting them when they are hurt or frightened, controlling them to keep them safe and help them become responsible people, giving them high ideals.

Children gain trust in themselves from being respected as human beings by their parents (or caregivers). This self-assurance helps them to be comfortable with themselves and with all kinds of people, for the rest of their lives. Respect from parents is what teaches children to give respect to their parents in turn.

Learning to be a man or woman. Boys and girls, by three years, focus on their parents' roles. A boy senses that his destiny is to be a man, so he watches his father particularly – his interests, manner, speech and pleasures; his attitude towards work; his relationships with his wife and with his sons and daughters; how he gets along with and copes with other men. A girl's need of a father at this time is not as obvious on the surface but is just as great underneath. Some of her relationships throughout life will be with males. She gets her ideas about what males are supposed to be like primarily from watching her father. The kind of man she eventually falls in love with and marries will probably reflect in one way or another the personality and attitudes of her father – for example, whether he's dominating or gentle, loyal or straying, pompous or humorous.

A mother's personality will be copied in many respects by her admiring daughter. How the mother feels about being a woman, a wife, a mother and a worker will make a strong impression on her daughter. How she gets along specifically with her husband will influence her daughter's future relationship with her own husband. A mother is her son's first great love. In obvious or subtle ways, this will set his romantic ideal. It will influence not only his eventual choice of a wife but also how he gets along with her.

Two parents are preferable. All things being equal, it is preferable for children to live with two parents (one may be a stepparent), if the parents love and respect each other. Two parents will be able to support each other emotionally. They will be able to balance or counteract each other's unjustified worries and obsessions about the children. The children will have a pattern of marital relations to guide them when they are adults. If the parents are of opposite sexes, then the children will know both sexes realistically as well as idealistically. If not, special efforts can be made to give children this helpful breadth of experience.

This is not to say that children can't grow up to be healthy without two parents; many do. If they lack a father, they create one – in their imagination – out of what they remember, what their mother has told them and the appealing characteristics of friendly men they see from time to time. This synthetic father can supply fairly well the masculine image they need. Similarly, a child without a mother creates one from memory, family stories and relationships with other women. Certainly it would be a great mistake for a parent to make a hasty, unsuitable marriage just to provide a child with a second parent.

PARENTS AS COMPANIONS

Friendly, accepting parents. Boys and girls need the chance to be around their parents, to be enjoyed by them and to do things with them. Unfortunately, working parents are apt to come home wanting most of all to relax after a long day. If they understand how valuable their friendliness is, they may feel more like making a reasonable effort to at least greet the children, answer questions and show an interest in anything they want to share. This is not to say that the conscientious parent should force himself or herself beyond the limits of endurance. Better to chat for fifteen minutes enjoyably and then say, 'Now I'm going to read my paper,' than to spend an hour grumpily playing.

A boy needs a friendly father. Sometimes a father is so eager to have his son turn out perfect that it gets in the way of their having a good time together. The man who is eager for his son to become an athlete may take him out at an early age to play catch. Naturally, every throw and every catch has its faults. If the father is constantly criticizing, even in a friendly tone, the boy becomes uncomfortable inside. It isn't any fun. Also, it gives him the feeling of being no good, in his father's eyes and in his own. A boy comes around to an interest in sport in good time if he's naturally self-confident and outgoing. Feeling approved of by his father and mother helps him more than being coached by his father. A game of catch is fine if it's the son's idea and if it's for fun.

A boy doesn't grow spiritually to be a man just because he's born with a male body. The thing that makes him feel and act like a man is being able to pattern himself after men and older boys with whom he feels friendly. He can't pattern himself after a person unless he feels that this person likes him and approves of him. If a father is always impatient or irritated with him, the boy is likely to feel uncomfortable not only when he's around his father but when he's around other men.

So a father who wants to help his son grow up comfortable about being a man shouldn't jump on him when he cries, scorn him when he's playing games with girls, or force him to practise athletics. He should enjoy him when he's around, give him the feeling he's a chip off the old block, share a secret with him, and take him on excursions sometimes when it's just the two of them.

A girl needs a friendly father, too. A friendly father plays a different but equally important part in the development of a girl. She patterns herself after him to only a limited degree, but she gains confidence in herself as a girl and a woman from feeling his approval. In order not to feel inferior to boys, she should believe that her father would welcome her in back-garden sports, on fishing and camping trips, and in attendance at football games, whether or not she wants to accept the invitation. She gains confidence in herself from feeling his interest in her activities, achievements, opinions and aspirations.

By learning to enjoy the qualities in her father that are particularly masculine, a girl is getting ready for her adult life in a world that is half men. The way she makes friendships with boys and men later, the kind of man she eventually falls in love with, and the kind of married life she makes are all influenced strongly by the kind of relationship she has had with her father throughout her childhood and by the relationship her parents enjoy with each other.

Mothers as companions. Boys and girls need their mother's companionship in more ways than just the time they spend together in their daily routines. They need opportunities for special activities with her, the same way they need them with their father. These could be trips to museums, films or sporting events, or time spent hiking, kicking a ball or riding bikes. The point is that it shouldn't be an obligation for the mother, but something both she and the children really enjoy.

What about single parents? Children benefit from positive relationships with both their mothers and the fathers. But what if, as is often the case, there is only one parent available, or if the parents are of the same sex? Must the child's psychological well-being inevitably suffer?

The answer to this question is a resounding no. While it is true that children need both male and female role models, those role models need not live in the same home. What children need most of all is nurturing and love, a consistent presence in their lives of someone who provides emotional support and teaches them the ways of the world. A child growing up with a single parent who can provide these necessities will be far better off than a child whose mother and father neglect his needs because of their own unhappiness. Most children from single-parent families find role models outside the home – a special uncle or aunt, perhaps, or a close friend of the family.

Children are adaptable. They don't need a perfect childhood (as if such a thing ever existed). They do need love and consistent care. When these are present, children do well in all sorts of different family constellations (see pages 741–762).

THE FATHER AS PARENT

Shared responsibility. As more and more women have become breadwinners for their families, men have been participating increasingly in all aspects of child care. As a society, however, we still tend to think of parenting as women's work. Other than breast-feeding, fathers can care for their children as well as mothers and contribute equally to their children's security and development. Everyone in the family benefits when parenting responsibility is shared,

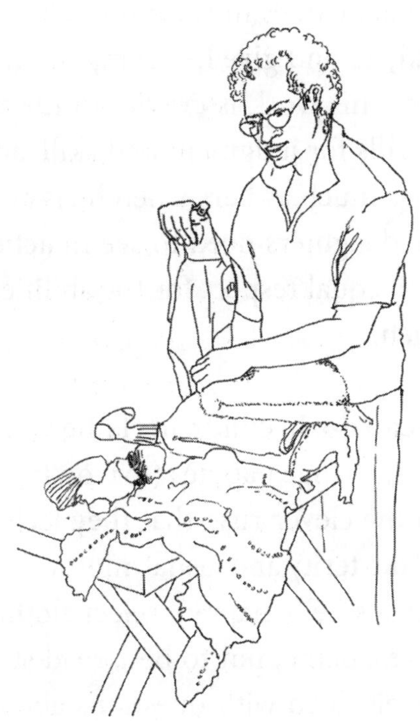

even if the division of labour isn't strictly fifty-fifty. At its best, parenting occurs in the spirit of equal partnership.

A father with a full-time job, even if the mother is staying at home, will do best by his children, his wife and himself if he takes on half or more of the management of the children (and also participates in the housework) when he is home from work and at weekends. The mother's leadership and patience will probably have worn thin by the end of the day, as would the father's if he were the one at home with the children all day. Children profit from experiencing a variety of styles of leadership and control by both parents, styles that neither exclude nor demean but enrich and complement the other.

When a father does his share of the work at home as a matter of course, he does much more than simply lighten his wife's workload and give her companionship. It shows that he believes this work is crucial to the welfare of the family, that it calls for judgment and skill, and that it's his responsibility as much as hers when he is at home. This is what sons and daughters need to see in action if they are to grow up with equal respect for the abilities and roles of men and women.

What fathers can do. In child care, fathers can give bottles, feed solid foods, change nappies (for too long fathers have got away with the clever ruse that they lacked the intelligence, manual dexterity and visual-motor skills to be capable of changing a smelly nappy), select clothes, wipe away tears, blow noses, bathe, put to bed, read stories, fix toys, break up quarrels, help with questions about homework, explain rules and assign duties. Fathers can participate in the whole gamut of domestic work: shopping, food preparation, cooking and serving, dishwashing, bed making, housecleaning and laundry.

There are increasing numbers of stay-at-home fathers married to women with full-time jobs, and these men assume the major share of care for the children and home while their children are small. Children in these families grow up just as emotionally and mentally healthy as children reared in more traditional families. Fears that boys in such families will somehow grow up as sissies or that girls will grow up unfeminine have no basis in fact.

DR SPOCK COMMENTS

I believe that both boys and girls should be raised with a deep conviction that the family is the richest and most enduring source of satisfaction in life. Then women could feel less pressure to accept men's traditional values, and men, freed from their narrow obsession with work and status, could begin to practise women's many skills and try to adopt their values. It will be a great day when fathers and mothers consider the care of their children as important to them as their jobs and careers, and when all career decisions are balanced with careful consideration of their effect on family life.

SELF-ESTEEM

Self-esteem, not self-satisfaction. Everybody, beginning in childhood, is entitled to a comfortable assumption that she is likable, that she is loved and that doing her best is good enough. But children don't need to feel satisfied with themselves and appreciated by those around them all of the time. Parents don't have to be constantly complimenting their children, whether they really deserve it or not, in order to be sure that their children are not being deprived of self-esteem.

Part of self-esteem is self-confidence. Praising a child can build self-confidence, but if the praise isn't genuine, the child will see straight through it. One way of helping your child build self-esteem is to help him cope with a range of emotions, both positive and negative. It's okay for a child to try something and not do well at it. The child who is showered with compliments, only to be insulted when a parent is angry, will not develop self-esteem. Rather, he will be anxious and insecure. Consistency and firm limits do more to build self-esteem than do hollow compliments.

The flip side is the parent who constantly finds fault or assumes the child has done, or is about to do, something wrong. Children who grow up under these conditions may develop a chronic sense of guilt and self-blame; their good behaviour is bought at a high price. In the matter of self-esteem, the first and most important step is not so much to build it up with a succession of compliments but to avoid tearing down the natural self-assurance with which children are born. Then you don't have to run the risks of conceit and excessive self-satisfaction that can result from too much praise.

·•· DR SPOCK COMMENTS

I find it easier to emphasize and clarify aspects of low self-esteem and its causes, perhaps because my mother was particularly eager to ward off conceit in her children, which she thought of as obnoxious in itself and likely to lead to more serious faults. I still recall today how, when one of her friends complimented me on my looks in adolescence, she hastened to say, after the friend left, 'Benny, you are not good-looking. You just have a pleasant smile.' All six of her children grew up feeling somewhat unattractive and underachieving.

The positive promotion of self-esteem. Children don't need compliments for every act of good behaviour or for every small achievement. Take the example of the child whose parents have been encouraging him to learn to swim by praising him to the skies every time he momentarily ducks his head underwater. After an hour of this he is still demanding, 'Watch me swim,' every minute, though he has made no real progress; he has only developed a greater appetite for praise and attention. Excessive compliments don't nurture independence (although they are much less destructive than the opposite, belittling and constant scolding).

Next to avoiding chronic scolding and belittling, the soundest way to foster self-esteem in your child is to show her an *enjoying love.* This means not just a devoted love that proves your readiness to make sacrifices for her, but an enjoyment of being with her, of hearing some of her stories and jokes, a spontaneous appreciation of some of her artwork or some of her athletic feats. You also show an enjoying love by occasionally suggesting an unanticipated treat, an excursion or even a walk together. Effective parents also enjoy setting limits, because they understand that this is an important part of teaching their children what they need to know. It's not that they enjoy making their children unhappy by denying them things, but they enjoy the whole process of helping a child grow and develop in every way.

Parents instill self-esteem by showing an attitude of respect for their children, such as one might show to a valued friend. This means not being rude, not being disagreeable and not being indifferent to her, but instead being polite and gracious. There is no reason for us to feel free to be rude, gruff or indifferent to our children just because they are younger.

The one mistake most often made by parents who do show respect for their children is a failure to expect respect from their children in return. Children, like adults, feel more comfortable and happier when dealing with people who are self-respecting and who naturally, as a result, show that they expect respect from others. You don't have to be disagreeable to convey this expectation. When a child belches loudly at the dinner table, it's more effective to remind him to please cover his mouth than to shout at him. Respect is a two-way street.

The press for achievement. We know that if you try hard enough, you can teach a two-year-old to read or even teach your one-year-old to recognize flash cards, but this is not a particularly wise thing to do. Some parents – armed with the hope that all it takes is the right playthings from infancy and the right mental stimulation at home and in school – try to fashion a precocious, brilliant child. But this particular kind of parental ambition, though understandable in a country where intelligence is so highly prized, is mistaken and apt to backfire. Mental capacity is only one aspect of a person, and may well fail to make him or her a success in life unless it is balanced with creativity, common sense and a genuine liking for others. There are always costs to pushing a child to succeed too early: the relationship between parent and child can become strained and overfocused on intellectual success rather than emotional closeness, and the child may neglect some areas of her development in an attempt to achieve mastery in one targeted area.

Trying to create a superkid is an understandable mistake. We all want our children to make the best use of their talents and to learn as much as they can. But there is no real evidence that pushing a child early on confers any later advantage. The first kid on the street to do something often doesn't end up any more competent than later bloomers. Attempts to push ahead one area – learning to read early, for example – almost always come at the expense of another important area of functioning, such as getting along with other children. Children develop best when their inborn talents and nature are allowed to blossom at their own pace.

BEYOND PARENTING

There is much beyond parenting that affects a child's mental health. Internal forces play a role, such as inherited mental and physical vulnerabilities and temperament. Other pressures arise within families: siblings are powerful shapers of a child's emotional landscape, for example. Still other dynamics play out in neighbourhoods and schools and in the society at large, areas where a parent's influence is often limited. Parenting is where you have the most control, but it's helpful to think about everything that impacts your child's mental health, because how you respond to these forces *can* make a difference.

Heredity. We know that many mental and emotional disorders are influenced by a person's genes, that is, by heredity. Depending on the illness, the strength of this influence can be modest or very great. For example, if both of a child's parents have manic-depressive (also called bipolar) disorder, the chances are better than fifty-fifty that the child will, too. Anxiety, obsessive-compulsive disorder and schizophrenia are all heavily influenced by heredity, as are attention deficit hyperactivity disorder (ADHD) and many other conditions.

In fact, it is likely that genes play a role in *every* mental health problem, either increasing or decreasing a child's susceptibility to different life challenges (what psychologists sometimes call the 'environment'). Differences in susceptibility explain in part why two children raised by the same parents in the same household often follow very different mental health paths. The other part, of course, is that even within the same family, the challenges (environment) can be quite different for different children.

Heredity also works in more subtle ways, by affecting a child's temperament, or style of behaving. One child is bubbly and outgoing; another is quiet and observant. One child seems to respond to any small change in temperature, noise or light level; another barely seems to notice. One child always starts with a positive outlook; another starts with the negative and has be won over to the positive.

Children who are often negative, intense and persistent have been said to have a difficult temperament, or worse, to be difficult children. But it's clear that temperamental patterns are either difficult or easy in relation to what is expected of a child. The temperaments of most six-year-old boys, with their high need for physical activity, are difficult in the context of most Year 2 classrooms, which demand a lot of sitting still. You can't choose your child's temperament, but by understanding and accepting it, you can choose to respond in ways that help your child learn to function well with you, with peers and with other adults.

Siblings. Parenting books often ignore the crucial role that siblings play in a child's growing up. But if you think about your own childhood, you'll probably agree that siblings – or the lack of them if you are an only child – had a tremendous effect on your personality. Perhaps you modelled yourself after an older brother or sister who seemed to be able to do everything right, or maybe you chose to do very different things in order to stake out your own territory. If

you were lucky, your siblings supported you, but if you had siblings who didn't (or don't) mesh well with your personality, you know how very difficult that can be.

There are ways for parents to take some of the edge off sibling jealousy (see page 793), but whether siblings really like each other or just tolerate each other depends a lot on chance. Siblings who are close in age and compatible in temperament can be lifelong best friends. Siblings whose temperaments clash may never feel truly comfortable and relaxed together.

Parents often reproach themselves because they have different feelings about each of their children. But they are expecting the impossible of themselves. Good parents love their children equally in the sense that they are devoted to each one, want the best for all of them, and will make any necessary sacrifices to achieve this. But since all children are quite different, no parent can feel just the same about any two of them. It's normal and inevitable that we should feel quite differently about each of our children, that we should be impatient with certain characteristics in some of them and proud of others. It is the acceptance and understanding of these different feelings, rather than feeling guilty about them, that will allow you to treat each of your children with the love and special attention he or she needs.

Birth order and spacing. It's fascinating how birth order seems to shape a person's personality. For example, oldest children tend to be task-oriented leaders and organizers. Youngest children are often spontaneous, self-involved and a bit irresponsible. Middle children have less clear-cut roles and often end up finding their identities doing very different things from the other members of their families. Only children tend to combine characteristics of oldest children (high-achieving, for example) and youngest children (attention-seeking, for example.)

These are only generalizations, of course. The dynamics within each family are unique. For example, if more than five years have passed between children, a youngest child might respond in some ways like an only child; if there is only about a year between children, they may act like twins. If the oldest child refuses to take over leadership of the siblings, a younger child may take on that role. A parent who is herself an oldest child might get along well with her own oldest but find her youngest child to be annoying in some ways (like her youngest sibling). As a parent, you may be able to understand and influence these forces, but you can't really control them.

Peers and school. After age six or seven, the peer group becomes more and more important. A child's manner of speaking and dress and what he likes to talk about are all likely to be coloured, if not determined, by the kids in the neighbourhood, at school and on TV. If baggy trousers and untied laces are in, there's nothing any parent can do to make shorts and loafers cool.

Sometimes neighbourhood and peer forces can actively threaten a child's mental health. For example, children who are bullied may face a greater risk of developing long-term behaviour disturbances (those who bully are also at risk). The child who has no friends at school is at high risk for depression; having even a single friend may make all the difference in the world. As a parent, you often have to step back and let your child work through the challenges of peer relationships. At other times, though, you may have to step in (more on page 1013).

RAISING CHILDREN IN A TROUBLED SOCIETY

British society has never been more stressful than now, at the beginning of the twenty-first century. On the one hand, our society remains excessively competitive and materialistic. We revere wealth, and take the lack of wealth as a sign of personal failure. At the same time, millions of middle-class jobs have disappeared and are unlikely to come back any time soon. Families are facing the multiple pressures of financial insecurity, neighbourhood deterioration and the depression that weighs on parents who no longer can find steady work, or sometimes any work at all. As hard as these pressures are on families in the middle, those at the lower end of the income ladder suffer even more. Military families face special pressures, as parents go away for long periods and sometimes return with lasting physical and psychological injuries. Worries about global environmental deterioration are growing. All of these pressures affect the lives of parents and children.

The news is not all bad, of course. As ever-expanding wealth seems more and more like an empty promise, people are finding value in spiritual pursuits and in their communities. They are planting gardens together, discovering the joys of low-tech entertainment and celebrating creativity. Trouble and disasters, poverty and pollution all bring with them opportunities for parents. When parents work towards making the world better, they give their children a double gift; they teach them the joy that comes with service. Parents convey this crucial life lesson best by leading the way themselves.

DR SPOCK COMMENTS

I believe that there are two changes needed to relieve these tensions and move towards a more stable society. The first is to raise our children with different, more positive ideals. Children raised with strong values beyond their own needs – cooperation, kindness, honesty, tolerance of diversity – will grow up to help others, strengthen human relations and bring about world security. Living by these values will bring far greater pride and fulfillment than the superficial success of a high-paying position or a new luxury car. The

> second change is for us to reclaim our government from the influence of giant corporate interests that care little for human individuals, the environment or world peace, and whose only aim is maximal profit. We must become much more politically active, so that our government will serve the needs of all citizens.

There are endless ways, large and small, to teach your children about caring for others and the world. When you drive at sixty miles per hour rather than seventy, and when you turn down the heat or turn off the light, talk about how you are saving fuel. When you see ugliness or injustice, speak out against it and let your children join you. Write letters to the editor. Work together with like-minded people in your community to take care of the less fortunate. Become involved politically. Some of the national groups working to improve children's lives are listed in the Resource Guide.

THE NATURAL WORLD

Watch a three-year-old explore the crack between two slabs of cement. A tiny spider crawling across a leaf fascinates her. Later she rolls down a grassy hill at the park, her face lit with pure joy.

Young children have a powerful connection to nature. Growing things of all kinds enthrall them. The slow-motion spectacle of a bean sprouting excites them. Given the chance, they gravitate to animals large and small. The moon and stars are characters in their imaginations. This

special bond between children and nature suffuses many of the great works of children's literature: *Charlotte's Web*, *Peter Rabbit*, *The Secret Garden*, *Goodnight Moon*.

Left to follow his own lead, a child outside naturally explores, pokes, prods, watches and learns. He learns, among other things, to interact with a world that follows its own rules, different from the mechanical laws that define the world indoors. He learns to create his own entertainment and enjoy his own company. He locates himself in the natural world.

In an era when children lived much of their lives out of doors, these gifts of nature were often taken for granted or left to poets to describe. It's only now, when so many children live in wholly artificial environments, that science has begun to measure the medical and psychological benefits of nature. Compared to their indoor peers, children who regularly play outside are less prone to obesity, asthma, depression, anxiety and ADHD. If nature could be put in a pill, doctors would prescribe it. (I am reminded that Dr Spock's mother used to send him outside to play for hours at a time, rain or shine; she was convinced it was good for him. She was right.)

Give your children time in the woods and other wild spaces. Take walks in the parks where you live, wandering with no goal other than seeing what's there. Go to national parks on holiday and take the nature walks. Find a group to go bird-watching with. Plant things.

The natural world can enhance your children's health and well-being. The connection runs in the opposite direction as well. Children whose love of nature is allowed to take root are apt to grow into allies of the natural world. They know why forests are worth fighting for and why it's worthwhile to turn off unneeded lights and recycle aluminium cans. As a parent, you can give the world to your children and your children to the world.

CHILD CARE

WORK IN THE FAMILY AND OUT

Most parents work, taking care of their children, making money or advancing their careers. The old rule that Daddy goes to work while Mummy stays with the children is just one of the options. In some families these roles are reversed. Often the arrangements are complicated and change from day to day and year to year. Each family has to make difficult choices balancing everyone's needs. It's not simply a matter of deciding to sacrifice for the sake of the child: children need happy, fulfilled parents if they are going to grow up to be happy, fulfilled adults. (In what follows, I use 'work' to mean a paid job or training, even though parenting is work, too.)

WHEN TO RETURN TO WORK

How long a maternity leave should you take? The basic six months seems right for many families. This gives your baby time to settle into pretty regular feeding and sleeping routines and to get used to the rhythm of her family. It also gives you time to adjust to your own physiological and psychological changes and to establish nursing and add a bottle or two during work hours. By six months most babies are showing more interest in the world around them, so the process of separating for several hours a day is more acceptable to most parents.

Whenever you return to work, it's normal to have mixed feelings. After a few weeks, many parents are eager to get back on the job, if only to have adults to talk with during the day. But they often also feel sad or guilty about leaving their babies. Or they simply want more time with them. If you have the option, listen to your feelings. If you feel you need more time at home with your baby, try to take it.

Maternity leave and rights. Mothers who are employees (as opposed to self-employed) are entitled to 52 weeks' maternity leave when they have a baby. The first 26 weeks are called Ordinary Maternity Leave (OML) and the following 26 weeks are called Additional Maternity Leave (AML). Your employer should assume that you are going to take the full 52 weeks – if you decide to go back to work earlier you should give them eight weeks' notice. You have the right to return to your old job after your OML, and the right to return to it after your AML as well, unless it is not reasonably practical. You also have the right to ask to return to work part time or with flexible hours. Your employer must consider this request seriously – if they don't give practical reasons for turning you down, it could be discrimination.

While you're on maternity leave you may be entitled to maternity pay, either under your contract of employment, or by law through Statutory Maternity Pay, which can be paid for up to 39 weeks. Adoptive parents are also entitled to 52 weeks' leave and to claim Statutory Adoption Pay. Self-employed women, as well as any mothers who don't meet the requirements for Statutory Maternity Pay, may be able to claim Maternity Allowance.

Working fathers can take one or two weeks' paternity leave after their partner has a child or when they adopt a baby. Dads may qualify for Statutory Paternity Pay during this leave. In addition to this, if the baby's mother has gone back to work without using up all her statutory maternity leave, fathers can take the remainder of the leave off instead. In this case, fathers can also take over the right to be paid any remaining Statutory Maternity Pay or Maternity Allowance.

CHILD CARE ALTERNATIVES

Arrangements in the first year. In the United Kingdom, many children under one year old spend at least part of their day in the care of someone other than their parents. Studies have shown that young infants can thrive in nonparental care without any apparent harm to their intellectual or emotional development. This is the general case for nurseries and childminders that are of high quality (see page 656). However, an individual baby might have difficulty adjusting to group care; for that baby, quiet one-to-one care may be what she needs to thrive. You're the best person to decide what will work for your child.

If you have misgivings about a particular nursery or childminder for your child, listen to your instincts and make other arrangements. Some parents are able to arrange their work schedules to allow one or the other to be at home most of the time; a childminder can fill in the rest. If this solution is not possible, there are four types of day care to choose from: care by relatives, in-home care, childminders and group care.

DR SPOCK COMMENTS

Should you send your child to day care? I think this is a very personal decision that must be based on your family's needs. If you want to send your infant to day care, I wouldn't feel at all guilty about it. He'll do just fine, so long as the quality of the care is high. In the long run, children do best when their parents are happy and fulfilled. It's much better for a child to attend a good nursery than to be at home with a parent who is lonely and miserable and who resents staying at home all day with the baby. On the other hand, if you do choose to stay home full-time with your baby for as long as possible, then that's a wonderful choice also. I think the advocates on both sides do a disservice to parents when they imply that there is only one way to handle the situation. The best situation is the one that works best for your family.

Altered work schedules. Often the best solution is one in which the parents' work schedules can be altered so that both can work a reasonably full shift and yet one or the other can be at home for most of the day. More and more businesses are offering flexibility in work hours.

Flexibility is often a win-win choice, because it increases worker satisfaction and productivity. In times of recession, many businesses decide to cut hours rather than lay people off; the ability to use these hours flexibly to meet family needs can be a silver lining to the dark cloud of decreased pay.

Of course, parents need to be together during sleeping times as well as for some of the children's waking hours. A nonparent caregiver can fill in any uncovered hours. A relative with whom the parents see eye to eye may be an ideal fill-in caregiver, if you have a willing relative who can take on the responsibility. Another solution is for one or both parents to cut down to part-time jobs for three years, until the child is old enough to attend preschool and a different solution can be found. Of course, this solution is out of reach for many families that require two full-time breadwinners to meet their expenses.

In-home caregivers (nannies). Some working parents engage a housekeeper or nanny to come to their home. If the nanny works several hours a day, this person may well become the second most formative influence on the young child's developing personality, after the parents. So parents should try to find a person who shows much the same kind of love, interest, responsiveness and control as they do.

Far and away the most important trait is the person's disposition. She should be affectionate, understanding, comfortable, sensible and self-confident. (Of course, a paid nanny could be male, too.) She should love and enjoy children without smothering them with attention. She should be able to control them without nagging or severity. In other words, she should get along with them happily. It is a help when interviewing a prospective nanny to have your child with you. You can tell how she responds to a child better by her actions than by what she says. Avoid the person who is cross, reproving, fussy, humourless or full of theories about raising children.

A common mistake that parents make is to look first of all for a person with a lot of experience. It's natural that they should feel more comfortable leaving a child with someone who knows what to do for colic or croup. But illnesses and injuries are a very small part of a child's life. It's the minutes and hours of every day that count. Experience is fine when it's combined with the right personality. With the wrong personality, it's worth very little.

Cleanliness and carefulness are more important than experience. You can't let someone make the baby's formula who refuses to do it correctly. Still, there are many rather untidy people who are careful when it's important. Better a person who is too casual than one who is too fussy.

Some parents focus on the education of a nanny. But education is less important than a nanny's personal qualities, especially for young children. Others are concerned that the nanny may speak little English. But in the vast majority of cases, children are not confused by the different languages of the nanny and parents. If the nanny stays with the child for years, the child may reap the benefits of having learned two languages at home.

Sometimes, inexperienced young parents settle for

a nanny about whom they don't really feel right because they've decided they can't do any better, or because the person talks a good line. Keep looking until you find someone you really like. When you find the right person, pay as much as you can afford (or perhaps a bit more), so that it is hard for that person to even consider working elsewhere. When you are away at work, the knowledge that your child is in excellent hands is worth a lot.

Concerns about nannies. If you've found a good nanny, your child will become attached to her. When this happens, it's natural to feel jealousy. But children who come to love their nannies don't love their parents any less. Try to be aware of your feelings and deal with them openly; if not, you may slip into being unfairly critical of the nanny. On the other hand, some nannies have a great need to take over the child, to push the parents aside, and to show that they always know best. They may be quite unconscious of this need, and they can rarely be reformed.

A common problem is that a nanny may favour the youngest child in the family, especially one who was born after she joined the household. If she can't understand the harm in doing this, she should not stay. Favouritism of this sort is destructive to the child who is favoured, as well as the children who are not.

As the parent, you need to stay in control. At the same time, it's important to feel that you and the nanny are partners. The most important questions for nannies and parents are whether they can be honest with themselves, listen to each other's ideas and criticisms, keep the lines of communication open, respect each other's good points and good intentions, and cooperate for the benefit of the children.

Care by relatives. It's great if there's a relative – a grandparent, for example – who can take care of your child. But all of the issues that apply to unrelated nannies, discussed above, also apply to family. It's very important that any family member who helps care for your child understands that you are still the parent: what you say, goes. As long as you have this understanding, then care by a relative can be a wonderful alternative.

Nurseries. Nurseries take care of children during their parents' working hours, perhaps 7.30 am to 6.30 pm. Some nurseries are subsidized by local authorities or by employers. At its best, a nursery offers the advantages of the preschool: an educational philosophy, trained carers and teachers, and full educational equipment.

Nurseries are usually open year-round apart from perhaps a week at Christmas. They offer a stable, structured setting and are required to follow country-wide standards for the teaching and care of under-fives. The level of training of the staff and the child-to-staff ratio are regulated and monitored. However, this type of care tends to be expensive. Staff turnover tends to be high, so it's unlikely that your child will be consistently cared for by the same person. There are great differences in the quality of nurseries, which are regularly inspected and graded.

Childminders. Childminders look after a small number of children in their home – they are a popular choice. Childminders may be more convenient and affordable than nurseries, and more flexible in their hours. A smaller, family-like atmosphere may feel more comfortable for a young child. Children have the opportunity to develop a trusting relationship with one person – a very good thing.

Childminders must be trained and registered. If you use an unregistered childminder, you can't be sure that basic health and safety measures are in place. If you choose a childminder, it's very important that you feel completely comfortable with the provider – or that the standard of care is as you would wish and you are welcome to drop in any time and stay as long as you want. Your child should be glad to go to the childminder, and when you pick your child up you should hear about what your child did during the day.

Is group care good for young children? There is a debate in the United Kingdom about the value or harm of group care for very young children. Some claim that group experiences are inappropriate for children in the first few years of life. They argue that every child needs one or two significant caretakers who are crazy about him, who give him their undivided attention, and who have a strong attachment to him. The opponents of group care worry that children raised at an early age by multiple caretakers will have difficulty with later interpersonal relationships. Finally, they contend that there is no better teacher for a child than an intensely involved parent.

Group care advocates tell a different story. They assert

that there are many proper ways to raise a young child. They point to other cultures where infants are raised by siblings and extended family without apparent ill effects. They remind us that there are no studies demonstrating high-quality group care to be in any way harmful to the emotional development of children. They worry that parents who work and send their infants to group care will feel needlessly guilty that they are somehow hurting their children.

Infants are resilient creatures up to a certain point, and there is no reason why high-quality group care should harm their development. Children need adults who are devoted to them, whether it's a single parent or a small group of nursery teachers. They need consistency in their relationships, but this can be provided at home and in many nurseries.

A few studies have looked at the differences between children who went to nursery and those who didn't; those studies show that high-quality group care – of small groups of children by carefully selected, well-trained staff – is not harmful for most children. Exposure to caring adults and other children in a safe, stimulating environment can promote curiosity and learning. On the other hand, if large groups of children are cared for by poorly trained staff, the experience may have the opposite effect. One study suggested that children who go to group day care for an extended period tend to be more oriented towards and responsive to their peers but less so to adults. Children who do not attend group care tend to be more oriented towards adults (often becoming the teacher's pet) and less responsive to their peers. Will this difference affect a child's later functioning in school, or persist into adulthood? Nobody knows.

Everyone does agree, though, that the quality of day care is critical for children's well-being. Responsive, nurturing, stimulating, consistent care is vital and can be provided only by stable, well-trained staff in a well-funded nursery setting. Unfortunately, the very best nurseries may be too expensive for the average family. The only solution is political pressure for government subsidy for quality child care programmes.

Child care as partnership. All of the adults who take part in caring for a particular child should see themselves as partners. Parents and nonparent caregivers need to share information and insights, and support each other. If your child has worked very hard in day care at a particular challenge – say, scribbling with a crayon – you ought to hear about it when you pick her up in the evening. In the same way, if your child has been up often during the night because of noisy thunderstorms, the child care provider needs to know about that in the morning.

When I was a young doctor studying child development, some of my most important lessons came from the teachers at my daughter's nursery. I would make a point of spending fifteen or twenty minutes there at the end of the day or sometimes in the morning, sitting on the floor with the teachers and children. I learned a lot about parenting by watching those very skilful professionals at work. If you can develop a relationship of cooperation and mutual respect with your child's caregiver, your child will benefit, and you'll benefit as a parent, too.

CHOOSING DAY CARE

Finding options. First you need to compile a list of what's available in your community. Start with friends who can give you personal recommendations. Contact your local authority Family Information Service (see www.direct.gov.uk for how to find them).

Relationships and turnover matter. Especially for young children, child care should strive to develop supportive relationships between children and their care providers. In order to feel safe, children need to trust the adults who care for them; caregivers need to know children thoroughly, and connect with them emotionally, in order to work out what they need from moment to moment. If a nursery manager tells you that children don't mind frequent changes in providers as long as the providers are all kindly, find a different nursery.

In practical terms, an emphasis on relationships means that each child should have one or two primary providers assigned to him, and every attempt should be made to keep the same primary providers through the year. Low provider turnover is crucial for two reasons: when providers change often, children can't form lasting relationships with them, and low turnover is a sign that caregivers are happy and feel well cared for themselves.

Calls and visits. Call the providers on your list to find out if they offer the kind of care you want. Ask for the names and phone numbers of families served by the provider. Call them and ask about the details of the care, including discipline techniques. Visit potential sites. Stay for a few hours in each one and watch for warm, nurturing interactions between the caregivers and children, appropriate supervision and safety measures, and whether activities are appropriate to the children's developmental levels. Are the children relaxed? Do they trust the staff and turn to them for help? Do they cooperate with other children? Is there a lot of fighting? A good relationship between staff and children will show in the relationships among the children.

Visit a nursery on a regular basis. Unannounced visits during the day will reassure you that all is well. Parents should feel welcome at the nursery and their visits should be allowed at any time.

Registration and inspection. All nurseries and childminders in the UK must be registered and regularly inspected. In England, they are inspected by Ofsted and must meet the standards laid down in the Early Years Foundation Stage. In Wales the inspectorate is the Care and Social Services Inspectorate Wales (CSSIW), while in Scotland it's Social Care and Social Work Improvement Scotland (SCSWIS). In Northern Ireland, inspections are carried out by Early Years Teams, part of local Health and Social Care Trusts. All these bodies lay down standards for children's care, development and teaching. Health and safety measures, premises and equipment, child-staff ratios and staff qualifications are all regulated and assessed. If a setting is found to be unsatisfactory, it will no longer be allowed to provide child care.

AFTER-SCHOOL CARE

After age five, and even more so after age eight, children seek and enjoy independence. They turn for their ideals and for companionship to adults who are not their parents (especially to good teachers) and to other children. Although they can get along comfortably for hours at a time without needing an adult's support, they still benefit from knowing that they belong somewhere, particularly after school. A motherly or fatherly neighbour may be able to substitute until one of the working parents comes home. After-school play clubs are valuable for all children, but particularly for those whose parents work.

Latchkey children. Because of the lack of affordable, good-quality after-school play centres or groups, there are thousands of latchkey children in our country. After school, they let themselves into their flats or houses with their own keys, and fend for themselves until a parent comes home from work.

A responsible, self-reliant child can do well caring for herself, provided that she feels secure and has enough to do. Careful planning can help both the parent and child to feel confident. It's important that latchkey children know how to reach their parents if they need to, and have a nearby adult to turn to in case of emergency. They need careful safety instructions – what to say when the phone rings or when a stranger knocks at the door, for example. They need to know what they *can* do – for example, how much TV is okay – and also what's off-limits.

It's important to find out how your child feels. Some are comfortable with caring for themselves for a short time; others are frightened. It's tempting to have older children look after younger ones. This can work well if the older child is responsible and the younger ones are compliant. If not, there can be a lot of tension and fighting; you may need to make other arrangements.

Although you might think that older children would do better in self-care, that's not always the case. Teens who have a lot of unsupervised time are more likely to engage in risky behaviours, such as smoking cigarettes, using drugs and alcohol, and having sex. Teens (like toddlers) often feel more comfortable with firm limits on their behaviour, even if they protest. Unless you're certain that your teen is level-headed and reliable, you might be better off finding a structured after-school programme.

BABYSITTERS

Babysitters are a boon to parents and can help a child to develop independence. It's important that you and your child should know your sitter well. For night sitting with a baby who doesn't wake, it may only be necessary for the sitter to be sensible and dependable. But for babies who wake and for older children, the sitter should be a person the child knows and likes. It's frightening to most children to wake and find a stranger. (I'll talk about sitters as if they are female, but males can be fine sitters as well.)

With a new sitter, stay home for the first couple of times you hire her. Watch her in action with your children to make sure that she understands and loves children and can manage them with kindliness and firmness. Try to find one or two reliable sitters and stick with them.

To keep things straight, it's sensible to have a permanent notebook for the sitter listing the child's routine, some of the things he may ask for (in his words), the telephone numbers of the doctor and of a neighbour to call in an emergency if you can't be reached, bedtime hours, what the sitter may help herself to in the kitchen, how to turn the boiler up or down, and the whereabouts of bedclothes, nightclothes and other things that may be needed. But most of all, you should know your sitter and know that your child trusts her.

Young or old? It's a matter of maturity and spirit rather than years. There are children as young as fourteen who are extremely capable and dependable, but it's unfair to expect such qualities in most people that age. And some adults may prove unreliable, harsh or ineffectual. One older person has a knack with children; another is too inflexible or too anxious to adapt to a new child. The British Red Cross offers babysitter training courses, which cover safety and first-aid procedures. It makes sense to select a sitter who has had this sort of training. With a young sitter it's also reassuring to know that the sitter's parents are at home and available in case a true emergency arises.

TIME WITH YOUR CHILD

Quality time. You don't have to do anything out of the ordinary to create quality time. Any routine activity – driving places, shopping, cooking and eating together, taking care of housework – can be an occasion for close, nurturing and lovingly responsive interactions. If your work hours are long, you might need to make special arrangements to make quality time possible. Under-fives can be regularly allowed to stay up late in the evenings if it is possible for them to regularly sleep late in the mornings or have a nap at day care. In two-parent families, the attention of one parent at a time can be quite satisfying to children.

Some parents misinterpret quality time to mean that it really doesn't matter how much time they spend with their children as long as the time they do spend is jam-packed with quality. But *quantity* is also important. Children need to simply be around their parents, watching them in action, learning from their day-to-day example, and knowing they are an important part of their lives.

On the other hand, quantity can be overdone. Conscientious, hardworking parents may take it as an obligation to be talking, playing and reading with their children long after patience and enjoyment have run out. Parents who regularly ignore their own needs and wishes in order to provide quality time for their children may come to resent the sacrifice, and then the spirit of friendliness evaporates. A child who senses that he can make his parent give him more time than the parent feels like giving is encouraged to become pesky and demanding. The trick is to find the right balance: to spend plenty of time with your children, but not at the expense of fulfilling some of your own personal needs.

Special time. Special time is a brief period – five to fifteen minutes is usually enough – that you set aside every day to spend with each child individually. What's special is not what you actually do, but the fact that your child gets your undivided attention. Turn your mobile phone off and the answering machine on. Special time shouldn't be taken away as a punishment. Your child deserves a little special time each day simply by virtue of being your child and being loved. If you're travelling on business, you can have special time by telephone – reading aloud, making up a story or just talking.

The temptation to spoil. Working parents may find that because they are starved for their child's company, and perhaps because they feel guilty about seeing her so little, they are inclined to shower her with presents and treats, bow to all her wishes regardless of their own, and generally let her get away with murder.

It's fine for working parents to show their child as much agreeableness and affection as comes naturally, but they should also feel free to stop when they're tired, consider their own desires, avoid giving presents daily, spend only what money is sensible, and expect reasonable politeness and consideration from their children – in other words, to act like self-confident, all-day parents. The child will not only turn out better but enjoy their company more.

DISCIPLINE

WHAT DISCIPLINE IS

Discipline means to teach. When most people use the word 'discipline', what they really mean is punishment. While punishment is a part of discipline, it is by no means the whole story. 'Discipline' comes from the word 'disciple' and really means 'to teach.' Discipline is more than just teaching a child to follow the rules. It's also teaching her to show consideration for others, to do the right thing even when no one is watching, and to question the rules and oppose those that are unjust.

As a parent, you could create a harsh system of punishments so that, like good little robots, your children would behave perfectly – at least if they thought you were watching. But what would be the effect on their spirits and feelings towards others? On the other hand, you could indulge their every whim and praise them regardless of their behaviour. Such children might have a certain measure of happiness, but most people wouldn't want to get within ten feet of them. The challenge of discipline is to teach children the how and the why of good behaviour, without undermining their sense of self-worth and independent judgment.

Why children behave. The main source of good discipline is growing up in a loving family – being loved and learning to love in return. We want to be kind and cooperative (most of the time) because we like people and want them to like us. (Violent criminals are often people who in childhood were never loved enough to make much difference to them. Many of them were also abused or were witnesses to significant violence and turmoil.) Children gradually lessen their grabbing and begin to share somewhere around the age of three, not primarily because they are reminded by their parents (though that may help a little) but because their feelings of enjoyment and affection towards other children have developed sufficiently.

Another vital element is children's intense desire to be as much like their parents as possible. In the three- to six-year-old period they work particularly hard at being polite, civilized and responsible. They pretend very seriously to take care of their doll children, keep house and go out to work, as they see their parents do.

Strict or casual discipline? This looms as a big question for many new parents, and remains a source of tension in many families. To some parents, a casual approach implies merely an easygoing style of management. To others, it implies permissiveness, foolishly overindulging a child, letting him do or have anything he wants. In this view, casual discipline makes for rude, spoiled children.

It turns out that strictness or casualness is not the most important issue. Good-hearted parents who aren't afraid to be firm when necessary can get good results with either moderate strictness or moderate casualness. On the other hand, a strictness that comes from harsh feelings or an excessive permissiveness that is timid or vacillating can lead to poor results. The real issue is what spirit the parent puts into managing the child, and what attitude is instilled in the child as a result.

Stick to your convictions. Parents who naturally lean towards strictness should probably bring up their children that way. Moderate strictness – in the sense of requiring good manners, prompt obedience and orderliness – is not harmful to children so long as the parents are basically kind and so long as the children are growing up happy and friendly. But strictness is harmful when parents are overbearing, harsh and chronically disapproving, or when they make no allowances for a child's age and individuality. This kind of severity produces children who are either meek and colourless or mean-spirited.

An easygoing style can also produce children who are considerate and cooperative, as long as the parents are not afraid to be firm about those matters that are important to them. Many excellent parents are satisfied with casual manners as long as the child's attitude is friendly. These parents may not be particularly strict about promptness or neatness, but they don't hesitate to correct a child for selfishness or rudeness.

Firmness and consistency. The everyday job of the parent is to keep the child on the right track by means of firmness and consistency. Though children do the major share in civilizing themselves through love and imitation, there still is plenty of work left for parents to do. In driving terms, the child supplies the power but the parents have to do the steering. Some children are more challenging than others – they may be more active, impulsive and stubborn than most – and it takes more energy to keep them on the right track.

Children's motives are good most of the time, but they don't have the experience or the stability to stay on the road. The parents have to be saying, 'We hold hands when we cross the street,' 'You can't play with that, it may hurt someone,' 'Let's go in now, because it's time for lunch,' 'We have to leave the wagon here because it belongs to Harry and he wants it,' 'It's time to go to bed so you'll grow big and strong,' and so on.

How well the guidance works depends on whether the parents are reasonably consistent (nobody can be completely consistent), whether they mean what they say, and whether they are directing the child for a good reason, not just because they're feeling mean or bossy. The parent's tone of voice matters. An angry or belittling tone is likely to evoke anger and resentment, rather than a desire to improve.

REWARD AND PUNISHMENT

Rules of behaviour. The same basic rules of behaviour work for animals, children and adults: behaviours that are rewarded happen more often over time; those that are ignored or punished happen less often. Immediate rewards and punishments work better than delayed ones. Once established, behaviours persist longer if they are rewarded intermittently rather than every time. If the rewards stop suddenly, the behaviour tends to happen more often for a while before it peters out. These rules aren't a recipe or a prescription for effective discipline. But effective parents understand them, or act as if they do.

It follows from these rules that if you want your child to start a new behaviour – saying 'Thank you,' for example – you should work out how to reward that behaviour, perhaps by praising him. If you want your child to stop a behaviour – belching at the dinner table, for example – you could work out a suitable punishment, and apply it every time your child belched at the table. For many behaviours, you could use rewards, punishments or both.

Reward or punish? In general, rewards are more fun than punishments, both for parents and for children. And, happily, they often work better. Punishments tend to make children feel resentful, so they aren't as motivated to do what you want. Rewards tend to make children feel more like pleasing you.

Often you can work out how to turn a punishment into a reward. Instead of punishing a behaviour (hitting, say), simply reward the opposite behaviour (playing nicely). Once you get into the habit of thinking this way, you'll notice that most of the behaviours you thought required punishment have opposites that you can reward. For example: rude table manners versus polite manners; being disagreeable versus being agreeable; being selfish versus being generous or considerate.

Effective praise. The most effective reward is usually praise or approval; the most effective punishment is usually ignoring or criticizing. Effective praise has two parts. You need to tell your child what she did and how you feel about it. Sometimes effective praise includes a third part, what good is going to come of it. For example, 'You picked up your clothes and put them all in the basket. That makes me feel proud of you. Now we have more time to play.' Just saying 'Good girl' doesn't work as well, because your child might not know what behaviour earned the praise. Random praise for no reason at all isn't effective, either, because 'being good' isn't really doing anything.

Effective criticism. Effective criticism has the same three parts as effective praise. It lets your child know what he did, how you feel about it and what the consequences are. For example, 'You threw your eggs on the floor. That makes me mad. Now we have to clean them up.' Notice how much more information this statement conveys than simply 'Bad boy!'

Discipline or behaviour modification? It might sound, from the above, that I am suggesting that parents always talk to their children in a very stiff way. But after a little practice, you forget about formulas for effective praise and criticism and just begin to communicate more clearly. In reality, a lot of the communication is nonverbal, conveyed in smiles, frowns and looks of delight or concern. Children are gifted readers of these gestures, particularly when they come from the important adults in their lives.

Teaching talk. Think of rewards and punishments as one way of teaching your child what he needs to know. Another way is simply talking with your child about what's going to happen and what the expectations are. If you're planning a trip to Grandma's house, you might say, 'Today we're going to Grandma's. When we get there, first we'll talk with Grandma and tell her about school or the fun things we're doing; then, after a little while, it'll be time to play.' Children are much more likely to behave well if they know what to expect and what's expected of them.

Staying positive. Just as praise works better than criticism most of the time, expectations are almost always more effective when they are phrased in a positive way. Compare these two statements, for example: 'We're going to have a good time at the supermarket; I expect you to listen and stay near me' and 'Don't go running off in the supermarket!' One of them paints a positive picture, the other a negative one. Children tend to act out the images: words of negation such as 'don't' or 'no' don't register strongly in a child's mind, and instead the child fixes on the very behaviour you're trying to prevent.

With a young child, you can often simply redirect the child from a prohibited activity (playing with the electric socket, for example) to one that is preferred (playing with blocks). You might say something like 'No, no, that's not safe,' but then you quickly follow up by pointing out a safe, approved activity.

Is punishment necessary? Many good parents feel that they have to punish their children once in a while. But other parents find that they can successfully manage without ever having to. A lot depends on how the parents were brought up. If they were punished occasionally for good cause, they naturally expect to have to punish in similar situations. And if they were kept in line by positive guidance alone, they are apt to find that they can do the same with their children.

On the other hand, there are also quite a few poorly behaved children. The parents of some of them punish a lot, and the parents of others never do. So we can't say either that punishment always works or that lack of it always works. It all depends on the nature of the parents' discipline in general.

Punishment is never the main element in discipline – it's only a vigorous reminder that the parents feel strongly about what they say. We have all seen children who were smacked and deprived plenty, yet remained ill-behaved.

DR SPOCK COMMENTS

Is punishment necessary? Most parents decide it is, at one time or another. But that doesn't prove that children themselves need a certain amount of punishment, the way they need milk and cod liver oil, to grow up right.

When it makes sense to punish. You don't sit by and watch a small child destroy something and then punish him afterwards. You stop him and redirect him. Punishment is what you resort to when your system of positive expectations and clear communication has failed. Maybe your son, sorely tempted, wonders whether you still mean the prohibition that you laid down a couple of months ago. Or maybe he is angry and misbehaves on purpose.

The best test of a punishment is whether it accomplishes what you are after, without having other serious effects. If it makes a child furious, defiant and worse-behaved than before, then it probably isn't working. If it seems to break the child's heart, then the cost is too high. Every child reacts somewhat differently.

There are times when a child breaks something out of carelessness. If he gets along well with his parents, he feels just as unhappy as they do, and no punishment is needed. In fact, you may have to comfort him. Jumping on a child who feels sorry already sometimes banishes his remorse and makes him argue.

Avoid threats as much as possible. They tend to weaken discipline. It may sound reasonable to say, 'If you don't keep out of the road with your bicycle, I'll take it away.' But in a sense, a threat is a dare – it admits that the child may disobey. It will impress him more to be firmly told he must keep out of the road if he knows from experience that his parents mean what they say. On the other hand, if you see that you may have to impose a drastic penalty, like taking away his beloved bike for a few days, it's better to give fair warning. It quickly destroys a parent's authority to make threats that aren't or can't be carried out. Scary threats, such as of monsters and police who take bad children away, are never really helpful and often lead to serious fears. Ditto for the threat to walk off and leave a dawdling child behind, because this threat undermines a central pillar of emotional security. You don't want your child to have to worry all the time about being abandoned.

Physical punishments (smacking). Hurting children in order to teach them a lesson is traditional in many parts of the world, though smacking is highly controversial in the UK. Smacking remains legal here, provided that it does not leave a mark, but there are frequent moves to ban corporal punishment in the home entirely.

There are several reasons to avoid physical punishment. For one thing, it teaches children that the larger, stronger person has the power to get his way, whether or not he is in the right. Some children then feel quite justified in beating up smaller ones.

When an executive in an office or a supervisor in a shop is dissatisfied with the work of an employee, he doesn't rush in shouting and whack him on the bottom. He explains in a respectful manner what he would like, and in most cases this is enough. Children are not that different in their wish to be responsible and to please. They react well to praise and high expectations.

In the olden days, most children were spanked on the assumption that this was necessary to make them behave. In the twenty-first century, as parents and professionals have studied children here and in other countries, they have come to realize that children can be well behaved, cooperative and polite without ever having been punished physically.

Parents often justify smacking on the grounds that they were smacked themselves and it didn't do them any harm. On the other hand, nearly all of these parents can remember having strong feelings of shame, anger and resentment in response to smackings. I suspect that these parents were able to grow up psychologically healthy in spite of the smackings, not because of them. Most scientific studies don't find that smacking, in itself, is either particularly harmful or particularly beneficial. The nature of the parent-child relationship – whether warm and loving or cold and harsh – is a much more powerful force in children's development.

Nonphysical punishments. There is a logic to many nonphysical punishments. If a baby grabs his mother's nose and yanks, he gets put down on the floor. The punishment is to be separated from his mother (although he's right at her feet). Parents who use this mild form of time-out quickly teach their infants to control the urge to take hold of everything if that thing is somebody's face. Another young child hits at her parent's face, just to get attention. This behaviour often gives rise to an ironic scene, with the parent slapping the child's hand while saying, 'No hitting!' A more effective response is to say, 'Ow! That hurts,' put the child down and find something else to be interested in for a couple of minutes. Instead of attention, the child's unpleasant behaviour has earned her just the opposite.

Another form of nonphysical punishment, effective for older toddlers, is time-out in a designated safe place or playpen for a few minutes. Consider the toddler who insists on trying to pull the little plastic safety plugs out of the electrical sockets – a definite no-no. This persistent child has ignored your spoken limit, and when you try to redirect her to another activity, she gleefully runs back to the socket. She thinks she is playing a great game. Instead of unwillingly joining the game, you can put the toddler in her safe place, say 'Time-out,' and leave her there for a couple of minutes. Most toddlers hate being taken away from whatever it is they are interested in, so you can expect wails of protest. But this mild form of punishment is an effective way of teaching your toddler that you mean business.

Time-out. A formal time-out procedure works well for preschool and young primary school children. Time-out means time away from attention and entertainment. At home, you can choose a time-out chair that is fairly isolated from the flow of activity – not so far away that you aren't aware of what your child is doing, but not right in the middle of things, either. When you announce a time-out, your child needs to sit in the time-out chair until you tell him it's time to get up. You can use an egg timer, set for one minute per year of age. Much longer than that, and a young child is apt to forget why he was put in time-out and simply feel sad or resentful. But if the child gets up before the timer dings, the timer gets reset and he has to serve his sentence again from the beginning.

At the end of the time-out, you can ask the child to tell you why he needed a time-out and what he's going to do differently. If he doesn't have an idea, tell him, and give him another short time-out to think about it. This procedure makes your child responsible for learning the lesson you're trying to teach.

Some parents find that putting a child in his room and telling him that he can come out when he feels ready to cooperate works well. A theoretical disadvantage of this technique is that it may make the bedroom seem like a prison. On the other hand, it teaches the child that being around other people is a privilege that can be lost, and that when one is angry enough, a good thing to do is to find a way to be alone for a bit, to calm down.

Natural punishments. It often works well if the punishment flows directly from the crime. If a child leaves toys all over the living room after you've asked him firmly to pick them up, the toys might be put away where he can't get at them for a few days. If a teenager refuses to throw her laundry in the basket, she may find herself without a clean shirt for school (a severe punishment for many teens, but not all). An older teen who stays out late without calling may lose the privilege of going out at night for a while, until he can show that he can handle himself responsibly. Effective punishments have a logic that even the child being punished has to acknowledge. They teach the crucial life lesson that actions have consequences.

Overreliance on punishment. When I meet a parent who says she has to punish her child all the time, I know that this is a parent who needs help. A few parents have extreme difficulty controlling their children. They say their child won't obey or that he's just bad. Often when you watch such a parent – let's say it's a mother – she doesn't appear to be really trying, even though she wants to and thinks she is. She frequently threatens, scolds or smacks, but she is inconsistent. She makes her child obey once, but five minutes later and again ten minutes later she seems not to notice; or she punishes but in the end never makes her child do what she said he had to do. Another just keeps shouting at the child that he's bad or asks a neighbour, right in front of the child, whether she has ever seen a worse one.

Parents like these unconsciously expect the child's bad

behaviour to go right on and believe that they can do nothing effective to stop it. They are inviting misbehaviour without realizing it. Their scolding and punishing are only an expression of frustration. In their complaints to neighbours, they are only hoping to get some comforting agreement that the child is truly impossible. These parents need help from an understanding professional.

TIPS FOR SETTING LIMITS

You can be both firm and friendly. A child needs to feel that her mother and father, however agreeable, have their own rights, know how to be firm and won't let her be unreasonable or rude. She likes them better that way. Their firmness trains her from the beginning to get along reasonably with other people.

Spoiled children are not happy creatures even in their own homes. And when they get out into the world, whether it's at age two or four or five, they are in for a rude shock. They find that nobody is willing to kowtow to them; they learn, in fact, that everybody dislikes them for their selfishness. Either they must go through life being unpopular or they must learn the hard way how to be agreeable.

Parents sometimes let their children take advantage of them for a while, until their patience is exhausted, and then become cross. Neither of these stages is really necessary. If parents have a healthy self-respect, they can stand up for themselves while they are still feeling friendly. For instance, if your daughter insists that you continue to play a game after you are exhausted, don't be afraid to say cheerfully but definitely, 'I'm all tired out. I'm going to read a book now, and you can read your book, too.'

Or maybe she is being very balky about getting out of the ride-on car of another child who has to take it home now. Try to interest her in something else, but don't feel that you must go on being sweetly reasonable forever. Lift her out of the car even if she yells for a minute.

Angry feelings are normal. When a child is rude to his parent – perhaps because he has had to be corrected or because he's jealous of his brother or sister – the parent should promptly stop him and insist on politeness. But at the same time, the parent can say that she knows he is cross at her sometimes – all children get mad at their parents sometimes. This may sound contradictory to you; it sounds like undoing the correction. Child guidance work teaches us that children are happier, as well as better-behaved, if their parents insist on reasonably good behaviour. But at the same time, it helps a child to realize that her parents know she has angry feelings and that her parents are not angry at her or alienated from her on account of them. This realization helps her get over her anger and keeps her from feeling too guilty or frightened because of it.

Making this distinction between angry feelings and angry actions works out well in actual practice. In fact, a cornerstone of mental health is to be able to recognize one's own feelings, and make reasonable decisions about whether or not to act on them. By helping your child find the words to describe her emotions, you are supporting the development of her emotional intelligence, a crucial ingredient in life success.

Don't ask if you mean to tell. It's easy to fall into the habit of saying to a small child, 'Do you want to sit down and have your lunch? Shall we get dressed now? Do you want to do potty? It's time to go out now, okay?' The trouble is that the natural response of the child, particularly between one and three, is 'No.' Then the parent has to persuade the poor child to give in to something that was necessary anyway.

It is better not to offer a choice if what you really mean is to give a direction. With young children, a nonverbal approach works well. When it's time for lunch, lead your child or carry him to the table, still chatting with him about the thing that was on his mind before. When you see signs that he needs to go to the toilet, lead him there or bring the potty to him without even mentioning what you're up to.

I'm not saying that you should swoop down on your child and give him the bum's rush. Every time you take a child away from something he's absorbed in, it helps to be tactful. If your fifteen-month-old is busy fitting one hollow block inside another at suppertime, you can carry him to the table still holding his blocks and take them away when you hand him his spoon. If your two-year-old is playing with a toy dog at bedtime, you can say, 'Let's put doggie to bed now.' If your three-year-old is chugging a toy car along the floor when it's time for the bath, you can suggest that the car make a long, long trip to the bathroom. When you show interest in what he's doing, it puts him in a cooperative mood.

As your child grows older, he'll be less distractible and have more concentration. Then it works better to give him a little advance warning. If a four-year-old has spent half an hour building a garage of blocks, you can say, 'Put the cars in soon now; I want to see them inside before you go to bed.' You might advise your child to 'find a good stopping spot', or offer to give him a 'five-minute warning' so he'll know when to wrap it up. This approach lets your child know that his playing is important; it gives him some sense of control within the limits you set. All this takes patience, though, and naturally you won't always have it. No parent ever has.

Don't give a small child too many reasons. When your child is young, rely most heavily on physically removing her from dangerous or forbidden situations by distracting her in favour of something interesting and harmless. As she grows a little older and learns the lesson, remind her with a matter-of-fact 'No, no' and then offer more distraction. If she wants an explanation or a reason, give it to her in simple terms. But don't assume that she wants an explanation for every direction you give. She knows that she is inexperienced. She counts on you to keep her out of danger. It makes her feel safe to have you guiding her, provided you do it tactfully and not too much.

You sometimes see a child between the ages of one and three who becomes worried by too many warnings. The mother of a certain two-year-old boy always tries to control him with ideas: 'Jackie, you mustn't touch the doctor's lamp, because you will break it, and then the doctor won't be able to see.' Jackie regards the lamp with a worried expression and mutters, 'Doctor can't see.' A minute later he is trying to open the door to the street. His mother warns him, 'Don't go out the door. Jackie might get lost, and Mummy couldn't find him.' Poor Jackie turns this new danger over in his mind and repeats, 'Mummy can't find him.' It's bad for him to hear about so many bad endings. It fosters a morbid imagination. A two-year-old baby shouldn't be worrying much about the consequences of his actions. This is the period when he is meant to learn by doing and having things happen. It's not that you should never warn your child in words, only that you shouldn't lead him out beyond his depth with ideas.

Then there is the overly conscientious father who feels he should give his three-year-old daughter a reasonable explanation of everything. When it's time to get ready to go outdoors, it never occurs to him to put the child's coat on in a matter-of-fact way and go out. He begins, 'Shall we put your coat on now?' 'No,' says the child. 'Oh, but we want to go out and get some nice fresh air.' She is used to the fact that her father feels obliged to give a reason for everything, which encourages her to make him argue for every point. So she says, 'Why?' but not because she really wants to know. Her father gives some reason, but she still wants to know why, and so it goes all day long. This kind of meaningless argument and explanation will not make her a more cooperative child or give her respect for her father as a reasonable person. She would be happier and get more security from him if he had an air of self-confidence and steered her in a friendly, automatic way through the routines of the day.

THE PROBLEM OF PERMISSIVENESS

When parents get unwanted results from too much permissiveness, it is not so much because they demand too little, though this is part of it, as it is because they are timid or guilty about what they ask.

If parents are too hesitant in asking for reasonable behaviour, they can't help resenting the bad behaviour that comes instead. They keep getting angry underneath, without really knowing what to do about it. This bothers their children, too. It is apt to make them feel guilty and scared, but it also makes them meaner and all the more demanding. If, for example, babies acquire a taste for staying up in the evening and the parents are afraid to deny

them this pleasure, they may turn into disagreeable tyrants who keep their mothers and fathers awake for hours. Parents are bound to dislike them for their tyranny. If parents can learn to be firm and consistent in their expectations, it's amazing how fast the children will sweeten up – and the parents will, too.

In other words, parents can't feel right towards their children in the long run unless they can make them behave reasonably, and children can't be happy unless they are behaving reasonably.

DR SPOCK COMMENTS

Though I've been accused of permissiveness, I don't consider myself permissive at all, and all the people who've used this book and spoken to me about it feel the same way. The people who call me permissive all admit that they haven't read the book and wouldn't use it. The accusation came for the first time in 1968, twenty-two years after the book came out, from a prominent clergyman who objected strongly to my opposition to the war in Vietnam. He said that my advice to parents to give instant gratification to their babies and children was what made these babies grow up to be irresponsible, undisciplined, unpatriotic young adults who opposed their country's war in Vietnam. There is no instant gratification in this book. I've always advised parents to respect their children but to remember to ask for respect for themselves, to give firm, clear leadership, and to ask for cooperation and politeness.

The parent who shies away from discipline. Quite a few parents shy away from guiding and controlling their children, leaving most of this work to their spouse. Mothers who aren't entirely sure of themselves may get into the habit of saying, 'Just wait until your father gets home!' Fathers may hide behind the paper or remain glued to the television set when a crisis occurs. When their wives reproach them, they explain that they don't want their children to resent them the way they often resented their own fathers. Instead they want to be pals with their children.

It's good for children to have friendly parents who will play with them, but children need parents to act like parents. They will have many friends in their lifetime, but only one set of parents.

When a parent is timid or reluctant to give leadership, the children feel let down, like vines without a trellis to grow on. When parents are afraid to be definite and firm, their children keep testing the limits, making life difficult for the parents and for themselves, until the parents are finally provoked into cracking down. Then the parents are apt to feel ashamed and back off again.

The father who avoids the disciplinary role simply forces his wife to discipline for two. In many such cases, the father does not end up with the friendly relationship he seeks. Children know that adults get irritated when they keep misbehaving. When they are dealing with a father who pretends not to notice, they feel uneasy. The children may imagine that he is concealing an anger that is much more dangerous than it really is. Some children may fear this kind of father more than the one who participates freely in their management and expresses his irritation. With an expressive father, children have opportunities to learn just what his displeasure means and how to deal with it. They find out that they can survive it, and this gives them a kind of self-assurance – just as they gain confidence when they overcome their fears and learn to swim or ride a bike.

Confusion about discipline. In traditional societies, where ideas about children stay the same generation after generation, most parents have no doubt about the best way to raise and discipline their children. By contrast, in many parts of the world, ideas about children are changing so rapidly that many parents are confused. Many of these changes have been driven by science. For example, psychologists have discovered that a warmly affectionate parenting style is more likely to produce well-behaved and happy children than is a coldly controlling style. Knowing this, some parents assume *all* that children need is love; that they should be allowed to express their aggressive feelings against parents and others; and that when children misbehave, the parents shouldn't get angry or punish them but should try to show more love.

Misconceptions like this are unworkable if carried very far. They encourage children to become demanding and disagreeable. They make children feel guilty about their excessive misbehaviour. They make parents strive to be superhuman.

Guilt gets in the way. There are many situations that give rise to persistent parental guilt: the mother who returns to her nine-to-five job without first settling in her own mind whether she thinks this is neglecting her child; parents who have a child with a physical or mental handicap; parents who have adopted a baby and can't get over the feeling that they have to do a superhuman job; parents who have been brought up with so much disapproval that they always feel guilty until they are proved innocent; parents who studied child psychology in college and therefore know about all the pitfalls and feel they have to be perfect.

Whatever the cause of the guilt, it tends to get in the way of easy management of a child. The parents are inclined to expect too little from the child and too much from themselves. They often still try to be patient and sweet-tempered when their overworked patience is exhausted and the child is getting out of hand and needs some definite correction. Or they vacillate when the child needs firmness.

A child, like an adult, knows when she is getting away with too much naughtiness or rudeness, even when her parents are trying to close their eyes to it. She feels guilty inside. She would like to be stopped. But if she isn't corrected, she's likely to behave worse and worse. It's as if she were saying, 'How bad do I have to be before somebody stops me?'

Eventually her behaviour becomes so provoking that the parents' patience snaps. They scold or punish her. Peace is restored. But the trouble with parents who feel guilty is that they are too ashamed of losing their temper. So instead of letting well enough alone, they try to undo the correction, or they let the child punish them in return. Perhaps they permit the child to be rude to them right in the middle of the punishment. Or they take back the penalty before it has been half paid. Or they pretend not to notice when the child begins misbehaving again.

In some situations, if the child does not retaliate at all, the parent begins to subtly provoke her to do so – without realizing, of course, what she or he is up to. All of this may sound too complicated or unnatural to you. If you can't imagine a parent letting a child get away with murder or, worse still, encouraging it, it only shows that you don't have a problem with guilt feelings. Guilt isn't a rare problem, however. A majority of conscientious parents let a child get out of hand occasionally when they feel they have been unfair or neglectful, but most soon recover their balance. However, when a parent says, 'Everything this child does or says rubs me the wrong way,' it's a pretty good sign that the parent feels overly guilty and is chronically submissive and permissive, and that the child is reacting to this with constant provocation. No child can be that irritating by accident.

If parents can determine in which respects they may be too permissive and can firm up their discipline appropriately, they may be delighted to find that their child becomes not only better-behaved but much happier. Then they can really love their child better, and the child in turn responds to this.

MANNERS

DR SPOCK COMMENTS

I think that teaching good manners should be part and parcel of all child rearing. Good manners give the right message to children, that there are certain acceptable ways to do things in our society, that showing courtesy towards others makes everyone happier and more loving.

Good manners come naturally. Teaching children to say please or thank you is really not the first step. The most important thing is to have them like people and feel good about their own worth as a person. If they don't, it will be hard to teach them even surface manners.

It's important for children to grow up in a family whose members are always considerate of each other. Then they absorb kindness. They want to say thank you because the people they look up to say it and mean it. They enjoy shaking hands and saying please. The example of parents' politeness towards each other and towards the children is crucial.

It's also very important for your children to see you treating people outside the family with kindness and consideration, particularly people who occupy a lower social position. When you act with genuine politeness towards the person who brings you your food or who cleans the floors, you are teaching your child the true meaning of manners.

Manners for young children. It's best to avoid making young children self-conscious with strangers. We're apt, especially with our first child, to introduce him right away to a new grown-up and make him say something. But when you do that to a two-year-old, you make him all embarrassed. He quickly learns to feel uncomfortable as soon as he sees you greeting somebody, because he knows he's about to be put on the spot.

It's much better in the first three or four years, when a child needs time to size a stranger up, to draw the newcomer's conversation away from him, not towards him. A child of three or four is likely to watch a stranger talking to his parent for a few minutes and then suddenly break into the conversation with a remark like, 'The water came out of the toilet all over the floor.' This isn't Lord Chesterfield's kind of manners, but it's real manners because he feels like sharing a fascinating experience. If that spirit towards strangers keeps up, he'll learn how to be friendly in a more conventional way soon enough.

PARENTS' FEELINGS MATTER

DR SPOCK COMMENTS

I think that idealistic young people approaching parenthood assume that if they are the right sort they will have unlimited patience and love for their innocent baby. But this is not humanly possible.

Parents are bound to get cross. When your baby has been crying angrily for hours, despite all your patient efforts to comfort her, you can't go on feeling sympathetic. She seems like a disagreeable, obstinate, unappreciative creature, and you can't help feeling angry – really angry. Or perhaps your older son has done something that he knows very well he shouldn't have done. Maybe he was so fascinated with a breakable object of yours or so eager to join some children on the other side of the street that he couldn't resist the temptation to disobey. Or maybe he was cross at you for having denied him something or angry at the baby for receiving so much attention. So he misbehaved from simple spite.

When a child disobeys a well-understood and reasonable rule, you can't simply be a cool statue of justice. Any good parent feels strongly about right and wrong. You were taught to feel that way back in your own childhood. It's your rule that has been broken. It's probably your possession that has been damaged. It's your child, about whose character you care a great deal, who has done wrong. It's inevitable that you feel indignant. The child naturally expects this, and is not hurt by it if your reaction is fair.

Sometimes it takes you a long time to realize that you are losing your temper. The boy may have been putting on a series of irritating acts from the time he appeared at breakfast – making disagreeable remarks about the food, half deliberately knocking over a glass of milk, playing with something forbidden and breaking it, picking on a younger child – all of which you have tried to ignore in a supreme effort to be patient. Then at the final act, which perhaps isn't so bad, your resentment suddenly boils over, shocking you a little with its vehemence. Often when you look back over such a series of exasperating actions, you can see that the child has really been asking for firmness all morning, and that it was your well-intentioned effort at patience that made him go from one provocation to another, looking for a check.

We also get cross with our children because of the pressures and frustrations we are feeling from other directions. A father, for example, comes home on edge from troubles that he's having in his work. He criticizes his wife, who then snaps at the older boy for something that ordinarily brings no disapproval, and he in turn picks on his younger sister.

Better to admit anger. So far we have been discussing the inevitability of parental impatience and resentment from time to time. But it's just as important to consider a related question: can parents comfortably accept their angry feelings? Parents who aren't excessively strict with themselves are usually able to admit their irritation. A naturally outspoken good mother whose little boy has been bedevilling her is able to say to a friend, half jokingly, 'I don't think I can stand being in the house with him for another minute,' or 'I'd enjoy giving him a thorough walloping.' She may not carry out any of these thoughts, but she isn't ashamed to admit them to a sympathetic friend or to herself. It relieves her feelings to recognize them so clearly and to blow them off in talk. It also helps her to see what she has been putting up with and to be firmer in putting a stop to it.

It's the parents who set impossibly high standards for themselves, who have angry feelings at times but can't believe that good parents should, who really suffer. When they detect such emotions stirring in themselves, they either feel unbearably guilty or try strenuously to deny them. But if a person tries to bury such feelings, they only pop up somewhere else – as tension, for example, or tiredness or a headache.

Another indirect expression of anger is overprotectiveness. A mother who can't admit that she feels antagonism towards her children may imagine instead all the awful things that could beset them from other directions; she worries excessively about germs, or about traffic. She tries to ward off these dangers by hovering over her children, which tends to make them too dependent.

Admitting your angry feelings helps you feel more comfortable, and it helps your child, too. In general, what makes a parent miserable makes the child miserable, too. When a parent believes that antagonistic feelings are too horrible to admit, the child absorbs the same dread of them. In child guidance clinics, we see children who develop fears of imaginary dangers – fear of insects, of going to school, of being separated from their parents – that prove on investigation to be a disguise for ordinary anger towards their parents, which these perfectionistic children dare not recognize.

Children are happier around parents who aren't afraid to admit their anger, because then they can be more comfortable about their own angry feelings. And justified anger that's expressed tends to clear the air and leave everyone feeling better.

When anger is not okay. Of course, not all the antagonism expressed towards children is justified. Here and there you see a harsh, unloving parent who abuses a child at all hours of the day, verbally or physically, with little reason and no shame. This constant flow of uncalled-for anger is very different from the irritation of parents whose conscientiousness and devotion to their children is plain to see.

A loving parent who feels angry most of the time, whether it's expressed openly or not, is suffering from a real emotional strain and deserves help from a mental health professional. The anger may be coming from some entirely different direction. An ongoing state of anger or irritation is often a sign of depression. Depression, which affects a great many parents – particularly mothers of young children – is a terribly painful condition. Thankfully, it is also very treatable (see page 831).

A frequent feeling of irritation towards one child in particular is apt to make a parent feel guilty, especially if there is no obvious reason. A mother says, 'This one always rubs me the wrong way. Yet I'm constantly trying to be sweeter to her and to overlook her bad behaviour.' Counselling may help this mother better understand herself and make the changes she knows she needs to make.

GRANDPARENTS

It's common to hear a grandparent ask, 'Why couldn't I have enjoyed my own children the way I enjoy my grandchild? I suppose I was trying too hard and feeling only the responsibility.'

Parents, who must take responsibility for improving their children, may need to be reminded from time to time of just how wonderful their children really are. With the perspective that comes with age, grandparents can often reassure parents that their children's difficult behaviours are really just bumps in the road, not mountain ranges to cross. Grandparents link children with their cultural heritage and the stories that make up their family saga. At times, too, grandparents may be called on to step in for parents who are away at work or ill. Grandparents who take on more permanent parenting responsibilities face special challenges.

Tensions are normal. In some families, all is harmony between parents and grandparents. In a few, disagreements are fierce. Often there is a little tension, most commonly concerning the care of the first child, but it wears off with time and adjustment.

The fortunate young woman who has lots of natural self-confidence can turn easily to her mother for help when she needs it. And when the grandmother makes a suggestion on her own, the mother finds that she can accept it if it seems good, or she can tactfully let it pass and go her own way. But most young parents don't have that amount of assurance at first. Like almost everybody else in a new job, they are sensitive about possible inadequacies, touchy about criticism.

Most grandparents remember this well from their earlier days and try hard not to interfere. On the other hand, they have had experience, they feel they've developed judgment, they love their grandchildren dearly and they can't help having opinions. They may have a hard time accepting all of the changes since the time when they cared for babies – out-of-home child care for infants, for example, or later toilet training. Even when they accept new methods, they may be bothered by what seems to them to be excessive zeal in carrying them out.

Young parents who have confidence in their own judgment can keep relations most comfortable by permitting or even inviting the grandparents to speak up about their opinions. Frank discussions are usually, in the long run, more comfortable than veiled hints or uneasy silences. A mother who is pretty sure she is managing the baby properly can say, 'I realize that this method doesn't seem quite right to you, and I'm going to discuss it again with the doctor to be sure that I've understood his directions.' This doesn't mean the mother is giving in. She certainly reserves the right to make her own decision in the end. She is only recognizing the grandmother's good intentions and evident anxiety. The young mother who shows reasonableness will reassure the grandmother not only in regard to the present problem but also in regard to the future in general.

A grandmother can help the mother do a good job by showing her confidence in her and by accepting her methods as far as possible. This puts the mother in a mood to ask advice when she is in doubt.

Grandparents as caregivers. When the children are left in the care of the grandparents, whether for half a day or for two weeks, there should be frank understanding and reasonable compromising. The parents must have confidence that the children will be cared for according to their beliefs in important matters. On the other hand, it's unfair to expect grandparents to carry out every step of management and discipline as if they were exact replicas of the

parents. It won't hurt children to be a little more respectful to the grandparents, to have their meals on a different schedule or to be kept cleaner or dirtier. If the parents don't feel right about the way the grandparents care for the children, they shouldn't ask them to take care of them.

Some parents are sensitive about advice. More than average tension may arise if the young mother (or father) has felt a lot of parental criticism throughout her childhood. This inevitably leaves her inwardly unsure of herself, outwardly impatient with disapproval, and grimly determined to demonstrate her independence. She may take to new philosophies of child rearing with unusual enthusiasm and push them hard; they seem like a wholesome change from what she remembers. They are also a way to show the grandparents how old-fashioned they are and to bother them a bit. Parents who find that they are constantly upsetting the grandparents should at least ask themselves whether they might be doing some of it on purpose, without realizing it.

The managerial grandparent. Occasionally there is a grandmother so constituted that she has always been too managerial with her own child and she can't stop even though her child is now a parent. Such a young parent may have a tough time at first keeping a perspective. For instance, a daughter dreads advice. When it comes, it makes her angry, but she dare not express her feelings. If she accepts the advice, she feels dominated. If she turns it down, she feels guilty. How can the mother in this situation protect herself?

In the first place, she can keep reminding herself that she is the mother now and that the baby is hers to take care of as she thinks best. She should be able to get support from the doctor if she has been made to doubt her own method. She is surely entitled to the support of her husband, especially if it's his mother who is interfering. If he thinks that in a certain situation his mother is right, he should be able to say so to his wife, but at the same time he can show his mother that he stands with his wife against interference.

The young mother will come out better if she can learn gradually not to run away from the grandmother and not to be afraid to hear her out, because both these reactions reveal, in a way, that she feels too weak to stand up to her. Harder still, she can learn how not to get boiling mad inside or how not to explode outwardly in a temper. You might say she's entitled to get angry, which is true. But pent-up anger and explosions are both signs that she has already been feeling submissive for too long out of fear of making the grandmother angry. A dominating grandmother usually senses these indirect signs of timidity and takes advantage of them. A mother shouldn't feel guilty about making her mother angry, if it must come to that. Actually, it shouldn't be necessary to blow up at the grandmother – or at least not more than once or twice. The mother can learn to speak up for herself right away, in a matter-of-fact, confident tone, before she gets angry: 'The doctor told me to feed her this way' or 'You see, I like to keep him as cool as possible' or 'I don't want her to cry for long.' A calm, assured tone is usually the most effective way to convince the grandmother that the mother has the courage of her convictions.

In those occasional situations that contain a lot of continual tension, it is often helpful for the parents, and perhaps the grandparents also, to consult a professional – a wise family doctor, a psychiatrist, a social worker or a sensible minister – in separate interviews, so that each can present the picture as she or he sees it. Eventually they can all come together for a final discussion. In any case, it should be understood that the responsibility and the right to make decisions ultimately belong to the parents.

Grandparents as parents. Many children are raised by their grandparents while their parents are incapacitated by mental illness or addiction. Grandparents often take on this responsibility with mixed feelings: love for their grandchildren, anger at their own children, and perhaps guilt and regret as well. The task can be wonderfully gratifying, but it is often exhausting. Grandparents in this situation may yearn for the regular relationship: that is, to 'spoil' their grandkids and then go home to a quiet house.

Custodial grandparents also often worry about what will happen if their own health should give out. Government agencies that provide support for children in foster care often do not extend the same level of support to grandparents who are acting as foster parents. On the other hand, a supportive family and community can make a huge difference. Many areas also have grandparent groups that provide parenting tips and camaraderie (see Resource Guide, page 1056).

SEXUALITY

THE FACTS OF LIFE

Sex education starts early whether you plan it or not. It is common to think that sex education means a lecture at school or a solemn talk by a parent at home. This is taking too narrow a view of the subject. A child is learning about the facts of life all through childhood – if not in a good way, then in an unwholesome way. The subject of sex is a lot broader than just how babies are made. It includes the whole matter of how men and women get along with each other and what their respective places are in the world.

DR SPOCK COMMENTS

I believe that sex is as much spiritual as it is physical, and that children need to know that their parents feel this way. This is what makes falling in love such an intense emotional experience. The lovers want to care for each other, please each other, comfort each other. They eventually want to have fine children together. If they are religious people, they want God to be part of their marriage. These aspirations are part of what makes for a firm and idealistic marriage.

The spiritual aspects of sex can't be explained to a one-year-old, of course, though the intense dependent love between him and his parents is laying the groundwork. But by the age of three, four and five, it is good for children to hear and see not only that their parents want to hug and kiss each other but also that they are kind, helpful and respectful to each other.

When parents answer children's questions about where babies come from, it's important for children to hear the parents speak feelingly about the part played by their devotion to each other, how they want to do things for each other, give things to each other, have children together and take care of them together, and how this goes along with the physical affection and wanting to put the seed from the penis into the vagina. In other words, parents shouldn't ever let the anatomical and physiological explanation of sex stand alone.

Sex education for babies. Sex education can start even before children can talk or ask questions. During bathing and changing, parents can get into the habit of talking comfortably about parts of the body, including their babies' genitals. 'Now we'll wipe your vulva,' or 'Let's get your penis cleaned up!' Using the right words – 'penis' or 'vulva' rather than 'wee-wee' or 'thing', for example – takes away some of the taboo aura from the genitals. In time, parents become more comfortable talking about sexual body parts without squirming – good preparation for the years ahead.

Children start to ask questions around age three. Children begin to get more exact ideas about the things that are connected with sex at around the age of two and a half to three and a half. This is the 'why' stage, when their curiosity branches out in all directions. They probably want to know why boys are made differently from girls. They don't think of it as a sex question; it's just another in a series of important questions. But if they gain the wrong impression, it will become mixed up with sex later and give them distorted ideas.

Where do babies come from? This question is also pretty sure to come up in the period around three. It's easier and better to begin with the truth rather than tell a fairy story and have to change it later. Try to answer the question as simply as they ask it. Young children are easily confused by too much information at one time. They understand more when information is given in small, simple explanations. For instance, you can say, 'A baby grows in a special place inside the mother called the uterus.' You don't have to tell them more than that for the time being.

Maybe in a few minutes, maybe in a few months, they want to know a couple of other things. How does the baby get inside the mother? How does it get out? The first question is apt to be embarrassing to the parent, who may jump to the conclusion that the child is now demanding to know about conception and sex relations. But they are making no such demand. They think of things getting inside the body by being eaten, and perhaps wonder if the baby gets in that way, too. A simple answer is that the baby grows from a tiny seed that was in the mother all the time. It will be months before they want to know or will be able to understand what part the father plays.

Some people feel that children should be told at the time of their first questions that the father contributes by putting his seed into the mother. Perhaps this is right, especially in the case of the little boy who feels that the man is left out of the picture. But most experts agree that it is not necessary to try to give a three- or four-year-old an exact picture of the physical and emotional sides of intercourse. It's more than children bargained for when they asked their question. All that's necessary is to satisfy their curiosity at the level of their understanding and, more important, to give them the feeling that it is all right to ask anything.

To the question of how babies get out, a good answer is something to the effect that when they are big enough they come out through a special opening that's just for that purpose, called the vagina. It's important to make it clear that it is not the opening for bowel movements or for urine.

A young child is very apt to stumble on some evidence of menstruation and to interpret this as a sign of injury. A mother should be ready to explain that all women have this discharge every month and that it doesn't come from a hurt. Something about the purpose of menstruation can be explained to a child of three or older.

Why not the stork? You may say, 'Isn't it easier and less embarrassing to tell them about the stork?' But even a child as young as three who has a pregnant mother or aunt may have a suspicion of where the baby is growing from observing the woman's figure and from bits of overheard conversation. It's apt to mystify and worry him to have his parent nervously telling him something different from what he suspects is the truth. Even if he doesn't suspect anything at three, he is surely going to find out the truth or the half-truth when he's five or seven or nine. It's better not to start him off wrong and have him later decide that you're something of a liar. And if he finds that for some reason you didn't dare tell him the truth, it puts a barrier between you and makes him uneasy. He's less likely to ask you other questions later. Another reason for telling the truth at three is that children at this age are satisfied with simple answers. You get practice and build a foundation for the harder questions that come later.

Sometimes small children who have been told where the baby is growing confuse parents by talking as if they also believe the stork theory. Or they may mix up two or three theories at the same time. This is natural. Small children believe part of everything they hear because they have such vivid imaginations. They don't try, as grown-ups do, to find the one right answer and get rid of the wrong ones. You must also remember that children can't learn anything from one telling. They learn a little at a time, and come back with the same question until they feel sure that they've got it straight. Then at every new stage of development, they're ready for a new slant.

Be prepared to be surprised. Realize ahead of time that your child's questions will never come in exactly the form or at the moment you expect. A parent is apt to visualize a scene at bedtime when the child is in a confidential mood. Actually, the question is more apt to be popped in the middle of the supermarket or while you are talking on the street with a pregnant neighbour. If it does, try to curb that impulse to shush the child. Answer on the spot if you can. If that is impossible, say casually, 'I'll tell you later. These are things we like to talk about when other people aren't around.'

Don't make too solemn an occasion of it. When children ask you why the grass is green or why dogs have tails, you answer in an offhand way that gives them the feeling that it is the most natural thing in the world. Try to get the same spirit of naturalness into your answers about the facts of life. Remember that even if this subject is charged with feeling and embarrassment for you, it is a matter of simple curiosity to them. Chances are the child will not be bothered if your response is straightforward.

Other questions – 'Why don't babies come until you are married?' or 'What does the father do about it?' – may not come until children are four or five or older, unless they observe animals or have friends with baby brothers or sisters. Then you can explain that the seed comes out of the father's penis and goes into the uterus, a special place different from the stomach, where the baby will grow. It may be some time before they try to visualize this situation. When they are ready for that, you can mention something in your own words about loving and embracing.

The child who hasn't asked. What about the child who has reached the age of four or five or more and hasn't asked any questions at all? Parents sometimes assume that this means the child has never thought of these questions. But most people who work closely with children would be inclined to doubt this. It is more likely that the child has gotten the feeling, whether the parents meant to give it or not, that these matters are embarrassing. You can be on the lookout for indirect questions and hints and little jokes that a child uses to test out parents' reactions.

For example, a child of seven who is not 'supposed' to know anything about pregnancy may keep calling attention to his mother's large abdomen in a half-embarrassed, half-joking way. Here is a good chance for the parents to explain. A little girl who is at the stage of wondering why she isn't made like a boy sometimes makes valiant efforts to urinate standing up. There are occasions almost every day, in a child's conversation about humans and animals and birds, when a parent on the lookout for indirect questions can help the child ask what she wants to know. The parent then has an opportunity to give her a reassuring explanation, even though she hasn't asked a direct question.

How schools can help. If the mother and father have answered earlier questions comfortably, children will keep on turning to parents as they grow older and want more exact knowledge. But the school has a chance to help out, too. Many schools and nurseries make a point of letting children in preschool or Reception take care of animals, such as rabbits, guinea pigs or white mice. This gives them an opportunity to become familiar with all sides of animal life – feeding, fighting, mating, birth and suckling of the young. It is easier in some ways to learn these facts in an impersonal situation, and it supplements what children have learned from their parents. But what they find out in school, they probably want to discuss and clear up further at home.

By Year 5 or 6, it is good to have biology taught in a simple way, including a discussion of reproduction. At least some of the girls in the class are entering puberty and need some accurate knowledge of what is happening. The discussion from a somewhat scientific point of view in school should help the child to bring it up more personally at home.

Sex education, including its spiritual aspects, should be part of a broad health and moral education from preschool right through school, ideally carried out harmoniously by parents and teachers.

TALKING WITH TEENS ABOUT SEX

Does sex education encourage sex? Many parents are afraid that talking about sex with their teenagers will be taken as permission for the teen to have sex. Nothing could be further from the truth. If anything, the more children learn about sexuality from talking with their parents and teachers and reading accurate books, the less they feel compelled to try to find out for themselves. Taking the mystery away from sex makes it less appealing to a teen, not more. Learning about abstinence – that is, effective ways to say 'No, thank you' – is also helpful. But there is good evidence from many studies that abstinence education alone rarely leads to a reduction in irresponsible and unsafe sexual activity. To be effective, education about sex and sexuality has to cover everything, including the biology of reproduction and contraception, the way sex is sold in the media, emotional and spiritual aspects of sex, religious and other values, and abstinence.

Talk, don't have 'the talk'. With adolescents, just as with younger children, it's best for talk about sex to come up easily from time to time rather than to be one big solemn lecture. It's easiest to talk with a teenager about sex if sex has been an open topic of conversation all along (see pages 163 and 193). One way to make sex a routine part of conversation is to comment on the sexual images that are everywhere on television and in newspapers and magazines. If your Year 8 child knows that you are comfortable talking about sex, then he won't be freaked out when you talk with him about sex when he's in the sixth form. A good time to talk about sex is when you're in the car together, perhaps driving your child to some fun activity. Having scenery to look at can help you both feel less self-conscious, and the car makes it hard for your teen to get up and walk away. These discussions should include talking about contraception, with specifics about both the boy's and girl's responsibilities. If you just can't find a way to get comfortable enough to talk about sex with your teenager, it's important to find another adult whom you both trust who can.

Go beyond fear. One mistake that is easy to make is to concentrate on the dangerous aspects of sex. Of course, the child who is moving into adolescence should know how pregnancy takes place and that there is a danger of disease in being promiscuous. For some, the fear of negative consequences will help them make wise decisions. But teens are famously constituted to take risks, believing that nothing bad can happen to them. For these teens, horror stories about AIDS and unwanted babies won't have much impact.

More than just warnings, teens need guidance in thinking through the psychological and relationship aspects of teen sex. What hopes or fears are motivating them? Do they see having sex as their ticket of admission into the popular crowd, or as a way to cement a tenuous relationship? Are they giving in to pressure or making an independent decision? Are they being honest and open in their relationships, or manipulative? Though advice is important, teens aren't usually great at listening to it. To help them think through the decisions they have to make, you should plan to do more listening than talking.

Teens are more likely to make wise decisions – to avoid reckless promiscuity or to put off sex altogether – if they have a solid foundation of self-respect, and if they have positive prospects for university or other careers to look forward to. Wise parents help their children make small decisions all through the growing-up years about how to choose their friends, how to spend their time and how to do the right thing. The common sense and values children learn in this way help them to navigate the rocky seas of adolescent sex.

Girls and puberty. The subject of puberty should come up before the first changes appear. In girls this is usually around age ten, but it can be as early as eight. Girls starting puberty need to know that during the next two years their breasts will develop, hair will grow in the genital region and under the arms, they will grow rapidly in height and weight, and their skin will change its texture and may become prone to spots. In about two years they will probably have their first menstrual period. (For more on puberty, see page 215.)

How you tell them about their menstrual periods makes a difference. Some mothers emphasize what a curse they can be, but it is a mistake to stress that part to a child who is still immature and impressionable. Other mothers emphasize how delicate a girl becomes at such times and how careful she must be. This kind of talk makes a bad impression, particularly on those girls who have grown up feeling that their brothers got all the advantages or who have been inclined to worry about their health. Girls and women can live perfectly healthy, normal, vigorous lives right through their menstrual periods. It is only the occasional girl who has cramps severe enough to keep her out of activities, and there are good treatments for them.

The best thing to emphasize about menstruation is that the uterus is being prepared for the growing of a baby. During the months she is waiting for her first period, giving the child a box of sanitary pads helps put her in the right mood. It makes her feel that she is grown up and ready to deal with life, rather than waiting for life to do something to her.

Boys and puberty. Boys need to be told about puberty before it starts, usually around age twelve but sometimes as early as ten. You should explain about the naturalness of erections and nocturnal emissions. Nocturnal emissions, which are often called wet dreams, are an ejaculation of semen (the fluid stored in the prostate gland) during sleep, often in the course of a dream of a sexual nature. Parents who know that nocturnal emissions are certain to occur and that boys will at times feel a strong urge to masturbate will sometimes tell the boy that these things are not harmful as long as they don't happen too often. The trouble is that adolescents easily become worried about their sexuality, easily imagine they are abnormal. Being told that 'this much is normal, that much is abnormal' is apt to make them more anxious. Boys need to be told that it's equally normal to have many or few nocturnal emissions, and that some perfectly normal boys have none at all.

HOW SEXUALITY DEVELOPS

DR SPOCK COMMENTS

We are sexual beings to our very core from the day we're born until the day we die. Sexuality is inborn, part of our nature, but exactly how that nature is expressed depends largely on familial, cultural and social values. Some cultures embrace human sexuality as a fundamental and natural part of day-to-day life.

Sensuality and sexuality. Sensuality refers to taking pleasure in the physical senses. Sexuality narrows the field to the reproductive organs. Babies are sensual creatures. They take great, uninhibited pleasure in their whole bodies, especially in certain areas like the mouth and genitals. They eat with gusto, smacking their lips when full, raising a ruckus when hungry. They delight in the pleasures of their body: being held, stroked, kissed, tickled and massaged. The pleasure principle reigns supreme.

Over time, and depending on how the world responds to their sensuality, infants begin to connect certain emotions and ideas with pleasurable sensations. If an infant who is rubbing her genitals is told, 'No! Don't do that! That's nasty!' she begins to associate that sensation with disapproval. While she may stop that behaviour, the desire for pleasure does not vanish, nor does the infant understand why this pleasurable activity is prohibited.

As children grow, they need to bring their enjoyment of sensual pleasures into line with what society accepts. They learn, for example, that it's okay to pick your nose or to scratch certain parts of the body, but not when other people are watching. An understanding of the idea of privacy develops gradually. A young child will say 'I want my privacy' in the toilet, but will think nothing of romping through the house with nothing on. Usually by the time they enter Year 2, children understand privacy more or less as adults do.

Masturbation. Between four and eight months of age, infants discover their genitals the same way they discover their fingers and toes – by randomly exploring all their body parts. They feel pleasure when they stroke their genitals, and as they get older, they remember these pleasurable sensations. So from time to time, they will intentionally stroke their genitals.

By eighteen to thirty months, children are becoming aware of gender differences, specifically focusing on the boy's penis and the girl's lack of one. This is how children see it, until they learn that girls have a vagina and a uterus in which to grow babies, which boys lack. This natural interest in the genitals at this time leads to an increase in masturbation.

By age three, children who haven't been forbidden and prevented from masturbating will do it from time to time. In addition to stroking their genitals with their hands, they may rub their thighs together, rhythmically rock back and forth, or make pelvic thrusting motions while sitting on the arm of a sofa or chair or lying on a favourite stuffed animal. Children at this age will also stroke their genitals to comfort themselves when they're tense or frightened.

Most school-age children continue to masturbate, although less openly and less frequently. Some masturbate a lot, some only a little. Children masturbate for pleasure, and they continue to use its calming, comforting effects to help deal with anxieties of all kinds.

Early sexual curiosity. Preschool-age boys and girls are often openly interested in each other's bodies and, if permitted, will spontaneously engage in show-and-touch. Playing house or doctor helps to satisfy sexual curiosity while also allowing children to practise being grown-up in more general ways. Among school-age children, comparing penis size among boys and appearance and size of the clitoris among girls is normal, part of the general process of seeing how you measure up to your peers. Some healthy children engage in these sorts of investigations; others do not.

How much modesty in the home? Standards of modesty vary from home to home. It's common for young children of both sexes to see each other undressed at times in the home, at the beach and in the toilet of a preschool, and there is no reason to think that this exposure has any ill effects. Children are interested in each other's bodies just as they are curious about many things in the world around them.

When young children regularly see their parents naked, however, there may be more cause for concern. The main reason is that young children's feelings for their parents are so intense. A boy loves his mother much more than he loves any little girl. He feels much more envy of his father and more in awe of him than he feels towards any boy. So the sight of his mother naked may be overstimulating, and the chance to compare himself unfavourably with his father every day may make him feel inadequate. This sense of inadequacy might stay with him long after he, too, has mature genitals. Sometimes a boy can be so envious, he may feel like doing something violent to his dad. Nudist fathers sometimes relate how their three- and four-year-old sons make snatching gestures at the father's penis during morning shaving; then the boy feels guilty and fearful. A little girl who regularly sees her father nude also may be too stimulated.

This isn't to say that all children are upset by parental nudity. Many may not be, especially if the parents are doing it out of a wholesome naturalness and not in a lascivious or showy way. Yet we don't always know the effect on the child, so I think it's wise for parents to keep reasonably covered once their children turn two and a half or three. Before that, it's helpful if children can accompany their parents into the bathroom, so they can see what the toilet is for. Occasionally a parent is caught off guard when a curious child comes into the bathroom. The parent shouldn't then act shocked or angry. It's only necessary to say, 'Will you wait outside until I get dressed?'

When should you start insisting on your privacy? Here, you are wise to pay attention to your own comfort level. At the point where you begin to feel uncomfortable with your child seeing you naked, that's a good time to start. If you are uncomfortable, your children will sense it. This increases the emotional content of the situation.

After the age of six or seven, most children begin to want a little more privacy for themselves, at least at times, and they are also much more capable of managing toileting and hygiene on their own. At this point, it makes sense to respect children's appropriate requests for privacy.

GENDER DIFFERENCES AND HOMOSEXUALITY

By age two, boys know that they're boys and girls know that they're girls, and they usually accept whichever sex they happen to be. Early on, it's common for boys to think that they can have babies, and for girls to think that they ought to be able to have penises. Such wishes are simply a sign of the young child's belief that anything is possible – if you want a penis, well, you can *have* a penis!

Gender identity develops as a result of both biological and social factors. Testosterone and oestrogen, the main hormones that determine whether the body develops as male or female, also affect the developing brain. On average, male brains are different from female brains. But the differences between the sexes in such things as aggressiveness or skilful use of language are actually much *smaller* than the differences between individuals. In other words, there are plenty of sensitive, peace-loving boys, and plenty of assertive and competitive girls.

How gender identity develops. The main thing that gives a boy a strong sense of male identity is not the toy cars or cowboy suits he's given, but his positive relationship with his father or other important men in his life. This relationship makes him want to grow up to be the same kind of person.

If a father anxiously turns down his son's request for a doll or otherwise shows his worry that the boy has 'girlish' tastes, the child's masculinity is not reinforced. If the father is confident in his own masculinity, he can help his son develop the nurturing side of fatherhood by supporting the doll play.

In the same way, a girl looks to her mother and other important women. A mother who encourages her daughter to explore many different activities, and does this herself, will raise a confident, strong daughter. But a mother who is overly anxious about her own femininity may put too much emphasis on her daughter's feminine development. If she only gives her dolls and cooking sets to play with and always dresses her in cute, frilly clothes, she is sending a distorted message about female identity.

It's also important for girls to forge a positive relationship with their fathers. If fathers neglect or ignore daughters, or refuse to play ball games with them or to include them in activities like camping and fishing, they might instill in them a sense of inferiority and reinforce role stereotypes. It is normal for little boys to want to play with dolls and for little girls to want to play with toy cars, and it's quite all right to let them. A boy's desire to play with dolls is parental rather than effeminate, and it should help him to be a good father. There is no harm in boys and girls wearing unisex clothes – jeans and T-shirts – if that's what they want, or for girls to have dresses if that's their preference.

As for housework, it's good for boys and girls to be given basically the same tasks. Boys can do as much bed making, room cleaning and dishwashing as their sisters. And girls can take part in gardening and car washing. This isn't to say that boys and girls can't swap certain chores or that it all has to come out exactly even, only that there should not be obvious discrimination or differentiation. The example of the two parents will have a strong influence.

DR SPOCK COMMENTS

I'm sure I became a paediatrician because I identified with my mother's intense love of babies. She had five more after me, and I remember my great pleasure in giving bottles and in soothing a fretful sister by pushing her up and down the porch in her white wicker carriage.

I think of girl patients who identified with a father who was a bird-watcher or an immunologist; the mother had no such interests. Identification is a matter of degree or interest or attitude, rather than 100 per cent male or female. In this sense, everyone identifies in some respect or degree with the opposite sex. This gives them understanding of the opposite sex as they grow up, and a richer, more flexible personality. It also benefits the society as a whole by allowing a mixture of attitudes in any occupation.

Homosexuality and homophobia. In our society, between 5 per cent and 20 per cent of adult men and women are gay or lesbian. Experts have difficulty calculating exact percentages because there is still considerable stigma attached to homosexuality. Also, the distinction between gay and straight is not as hard and fast as one might think. Quite a few people who identify themselves as straight have, or have had, sexual relations with people of their own gender. A sizable number are bisexual. Many feel homosexual attraction but limit their behaviour to the heterosexual sphere. Human sexuality, like so much else, falls along a continuum.

Gays and lesbians are now more visible in our popular culture, in films, magazines and television, and among musicians, fashion designers, athletes and even politicians. Despite this visibility, or maybe because of it, many people still have an unreasonable fear of homosexuality. Homophobia may arise out of a fear of differentness, or perhaps from the fear that they might harbour homosexual desires themselves. In its most violent form, homophobia leads to hate crimes and to laws that limit the freedoms of gays and lesbians.

Some parents fear that contact with gay or lesbian teachers may cause children to become gay, but there is absolutely no evidence that the sexual orientation of either gay or heterosexual children can be changed or influenced through example. There is increasing evidence that a person's basic or primary sexual orientation is set by the very earliest years of development, if not antenatally.

If your child asks about gays and lesbians, or even if you're just talking about sex in general, I think you can explain quite simply that some men and women fall in love with and live with people of the same sex. If homosexuality is considered a sin in your family's religion, you will need to be especially sensitive in how you handle the issue, since there is a chance that a child of yours may grow up to be homosexual. In that case, you will want to have talked about the issue in such a way that your child feels comfortable confiding in you and seeking your support, and is not overcome with shame.

Homophobia can kill. A child with homosexual leanings who grows up in a family or culture that condemns homosexuality is at high risk for serious mental and physical health problems. Teens whose families reject their homosexuality report severe depression more than six times as often as their heterosexual peers, and suicide attempts more than eight times as often.

Worries about gender confusion. It's normal for boys to enjoy baking and cleaning and playing with dolls, to occasionally play at being mummies, and even to pretend to have babies themselves. If a boy *exclusively* wants dresses and dolls, prefers to play *only* with girls, and consistently says he wants to be a girl, it is reasonable to be concerned about his gender identity. If a girl wants to play a lot with boys and occasionally wishes she were a boy, she's most likely reacting to taunts about girls not being good or strong or clever enough, and testing her own limits, or she may be showing a positive identification with her father or brother. However, if she wants to play *only* with boys and is *always* unhappy about being a girl, it's wise to take her for a consultation with a professional, who can help clarify the issues and support her and her family.

When a child is persistently adamant about wanting to be the other sex, a psychiatrist or psychologist may make the diagnosis of gender identity disorder (GID). It's very likely that in the future GID will be found to have biological or genetic causes. Whatever the cause, gender confusion is likely to be a source of pain and confusion for the child, and worry for the family.

When parents think that their little boy is effeminate or their little girl is too masculine, they may wonder whether the child will grow up to be homosexual. Because of prevailing prejudices against homosexuality, this can create worry and anxiety. However, sexual orientation – homosexual or heterosexual – is a different issue from gender identity. Many children with GID do grow up to be homosexual; many do not. With all of these issues, the parents' willingness to understand and support the child is what makes a positive long-term outcome possible.

ABUSIVE SEX

Parents who want their children to grow up sexually healthy face an uphill battle. From pervasive Internet pornography to mainstream billboards, commercials and TV dramas, our culture consistently mixes sexuality with violence and domination. Many children grow up witnessing the same confusing scenes in their homes. A boy who sees his father acting in controlling, violent ways towards his mother learns negative lessons about relations between the sexes that are hard to unlearn. A girl who sees her mother being pushed around may have a hard time imagining herself as an independent and respected adult. The ultimate mixing of sex and power occurs when an adult coerces a child into sexual behaviour. See page 769 on sexual abuse.

It's important to make your home a haven from the negative images of sexuality. That means limiting or completely doing without TV, Internet and other media that are saturated with violent sex (see page 723 on media); talking with your children about how sex is portrayed for commercial purposes; and, most important, demonstrating healthy sexuality in your own life.

THE MEDIA

LIVING WITH THE MEDIA

Should you worry? Are television, films, and popular music harmful to children, or simply amusements? Parents in every generation tend to view their children's music and other entertainment with alarm, while accepting as harmless the songs and stories of their own youth. People naturally value what they grew up with and reject anything new. Popular music and other media create experiences that can be shared on the school bus and in the school halls. This kids' culture is a healthy part of the normal process by which children and adolescents carve out independent identities and search for their own answers to life's eternal challenges.

On the other hand, it's obvious that the media can have powerful and disturbing effects on children's behaviour. With the rise of social networking sites, the electronic media increasingly pose additional risks.

TELEVISION

A high-risk medium. Of all the media, television has the most pervasive influence on children. Children aged five to sixteen spend an average of two and a half hours a day watching television. Each year teenagers witness an estimated ten thousand murders, assaults and rapes, twenty thousand adverts and fifteen thousand sexual situations (of which only a tiny fraction – less than 2 per cent – include birth control). Nearly two-thirds of children age five to sixteen have televisions in their bedrooms in the UK.

There is no question that some programmes provide wonderful learning experiences for children. These are the programmes that educate in a fun way, that teach values of caring and kindness, and that appeal to the child's higher instincts. The UK is lucky enough to have some excellent television programmes aimed at younger children – older children and teenagers are not always so lucky.

Another subtle but worrisome effect television has on its viewers is its tendency to promote passivity and a lack of creativity. Watching television requires little mental activity on the viewer's part. You simply sit and let the images flow by. Some research suggests that this sort of nonparticipatory viewing fosters a short attention span, making it hard for children to apply themselves in school.

Obesity is another unwanted side effect of too much television. Children burn few calories while watching TV. Research has shown a direct link between television and obesity: the more a child watches, the greater the chance he'll be seriously overweight. At the same time, television probably encourages the development of eating disorders by presenting a distorted version of reality in which the women are unnaturally thin and the men are improbably buff. No wonder so many teens feel unattractive by comparison.

Violence is another real concern. After exposure to on-screen violence, children are more likely to physically attack their peers and to feel more vulnerable to attack themselves. In other words, exposing children to typical TV fare puts them at risk, just as surely as playing in the street, or riding in the car without a seat belt.

DR SPOCK COMMENTS

We are leaving our children in the care of an electronic babysitter for twenty-three hours of every week. This sitter tells our children that violence is an acceptable way to solve problems; that sex is especially exciting when it occurs without love and, besides, there are no real negative consequences anyway; and that owning the latest products is a measure of success and happiness. There seems to be very little similarity between the world the electronic babysitter is selling to our children and the world we would like to see. Why would parents entrust their children to such a caretaker?

Why is most television so bad? Many people incorrectly believe that the product line of the commercial television industry is the adverts. In fact, the product sold by the television companies is the viewer's attention. The more of this product they accumulate, the more money they make from their adverts. Since television is a means to catch your attention (and not to educate, edify or entertain, unless that catches your attention), it becomes clear why many programmes, particularly those on commercial channels, try to appeal to the broadest base of viewers, which usually translates into sensationalism.

That television is designed specifically to capture and hold the viewer's attention explains why watching television is possibly the worst thing to do right before bed. Rather than putting you to sleep, the television keeps you up until you are so exhausted that you simply cannot hold your eyes open. Most of the children I see with severe problems falling asleep are actually keeping themselves awake by watching television.

Do you need a television? Very few parents choose to live entirely without TV. But the ones who do always seem happy with that decision. Children who never get into the habit of watching television don't miss it. They simply fill their days with other activities. Parents often think that television makes their lives easier, because it keeps their children occupied for blocks of time. But when you figure in all the hours spent arguing about how much children can watch and what shows they can and cannot watch, then add in the hassles of getting the children to stop watching so they can do homework or housework, it probably takes less effort to not have a television at all.

Take control. Assuming that you're among the majority who choose to live with television, what's most important is that you take control of the television. First and foremost, if there's a television in your child's bedroom, remove it. Put the television out in the open, where you can easily monitor what and how much is being watched.

Some children are glued to the set from the minute they come home in the afternoon until they are forced to go to bed at night. They don't want to take time out for supper, for homework or even to say hello to the family. Parents are sometimes tempted to let their children watch endlessly because it keeps them quiet.

It's better for the parents and child to come to a reasonable but definite understanding about which hours are for outdoors and friends, which are for homework and which are for television viewing. A maximum of one or two hours after homework, chores or other responsibilities is a reasonable limit for most families.

For very young children the solution is easy because your control is close to absolute. Pick wonderful DVDs for them to view over and over again. They won't even realize that the television can be used in any other way. When they do watch television, make sure you approve of the programmes, and there is plenty of educational television available for this age group on the non-commercial channels. If you use television at all as a babysitter, then it is entirely proper for you to make sure that it meets with your approval, as you would make sure with any babysitter. For example, you can, and probably should, flatly forbid children to watch violent programmes.

Young children can only partly distinguish between drama and reality. You can explain, 'It isn't right for people to hurt each other and kill each other, and I don't want you to watch them do it.' Even if your child cheats and watches such a programme in secret, she'll know very well that you disapprove, and this will protect her to a degree from the coarsening effect of violent scenes. Most likely, your children will be secretly relieved that you are keeping them away from violent shows. A very large percentage of children report being seriously scared by things they see on television. Who needs that?

For older children, who may watch when you are not there, parental controls can be a blessing. Many digital boxes and digital TVs have a parental lock facility that allows you to control which channels can be viewed.

An older child is likely to bristle at your attempts at censorship: 'Everybody else watches these cartoons. Why can't I?' When this happens, you can simply stick to your guns. While it's true that children will undoubtedly watch the forbidden programmes at friends' houses, you are still giving the message that this programme does not conform to your family's values and that's why you don't want them to watch it.

Watch TV with your child. A good way to handle the unwholesome messages on TV is to watch with your child and help her to become a discriminating, critical viewer. You can make comments on whether what you've just seen together bears any resemblance to the real world. If you've just seen a fight where someone gets punched and merely shrugs it off, you can say, 'That punch in the nose must have really hurt. Don't you think it did? Television isn't at all like real life, is it?' This also teaches empathy with the victim of violence rather than identification with the aggressor. When viewing an advert, you might comment, 'Do you think what they are saying is true? I think they just want you to buy their product so they can get rich.' You want your child to view adverts for what they are and begin to understand their manipulative intent. When viewing a scene with sexual content, you can comment, 'That's not what it's like in real life at all. Usually that happens after people have known each other for a long time and really love each other.'

You can use TV viewing to help your child learn to make sense of the world in a more realistic and wholesome way and to see TV for the fantasy it is. As these lessons are learned, your child can become immunized against wholesale acceptance of the media's messages.

Get involved. A simple step is to write letters to the television networks about what you like and don't like in children's programming. When the networks receive one letter, they assume that there are ten thousand people out there who feel the same way. So you *can* have an impact.

DR SPOCK COMMENTS

In my opinion, not having a TV at all seems to be a logical solution. That way, children and the family cannot rely on passive entertainment and, as mankind did for thousands of years, learn to creatively and actively broaden their interests by reading, writing or conversing with one another.

VIDEO GAMES

What makes video games so engrossing, and so potentially dangerous to children, is that they provide instant feedback. Point your cursor in the right direction, press a button at the right time, and something blows up – *and* you get points for it. They hold children's attention by automatically adjusting the level of difficulty so that the task is always challenging without being truly frustrating, and by providing frequent rewards (points). In other words, video games are ideal teaching tools. Unfortunately, what they often teach children is how to shoot quickly and accurately. As technology improves and the screens become more and more lifelike, children practise shooting images that look more and more like real people. And the more they practise this shooting, the less horror and disgust they feel over the idea of killing people. It's not that they become cold-blooded exactly, just less tenderhearted. When they think of bullets flying, their main emotion is excitement, not fear or revulsion. Video games, much more than violent films, have the ability to capture children's imaginations and train their emotions to accept violence, because with video games children are active participants.

Even nonviolent video games can capture children's imaginations so completely that they actually become obsessed with them, unable to think about anything else, including schoolwork. Children talk about feeling trapped and helpless in the face of the video game obsession, and they completely break down if their parents take the games away. This problem has got much worse with the increasing availability of handheld, battery-operated games.

Is there anything positive about video games? All of the practice making precise hand and finger movements in response to visual inputs does seem to train children's eye-hand coordination in a way that prepares them for jobs that require quick reactions (being a fighter pilot, for example, or a London cabbie). For boys whose social skills are underdeveloped and who are no good at sport, skill at video games is an alternative path to prestige and peer acceptance. Certainly, if the talk of the playground is all about the latest blow-'em-up video game, it's hard to be the one kid who isn't allowed to play.

Of course, not all video games are violent and destructive. Some allow children to experiment with building things – houses, cities or roller coasters, for example. Others stretch a child's visual skills or logical thinking, and some even make it more fun to learn maths or reading. It's not hard to tell these more peaceful games apart from the shoot-to-kill variety. A glance at the box is usually all it takes.

The key with video games, just like with television, is for parents to take control. Most children can probably handle limited exposure to action video games without ill effect. Parents have to be ready to step in and set a limit, however, so the video game playing doesn't get out of hand. If your child is inclined to protest vigorously against limits, you might be better off just saying no altogether. If your child is fascinated by force – he's constantly practising karate kicks or machine-gunning the air – I'd suggest that you cut his exposure to violent video games to zero. His head is already working overtime with images of fighting. Better to feed his imagination with nonviolent ideas: roller coasters are exciting, without the bullets.

FILMS

Scary films. Movie viewing is a risky business for children under the age of seven. For example, you hear about an animated feature that sounds like perfect entertainment for your small child. But when you watch it, you find that there is an episode in the story that scares the wits out of him. You have to remember that a child of four or five doesn't distinguish clearly between make-believe and real life. A witch on the screen is just as alive and terrifying to a child as a flesh-and-blood burglar would be to you.

The only safe rule is not to take a young child to a film unless you, or someone you know and trust, has seen it and is positive that it contains nothing upsetting. Even then, young children should always go with a sympathetic adult who can explain any disturbing scenes and comfort the child when necessary.

What films are appropriate for children? There are no hard-and-fast rules. The answer depends on your child's maturity, her response to scary stories, and your family's values. Do you want to avoid violence altogether or just certain kinds, like very graphic violence? When do you think a child is mature enough to be exposed to sexual scenes, and what is acceptable in those scenes?

If you err, it should probably be on the side of being overly restrictive about which films you allow your children to see. It is much more harmful for a child to be exposed to an upsetting or inappropriate scene that she is not ready for than to be denied access to a film she is actually mature enough to watch. When used as a point for discussion, conflicts about which films are appropriate allow you to hear your child's side of the argument and why she feels she is totally ready and absolutely must see this film. You can then discuss your view that loveless or brutal sex is not good at any age. Your child still won't like it, but you'll be teaching her your values in a very direct way and learning more about your child's world.

ROCK AND ROLL, RAP

·◆· DR SPOCK COMMENTS

I remember well that in the early days of rock and roll parents worried about Elvis Presley's dancing on television. He was shown only from the waist up, lest his gyrating hips corrupt the multitudes of youthful viewers. A decade later the records of the Beatles were burned because of their allegedly depraved effects on the minds of adoring teens.

If there is one common thread to the music of teenagers over the decades, it is to turn society's staid old music on its head and to rebel against the status quo. If the music of teenagers isn't found offensive by adults, it probably won't be very successful. Music, among other things, is a means by which each new generation differentiates itself from the old and provides itself with a bond of shared musical culture and identity.

This is not to say that offensive music is only in the ear of the beholder. It is distressing to hear lyrics that glorify aggression and disrespect towards women and aggrandize drug use. But is there a way to prevent your children from hearing such songs? You can certainly sit down with them and ask them questions about the songs: 'Why does this song call women disparaging names? Why do the lyrics show such disrespect for the police? What do you think these sexy lyrics actually mean?' During such discussions with your child you can also clarify your view on the song's message: 'I don't like songs that say drugs are good.' You need to be thoughtful and respectful towards the music, even if you think it sounds like a band of screech owls, and you should also voice your views in a way that is not disrespectful of your child and his generation. If you appear to reject the music from the start, your child is likely to pigeonhole you as being hopelessly out of it and discount anything you have to say.

Studies have shown that for the majority of children, most offensive lyrics go in one ear and out the other. Unlike films and TV, there isn't much evidence that offensive lyrics really have much effect on most children's well-being. But the coarsening, offensive nature of some lyrics should not go unnoticed and undiscussed by you. It's yet another opportunity to enter into your children's culture and try to help them to clarify their ideas and thoughts about their most important art form.

Music videos. The majority of households receive digital television, and with it, music videos. Many of these contain sexual images, very often bordering on pornography. Violence is common, including violence against women. By pairing these gripping images with catchy tunes, music videos seem to be able to take hold of the imagination in a powerful way. It should not come as a surprise, therefore, that exposure to music videos has been tied to aggression and approval of teen sex. Limiting exposure by blocking music channels is one solution; watching with your teen and using the opportunity to educate is another. Some music videos do portray responsible behaviour and non-violent conflict resolution. When you run across them, let your teens know that you approve.

THE INTERNET

For children, the Internet provides an exciting opportunity for independence and freedom in a world that seems safer than it really is. It gives them access to unlimited information and allows them to connect with like-minded peers. For example, there are chat rooms where children with specific interests or particular disabilities can talk to others with the same interests or disabilities anywhere in the world. The Internet allows children to break through isolation.

But along with these very real advantages comes danger, especially for children. Unfortunately, in the virtual world of the Internet there are real individuals who prey on children's innocence and immaturity. A children's chat room, for example, can turn into a lewd monologue by an adult posing as a child if not properly moderated. Websites devoted to violence or pornography are easily accessible; a child who spends any time surfing the Web is likely to stumble on several. Social networking sites – Facebook and MySpace are the most popular – connect children and teens with infinite numbers of strangers. Online 'friends' aren't necessarily friends at all, but may be acquaintances several times removed, or aliases for cyberstalkers. Teens often post personal information, including phone numbers and addresses, without realizing the mischief and danger this can cause. As more and more children access the Internet through their mobile phones, parents lose their ability to monitor and control their children's virtual activities. The Internet becomes a world without parents.

A less dramatic risk, but in some ways an equally concerning one, is the great amount of advertising on the Internet. Corporations spend billions creating exciting sites designed to sell their products and brands. Exposure to these sites fosters materialism and the illusion that big corporations are entirely benign entities.

Learn about the Internet yourself. Let your child teach you about the Internet, if he already knows, or learn about it together. That way, at least for a time, you can surf together, talking about what and where you want to go, discussing what to do and not to do, and stating your expectation of good manners. By sharing this experience, you will have the opportunity to talk things over in a way you'll miss if you never learn the first thing about the Internet. You'll get to know what kind of chat rooms and information sites are out there and how they operate. Set up your own Facebook page, so that you come to understand how it works. Read more about Internet safety (see page 739). This knowledge will allow you to better judge what sites pose a threat to your child and when you are being unjustifiably old-fashioned and insecure.

Supervise and set limits. It helps for parents to spell out the basic ground rules for their children, then provide enough supervision to ensure that those rules are being followed. For a teenager, supervision may mean occasionally glancing at the screen while your teenager is online. Preteens require more direct contact and discussion of what they are doing on the Internet. When younger children use the Internet, you should be at their side for much of the session. Chat rooms, unless well supervised, are not appropriate for young children.

If your child uses social networking sites, you should visit their pages regularly to make sure they conform to your safety standards and values. Teens sometimes establish two pages, one for their parents to see and one to actually use. Networking, like gaming and chatting, can become an addiction. The hallmark is an inability to stop, even when other aspects of life are clearly suffering.

What are fair time limits? Like television, you should set a time limit on how long the Internet can be accessed each day. It's unhealthy for a child to be lost in the virtual world of his computer while neglecting real-life conversations, experiences and friends. Having the computer in a public room, rather than a bedroom, makes it easier to supervise and set limits.

Supervision becomes vastly more difficult when children have their own Wi-Fi-enabled laptops and handheld devices. There are programmes that track the sites that have been visited. I suspect, though, that an inventive teen can easily enough find ways around this (not least of which is simply using a friend's device). You might decide that your child does not need a mobile phone, or perhaps needs one that doesn't also access the Internet. But there will still be times when you won't be there staring over your child's shoulder; the only real answer is communication, education and trust.

Ground rules for Internet safety. Just as there are safety rules for crossing the road, riding a bike or driving in the car, there are rules children need to follow to stay safe online.

1. Never post personal information – your address, your phone number, or the name of your school – or send it to anyone you haven't already met in person.
2. Never tell anyone else your password. Although chat room correspondents may seem like your friends, they are really strangers. You need to be as careful with these strangers as with those you meet on the street.
3. If a message makes you feel uncomfortable in any way, stop and tell an adult.
4. Use good 'netiquette' – treat people with politeness and consideration. Inappropriate or rude communications are not acceptable, even if you're anonymous.
5. Only post comments or pictures that you'd be comfortable showing to your head teacher or your grandmother. Once it's posted, you lose control of the material, because someone else can copy it and pass it along. Deleting material from your page doesn't delete it from the online world.

Sex on the Internet. The Internet is awash with pornography. You can avoid much of it by using parental control features on commercial online services or by purchasing blocking software. Many online services offer a way for parents to give children access only to carefully screened and supervised children's sites and chat rooms. Some software keeps logs that allow you to see exactly where your child has been.

Still, you're not likely to be able to shield your child completely. Rather than trying to pretend that the porn isn't there, you can take the opportunity to teach. Before your child goes online alone, talk about what she's likely to find. Explain that pornography is a business: some adults pay money to see pictures of other adults naked. Help your child understand what's wrong with this mixing of commerce with sexuality. Let your child know what you expect her to do if she runs across a sex site (leave the site, turn off the computer, tell you). Talk with teens about pornography's damaging effects on the people who make it (who are often victims of sexual abuse or addicts supporting their habits) and on people who try to model their own sex lives after it.

Remember, talking about sex doesn't make children engage in it. Instead, when you can discuss sex in a matter-of-fact way, it takes away some of the thrill of mystery and discovery that so often surrounds the topic. Also, you let your child know that you are approachable and askable (see pages 708–722 for more on talking about sex).

Technology can help protect your child from much of the worst Internet rubbish, but there is no substitute for instilling a sense of responsibility and values in your child so that he will make the right choices on his own.

DIFFERENT TYPES OF FAMILIES

As our society has opened up, we've learned that children can thrive in many different kinds of families – families with one parent, families with two mummies or two daddies, and many other variations. The power of shame and stigma has waned, so merely being different is less stressful. The freedom to create families outside the traditional mould means that more people can now devote their hearts and talents to the raising of children.

DR SPOCK COMMENTS

It's been said that the family as an institution in America is dying. I don't think that's true. The family has certainly been changing. Since the mid-1980s fewer than 10 per cent of American families have been made up of a father who goes out to work, a mother who stays at home, and two children. But the family, whomever it may include, is still the centre of our daily lives.

ADOPTION

Reasons to adopt. A couple should decide to adopt only if both of them love children and very much want a child. All children, whether biological or adopted, need to feel that they belong to their parents and are loved deeply and forever. An adopted child can easily sense a lack of love in one or both parents because she may not be as secure to begin with, having been through one or more previous separations. She knows that she was given up for some reason by her biological parents, and she may fear secretly that her adoptive parents might someday give her up too.

You can see why it's a mistake to adopt when only one parent wants to, or when both parents are thinking of it only for practical reasons, such as to have someone to take care of them in their old age. Occasionally a woman who is afraid that she's losing her husband will want to adopt a child in the futile hope that this will keep them together. Adoption for these reasons is unfair to the children.

Parents with an only child sometimes consider adopting another to provide company. It is a good idea to talk this over with a mental health professional or the adoption agency before proceeding. The adopted child is apt to feel like an outsider compared to the other child. If the parents lean over backward to show affection for the newcomer, it may upset rather than help their biological child. This is a potentially risky business for all concerned.

There can be pitfalls, too, in adopting to 'replace' a child who has died. Parents need time to work out their grief. It is unfair and unsound to want to make one individual play the part of another. She is bound to fail at the job of being a ghost. She should not be reminded of what the other child did, or be compared with her either out loud or in the parents' minds. Let her be herself. (This applies also to a child who is born after an older one dies.)

At what age should a child be adopted? For the child's sake, the younger the better. Even though early placement is not possible for thousands of youngsters living in foster homes and institutions, these older children can also be successfully adopted. The majority of children adopted in the UK are not infants. The agency will help older children and parents decide if adoption is right for them.

DR SPOCK COMMENTS

A couple should not wait until they are too set in their ways to adopt. They've dreamed so long of a little girl with golden curls filling the house with song that even the best of children turn out to be a rude shock. It is not a matter of years alone but of an individual's capacity to give a particular child what she needs.

How to adopt. The adoption of children can be a gruelling experience. Because there are more potential adopters than adoptees, the selection agencies can be extremely choosy. You will need to be prepared for lots of frustration and disappointment.

There are roughly two hundred or so authorized adoption agencies, which, by law, are not allowed to charge a fee for their services. Private adoption is illegal in Britain, and even adoptions within families require an adoption order by a court, dependent on a report supplied by the social services. For more information, you should contact the British Agency for Adoption and Fostering. Most of the children waiting to be adopted are older. This means that most of the people who want to adopt babies or very young children will be unable to do so or will have to wait for a long time. They may be tempted to adopt a baby privately. This, however, is illegal. For information on international adoption, see page 749.

Children with special needs. Increasingly, unmarried parents are keeping and raising their children, leaving fewer very young infants available for adoption. However, other children are waiting for parents. They are for the most part school-age. They may have a brother and sister from whom they don't want to be separated. They may have some physical, emotional or intellectual handicap. They may be war orphans. They are as much in need of love and can be as rewarding to parents as any other child.

They do have some special needs, however. Since they are older, they may have had more than one foster care situation. Having already lost parents (biological, then foster), they may be insecure and fearful of being rejected again. Children express this in a variety of ways, sometimes testing to see if once again they will be sent back. These anxieties present adoptive parents with special challenges. As long as parents know what to expect, the process of adopting such children can be especially rewarding. It's the responsibility of adoption agencies to focus their attention on finding homes for children with special needs, even more than on finding babies for adoptive parents.

Nontraditional parents. In the past, most adoption agencies would only consider married, two-parent families without biological children. Now many agencies welcome single parents, parents in committed gay and lesbian partnerships or marriages, parents whose race is different from the child's, and other nontraditional applicants. Childhood passes quickly, and a permanent parent *now* is of more value than the possibility of two parents some time in the future. Furthermore, agencies have learned that when it comes to adopting successfully, the outward characteristics of families matter less than the inward character of the parents. There may also be other good reasons: certain children have been emotionally bruised in such a way that it is better for them to have one parent of a particular sex, and other children have such a tremendous need for attention and care that the absence of a spouse allows a single parent or a nontraditional family to give the child what he needs.

Open adoption. In recent years, it has become increasingly common for the birth mother (and sometimes the birth father) and the adoptive parents to share information, ranging from getting a general description of each other conveyed by a social worker to actually meeting. And in some cases an arrangement is made for the birth mother to keep up with the child – for example, receiving a snapshot of the child and a letter from the adoptive parents once a year or more often.

Openness often works out well for all parties involved. Many children seem to be able to handle having both a birth mother and 'a mother who takes care of me'. Knowing their birth mother spares children the pain of wondering, 'What is she like? What would she think of me?' Even if the reality is sad – the mother may have serious problems of her own, for example – the unhappy reality often seems less disturbing to the child than an idealized (or demonized) fantasy.

Telling the child. When should an adopted child be told she is adopted? She's sure to find out sooner or later from someone, no matter how carefully the parents think they are keeping the secret. It is practically always a very disturbing experience for an older child, or even an adult, to discover suddenly that she is adopted. It may disturb her sense of security for years.

The news shouldn't be saved for any definite age. From the beginning parents should let the adoption come up naturally in their conversations with each other, with the child and with their acquaintances. This will create an atmosphere in which the child can ask questions whenever the subject begins to interest her. She will find out what adoption means bit by bit, as she gains understanding.

Some adopting parents make the mistake of trying to keep the adoption secret; others err in the opposite direction by stressing it too much. If they go too earnestly at the job of explaining to the child that she's adopted, she may begins to wonder, 'What's wrong with being adopted, anyway?' But if they accept the adoption as naturally as they accept the colour of the child's hair, they won't have to make a secret of it or keep reminding her of it.

Answering children's questions. Let's say that a child around three hears her mother explaining to a new acquaintance that she is adopted, and asks, 'What's "adopted", Mummy?' She might answer, 'A long time ago I wanted very much to have a little baby girl to love and take care of. So I went to a place where there were a lot of babies, and I told the lady, "I want a little girl with brown hair and blue eyes." So she brought me a baby, and it was you. And I said, "Oh, this is just exactly the baby that I want. I want to adopt her and take her home to keep forever." And that's how I adopted you.' This makes a good beginning because it emphasizes the positive side of the adoption, the fact that the mother received just what she wanted. The story will delight the child, and she'll want to hear it many times.

Children who have been adopted at an older age will need a different approach. They may have memories of their biological and foster parents. Agencies should help both the child and the new parents handle this. It is important to realize that questions will surface repeatedly during different stages of this child's life. They should be answered as simply and honestly as possible. Parents should allow the child to freely express her feelings and fears.

Between the ages of three and four, an adopted child is apt to want to know where babies come from. It is best to answer truthfully but simply enough so that the three-year-old can understand easily (see page 703). But when you explain that babies grow inside the mother's abdomen, it makes the child wonder how this fits in with the story of picking her out at the agency. Maybe then, or months later, she asks, 'Did I grow inside you?' Then you can explain, simply and casually, that she grew inside another mother before she was adopted. This is apt to confuse her for a while, but she will get it clear later.

Eventually a child will raise the more difficult question of why her biological parents gave her up. To imply that they didn't want her would shake her confidence in all parents. Any sort of made-up reason may bother her later in some unexpected way. Perhaps the best answer and nearest to the truth might be, 'I don't know why they couldn't take care of you, but I'm sure they wanted to.' During this period when the child is digesting this idea, she needs to be reminded, along with a hug, that she's always going to be yours now.

Information about the birth parents. Most adopted children are intensely curious about their biological parents. In former times, adoption agencies told adopting parents only the vaguest generalities about the physical and mental health of the biological parents. They completely concealed their identities. This was partly to make it easy for the adopting parents to answer 'I don't know' to the extremely difficult questions a child would ask about her origin and about why she was relinquished. And it was even more to protect the privacy of the biological parents, who in most cases were unmarried and who, in their subsequent separate lives, may have kept the early pregnancy a secret.

Today, many adoptees contact their birth mothers. In some cases, when this has led to a visit, it has had a beneficial effect on the turbulent feelings and obsessive curiosity of the adopted individual. In other cases, however, such a visit has been disturbing to the adoptee, to the adopting parents, and to the biological parents as well. Any decision needs to be discussed at length with the agency people, with all its pros and cons.

The adopted child must belong completely. The adopted child may have the secret fear that her adoptive parents, if they change their minds or if she is bad, will someday give her up, just as her biological parents did. Adoptive parents should always remember this and vow that they will never, under any circumstances, say or hint that the idea of giving her up has ever crossed their minds. One threat uttered in a thoughtless or angry moment might be enough to destroy the child's confidence in them forever. They should be ready to let her know that she is theirs forever at any time the question seems to enter her mind – for instance, when she is talking about her adoption. But it's a mistake for the adopting parents to worry so much about the child's security that they overemphasize their talk of loving her. Basically, the thing that gives the adopted child the greatest security is being loved, wholeheartedly and naturally.

International adoption. About 350 children from around the world are adopted into the UK every year. The opportunity to adopt a baby from overseas is the answer to many parents' prayers. But internationally adopted children and their families face some special challenges. Many of the children arrive malnourished, with missed immunizations and with other medical conditions – issues that are usually dealt with easily. However, many also have developmental and emotional issues that can be harder to treat.

Most internationally adopted children have led hard lives. Many have lived in institutions that barely met their physical and emotional needs, while those who have had loving foster parents have had to endure the pain of separation. Generally, the longer a child has lived in an orphanage or similar institution, the greater the chance of lasting physical, intellectual and emotional damage. But it's important to remember that most internationally adopted children grow up to be emotionally as well as physically healthy. They may feel disoriented or experience grief at first, but most make strong, loving connections with their new families. Nearly all show signs of delayed growth and development by UK standards, but most catch up within two or three years.

A lot depends on changing historical and political conditions in the child's country of origin. A country might rule, for example, that foreigners can adopt only children with severe physical disabilities. A few months later, though, the law may change. Because of these variables, an adoption agency that specializes in international adoptions – or in the specific country being considered – can be a tremendous help to parents.

Internationally adopted children often look different from their adoptive parents, and so may face insensitive comments or outright prejudice. For children old enough to speak who don't know English, the trauma of suddenly not being able to communicate adds to the stress of the adoption. Because the children's biological heritage links them to a different culture, their relationship to that culture becomes an issue for the parents to grapple with when the children are young, and for the children themselves when they are older.

For many parents, the act of adopting a child from a different country has political and ethical implications, too. The parents understand that they have benefited, in part, from the terrible conditions in the child's country of origin. Their child has a chance to lead a better life, but at the cost of being taken away from her own land and culture. Some families translate these concerns into action, perhaps by sending money and supplies to help other children who were left behind.

Many children adopted from overseas end up doing wonderfully, but some do not. Developmental-behavioural paediatricians and other experts can help parents weigh the risks. Only the parents know how strong their need is for a child and how much uncertainty and difficulty they can bear. Parents who choose to raise a child who may have severe problems are heroes. But parents who search their souls and decide that they cannot raise such a child have also acted courageously.

SINGLE-PARENT FAMILIES

DR SPOCK COMMENTS

No question that parenting is a tough job, no matter how you look at it, and being a single parent makes the job that much tougher. You don't have a supportive

> partner to ease the relentless day-to-day responsibilities of raising children. Everybody and everything depends on you. You don't get a real break or holiday. If you are the only breadwinner, financial worries add to your burden. It sometimes feels as if you just don't have enough physical and emotional energy to keep it all going.

In the UK, a quarter of families are headed by a lone parent. Over their lifetimes many children will spend some time in a single-parent household, either because of divorce (see page 779) or because their parents never married. Most single parents are mothers, and many have incomes below or close to the poverty line.

Being a single parent is no picnic, but it does have its rewards. You and your children may achieve a special closeness. You may discover strengths that you never knew you possessed and come out of the experience a stronger, wiser person. When things go well – as they often do – there can be a great sense of accomplishment.

Pitfalls of single parenting. One potential pitfall is an unwillingness to set firm limits. Many single parents feel guilty because their children are not growing up with two parents. They worry that their children are missing something essential, and they regret not being able to spend more time with their children. The temptation is strong for parents to indulge their child, giving in to the child's every whim.

This isn't helpful. In fact, it's not wise for the parent to focus on the child for most of the time they are together, as if the child were a visiting princess. The child can be working on a hobby, doing homework or helping with the housework most of the time, while the parent does likewise. This doesn't mean that they have to be out of touch. If they are in tune with each other, they can chat and comment off and on as the spirit moves them.

Another pitfall for single parents is to treat their children as their best friends, telling them their deepest feelings. A single parent will sometimes have her school-age child sleep with her, not because the child is frightened or lonely, but because the parent wants company. Children can take on extra housework and provide some emotional support to a distressed parent, but they can't take on an adult role without serious consequences for their growth and development.

The mother as single parent. Let's take the example of the child who has no father at home. It would be foolish to say that the father's absence makes no difference to this child or that it's easy for the mother to make it up to him in other ways. But if the job is handled well, the child can grow up well adjusted.

The mother's spirit is the most important element. A single mother may feel lonely, tied down or cross at times, and she will sometimes take her feelings out on the child. This is natural and won't hurt him too much.

The important thing is for her to go on being a normal human being, keeping up her friendships, her recreations, her career and her outside activities as far as she can, and not have her life totally revolve around her child. This is hard if she has a baby or child to take care of and no one to help her. But she can ask people in or take the baby to a friend's house for an evening if he can adjust to sleeping in strange places. It's more valuable to him to have his mother cheerful and outgoing than to have his routine perfect. It won't do him any good to have her wrap all her activity and thoughts and affection around him.

Children need to be friendly with other men if the father is not there. With babies up to the age of a year or two, a good deal is accomplished if they can just be reminded frequently that there are such creatures as agreeable men, with lower voices, different clothes and a different manner from women. A kindly grocer who just grins and says hello helps, even if there are no closer friends. As children grow to age three and over, the kind of companionship they share with men is increasingly important. They need chances to be with, and feel close to, men and older boys. Grandfathers, uncles, cousins, scoutmasters, male teachers, a priest or minister or rabbi, and family friends can serve as substitute fathers if they enjoy the child's company and see him or her fairly regularly.

Children of three or over are likely to build up an idealized image of their father, whether they remember him or not. The other friendly men they see and play with give substance to the image, influence their conception of their father, and make their father mean more to them. The mother can help by being hospitable to male relatives, sending her son or daughter to a summer camp that has some male staff, picking a school (if she has a choice) that has some male teachers, and encouraging a child to join clubs and other organizations that have male leaders.

The boy without a father particularly needs opportunities and encouragement to play with other boys every day, if possible, by the age of two. The temptation of the mother who has no other equally strong ties may be to make her son her closest spiritual companion, getting him interested in her preoccupations, hobbies and tastes. If she succeeds in making her world more appealing to him and easier to get along in than the world of boys, where he would have to make his own way, he may grow up with predominantly adult interests. It's fine for a mother to have plenty of fun with her boy, provided she also lets him go his own way, and provided she shares in *his* interests rather than having him share too many of hers. It helps to invite other boys to the house regularly and to take them along for treats and on trips.

The father as single parent. Everything about a mother raising a child alone applies to a father raising a child alone. But often there's an additional problem. Few fathers in our society feel completely comfortable in a nurturing role. Many men have been brought up believing that being a nurturing person is soft and therefore feminine. Consequently, many fathers find it hard, at least at first, to provide the gentle comforting and cuddling that children need, especially young children. But with time and experience, they can certainly rise to the task.

STEPFAMILIES

It's no accident that so many fairy tales have an evil stepmother or stepfather as the villain. Stepfamily relationships often lend themselves to mutual misunderstandings, jealousy and resentment. After a divorce, a child may form an unusually close and possessive bond with the custodial parent. Then along comes a strange man who takes away the parent's heart, bed and at least half of her attention. The child cannot help resenting this intruder, no matter how hard the stepparent tries to form a good relationship.

The resentment often takes extreme forms. This gets under the stepparent's skin and he is likely to feel the urge to respond with equal hostility. The new relationship between the adults quickly becomes strained because it feels like a no-win, either-or choice. The main thing for stepparents to realize is that this hostility, on both sides, is almost inevitable and not a reflection of their worth or of the eventual outcome of the relationship. The tension often persists for months or years and only gradually lessens. In rare other situations, the new parent may be much more easily accepted.

DR SPOCK COMMENTS

Years ago, with what I thought was great wisdom, I wrote a magazine article about stepparenting. Then in 1976 I became a stepfather and realized that I was quite incapable of following my own advice. I had advised stepparents to strictly avoid trying to be disciplinarians, but I kept reproaching my eleven-year-old stepdaughter for her consistent rudeness, and I kept trying to make her conform to a few rules of mine. This was one of the most painful relationships I ever experienced, and the one that taught me the most.

Why is stepparenting so hard? There are plenty of good reasons why life in a stepfamily is stressful, at least initially:

- *Loss.* By the time they enter a stepfamily, most children will have experienced significant loss: the loss of a parent, and perhaps the loss of friends because of a move. This sense of loss affects a child's early response to the new stepparent.
- *Loyalty issues.* The child may wonder, 'Who are my parents now? If I show affection to my stepparent, does it mean I can't or shouldn't love the parent who is no longer with me? How can I split my affections?'
- *Loss of control.* No child ever makes the decision to have a stepfamily; the decision is made for him by adults. He feels buffeted by forces and people over whom he has no control.
- *Stepsiblings.* All of these stresses can be made worse by the presence of stepsiblings. The child wonders, 'What if my mother or father loves my stepbrother more than me? Why do I have to share my possessions, or my room, with this complete stranger?'

Positive aspect of stepfamilies. While difficulty is standard in the beginning, most family members eventually adapt to the new circumstance. This takes time.

Stepsiblings and stepparents often establish close, long-lasting relationships. After all, each has the shared experience of a disrupted and reconstituted family. The 'dual citizenship' of living in two separate families can enrich a child's understanding and acceptance of diversity and cultural differences.

Tips for stepparenting. There are some general principles that may or may not be helpful and that are certainly difficult to apply. The first is for the parents to agree ahead of time on how they'll handle the children and to have realistic expectations of what the new family will be like.

It's important for the parents to understand that children need plenty of time to get used to the new arrangement. Parents need to be consistent with the children about family rules regarding bedtime, housework and homework, and allow time for them to accept these rules.

It is better for a stepparent to avoid moving into the guiding and correcting role of a full parent too soon. A stepparent who tries to enforce such things as housework, bedtime and curfews too soon is sure to be judged as a harsh intruder, even if enforcing the same rules as the natural parent.

On the other hand, it's not good for parents to be submissive when the stepchild intrudes into their territory, for instance, and abuses one parent's possessions. The parent should set a limit in a friendly but firm way: 'I don't like it when you hurt yourself or your things, and I don't like it when you hurt my things, either.' You can't make an issue of every hostile look; you'd be grouchy all day. So ignore the small slights and save your comments for major infractions of the rules.

When to seek help. Too often, the stresses that come along with stepparenting end up straining marriages to the breaking point or beyond. So it is wise to seek professional help at the first signs of real trouble, rather than waiting for the problems to grow. The help may take the form of guidance or direction for the parents on how to proceed, marital or family therapy, or individual counselling for one or more of the children. Stepparent groups can be helpful, too. For more on stepfamilies, see 'Divorce', page 779.

GAY AND LESBIAN PARENTS

A growing number of gay and lesbian couples are choosing to become parents. The experience of being a gay or lesbian

parent is different depending on where you live. Some communities are accepting; others so vilify nontraditional families that you might not feel comfortable even discussing the issue outside the family.

Effects on children. There have been many studies looking at the development of children of gay and lesbian parents, and the results all line up: there are no significant differences between children raised by heterosexual parents and those raised by gay or lesbian parents. What matters is not the parents' gender or sexual orientation but how loving and nurturing they are. Since gay men and women can be as warm and caring (or as dysfunctional) as heterosexual parents, it is not surprising that the mental health of their children is comparable.

Compared to children in heterosexual households, the children of gay and lesbian parents are equally likely to play with same-sex peers when they are in school and choose opposite-sex romantic partners when they are older. As a group, they are more tolerant of different sexual orientations and more sensitive to minority status. They are less likely to be victims of sexual abuse. Surprisingly, perhaps, they are no more likely to be teased at school than other children.

Legal issues. For gay and lesbian parents who are not their child's biological or adoptive parent, there is the issue of getting legal parental responsibility. Parental responsibility means that you can have your say in your child's healthcare and education – for example, you would be able to give consent for their treatment in hospital. Even if you are in a civil partnership with one of the child's biological parents, this does not necessarily give you parental responsibility. There are various options for getting parental responsibility, including making a parental responsibility agreement, applying for a court order and adoption, depending on your circumstances. Contact your Citizens Advice Bureau for advice.

Finding support. There are many books written for gay and lesbian parents that you might find useful. Many communities offer support groups for children (and parents) to share their experiences with others in similar circumstances (see pages 1054–5). There are also some terrific books for children that address issues of gay and lesbian families.

Help for heterosexuals. Awareness about gay and lesbian parents has grown so much in recent years that many heterosexual parents feel comfortable with the issue. But others still have concerns. Will it be confusing to a child with a mummy and daddy to be friends with a child who has two mummies or two daddies? I think the answer is simply no. Children are remarkably able to accept plain facts when they are presented plainly.

What *can* be confusing is when a child is taught that homosexuality is wrong, and then meets parents who seem to be very nice and who have great kids, and who turn out to be gay or lesbian. In that case, the child may have a hard time reconciling what she knows from firsthand experience with what she has been told is true.

Opposition to gay and lesbian parenting often arises from the fear that such parenting fosters homosexuality. However, sexual orientation appears to be controlled by biology (see page 720). Sometimes the opposition comes from a religious conviction that homosexuality is sinful. Such doctrines put tremendous pressure on children who do not fit the heterosexual mould, and put them at risk for a range of mental health problems, including suicide (see page 720). Parents may struggle to reconcile their faith with their need to provide love and security to their children.

DR SPOCK COMMENTS

The existence of gay and lesbian families offers you an opportunity to teach your child about different types of families and to value what is really important – not whether other families are different from yours, but whether they uphold those values your family respects: kindness, consideration and warmth. Such lessons in tolerance and acceptance of diverse family structures will serve your child well in dealing with the exploding cultural diversity of the world of the twenty-first century.

STRESSES AND TRAUMAS

Ordinary life for a child in the twenty-first century can be extraordinarily stressful. Television opens children's eyes to terrorism, earthquakes, wars and global warming. For many children, however, the disasters are closer to home. Physical and sexual abuse take a terrible toll. Domestic violence often devastates children, even if they are not physically harmed themselves. Children may have to cope with such stresses as the death of a family member, a parent's going away temporarily, or the lasting separation of divorce. Economic instability and unemployment add to the strains many children feel.

When you think about all this, what is amazing is that so many children grow up strong, loving and optimistic. This resilience comes from a powerful inner drive towards happiness and health and from relationships – or even a single relationship – with adults who care for them and believe in them.

THE MEANING OF STRESS

Stress is a physical response. The body responds to threatening situations by releasing the stress hormones adrenaline and cortisol. In small doses these hormones help with concentration and endurance (think of doing a long, hard maths test). At high levels they trigger the so-called flight-or-fight response (think of being attacked by a vicious dog): the pulse races, blood pressure shoots up, muscles tense, noncritical functions such as digestion shut down, concentration narrows to a pinpoint focus, and time seems to move more slowly.

Stress affects the brain. After a severe stress, a special neural connection is forged between the threatening stimulus and the stress response system. As a result, the next time the same stimulus shows up – perhaps it was a mugger in a face mask – the response occurs even faster. This special connection, however, also means that anything like the original threatening stimulus – a completely harmless face mask, for example – can trigger an inappropriate stress response. This is what happens in people with post-traumatic stress disorder, or PTSD. PTSD is common among soldiers returning from combat (it used to be called 'shell-shock'), but it also occurs in children who have experienced violence or other severe trauma. Along with the stress response often come vivid memories of the original traumatic event, which can plague children while awake and create vivid, horrifying nightmares while asleep.

Vulnerability to stress. Not everyone responds the same to stressful situations. About one child in seven is particularly vulnerable to stress. Even as babies, they respond to any new person or thing with a greater release of stress hormones. As older children, they tend to be more cautious or shy, taking longer to feel comfortable in any new situation, and they often develop fears or other anxiety-related problems. This vulnerability to stress is inborn, and scientists are on their way to discovering the responsible gene or genes; it often runs in families. Stress-vulnerable children are more likely to develop symptoms in response to any severe stressor, such as being chased by a dog or experiencing an earthquake.

If you know that your child has a special vulnerability to stress, you can help him develop coping skills by exposing him only to stresses that he can handle. For example, you might decide to turn off the television when the news is all about a war or earthquake, and instead talk about the situation over dinner – a much less intense exposure. Each time your child succeeds in handling a mildly stressful situation, his coping skills and confidence grow.

TERRORISM AND DISASTERS

The events of September 11 2001 are dramatic recent proof that the world is a dangerous place. Since then, there have been countless reminders. Each tornado, earthquake or act of terrorism undermines the illusion of safety for the families and children most immediately affected as well as those who witness the event in the media.

Children who experience disaster either directly or through repeated exposure to graphic images on television are likely to show signs of stress. After the September 11 attacks, for example, many American preschool children drew pictures of aeroplanes in flames, or made block buildings and crashed toy aeroplanes into them. Play of this kind is one way that young children take control of frightening realities. A sign of healthy coping is that the child eventually begins to create happy endings. The aeroplane lands safely; the building doesn't fall down; the child comes away looking relieved. The play of a child who has been traumatized is different: the planes continue to crash, the buildings fall over and over, and the child comes away exhausted and even more worried than before. This kind of repetitive, compulsive play is a sign that a child needs the help of a skilled psychologist or therapist.

Responding to disasters. Disasters, both natural and man-made, threaten the basic contract between parents and children, which is that parents will keep their children safe. So, it is very important that parents reassure their children that the adults – Mummy, Daddy, the prime minister – are doing whatever needs to be done to make sure no one else is hurt. Parents also need to protect their children from being further traumatized by repeated exposure to televised images of the event. As hard as it was to turn off the television after September 11 or during coverage of more recent battles and disasters, that is exactly what wise parents did.

The specific reason for a child's anxiety may be different from what you'd expect; a good general rule is to listen carefully to your child first, then try to answer the specific questions or concerns your child has. Children take security from familiar surroundings and routines, so that a quick return to the comforting patterns of everyday life – breakfast, school, the bedtime story – is very helpful.

Finally, it's important to pay attention to your own stress responses. Children follow their parents' lead. If you are terribly upset, your child will pick up on it. It's good to talk about your feelings in simple terms, so that your child knows what it is that is upsetting you (otherwise he's likely to imagine that *he* is). And it's very important to reach out for help to friends, family members, clergy or others in the community. If stress symptoms persist, in you or your child, a professional can often help (see page 940).

PHYSICAL ABUSE AND NEGLECT

Anger at children. Most parents get angry enough at their children once in a great while to have the impulse to hurt them. You may feel angry at a baby who continues to cry for what seems like hours when you have done everything possible in the way of comforting her, or at a child who has broken some precious possession right after you have asked him to put it down. Your rage boils up, but in most cases you control yourself. You may feel ashamed and embarrassed afterward. When such incidents occur again and again, it's a sign that you may need help from your doctor.

DR SPOCK COMMENTS

I remember when I was a medical student, picking up my own endlessly crying six-month-old baby in the middle of the night and yelling, 'Shut up!' at him, barely able to control myself from physically hurting him. He hadn't slept through the night for weeks, and his mother and I were exhausted and at our wits' end.

The roots of child abuse. Abuse and neglect refer to actions that threaten, or fail to protect, a child's basic physical and emotional well-being. Anything that increases stress in a family increases the risk of abuse. Poverty, addiction and mental illness are linked to abuse and neglect, but children throughout society are affected. Children who have physical or mental disabilities or special needs are also more vulnerable to abuse. Many abusive adults were abused, neglected or molested in their own childhood. They need therapy, individually and perhaps in groups. About one-third of children who are victims of abuse grow up to be abusers themselves.

Laws against abuse. The purpose of the laws on child abuse and neglect is to protect children. The law aims to help parents through counselling to understand and cope with the pressures on their lives. The preference is almost always to keep the child in his home while the parents are in treatment, though if the risk is too great, the child is placed in a foster home until the family is ready to care for him again.

Physical abuse and culture. In many parts of the world, slapping, smacking and whipping are considered good parenting, not abuse. In the United Kingdom, physical punishment that leaves a mark is illegal and is likely to be reported. The fear that children may be taken away can be paralyzing. One mother told me, 'My children don't respect me, because they know there is nothing I can do!'

Other parenting practices are sometimes mistaken for

abuse. One example is cupping, a common practice in Southeast Asia that involves placing a warmed glass over the child's skin. As the air in the glass cools, it sucks the skin into the glass, raising a welt. The purpose of this treatment is not to punish but rather to take away illness.

SEXUAL ABUSE

It's important to realize that a great majority of sexual molestations of children are carried out not by depraved strangers but by family members, stepparents, friends of the family, babysitters or other people already known to the children. Girls are most at risk, but boys are also victimized.

What to tell children. One recommendation that has been made is to have talks by police officers in schools, warning children of strangers who offer sweets and rides. But such talks, if carried out by authorities without special training, can encourage excessive morbid fears.

To make warnings less frightening, you can tell a young child (three to six years old) that an older child may want to touch her private parts, her clitoris or vagina, but she shouldn't let him or her. (See pages 193 and 701 on talking about the genitalia.) This can be brought up in connection to bathing and toileting, activities where parents normally touch children's sensitive areas, or in response to a question, or after a child has been discovered 'playing doctor'. Repetition helps.

You can teach your child to say, 'I don't want you to,' and

then tell you what happened. You can add, 'Sometimes a grown-up may want to touch you, or want you to touch him, but you should not. Tell him you don't want him to. Then tell me. It won't be your fault.' This last is mentioned because children characteristically don't report these incidents since they feel guilty, especially if the molester is a relative or family friend.

When to suspect. Sexual abuse is difficult for parents to suspect and for doctors to diagnose because shame, guilt or embarrassment leads to silence and because physical signs of abuse are usually absent. If there is genital or rectal pain, bleeding, trauma or signs of infection, you should seek medical evaluation. It's important to know that most mild vaginal infections in girls before puberty are not a result of sexual abuse.

Children who have been sexually abused often exhibit inappropriate sexual behaviours, such as imitating adult sex acts in front of other children. This is very different from normal sexual exploration, playing doctor or 'You show me yours, and I'll show you mine.' A child who masturbates compulsively or publicly may be replaying traumatic experiences.

Other behaviours found to be associated with sexual abuse in children and adolescents are less specific, including withdrawal, excessive anger or aggression, running away from home, fears (especially of situations related to the abuse), changes in appetite, sleep disturbances, a recent onset of bed-wetting or soiling, or a decline in school performance. Of course, these behaviour changes occur in children and adolescents as a result of many other stresses. In fact, in most cases they are *not* signs of sexual abuse. The point is to keep the possibility of sexual abuse in mind but not to obsess about it to the extent that you are constantly anxious.

Getting help. If you suspect sexual abuse, call your doctor. There are specialized teams of doctors, psychologists and social workers who evaluate children who may have been victims of sexual abuse. The point of these evaluations is to find out if abuse occurred and to gather evidence that can be used in court to convict the abuser, all without further traumatizing the child. Part of the evaluation is also to check for any medical problems, such as infection, that may need treatment.

Sexually abused children often struggle with feelings of shame and guilt. Parents can help by frequent reassurance that the child is not at fault, and that the parent will make sure that the abuse never happens again. It is crucially important that a child who has been a victim sees that her parents are standing up for her and doing everything they can to protect her in the future.

Any child who has been the victim of sexual abuse needs psychological evaluation. Treatment can often be brief, but it may need to be repeated later on because issues related to the abuse are bound to resurface. Psychological recovery from sexual abuse is possible but often takes many years.

DOMESTIC VIOLENCE

Every family has disagreements. Sometimes arguments turn into shouting, followed by threats, pushing, hitting and more extreme violence. Many children who witness these scenes suffer psychological damage, even if they aren't physically harmed. Often it's the father who is the attacker, although not always. During the fight the child may cower in a corner, feeling terrified, enraged and powerless. Afterward he's apt to become clingy, as though afraid to let his mother out of his sight. Still later the child seems to change sides, taking on the characteristics of the abuser. He hits his mother and showers her with the very same curses that his father used. Psychologists call this behaviour identification with the aggressor; it's a sign of emotional trauma.

In addition to aggression, young children who witness domestic violence often have problems sleeping and paying attention in school; they are also prone to developing growth problems, because it's hard to feel like eating when you are terrified. Child abuse and domestic violence often go together.

What you can do. The first thing is that the violence must stop. This often means that the mother and children leave the home, a terribly difficult decision but often unavoidable. (Although I mention mothers here, because they are most likely to be the victims, men can be victims of domestic violence as well.) The Refuge freephone hotline,

0808 2000 247, is a twenty-four-hour source for immediate help and referral to a safe house in your area. The website, refuge.org.uk, provides specific information to help you find safety, make legal plans and get support. Children who have behaviour problems as a result of exposure to domestic violence often need professional help to get past the trauma and recover their ability to feel safe and enjoy life (see page 940).

DEATH

A fact of life. Death is a fact of life that every child must grapple with. For some, the death of a goldfish is their first exposure; for others, it is the death of a grandparent. In many cultures, death is viewed as a natural occurrence, and no attempt is made to isolate it from everyday life. Our culture, on the other hand, remains very uneasy about the whole thing.

DR SPOCK COMMENTS

If adults are uncomfortable with the notion of death, it is no wonder that many are even more perplexed about how to help children deal with it. Some would just as soon deny the whole thing. That dog lying motionless at the side of the road? 'He's just resting. He's fine. What did you learn in school today?' Others choose to avoid the concrete and focus solely on the ethereal: 'The angels came and took Grandpa and now he's up in heaven with Grandma.' Still others duck the question altogether: 'Don't you worry about what death is. No one is going to die soon. Where do you get such ideas?'

Helping young children understand death. In the preschool years, children's ideas about death are influenced by the magical tendencies of their thinking. Children this age may believe, for example, that death is reversible and that the dead person will come back some day. They also tend to feel responsible for everything that happens in their world, including death, and may fear punishment for unkind thoughts they had about the dead person or animal. They may also view death as catching, like a cold, and worry that someone else will soon die.

Since this is the age when children take everything quite literally, it's especially important not to refer to death as 'going to sleep'. Many children will then become terrified of going to sleep and dying themselves or else say: 'Well, wake him up!' 'We lost Uncle Archibald' can strike terror into the heart of any child who himself has got lost. I remember one child who developed a fear of flying after hearing that a dead relative had 'gone to his home in the sky'.

Young children think in very concrete terms: 'How will Uncle Bob breathe if he's in the ground?' Parents can help a child by being equally concrete: 'Uncle Bob won't breathe any more. He also won't eat with us any more or brush his teeth. Being dead means that your body stops working completely; you can't move or do anything. Once you are dead, you cannot become undead.' Young children need to hear, sometimes several times, that they in no way caused the death.

Even as young as three or four, children can understand that death is a part of the life cycle. Things and people have beginnings, they start small, they grow up, they get old and they die. That is how things work.

Death and faith. All religions provide explanations of death. Whether these involve heaven and hell, reincarnation or spirits moving about the earth, I think it is important for parents to clarify to their children that these beliefs are built on faith, which is a special way of understanding the world. Children need to learn to treasure their own faith, while at the same time accepting that other people's faiths may lead them to see things differently.

Funerals. Many parents wonder whether to allow a young child to attend the funeral of a relative or close friend of the family. I think that a child from the age of three onward can attend a funeral and perhaps accompany the family to the cemetery for the burial, as long as the child wants to go to the funeral and the parents prepare him for what will happen. Children get from funerals what adults do: a confirmation of death's reality, and a chance to say goodbye in the company of friends and family.

It's important that an adult whom the child knows well is with the child the whole time to offer comfort, answer questions and take the child home if he becomes too upset.

Dealing with grief. Some children show their grief by crying; others may become hyperactive, or clingy; others may seem utterly unaffected, although later it becomes clear that they were also grieving. Parents can help their child deal with grief by acknowledging that losing a friend or grandparent is very sad and that it is sad to know that that person won't be coming back. As a parent, you do not need to pretend that you yourself are not upset or sad. By letting your child see that you have strong feelings, you make it okay for the child to accept her own feelings, too. By handling your feelings appropriately – for example, by talking about them – you teach your child how to deal with sadness and grief.

If a child asks about your dying. Probably the scariest thing for a child is the death of a parent. If there has been a death recently that has affected your family, or if your child asks you earnestly about death, you can almost assume that underlying it is the concern that you might die.

Here a blanket reassurance is in order. You can state that you will not die until your child is all grown up and (if you're lucky) has children of his or her own. Then, when you are a very old grandparent, it will be time for you to die. Most children are comforted by having this terrifying event put off into an unimaginably distant future. They know they aren't grown-ups yet, so they don't have to fear your dying. Although you can't be absolutely certain that you will live that long, this is not the time to go into all of the possibilities. Your confident promise to stay alive is the reassurance your child needs.

SEPARATION FROM A PARENT

Children draw their sense of security from their relationships with their parents. When young children have to be separated from a parent, even for a relatively short time, the stress of the separation can cause long-term difficulties. In a young child's mind, 'only a few days' can seem like forever.

Traumatic separations. If a mother goes away for a number of weeks – to care for her ailing mother, for instance – her baby of six to eight months is likely to go into a depression, especially if the mother has been the only caretaker up to that time. The baby becomes visibly depressed. She loses her appetite, lies on her back rolling her head from side to side, and no longer tries to explore her environment.

Around two years of age, separation from the mother no longer produces depression; instead it results in anxiety. Commonly a mother is called out of town by an emergency or decides to take an all-day job without preparing the child for the change to out-of-home care, or perhaps a child has to stay alone in the hospital for several days.

The child may seem fine while the mother is away, but when she returns all the pent-up anxiety breaks out into the open. The child rushes to cling to her mother and cries out in alarm whenever her mother goes into the next room. At bedtime she clings to her mother with a grip of steel and can't be put down. If the mother finally gets free and heads for the door, the child unhesitatingly scrambles over the side of the cot, though she has never dared do this before, and rushes after her. It's a truly heartrending picture of panic. If the mother succeeds in getting the child to stay in her cot, the baby may sit up all night.

Instead of becoming clingy, a child may punish her mother by refusing to recognize her when they are reunited. When she decides to recognize her mother again, she may scream at her in a rage or begin hitting her. (Of course, a father's sudden absence can trigger the same behaviours, if the father is the main caregiver.)

What you can do. For a younger child, try to keep the separation as short as possible; have a family member take care of the child, rather than a stranger. Tape a photo of the absent parent where it can be seen from the cot; have an article of the parent's clothing for the child to cuddle with (beware, though, of suffocation risks with infants); make a tape recording of the parent telling favourite stories or singing favourite songs.

For older children, make a calendar and check off each day until the parent returns; talk about what you'll all do together then; have frequent telephone calls or letters. For separations that are months in length, tie the parent's return to an expected change in the seasons or to another milestone the child will recognize. So instead of saying 'Daddy will be back in June', say 'First we'll have winter, then the weather will warm up and flowers will start coming out, and after that, Daddy will be home.' Read stories about families that have to be apart but then come together again (my favourite is the classic *Make Way for Ducklings*, by Robert McCloskey). If the date of the parent's return is uncertain (as when one parent must serve in the army overseas), it is even more important to exchange letters, phone calls and emails, to remember what you did when you were all together and talk about the good times to come.

DIVORCE

Divorce was rare in the United Kingdom until the 1970s; now it ends almost one half of marriages. In the UK, there are currently around 140,000 divorces a year. You can read about friendly divorce in fiction and see examples of it in films, but in real life most separations and divorces involve two people who are angry with each other. Divorce is often very hard on children. In most cases, it brings with it lowered living standards; often children have to move away from friends and school; parents are often upset or depressed, making them less able to support their children; children may blame themselves (unrealistically) for the breakup and may feel that they cannot be loyal to one parent without being disloyal to the other. On the plus side, divorce may release children from a toxic household. On the negative side, the emotional fallout can damage children for decades.

Stages of separation. Divorce is a milestone in a process that typically stretches over years. The end of the marriage may begin with a gradual buildup of differences and grievances, or with a sudden rupture due to violence or infidelity. During this period, children endure confusing, anxiety-provoking silences or full-throated battles; there may be interludes when everything seems fine, only to fall apart again. The parents are likely to be as confused and worried as their children. There may be periods of separation and reconciliation. Finally it becomes clear to one or both of them that the marriage is beyond saving. Some time after this, the actual divorce begins.

Recovery from the divorce also follows a predictable sequence. After a period of disruption and uncertainty, things fall into a routine of regular visits or moving back and forth between households. The children eventually let go of their hopes that their parents will reunite; the parents recover from their emotional shock and begin to rebuild their social lives. At some point the children may acquire stepparents and perhaps stepsiblings as well; it may be a joyful development or a stressful one.

This sequence plays out, with variations, thousands of times a year. It's remarkable, really, that children often come through the process mostly or even completely intact. That says a lot about children's resilience and parents' will for their children to thrive, even though their marriages have died.

Marriage counselling. When a marriage is in trouble, long before it fractures completely, it makes sense for parents to give marriage counselling or family therapy an honest try. It's best, of course, if both husband and wife go into counselling on a regular basis, to get a clearer view of what has gone wrong. Even if one spouse refuses to acknowledge his or her role in the conflict, it may still be worthwhile for the other to get counselling on whether and how to save the marriage. After all, there were strong positive attractions in the beginning, and many divorced people say later that they wish they had tried harder to solve the problems and make a go of it.

Telling the children. Children are always aware of and disturbed by conflicts between their parents, whether or not divorce is being considered. It is good for them to feel that they can discuss these situations with their parents, together or singly. They need to get a more sensible picture than their morbid imaginations may suggest. Also, they need to believe in both their parents in order to grow up believing in themselves. For this reason, it's wise for the parents to avoid bitterly heaping blame, which is a natural temptation. Instead, they can explain their quarrels in general terms, making it clear that they are trying to work things out so that everyone in the family can be happier.

It is wise to keep children from hearing the word 'divorce' shouted in anger. When the parents are certain that they cannot make the marriage work, the coming divorce should be discussed with the children, not just once but again and again. To young children the world consists of the family, which to them is mainly the father and mother. To suggest breaking up the family is like suggesting the end of the world. So the divorce has to be explained much more carefully to them than it would be to an adult.

Children usually want to know where they will live and with whom, where they will go to school, what will happen to the parent who moves away. They need to hear over and over again that both of their parents will always love them, and that it wasn't anything they did that made their parents divorce. Young children are very egocentric and will imagine that it was their actions that caused the parents to separate. They need many opportunities to ask their questions, and they need patient answers at a level they can understand. Parents might be tempted to give too much information; it's better to listen carefully and try to answer just what the child is asking.

Emotional responses. In one study children under six most often showed fears of abandonment, sleep problems, regression in bed-wetting and temper tantrums, and aggressive outbursts. Children of seven and eight expressed sorrow and feelings of aloneness. Nine- and ten-year-olds were more understanding about the realities of divorce, but they expressed hostility towards one or both parents and complained about stomachaches and headaches. Adolescents spoke of the painfulness of the divorce and of their sadness, anger and shame. Some girls were handicapped in developing good relationships with boys.

The best way to help children is to give them regular opportunities to talk about their feelings and to reassure them that it's okay to feel the way they do. When parents are in too much pain themselves to be able to have these discussions, it's important to find a professional counsellor whom the children can see regularly. Emotional responses are to be expected in parents and children alike; counselling or therapy often, if not always, has a role to play.

Parents' reactions. Mothers who gain custody of the children usually find the first year or two after divorce very difficult. The children are more tense, demanding and complaining. The mother is apt to feel tired out from working at a job and caring for the home and the children single-handedly. She may miss adult companionship, including the social and romantic attention of men. Worst of all, most mothers say, is the fear that they will not be able to earn a satisfactory living and to run the family. This is a realistic fear, as poverty often follows on the heels of divorce. Fathers who get custody of their children have similar problems, although the prospect of poverty is often less stark.

Some people imagine that divorced fathers without custody have a high old time and think of all the dates they can arrange, with no family responsibilities except child support payments and visitation. However, studies show that most of these fathers are miserable much of the time. If they get involved in casual affairs they soon find that these are shallow and meaningless. They are unhappy not to be consulted about both important and unimportant plans for the children. They miss the company of their children. Even more, they miss having their children ask them for advice or for permission, which is part of what a father is for. Their children's weekend visits often settle into a routine of fast food and films, which may satisfy the children's needs for pleasure but not their own need for a real relationship. Fathers and children may also find conversation difficult in this new situation.

Custody. After several decades in which custody was routinely awarded to the mother unless she was clearly unfit, courts are increasingly seeing fathers as capable of assuming primary responsibility for their children. Custody battles often keep parents from focusing on what would be best for the children.

The factors to consider are these: who has been providing most of the care, especially in the case of babies and small children who will badly miss their accustomed caregiver? What kind of relationship does each child have to each parent? What is each one's expressed preference, especially in later childhood and adolescence? How important is it for each child to live with a brother or sister?

When a child or teen finds tensions building with the custodial parent, she may start thinking that the grass is greener on the other side. Sometimes it is better for this child to live with the other parent, at least for a while. But a child who moves back and forth several times may be trying to leave her problems behind rather than solve them. It's better to try to get to the bottom of what's troubling her.

Joint custody. In the past it has usually been assumed that the divorcing parents will be adversaries with regard to custody, child support and property settlement. The more this battling attitude can be avoided, especially in the question of custody, the better for the children. In recent years, there has been a movement for joint custody, to keep the noncustodial parent (more frequently the father) from getting the short end of the stick in visitation rights and, even more important, to keep him from feeling divorced from his children, a feeling that often leads to a gradual withdrawal from contact with the children.

When speaking of joint custody, some lawyers and parents mean an equal sharing of the children, such as four days with one, three with the other, or one week with one and then a week with the other. This may or may not be practical for the parents or comfortable for the children. School age children have to keep going to the same school, and the same may be true for nursery or preschool. Children like and benefit from routine.

It's more positive to see joint custody as a spirit of cooperation between the divorced parents with regard to the children's welfare, which means first and foremost that they consult with each other about plans, decisions and responses to the children's major requests, so that neither parent feels left out. (It may be very helpful to have a counsellor, one who knows the children, to help the parents come to some decisions.) The second priority is to share the children's time in such a way that each parent keeps as closely in touch with them as possible, which will have to depend on such factors as the distance between the parents' dwellings, the capacity of the dwellings, the location of the school and the preferences of the children as they grow older. Obviously, if one parent moves across the country, the visits will have to come at holiday times, though the parent can still keep in touch by letter, phone and computer.

Joint physical custody is when children split their time between parents; joint legal custody means that both parents have a say in major decisions in the child's life, involving such things as school, summer camp and religious matters. In either case, joint custody can have significant positive ramifications if the parents can work together for the benefit of their children. In general, children have a better social, psychological and academic adjustment when both parents remain involved in their lives.

DR SPOCK COMMENTS

Joint custody lets both parents know that they are important in their child's life. Although it is a contract bound by the legal system, the most important thing here is the spirit of cooperation between the parents.

Visitation. Five days with the mother and weekends with the father has a practical sound and is a common schedule, but the mother may well want some weekend time with the children, when she can be more relaxed, and the father may want an occasional weekend without them. Much the same considerations may apply to school holidays. As the children get older, friends, sports or other activities may draw them to one home or the other. So any schedule is apt to require flexibility.

It is vital that noncustodial parents not casually break their appointments for visits. Children are hurt when they get the impression that other obligations are more important. They lose faith in the negligent parent and in their own worth. If appointments have to be cancelled, this should be done ahead of time and substitutions made if possible. Most important of all is that the noncustodial parent should not break contact frequently or erratically.

Some noncustodial fathers and mothers feel shy or awkward when visitation time comes. They often respond by simply providing treats – meals out, films, sporting events, excursions. There is nothing wrong with these occasionally, but parents shouldn't think of treats as essential on every visit; such behaviour would signal that they are afraid of silences, and it will make these treats more obligatory every week.

The children's visits can generally be as relaxed and as humdrum as staying in their regular home. That means opportunities for activities such as reading, doing homework, bicycling, roller skating on the pavement, playing ball, fishing or working on hobbies such as model building, stamp collecting or carpentry. Parents can participate in those activities they enjoy, which provide ideal opportunities for casual conversation.

Younger children are often irritable when they make the transitions from one parent to the other. Especially on their return from a visit with the noncustodial parent, children may be cranky from tiredness. Sometimes it's simply that the child is having difficulty shifting gears out of one setting and into another. Each departure and return may remind the child, at least subconsciously, of the original departure of the noncustodial parent. Parents can help by being patient during the transitions, by being absolutely reliable about time and place of pickup or drop-off, and by trying to keep these exchanges as free of conflict as possible.

Grandparents after a divorce. It's also important for the children to maintain as much contact with their grandparents as they had before the divorce. It can be very difficult to stay in touch with the parents of your ex-spouse, especially if you or they feel hurt or angry. Sometimes the custodial parent may say, 'The children can see your parents during their visitation time with you. I won't have anything to do with your parents.' But birthdays, Christmas and special occasions are never so conveniently arranged. Try to remember that grandparents can often be a great source of support and continuity for the children, so keeping in touch will be worth the extra effort. The grandparents' own emotional need to stay in touch with their grandchildren should also be respected.

Avoid trying to bias the children. It's vital that one parent not try to discredit or even criticize the other with the children, though this is a great temptation. Both parents feel a little guilty about the failure of the marriage, at least unconsciously. If they can get their friends, relatives and children to agree that the ex-spouse is at fault, they can lessen the guilt. So they are tempted to tell the worst possible stories about their ex, leaving out any mention of their own contribution. The trouble is that children sense that they are made up of both parents, and if they come to accept the idea that one was a scoundrel, they assume that they've inherited some of that. Besides, they naturally want to retain two parents and be loved by both. It makes them feel uncomfortably disloyal to listen to criticism. It's equally painful for children if one parent involves them in keeping secrets from the other parent.

By adolescence, children know that all people have imperfections, and they are not so deeply affected by the faults of their parents, though they can be very critical. Let them find the faults for themselves. It's better policy for one parent not to try to win the children's allegiance by criticizing the other. Teenagers are prone to turn hot and cold on slight provocation. When they become angry at the parent they've favoured, they may do an about-face and decide that all the unfavourable things they've heard in the past about the other parent were unfair and untrue. Both parents will have the best chance of retaining their children's love for the long haul if they let them love both, believe in both and spend time with both.

It's a mistake for either parent to pump the children about what happened while they were visiting the other parent. This only makes children uneasy, and in the end it may backfire and make them resent the querying parent.

Dating for the parent. Children whose parents have been recently divorced consciously or unconsciously want them to get back together and think of them as still married. They often feel that dating represents faithlessness on the part of their parent and an unwelcome intrusion on the part of the date. So it is best for parents to go slowly and be tactful in introducing their dates to their children.

Let the fact that the divorce is permanent sink in for a number of months. Be alert to the children's remarks. After a while you can bring up the topic of your loneliness and drop the idea that you may want to have a friend to date. It's not that you are allowing your children to control your life forever; you are simply letting them know that dating is a possibility, and doing so in a way that is more comfortable for them than being presented with a person in the flesh.

If you are a mother who has been living with young children who rarely or never see their father, they may beg you to marry and give them another daddy. Nonetheless, they will probably show evidence of jealousy as soon as they see the growing closeness between you and a man. A similar thing happens to a father who's had custody of his young children. Don't be surprised by your children's strong and contradictory feelings; they are normal.

Long-term effects on children. Children who have been through a divorce never come out untouched, but many are able to go on to have happy, fulfilled lives. Others struggle for a long time with feelings of anger, loss or uncertainty. Children who are able to continue to have loving relationships with both parents do the best. Where this is not possible, help over the years from professional counsellors or therapists can make recovery possible.

SECTION V

Common Developmental and Behavioural Challenges

SIBLING RIVALRY

JEALOUSY BETWEEN SIBLINGS

There is bound to be some jealousy between siblings. If it is not severe, it probably helps children to grow up more tolerant, independent and generous. One way children learn to deal with their jealous feelings is take on some of the nurturing qualities of their parents. In many families, jealousy gets turned into friendly competition, mutual support and loyalty.

You might also know other families where the children never really liked each other very much, and may not have much to do with each other even as adults. Parents affect how sibling relationships develop, and luck also plays a role. Some siblings naturally enjoy each other's company – they'd be friends even if they weren't from the same family. Other siblings start out with very different personalities – one likes noise and excitement, while the other craves peace and quiet – and so have a harder time getting along.

Equal love, different treatment. In a general way, the more agreeably parents get along with each other, the less sibling jealousy there is. When all the children are satisfied with the warm affection they receive, they have less reason to begrudge the attention their parents give to their brothers and sisters. What makes each child secure in the family is the feeling that his parents love him and accept him for who he is.

Parents can love their children equally without treating them exactly the same. A useful principle is, 'Everybody in the family gets what they need – and sometimes we all need different things.' A younger child needs an earlier bedtime. An older child needs more responsibility for housework.

When parents or relatives try to treat different children *equally* rather than individually, jealousy often intensifies. A harassed mother who is trying hard to treat her jealous children with perfect justice may say, 'Now, Susie, here's a little red fire engine for you. And Tommie, here is one exactly like it for you.' Each child then, instead of being satisfied, suspiciously examines both toys to see if there is any difference between the two. It's as if the mother said, 'I bought this for you so you wouldn't complain that I was favouring your brother,' instead of implying that 'I bought this for you because I knew you'd like it.'

Avoid comparisons and 'typecasting'. The fewer comparisons, complimentary or uncomplimentary, between siblings the better. Saying to a child, 'Why can't you be polite like your sister?' makes him resent his sister and the very idea of politeness. If you say to an adolescent girl, 'Never mind if you don't have dates like your sister. You're much cleverer than she is, and that's what counts,' it belittles her unhappiness at not having dates and implies she should not be feeling what, in fact, she is feeling. This is a setup for further rivalry.

It's tempting for parents to typecast their children. One child is 'my little rebel', while the other is 'the angel'. The first child may begin to believe that she always has to buck authority or risk losing her identity in the family. And even though the 'good child' may sometimes feel like doing something naughty, she may fear that she has to continue to play her assigned role or risk losing her parents' love. And she may resent the 'rebel' for having a freedom she lacks.

Sibling fights. It generally works better if parents keep out of most of the fights between children who can stand up for themselves. When parents concentrate on pinning the blame, it leaves one warrior feeling more jealous.

To a greater or lesser degree, children's jealous squabbles come about because each would like to be favoured by the parents. When parents are quick to take sides, in the sense of trying to decide who is right and who is wrong, it encourages the children to fight again soon. The fight then becomes a tournament to see who can win Mum's allegiance, at least this time. Each wants to win the parents' favour and see the other scolded.

If you do feel you have to break up a fight – to protect life and limb, to prevent rank injustice or simply to restore quiet – it's better simply to demand an end to the hostilities, refuse to listen to arguments, act disinterested in who is right and who is wrong (unless a flagrant foul has been committed), concentrate on what's to be done next and let bygones be bygones. You might suggest a compromise, distraction might save the day, or the children might need to be separated and sent to neutral, boring and very separate locations.

When sibling fighting is severe and getting worse, that is often a sign that family therapy may be needed (see page 944). Older children who are left to take care of their younger brothers and sisters may resort to violence or threats to establish their control. In these situations, you may need to put someone else in charge (e.g., a hired sitter or an adult relative), or enroll the children in an after-school club (see page 647).

THE MANY FACES OF JEALOUSY

Recognizing sibling jealousy with a new baby. If a child picks up a large block and hits the baby with it, the mother knows well enough that it's jealousy. But another child is more polite. He simply observes the baby without much enthusiasm or comment. One child focuses all his resentment against his mother, grimly digging the ashes out of the fireplace and sprinkling them over the living room rug in a quiet, businesslike way. Another with a different makeup mopes and becomes dependent, loses his joy in the sandpile and his blocks, and follows his mother around, holding on to the hem of her skirt and sucking his thumb.

Occasionally you see a small child whose jealousy is turned inside out. He becomes preoccupied with the baby. When he sees a dog, all he can think of to say is, 'Baby likes the dog.' When he sees his friends riding trikes, he says, 'Baby has a tricycle, too.' In this circumstance, some parents might say, 'We found that we didn't have to worry about jealousy at all. Johnny is so fond of the new baby.' It is fine when a child shows love for the baby, but this doesn't mean that jealousy isn't there. It may show up in indirect ways or only in special circumstances. He may hug the baby just a little too tightly. Perhaps he's fond of her indoors but is rude when strangers admire her on the street. A child may show no rivalry for months until one day the baby creeps over to one of his toys and grabs it. Sometimes this change of feeling comes on the day the baby begins to walk.

Being oversolicitous of the baby is just another way of coping with the stress. At its root is the same cauldron of mixed feelings – love and jealousy – that drive other children to regress or indulge in wrathful fits. It's wise to go on the assumption that there is always some jealousy and some affection, whether they both show on the surface or not. The job is not to ignore the jealousy, try to forcibly suppress it or make the child feel deeply ashamed about it, but to help the feelings of affection to come out on top.

Handling different kinds of jealousy. When the child physically attacks the baby, a parent's natural impulse is to act shocked and to shame him. This doesn't work out well for two reasons. He dislikes the baby because he's afraid that his parents are going to love her instead of him. When they threaten not to love him any more, it makes him feel more worried and cruel inside. Shaming also may make him bottle up his feelings of jealousy. Jealousy does more harm to his spirit and lasts longer if it is suppressed than if it is allowed to stay out in the open.

As a parent in this situation, you have three jobs: to protect the baby, to show the older child that he is not permitted to put his mean feelings into action, and to reassure him that you still love him and that he is really a good boy. When you see him advancing on the baby with a grim look on his face and a weapon in his hand, obviously you must grab him and tell him firmly that he can't hurt the baby. (Whenever he succeeds in being cruel, it makes him feel guilty and more upset inside.)

This situation gives you an opportunity to teach your child that his feelings are understandable and acceptable; it is the acting on those feelings that is not permitted. You can turn your grab into a hug and say, 'I know how you feel sometimes, Johnny. You wish there weren't any baby around here for Mummy and Daddy to take care of. But don't you worry, we love you just the same.' If he can realize at a moment like this that his parents accept his angry feelings (but not his angry actions) and still love him, it is the best proof that he doesn't need to worry.

As for the child who intentionally spreads dirt around the living room, it's natural for you to feel exasperated and angry, and you will probably reprove him. But if you realize that he did it from a deep sense of despair and anxiety, you may later feel like reassuring him. Try to remember what may have happened that sent him over the edge.

Withdrawal is concerning. The child who mopes in his jealousy needs affection, reassurance and drawing out even more than the child who eases his feelings by being naughty. With the child who doesn't dare show directly what's bothering him, it may actually help him to feel better if you can say understandingly, 'I know that sometimes you can feel angry at the baby, and angry with me because I take care of her,' and so on. If he doesn't respond after a while, consider hiring a temporary helper for the baby if you can afford one, and see if he can recover his old zest for life through more individual attention for a short while.

It is worthwhile to consult a children's psychiatrist or psychologist, or a paediatrician with special expertise in child behaviour and development, about the child who cannot seem to get over his jealousy, whether it takes the form of constantly misbehaving or moping or being obsessed with the baby. The therapist may be able to draw the jealousy to the surface so that the child can realize what's worrying him and get it off his chest.

If the jealousy comes out strongly only after the baby is old enough to begin grabbing the older child's toys, it may help a great deal to give him a room of his own, where he can feel that he and his toys are safe from interference. If a separate room is out of the question, find a big chest or cupboard for his things, one with a latch that the baby can't work. Not only does this protect his toys, but having a latch that only he can operate gives him a great sense of importance and control. (Beware of toy chests with heavy lids, however, as these are sometimes a cause of serious injury.)

Sharing toys. Should an older child be urged or compelled to share her toys with the baby? If you force your child to share her toys, chances are her resentment will grow, even if she does what you tell her to. Instead, try suggesting that she give the baby a plaything that she has outgrown. This may appeal to her pride in her relative maturity so she can demonstrate a generosity of spirit towards the baby that is not really there. But for generosity to have any meaning, it must come from inside – the person must feel secure, loving and loved first. Forcing a child to share her possessions when she is feeling insecure and selfish only makes her feel more put upon and undervalued.

Generally speaking, jealousy of the baby is strongest in the child under five, because he is much more dependent on his parents and has fewer interests outside the family circle. The child of six or more is drawing away a little from his parents and building a position for himself among his friends and teachers. Being pushed out of the limelight at home doesn't hurt so much. It would be a mistake, though, to think that jealousy doesn't exist in the older child. He, too, needs consideration and visible reminders of love from parents, particularly in the beginning. The older child who is unusually sensitive or who has not found his place in the outside world may need just as much protection as the average small child. Stepchildren whose relationships in the family might be shaky anyway may need extra help and reassurance. Even the adolescent girl, with her growing desire to be a woman, may be unconsciously envious of her mother's new parenthood or pregnancy. Teens often seem scandalized to learn that their parents have a sex life. A typical remark is, 'I thought my parents were beyond that sort of thing.'

Feeling guilty doesn't help. There's one caution to add here that may sound contradictory. Conscientious parents sometimes worry so much about jealousy and try so hard to prevent it that they make the older child less secure rather than more so. Parents may reach the point where they feel positively guilty about having a new baby, feel ashamed to be caught paying any attention to her, and fall all over themselves trying to appease the older child. If a child finds that his parents are uneasy and apologetic towards him, it makes him uneasy, too. His parents' guilty behaviour reinforces his own suspicion that there is dirty work afoot and inclines him to be meaner to both baby and parents. In other words, the parents should be as tactful as possible with the older child but should not be worried, apologetic, submissive or lacking in self-respect.

JEALOUSY OF THE NEW BABY

DR SPOCK COMMENTS

Imagine this scenario: your partner comes home one day with another woman and says to you: 'Dear, I love you as much as I always have, but now this person is going to live with us, too. By the way, she is also going to take up a lot of my time and attention because I'm crazy about her and she is more helpless and needy than you are anyway. Isn't that wonderful? Aren't you delighted?' How nice do you think you would be? I heard of a child who ran to the door when the visiting nurse was leaving and called out, 'You forgot to take your baby.'

Feelings of rivalry are often more intense in a firstborn child, because he has been used to the spotlight and has had no competition. A later child has already learned to share his parents' attention since his birth. He can see that he's still just one of the children. This doesn't mean that second and third children don't have deep feelings of rivalry towards the next child. They do. More depends on how the parents handle the situation than whether the child is firstborn.

Jealousy can be helpful as well as hurtful. Jealousy stirs up strong emotions, even in grown-ups. They can be more disturbing to the very young child because she doesn't know how to deal with them. Though it can't be completely prevented, you can do a great deal to minimize jealousy or even convert it into positive feelings. If your child comes to realize that there is no reason to be so fearful of a rival, it strengthens her character so that she will be better able to cope with rivalry later in life, both at work and at home.

What is important is not that the child feels jealous, which is normal, but just how he handles the feeling. Putting his feelings into words helps him master them. You can say, 'I know you are angry and jealous, but hurting the baby won't help.' You can add, 'And I love you too. I love you and the baby.' If a two-year-old slaps the baby, for example, you can guide the older child's hand into a caress and say, 'He loves you.' The older child's feelings are a mixture; you can help the love to come out on top.

The first weeks and months. Ways to help prepare an older child for the birth of a sibling have been discussed in an earlier chapter (see 'Helping Siblings Cope', page 26). The first weeks and months are also times when tactful parenting can help. Play down the new baby in the early weeks. Don't act too excited about her. Don't gloat over her. Don't talk a lot about her. As far as is convenient, take care of her while the older one is not around. Fit in her bath and some of her feedings when he is outdoors or taking his nap.

Many young children feel the greatest jealousy when they see the mother feeding the baby, especially at the breast. Give him a bottle or a turn at the breast, if he wishes. It's a little sad to see an older child trying a bottle out of envy of the baby. He thinks it's going to be heaven. But when he gets up his courage to take a suck, disappointment spreads over his face. It's just milk, after all, coming slowly, and it has a rubber taste. He may want a bottle off and on for a few weeks, but there's not much risk that he'll want to go on with it forever if the parents give it to him willingly and if they do other things to help him learn to deal with his jealousy. If he's around when you feed the baby, he should be allowed in freely. But if he is playing happily downstairs, don't attract his attention to what's going on. The goal is not to avoid rivalrous feelings altogether – that is impossible – but rather to minimize them in the first weeks, when the awful reality of the situation for the older sibling is beginning to sink in.

Other people play a part in jealousy, too. When a family member walks into the house, he should suppress the impulse to ask the child, 'How's the baby today?' Better to act as if he has forgotten there is a baby, sit down and pass the time of day. Later he can drift over to have a look at the baby when the older one is interested in something else.

Grandparents who make a big fuss over the baby can be a problem, too. If the grandfather meets the older sibling in the front hall with a big package tied up in satin ribbon, and says, 'Where's that darling baby sister of yours? I've brought her a present,' the brother's joy at seeing his granddad turns to bitterness. If parents don't know a visitor well enough to coach her in how to act, they can keep a box of inexpensive presents handy and produce one for the older child every time a visitor comes with a gift for the baby.

Helping your child feel more grown-up. Playing with dolls may be a great solace to the older child, whether girl or boy, while the mother cares for the baby. He wants to warm his doll's bottle just the way his mother does and have reasonable facsimiles of the clothing and equipment that his mother uses. But doll play shouldn't take the place of having the child help care for the real baby; it should only supplement it.

A great majority of young children react to a baby's arrival by yearning to be a baby again, at least part of the time. This developmental regression is quite normal. They may, for example, lose ground in toilet training and begin to wet or soil themselves. They may lapse into baby talk and act helpless about doing things for themselves. I think parents are wise to humour the craving to be a baby at those moments when it is very strong. They can even good-naturedly carry the child up to his room and undress him, as a friendly game. Then he can see that he is not being denied these experiences, which he imagines are delightful but which may prove disappointing.

The drive to continue to grow and develop usually soon overtakes the desire to regress, as long as the temporary regressions are handled sympathetically and good-naturedly. For your part, you can help by not paying so much attention to these episodes of regression and by appealing, most of the time, to the side of your child that wants to grow up.

You can remind him of how big, strong, clever or skilful he is, how much more he is able to do than the baby. That's not to say that you should be constantly giving him overenthusiastic sales pitches, but you should remember to hand him a sincere compliment whenever it is appropriate. And I'd avoid pushing him too hard to be a grown-up. After all, if you are constantly calling all the things that the child temporarily yearns to do 'babyish' and all the things that he's temporarily reluctant to do 'grown-up', he can only conclude that he wants to be a baby.

It's also important to avoid making direct comparisons that imply that you prefer the older child to the baby. To feel that he is favoured may gratify a child temporarily, but in the long run he will feel insecure with parents who are partial, because he worries that they might change their preference. The parents should, of course, let their love for the baby be evident. But all the same, it is very helpful to give the older child chances to feel proud of his maturity and to remember that there are lots of disadvantages to being a baby.

Turning rivalry into helpfulness. One of the ways in which a young child tries to get over the pain of having a younger rival is to act as if he himself is no longer competing in the same league as the baby. Instead, he becomes a third parent. When he's feeling very angry with the baby, he may act the role of the disapproving parent. But when he's feeling more secure, he can be the kind of parent you are, one who teaches the baby how to do things, gives him toys, wants to assist in feeding and bathing and clothing him, comforts him when he's miserable, and protects him from dangers.

You can assist his role-playing by suggesting how he can help you at times when it wouldn't occur to him, and by showing real appreciation for his efforts. Sometimes it's not even pretend help: parents of twins, who are often desperate for assistance in caregiving, are frequently amazed to find how much help they received from a child as young as three years with tasks like fetching a bath towel, a nappy or a bottle from the kitchen.

A small child almost always wants to hold the baby, and parents are apt to hesitate for fear he may drop her. But if the child sits on the floor (on a carpet or blanket), in a large stuffed chair or in the middle of a bed, there's little risk, even if the baby is dropped.

In such ways the parents can help a child to actually transform resentful feelings into cooperation and genuine altruism. The stresses and strains of coping with a new sibling can be transformed into new skills in conflict resolution, cooperation and sharing. Learning to cope with the challenges of not being the only show in town is a lesson that can pay off all through life.

SIBLINGS WITH SPECIAL NEEDS

If the new baby has colic or for some other reason needs lots of extra attention, the older child will need extra reassurance that his parents love him just as much as before. It may be helpful for the parents to divide their chores up to be sure that one parent is always available to the older child. He'll also need to be reassured that nothing he thought or did is responsible for the baby being sick. Remember that young children are prone to think that everything that happens in the world is because of them.

Siblings of children who have special needs – a chronic medical condition, say, or a developmental problem such as autism – also need special attention. Parents need to take care that the siblings *without* special needs feel included in the family and important in their own right. It is good for a healthy child to be able to help out in the care of a brother or sister with a chronic illness, but the healthy child also needs time and support to do normal childhood things – to have friends, play football, take piano lessons and just muck around. And the healthy child needs at least some of the parents' time all to himself.

Meeting the special needs of one child and the everyday needs of his siblings puts great demands on a parent and on a marriage. There will be times when *someone's* needs aren't met. The point is, it shouldn't always be the healthy child who has to make that sacrifice. Finding the right balance is a great challenge. Help from outside the nuclear family – from other relatives, friends, professionals and community programmes – often makes it possible.

Among the siblings of children with special needs, a certain number grow up angry or sad, burdened with emotional or behavioural problems. Many others, however, develop maturity, generosity, perspective and a sense of purpose that serve them well throughout life.

ACTING OUT

TEMPER TANTRUMS

Why tantrums? Almost all children have temper tantrums between one and three years (see pages 156 and 173). They're developing a sense of their own will and individuality. When they're thwarted, they know it and feel angry. Yet they don't usually attack the parent who has interfered with them. Perhaps the grown-up is too important and too big. Also, their fighting instinct isn't very well developed yet.

When the feeling of fury boils up in them, they can't think of anything better to do than take it out on the floor and themselves. They flop down, yelling, and pound with their hands and feet; sometimes they might even hit their heads. The typical tantrum lasts between thirty seconds and a couple of minutes, rarely more than five minutes. It seems like much longer. At the end, a child often feels sad and wants comforting. After that, the episode is forgotten (by the child, at least).

A temper tantrum once in a while doesn't mean anything; a child is bound to be frustrated sometimes. A surprising number of tantrums are a result of fatigue or hunger, or of putting a child into a situation that exceeds his capabilities. (Most supermarket tantrums fall into this category.) If the tantrum is of this sort, a parent can ignore the apparent cause and deal with the underlying problem: 'You're tired and hungry, aren't you? Let's get you home and fed and to bed, and you'll feel a lot better.'

You can't dodge all temper tantrums. Sometimes you can see a tantrum coming and head it off by redirecting your child to a less frustrating activity. But you can't always respond quickly enough. When the storm breaks, try to take it casually. Don't give in and meekly let your child have her way or she'll be throwing tantrums all the time on purpose. Don't argue with her, because she's in no mood to see the error of her ways. Getting angry yourself only forces her to keep up her end of the row. Give her a graceful way out. One child cools off quickest if the parents fade away and go about their own business matter-of-factly, as if they can't be bothered. Another with more determination and pride sticks to her yelling and thrashing for an hour unless her parents make a friendly gesture. As soon as the worst of the storm has passed, they might pop in with a suggestion of something fun to do, and a hug to show they want to make up.

It's embarrassing to have a child throw a tantrum on a busy pavement. Pick her up, with a grin if you can manage one, and lug her off to a quiet spot where you can both cool off in private. Any parent who is watching will know what is going on and feel sympathetic. The key is your ability to handle your child's upset without getting too upset yourself.

Frequent tantrums. A child who has frequent temper tantrums may have inborn traits of temperament that increase frustration. For example, she may be very sensitive to any change in temperature or sound, or to the feel of different clothes on the skin. One child has a tantrum every time her parents put her socks on unless the seams at the toes are in exactly the right place. Another child has the trait of high persistence. Once she gets started doing something, it's very hard to tear her away. This child might be very successful in school, where high persistence often earns high marks. But as a young child, the persistence guarantees a couple of tantrums a day.

Another temperament trait that results in frequent tantrums is high intensity of expression. Children with this trait are very dramatic. When they're happy, they shout with glee; when they're upset, they wail in despair. Another kind of tantrum-prone child is very sensitive to new people and places. It takes this child several minutes before he feels comfortable. If he's pushed to join the group before he's ready, he may break down into a tantrum.

If your child is having frequent temper tantrums, ask yourself the following questions: Does she have plenty of chances to play freely outdoors? Are there things for her to push and pull and climb on there? Indoors, has she enough toys and household objects to play with, and is the house childproofed? Do you, without realizing it, arouse balkiness by telling her to come and get her shirt on instead of slipping it on without comment? When you know that she needs to use the toilet, do you find yourself asking her if she wants to go to the bathroom instead of leading her there? When you have to interrupt her play to get her indoors or to meals, do you give her a minute or two to finish up and find a good stopping place? Do you get her mind on something pleasant that you're about to do? When you see a storm brewing, do you meet it head-on, grimly, or do you distract her with something else?

Learned tantrums. Some children have learned that tantrums are the best way to get what they want or to avoid unpleasant tasks. It can be hard to sort out these manipulative tantrums from tantrums caused by frustration, hunger, tiredness or fear. One hint is that manipulative tantrums tend to stop right away once the child gets what he wants. Another hint is that the child may work up to the tantrum by whining in a demanding way. The answer to these tantrums, of course, is for parents to stick by their guns. When they say 'No biscuits now', they shouldn't change their mind five minutes later in response to a tantrum.

To make this strategy work, you have to pick your battles carefully. If you feel strongly that biscuits before dinner are a bad idea, then by all means lay down a 'no biscuits' rule, and stick to it. But if you don't feel strongly about biscuits, consider saying yes *before* the tantrum, because if you wait until after the tantrum to say yes, you end up rewarding your child for having a tantrum. That just results in more tantrums.

A lot of parents find that their children throw tantrums about biscuits, but rarely if ever when it comes to getting buckled into their car seats. Why? Because the parents are absolutely consistent when it comes to the car seats, so the children know there is no point in bucking that rule.

Tantrums and language delay. Delayed language development often goes with tantrums, frequently in boys. A child may become frustrated because he can't make his needs and wants known. He may feel cut off from other children and adults – a very lonely and frustrating feeling. When he's upset, he can't use words to express his frustrations; he can only act out his rage.

As children grow older, they learn to talk to themselves to calm themselves down. If you think about it, you probably talk to yourself, too, either out loud or silently, when you need to calm down or reassure yourself. A child who has underdeveloped language skills can't use this very powerful self-comforting and self-control strategy. So negative emotions are more likely to blow up into tantrums.

Tantrums as a sign of other problems. By age four or five, most children are down to the rare tantrum, maybe one or two a week. But one child in five continues to have tantrums that occur three or more times a day, or long tantrums that regularly persist for more than fifteen minutes.

Causes of frequent tantrums in older children include developmental problems, such as intellectual disabilities, autism or learning disabilities. Chronic medical problems, such as allergies or eczema, may decrease a child's frustration tolerance. Certain medications may put children on edge. When children have been seriously ill, parents often have a hard time setting limits. Frequent tantrums may be the unhappy result.

A child who regularly hits or bites himself or other people while having a tantrum is showing signs of serious emotional upset. When in doubt, use your own feelings as a guide. If you find your child's tantrums annoying or sometimes amusing (although you should not let your child see this), then you're probably handling them just fine. If you find yourself feeling very angry, ashamed or upset by your child's tantrums, or if you worry that you might lose control yourself, then there is a real problem. Any time tantrums are not responding to basic good parenting and the passage of time, it makes sense to seek the help of an experienced professional (see page 940).

SWEARING AND BACK CHAT

Potty talk. Around four years of age, many children go through a phase of revelling in toilet words. They cheerfully insult each other with expressions like 'You great big poo' and 'I'll flush you down the toilet', and think they are very witty and bold. You should consider this a normal development, one that usually soon passes.

In my experience, the young children who continue to delight in using naughty words are those whose parents are openly shocked and dismayed and who threaten dire consequences for continued use of toilet language. The child thinks: 'Hey, this is a pretty good way to stir things up. This is fun! This gives me power over my parents!' This excitement outweighs any unhappiness she might feel about making her parents angry.

The easiest way to stop a young child from using naughty words is to simply ignore them, or say something very low-key, such as 'You know, I don't like that kind of talk.' If her words float out into space and nothing comes back, the child is apt to lose interest.

School-age swearing. As they grow older, all children learn swear words from their friends. Long before they know what the words mean, they know that they are naughty. Being human, they repeat them to show that they are worldly-wise and not afraid to be a little bad. It's usually quite a shock to conscientious parents to hear these words coming from the mouths of their supposedly sweet innocents.

What's a good parent to do? As with the three- or four-year-old, it's better not to act horribly shocked. For timid children, seeing that their parents are shocked has too strong an effect; it worries them, makes them afraid to be around children who use bad words. But most children who find they have shocked their parents are delighted, at least secretly. Some of them go on swearing endlessly at home, hoping to get the same rise. Others, stopped at home by threats, use their bad language elsewhere. The point is that when you show children that they have the power to scandalize the whole world, it's like handing them a full-size cannon and telling them, 'For goodness' sake, don't set it off.'

On the other hand, you don't have to sit mute and just take it. You can just tell your child firmly that you and most people don't like to hear those words and you don't want them to use them. End of discussion. If your child persists, in a challenging way, you can use time-out as a reasonable consequence (see page 676).

Teenagers. Some teenagers liberally interject swear words into many of their conversations. These expletives serve multiple purposes: to express disgust or contempt (a common feeling in many teens), to underline the importance of the topic, to discharge emotion or to show frank disregard for what they think of as arbitrary and old-fashioned societal taboos. But swearing at this age primarily serves as a mark of belonging to one's peer group.

You will lose any debate about whether swearing is good or bad, and your child already knows that some behaviours make you unhappy. But it is reasonable for you to request that your teen limit his swearing to times when it won't offend others or prove harmful to himself – for example, no swearing in your presence, no swearing in front of his little brother and no swearing at school. As with younger children, if you make a big deal about the swearing, you will probably only end up giving your teen an easy way to show his independence and to feel powerful. With teens, in particular, it's helpful to focus on what they are saying, rather than how they are saying it.

Back chat. With back chat, as with swearing, the key is to focus on what the child says, not how she says it. Young children often try talking back as a way to test limits and exert power (see page 172). It's helpful to let the child know that you have heard her, but then make sure that your rules still stand: 'I know you don't want to stop now, but it's time to tidy up' (while helping the child to get started tidying up).

If you are reasonably polite to your child, you have the right to expect a reasonable amount of politeness in return. Sometimes children need to be told or reminded that the way they are expressing themselves is rude. A clear, unemotional statement often works best: 'When you talk to me in that tone of voice, it makes me feel that you don't respect me, and that makes me angry.' Another approach is to ask the child what he meant by his tone of voice: 'Were you meaning to sound sarcastic just now? I just want to be sure I really understand what you want to tell me.'

BITING

Biting babies. It's natural for babies around one year to try to take a bite out of their parent's cheek. Their teething makes them want to bite anyway, and when they feel tired they're even more in the mood for it. It doesn't mean much, either, when a child between one and two bites another child, whether it's in a friendly or angry spirit. Children at that age can't express complex feelings in words, so their frustration or desire to dominate comes out in primitive ways, like biting. Additionally, they can't really put themselves in another's shoes; they usually don't even realize how much it hurts the other child.

A parent or other caregiver can say firmly, 'That hurts! Be gentle,' and then put the child down on the floor briefly or remove him from the playgroup for a moment. The idea is simply to give him the message that this behaviour makes you unhappy, even if he is too young to understand exactly why.

Toddlers and preschoolers who bite. If biting is a problem between ages two and three, you have to decide if it is an isolated problem or not. Consider how often the biting occurs and how the child is getting along otherwise. If he is tense or unhappy much of the time and keeps biting other children for no good reason, it's a sign that something is wrong. Perhaps he is being disciplined or restricted too much at home and is frantic and high-strung. Perhaps he has had too little chance to get used to other children and imagines them to be dangerous and threatening. Perhaps he is jealous of a baby at home and carries over the fear and resentment to all other small children, as if they were competitors, too.

When biting is accompanied by many other aggressive and worrying behaviours, it is often a symptom of a larger problem. It is that larger problem, rather than the biting, that needs attention.

Usually, however, biting comes unexpectedly in an otherwise model citizen. Parents are apt to worry that their sweet child may grow up to be a cruel adult. But in this case it's most likely a normal developmental challenge, not the mark of a psychological problem. Even the gentlest of children can have a brief biting phase.

What to do about biting. If you can, prevent the biting before it starts. Are there predictable times it occurs? If so, a little more adult supervision during those times may be quite useful. Is your child often frustrated because he is the least competent member of his playgroup or because your limit-setting is inconsistent? You may need to consider changing his daily routine. Also be sure to give him lots of positive attention when he is behaving well. Some children only get their parents' full attention after they've broken something or bitten someone. It's much more effective to give high-intensity attention in response to positive behaviours.

When you see your child's frustration growing, try to redirect him to another activity. If your child is old enough, you can discuss the problem at another time and ask him to help you think about how it hurts and what else he could do when he has the urge to bite.

If the biting has already occurred, it's helpful to attend to the child who was bitten first, and ignore the biter. After comforting the victim, give your child the firm message that biting makes you unhappy. Tell him not to do it again. Then sit with him for a few minutes while the message sinks in. Hold his hand or hug him firmly if he tries to go away. Avoid long lectures.

Bite back? Some parents who have been bitten by an infant or a one-year-old ask if they should bite back. No. You can control your child better by staying in charge as a friendly boss. When you bite or slap a very young child he's apt to keep it up, either as a fight or as a game or because he believes that if you are capable of such behaviour, why shouldn't he be? Biting a child to show him how it feels to be bitten usually breeds anger or fear rather than empathy. The best response is to keep from being bitten again by drawing back when he gets that gleam in his eye. Show him clearly that you don't like it and won't let it happen.

Biting after three. Biting usually stops by the third birthday or a little after. At that time the child has learned to use words to express his desires or vent his frustrations. He also has a better ability to restrain his impulses. If children this age continue to bite, it may be a sign of a bigger developmental or behavioural problem. An experienced doctor or other professional might be able to help work out if this is the case.

HYPERACTIVITY (ADHD)

What is hyperactivity? It's normal for young children to be hyperactive, in the sense of having boundless energy and no common sense. When people use hyperactivity to mean a psychiatric or neurologic disorder, they are referring to attention deficit hyperactivity disorder, or ADHD. According to the standard definition, ADHD includes three main parts: inattention, impulsivity and hyperactivity. That is, a child with ADHD has (1) poor ability to focus and sustain attention on tasks that aren't terrifically interesting; (2) difficulty controlling impulses, such as the impulse to call out in class or to jump off the garage roof; and (3) difficulty sitting still without fidgeting in class or at the dinner table.

These problems need to be severe enough to interfere seriously with a child's life. A child who is doing okay in school and at home does not have ADHD, even if he has endless energy, clowns around in class, or daydreams a lot. Also, by definition, the problems are present before the child turns seven.

ADHD is very hard on children and families. The children constantly get into trouble; their parents find themselves shouting and punishing much more than they would like; the children's friendships are usually brief. Sadness, loneliness, low self-esteem and anger are common results.

ADHD – inattentive subtype. Children with this condition have difficulty focusing and sustaining attention; they are disorganized and easily distracted but not particularly impulsive or overactive. They have many of the same problems as children with full-blown ADHD, but their problems may go unrecognized because they don't cause a lot of disruption. More of them are girls. (Sometimes this condition is also called attention deficit disorder, or ADD, but this term can be confusing because it used to apply to the full ADHD disorder.)

Does ADHD exist? Nearly every professional agrees that there are *some* children who are extremely hyperactive, impulsive and inattentive because there is something wrong in their brains. Where experts disagree is in the matter of how many such children there are. Using the standard psychiatric definition, a large number of children in the United Kingdom – perhaps 5 per cent – have ADHD. It's hard to believe that so many children have a brain abnormality.

One problem with the diagnosis of ADHD is that it relies on parents and teachers answering questions that are open to differing interpretations. For example, one of the criteria is that a child 'often has difficulty organizing tasks and activities'. But the terms 'often', 'difficulty', and 'tasks and activities' aren't defined. Does 'often' mean once every day, or all day long? Is fixing a bicycle – something many children with ADHD do quite handily – a task, or does that term only apply to schoolwork? Schoolwork is *supposed* to be challenging; if a child is having difficulty completing her advanced calculus homework, does that count? It's not surprising that teachers and parents often don't agree in their assessments of whether a particular child is hyperactive. There is no completely objective way to make the diagnosis.

So although it is clear that there are many children who are struggling in school and at home, and whose problems fit the description of ADHD, it's not clear how many of them have abnormal brains. I suspect that many of them have brains that are perfectly healthy but simply are not well suited to doing what we now require all children to do, namely, sit still, listen and follow directions for paper-and-pencil tasks all day long.

Does poor parenting cause ADHD? There's no evidence that it does. Some parents of children with ADHD have excellent parenting skills; many have average skills; and a few have very limited skills. A child who is spoiled – who has never learned to take no for an answer or to wait for what he wants – can look like he has ADHD. But most children with ADHD grow up with reasonable limits and discipline, yet do not learn to control themselves normally.

Things that look like ADHD. Many different problems can mimic ADHD. Some of these are inside the child, for example, seizures that cause a child to black out for a few seconds many times a day. Other problems are outside the child, such as a school curriculum that is much too hard or much too easy for him. Often there are several different problems going on all at once: children with emotional and learning problems, who live in stressful homes and whose school classrooms are out of control.

Some of the conditions that can look like ADHD include:

- Psychiatric problems, including depression, anxiety, obsessive-compulsive disorder, response to trauma or grief and others.
- Problems of hearing and vision.
- Learning disabilities. For example, children with reading difficulties often act out in classes – see page 1005. Quite often learning disabilities appear together with ADHD; at other times, learning disabilities are mistaken for ADHD.
- Sleep disorders. Overtired children are often inattentive and may act impulsively; see page 883.

- Medical problems, such as seizures or side effects of medications.

It's hard for anyone, even a skilled doctor, to sort through all the possibilities. It can be tempting to simply call it ADHD and prescribe medication. But the usual medications for ADHD improve attention in most people, regardless of whether or not they have ADHD. So if a child improves on medication, it does not mean he necessarily has ADHD. These medications may also make some conditions worse. Or they may fool parents and doctors into thinking that they are helping, when the real issue is not being addressed. For example, a child who has a learning disability may sit more quietly when he takes ADHD medication, but he still won't learn well. So it is very important that parents and doctors take time and care when diagnosing ADHD.

ADHD or bipolar disorder. Increasingly, school-age children are being diagnosed with bipolar disorder, which used to be called manic-depression. In adults, this condition is marked by well-defined episodes of elevated energy and mood (mania) alternating with decreased energy and mood (depression). In children, these cycles may be very short, and the manic phase can appear as extreme anger. In practice, it is often hard to tell if the problem is severe tantrums, ADHD with impulsive outbreaks of anger and aggression, or truly bipolar disorder.

The medications for bipolar disorder tend to be powerful, with potentially severe side effects. For example, one of these medications, risperidone, is known to cause dramatic weight gain and to increase the risk of diabetes. Psychotropic medications can make a huge difference for children who truly need them, but they should only be prescribed by doctors who have special training, such as psychiatrists or developmental-behavioural paediatricians.

How doctors diagnose ADHD. There is no blood test or brain scan to diagnosis ADHD, so doctors have to rely on information from parents and teachers, as well as their own observations. Those observations aren't always reliable. Children with ADHD are often on their best behaviour in the doctor's surgery. (Children with ADHD *can* behave appropriately – they just can't do it consistently.)

A doctor diagnosing ADHD should obtain information from at least one parent and one teacher, either by interview or through questionnaires or written descriptions. The doctor should review the child's developmental and psychiatric history, review the family history, interview the child and do a thorough physical examination. A doctor who makes a diagnosis of ADHD after spending fifteen minutes with a child is not giving state-of-the-art care.

Often, a paediatrician or family doctor will work together with a psychologist or psychiatrist to diagnose ADHD. The process may involve psychological testing and a detailed learning assessment.

Treatments for ADHD. There are many kinds of treatment available to children with ADHD. Most children need more than one treatment modality. It's a mistake, for example, just to treat the child with medications without trying to change the way parents and teachers deal with his challenging behaviour.

The diagnosis of ADHD does *not* automatically mean that a child has to be on medication. On the other hand, there is plenty of evidence that medication is the most effective treatment for the core symptoms of ADHD, the inattentiveness, impulsivity and overactivity. For example, in a large study, children who were given medication and psychological treatments did not do much better, in terms of their core ADHD symptoms, than children who got medication alone.

But psychological counselling and other nonmedication therapies are still very important for two reasons. First, they help children cope with problems brought on by the ADHD, such as difficulty making friends and dealing with frustration. Second, nonmedication therapies are important to help children with the learning problems and behaviour problems that often go along with ADHD but which are not part of the core ADHD symptoms. For example, many children with ADHD have learning disabilities as well. Medication for ADHD does not treat the learning disabilities; for those, special education is required.

Medications for ADHD. The medications most often used to treat ADHD are stimulants. Like caffeine, stimulants increase alertness by stimulating parts of the brain that are active during focused attention. Also like caffeine, stimulants cause the heart to beat faster and can create a feeling of anxiety or being wired. Stimulants are sometimes confused with tranquillizers or narcotics, but they are very different in what they do and how they affect the brain. The main stimulant is methylphenidate (the medication in Ritalin, Concerta XL and Metadate, among others). Other kinds of medication besides stimulants are sometimes used for ADHD. But stimulants work for nearly eight out of ten children with ADHD.

Are stimulants safe? Many parents are afraid to use medication to treat ADHD. It is reasonable to have concerns about any medication that affects how a child's brain works, especially if the child may take it for many years. However, many of the fears that parents have are based on misinformation. For example, it does not appear that stimulants are addictive the way drugs such as heroin or cocaine are. Children who suddenly stop taking stimulants do not develop cravings or withdrawal symptoms. Some people abuse stimulants to get high, but children who take stimulants to treat ADHD report feeling calmed down by the medication, not jazzed up.

Children with ADHD do go on to develop alcoholism and other addictions more often than other children, but it's not clear that the medication is to blame. In fact, children with untreated ADHD may turn to alcohol or drugs as a way to deal with feelings of sadness and hopelessness that result from their endless troubles in school, at home and with peers. Medication treatment for ADHD may make it *less* likely that teens will abuse illegal drugs.

Stimulants do have side effects, such as stomachaches, headaches, decreased appetite and sometimes sleep problems. But for the most part, these are mild and go away once the dose is adjusted. Children taking stimulants should not be spacey or act like zombies. These are symptoms of overdosing. I know medication is working when I ask a child how it makes him feel, and he responds, 'I feel like myself.' A key to the safe use of medication – any medication – is close monitoring. Children on medication for ADHD should see the doctor at least four times a year, more often in the beginning while adjusting the dose.

Children who start medication for ADHD do not have to stay on it for their entire lives, although many do choose to continue through adolescence. As children get older their physical hyperactivity tends to diminish but their difficulty focusing often continues, and medication continues to help them. Those who exercise a great deal of self-discipline can do well off medication.

What happens to children with ADHD? With good medical care and education, children with ADHD should be able to succeed. As they grow, the traits that caused them so much trouble in school – spontaneity, energy, the ability to think about three things at once – may serve them very well in the workplace. Children who have other problems along with their ADHD, such as depression or severe learning disabilities, face a tougher road and need more support.

How can you tell if your approach to ADHD is working? A child who feels good about himself, has friends and likes school is doing well. A child who feels bad about himself and who frequently says that he's 'stupid' or that the other kids don't like him needs more help. Over time, low self-esteem can become a bigger problem than the ADHD itself.

What you can do. If you think your child might have ADHD, talk with your doctor, or find another professional who can help you (see page 940). The Resource Guide (page 1060) lists a parent support organization that can be very helpful. As with any chronic developmental or medical condition, the more you know, the better you'll be able to work with doctors, teachers and other professionals to support your child's healthy development.

SADNESS, WORRIES AND FEARS

Sadness, worries and fears are part of childhood. A toddler feels sad and stops eating when her mother is called away on business for a couple of days; a four-year-old worries that his angry thoughts might truly harm his father, or cause his father to harm him; a five-year-old panics at the thought of going to the dentist. These are all normal emotional strains; most children overcome them and grow stronger.

Sometimes, however, the emotions are too intense for the child to handle. A parent leaves for good, perhaps to another city or to prison; or something truly terrifying occurs, such as physical violence against a parent, a stabbing or a violent attack at school. These traumas are more common in the lives of children growing up in poverty, but they happen everywhere. Other emotional stresses may be less dramatic: an emotionally abusive sibling, an unrecognized learning disorder, a parent whose depression or worries about work take her away emotionally for days at a time.

When children are overwhelmed by sadness, worries or fears for whatever reason, they may develop depression or an anxiety disorder. These problems aren't rare, but they often go undiagnosed.

DEPRESSION

Depression in a child or adolescent is often easy to spot if you know what to look for. A very young child might appear listless and stop eating. A school-age child might develop stomachaches or headaches, causing days missed from school. (The first thing to do, of course, is to have the doctor check for other illnesses.) Rather than being sad, a child with depression might be irritable, constantly angered by the littlest things. Like depressed adults, children with depression lose interest in doing things they used to think were fun; nothing excites them. They may lose energy and the ability to concentrate on schoolwork. Grades often drop. They often eat and sleep much more than usual, although sometimes the opposite occurs. If you question the child gently, she might admit that she thinks she is to blame for everything being bad, and she is sure that things can never get better; she may have thought of killing herself.

Depression runs in families. It's good to know this, because it may alert you to the signs. Boys and girls are equally affected when they are young; among adolescents, depression is more likely in girls. Teenage boys, when they are depressed, are at especially high risk of killing themselves, particularly if they drink or take drugs.

Rarely, an older child bounces between periods of depression and periods of extremely high energy during which he feels superhumanly happy, attractive, intelligent and strong. This is manic-depressive or bipolar disorder. Younger children may also have bipolar disorder, although the symptoms are somewhat different and psychiatrists may disagree about the diagnosis.

Depression can be treated. Two specific forms of talk therapy – cognitive behavioural therapy and interpersonal therapy – work well. Medications can also help. There are concerns that antidepressant medications may increase the risk of suicide, but many experts feel that the opposite is true. In any case, you don't need to decide about medication right away; the most important thing is to begin treatment of some sort. With treatment most children recover; however, depression often comes back and needs to be treated again.

ANXIETY DISORDERS

Anxiety takes different forms in children. Fears are normal in preschool children (see page 188). An eight-year-old boy may worry that something bad will happen to his mother while he is away at school, to the point that he can't concentrate on his lessons. A ten-year-old girl is so terrified she will be called on in class that she throws up. A twelve-year-old simply worries all the time, about everything. He can't sleep, and his body aches from the tension.

Other anxiety disorders include panic attacks, where a teenager suddenly has the intense feeling that he is dying or going crazy, and obsessive-compulsive disorder, where a child engages in rituals – turning the light off and on a certain number of times, or washing her hands repeatedly – in response to the feeling that something dreadful will happen if she doesn't. Extreme fears that prevent a child from doing normal things, such as riding in lifts or being in crowds, are related disorders.

Two things should tip you off to the possibility of an anxiety disorder. One is an anxiety problem in the family. Anxious parents may pass on genes that set their children up for anxiety problems, and they may also unwittingly teach their children to be anxious. The other tip-off is the presence of signs of any other behavioural or emotional disorder – ADHD, say, or depression – since anxiety often occurs as part of a larger picture.

Like depression, anxiety is treatable, with either medication, talk therapy or both. When anxious parents have their own anxiety treated, the children also often improve as well.

Fear of talking. A surprising number of children have a dread of talking outside the home or to people outside the family. At home they chat away normally, but if a stranger comes to visit, they immediately fall silent. At school they may be so silent that their teachers think they are seriously delayed. Unlike a normally shy or slow-to-warm-up child, a child with *selective mutism* never feels comfortable enough to talk and interact with people outside her comfort zone. Attempts to bribe, pressure or entice these children to talk just add to their anxiety and make the problem worse. Specialized therapy can help, however (see the Resource Guide, page 1069).

MESSINESS, DAWDLING AND WHINING

MESSINESS

Let them get dirty sometimes. Children love to get dirty, and it's good for them. They love to dig in earth and sand, wade in mud puddles, splash in water in the sink. They want to roll in the grass and squeeze mud in their hands. When they have the chance to do these delightful things, it enriches their spirit and makes them warmer people, just the way beautiful music or falling in love improves adults.

Small children who are always sternly warned against getting their clothes dirty or making a mess, and who take these warnings to heart, will become inhibited and mistrustful of the things they enjoy. If they become really timid about dirt, it can also make them too cautious in other ways, and can keep them from developing into the free, warm, life-loving people they were meant to be.

I don't mean to give the impression that you must always let your children make any kind of mess that strikes their fancy. But when you do have to stop them, don't try to scare them or disgust them; just substitute something else a little more practical. If they want to make mud pies when

they have their Sunday clothes on, have them change into old clothes first. If they get hold of an old brush and want to paint the house, set them to work with a bucket of water for 'paint' on the shed or the tiled floor of the bathroom.

Messes around the house. Once children are old enough to make messes, they're old enough to begin learning to tidy up. At first they need a lot of help; later, they can take on more of the task themselves. A child who leaves messes may have learned that someone else – Mummy, perhaps – will clean it up. She needs to hear clear, consistent expectations. Another child is simply overwhelmed. He needs help organizing the task into manageable pieces: 'First, find all the wooden blocks and put them in the block box.'

If children refuse to clean up their messes, it's reasonable for them to lose the privilege of playing for a few days with the toys that they left around (see page 674 on nonphysical punishments). If you've stored away a lot of your child's toys, there are simply fewer toys around to trip over. If you store toys for longer periods, when the toys come out of the cupboard they are 'new' again, and therefore much more fun for a while.

The messy room. A child's bedroom is a different story. If a child has her own room, it's good for her to take responsibility for it. From a parent's point of view, that may mean keeping quiet about a level of disorder that would be unacceptable in the public parts of the home. Setting aside vermin, fire hazards and a floor so cluttered that it's impossible to walk, a messy room harms no one but its occupant. A child who always has to search around for her favourite trousers or socks that match eventually learns to put things where they belong.

Giving your child responsibility doesn't mean that you can't remind her gently from time to time about the room, or even offer to help out. After a certain level of messiness, many children simply don't know where to start. But the problem belongs to your child, so the solution should, too.

DAWDLING

If you ever have seen a parent trying to jump-start a dawdling child in the morning, you vow that you will never get in that fix. The parent urges him, warns him and scolds him to get out of bed, get washed, get dressed, eat his breakfast, start for school.

All children tend to slow down when doing tasks that

aren't fun. Some are more easily distracted and thus less goal-directed than others. They become habitual dawdlers in response to constant pushing by their parents: 'Hurry up and finish your lunch' or 'How many times do I have to tell you to get ready for bed?' It's easy to fall into the habit of prodding children, but it can build up an absentminded balkiness in them. Parents feel they have to nag or the child won't get anywhere. The child assumes that there's no reason to move until the parent's irritation reaches a certain point. It becomes a vicious circle.

DR SPOCK COMMENTS

You may have the impression that I think children should not be held to any obligation. On the contrary. I think they should sit down at the table when the meal is ready and get up in the morning at the proper time. I'm only making the point that if they are allowed to use their own initiative most of the time, are reminded in a matter-of-fact way when they've clearly failed to do something on their own, are not prodded unnecessarily in advance, and are not hurried all the time, they usually find strategies to overcome their slow-starting nature.

Early teaching. Young children function best when they follow routines. For everyday tasks such as getting up in the morning or getting ready to go outside, lead your child through the same steps in the same order each time. If you've ever watched snack time at a well-run preschool, you know how efficient young children can be when they are running through familiar patterns. As your child begins to remember the routine on his own, step out of the picture as quickly as you can. When he slips back and forgets, lead again.

When he goes to school, let him think of it as his job to get there on time. It may be better to quietly allow him to be late to school once or twice, or to miss the bus and school altogether and find out for himself how sorry he feels. A child hates to miss things even more than his parent hates to have him miss them. That's the best spring to move him along.

Dealing with dawdling. An older child who dawdles may be disorganized or distractible. She starts out with the intention of getting dressed, but on the way to her dresser she finds a toy that needs playing with, a doll that has to be put to bed, and a book that needs reading. Fifteen minutes later, she's still in pajamas, happily playing. One strategy is to help the child make a chart, using pictures or words (if she can read and write), outlining the different steps that must be done to, say, get ready for school in the morning. Cover the list in clear plastic, so that the child can use a dry-erase marker to check off each step as she completes it. Set a timer, and let her try to get through her list before it dings. Give her a simple reward for 'beating the clock'. The best rewards follow naturally; in this case, getting dressed and ready on time without having to be nagged means that there is time for a few minutes of reading aloud (by you), video gaming or even television before it's time to leave for school.

WHINING

The whining habit. Young children whine when they're tired or uncomfortable and often when they are working themselves up to a tantrum (see page 809). A few children get into the habit of whining all day for a whole variety of reasons: to get special treats or privileges, because they're bored or jealous, or because things aren't going just right. They seem constantly dissatisfied and unhappy, and they make those around them miserable as well. There's a quality to their whining not just of distress but also of coercion: they're going to keep up until you give them what they want.

A child who persistently whines at one parent – her mother, say – may act much more grown-up with her father and at school. Often, too, a parent who has two or more children will tolerate whining in only one. In these cases, the whining may not reflect simply a habit or a mood in the child but also an attitude towards that parent. The child's demanding and complaining, and the parent's resisting, pleading, yelling and (often) giving in, follow a predictable pattern. Neither seems to be able to break the cycle.

DR SPOCK COMMENTS

I remember spending a day with a family in which the mother was a no-nonsense person with three of her four children. They were polite, cooperative, independent, cheerful individuals, but the five-year-old girl bugged her mother endlessly. She complained of boredom, hunger, thirst and cold, when she herself could easily have found remedies for these small needs.

The mother would ignore her for a while. Then she'd suggest that the girl get what she wanted. But she'd say it in an indecisive or apologetic tone. She never got masterful, even after an hour of steady whining. Sometimes she would even begin to whine back to 'quit the whining'. The end result: a nonproductive, mewling duet.

In one sense, such whining is not a serious disturbance. But it's certainly a pain in the neck to the other members of the family and to their friends, and it can lead to a mountain of frustration in the parent who hears it most often.

What to do about whining. There are definite, practical steps you can take if your child is a habitual whiner. First, ask yourself whether your attitude is feeding the whining. You may be using some expression of evasiveness, hesitation, submissiveness or guilt, mixed with the inevitable irritability that comes from feeling victimized. This is the most difficult step, because parents are usually quite unaware of anything except their impatience and the child's constant demands.

If you can't see any uncertainty in your behaviour, ask yourself how you may be unwittingly rewarding the whining – for example, by paying too much attention to it or by finally giving in to stop the onslaught.

If your child whines for special privileges, the solution is to make as many rules as necessary to cover all the usual pleas and then stick to them with determination and consistency. Bedtime is always to be at a certain hour; only certain television programmes may be viewed; friends may be invited for a meal or an overnight stay only at a certain frequency. These are the family rules, etched in stone by benevolent dictators. There are just no arguments about them. At first, when you stop giving in to the whining, you can expect it to increase in frequency and intensity. Then, after you have held your ground, it will go away.

If your child whines that he has nothing to do, it's smarter not to be drawn into suggesting a variety of possible activities, which a child in this mood will scornfully and with relish shoot down, one by one. You can toss the responsibility back to the child without getting bogged down in futile arguments by saying, 'Well, I've got a tonne of work to do, but then I'm going to do some fun stuff afterward.' In other words, 'Follow my example: find things to do for yourself. Don't expect me to amuse you or argue with you.'

You can also simply tell your child that you don't respond to requests made in a whiny tone of voice. You can say simply, 'Please stop whining right now!' If your child persists in annoying you, threatening to make you miserable unless you give in, you can impose a time-out (see page 676).

It's fine to give children reasons: 'We're not having pizza for dinner because we just had pizza for lunch' or 'We have to go home now so we can take our naps.' But sometimes (often!) parents just have to make a decision, and children just have to live with it. 'We're not buying that toy today, because we're not buying toys today.' Confident parents don't engage in endless arguments with their children about the limits they've set. If allowed, children will keep these conversations going forever and probably outnegotiate the parent at every turn. State your case, set your limits and end the conversation pleasantly but decisively.

It's fine for children to ask for something special occasionally, and fine for parents to give freely what they ask for, as long as they think the request is reasonable. But it's also important for children to learn to accept 'No' or 'Not today' as an answer. Demanding whining is a sign that your child still needs to learn this key lesson. If you catch yourself feeling bad about being tough on your child or wondering if you aren't somehow hurting him by not giving in to his demands, remind yourself that your child is strong (strong enough to make your life miserable at times), and a tough parent is what your child needs in order to move forward. Saying no is an act of love.

HABITS

THUMB-SUCKING

What thumb-sucking means. Thumb-sucking is quite different in babies from what it may indicate in older children. Many babies suck their thumbs, fingers or fists even before they are born. Sucking is how babies get nutrition, and it also helps them relieve physical and emotional tension. Babies who nurse more tend to suck their thumbs less, because they are already getting plenty of sucking. Not all babies are born with the same urge to suck. One baby never nurses more than fifteen minutes at a time and yet never puts a thumb in her mouth. Another baby, whose bottles have always taken twenty minutes or more, needs still more time sucking. A few begin to thumb-suck in the delivery room and keep at it; others thumb-suck early but soon give it up. Most babies who thumb-suck start before they are three months old.

Thumb-sucking is different from the thumb, finger and hand chewing that almost all babies do from the time they begin to teethe (commonly at around three or four months). During his teething periods, the baby who is a thumb-sucker is sucking one minute and chewing another.

Thumb-sucking in the older baby and child. By the time a baby is six months old, thumb-sucking is turning into something different. It is a comforter that she needs at special times. She sucks when she is tired, bored or frustrated, or to put herself to sleep. When she can't make a go of things at the more grown-up level, she retreats to early infancy, when sucking was her chief joy. It's very rare for a child beyond the age of a few months or one year to begin to thumb-suck for the first time.

Is there anything that the parents need to do? Probably not, if the child is generally outgoing, happy and busy and if she sucks mainly at bedtime and occasionally during the day. Thumb-sucking by itself is not a sign of unhappiness, maladjustment or lack of love. In fact, most thumb-suckers are very happy children; children who are severely deprived of affection don't thumb-suck.

If a child is sucking a great deal of the time instead of playing, parents should ask themselves whether there is anything they ought to do so that she won't need to comfort herself so much. Another child may be bored from not seeing enough of other children or from not having enough things to play with. Or perhaps she has to sit in her playpen for hours. A boy of a year and a half may be at loggerheads with his mother all day if she is always stopping him from doing the things that fascinate him instead of diverting him to playthings that are permissible. Another boy has children to play with and freedom to do things at home, but he's too timid to throw himself into these activities. He thumb-sucks while he watches. The point of these examples is only to make it clear that if anything needs to be done for excessive thumb-sucking, it is to make the child's life more satisfying.

Sometimes in an older child, thumb-sucking is simply a habit, a pattern of behaviour that repeats for no good reason. The child wants to stop, but his fingers seem to end up in his mouth of their own accord; he's not really aware that he's doing it.

Health effects of thumb-sucking. The physical problems caused by thumb-sucking are mild. Thickened skin on the favourite thumb or finger is common and will go away on its own. Minor infections around the fingernail also occur and are usually easy to treat (see page 501). The most concerning problems are orthodontic. It is true that thumb-sucking often pushes the upper front baby teeth forward and the lower teeth back. How much the teeth are displaced will depend on how much the child sucks her thumb and, even more, on what position she holds her thumbs in. But dentists point out that this tilting of the baby teeth has no effect on the permanent teeth, which begin coming in at about six years of age. In other words, if the baby gives up thumb-sucking by six years of age, as happens in a great majority of cases, there is very little chance that it will displace the permanent teeth.

Preventing thumb-sucking. You don't need to be concerned when babies suck their thumbs for only a few minutes just before their feeding time. They are probably doing this only because they're hungry. It's when babies try to suck their thumbs as soon as their feeding is over or when they suck a lot between feedings that you might think of ways to satisfy the sucking craving.

If your baby begins to try to suck her thumb or finger or hand, it's best not to stop her directly but to try to give her more opportunity to suck at the breast, the bottle or the dummy. If your baby hasn't been a confirmed thumb-sucker from birth, the most effective method by far to prevent the habit is the ample use of the dummy in the first three months. If you're bottle-feeding, think about using a nipple with a smaller hole, so your baby gets to do a lot of sucking during feeding. If you're breast-feeding, think about letting your baby nurse longer, even after she's got most of the milk she needs.

With a thumb-sucker, it's better to go slowly in omitting feedings. It's not just the length of each feeding but also the frequency of feedings over twenty-four hours that determines whether a baby satisfies the sucking instinct. So, if a baby is still thumb-sucking even though you have made each breast- or bottle-feeding last as long as possible, it is sensible to go slowly in dropping other feedings. For example, if a three-month-old baby seems willing to sleep through the late evening feeding at the parents' bedtime but is doing a good deal of thumb-sucking, you might wait a while longer before dropping the late evening feeding – perhaps a couple of months, provided the baby is still willing to drink when awakened.

Methods that don't work. Why not tie babies' arms down to keep them from thumb-sucking? This would cause them a great deal of frustration, which could produce new problems. Furthermore, tying down the hands usually doesn't cure the baby who is thumb-sucking a lot, because it doesn't respond to the baby's need for more sucking. A few despairing parents use elbow splints or put bad-tasting liquid on the baby's thumbs, not just for days but for months. And the day they take off the restraint or stop the liquid on the thumb, the thumb pops back in the mouth.

The one time bitter-tasting liquids can be helpful is for the very motivated older child who needs something to alert him when his thumb goes into his mouth unconsciously. The child should be in charge of painting his own thumbs. Success is much more likely if he feels in control of the process.

Breaking the habit. Elbow splints, mitts and bad-tasting stuff on the thumb won't stop the habit any more often in older children than they do in small babies. These approaches may even prolong the habit by setting up a power struggle between the determined sucker and his parents. The same applies to scolding a child or pulling his thumb out of his mouth. What about the common ploy of handing a child a toy when he starts to thumb-suck? It certainly is sound to have enough interesting things around for them to play with so that he won't be bored. But if every time his thumb goes in the mouth you jump towards him and poke any old toy into his hands, he'll soon catch on.

What about bribery? If your child is one of the rare ones who is still thumb-sucking at the age of five and you are beginning to worry about what it will do to the permanent teeth when they come in, you will have a fair chance of succeeding if the bribe is a good one. A girl of four or five who wants to get over her thumb-sucking may be helped by having her fingernails painted like an older girl's. But practically no child of two or three has the willpower to deny an instinct for the sake of reward. You're apt to make a fuss and get nowhere.

If your child is thumb-sucking, see to it that his life is good. In the long run it will help him if you remind him that someday he will be grown-up enough to stop. This friendly encouragement makes him want to stop as soon as he is able. But don't nag him.

Most important of all, try to stop thinking about it. If you keep on worrying, even though you resolve to say nothing, the child will feel your tension and react against it. Remember that thumb-sucking goes away all by itself in time. In the overwhelming majority of cases, it is over before the adult teeth appear. It doesn't go away steadily, though. It decreases rapidly for a while, and then comes back partway during an illness or when the child has a difficult adjustment to make. Eventually it disappears for good. It rarely stops before three years. It usually peters out between three and six.

Some dentists use metal wires attached to the upper teeth to make thumb-sucking not only unpleasant but virtually impossible. This measure should be a last resort. Not only is it expensive, but it takes all control away from the child at an age when it's important for children to feel that they can be in control of their bodies.

OTHER INFANT HABITS

Stroking and hair pulling. Most of the babies who suck their thumbs past the age of one also do some kind of stroking at the same time. One little boy rubs or plucks a piece of blanket, a nappy, a piece of silk or a woolly toy. Another strokes his earlobe or twists a lock of his hair. Still another wants to hold a piece of cloth right up close to his face and perhaps stroke his nose or lip with a free finger. These motions remind you of how younger babies used to gently feel their mother's skin or clothing when they were nursing at the breast or bottle. When they press something against their faces, they seem to be remembering how they felt at the breast.

Occasionally an infant gets into the habit of stroking and tugging on strands of his own hair. The result can be unattractive bald spots for the baby and worry for the parents. This behaviour is just a habit, not a sign of emotional or physical disturbance. The best treatment is simply to cut the hair short so that there is nothing for the baby to grab hold of for a while. By the time the hair grows back, the habit is usually gone.

In older children, compulsive hair pulling is more likely to be a sign of anxiety or psychological tension, so consultation with a psychologist or other professional makes sense (see page 940). Medical tests might also be required to rule out other causes for hair loss.

Ruminating. Rarely, a baby or young child gets into the habit of sucking and chewing on her tongue until her last meal comes up, a practice known as ruminating. Some cases begin when thumb-sucking babies have their arms restrained; they turn to sucking their tongues instead. I would certainly advise letting such babies have the thumb back immediately, before the ruminating becomes a habit. Be sure also that the baby has enough companionship, play and affection. Rumination may signal unusually high tension in the infant-parent relationship. Professional guidance can help (see page 940).

RHYTHMIC HABITS

Body rocking, head banging. It's common for a child between about eight months and four years to rock his body or bang his head from time to time. A baby lying in her cot may roll her head from side to side or get up on all fours and jounce back and forth against her heels. With each forward movement her head may hit against the cot; it looks painful, but it clearly isn't, and it's never hard enough to cause brain injury (although it sometimes raises a lump). A baby sitting on a sofa will rock hard against the back and let it bounce her forward again.

What's the meaning of these rhythmic movements? They usually appear during the second half of the first year, when babies naturally acquire a sense of rhythm. Like thumb-sucking or the stroking of a soft toy, rocking and banging seem to be self-comforting behaviours. They usually occur when the child is sleepy, bored or upset, or in response to physical discomfort from teething, for example, or an ear infection. Perhaps these behaviours represent a desire to reproduce the experience of being rocked and carried by a parent.

The same movements, especially head-banging, occur frequently and intensely in some children who are emotionally neglected or physically abused, and in some with autism or other developmental disorders. If you see such behaviour occurring with great regularity, it's reasonable to discuss it with your doctor.

NAIL-BITING

What it means. Sometimes nail-biting is a sign of tenseness; sometimes it's just a habit that doesn't mean anything in particular. Nail-biting is more common in relatively high-strung children who are inclined to worry a lot, and it tends to run in families. Children often bite their nails when they are anxious – for instance, while waiting to be called on in school or while watching a scary episode in a film.

A good general approach is to find out what some of the pressures on your child are and try to relieve them. Is she being urged, corrected, warned or scolded too much? Are your expectations for schoolwork and extracurricular achievements too high? Is she putting herself under too much pressure? Is she getting along with peers? Ask her teachers what they see in the classroom and the lunchroom. If film, radio and TV violence makes her jittery, it's wise to make such programmes off-limits. (Actually, that's probably a wise decision for all children.)

Prevention strategies. School-age children are often motivated to stop nail-biting because they sense disapproval from peers or because they want nicer-looking nails. You can support this positive motivation by offering suggestions. But it's best to let your child be in charge of the campaign. The problem belongs to your child, and the solution should, too.

Nagging or punishing nail-biters usually doesn't stop them for longer than half a minute, because they seldom realize they are doing it. In the long run, it may increase their tension or encourage them to think of the biting as their parents' problem, not their own. Bitter medicine on the nails can work, if the child asks for it as a way to remind himself that he wants to stop the nail-biting. But if it's put on against his will, the child is bound to think he's being punished. That only gives him another thing to feel tense about and may prolong the habit.

Take a broader view. If your child is otherwise reasonably happy and relaxed, you don't need to make too much of nail-biting. But when nail-biting is one of a host of worrying behaviours, then it makes sense to seek professional help (see page 940). It is the cause of the child's anxiety, not the nail-biting itself, that should be of greatest concern.

STUTTERING

What causes stuttering? Between two and three years of age, almost every young child goes through a period when talking is an effort and the words sometimes don't come out right; they may repeat words, or hesitate and then rush ahead too fast. This is all part of normal speech development. About one child in twenty has more difficulty, repeating many words or partial words, lengthening some and entirely blocking others. Some children also show signs of facial stress. Fortunately, mild to moderate stuttering like this usually goes away by itself. Only about one child in one hundred ends up with a long-standing stuttering problem.

We don't really know what causes persistent stuttering. Stuttering is much more common in boys than girls (like many other speech and language problems). It often runs in families, suggesting that genetics plays a role. And brain scan studies have found some differences in the size of certain brain areas in adults who stutter. It used to be thought that stuttering was a sign of stress. That makes sense, because children who stutter almost always stutter more when they are under stress. But many children experience severe stresses without ever stuttering, and many who stutter are otherwise quite well adjusted.

A tongue tie (when the fold of skin that runs from the middle of the underside of the tongue to the floor of the mouth appears to be too short to allow free movement of the tongue) has nothing to do with stuttering.

·•· DR SPOCK COMMENTS

One little boy began to stutter when a new baby sister was brought home from the hospital. He didn't show his jealousy outwardly. He never tried to hit or pinch her. He just became uneasy. A girl of two and a half began to stutter after the departure of a fond relative who had been with the family a long time. In two weeks her stuttering stopped for the time being. When the family moved to a new house, she was quite homesick and stuttered again for a period. Two months later her father was called into the army. The family was upset, and the little girl started stuttering again.

Responding to stuttering. When your child talks to you, give him your full attention so that he doesn't get frantic. Telling a child to slow down or asking him to repeat himself often just increases his self-consciousness, making the stuttering worse. Instead, try to respond to what the child is saying rather than how he says it. Train yourself to speak in a relaxed, unpressured way, and help others in the family to do the same. (Slowing way down doesn't help, though; it's best to be natural.) Stuttering gets worse when children feel they only have a few seconds to make themselves heard. Instead, make it a family rule that everyone takes turns and gives the others time to express themselves.

Anything you can do to lower your child's stress level is likely to help. Does he have plenty of chances to play with other children? Does he have toys and equipment enough, indoors and out? When you're playing with him, let him take the lead. Play quietly sometimes, simply doing things without necessarily talking at the same time. A regular daily schedule, less pressure to perform and less rushing around are all helpful. If your child was upset by being separated from you for a number of days, try to avoid further separations for a couple of months. If you think you have been talking to him or urging him to talk too much, try to train yourself out of it.

When to get help. Since most children who stutter get better on their own, it can be hard to know when to refer a child for special help. A good rule of thumb is to get help right away for severe stuttering and for any stuttering that hasn't shown signs of getting better after about four to six months.

When is stuttering severe? In severe stuttering, the child is often very concerned and self-conscious and may avoid speaking altogether; there's usually a lot of muscle tension in the face, and the voice pitch may go up (another sign of tension). He stutters pretty much all the time, even when relaxed. When you're with a child who has a severe stuttering problem, you probably feel tense yourself. Here, as with so many parts of parenting, it's wise to trust your instincts: if a child's speech difficulty makes you feel uncomfortable, that's a sign to get help.

With severe stuttering, work with a trained speech therapist can help, the sooner the better (see the Resource Guide, page 1070). There are special techniques to teach a child to speak more fluently. Even if speech therapy can't fix a child's stuttering, it may keep it from getting worse. A good therapist can help the child and the family understand the problem and adapt to it in healthy ways.

TOILET TRAINING, SOILING AND BED-WETTING

READINESS FOR TOILET TRAINING

First, relax. Everyone talks about the child's readiness to be trained, but parents have to be ready, too. Many feel anxious about the whole business. You might have heard about children who are four or five who refuse to use the toilet, or younger children who can't get into preschool because they're still in nappies. On one hand, it's easy to regard toilet training with grim determination as a test which might be failed. On the other hand, you might worry that if you try too hard it will make your child rebellious or cause emotional problems.

In reality, you probably have nothing to worry about. Most children learn how to use the potty sometime between age two and a half and three and a half. Some start as early as eighteen months, others as late as thirty-six. As a group, those who start younger don't finish any sooner; girls finish a couple of months before boys do. Whenever you start toilet training, it's best to avoid the extremes. Harsh punishments often backfire, while a completely hands-off approach runs the risk that your child will decide that nappies are the way to go. If you steer a middle course and adjust your training to your child's motivation and level of maturity, you're likely to come out fine in the long run.

DR SPOCK COMMENTS

Many people have the idea that the only way that a baby becomes trained is by the parents' strenuous efforts. This is the wrong way to look at it. Generally speaking, babies themselves gradually gain control of their own bowels and bladders as they grow.

Toileting and development. Toilet training normally happens at a time when young children are developing a sense of themselves as individuals. At this age, around two or three, they want independence and control over everything they do. They are just learning what's theirs and that they can decide whether to keep it or give it away. They are naturally fascinated by what comes out of them and pleased by their own growing mastery over when it comes out and where it goes.

Learning to use the toilet gives children control of two orifices of the body that previously functioned automatically. This new control makes them feel proud, so proud at first that they try to perform every few minutes. In learning to use the toilet, they are accepting the first serious responsibility assigned to them by their parents. Successful cooperation on this project gives parents and children new confidence in each other. The child who previously enjoyed making messes with food and BMs (bowel movements) now begins to take satisfaction in cleanliness.

You may think of this shift as primarily meaning no

more soiled nappies. That's important, all right. But the preference for cleanliness that a child gains means a lot more than that. It's actually the foundation for a lifelong preference for unsticky hands, for clean clothes, for a neat home, for an orderly way of doing business. Toilet training plays a part in the formation of a child's character. If you take advantage of your child's natural desire to become more grown-up and self-sufficient, the process will be a lot easier for both of you.

Early toilet training. In the first year a baby shows very little awareness of bowel function. When her rectum becomes full, particularly after a meal when the intestines are active, the stool presses against the inner valve of the anus and causes it to open somewhat. This stimulates a squeezing, pushing-down action of the abdominal muscles. The baby, in other words, does not decide to push the way an older child or adult does; it happens automatically. The bladder also works on autopilot in much the same way.

Even though small babies can't consciously control when they go, they can be trained to urinate and move their bowels on cue. Early training is standard practice in many parts of the world; it makes great sense where access to nappies is limited and where infants are more or less constantly held by their mothers. In fact, similar training methods were common in the United Kingdom a few generations ago. The process is simple enough. The mother senses when the baby is about to have a BM (often a few minutes after the baby has eaten) and sits the baby on a toilet or potty. Over time, the baby comes to associate sitting on the potty with relaxing his anal opening.

A similar technique can be used to train a baby to urinate on cue. When the mother senses that the baby is about to urinate, she holds the baby in a particular position (over a sink, for example), and makes a 'psssh' sound. The baby learns to link the position, sound and act of passing urine. After that, if the mother holds the baby in the right position and makes the right sound, the child urinates by reflex.

This process is truly toilet *training* rather than learning, because the baby is not conscious of what she herself is doing, at least not at first. It takes a lot of attention and persistence to train a child in this manner, and it's very important that the parent remain calm and positive. If the parent becomes frustrated or impatient, the negative emotion is bound to become attached, in the child's mind, with the act of being put on the potty – just what you don't want to have happen.

Bowel control between twelve and eighteen months. At this age children gradually become conscious of when a bowel movement occurs. They may pause in their playing or change facial expression momentarily, though they are nowhere near ready to notify a parent.

As they gaze fondly at their BM in their nappy, they are likely to develop distinctly possessive feelings for it. They are proud of it as a fascinating personal creation. They may sniff the smell appreciatively, as they have been taught to sniff a flower. Such positive pride in the movement and its smell and the enjoyment of messing in it if the opportunity arises are characteristic reactions of this period.

One aspect of this possessiveness, as parents who have succeeded in catching movements have discovered early in the second year, is a reluctance about giving up the BM to the potty and to the parent. Another aspect is anxiety about seeing the BM flushed away in the toilet; to some small children this is as disturbing as if they saw their arm being sucked down the toilet.

Later, after about eighteen months, a child's possessive feelings toward his BMs naturally give way to a preference for being clean. You don't need to teach a child to be disgusted by body functions. The natural preference for being clean helps motivate a child to become trained and stay trained.

Indirect signs of readiness. Beginning in the second year, other aspects of readiness appear that we don't ordinarily associate with toilet training. Children now feel an impulse to give presents, and take great satisfaction from this – though they usually want them right back again. Their contradictory feelings may show in the way they hold out one of their toys to a visitor but refuse to let go of it. It's at this age that children become fascinated with putting things in containers and watching them disappear and reappear. Toddlers take great pride in learning any skill that they can carry out independently, and they enjoy being praised for their accomplishment. They gradually imitate more and more of the activities of their parents and older brothers and sisters. This drive can play an important part in training.

Balking. Often, a child who took to the idea of using the potty seat early in the second year will back off suddenly. He sits down willingly but doesn't have a BM. Then, right after getting up, he moves his bowels in a corner of the room or in his pants. Parents sometimes say, 'I think my child has forgotten what it's all about.'

I don't believe children forget that easily. I think that their possessive feelings about their BMs have become temporarily stronger and that they are simply unwilling to give them up. Early in the second year they have an increasing urge to do everything for themselves, in their own way, and toileting may seem too much like the parents' scheme. So they hold the movement in, at least until they can get away from the potty, which symbolizes giving it up and giving in.

If this resistance persists for many weeks, children may hold back not only when on the potty but for the rest of the day if they can manage it. This is a psychological type of constipation. Balking can occur at almost any point in the toilet training process, but it is more apt to occur between twelve and eighteen months, rather than later. Balking may be a signal for you to wait at least a few months, in order to let your child feel that it is he who has decided to control his bowels and bladder, rather than that he is giving in to parental demands.

Readiness between eighteen and twenty-four months. At this age, most children show more definite signs of readiness. They often show a new desire to please the parents and fulfill their expectations – very helpful for toilet training. At this age, children begin to take great pride in learning any skill that they can carry out independently, and they enjoy being praised for their accomplishments. They gain the idea that certain things belong in certain places, and they begin to take interest in putting away their toys and clothes.

Body awareness is increasing, so they have a greater sense of when a movement is coming or being passed. They may stop playing for a few seconds, or they may act a bit uncomfortable afterward. They may make a sign or sound to the parent to indicate that the nappy is soiled, as if asking to be cleaned up. You can help by gently reminding your child to tell you if he has had a BM. At first he's apt to tell you when it's already too late. But with practice, he'll notice the feeling of pressure in the rectum that signals that a BM is ready. Without this body awareness, it's hard to learn to use the toilet independently.

In addition, children's ability to move around is now much improved. They can walk and climb almost anywhere, and certainly can get onto the potty and sit steadily. They are able to pull their nappy or pants down by themselves.

A child who has arrived at these developmental milestones is probably ready to learn the fine art of bowel and bladder control.

A GENTLE TRAINING APPROACH

Training without force. If you wait until they are ready, children can learn to use the potty without being forced. Training children when they are ready makes the whole process more relaxed and pleasant, without a lot of power struggles. Children who train this way often end up feeling quite proud of themselves, and ready to take on the next developmental challenge. In the 1950s, T. Berry Brazelton showed that these children rarely develop bed-wetting and soiling problems. Such problems were quite common among children who had been subjected to the harsher and more controlling training approaches that were then standard practice.

Following this gentle approach, most children are out of nappies somewhere around age two and a half, and dry at night around age three to four. They key is, children decide of their own free will to gain control over their bladder and bowels when they feel able, because they want to be grown-up. This method requires that the parents trust in their children's desire to mature and that they be willing to wait without impatience.

But remember, this does not imply an absence of expectation on the parents' part. Once a decision to train the child is made, at about age two to two and a half, the parents' attitude is always the same – a consistent, kind expectation that the child will use the toilet as older children and adults do. This is expressed as mild praise when the child is successful and encouragement, not anger or criticism, when he chooses not to comply or has an accident.

The adult toilet or a potty? You can buy child-size toilet seats that fit over the regular adult seats. But these put the child high up in the air – an uncomfortable position in which to try to relax and let go. You'll need to find a seat with footrests, and get a sturdy step stool so your child can climb up by himself.

A better solution is to use a child's small plastic potty. Children feel friendlier towards a small piece of furniture that is their own and on which they can sit down by themselves. Their feet stay on the floor, and there is no height to make them feel insecure. For boys, don't use the urine guard that comes with the seat. All too often, it hurts a boy when he is getting on or off. Then he won't use the seat again.

The first stage. To begin, let your child become familiar with the potty, without any pressure to perform. If you allow your child to see you use the toilet, he'll know what it's for and may want to mimic this grown-up activity. You can use tactful suggestions and flattery, but don't show disapproval for failure. If your child does sit on the potty, don't try to make him stay any longer than he wants to; that's a sure way to make the potty seem like a punishment. Let him get used to the potty for at least a few weeks as an interesting piece of furniture to sit on with all his clothes on if he wishes, rather than as a contraption to take his BMs away.

The second stage. When your child has accepted the potty, you can suggest casually that he use it for BMs, the way his parents use the toilet seat. Pretend that it doesn't matter much to you. Children at this age are easily alarmed by being hurried or pushed into an unfamiliar situation. You can show how you sit on the grown-up toilet seat, and he can sit on his potty while you are sitting on the toilet.

Let your child get up and leave the seat immediately if he wants. The experience of sitting will be helpful, no matter how brief it is. The child should think of sitting on the seat not in any sense as an imprisonment but as a voluntary ritual carried out with pride.

If the child has not been willing to sit down without a nappy, allow a week or so before suggesting it again. You can explain again how Mummy and Daddy, and perhaps one or two of the child's older acquaintances, use their toilet that way. It often helps to have your child watch a friend perform. (If he has an older brother or sister, he will probably already have watched.)

After the idea of depositing the BM or urine in the potty has been discussed a couple of times, you can take off the child's nappy at a time when a movement is most likely, lead him to the seat, and suggest that he try it. It is okay to use praise or small rewards to encourage your child to sit, but don't spend a lot of time urging or pushing him if he doesn't want to. Try another time or another day. Someday, when the BM does go into the potty, he'll understand better and may want to cooperate.

After a BM in the nappy, lead the child to the seat and show him the BM while you put it in the potty. Explain again that Mummy and Daddy sit on their seat to have their BMs, that he has his own seat, and that someday he will do his BM in it just like them.

If you have had no success in catching a movement or urination, drop the business again for a few weeks and then try gently once more. Take an upbeat attitude without making it a big deal or applying a lot of pressure.

At this stage don't flush the BM from the nappy down the toilet until the child has lost interest and gone on to something else. Most one- to two-year-olds are fascinated with the flushing at first and want to do it themselves. But later some of them become frightened by the violent way the water flushes the movement away, and they become afraid to sit on the seat. They probably fear that they might fall in and be swirled away in a watery rush. Until two and a half years, it's a good idea to empty the potty and flush the toilet after the child has left the room.

The third stage. When your child begins to be interested and cooperative, take him to the seat two or three times a day, especially if he gives the slightest signal of readiness to urinate or have a BM. Even if a boy just has to urinate, I recommend that he sit rather than stand at this stage. If he manages to pass some urine or BM in the right place, praise him for being so grown-up – 'just like Daddy' or Mummy, brother, sister or admired friend – but don't overdo it. At this age a child doesn't like to be too compliant.

When you're sure your child is ready for the next step – going by himself – let him play for periods without any clothes on from the waist down. Put the potty nearby, indoors or out, explaining that this is so that he can go all by himself. If he is not resistant, you can remind him every hour or so that he may want to go all by himself. If he gets bored or resistant or has an accident, put him back in nappies and wait.

Is this the right method for you? As you know from visiting the bookstore, there is now a small industry in books about toilet training. Many of them promise fast results. Why wait patiently when you can get the process over with right away? Why not just tell your child what you want him to do, and expect him to do it?

If your child is very obedient, a simple demand for potty performance might work. However, if your child often tries to resist your demands – a very normal behaviour for toddlers and young preschoolers – toileting can easily become the focus of a power struggle.

This is a struggle that you are bound to lose. Young children are more powerful than their parents when it comes to two things: what goes into their bodies and what comes out. If a child is determined not to eat the food that's in front of him or to hold on to his bowel movements, there isn't a lot a parent can do about it. When a child holds back, the bowel movements often become hard and dried out, and therefore painful to pass (see page 583). The child then has a new motivation to resist the toilet – and so the problem just gets worse.

Many parents feel they have to train their children early so that the children can begin nursery. However, nursery staff are often quite experienced with toilet training and can be a great help. This is a perfect example of a developmental challenge that is easier to tackle when parents and day care providers work as a team.

Fear of painfully hard movements. Sometimes a child has a spell of unusually hard movements that are painful to pass. Collections of small, hard pellets are rarely painful. It's usually the hard movement in one large piece with a wide diameter that is to blame. As it passes, this movement may tear a tiny slit, or fissure, in the edge of the stretched anus, which may bleed a little. (If you notice blood in your baby's nappy, let the doctor know about it.) Each time another movement passes it opens the fissure again. This is quite painful, and may keep the fissure from healing for weeks.

You can easily see how a child who has once been hurt may develop an aversion to having BMs. If the child does succeed in holding back the movement for several days, it is more likely to come out large and hard. A vicious cycle develops, leading to worse and worse constipation. Constipation is the number one cause of toileting refusal in young children. The key is to take care of the constipation before trying to make any progress toileting. During this process, it helps to keep reassuring the child that you know he is worried for fear another movement will hurt the way the previous one did, but that he doesn't need to worry any more because the movements are now going to be kept soft. For instructions on treating constipation, see page 586. If constipation is severe, you'll probably need a doctor's help to deal with the problem.

BLADDER CONTROL

Simultaneous bowel and bladder control. One of the advantages of the gentle approach described above is that when children feel ready to control themselves, they usually achieve bowel and bladder control almost simultaneously. By the first part of the third year, there is sufficient readiness – in terms of awareness and of physical competence – for both bowel and bladder control. All that is then necessary is the child's wish to be grown-up in these respects; very little special effort is required on the parents' part to achieve bladder control.

Attitudes toward BMs and urine. There are interesting differences in children's attitudes toward their BMs and their urine that may help you to understand their behaviour. Children rarely make an issue of daytime urination. It seems that urine doesn't matter to them as a possession the way BMs do. For most children, complete bladder control tends to come at the same time or slightly later than bowel control. It may be that it's easier to hold on to a solid than to hold on to a liquid.

Bladder function tends to mature by itself, irrespective of training efforts. The bladder empties itself frequently in the first year. But by fifteen to eighteen months it begins to retain urine for a couple of hours, even though no training has been started. In fact, an occasional baby becomes spontaneously dry at night by a year of age. The bladder retains urine for longer periods during sleep than during wakefulness, and dryness may be discovered after a two-hour nap months before daytime control is achieved.

There may continue to be occasional accidental wettings in the daytime for several months after children have gained general control of urine. This happens when they are preoccupied with play and don't want to interrupt it.

Easily removed pants. When your child can successfully control his BMs and bladder, put him in pants that he can pull down by himself. This further step towards independence will lessen the chance of backsliding. But don't use pants before the child is generally succeeding; they won't do any good for a child who is not succeeding, and you will have wasted their value as a mark of independence. Pull-ups, which are also called disposable training pants, are nappies made to resemble underpants. They probably slow down the process of toilet training by giving children the gratification of being out of nappies without having done the work to master their bodily functions, and because they are so absorbent, they remove the sensation of wetness that normally motivates a child to use the potty.

Inability to urinate away from home. It sometimes happens that a child around two has become so well trained to his own potty chair or toilet seat that he can't perform anywhere else. You can't urge him or scold him into it. He will probably wet his pants eventually, for which he shouldn't be scolded. Keep this possibility in mind when you take him travelling, and bring along his own seat if necessary.

If he is painfully full, can't let go, and you're visiting at a friend's home or staying at a hotel, try having your child sit in a warm bath for half an hour, letting him know it's okay to urinate in the bathtub. This will probably work.

It's better to get a child used to urinating in different places early. There are portable urinals for boys and for girls to which they can become accustomed at home and which can then be taken along when they visit. Some children are more comfortable in nappies when they're away from home, so you may want to give them that choice.

Standing up to urinate. Parents are sometimes worried because a two-year-old boy won't urinate standing up. It's fine for boys to sit down to urinate until they are very comfortable on the potty. The longer they sit for urinating, the less likely they are to miss the toilet. A boy is bound to get the idea sooner or later when he sees his father or older boys standing.

Staying dry at night. Many parents assume that children learn to stay dry through the night only because the parent takes him to the toilet late in the evening. They ask, 'Now that he is reasonably dry in the daytime, when should I begin to toilet-train him at night?' This is a mistaken idea, making night dryness sound like too much of a job. It's closer to the facts to say that a child just naturally becomes dry at night when his bladder becomes mature enough, provided he isn't nervous or rebellious.

Most children become dry at night around three years

of age, although roughly one in five still wets the bed at age five. Boys tend to be later than girls, high-strung children later than relaxed ones. Slowness in becoming dry at night is often a family trait (see page 877 on bed-wetting).

DR SPOCK COMMENTS

I don't think it is necessary for parents to do anything special about night training beyond expressing the consistent expectation that the child will make an effort to be dry at night. The natural maturing of the bladder plus the idea that urine belongs in the toilet will take care of most cases. Of course, it helps a little if the parents share in children's pride when they begin to have dry nights.

Teach proper wiping and hand-washing. When your daughter shows an interest in wiping, you'll have to negotiate letting her wipe first with you finishing up until she can do a complete job by herself. This is the time to start teaching little girls to wipe from front to back to prevent bladder infections. Boys often need help with hygiene, too.

Hand-washing is part of going to the toilet. A step stool helps young children reach the sink. Little hands need small bars of soap, the size you find in hotel bathrooms. To wash effectively takes at least 20 seconds of brisk rubbing with soap suds, a fairly long time. To help make the time pass pleasantly, and to get your child into the habit of washing for long enough, make up a hand-washing song to sing while washing, or tell a story about each finger. It takes about 20 seconds to sing the ABC song once or 'Happy Birthday' twice.

SETBACKS IN BOWEL AND BLADDER CONTROL

Expect setbacks. Mastery of bowel and bladder functions occurs in little steps for most children. You can expect plateaus and setbacks to be scattered among the gains. Emotional upsets, illness, travelling and a new baby can all cause setbacks even in a child who seemed fully trained. Avoid scolding and punishing when this happens. When accidents occur, reassure your child that he'll regain control soon and that you know he still wants to be grown-up in this respect.

Backsliding on BMs. Many children refuse to have their BMs on the potty after they have trained themselves for urine; this happens more often to boys. They may hide in a corner when they have to have a BM, or insist on having a nappy on. Some appear afraid of the toilet. Constipation is a common problem, and in fact precedes the toileting refusal more often than not; this needs to be taken care of as a first priority (see page 583).

It can be terribly frustrating to parents, who know that their child *could* use the potty if only he *would.* Sticker charts, rewards, threats, bribes, pleading – all are likely to fail. What works is for the parent to take away all the pressure for potty performance and give the child back his nappies or pull-ups. Let him know that you're confident he'll be able to use the potty when he's ready to, and leave it at that. This approach works within a matter of a few months in the great majority of cases. If toileting refusal continues past four years of age, it's best to consult with a paediatrician or psychologist who is experienced in helping families with toilet training problems.

SOILING

Normal accidents. It's normal for a young child to have an occasional accident. The child may have forgotten to wipe well, or he may have been so busy playing that he ignored the feeling of fullness in his rectum until it was too late. The answer for these problems is obvious: a gentle reminder about wiping and making it a habit to take a toilet break a couple of times a day ought to do the trick. For a very busy child, it helps to have a magazine rack or a small stack of picture books in the toilet, so there's something to do while sitting on the potty for a few minutes.

Soiling in the older child. After about age four, soiling is a more serious problem. In the typical case a school-age boy who has been using the toilet normally for years begins passing stool in his underpants. What is bewildering to the family is that he barely seems to notice it has happened and claims to have had no sensation of passing the stool; even more incomprehensibly, he denies smelling it.

Of course, other children do notice the odour, and may tease the child unmercifully or shun him. So soiling is really a psychological and social emergency, because of the shame and humiliation it can cause. Children with this problem often pretend they don't care about it, but they are simply trying to protect themselves from the distressing reality. The medical term for this problem is *encopresis.*

In most cases, encopresis is the result of severe constipation. As the stool sits in the colon it forms chunks of dry, claylike material that build up, stretching the intestines. When the rectum and the muscles that close off the anus are chronically overstretched, they no longer contract effectively. The child loses the sensation of fullness and the ability to hold stool in. Liquid stool makes its way between the chunks of dried stool and drips out of the partly open anus, and smaller chunks may come out without the child noticing. As for not smelling the stool, that is a normal reaction: children and adults normally do not smell their own body odours (bad breath, for example).

The treatment is, first and foremost, to take care of the constipation (see page 586). It is also very important to explain to the child what is going on and why he is not to blame. Exercises to strengthen the abdominal muscles (for more effective pushing) and regularly scheduled time on the toilet help the child pass stool every day and give him a way to take some control of the situation. No one in the household should be allowed to shame, embarrass or criticize the child, on the general principle that family is about supporting each other, never hurting. An attitude of 'we're all in it together', with child, parent and doctor playing on the same team, is most helpful.

Rarely, soiling occurs without constipation. The child

passes normal BMs in his pants, rather than stains or chunks. This form of encopresis is more likely to reflect an underlying emotional disturbance or response to severe stress. Getting help from a child behaviour professional (see page 940) can make a big difference.

BED-WETTING

Everybody wets the bed until they learn how to stay dry. Most girls have mastered nighttime dryness by about four, most boys by five. No one knows for sure why girls develop earlier. At age eight, about 8 per cent of children – one in twelve – still wet the bed. So if you have a Year 4 who wets the bed, you can reassure him that there is most likely at least one other child in his classroom who has the same problem.

Bed-wetting patterns. A child who has never consistently been dry at night has what doctors call *primary nocturnal enuresis.* This is the most common pattern. The causes and treatments are discussed on the following page.

Less commonly, a child who has been dry at night for several months suddenly starts wetting again. Doctors call this pattern *secondary nocturnal enuresis* and look for medical causes such as bladder infections and diabetes. Sometimes a young child starts bed-wetting again in response to a normal stress. It could be the birth of a sibling, a move or some other change. In these cases, patience and reassurance often do the trick. In a few weeks, the child feels better and is able to take charge of nighttime dryness again. Severe psychological stress such as sexual abuse can also cause a child to start wetting; it's important to keep this in mind, but understand that other, less concerning causes are more likely.

A third pattern involves daytime wetting. A child may have continual dampness in the underpants, may pass urine with coughing or laughing, may drink a lot and pass large quantities of urine, or may have frequent urges but not pass much at any given time. All of these symptoms call for medical assessment (see page 602 for more details).

Causes of bed-wetting. When a child has never learned to stay dry at night (that is, primary nocturnal enuresis), there is rarely a medical cause that can be treated. However, the problem *is* medical in the sense that genes play a role. There is often a history of bed-wetting in the parents; if both parents wet the bed into late childhood or adolescence, their offspring are very likely to have the same problem. Parents often believe that children who wet the bed are especially deep sleepers; however, doctors who study children's sleep patterns have not found evidence that this is true. Most children who wet the bed do not appear to have smaller bladders than other children. But it may be that their bladders are more prone to empty themselves before they are completely full.

It's not at all uncommon for a child with bed-wetting to have constipation. The bladder sits right next to the rectum within the pelvis. When the rectum is chronically packed full of hard stool, it puts pressure on the bladder and makes it difficult for the urine to get out. As a result, the bladder tends to squeeze extra hard in response to a small volume of urine, rather than simply stretching to hold more. Treating the constipation (see page 586) often fixes the problem. By the same token, attempts to treat the bed-wetting without first dealing with the constipation often fail.

For the most part, though, the cause of bed-wetting is simply that the child has not yet learned how to stay dry at night. With the passage of time, in any given year about one in seven children who used to wet will become dry all on their own. For those who don't, there are effective ways to speed the process along.

Learning to stay dry. If a child has learned how to ride a bicycle, he can use that experience to help understand the process of staying dry. Once the brain has been trained to balance the bike, you don't have to think consciously about it any more; you simply hop on and ride. It's the same with staying dry. Once the brain has been trained, you simply fall asleep. The autopilot does the rest.

It helps, too, to have an idea of how the body normally works. Holding in urine involves the action of two separate muscles that function like valves. The outer muscle is under conscious control: it's the one you tighten up when you're trying to hold on until you get to the next service station. The inner muscle is under unconscious control: it's the one that keeps you dry without your having to think about it all the time. As the bladder fills up with urine, it sends nerve signals to the brain. The brain then either sends back signals that keep this inner valve closed or creates an uncomfortable feeling that tells you to find a bathroom or (if you're asleep) wakes you up. What children need to learn in order to stay dry at night is to pay attention, even while they're sleeping, to the signals coming from their bladders.

Treatments for bed-wetting. Commonsense treatments include reminding your child not to drink a lot in the hour or two before bedtime and putting a nightlight in the hall so it's easy for him to get to the bathroom. Some parents insist that their child not drink anything at all after dinner, but this more drastic measure is often uncomfortable for the child and rarely works anyhow. Avoiding caffeine-containing drinks such as colas and tea is also very helpful, since these increase urine production.

Children who have wet the bed for years get used to sleeping on damp sheets. They need to get used to the feeling of a dry bed so that they'll be motivated to keep it that way. A good strategy is to make up your child's bed like a sandwich: put down a plastic mattress cover, then a cloth sheet, then another plastic sheet, then a final cloth sheet. If the child wakes up in a damp bed, he can simply pull off the top sheet and the plastic one under it, put on a pair of dry pajamas and climb back into a warm, dry bed. In the morning, the child can help with the washing and remake the sandwich bed for the following night. Taking responsibility in this way helps a child realize that the bedwetting is *his* problem to solve, not simply an annoyance to his parents.

Medications for bed-wetting include imipramine and desmopressin (DDAVP). Both of these medications can be quite effective in temporarily decreasing bed-wetting, but there are disadvantages. Both can be very dangerous when taken in overdose. Desmopressin is quite expensive. And neither actually solves the problem. Once a child stops taking the medication, there is a very strong chance that the bed-wetting will return.

A better solution relies on the brain's ability to learn. Following the explanation given on page 879 (see 'Learning to Stay Dry'), the child can be coached to visualize his bladder filling up with urine, then sending a message (in this era, probably an instant message or a tweet) up to the brain. Some children like to imagine a little person at a monitor up in the brain. When the message comes in that the bladder is full, the little person jumps up and rings a bell, waking the child up. Children who visualize this scene several times as they are falling asleep often find that they wake up before they wet. (What happens when we sleep depends on what we're thinking about during the day; parents have all had the experience of putting a sick child to bed, then waking at every tiny cough or sneeze.) Psychologists and behavioural paediatricians who are trained in hypnotherapy often help children control their bed-wetting using this imaginative approach.

Another learning technique involves the use of a bed-wetting alarm. These devices use an electronic sensor to detect the presence of urine, then buzz, beep or vibrate to wake the child up. The child learns to rouse at the very first sign of wetting, and then begins to rouse just before the urine flows. Bed-wetting alarms can lead to dryness in nearly three-quarters of children after a month or two of use, and in most cases the improvement is permanent. Bed-wetting alarms cost £40 to £120. Sometimes the alarms are combined with visualization or medication. You can buy them online.

A major advantage of approaches based on learning rather than medication is that they let a child take credit for solving his own problem. The next time he faces a difficult challenge, you can remind him of his past success. In this way, bed-wetting becomes an opportunity for growth.

SLEEP PROBLEMS

NIGHT TERRORS AND SLEEPWALKING

Night terrors. It's common for a child of three or four to sit up in bed, eyes wide open, crying or talking in a confused way. When his parents go to comfort him, he struggles and cries louder. After ten or twenty minutes he settles down. In the morning he has no memory of the event. Night terrors usually happen in the first half of the night, when most deep sleep takes place. They seem to be caused by the immaturity of the brain, because most children grow out of them by age five or six. They aren't dangerous, although they can be upsetting to parents. Sometimes they seem to be triggered by stress – for example, when starting in a new classroom. It's always sensible to remove any sources of high stress if possible. In severe cases, medication may help.

Sleepwalking and sleep talking. These problems have a lot in common with night terrors. They start with the child in deep sleep, and the child has no memory of them when she awakens. They're not dangerous in themselves, but sleepwalking can lead to injury if a child stumbles into something or falls downstairs. Safety gates or even a latch on the child's bedroom door may be what it takes to keep a child safe. Medicine is rarely needed or helpful.

INSOMNIA

Difficulty falling asleep. Young children often fight sleep because it's hard to say goodbye to all the exciting things in the world, or because they are uncomfortable separating from their parents at bedtime (for more on these typical problems, see pages 157 and 187). In older children and teens, the most common cause of insomnia is television in the bedroom. At first the television may seem to make falling asleep easier, but it quickly becomes a habit that is hard to break. Rather than relaxing into restful sleep, the child stays awake until he simply cannot hold his eyes open any longer, well past the point of normal tiredness.

The best treatment for this problem is to keep television out of the bedroom, or remove it if it is already there. You can expect an angry child at first, but this is no time to waver or give in. To wean a child from television dependence, try reading aloud or using recorded books. The child can listen with her eyes closed and drift off to sleep to a familiar story or poems.

Medication often isn't effective for inducing sleep in children, or it works only for a while. Doctors may prescribe medication for the insomnia that is part of another condition, such as ADHD.

Midnight waking. Children who wake in the middle of the night and can't fall back asleep have a different form of insomnia. In young children, the problem is often a habit (see page 101). In an older child, depression may interfere with sleep; chronic medical conditions such as allergies may also be at fault. Children can suffer from restless leg syndrome, with leg pains and sleeplessness. A few children wake in the middle of the night and eat compulsively.

What to do. Look for new sources of stress during the day, as these often interfere with falling or staying asleep. It could be something as serious as bullying in school or as innocent as wanting to be friends with someone who isn't interested; reduce the stress if you can. Stick to a predictable bedtime routine: television off a good hour or two in advance, bath, pajamas, brushing the teeth, stories, prayers if they are part of your family tradition, kisses. Protect your child from disturbing television images, whether from horror shows, kids' cartoons or the news. Try to have peaceful evenings at home. If these commonsense approaches don't help, let your child's doctor make certain there is no medical cause for the problem.

DISORDERS OF FEEDING AND EATING

FEEDING PROBLEMS

How feeding problems start. Why do so many children eat poorly? Most commonly it's because so many parents are conscientious about trying to make them eat well! You don't see many feeding problems in puppies or among young humans in places where mothers don't know enough about diet to worry. Some children are born with a wolf's appetite that stays big even when they're unhappy or sick. Others have appetites that are more moderate and more easily affected by their health and spirits. Almost without exception, babies are born with enough appetite to keep them healthy and to keep them gaining weight at the proper rate.

The trouble is that children are also born with an instinct to get balky if pushed too hard, and an instinct to get disgusted by food with which they've had an unpleasant experience. There's a further complication: children's appetites change, almost by the minute. For a while a child may feel like eating a lot of butternut squash or a new breakfast cereal, but next month the same foods disgust her.

If you understand this, you can see how feeding

problems might begin at different stages in a child's development. Some babies become balky in their early months if their parents often try to make them finish more of their bottle than they want. Some develop problems when the first solid food is introduced. Perhaps they have a hard time learning to swallow it without gagging and are not given a chance to get used to it gradually, or they are pressured to eat when they are not in the mood. Many become more picky and choosy after the age of eighteen months because their rate of weight gain normally slows down then, because they become more opinionated and perhaps because of teething. Urging them to eat reduces the appetite further and more permanently. A very common time for eating problems to begin is at the end of an illness. If an anxious parent begins pushing food before the appetite returns, the pressure may quickly increase the child's disgust, which can then become a fixed feature.

Not all eating problems start merely because of parental urging. A child may stop eating because of jealousy of a new baby or worries of many kinds. But whatever the original cause, the parents' anxiety and urging usually make the problem worse and keep the child's appetite from returning.

Parents have feelings, too. And they are strong feelings by the time they have a chronic feeding problem on their hands. The most obvious one is anxiety: that the child will develop a nutritional deficiency or lose resistance to ordinary infections. The doctor tries to reassure them again and again that children with eating problems are not more susceptible to diseases than other children are, but this is hard for them to believe (and indeed, when poor eating continues long enough, it *does* weaken the immune system). The parents are apt to feel guilty, imagining that their relatives, their in-laws, the neighbours and the doctor consider them neglectful parents. They don't, of course. It's more likely that they understand because they have at least one child in the family who's a poor eater, too.

Then there's the parents' inevitable feeling of frustration and anger at a child who can completely foil their efforts to do right by her. This is the most uncomfortable feeling of all, because it makes conscientious parents feel ashamed of themselves.

It's an interesting fact that many parents whose children have eating problems recall having had an eating problem themselves in their own childhood. They remember only too well that urging and forcing worked in the wrong direction, but they find themselves powerless to do otherwise. In such cases, the strong feelings of anxiety, guilt and irritation are partly leftovers from the same feelings implanted in their own childhood.

There's rarely danger for the child. It's important to remember that children have a remarkable inborn mechanism that lets them know how much food, and which types of food, they need. It is rare to see serious malnutrition result from a child's picky eating habits. Working together with a supportive physician can relieve some of the pressure and worry that comes with caring for a very picky eater. A daily multivitamin can also help ensure that a child is getting the vitamins and minerals he needs.

Treating feeding problems. The aim is not to *make* the child eat, but to let her natural appetite come to the surface so that she *wants* to eat. Try hard not to talk about her eating, either threateningly or encouragingly. Don't praise her for taking an unusually large amount or look disappointed for eating little. With practice, you should be able to stop thinking about it. That's real progress. When your child feels no more pressure, she can pay attention to her own appetite.

Her appetite is like a mouse and the parents' anxious urging is the cat that has been scaring it back into its hole. You can't persuade the mouse to be bold just because the cat looks the other way. The cat must leave the mouse alone for a while.

DR SPOCK COMMENTS

Once an eating problem is established, it takes time and understanding and patience to undo. The parents have become anxious. They find it hard to relax again as long as the child is eating poorly. And yet their concern and insistence are the main things that are keeping the child's appetite down. Even when they reform, by a supreme effort, it may take weeks for the child's timid appetite to come back. She needs a chance to slowly forget all the unpleasant associations with mealtime.

You sometimes hear the advice, 'Put the food in front of the child, say nothing, take it away in thirty minutes, no matter how much or how little has been eaten. Give nothing else until the next meal.' It is true that usually when children are hungry they will eat. So this is all right if it is not done in anger or as a punishment and if it's carried out in the right spirit – that is to say, if the parent is really trying not to fuss or worry about the child's eating and remains agreeable. But angry parents sometimes apply the advice by slapping the lunch plate in front of the child, saying grimly, 'Now, if you don't eat this in thirty minutes, I'm going to take it away and you won't get a thing to eat until supper!' Then they stand glaring at her, waiting. Such threatening hardens the child's heart and takes away any trace of appetite. The balky child who is challenged to an eating battle can always outlast a parent.

You don't want your child to eat because she has been beaten in a fight, whether you have been forcing her or taking her food away. You want her to eat because she feels like eating.

Start by offering the foods she likes best. You want her mouth to water when she comes to meals, so much so that she can hardly wait to begin. The first step in building up that attitude is to serve for two or three months the wholesome foods she likes best, omitting all the foods that she actively dislikes and offering as balanced a diet as possible.

If your child dislikes only one group of foods or another but eats most kinds fairly well, you can substitute one food for another – fruits for vegetables, for example – until a child's appetite swings around or until her suspiciousness and tenseness at meals abate.

Accept your child's food choices. A parent might say, 'Those children who dislike just one type of food aren't real

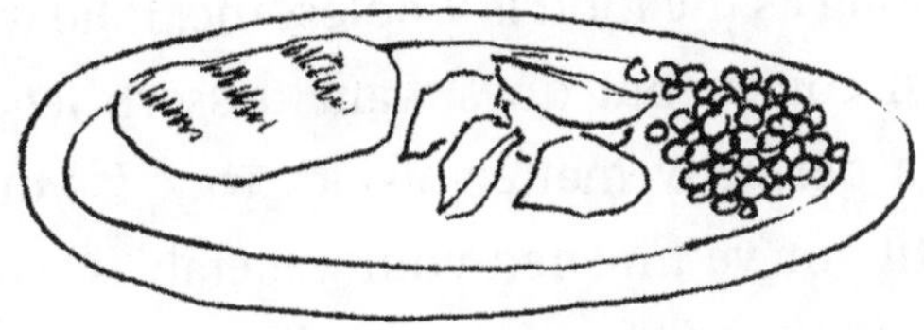

problems. Why, my child likes only peanut butter, bananas, oranges and cola. Once in a while he'll take a slice of white bread or a couple of teaspoons of peas. He refuses to touch anything else.'

This is a more difficult feeding problem, but the principle is the same. You could serve him sliced bananas and a slice of enriched bread for breakfast; a bit of peanut butter, two teaspoons of peas and an orange for lunch; a slice of enriched bread and more banana for supper. Let him have seconds or thirds of any of the foods if he asks for them. Give him a multivitamin as nutritional insurance. Serve different combinations of this diet for days. Hold firm on soft drinks and other junk foods; if his stomach is awash with syrup, it takes away what little appetite he has for more valuable foods.

If at the end of a couple of months he is looking forward to his meals, add a couple of teaspoons (no more) of some food that he sometimes used to eat (not one he hated). Don't mention the new addition. Don't comment whether he eats it or leaves it. Offer this food again in a couple of weeks, and meanwhile try another. How quickly you add new foods will depend on how his appetite is improving and how he's taking to the new foods.

Make no distinctions between foods. Let him eat four helpings of one food and none of another if that's what he prefers, as long as the food is wholesome. If he wants none of the main course but does want dessert, let him have dessert in a perfectly matter-of-fact way. If you say, 'No dessert until you've finished your vegetables,' you further take away his appetite for the vegetable or the main course and you increase his desire for desserts. This result is the opposite of what you want. The best way to handle the dessert problem is not to serve any dessert except fruit more than a night or two a week. If a nonfruit dessert is served, it should be given to all family members.

It's not that you want children to go on eating lopsided meals forever. But if they have a feeding problem and are already suspicious of some foods, your best chance of having them come back to a reasonable balance is to let them feel that you do not care one way or the other about what they eat.

It's a great mistake for the parent to insist that children who have feeding problems eat 'just a taste' of a food they are suspicious of, as a matter of duty. If they have to eat anything that disgusts them, even slightly, it lessens the chance that they will ever change their minds and like it. And it lowers their enjoyment of mealtimes and their general appetite for all foods. Certainly never make them eat at the next meal food that they refused at the last meal. That's looking for trouble.

Serve less than they will eat, not more. For any child who is eating poorly, serve small portions. If you heap her plate high, you will remind her of how much she is going to refuse and you'll depress her appetite. But if you give her

a first helping that is less than she is going to eat, you will encourage her to think, 'That isn't enough.' You want her to have that attitude. You want her to think of food as something she is eager for. If she has a really small appetite, serve her miniature portions: a teaspoon of beans, a teaspoon of vegetables, a teaspoon of rice or potatoes. When she finishes, don't say eagerly, 'Do you want some more?' Let her ask, even if it takes several days of miniature portions to give her the idea. It's a good idea to serve the miniature portions on a very small plate, so that the child doesn't feel humiliated by sitting in front of tiny portions of food on a huge plate.

Stay in the room . . . or leave. Should the parents stay in the room while the child is eating? This depends on what the child is used to and wants, and how well the parents can control their worry. If they have always sat there with him, they can't suddenly disappear without upsetting him.

If they can be sociable and relaxed, and get their minds off the food, it's fine for them to stay, whether or not they are eating their own meal. If they find that even with practice they can't get their minds off the child's eating or can't stop urging him, it may be better for them to retire from the picture at the child's mealtime – not crossly, not suddenly, but tactfully and gradually, a little more each day, so that he doesn't notice the change.

No acts, bribes or threats. Certainly, you shouldn't bribe your child to eat: a little story for every mouthful or a promise to stand on your head if he finishes his spinach. Although this kind of persuasion may seem effective at the beginning, in the long run it dampens a child's appetite more and more. You have to keep upping the ante to get the same result, and end up putting on an exhausting vaudeville act for five mouthfuls.

Don't ask a child to eat to earn his dessert, a sweetie, a gold star or any other prize. Don't ask him to eat for Aunt Minnie, to make his mother or father happy, to grow big and strong, to keep from getting sick or to clean his plate. Children should not be threatened with physical punishment or loss of privileges in an attempt to get them to eat.

Let's state the rule one more time: don't ask, bribe or force a child to eat. There is no harm in a parent's telling a story at suppertime or playing music, if that has been the custom, so long as it is not connected with whether the child is eating or not.

·✦· DR SPOCK COMMENTS

I remember a mother who had been embroiled in a feeding problem with her seven-year-old daughter – urging, arguing, forcing. When the mother understood that the child probably had, underneath, a normal appetite and a desire to eat a well-balanced diet, and that the best way to revive it was to stop battling over meals, she swung to the opposite extreme and became apologetic. The daughter by this age had a lot of resentment in her from the long struggle. As soon as she realized that her mother was all meekness, she took advantage of her. She would pour the whole sugar bowl on her cereal, watching out of the corner of her eye to see her mother's silent horror. The mother would ask her before each meal what she wanted. If the child said, 'Hamburger,' she obediently bought and served it. Then the child, would say, 'I don't want hamburger. I want frankfurters,' and the mother would run to the shop to buy some.

There is a middle ground. It's reasonable for a child to be expected to come to meals on time, to be pleasant to other diners, to refrain from making disparaging remarks about the food or declaring what she doesn't like, and to eat with the table manners that are reasonable for her age. It's fine for the parents to take her preferences into account as much as is possible (considering the rest of the family) in planning meals, or to ask her occasionally what she would like, as a treat. But it's bad for her to get the idea that she's the only one to be considered. It's sensible and right for the parents to put a limit on sugar, sweets, cola, cake and the other less wholesome foods. All this can be done without argument as long as the parents act as if they know what they are doing.

NEEDING TO BE FED

Should the parents feed a poor eater? A child who is given proper encouragement will take over his own feeding somewhere between twelve and eighteen months. But if the parents have continued to feed him until age two or three or four, probably with a lot of urging, it won't solve the problem simply to tell him, 'Now feed yourself.'

The child now has no desire to feed himself; he takes being fed for granted. To him, being fed is an important sign of his parents' love and concern. If they stop suddenly, it hurts his feelings and makes him resentful. He is liable to stop eating altogether for two or three days – and that's longer than any parents can sit by and do nothing. When they feed him again, he has a new grudge against them. When they try another time to give up feeding him, he knows his strength and their weakness.

A child of two or more should be feeding himself as soon as possible. But getting him to do it is a delicate matter that may take several weeks. You mustn't give him the impression that you are taking a privilege away. You want him to take over because he wants to.

Serve him his favourite foods, meal after meal and day after day. When you set the dish in front of him, go to the kitchen or into the next room for a minute or two, as if you had forgotten something. Stay away a little longer each day. Come back and feed him cheerfully with no comments, whether or not he has eaten anything in your absence. If he gets impatient while you are in the next room and calls you to come and feed him, come right away with a friendly apology. He probably won't progress steadily. In a week or two he may get to the point of self-feeding at one meal and insisting that you feed him at others. Don't argue at all during this process. If he eats only one food, don't urge him to try another. If he seems pleased with himself for doing a good job of self-feeding, compliment him on being a big boy, but don't be so enthusiastic that he gets suspicious.

Suppose for a week or so you have left him alone with good food for as long as ten or fifteen minutes and he's eaten nothing. Then you ought to make him hungrier. Gradually, over three or four days, cut down to half what you customarily feed him. This should make him so eager that he can't help starting to feed himself, provided you are being tactful and friendly.

By the time the child is regularly feeding himself as much as half a meal, I think it's time to encourage him to leave the table rather than feed him the rest of the meal. Never mind if he has left out some of his foods. His hunger will build up and soon make him eat more. If you go on feeding him the last half of the meal, he may never take over the whole job. Just say, 'I suppose you've had enough.' If he asks you to feed him some more, give him two or three more mouthfuls to be agreeable and then suggest casually that he's through.

After he has taken over completely for a couple of weeks, don't slip back into the habit of feeding him again. If someday he's very tired and says, 'Feed me,' give him a few spoonfuls absentmindedly, and then say something about his not being very hungry. A parent who has worried for months or years about a child's eating, who spoon-fed him much too long and finally let him feed himself, has a great temptation to go back to feeding him again the first time he loses his appetite or is sick. Then the job has to be done all over again.

GAGGING

The child beyond the age of a year who can't tolerate anything but pureed food has usually been fed forcibly, or at least urged vigorously. It isn't so much that she can't stand lumps. What makes her gag is having them pushed into her. The parents of gagging children usually say, 'It's a funny thing. She can swallow lumps all right if it's something she likes very much. She can even swallow big chunks of meat that she bites off the bone.'

There are three steps in curing a child who gags. The first is to encourage her to feed herself completely (see the section preceding). The second is to get her over her suspicion of foods in general (see page 886). The third is to go unusually slowly in coarsening the consistency of her food. Let her go for weeks or even months, if necessary, on pureed foods, until she has lost all fear of eating and is really enjoying it. Don't even serve her meats, for instance, during this time if she cannot enjoy them finely minced.

In other words, go only as fast as the child can comfortably take it. A few babies have such sensitive throats that they gag even on pureed foods. In some of these cases, the cause seems to be the pasty consistency of the food. Try diluting it a little with milk or water. Or try chopping vegetables and fruits finely without mashing them.

In most hospitals there are speech and language pathologists or occupational therapists who specialize in problems of gagging and swallowing. Working with one of these specialists can be very helpful.

THIN CHILDREN

Thinness has various causes. Some children seem to be thin by heredity. They come from thin stock on one or both sides of the family. From the time they were babies they have been offered plenty to eat. They aren't sickly and they aren't nervous. They just never want to eat a great deal, especially of rich foods.

Other children are thin because their appetites have been taken away by too much parental urging (see page 889). Other children can't eat for other nervous reasons. Children who are worrying about monsters, death or a parent's going away and leaving them, for example, may lose a lot of their appetite. Angry arguments or physical fighting between parents can be terribly upsetting for children, taking away their appetites. The jealous younger sister who is driving herself all day long to keep up with her older sister burns up a lot of energy and gives herself no peace at mealtime, either. As you can see, the tense child is thinned out by a two-way process: the appetite is kept down, and the restlessness uses up extra energy.

Hunger. Many children throughout the world are malnourished because their parents can't find or afford the proper food. Even in the wealthy United Kingdom, over 2 million children experience periods of time when they cannot count on having enough to eat. Not only does this food insecurity interfere with children's growth, it also plays havoc with their ability to learn in school. Hungry children can be overweight if the only foods the family can afford are starchy, low-cost and high-calorie but poor in nutrition. As unemployment and housing repossessions continue to squeeze many UK families, one positive effect may be a lessening of the shame that has gone with needing to ask for help. In our current economy, many self-sufficient and hardworking people need assistance. (See page 390 for low-cost meal ideas.)

Illness. Health visitors and doctors can monitor children's growth at each appointment, and a pattern of poor weight gain over time triggers a search for chronic diseases that might be responsible. Children who become thin during an acute illness usually recover their weight promptly if during convalescence they are not urged to eat until their appetite recovers.

Significant loss of weight is serious. If a child suddenly or slowly loses a lot of weight, he must be seen by a doctor promptly. The most common causes of weight loss are diabetes (which also produces excessive hunger and thirst and frequent urination), worry about serious family tensions, tumours and obsession in adolescent girls with the need to diet. (See page 906 on anorexia nervosa.)

Care of a thin child. If you have got caught up in a power struggle with your child over feeding, try to relax and take the pressure off your child and yourself (see page 889).

Eating between meals is helpful for those thin children whose stomachs never seem to want to take much at a time but who are quite willing to eat often. It doesn't help to allow constant snacking; children who do that develop poor eating habits. Instead, offer one nutritious snack after breakfast, another after lunch and a third at bedtime. It's tempting to give a thin child high-calorie, low-nutrition junk foods for snacks, either as a bribe or to have the comfort of seeing him eat something. But it's better to offer foods with more nutritional value than just calories.

A healthy child may stay thin despite a large appetite. In many of these cases, the child prefers relatively low-calorie foods, like vegetables and fruit, and shies away from rich desserts. If your child doesn't seem to have any kind of problem, has been slender since infancy, but gains a reasonable amount of weight every year, relax. She or he is meant to be that way.

OBESITY

In the sixty plus years since this book was first published, children's genes have not changed, but obesity has become a worldwide epidemic. More children are seriously overweight than ever before, and more are developing the form of diabetes that used to affect only obese adults. Plump babies often grow up to be lean children and adults. But by age six or seven, when children are normally at their thinnest, a child who is obese is unlikely to simply grow out of the condition. By adolescence, obesity is usually a life-long condition.

What is obesity? It's hard to measure body fat precisely, but a measurement called body mass index (BMI), which combines height and weight, gives a pretty good estimate of fatness. The NHS website (www.nhs.uk) has a useful BMI calculator. The standard definition for obesity in a child is a BMI that falls at or above the 95th percentile, meaning that the child's BMI is higher than ninety-five out of one hundred boys or girls of the same age. By this definition, five out of one hundred children should be obese. In reality, something like sixteen out of a hundred are, and in some communities the numbers are higher yet.

Sometimes it's very obvious that a child is carrying too much weight. Other children just look large; it's only when you consult the charts that you see they are much heavier than they should be. We're now so used to seeing overweight children that our idea of what's normal has shifted. For example, a six-year-old boy is supposed to look skinny; if he looks well-proportioned or stocky by the standards of a boy of ten or twelve, he's probably obese. A few children have high BMIs not because of fat but because they are very muscular; it's not hard to tell who these young athletes are.

Causes of obesity. People become obese when they consistently eat too much and exercise too little. That's simple enough, but the underlying causes are very complicated. Among them are changes in how food is grown, sold and marketed; the way our society has organized work and play; the foods that are sold and served in schools, and the physical education and sports that are offered; the growth in electronic entertainment; and public policies that encourage car-use.

Many people think the cause of obesity is thyroid or other hormonal trouble, but this is rarely the case, especially if the child is of at least average height. There are several genetic diseases that cause obesity, but there are also non-disease-related genes that determine a person's characteristic metabolic rate, usual activity level, appetite, tendency to feel full or satisfied and the intensity of pleasure or reward obtained from eating, among many other factors. Certain genes set people up to become obese. A child who inherits a high number of such genes begins life with a medical vulnerability that, given the ready availability of high-calorie foods, will blossom into obesity.

Scientists are looking into the possibility that other factors, including a very large number of synthetic chemicals, may trigger obesity, at least in some people. So far, we know of this effect for certain chemicals (bisphenol A, or BPA, for example) in laboratory animals, but the evidence is not conclusive yet for humans. I suspect that the coming years will expose the role of toxic chemicals in obesity as well as in cancer and other problems. In the meantime, there is one toxic substance that is well known to increase obesity in children: television. Some medications are also known triggers of obesity, including medications used to treat serious emotional disturbances in children.

Effects of obesity. It's common knowledge now that obesity greatly increases the risk of diabetes, heart disease, high blood pressure and stroke. In children, obesity also causes headaches, chest pain from acid reflux, stomachaches, constipation and pains in the back, hips, knees, ankles and feet. Obese children are prone to develop obstructive sleep apnea, a condition in which they snore and are chronically sleep-deprived despite spending many hours in bed. Some of these children are obviously sleepy during the day, while others are irritable or have problems paying attention in school. Obesity makes asthma worse, and a combination of overweight, knee pain and shortness of breath leaves many obese children disabled. They can't play like normal children. It's easy for them to be caught up in a cycle of inactivity that leads to more weight gain, and in turn to more inactivity. Even though obesity is no longer rare, it's still a cause of teasing, shame, isolation and low self-esteem in children. These are high costs, even without the long list of physical harms.

Preventing and treating obesity. You can't change your child's genes, but there are many choices you can make that will reduce your child's likelihood of obesity. You can breast-feed your baby for six months or a year; feed your family a diet based mainly or entirely on plants (see page 374 for the benefits of vegetarian and vegan diets); limit your child's exposure to television or do without it entirely; regularly enjoy pleasant family dinners together; make your home a 'no-buy zone' for foods that are highly processed and high in fats and refined sugar (especially high-fructose corn syrup); buy high-quality fruits and vegetables; spend time each day doing active things with your children; and find fun after-school activities for them that will get them moving.

If obesity runs in your family, it is especially important for you to choose a healthy lifestyle for yourself and your children. If there are members of your family who are thin, remember that healthy eating and exercise are beneficial for all children, not just those who are overweight. Parental leadership is the key in this, as in so many other areas of family life.

If you have a child who is already obese, the first place to start is with the same healthy, familywide lifestyle changes. Beyond that, you may want to seek help from a doctor or dietician who is experienced in guiding children and families to make the necessary changes to slow or reverse excess weight gain. A child who shows a willingness to cooperate in making healthy lifestyle changes should certainly be encouraged to talk with the doctor, preferably alone. Having this kind of discussion with a professional may give the child the feeling of running her own life like a grown-up. Anyone can take dietary advice better from an outsider. Children do not need any medicine for reducing. The treatment is a change in eating patterns, from fatty foods to healthy foods, paired with a gradual, steady increase in physical activity.

Dieting, pills and surgery. There is no end to odd diets and pills, many of them advertised as 'all-natural', that claim to make weight loss easy. The bottom line is, none of them works well. Ultra-low-carbohydrate diets don't work better, in the long run, than sensible eating. These and other diets that cut out whole classes of nutrients pose a real risk of interfering with normal growth and development.

The most thoroughly researched weight loss medications can claim at best a reduction of 5 per cent or 10 per cent in the weight of obese adults; there isn't much research in children. Children taking stimulant medication often lose weight, but they quickly gain it back once off the medication; in any case, the use of these medications for children without ADHD is unethical. Other weight-loss medications have been found to have serious side effects. Except under rare circumstances, then, pills are not a solution.

Finally, weight-loss surgery is increasingly being offered to extremely obese children. It is available only to children who meet strict criteria. It is somewhat dangerous (although the death rate from the operation has been falling, as surgeons gain experience). Most important, for the surgery to work, the child has to stick to a regimen of healthy eating and exercise for life, otherwise the weight will come back.

EATING DISORDERS

At the same time that more and more children are obese, many girls feel intense pressure to be unnaturally thin, and boys to be unnaturally muscular. As early as age ten or eleven a majority of girls believe that they need to diet, and eating disorders – anorexia nervosa and bulimia – are a serious concern.

The main feature of anorexia is compulsive dieting with severe weight loss, while bulimia involves out-of-control eating (bingeing) followed by self-induced vomiting, laxative abuse or other extreme measures to limit weight gain. Together, these disorders affect somewhere between 2 per cent and 9 per cent of women, mainly in their teens and early adult years (the actual numbers are hard to know, since people with eating disorders often hide them). Perhaps one person in ten with an eating disorder is male.

Scientists don't know exactly why some people develop these disorders. Most likely the causes include inherited vulnerability, childhood experiences and immersion in our body-obsessed culture.

Addicted to thinness. One way to look at eating disorders is as a form of addiction – not to a drug, but to the act of dieting or bingeing on food. Eating disorders may start out as something that seems positive – losing weight, getting in shape – but then the addiction takes over. Just as the alcoholic is always thinking about how to get his next drink, the anorexic is always thinking about how to lose the next few ounces, and the bulimic is always resolving to escape the destructive binge-purge cycle.

A person with an eating disorder cannot simply decide to stop having the disorder, any more than an addict can simply decide to stop using. While some women say that they have overcome eating disorders on their own, most require professional treatment, often by a team including physicians, psychologists, nutritionists and others. Recovery is rarely quick or easy, but people *can* recover.

Psychological changes. Anorexia nervosa is about more than just dieting too much. A girl or woman with anorexia nervosa believes that she is overweight, even though she is obviously too thin. An extreme fear of gaining weight dominates her thoughts. Being fat is the worst possible fate she can imagine; nothing else is nearly as important. In medical terms, 'anorexia' refers to a loss of appetite. But many people with anorexia nervosa wage a constant fight against hunger. They often obsess about food, cooking elaborate meals that they do not eat. Some exercise compulsively – two or three times a day.

People who develop anorexia may be outwardly successful – getting good marks, for example – but often feel inwardly inadequate. They may have trouble expressing emotions, particularly anger. They tend to feel that they are not in control of most aspects of their lives, but that weight loss is something they *can* control. People with the disorder may alienate their friends and family, who see the person's self-destructive behaviour but cannot talk them out of it.

Physical changes. In anorexia, the abnormal loss of body fat drives hormone levels down, and menstrual periods cease or do not start at all. (Males with anorexia also have abnormal sex hormone levels.) As the state of undernourishment worsens, the bones lose calcium and weaken; there is damage to organs throughout the body, including the heart and other muscles. About one in ten people with anorexia nervosa dies as a result of the disease. In bulimia, frequent vomiting damages the teeth and affects blood chemistry.

Treatment. Because anorexia is a complex disorder, with physical, psychological and nutritional components, it is best treated by teams that include psychologists, psychiatrists, family therapists and nutritionists. The first priority is weight gain. People who are severely underweight typically need to be hospitalized to ensure that they put on pounds safely. Psychotherapy focuses on helping the person change how she thinks about her body and what it means to be attractive and successful. She needs to learn to express her feelings in nondestructive ways. Medication can help treat depression or other psychiatric problems that go along with the eating disorder.

Preventing eating disorders. If your child tends to be on the heavy side, talk about being healthy rather than losing weight. Make sensible eating and exercise a whole-family affair. Pressure on a child to slim down usually backfires, leading to overeating, but it can also trigger an eating disorder in a child who is driven to please.

Respect your child's natural body type. If your child has a medium build, let her know that you think she is perfect. If people in your family tend to have a rounder physique, there is little to be gained from trying to reshape your child. As parents, we absorb the same thin-is-beautiful message that is everywhere in our culture. It's important that we keep these attitudes to ourselves.

Never tease your child about being chunky or pudgy. You don't mean harm, of course, but children can be extremely sensitive to this sort of joking. They take the message to heart, and the idea develops that they really do need to diet. Similarly, if your child is naturally slender, don't go on and on about how wonderful it is to be thin. Naturally thin children may be at increased risk of developing anorexia nervosa because it is easier for their bodies to burn calories. If they receive a lot of praise or admiration for being thin, the temptation to embrace thinness as an end in itself can be strong.

Talk with your children about how TV, films and print advertisements glorify thinness. 'Look at that actress,' you might say while watching TV together. 'She's really thin! Most real people who are healthy aren't that skinny.' It's up to you to counteract the attempt by businesses to sell their products by promoting one particular ideal of beauty that focuses on thinness. Even children's cartoons tend to glorify one particular body shape (tiny waist and large breasts in female characters; in males, huge shoulders and chest and again a very small waist). Children absorb this beauty ideal. This is yet another good argument for limiting (or eliminating) TV viewing for young children.

Pay attention to hints that your child is thinking a lot about weight. If she seems fascinated by fashion models or rail-thin celebrities, try to encourage other interests – for example, art or music. If she begins talking about dieting, change the focus, if you can, to being healthy rather than getting thin. Even for children who are chunky, dieting is rarely the best answer; healthy eating and activity are.

Pay special attention if your child is involved in ballet or in sports like gymnastics or wrestling, because of the importance of weight limits. For children and teenagers, coaches should see it as their first duty to ensure that their young athletes are healthy. They should not be suggesting weight-loss diets, and should work with parents to watch for signs of unhealthy dieting.

A child who develops an eating disorder is often a perfectionist. He may be more successful than his classmates but less happy. With such a child, try to lower the pressure to succeed. Steer your child towards team sports, because these activities tend to put children under less pressure. If your child takes dance or music lessons, look for a teacher who emphasizes joyful self-expression rather than perfect technique. Appreciate your child's good grades, but be sure to openly recognize other things about her as well – her good sense or her loyalty to friends, for example – so she learns that high marks are not the most important thing about her.

Examine your own behaviour. If you are constantly dieting, you're teaching your child that weight is something to be fought and controlled. If you do need to lose weight, it's probably best to make your diet part of a comprehensive plan to lead a healthier life, not just something you're doing to look good. Focusing on good health is a better message for your child and will probably be more effective in the long run for you, too.

CHILDREN WITH SPECIAL NEEDS

AN UNEXPECTED JOURNEY

Having a child with special needs sets a family on an unexpected journey. The road is steeper, the signposts less clearly marked, and the destination less familiar than for other families. The journey may begin with an unsettling worry that something is just not as it should be, or it may begin with a sudden injury or illness or the birth of a child with a physical malformation. However it begins, the first steps take parents through an emotional landscape defined by loss. Here they may encounter valleys of sadness or numbness, quicksands of guilt and peaks of anger.

Moving on, parents are confronted by new barriers, both practical and emotional. On the practical side, there is the challenge of finding good medical and educational care for a child with special needs. On the emotional side, there is the challenge of throwing one's whole heart into the care of a special child while still having emotional energy and time for one's other children, one's partner and oneself.

The journey can seem lonely, but it doesn't have to be. Approximately one-third of children in the United Kingdom have a chronic medical or developmental condition; one child in ten has a condition that is of at least moderate severity; one in a hundred has a severe disability. One in a hundred may not sound like a lot, but it means that many thousands of children and families are travelling the same road. These families, and the professionals who support them, make up a strong community, well supplied with knowledge, wisdom and commitment. If there is one piece of advice that surely applies to any parent of a child with special health or developmental needs, it is to reach out to this community for help and support. Each family follows its own path, but the way can be smoother if you let families that have gone before serve as guides.

Parents have taught me this about the journey: the terrain may be stark and rough, but you may be surprised to discover spots of startling beauty and deep springs of sweetness that sustain you. Chances are you will find that you and your family have strengths you had not imagined.

Who are the children with special needs? In the past, it was common to talk about 'handicapped children' or to label a child by the name of his condition – a 'Down's syndrome kid' or an 'autistic child'. We know, though, that children are individuals, not just diagnoses. So we talk about a child with a disability rather than a disabled child, or a child with special health care needs (CSHCN for short). Changing how we talk about these children changes how we think about them and how we treat them.

A wide range of children fall under this heading. They include children with common medical conditions such as asthma and diabetes, moderately uncommon conditions such as Down's syndrome and cystic fibrosis, and rare conditions such as phenylketonuria. Among CSHCNs are children with complications of prematurity such as cerebral palsy, deafness or blindness; children whose brains have been damaged by trauma or infection; and children with physical malformations such as cleft palate, dwarfism or disfiguring birthmarks. Altogether, there are probably three thousand different conditions that comprise special health care needs.

Each condition carries its own set of problems and therapies. And of course, the children who have these conditions and their families all have their unique strengths and weaknesses, so that it is often unrealistic to talk about children with disabilities or CSHCNs as though they were a single large group. Still, there are some generalizations that apply.

COPING WITHIN THE FAMILY

Different parents cope differently. One parent becomes very analytical and tries to learn everything possible about her child's condition; another is content to let somebody else be the expert. One parent shows a lot of emotion; another puts on a stoic face and seems to feel very little. One parent blames himself and becomes depressed; another blames others, or the world at large, and becomes furious. One feels hopeless; another dives into political advocacy.

Within a family, parents' different coping styles may become an added source of stress. There's still the expectation in our culture that real men don't cry. However, a father's lack of outward emotion might seem to the mother like callousness. The father, for his part, may feel that the mother is making things worse by being overemotional. It's important to be aware of these potential differences in style and look past them to the underlying reality, which is that both parents care deeply. When parents can understand and accept each other's different coping styles, both can feel supported and stronger.

Expect grief. Grieving is normal and understandable. Parents have to mourn the loss of the perfect child they expected before they can learn to accept the actual child they have. We talk about the stages of grief – denial, anger, bargaining, depression and acceptance – as though everyone passes through these in just that order. The reality for most parents is that all of these reactions are present, to one degree or another, at the same time. So you may find yourself feeling angry or depressed for no apparent reason – at the supermarket, say – until you realize that your grief has for some reason emerged at this time.

Grief becomes worrying when a father or mother seems to be locked into it with no room to move on – the parent who is angry at everybody, who is so depressed as to be unable to get out of bed in the morning, or who cannot acknowledge the reality of the child's circumstances. Although such responses are common early on, it's concerning if they stop a parent from functioning or persist month after month without fading.

It's normal to need to be alone for a time, but it's not healthy to stay isolated. Grief starts to pass once it is shared.

The ability to grieve together with a partner, friends, family, church or a professional is a good sign of resilience. People are not meant to suffer alone.

Watch out for guilt. Another common reaction by a parent to a child with a disability is guilt. A parent thinks, 'It must be something I did wrong,' and is endlessly preoccupied with what that might have been, despite reassurances from professionals that the condition was simply a matter of bad luck. One parent believes deep down inside that her child's malformed hand was caused by the aspirin she took during her pregnancy (although it had nothing to do with it). Another recurrently relives the scene of an accident and berates himself: 'If only I had not let him ride his bicycle on that street, this never would have happened.'

The problem with guilt is that it leaves no way forward. The preoccupation with the past saps the energy that a parent needs to cope with the present. Guilt can even become a handy excuse: 'It's all my fault, so I can't be expected to do anything about it.' Don't fall into this trap, and if your partner has fallen in, confront him and drag him out.

DR SPOCK COMMENTS

There is no perfect way to be a parent of a child with disabilities. There are always trade-offs: sometimes you just need to get away for your own peace of mind; sometimes you feel that you're neglecting one family member while you attend to the needs of another; sometimes you feel as if you're just not up to the task.

This is all par for the course; you can't do it all. The good news is that you don't need to do it all – after all, no one ever has.

Beware of specialization. It often happens that one parent takes the lead in the care of the child with the disability, going to all the appointments and parent support group meetings and learning everything about the condition. The problem with this kind of specialization is that the other parent – often the father – may feel more and more left out, and less and less comfortable taking care of the child. The father may also find that he has less and less to say to the mother, who is wrapped up in the world of the disability. If this unhealthy situation persists, it can destroy a marriage.

The best way to avoid this trap is for each parent to take turns providing care for the child with special needs. If one parent stays home to care for the child during the day while the other goes off to a job, the parent with the job should make sure that he or she cares for the child for blocks of time after work and at weekends, and takes time off from work now and then to go to appointments and meetings. It may seem unfair – after all, the parent with the job is probably working hard all day long, too, and deserves to relax – but unfair or not, it's really necessary if parents are to stay together and function as a team.

Save time for siblings. Children with disabilities require extra effort, physically and emotionally. But if a child's disability becomes the sole focus for the family, the other siblings are bound to feel resentment. They may wonder why it takes a problem to engage their parents' attention. Some start to cause trouble themselves, as if to say, 'Hey, I'm your child also. What about me?' Others become hyperresponsible, as though by being perfect they can somehow make up for their sibling's imperfection and win their parents' love. Neither of these responses leads to long-term mental health.

All children have needs, even if they aren't special needs. They need love and attention every day. That doesn't mean parents necessarily have to spend lots of time with them – just enough to let each child know that he is important. Many times a school play or football game has to take a backseat to an emergency medical appointment. But it's good if *sometimes* the routine doctor's appointment is what ends up being rescheduled.

It's also helpful to offer to involve healthy siblings, if they wish, in some of a child's evaluation or therapy sessions. This takes some of the mystery out of the attention the child with a disability is receiving. But if a sibling doesn't want to tag along to the clinic or the therapist's office, honour that preference when you can. A child who feels he has some say in the matter is much more likely to offer his assistance freely and with a good heart.

It isn't easy being the sibling of a child with a disability. But it can be a positive experience, teaching empathy and compassion, tolerance for differences among people, courage and resilience.

Nurture your adult relationships. Your relationship with your spouse requires care and attention. The statistics are thought-provoking: when a severe disability makes its appearance, about a third of marriages crumble under the strain, a third remain the same and a third are strengthened and enriched as parents meet the challenges together. For relationships to grow requires open communication and mutual trust. Most of all, it takes work and a commitment to invest energy in the relationship itself.

Your relationships with friends and your community are likely to change also. Having a child with a disability can be a profoundly isolating experience, if you let it. Or it can enrich your relationships with your circle of friends. Many parents learn who their real friends are: those who offer love and support, not those who shy away. You can be the best possible parent only when you don't neglect the other important things in your life. You need and deserve to have friends, have fun and now and then get away from your daily responsibilities.

Respite equals freedom. In one study, parents of a child with a disability were asked what the biggest area of need in their lives was. It was respite: someone to take care of their child for a time so that they could go to a film, do some shopping, or visit friends. Respite can come from professional agencies, friends, one's church or synagogue and family. Don't feel that you should never leave your child. She needs to learn to separate from you, just as any child does, and you need to feel comfortable when she is in the care of others.

Take care of yourself. You can provide the best care for your child when you feel happy and fulfilled as a person.

No one can tell what that will take. For some parents it means finding excellent services for their child and going back to work. Others choose to devote more of their time to their children. Regardless of how you decide to focus your energies, there are bound to be family members and friends who think you ought to have made different choices. You can't please them all, so it's best not to put too much weight on their opinions. There is no right or wrong decision here, just whatever will work best for you.

TAKING ACTION

Having a child with a disability or special health care needs can easily bring on feelings of helplessness and despair. The antidote to those feelings is to take action. There is a lot you can do.

Learn all you can about your child's condition. The more you understand about it, the less mysterious it will be, the better you will be able to understand the doctors, and the more you will be able to help the therapists. Connect with the national organizations that deal with this problem; read books; talk to professionals and other parents.

Get organized. The demands on parents of children with disabilities can be overwhelming: doctor's appointments, therapy sessions, diagnostic tests, school visits and so on. You will need to become efficient if these responsibilities are not to take over your life. Many parents keep a loose-leaf binder filled with information about what has been done and what has happened, and bring it with them to all appointments. If your child has multiple appointments, try to schedule them together; many clinics and hospitals aim to provide one-stop shopping.

Find a medical home. A child with special health care needs benefits if she has one doctor – usually a GP – who understands her condition, knows the available medical and social service resources, and can coordinate her care. This doctor should know the child and family well, including their strengths and weaknesses, and should help the parents take steps that support the health of the entire family. Of course, every child would benefit from individualized, supportive, family-centred care. But for children with special health care needs, a 'medical home' is a necessity.

Join a parent support group. Parent groups can provide education, tips for finding the best doctors and therapists, and personal support. There are national organizations for most medical and developmental conditions. Some are listed in the Resource Guide (starting on page 1060) or you can find them online, at your local library or through your doctor.

Advocate for your child. You may find that you have to negotiate between large bureaucracies and multiple professionals. The local school system may not offer a programme that meets your child's special needs. Some communities are insensitive to the needs of people with disabilities and don't provide appropriate support. In such cases an insistent, knowledgeable parental voice can make all the difference. Many communities have organizations whose main purpose is to educate and empower parents to be effective advocates. Ask your child's doctor, or go through the national organizations listed in the Resource Guide (page 1045).

Don't be discouraged if your first efforts meet resistance. With practice, you'll become more and more effective. You also don't have to do it alone. The only voice more powerful than that of a persistent parent is the voice of a *group* of persistent parents. Join up with a national coalition of parents to make your single voice part of a chorus to influence legislators and the courts.

Get involved in your community. Many communities and religious groups rally in support of their members with disabilities. Introduce your child to your neighbours, to people in your place of worship, to the community as a whole. Help them to understand the needs of children with disabilities. You will be gratified at the outpouring of support from your community when they get to know your child as a person.

EARLY INTERVENTION AND SPECIAL EDUCATIONAL NEEDS

Early intervention. In the UK, the government aims to have a system in place to coordinate early intervention services for children with special needs. These services include such things as occupational therapy, physical therapy, and speech and language therapies. For any child under school age, early intervention is crucially important. Your child's doctor ought to be able to set the ball rolling.

Special Educational Needs. In England and Wales, the term Special Educational Needs (SEN) has a legal definition and is used to refer to children who have disabilities or learning difficulties that make it harder for them to access education or to learn than most children of the same age. You can apply to your local authority to have your child assessed for SEN, or the school or preschool can request the assessment. If it turns out that your child needs a lot of extra help in school in order to make good progress, the local authority will draft a 'statement of needs' for your child that includes all of the relevant information. In Scotland, the Additional Support for Learning Act defines the law relating to children with special educational needs: children may be said to have SEN or Additional Support Needs (ASN).

The aim across the UK is for most children with Special Educational Needs to be schooled in a mainstream school, perhaps with the help of outside specialists if needed. Many ordinary schools have special provision for children with particular needs, such as good access for physically disabled pupils or special teaching for children with dyslexia or hearing difficulties. You can ask for your child to attend a special school if you think that is best, or your local authority may recommend a special school if it feels that the schools in your area cannot meet your child's needs. You may want to discuss your child's needs with their school or preschool's Special Educational Needs

Co-Ordinator (SENCO) to ensure that your child can participate in the school's academic and social activities to the greatest extent possible.

When it's done well, mainstreaming benefits all children, both those with disabilities and those without. When it's done poorly, without adequate provision for children's special needs, it can mean simply that a child with special needs does not have his needs met and therefore does not learn. The SEN Codes of Practice aim to give parents the power to ensure that their children are educated appropriately.

INTELLECTUAL DISABILITY

Labels and stigma. Over the years, people have used many different terms to describe children and adults whose intellectual abilities are significantly below average: 'slow', 'delayed', 'cognitively impaired' and 'mentally retarded'. These terms have each accumulated a heavy load of stigma, to the point that they are now insults. The new term, intended to minimize stigma, is 'intellectual disability'. In addition to changing the words we use, we need to change how we think about this problem. Intellectual disability (ID) is a condition, like blindness or deafness, that makes it difficult for people to function in school and society without special assistance. When they receive that assistance, they can live lives that are full, satisfying and productive. They can love and be loved. They can contribute to their communities.

Developmental delay and ID. Many typically developing infants and young children are slow to reach milestones such as walking independently or using full sentences. A child who is very slow may be labelled 'developmentally delayed'. The label doesn't say much about why the delay exists or what it means for the future. Young children often show uneven progress in their development, and many children with developmental delays eventually catch up, often without help from therapists or other professionals.

Others remain delayed, and over time it becomes clear that they are learning and developing many skills at a slower rate than most other children. Eventually these children are likely to be diagnosed as having intellectual disability. Young children with more severe delays, or with medical conditions that are known to affect brain development, may be diagnosed with ID within the first year or two of life, but others may not be diagnosed until they are in school.

How ID is diagnosed. A child with ID will have scored very low on a standard intelligence test performed by a specially trained professional. In addition – and just as important – the child will show impaired ability to carry out everyday activities, such as self-care (feeding, grooming, dressing), communicating needs and ideas, school and work. In the past, children were categorized as having mild, moderate or severe ID on the basis of their IQ score. Professionals now focus more on the amount of support a child needs in order to get along in life. Does the child need special support only some of the time, in some situations (for example, in school), or most of the time, in most settings? Instead of being just a label, the diagnosis of ID becomes a description of the kind and intensity of help a child needs to make progress and function in life.

Causes of ID. When intellectual disability is severe, it's often possible to find an underlying cause. Examples include lissencephaly, a condition in which the brain fails to form normally, or rubella (German measles), a viral infection that is mild in childhood but which can cause brain damage to the developing foetus. Many genetic conditions, such as Down's syndrome (see page 936), result in intellectual disability.

When intellectual disability is mild, however, it is often impossible to pin down a cause. We know that many different things can affect the developing brain, such as exposure to lead or mercury (see page 20), or malnutrition early in life. Exposure to alcohol during pregnancy is a well-known cause of ID, and cigarette smoking during pregnancy can have similar, if less dramatic, effects. Within a large group of children, we know that these exposures lower the average IQ score. But for a particular child, we often can't know that this or that exposure was *the* cause of the ID. A lot of intellectual disability remains idiopathic, which simply means that we don't know the cause.

Children with mild intellectual disability often come from homes that offer relatively little intellectual stimulation. It's not clear that the lack of stimulation *causes* the disability; it's more likely that several factors are at work. However, it is clear that attendance at a high-quality preschool promotes the intellectual development of children from less stimulating homes. Encouraging parents to read aloud to their babies and giving them picture books to get them started also increases young children's language development, a key part of IQ. The brain is a very adaptable organ; given the right stimulation, it can grow in surprising ways.

What children with ID need. Being accepted and loved enables *all* children to make the most of their abilities. Like all children, children with ID need stimulation and challenges that fit their level of ability, even if that means challenges that are below the child's chronological age. For example, a child of seven or eight may need opportunities to play make-believe, while his typically developing agemates have moved on to board games. Children with ID need playmates they can enjoy and keep up with, even if they are much younger. In school, they need to feel that they belong and can accomplish something. Like all children, when they are given challenges that match their abilities, they delight in learning. A child with ID who is learning is happy, like any other child.

DR SPOCK COMMENTS

Parents of a child of average intelligence don't have to ask a doctor or read a book to find out his interests.

They simply watch him playing with his own possessions and with the possessions of neighbours and sense what else might appeal to him. They observe what he is trying to learn and help him tactfully. The same should hold true for children with intellectual disability: you watch to see what he enjoys. You get him the playthings that are sensible. You help him locate the children he has fun with, every day if possible. You teach him the skills he wants assistance with.

ID and SEN. It is important that all children with ID are assessed to obtain a statement of their needs (see page 923). Then you can start to make appropriate decisions about their schooling. It is not ideal to delay a child's preschool attendance because of intellectual disability, because an appropriate preschool can be extremely beneficial.

The child with more severe ID. A child who at eighteen months or two years is still unable to sit up and who shows little interest in people or things presents more complicated problems. She will have to be cared for like a baby for a long time. Whether this occurs at home or in a residential setting depends on the degree of disability, the temperament of the child and the ability of the family to meet her needs and manage the strains involved in caring for her. In the past, the assumption was that children with intellectual disability would all be sent to special schools. Now the assumption is that children with intellectual disability will live at home and attend regular schools with the supports they need.

Adolescence and the transition to adulthood. Children with intellectual disability grow up. In adolescence, they face the same conflicting desires and fears that enchant and bedevil other teens, but with added challenges. With limited independence, the mechanics of socializing – going out to the cinema, hanging out with friends – may be harder. And it may be difficult for them to understand the social rules that govern relationships between the sexes. It doesn't help that many people assume that a person with intellectual impairments doesn't, or shouldn't, have sexual feelings. If early and continuing education about sexuality and human relationships is important for typically developing children (see page 701), it is even more important for children with cognitive disabilities.

Worries about how a child with intellectual disability will find a place in the adult world haunt many parents. Young people can gain access to special programmes to help them make the transition to further training, appropriate jobs and suitable living arrangements. Throughout the teen years, the process of setting educational and life goals and evaluating them serves a double purpose: it ensures that children with ID receive the help they need, and it encourages them to take control, as much as they can, of their own destinies.

DR SPOCK COMMENTS

Many useful and dignified jobs can be performed well by people who have less than average intelligence. It's the right of every individual to grow up well enough adjusted and well enough trained to be able to handle the best job that he has the intelligence for.

You can find much more information on all of the topics touched on above. The Resource Guide (page 1045) is a good place to start.

AUTISM

A time of hope and concern. Awareness about autism has never been greater. We now understand that autism is caused by abnormal development of the brain, not abnormal parenting, and that early, intensive special education can help children with autism learn to communicate and think more flexibly. With greater availability of high-quality treatment programmes, professionals are making the diagnosis at earlier and earlier ages, greatly increasing the chances of improvement.

On the negative side, the number of children with autism seems to be rising. I say *seems*, because we still are not sure how much of the rise is the result of increased awareness and how much is due to an actual increase in autism. The popular theory that autism is caused by immunizations seems very unlikely (see page 441). But there are many other possible causes, and not all have been thoroughly researched. And while early, intensive education is helping more children, many parents still cling to the hope that miracle treatments can deliver an instant cure. When those hopes turn out to be false, as they almost always do, the disappointment can be severe. It is realistic to expect that a child with autism will make significant progress, and he may well function independently and even excel; it is also likely that he will continue to experience special challenges throughout life.

We know more about autism now than ever before, but we still have a great deal to learn. The paragraphs following can only offer a brief introduction. If a child of yours, or one you love, has autism, you'll want to learn much more. The Resource Guide should get you started (see page 1061).

What is autism? Children with autism have abnormal development in three main areas: communication, relationships, and interests and behaviours. Although typically developing children sometimes have difficulties in one or another of these areas, it is the overall pattern of problems that constitutes autism. Here are some examples:

Communication. Children with autism may not babble at the expected time (around six to twelve months) and often are late to say words. If they do speak, they often repeat words meaninglessly and cannot carry on a conversation. Children with autism also have problems with nonverbal communication. They don't use eye contact to show that they are listening, or point to things to show that they find them interesting.

Relationships. Infants with autism may not cuddle normally or reach out to be picked up; some are upset by tickle games that most babies find delightful. Children with autism often ignore peers or interact in unwanted ways because they can't read the social cues that mean 'I'm ready to play now' or 'leave me alone'. They may be affectionate with their parents, but in odd ways, such as backing up into someone as a way to request a hug.

Interests and behaviours. Children with autism often become fascinated by a small number of behaviours that they repeat over and over. One child lines up toy cars in the same order, or perpetually flicks the lights off and on. Another child puts a DVD into the player and takes it out again, for hours at a time. Any attempt to change the routine may trigger a tantrum. Spinning objects often seem to hold a special fascination. Children with autism often spin their own bodies, flap or twist their hands, or rock back and forth repetitively. They may react unexpectedly to sounds, odours or touch. For example, many love the feeling of being held tightly, but hate being touched lightly.

The range of autistic problems. Experts recognize a spectrum of autistic disorders, ranging from mild to very severe. The terminology can be confusing: 'pervasive developmental disorders' is sometimes used to describe the whole autism-related spectrum, but 'pervasive developmental disorder' (PDD or PDD-NOS, 'not otherwise specified') refers to an autistic disorder that does not have all the symptoms of full-blown autism, and is sometimes called high-functioning autism.

Asperger's syndrome is a type of autism in which children can speak correctly but struggle with the finer points of social language use. For example, the intonation of their speech sounds flat or singsong, or they speak like little professors but find it next to impossible to make small talk.

Increasingly, children are being diagnosed with Asperger's syndrome who have mildly abnormal social relationships and other behavioural quirks. At the mild end of the spectrum, the line between syndrome and difference is blurred.

At the more severe end, autism often co-occurs with severe intellectual disability, hearing problems or persistent seizures. Although such children may never learn to communicate verbally, sensitive teachers and therapists can often help them establish other means of communication and connection.

Along with the core problems of communication, relationships and interests, children with autism often have symptoms of depression, anxiety, anger, or attention deficit. Effective treatment addresses both the core issues and associated problems.

Is there a basic problem in autism? There are many theories. One that makes sense to me is that autism affects the way the brain processes information coming in from the senses, perhaps like a television set with bad reception. Some of the signal gets through okay, other bits are distorted, and other bits are lost altogether. It's possible that the core difficulties in autism – with communication, relationships and behaviours – are responses to these mixed-up signals, the child's attempt to cope with a confusing and frightening world.

Some of the more dramatic symptoms, such as violent temper tantrums, might be expressions of the extreme frustration and unhappiness that come from being cut off from other people. The love of spinning, another common symptom, might reflect abnormalities in the child's vestibular sense, the sense that normally controls balance. The child may avoid eye contact, preferring instead to look at a small number of very familiar objects, because the human face provides too much information all at once – something the child with autism finds overwhelming and upsetting. Or it may be that children with autism lack the ability to make sense of the information conveyed in facial expressions, an ability that typically developing children acquire very early in life (or perhaps they are born with it). In this case, children with autism avoid eye contact not because it is upsetting but because it isn't interesting; it doesn't tell them anything. New research suggests that this may be the case.

If autism distorts the way a child sees, hears, feels and tastes, then all of the everyday sensations that normally connect children with their parents – shared glances, cuddling, music – might instead set the child with autism apart. The challenge in treating autism is to get past the garbled sensory input and connect with the child, overcome the child's defensive behaviours and teach the child the skills to communicate ideas and feelings.

Early signs of autism. Early detection of autism greatly improves the outlook. Very early in infancy, parents may have a vague feeling that something just isn't right. Looking back later, they may realize that their baby didn't gaze into their eyes like other infants, or never really liked tickling games. Other early signs include, by twelve months, not pointing at objects with a single finger in order to direct the parent's attention; by fifteen months, not using any words to communicate wants or simple ideas; or by two years, not putting two words together to make simple sentences. None of these warning signs is definitive for autism (hearing loss, other developmental problems and variations of normal development sometimes look the same). Still, if you notice any of them, you should seek a developmental evaluation for your child and not simply accept reassurance that he will 'grow out of it'.

Therapies for autism. The mainstay of autism therapy is early, intensive education with a focus on communication. Programmes that have been shown to improve children's language and relationship skills usually involve effort several hours a day, seven days a week. Applied behaviour analysis is the best-researched treatment approach; professionals trained to provide this specialized therapy may identify themselves as board-certified behaviour analysts (BCBAs). Children may be involved in more than one programme and also have tutors or hired assistants with varying levels of training working with them. A number of disciplines, including speech and language therapy, physical therapy and occupational therapy, can contribute to the total treatment package.

Given the great intensity of this effort, it is almost inevitable that one parent will devote all of her time to the care and education of the child with autism. Finding a balance, so that others in the family also stay involved and all family relationships are nurtured, is a critical challenge.

No medication has been found to cure the underlying

problems in autism. Various medications are used, however, to reduce symptoms of rage, anxiety or obsessiveness, which may make family life intolerable or interfere with the child's education. Many parents turn to complementary and alternative medicine looking for a cure. There they find an often confusing plethora of theories and therapies, some of which make more sense than others. None, however, has stood up to scientific scrutiny as yet. Many children are put on gluten-free, dairy-free diets and given large doses of B vitamins. Such dietary changes are difficult to maintain but not dangerous.

More controversial are treatments that involve giving children medications intended to rid the body of heavy metals such as mercury. Chelation therapy, as this approach is called, is costly, often painful, potentially dangerous and utterly unproven. Parents are not wrong to want to do everything possible for their children who have autism, but they also should hold themselves to the medical dictum: 'First, do no harm.'

Parents of a child with autism need to learn a great deal to manage their children's education. The Resource Guide (page 1061) lists a reliable starting point.

DOWN'S SYNDROME

A child born with Down's syndrome faces both developmental challenges and medical risks. Early on, feeding problems and developmental delays are common. Most children with Down's syndrome have intellectual disability, ranging from mild to severe. They grow slowly and are prone to problems with hearing, vision problems, ear and sinus infections, disturbed sleep, low thyroid hormone, heart problems, severe constipation, joint problems and others. Any particular child may have none, a few or many of these problems.

Still, life can be full and satisfying for a child with Down's syndrome, and for his family. This positive outlook is due, in large part, to courageous parents who have refused to hide their children away, demanding that society grant full rights to children and adults with Down's syndrome and all other disabilities.

Definition and risk. A syndrome is simply a group of physical symptoms that often occur together. 'Down' refers to John Langdon Down, who first described the syndrome back in 1865. Nearly one hundred years later, the cause was discovered: extra genetic material from chromosome number 21. Most people with Down's syndrome have three copies of this chromosome, rather than the normal two. The term 'trisomy 21', another name for the syndrome, simply means three copies of chromosome 21. Rarely, the cause is a small piece of an extra chromosome 21 that has moved over to another chromosome – in genetics terms, a translocation. A translocation increases the chance that a second child in the same family will have Down's syndrome.

One child in eight hundred is born with Down's syndrome, making it common as genetic disorders go. Among older mothers, the chance that one of their eggs will contain an extra chromosome 21 rises, and with it the chance of having a child with Down's syndrome. By age thirty-five, a mother has one chance in 250 of having a child with Down's syndrome.

Diagnosis of Down's syndrome. The diagnosis can be made during the first trimester of pregnancy by testing the amniotic fluid (amniocentesis) or part of the placenta (chorionic villus sampling). Most obstetricians recommend one of these tests for mothers age thirty-five and over. Antenatal ultrasounds may also suggest the diagnosis.

At birth, the physical examination can also suggest Down's syndrome, but a final diagnosis depends on a blood test. It can take a week or two for the results to come back from the lab.

Treatment. There is no medication, diet, supplement or other treatment that can cure Down's syndrome. Wonder drugs and revolutionary therapies appear with regularity; so far none has stood up under scientific study. Parents have to balance the resolution to try everything against the emotional drain and expense of one disappointment after another. It's important that parents accept the children they have, even while looking for ways to make their lives better.

Children with Down's syndrome benefit from having a medical home (see page 921): a committed doctor who can help parents anticipate the various health issues that are bound to come up, and access the specialists and therapists they need. It's worth the effort to find a doctor who has special expertise and experience working with children with disabilities, Down's syndrome in particular. For example, such a doctor is more likely to have access to special growth charts that can aid in the detection of growth difficulties in children with Down's syndrome.

Educational planning should be tailored to a child's particular interests, temperament and learning style. This is true for all children, of course, but it's especially critical for children with Down's syndrome. Inclusion in regular classes often works well but usually requires special support from a knowledgeable educational specialist or school psychologist.

The care of children with Down's syndrome works best when parents, doctors and teachers work together. The leaders of the team, inevitably, are the parents. Participation in a parent support group can give them the information and encouragement they need to be effective leaders for their children's care. The Resource Guide (page 1064) can help you access groups in your area.

OTHER SPECIAL NEEDS

This chapter describes a very few of the conditions that create special medical and developmental needs. Attention deficit hyperactivity disorder is discussed in the chapter 'Acting Out' (page 820); learning disabilities are tackled in the section 'Learning and School' (page 949). For many other common and uncommon problems, including deafness, Tourette's syndrome, cystic fibrosis and others, the Resource Guide (see pages 1060–1072) can get you started.

GETTING HELP

WHY PEOPLE SEEK HELP

Many different professionals are trained to understand and treat the behavioural and emotional problems of children. Back in the nineteenth century, psychiatrists were mainly concerned with caring for the insane, and some people still hesitate to consult with any type of mental health professional. But mental health professionals have learned that helping with everyday problems is often the best way to do the most good. There's no reason to wait until a child is severely disturbed before seeing a child mental health professional, any more than there is to wait until he is in a desperate condition from pneumonia before going to the doctor.

FIRST STEPS

When you need help, your doctor may be the best place to start. Many communities have clinics that provide counselling for children and families; they are listed in the phone book under 'Family Services', 'Counselling', or 'Mental Health'. Religious leaders often provide counselling themselves, or can help connect you with other professionals. Or you can call a hospital nearby and ask the switchboard to connect you with the right department.

Depending on your particular needs, one type of professional might be better than another. The paragraphs below give brief descriptions of many of the professionals most likely to be of help. To learn more, and locate professionals in your area, you can contact the professional societies that are connected with each field; contact information is listed in the Resource Guide (page 1060). Another good place to start is your local authority's Family Information Service.

TYPES OF THERAPY

It's important to realize that there are many different types of therapy. The old cliché of lying on a couch and talking about your dreams while a bearded psychoanalyst takes notes is just that, an old cliché. Insight-oriented therapies do attempt to bring patients to a deeper understand of their personal histories and motivations, including early childhood experiences. But other therapies focus much more on the here and now, seeking to change behaviour by changing how patients think about themselves and others, an approach known as cognitive behavioural therapy, or CBT. Research in the past few years has shown that CBT can be surprisingly powerful. For example, a child suffering from depression can learn to recognize the negative, overly critical thoughts he repeats to himself, and substitute more realistic and hopeful ones.

Young children, who have a hard time putting feelings into words, often benefit from play therapy. Older children may benefit from art therapy or narrative therapy, in which they learn to create narratives or stories that help them cope. For children with problematic behaviours, a behavioural approach, focusing on identifying triggers and consequences of negative and positive behaviours, can be very effective. Most behaviour therapies include a component of parent training, that is, specific instructions and coaching to help parents intervene effectively to change their children's behaviour.

Family therapy can often be extremely helpful, sometimes in combination with one of these individual approaches. There are many options out there. When you are considering starting to work with a therapist, ask about the therapeutic approach to make certain it is something that feels comfortable to you.

CHOOSING A PROFESSIONAL

Ask friends and family for a recommendation. Talk with the professional before bringing your child and see how you feel. It's important that both you and your child feel comfortable. Many therapists work within the NHS, or you may choose to take the private route.

Developmental and behavioural paediatricians. These are doctors who have done the usual paediatrics training plus two or three more years studying and taking care of children with developmental and behavioural problems. Some specialize mainly in developmental problems, such as intellectual disability or autism; others specialize mainly in problems of behaviour, such as bed-wetting or ADHD.

Most developmental and behavioural paediatricians have experience in assessing and treating common behavioural and emotional problems of children. Like psychiatrists, they are trained in the use of medications to treat behaviour, although certain very severe problems, such as bipolar disorder, are probably best handled by psychiatrists.

Psychiatrists. These are medical doctors who specialize in mental and emotional disorders. A child and adolescent psychiatrist has additional training in handling the particular problems of children and adolescents. Psychiatrists often work as part of teams, prescribing medications while other professionals – psychologists or social workers, for example – provide counselling or talk therapy. Certain severe conditions, such as anorexia nervosa, bipolar disorder and major depression, are probably best treated with the help of a child psychiatrist.

Psychologists. Psychologists who work with children are trained in such areas as intelligence testing and aptitude testing, the causes and treatment of learning and behaviour problems, and emotional problems. Others specialize in the problems of children facing chronic medical illnesses and repeated hospitalizations, often in collaboration with child life professionals. Psychologists are often the best resource for cognitive behavioural therapy (CBT) to treat anxiety or depression in children. To practise as a psychologist, a person must have completed undergraduate and postgraduate training (including working with clients under the supervision of a seasoned therapist).

Social workers. These professionals have gained an undergraduate degree in social work, and many have undertaken further training on top of that. Social workers can evaluate a child, his family and his school situation and can treat behavioural problems in both the child and the family. Many social workers also have advanced training in family therapy.

Psychoanalysts. These are psychiatrists, psychologists or other mental health professionals who treat emotional problems through exploration of unconscious conflicts and defences as they have developed over time, and through the patient's relationship with the analyst. Child psychoanalysts (like psychologists) often use play and art as well as talk to communicate with their young patients, and they often work with the parents as well. Psychoanalysts must be registered with the British Psychoanalytic Council (www.psychoanalytic-council.org).

Family therapists. The main insight of family therapy is that everyone in the family is connected. A child's difficult behaviour often causes difficulties in the family as a whole, and problems in the family often result in troubled behaviour in a particular child. Frequently the best way to improve the child's behaviour is to help the whole family function better.

Family therapists can be psychologists, psychiatrists, social workers or other professionals who have completed additional training in family therapy.

Professional counsellors and school counsellors. The qualifications for a professional counsellor are usually an undergraduate degree and a postgraduate diploma involving supervised practice. They should be on the UK Register of Counsellors (UKRC) or have British Association for Counselling and Psychotherapy (BACP) accreditation. If your school offers a counsellor, check that they have appropriate training and accreditation.

Speech and language, occupational and physical therapists. Therapists in these fields can be exceptionally helpful in the assessment and treatment of children with both developmental and behavioural difficulties. All apply a variety of techniques involving education, specialized exercises and hands-on manipulation. The best of these therapists also work with parents, to help them continue the treatments in between sessions. There is a fair amount of overlap between these professions in terms of the problems they address and the techniques they employ. This makes sense, because when it comes to children, all of the systems – moving, playing, handling objects, paying attention, eating and communicating – are interconnected. Training for these professions involves at least an undergraduate degree and professional accreditation, and many have further advanced training.

WORKING TOGETHER

Parents should plan to work together with the professionals they choose. Some therapists limit a parent's involvement to bringing the child and taking him home again. Most, however, invite parents to take a much more active role. In family therapy, the whole family becomes the patient.

It's reasonable, early on, to agree with the professional on the main goals of the therapy. What changes can you expect, and when? Then from time to time you can check in and see if you are getting where you hoped to be. For specific issues such as bed-wetting or tantrums, a few sessions may be all that's needed; other problems may take longer. Often children and parents benefit from working with the same professional on and off over a period of years.

One of the advantages of clarifying your expectations early on is that it helps you make decisions when things aren't going well. You can't expect instant changes for problems that have developed over a long time, and problems often seem to get worse before they get better. Once you've chosen a professional to work with, it makes sense to stick with that person for a time, even if there are periods of uncertainty. On the other hand, if months have gone by without positive change and your expectation was that changes would appear, it's fine – necessary, really – that you talk with the therapist about trying a new approach, or a new therapist.

A setback, even a change from one professional to

another, is not the end of the world. What's most important is that you and your child continue to believe that things can get better. In the long run, an attitude of hopeful activism often makes all the difference.

SECTION VI

Learning and School

LEARNING AND THE BRAIN

THE NEW BRAIN SCIENCE

We now know enough about the brain to begin to understand how babies and children learn. We understand, for example, why babies learn best when they have a chance to use their bodies and all of their senses: touching, seeing, moving, smelling, hearing and tasting. We understand why they repeat a certain behaviour over and over – shaking a rattle, or listening to the same story – then suddenly lose all interest. And we know why it is easier for them to learn certain skills at certain ages, such as picking up a second language before age ten. We are also beginning to use our knowledge of how the brain changes in order to design new therapies for children with learning disabilities.

The new brain science can be boiled down to a few principles: all thinking involves activity of the brain. As the brain acts, it changes, becoming more efficient at whatever it is doing. Although it never stops changing, the brain becomes less flexible with age. Experiences in the first years of life are, therefore, important in getting the brain off to a good start, setting the stage for learning throughout life.

Genes and experience. For decades, scientists believed that a baby's brain developed according to a detailed plan carried in her genes. Now we know that genes only draw the outlines; experience fills in the details. A child's experiences shape how her brain is wired, and therefore how it functions.

One reason that experience and not genes must determine how the nerves in the brain connect up with each other is that the brain is simply too complicated. The human brain contains about a hundred billion nerve cells (neurons), and each connects to about ten thousand other neurons. If you multiply these numbers together, you come up with ten trillion connections. The twenty-six chromosomes that make up the human genome simply cannot contain enough information to spell out each of those connections.

Instead, genes are responsible for creating the overall structure. Early in development, they cause neurons to divide and grow at an enormous rate, to move out into approximately their final positions, and to begin to connect up with each other. The parts of the brain that control basic body functions such as breathing or the heartbeat develop early – they have to. But other functions, such as the ability to understand language and to speak, emerge much later. These functions, and the complicated neural circuits that make them possible, develop under the control of experience.

In other words, we are born with unfinished brains. This is a very good thing. If our brains were finished at birth, they wouldn't be able to adapt as readily to different surroundings. For example, a child who grows up hearing Chinese develops the neural circuits required to process the sounds of Chinese. By twelve months old, he has already largely lost the ability to perceive some sounds in English. In the same way, the child who grows up hearing English loses the ability (the circuits) to process some of the sounds of Chinese, even as he is becoming much more skilful in handling the sounds of English. This kind of adaptation affects other senses as well. For example, children who grow up in modern houses become better at perceiving straight lines and squared-off angles than children who grow up in rounded huts.

Use it or lose it. How is the brain able to adapt itself so well? An important part of the answer lies in a simple rule that affects the connections between neurons: use it or lose it. All thinking depends on nerve cells connecting with each other across tiny gaps called synapses. And each time two nerves make a particular connection, that synapse grows stronger. As the brain develops, stronger synapses remain while weaker ones are pruned away, as a gardener prunes a rosebush.

Early on, the brain makes many more synapses than it needs. In the course of learning, many of these synapses are pruned away. A twenty-one-year-old Oxford graduate has fewer synapses than a two-year-old baby. By cutting out unnecessary, unused synapses, the brain makes itself faster and more efficient. At the same time, though, it becomes harder for the brain to adapt in completely new directions. So, for example, our Oxford graduate can readily learn complicated concepts in history (an area she has studied) but has a very hard time learning the sounds of Mandarin Chinese, something that requires her brain to work in an entirely new way (and something our two-year-old can do with relative ease).

So babies need to be exposed to a wide range of experiences for their brains to develop with the greatest flexibility. They need things to feel, bang, taste, draw with, build with, take apart, jump on, jump off, hold, throw – a full range of stimuli. They need to hear lots of language and have the experience of being listened to. As they grow, the neural connections strengthened by their early experiences allow them to acquire all kinds of new information.

Again! Again! The use-it-or-lose-it principle helps to explain why babies and young children tend to repeat certain activities again and again. At ten months, for example, a baby grabs the bars of his cot and, using all the strength in his chubby arms and legs, pulls himself up to standing. Unsure of what to do next, he lets go, bumping back down on his bottom; a minute later he is pulling up again. This continues until he starts fussing or falls asleep exhausted.

This baby is not only exercising his muscles, he's exercising his brain. Each time he repeats the process of pulling up and standing, he strengthens a particular set of synapses that eventually will give him the balance and coordination he needs to walk. Once he has mastered the skill of standing on his own, the pulling-up routine loses all interest for him, and he moves on to his next project.

You can see this sort of repetition in every area of development. Babies have a strong internal drive to learn. It may be helpful for you to know that your baby's obsessive interest in putting blocks into a bucket or hearing the same story five hundred times is evidence that his brain is busy wiring itself up.

Learning and emotion. We're used to thinking about emotions as being very different from logic. In fact, they are closely connected. When a baby is learning, he's generally attentive, involved and happy. Positive emotions are the fuel that power children's exploring and learning. In another way, emotions both positive and negative make learning possible. Children only pay attention to things that evoke positive or negative emotions. (Later, we learn to make ourselves pay attention to certain things because we know we have to, but we never learn them as well as when we're emotionally involved.) In the brain, the neural systems that produce emotions are very closely connected to the systems that produce logical thought. When (as rarely happens) those systems are disconnected, so that a person now thinks without feeling, it creates a very severe learning disability.

In babies and young children, a good sign that they are learning is that they are laughing, smiling and cooing, or simply looking with a very intent gaze. All of the loving you give a baby – the rocking, holding, tickling, singing and talking – feeds her emotional growth, and at the same time strengthens her desire and ability to learn.

HOW CHILDREN THINK

Piaget's insights. How do babies and children learn to make sense of the world? Some of the earliest, and still best, answers came from a Swiss psychologist named Jean Piaget. Piaget initially developed his theories simply by making careful observations of his three young children. He then spent the rest of his life trying to prove these theories through careful scientific study, but it was watching the day-to-day development of children that got him started. You can do the same.

Piaget believed that human development proceeds in stages that are the same for everybody. Through a careful description of these stages, he explained how an infant with little ability to think abstractly comes to be able to reason logically, create hypotheses about how things work and invent new ideas and behaviours that he has never seen or heard before.

Little scientists. Piaget viewed infants and children as little scientists. He believed we are born with a drive to make sense of the world and that we do so by constantly conducting experiments. A four-month-old who keeps dropping food off the high chair and then looking for it is experimenting with the idea of gravity. He's also experimenting with the idea that objects continue to exist even if they're out of sight, a concept psychologists call *object permanence.*

Until the baby engages in this experiment and repeats it many times, nothing really exists for him except what he is seeing and hearing and touching at that moment. Out of sight is out of mind. Infants begin to learn object permanence in the first months by trial and error. At three months, the infant drops the dummy or bottle by accident and is surprised to see it on the floor a few seconds later. This happens again, and then again. Slowly it begins to dawn on him that the object on the floor is the same one that was just in his hand.

When his research on dropping things is completed to his satisfaction, he gets the idea that if he just saw something and now it's gone, it must be on the floor. If it's not on the floor, then it probably no longer exists. It is not until the next stage, at about eight months, that the infant's ideas about object permanence become more sophisticated and he begins to search elsewhere for missing objects.

Infants love to play peekaboo for the same reason: the face is there, then it's not, and then it is. The infant's capacity to continue this game is boundless because it is exactly one of the questions he is working on at that stage of his development. Once he is satisfied that faces continue to exist even if he can't see them, peekaboo falls by the wayside and a new game, one that is appropriate to his current developmental questions, arises.

Sensorimotor thinking. Piaget called the first two years of life the sensorimotor period. By this he meant that infants and toddlers learn by doing, by exercising their senses and motor (muscle) abilities. If a baby learns to hold a rattle, she has the idea that rattles are for holding. When she shakes the rattle, bangs it on her high chair and puts it in her mouth, she's showing that she has more ideas about rattles. If you take the rattle and hide it under a cloth, does she pull the cloth away to get at the rattle? If so, she has the idea that objects (or at least rattles) can be hidden and found. (At this point, it becomes harder to take things away from her when you no longer want her playing with them.)

Another concept babies are learning about is cause and effect. At four or five months, if you tie one end of a string to a baby's ankle and the other end to a mobile hanging over the cot, the baby will quickly learn to move his leg to make the mobile move. (Be sure you take the string with you when you go, so that it can't get wrapped around your baby's arm or neck.) Babies later learn to use objects to achieve desired effects, such as using a stick to get a toy that is out of reach. Later, they discover that hidden causes can have effects. Wind-up toys are a good example of hidden causes. Between eighteen and twenty-four months is when most babies figure out how to make them work.

During the sensorimotor period, babies begin to understand words and use them to refer to objects and communicate their needs. But it's not until toddlers are able to start putting words together into interesting combinations – 'Brick in!' or 'Biscuit all gone!' – that words become a flexible tool for thinking. When that happens, the sensorimotor period comes to an end.

What's important for parents to understand is that thinking develops in stages. It's a mistake to try to rush the process, skipping over sensorimotor learning and going straight to more advanced verbal learning. All the banging, smearing and messing around that babies do is necessary to prepare their brains to take the next step.

Preoperational thinking. Piaget used the word 'operation' to mean reasoning in a logical way. He thought of preschool-age children, between about two and four, as preoperational because children that age don't think logically. For example, a three-year-old might well think that rain falls because the sky is sad, or that she got sick because she was bad. A child in the preoperational stage can only see things from her own point of view. She's self-centred, but not necessarily selfish. For example, if her father is unhappy, she might bring over her own favourite stuffed animal to try to comfort him – after all, it works for her.

A young child's ideas about quantity are also illogical. Piaget showed this in a famous experiment in which he gave young children a low, wide dish full of water. Then he poured the water into a tall, narrow glass. Almost all of the children said that the glass held more, because it looked bigger. The fact that the same water could be poured back and forth between the dish and the glass didn't change the children's minds. Any poor doctor who has tried to convince a two-year-old that the needle he is about to use is really very small knows that to a child in the prelogical phase, the actual size of an object is not nearly as important as how big it *seems*. The same sort of confusion causes many young children to fear that they could be swept down the bathtub drain.

Concrete operations. Most children during the early school years, from about age five to nine or ten, are capable of logical thinking but not abstract thinking. Piaget called these early logical thoughts *concrete operations*: logical reasoning applied to things you can see and feel. This kind of thinking also shows up in children's approach to right and wrong. A six-year-old is likely to feel that a game can only be played by one set of rules. It would be wrong to change the rules, even if all the players agreed, because rules have to be followed. A nine-year-old might consider breaking a window with a wildly thrown cricket ball to be a more serious crime than stealing a chocolate bar, because the window costs so much more. The fact that the window breaking was completely unintentional, while the candy

theft was premeditated, would not necessarily figure in this concrete-operational reasoning.

Another area where a concrete-operational child might have difficulty is in working out other people's motivations. It's fascinating to read a story to a young school-age child and then ask her to explain why certain characters did what they did. You'll quickly discover that what may seem obvious to you is actually very hard for your bright eight-year-old to grasp. I recommend trying this with a classic like *Charlotte's Web* by E. B. White.

Abstract thinking. Towards the end of primary school, children begin to think more about abstract qualities such as justice or destiny. Their thinking becomes much more flexible, allowing them to imagine many different solutions to a physical or social problem. They start to be able to reason from principles to particulars and back again. Abstract reasoning of this sort often leads teens to question their parents' teachings and values, making for sometimes heated dinnertime conversation. It can also lead teens to develop a high level of idealism, which can become a powerful political force.

Not all teens reach this state of *formal operations*, as Piaget termed it. They may use abstract thinking in some areas but not in others. For example, a fifteen-year-old who loves computers may think abstractly about firewalls and file-sharing protocols, but quite concretely when it comes to friendships with girls. In some ways, he might even be *pre*operational. For example, he might harbour the utterly illogical belief, common among teens, that he is invulnerable. Therefore, he smokes cigarettes and gets into cars with other teens who have been drinking.

Paying attention to your child's level of thinking – pre-operational, concrete operational or formal operational – may allow you to communicate more effectively.

Children are different. An understanding of cognitive development leads to an important point: children are not merely little adults. They understand the world in a fundamentally different way from the way most adults do. Depending on their cognitive stage, they may be more self-centred, more rigid or more idealistic. What makes perfect sense to us may make little or no sense to a child.

DR SPOCK COMMENTS

In my experience, parents sometimes have problems with their children because they don't really appreciate how fundamentally differently they and their children see the world. Consequently they think their child is capable of more understanding than he really is. This is why they sometimes offer a long intellectual explanation to a two-year-old of why she should share. Although sharing is not part of any child's way of seeing the world at that stage, that doesn't mean that it won't be later on. This same misunderstanding causes some adults to tell teenagers not to smoke because they might get lung cancer and die in forty years. Much better to speak to teens about immediate consequences, like bad breath, decreased endurance and looking stupid. That's what really counts in their world.

MULTIPLE INTELLIGENCES

The theories of Piaget, described on page 956, explain a lot about children's thinking, but they don't tell the whole story. We now know from ingenious experiments that very young babies are capable of feats of memory, and even of simple mathematics, that we never thought possible.

Another great advance has been the realization that the verbal-analytical intelligence Piaget talked about, which is the kind measured by the standard IQ tests, is only one of several kinds of intelligence. In fact, everyone has multiple intelligences. Other types of intelligence include spatial, musical, bodily-kinesthetic (movement), interpersonal (relationships with others), intrapersonal (self-understanding and insight into others) and naturalist (understanding and classifying objects in nature).

Uneven intelligence. The theory of multiple intelligences makes sense when you think of intelligence as the processing of information by the brain. Information of all sorts flows through the brain all the time – for example, information about tones and rhythms in speech or music, or about the position of one's body in space. Different parts of the brain process this information and combine it in different ways. It's possible for one area of the brain to be working quite well, while another is not. For example, people who have damage to the part of the brain that controls speech may not be able to talk, but they may be able to sing words, since their musical ability is housed in another location and is unimpaired.

Even people without brain damage aren't equally endowed in all the different intelligences. One child learns best by listening, another by watching, another by holding something physical in her hand, and still another by acting out a concept with her whole body. Someone can be verbally gifted but completely at a loss when it comes to working out how to drive across town. When these inequalities in intelligence are very marked, they can create learning disabilities (see page 1005).

Think about your own abilities and limitations and you're sure to realize that you're more gifted in some areas than others. In my own case, I am a good public speaker, but I can't hit a baseball to save my life. I can play a musical instrument, but I've never been able to draw a horse that actually looks like one (although I once tried for several months).

As you pay attention to your child's different intelligences, you may realize that some of the things you thought he was avoiding out of laziness are actually more difficult for him than you suspected. You may also recognize areas in which your child is gifted, even though these gifts may not translate to higher grades. By expanding your focus to include multiple intelligences, you can appreciate and nurture more of your child's strengths, and more of your own.

Everything you do to keep your child safe and healthy, to teach reasonable behaviour and to have fun together prepares your child to succeed in school. It's important, too, for young children to have opportunities to play with their peers, and to begin to feel comfortable with adults who are not their parents. Beyond this, the qualities that make a child ready for school include a basic level of developmental maturity, especially listening and speaking skills, and an eagerness to find out things. Children also need to have an understanding of the usefulness of the printed word, a familiararity with the letters of the alphabet and a love of stories.

A few children go straight to school, having spent their first four years entirely at home. But for most, school readiness is a team effort, with parents and preschool staff working together to help children get off to a good start.

READING ALOUD

The goal of education is not just for children to be able to read and write, but for them to become literate. Literate adults use reading to learn about things that interest them, and writing to share their ideas. Literate children view reading and writing as exciting and worthwhile in their own right. They tend to have rich imaginations and many interests. Literacy widens a child's world. And very often, literacy starts with a parent reading aloud.

If you were lucky enough to have been read to when you

were a child, there's a good chance that you will naturally share the pleasure with your child. Even if you weren't, you've probably heard that reading aloud is a good thing to do.

Why read aloud? It is true that some children do well in school without ever having been read to by their parents. But the chances that a child will succeed at reading and writing go way up if that child starts school already having had a lot of experience with the printed word, and feeling very positive about books.

When you sit down with your child and a book, many wonderful things happen. By talking about the pictures, you expose her to lots of new and interesting words. By reading and rereading, you give her many opportunities to learn how the words come together in interesting sentences. You build up her listening and attention skills. And you help her begin to see the connections between the let-

ters she sees and the words she hears. Most of all, it's the joyful interaction with a loving parent that brings picture books to life for children and makes being read to such a powerful experience.

Bilingual families. Children who grow up hearing two languages have a real advantage. While they often take a bit longer to start expressing themselves clearly, once they get going they quickly become fluent speakers in both languages.

Parents living in the United Kingdom who don't speak English well themselves should talk with their children and read to their children in their native language. It's much more helpful for a child to hear a language – *any* language – spoken well than to hear English spoken badly. A child who learns Spanish or Russian at home can quickly pick up English in preschool. A child who never learns to speak any language well (because he did not have the chance to hear a language spoken well) has a much harder time.

Many picture books are now available in Punjabi and other languages. Also, many have English and a second language printed on the same page – a great way for parents and children to learn.

Reading to newborns. Babies who are read to enjoy the sound of the reader's voice and the feeling of being held. Parents often start reading aloud while they're still pregnant, so that their babies are born already knowing and loving the sound of their mother's reading voice, which is distinct from conversational speech.

Reading to newborns exposes babies to a lot of human speech. Listening as their parents talk to them is one very important way that babies begin to learn language. And strong language skills are among the best predictors of later reading and writing abilities. Listening also calms babies down; you can watch their bodies become still as they focus their attention.

If you want to read to your new baby, it doesn't much matter what you read. Choose something that interests you – gardening, sailboats or a novel. Even better, choose something that you and your spouse or partner both enjoy, and take turns reading to each other while you cuddle with your new baby.

Sharing books with babies. By six months, your baby is apt to react to a new, brightly coloured book with excitement. He reaches for it, pats at it, growls or 'talks' in an excited way. He holds it, waves it about, bangs it and chews on it. Don't be worried by this gleeful manhandling. Children learn to respect and take care of books gradually, as they come to understand their special value.

Pick board books with simple, bright pictures. Photos of other babies are a favourite. Pick some simple poetry that rhymes. If your baby likes it (and many do), read your own grown-up book out loud, stopping frequently to talk with your baby. Babies this age don't understand the words, but they like the sounds.

Somewhere around nine months of age, babies begin to

develop wills of their own. They want to feed themselves, and they often want to be in charge of their books. If reading time begins to resemble a battle, change your tactics. Try using two books, one for your baby and one for you. Read for shorter periods. It's okay to use the book as a plaything for some of the time, letting your child take it, flip the pages, bang it. While you're doing that, you might discover a special picture now and then and show it to your baby, letting your voice convey your excitement.

Try playing peekaboo with the pictures by covering a favourite character, then asking, for instance, 'Where's the doggie?' If there's a poem, read it rhythmically. Move your body (and the baby in your arms) in time with the words. If the book has pictures of babies, touch the pictures and then touch your baby in the same place.

Some babies love to listen for a long time (five to ten minutes or more). More active babies may only pay attention for a minute or less. The amount of time is not important. Enjoying each other and the book is. If your baby seems bored, or if *you* are, pick a different book or do something else.

Toddlers and books. Between nine and twelve months of age, some babies begin to understand that things have names. Once they have this idea firmly established, they want to hear the names of everything. A picture book is the perfect vehicle for naming games. With a familiar picture book, ask, 'What's that?' Pause for an instant and then give the answer. If your baby loves this game, it is because his mind is open to learning. You won't hear him saying these words right away, but over the next year or two, you're likely to be amazed at his vocabulary.

As time goes by, toddlers pay more attention to what the pictures show. A twelve- to fifteen-month-old may be content to hold the book upside down. Starting around eighteen months, many children will turn the book around so that the pictures are right side up.

Many younger toddlers are in love with movement. Those who are not walking yet still love the rocking, tickling and hugging that go along with reading aloud. Those who are walking may only sit still for a few minutes at a time, but they often enjoy listening from across the room. Mobile toddlers will often carry a book around or bring it to a grown-up to read. A toddler who is discovering his own will may insist on picking the same book over and over, protesting if you make a different selection.

To avoid a power struggle, store books on a low shelf so that your toddler can get them out and put them back herself. Put only three or four books out at a time; too many makes the choice overwhelming and just increases the number of books you'll have to pick up off the floor.

By eighteen months, many toddlers are walking steadily. A favourite activity now becomes walking while carrying something, often a book. A toddler who knows that a book is a ticket to attention from parents will walk over and deposit one on a parent's lap, often accompanied by the demand, 'Read!'

Reading with an older toddler. As they approach their second birthday, toddlers are making great strides in language development. Books help teach language by giving the older toddler many opportunities to name things and get feedback from a grown-up. The parent points at a picture and asks, 'What's that?' Then, depending on what the toddler responds, the parent either says the name of the object and praises the child or offers a kind correction: 'Nope, that's not a dog, that's a horse!'

What makes this sort of back-and-forth teaching so powerful is that it happens over and over. For a young child, repetition is a key to learning. That the same pictures come up again and again paired with the same words on the same page allows him to feel a measure of control over the book. The child expects a particular picture or word to show up on the next page – and it does!

At the same time your toddler is conquering new words, he also is working out how they come together to make sentences and how sentences make stories. You won't see the results of this learning for many months. But by two and a half to three years, you may notice your child using complex storylike phrases in his play, such as 'Once upon a time' or 'What's going to happen next?' The seeds of rich language are planted early through much experience with books and stories.

The wrecking crew. Babies and toddlers are rough on books. Many bent pages can be expected, and even a tear here and there. Scribbling on the pages of a book is something almost every toddler does at least once or twice in her literary career. While it looks destructive, it's often a toddler's way of getting into the book.

A gentle reminder that books need a little tender loving care works better than scolding (which might just convince your toddler that books are too much trouble altogether). Even better, get some scrap paper and some crayons and let your toddler scribble to his heart's content on these pages. The first step on the road to writing is scribbling. If you look at your toddler's artistic creations over time, you might well start to see letterlike shapes.

Different learning styles. One toddler who is very visual in her approach to the world might spend long minutes studying the pictures in a book. Try a book with a partially hidden character. A visually oriented toddler will delight in finding the approaching lion on each page of Clare Beaton's *How Loud Is a Lion?*

A verbally oriented toddler will love to listen to the sound of words. Poetry is especially attractive because of the rhyme and rhythm. A story with a repeated chant ('Fee-fi-fo-fum' in *Jack and the Beanstalk*) delights many toddlers and, because it is predictable, they can join in the reading.

Many young children learn best by moving their bodies and by touching. If there is motion in the story (a boat rocking on the waves, a baby on a swing, a horse galloping or a mum stirring soup), you can act out the motion with your toddler. Talking, touching, moving and playing make the book come alive to all of your toddler's senses.

All children learn best when they are actively involved. They love the opportunity to act out parts of the books they're listening to. So if you're reading a story about magic genies and flying carpets, you might want to dig out an old teapot and a rug or a sheet. Your child will know just what to do.

Reading with preschoolers. Preschool children have wonderful imaginations. In their minds, magic really happens. Because they don't have a lot of experience of how the world works, young children are able to believe many things that older children reject, like Santa Claus. In a sense, they live in a world that their imagination creates.

It's natural, then, that preschoolers love storybooks. Listening to a story, one child's expression is utterly absorbed, her eyes wide. Another child needs to keep moving around (the restless energy of some preschoolers is really a force of nature) but still manages to catch every word. You know that a child is caught up in the imaginative world of a book when she responds with real emotions to events in the book. Characters from the book are apt to come alive in her play. Words from the book sneak into her vocabulary.

Like all of us, preschool children want to feel a sense of control. One way is being able to choose the book. Although some preschoolers can handle choosing one book from a shelf full of them, many need smaller choices (say, one of three books) to feel comfortable. Another way preschoolers enjoy a sense of control is by partially memorizing books.

When a child chooses the same book over and over, it's a sign that there is something in that book that is very important to her. It may be an idea (for example, the idea of overcoming an obstacle, as in *Three Billy Goats Gruff*) or a visual image (perhaps the picture of the troll under the bridge), or even just a single word. Whatever it is, once the child completely understands it, she usually moves on to a new book.

There are many ways to enjoy books with your pre-school child:

- Have books all over the house – in the living room, in the toilet, by the kitchen table and especially in her bedroom.
- Make bedtime or waking up in the morning – or both – regular times for reading together. Let your child tell you when she's had enough; also, stop when *you* have had enough. It's great if children love books, but it's always the grown-up's job to set limits.
- Limit TV viewing. I personally feel that a no-TV diet is best for preschoolers. The vivid images on TV (even, or especially, in cartoons) tend to overwhelm their sensitive imaginations, so there is no space left for the quieter but still compelling images from books.
- Use your public library. In addition to a huge selection of books, many libraries offer story hours, play groups and child-size tables and chairs for comfortable perusing. An outing to the library can feel special, even if it happens every week.
- Don't feel that you have to keep reading to the bitter end. If your child loses interest, the best thing to do is

to stop and perhaps try a different book. It may also be that the book has touched on issues that are emotionally charged for your child. Squirming or falling asleep may be your child's way of saying, 'I've heard enough for now.'

- Invite your child to participate. Children learn most from reading aloud, and probably benefit the most emotionally, if they participate actively. That may mean making comments or even interrupting the reading to talk about an idea or feeling that comes up. Reading aloud shouldn't be a performance; it should be more like a discussion.
- Make up stories yourself and encourage your preschooler to help you. If you come up with a story you really like, write it down. You can make your own storybook, then read it aloud.

Reading aloud with an older child. Reading aloud doesn't have to end just because your child gets older. If it's something you both love to do together, there are many good reasons to continue. Sharing pleasant and interesting experiences makes your relationship stronger. Having a reservoir of positive feelings helps you and your child cope with disagreements and other tensions that are an inevitable part of growing up.

Reading aloud keeps interest high. Between Reception and Year 3 or 4, children are still developing their basic reading skills. During that time, many of the books that are simple enough for them to read themselves are too simple for them to find interesting. But by reading aloud together, you can help your child enjoy more difficult books that are likely to keep her engaged until her reading ability catches up with her interests.

Reading aloud is especially important if your child is having difficulty learning to read. Some children find reading easy. Others, equally bright, find it quite challenging at first, often because their brains are taking longer to reach the level of maturation needed for reading. In time – most often by the end of Year 3 – they catch up and do just fine. But until that happens, reading is likely to be difficult, and many children sour on it. If they have parents who read to them, however, they're much more likely to continue to love books and to stick with it, work hard and eventually gain the skills they need for independent reading.

Reading aloud also builds listening skills. It's a good idea to stop from time to time and talk about the story with your child. First of all, you want to make sure that she is following the story. If not, you can help explain the plot, a character's motivations, a hard word or whatever else is puzzling her. When you ask open-ended questions, you strengthen your child's ability to think about what she hears and make sense of it. Ask why a particular character did what he did, or ask your child what she thinks is going to happen next.

Reading aloud builds vocabulary. There are words in books that you almost never hear in everyday speech. One of the best children's books of all time, *Charlotte's Web* by

E. B. White, is written mostly in plain English. But even here, you find interesting words like 'injustice,' 'terrific,' and 'humble.' Don't be surprised if you hear your child using some of these 'book words' when she speaks. Many children love to play with new words, and in the process they are building skills that will help them throughout their school careers.

Stories are the building blocks of imagination. Children take bits and pieces of the stories they hear and use them in their own make-believe. So if you want your child to have a rich imagination, let her hear lots of good stories. The same thing happens when children watch television: they build the stories into their play. But because the images on television are so much more vivid than the word images in books, children don't need to use their imagination as much. Consequently, during playtime they often simply copy what they see on television rather than creating their own stories.

Books help teach character. Many educators and psychologists believe that books are one of the best ways children learn about right and wrong. As they see how characters react in a given situation – how they treat their friends, for example, or what they do when they want something that isn't theirs – children get a clearer picture of what's admirable behaviour and what's not. The messages in books can be a compelling and enjoyable way to reinforce the values you're trying to teach your child at home.

Choosing nonracist, nonsexist books. Books carry

powerful messages, both in what they say and in how they say it. Books that portray people of all colours, cultures and ethnicities with respect and avoid sexual stereotypes help children take an accepting and positive view of themselves and the rest of humanity. Look for children's books that embrace the reality of our multicultural society.

In judging a book, look at the story line. Do people of colour or females play important, leading roles? Are cultural beliefs and practices portrayed accurately? Are different lifestyles depicted in a positive light? Look at the characters. How are individual characters presented? Who has the power? Who are the heroes in the story? Who are the villains? Look at the illustrations. Are characters drawn in a way that avoids stereotypes? Do people have a variety of facial features and other physical characteristics, as well as different colours of skin?

What messages does the story send? Does it glorify violence or revenge? Stories in which the hero's only virtue is brute strength do not help children value their own positive qualities. By contrast, heroes who also show compassion, resourcefulness and courage allow children to feel that they might be like those heroes in their own small way.

PRESCHOOL

The philosophy of preschool. The purpose of preschool or nursery school (two terms for the same thing) is not just the custodial care of children. Nor is it just to prepare them for the three R's of primary school. It is, above all, to give young children such a wonderful first experience of school that they want to learn for the rest of their lives.

Good preschools expose young children to a range of experiences that nurture sensitivity, creativity and competence. These include dancing and making rhythmic music, painting pictures, finger painting, clay modelling, building with blocks, vigorous outdoor play and playing house, which is really playing family. Ideally, there are quiet corners for individual play and for those times when a child feels the need to rest. Preschool tries to nurture a broad variety of capabilities – academic, social, artistic, musical and muscular. The emphasis is on initiative, independence, cooperation (discussing and sharing play equipment instead of fighting over it) and incorporating the child's own ideas into play.

The term 'preschool' means, literally, 'before school'. But preschool isn't something that occurs before school; it *is* school. The focus of preschool should be not on preparing a child to succeed at 'real' school later but on her educational needs right now.

What do children learn in preschool? Many three- and four-year-olds are already old hands at being away from home; others must learn to feel comfortable. Regardless of their past experiences with care outside the home, children face similar challenges when they enter preschool. They all need to learn to control their feelings and also to express them. They need to get along in a group and also to take their own ideas and run with them. They need the opportunity to be leaders and also to let others lead.

Three- and four-year-olds are naturally very curious about the world around them, and they are capable of learning a great deal about its workings: how seeds sprout, how water flows, how clay feels when it's pushed and pulled, how colours change when paints mix, what makes one block tower balance and another fall over, and so on. Good preschools give students plenty of hands-on opportunities to explore their world.

More fundamentally, children in preschool learn how to learn. In a good nursery or school, they come to view learning as creative exploration, not dull memorization, and they come to view school as a place where they feel comfortable and safe.

Readiness for preschool. Every child faces unique challenges in growing up. Skilled preschool teachers and staff are trained to work with children who have different strengths and needs.

At the beginning of preschool, many children use simple three- to five-word sentences. They can express their needs and tell what happened in the recent past. They understand most of what's said to them and can follow three-part directions. They can listen to a story for several minutes, then talk about it. However, they are apt to misunderstand many phrases that make perfect sense to adults. For example, if you say you are 'hungry enough to eat a horse', a three-year-old might point out seriously that there aren't any horses around.

At age three, children often mispronounce words. In general, you should be able to understand about three-quarters or more of the words they say. Children who have articulation problems or who stutter (a common difficulty at this age; see page 853) may become frustrated when people don't understand them. A patient teacher can be very helpful, as can a skilled speech therapist.

Some preschools require children to be comfortable using the toilet before starting in school, but not all do. Being around peers who go to the toilet like grown-ups is a huge incentive for children who still rely on nappies. Most work hard and master toilet skills within a few weeks. Many young children still need help with wiping, or at least a reminder to wipe well and wash their hands. Preschool staff understand that being able to use the toilet independently is a major milestone for a young child, and gladly work with parents to help him achieve this goal.

Eating, even if it's just a mid-morning snack, is a part of every preschool session. By age three years, children are usually able to manage finger foods and drinking from a cup, and they understand basic table manners. Children with developmental disabilities (such as cerebral palsy, for example) may need individual help during snacks.

Preschool children learn basic dressing and undressing: putting on a coat, for example, and slipping on boots. Teachers expect to help with buttons, zips and press studs. It's also okay if some children need more assistance for a while.

What a good preschool looks like. Your child could attend preschool in the same nursery where she has always had her day care, in a dedicated private preschool, a children's centre or in the preschool of your local primary school. Wherever you decide she will spend her preschool hours, all three- and four-year-olds are entitled to fifteen hours of free nursery education for thirty-eight weeks of the year. If your child is already in a private nursery, ask your nursery manager for details of how the early education grant will reduce your monthly bill.

A good preschool teacher is many things: a nurturing caregiver, an instructor sowing the seeds of learning, a physical education coach, a guide to the creative worlds of art, music and literature. The more you understand about what a preschool teacher actually does, the better able you'll be to look for excellence and to appreciate it when you find it. One important clue to a teacher's approach to learning is evident even before her young charges set foot in the preschool: the setup of her classroom.

A preschool classroom shouldn't look like a classroom for older children. Instead of desks or tables in regular rows, there should be areas for different activities: painting, block building, make-believe, reading and playing house.

In a typical preschool, children have ample opportunities to move from space to space, and to step outdoors, according to their interests. An important part of their education is to learn how to decide on an activity, and then stick with it for a while. Good teachers keep tabs on their students – where they are in the room and how engaged they are in their activities. If a child is having a hard time choosing, the teacher helps him settle into an activity. If a child is stuck in the same activity for too long, the teacher helps him make another choice.

Many aspects of the room also change daily. One day the art area features finger paints. A day or two later, there may be an assortment of materials for mosaics. Another day there are sheets of paper stapled together to make books. How long an activity lasts depends on the children's interest.

In addition to the regular activity areas, some parts of the room reflect projects or special areas of focus for the class. One month there is a grocery store, with children shopping, making change and taking inventory; the next month, a post office appears; after that, it might be a bakery.

The different areas in the room connect with other things the class is doing. For example, after discussing food from around the world, the children might transform a part of the room into a restaurant. These special areas also reflect the values and concerns that the children are developing: a focus on the environment, perhaps, featuring an indoor garden and items collected on a nature walk.

In planning and making these changes, the teacher listens to the children. She understands that the classroom is not hers, but rather is theirs. As the children think and talk about their space and how they use it, they are learning important lessons about negotiation and cooperation.

The teacher arranges the environment outside the classroom as well. All preschools need to have outdoor spaces for active play. A thoughtfully designed garden has safe areas for running, climbing, riding and imaginative play. The teacher keeps track of each child, noticing who is doing what and for how long. She offers direction where needed and sometimes joins in the play, but she also knows when to observe quietly.

The first days at preschool. An outgoing three-year-old takes to preschool like a duck to water and doesn't need a gentle introduction. It may be quite different with a sensitive child who still feels closely attached to his parents. If his mother leaves him at school the first day, he may not make a fuss right away, but after a while he may miss her. When he finds she isn't there, he may become frightened. The next day he may not want to leave home.

With a dependent child like this, it's better to introduce him to preschool gradually. For several days, his mother might stay nearby while he plays and then take him home again after a time. Each day, the mother and child stay for a longer period. Meanwhile, he is building up attachments to the staff and other children that will give him a sense of security when his mother no longer stays.

Sometimes a child seems quite happy for several days, even after his mother has left him at school. Then he gets hurt and suddenly wants her. In that case, the staff can help the mother decide if she should come back for a number of days. When a mother is staying around the school, she ought to remain in the background. The idea is to let the child develop his own desire to enter the group, so that he forgets his need for his mother.

Sometimes the mother's anxiety is greater than the child's. If she says goodbye three times over with a worried expression, he may think, 'She looks as if something awful might happen if I stay here without her. I'd better not let her go.' It's natural for a mother to worry about how her small child will feel when she leaves him for the first time. Staff can often provide good advice in this situation: they've had lots of experience with it. A discussion before the beginning of school gives the teacher a head start in getting to know each child, and helps parents and staff trust each other and work together smoothly right off the bat.

A child who starts with some genuine anxiety about separating from the parent may learn that this gives him control over a highly sympathetic parent. He may then progressively exploit this control.

When the staff are kind and understanding but a child becomes reluctant or fearful about returning to school, I think it is usually better for the parents to act quite confident and firm and explain that everybody goes to school every day. In the long run, it's better for the child to outgrow his dependence than to give in to it. If the child's terror is extreme, the situation should be discussed with a child mental health professional.

Reactions at home. Some children find the early days and weeks of preschool to be hard work. The large group, the new friends and the new things to do get them keyed up and worn out. If your child is too tired at first, it doesn't mean that she can't adjust to school, only that you have to compromise for a while until she is used to it. Discuss with her teacher whether it would be wise to cut down her preschool time temporarily. In one case, coming to school in the middle of the morning is the best answer. Taking the easily tired child home early works less well, because she hates to leave in the middle of the fun. Keeping the child at home one or two days a week may be the answer to this temporary problem. Some small children starting preschool preserve their self-control in school in spite of fatigue, but let loose on the family when they come home. This calls for extra patience and a discussion with the teacher.

A well-trained preschool teacher ought to be, and usually is, a very understanding person. A parent shouldn't hesitate to talk over the child's problems with the teacher, whether or not those problems are connected with school. A teacher gets a different slant and has probably faced the same problems before in other cases.

Pressures in preschool. Education is competitive, and preschools are not immune. Ambitious parents often see the right preschool as the necessary first step on the path to an Oxbridge degree. Some private preschools have responded to the pressure for future success by incorporating academic structure, curriculum and teaching practices. A certain part of each day may be set aside for what is often called seat work (staying in your chair for an extended period of time and concentrating on an assigned task). All of these efforts are intended to prepare children for the next rung of the educational ladder.

What's wrong with this approach? Most young children are eager to please their teachers. After a lot of repetitive drilling, even a three-year-old will be able to read several words by sight. Some of the more advanced will be able to sound out simple words. Many of the children will be very impressive when they start in Reception.

However, by the end of Year 1 they won't be any better at reading than any other children. They will have spent a lot of time and effort with no lasting benefit. On the other hand, many of them may have decided that reading and maths are terribly boring and hard, nothing they would ever do voluntarily. Of course, children should be taught their letters and numbers in preschool, but these academic elements need to be part of experiences that are meaningful for children.

For example, rather than relying entirely on flashcards and rote drills, teachers may read stories out loud and encourage children to respond creatively; they may call children's attention to signs and labels in the classroom and include elements of writing, reading and counting in a wide range of activities. For example, if the classroom has a pet hamster or rabbit, every child will know how to read the animal's name on the sign above the cage. The teacher might make a calendar showing feeding times, then have the children sign up to feed their pet, counting the days until it's their turn. In these ways, children learn print and number concepts in the context of real-life experiences.

While knowledge of letters and numbers is important, an overly academic approach to preschool can get in the way of play, which is the way children develop social skills and exercise their creativity. An excessively skill-and-drill approach to preschool education teaches young children that learning is something you do out of a sense of duty. A more balanced approach, which includes plentiful opportunities to play, teaches children to love learning.

SCHOOL AND SCHOOL PROBLEMS

A dedicated school principal once said to me, 'Every child has gifts; it's our job to help discover and nurture them.' I think this comes close to defining the heart of education. In fact, the word 'education' stems from Latin words that mean 'to lead out' – that is, to draw out the child's inner qualities and strengths. That is very different from the notion that teachers need to pour knowledge into children, as if they were empty jars waiting to be filled. John Dewey, a famous educator from a century ago, said, 'True education frees the human spirit.' I believe that.

WHAT SCHOOL IS FOR

The main lesson learned in school is how to get along in the world. Different subjects are merely means to this end. One job of a school is to make subjects so interesting and real that children want to learn and remember information for the rest of their lives.

There's no use in knowing a lot if you can't be happy, get along with people and do fulfilling work. The good teacher tries to understand each child in order to help him develop into a well-rounded person. The child who lacks self-confidence needs chances to succeed. The troublemaking show-off has to learn how to gain the recognition he craves through doing good work. The child who doesn't know how to make friends needs help in becoming sociable and appealing. The child who seems to be lazy needs to have her enthusiasm sparked.

DR SPOCK COMMENTS

In the old days, it used to be thought that all a school had to do was teach children how to read, write, add and memorize a certain number of facts about the world. I heard a teacher tell how, in his own school days, he had to memorize a definition of a preposition that went something like this: 'A preposition is a word, generally with some meaning of position, direction, time or other abstract relation, used to connect a noun or pronoun, in an adjectival or adverbial sense, with some other word.' Of course, he didn't learn anything when he memorized that. You learn only when things have meaning for you.

How teachers make school interesting. A school can go only so far with a cut-and-dried programme in which everyone in the class reads from page 7 to page 23 in the textbook at the same time, and then does the examples on page 128 of the arithmetic book. This works well enough for the average child who is well adjusted anyway. But it's too dull for the bright pupils, and too speedy for the slow ones. It gives the boy who hates books a chance to stick paper clips in the hair of the girl in front of him. It does nothing to help the girl who is lonely or the boy who needs to learn to cooperate.

When teachers start with a topic that children are interested in, they can use it to teach all manner of subjects. Take the case of a Year 3 class in which the term's work centres on ancient Egypt. The more the children find out about mummies, the more they want to know. The textbook tells a story, and the children really want to know what it says. For arithmetic, they study what the Egyptians used for money. Then arithmetic isn't a separate subject at all, but a useful part of life. Geography isn't spots on a map; it's the pyramids and temples. In science the children make dye from berries and use it to dye cloth, or discuss how the Nile affected Egyptian beliefs.

People are sometimes uneasy when schoolwork seems too interesting, feeling that a child needs mostly to learn how to do what's unpleasant and difficult. But if you stop and think of the people you know who are unusually successful, you'll see that they are usually the ones who love their work. In any job there's plenty of drudgery, but you do it because you see its connection with the fascinating side of the work. Darwin was a wretched student in school. But later he became interested in natural history, performed one of the most painstaking jobs of research that the world has ever known, and worked out the theory of evolution. A boy in secondary school may see no sense in geometry, hate it and do badly in it. But if he is later studying to be an air navigator, sees what geometry is for and realizes that it could save the lives of the crew and passengers, he works at it like a demon.

Effective teachers understand that every child needs to develop self-discipline to be a useful adult. But you can't snap discipline onto children from the outside, like handcuffs; it's something that children have to develop inside, by first understanding the purpose of their work and feeling a sense of responsibility to others in how they perform it.

Linking school with the world. A school wants its pupils to learn firsthand about the outside world, so that they will see the connection between their schoolwork and real life. It arranges trips to nearby industries, asks people from the community to come in and talk, encourages classroom discussion. A class that is studying food may have an opportunity to observe some of the steps in the growing, harvesting, transportation and marketing of vegetables. A class that is studying government might visit the Houses of Parliament or City Hall.

Another thing that a good school wants to teach is democracy, not just as a patriotic ideal but as a way of living and getting things done. A good teacher knows that she can't teach democracy out of a book if she's acting like a dictator in her classroom. She encourages her pupils to decide how to tackle certain projects and overcome the difficulties they will run into. She lets them work out among themselves who is to do this part of the job, who that one. That's how they learn to appreciate each other and get things done, not just in school but in the outside world, too.

When teachers tells their pupils what to do every step of the way, the children will work while she is in the room.

When she leaves, though, a lot of them will start fooling around. They decide that lessons are the teacher's responsibility, not theirs. Children who help to choose and plan their own work and cooperate with each other in carrying it out accomplish almost as much when the teacher is out of the room as when she is present. They know the purpose of their work and the steps to accomplish it. Each one wants to do a fair share because each is proud to be a respected member of the group and feels a sense of responsibility to the others.

This is the very highest kind of discipline. This training, this spirit, is what makes the best citizens and the most valuable workers.

How school helps a child with difficulties. A girl in Year 1 or 2 who is having difficulty learning to read, for example, will benefit from a teacher who is interested in helping her not only to read and write but also to find her place in the group. Such a scenario might play out in the following manner. The teacher learned in a conference with her mother that she used tools well and loved to paint and draw. He saw ways to use her strong points in the class. The children were painting a large picture of Egyptian life to hang on the wall, and constructing a model of a pyramid and town. The teacher arranged for the girl to have a part in both these projects. Here were things she could do well without nervousness.

As the days went by, she became more and more fascinated with Egyptians. In order to paint her part of the picture and make her part of the model correctly, she needed to find out more from books. Now she wanted to learn to read, and she tried harder. Her classmates didn't look down on her because she couldn't read. They thought more about how she was such a good painter and model builder, and often asked her to help them. As her confidence grew, so did her receptivity to new skills.

LEARNING TO READ

The question of how best to teach children to read has been controversial. Early in the twentieth century, the received wisdom was that children should not be exposed to reading too early, lest it confuse their immature brains. Later, in the 1960s, researchers realized that even very young children learned a lot about how literacy works simply by observing their parents. Furthermore, children given crayons and paper often experimented with making letters and words. They also learned to read familiar words on cereal boxes and street signs long before receiving any formal lessons. Educators were so enamoured with these discoveries – sometimes called *emergent literacy* – that some even thought formal teaching might be unnecessary altogether.

In recent decades, educational research has come back to the idea that children need to be taught how the alphabet works: how letters stand for sounds, and how those sounds come together to form words. This emphasis on phonics has not replaced the insights of emergent literacy. Instead, educators realize that children need exposure to both kinds of learning. They need to be read to; they need to make up their own stories and dictate them to parents and teachers, then read them back; they need lots of time to play with letters and words.

PHYSICAL EDUCATION

Physical health means more than just the absence of disease. It means having a body that is strong, flexible and coordinated, and having the skills to use that body in joyful ways. Many three- and four-year-old children already demonstrate these fundamentals of physical health. But as children get older and spend long hours sitting in schools and doing homework, physical fitness often declines. Few schoolchildren now have daily PE lessons as they sometimes did in the past.

Benefits of physical education. In the past, the focus of PE classes was to train children to participate in competitive sports. More recently, the focus has shifted to developing healthy habits and fitness. The hope is that children will make regular physical activity part of their lives. Regular physical activity improves children's attention and moods. Exposure to a variety of different physical activities – such as swimming, running, gymnastics and other sports – helps children discover the activities that most appeal to them. With increasing coordination and endurance, they tend to enjoy the activities even more and are more likely to continue them.

In PE classes, children also learn sportsmanship and

teamwork. They learn to support classmates who aren't as skilled as they are. For children who have academic difficulties or learning disabilities, physical education provides an opportunity to excel and to build up their self-esteem. For many children, vigorous, skilful physical activity provides an important avenue for self-expression. While some children draw pictures or write in their diaries, others find more physical outlets for their emotions. Children benefit greatly from a PE teacher or coach who understands this emotional side of physical activity and sport, and who forms a supportive relationship with the child.

PARENTS AND SCHOOLS

Children learn best when parents and teachers work together. Children respect their teachers when they see that their parents respect them. It's easy to maintain a positive relationship with the school when your child is doing well, but it's even more important when your child is struggling or when there are things about the school that need improvement.

Parents in schools. More than just attending parents' evenings (which are certainly important), make an effort to get to know your child's teachers. Volunteer to help in the classroom; participate in field trips and special events. Teachers communicate more easily with involved parents. If your child has any academic, behavioural or social difficulties, you'll hear about them early on, when they're easier to fix.

What's more, solutions that include both parent and teacher input are almost always more effective.

Parent groups such as PTAs and boards of governors make great contributions to schools. Parents working together can provide the school with vital feedback about the lives of the students. What concerns do their children voice at home? Which parts of the school experience are strong, and which could be stronger? When you give your time and efforts to the PTA, you gain a certain standing in the school community. The teachers and the head are more likely to see you as an ally and make sure your child's needs are met.

As you work with the teachers and administration, you'll gain the confidence to share important personal information. If something upsetting has happened at home, such as the death of a grandparent or a divorce, it's helpful to let your child's head and teachers know so that they can be supportive and watch for signs of stress.

Supporting school at home. Parent involvement also means creating a home environment that supports learning. Most children need a well-lit, quiet place to work (although some children concentrate better with noise around them), and they need sufficient time. That may mean limiting some social engagements, or even other learning activities. Some children are so overscheduled with music lessons, sport practice, art lessons, religious schooling and other obligations that homework gets compressed into a last-minute, late-night rush. Creating a supportive environment might also require you to limit television, video games and recreational use of the computer.

Be a role model for learning. Children approach learning more positively when they see their parents making efforts to continue to learn. This applies just as much to parents who have a high degree of education as to those who do not. Set high but realistic expectations. As one colleague put it, 'My children know that they have to do their best. Since their best is A's, they know I expect A's.' For other children, realistic expectations mean earning solid B's or working hard in special education courses. Regardless of their level, children succeed when they set rigorous but attainable goals for themselves.

Parents as advocates. Some parents feel helpless in the face of an educational system that seems big, impersonal and unresponsive. Other parents feel empowered to take a leadership role when it comes to their children's education. Leadership doesn't necessarily mean being completely in charge, however. Effective parents know that they need to work together with teachers and heads, and sometimes with doctors or therapists. They know how to be pleasant and thoughtful, but also how to insist that their children receive an excellent education. They know their rights and join with other effective parents. They become a force for the positive education of their children. Not all school personnel are thrilled about these empowered parents (who tend to make demands and ask a lot of questions, after all), but generally administrators respect them and work hard to meet their expectations.

Your educational history. As a parent, your point of reference is bound to be your own school days. If you were lucky enough to go to a good school, you may now have very high standards for your child's school. On the other hand, your school experiences may have been largely negative. In this case, it's important to remain open-minded and optimistic that your child can have a better experience. Your active, committed, thoughtful cooperation with the school can help bring that about.

HOMEWORK

Why homework? In the early years, the main purpose of homework is to get children used to the idea of doing schoolwork at home; it also helps them develop time-management and organization skills. Later, homework has three main goals: to give children practice in using skills or concepts they learned in class; to prepare them for the next class; and to give them an opportunity to work on a project that is time-consuming or requires outside resources (such as the library, the Internet or you, the parents).

Children who do more homework score better on standardized tests. It stands to reason that when teachers set high expectations for learning, including relatively high homework demands, children learn more.

How much is enough? There are no hard-and-fast rules about how much homework should be assigned. However, as a general guideline, homework should take no more than an hour a week in Years 1 and 2, one and a half in Years 3 and 4, thirty minutes a night in Years 5 and 6, forty-five to ninety minutes in Years 7 and 8, building to one to two hours in Year 9.

Some schools assign much more than others, but this doesn't always guarantee higher achievement, especially in primary school. Beyond a certain point, homework may not only be overwhelming but may squeeze out other valuable activities, such as play, sport, music lessons, hobbies and relaxation. More is not always better. If your child routinely needs to spend much more time on homework than you think she should, talk with the teacher. The homework expectations may be unrealistic, or your child may be experiencing special difficulties that need to be addressed head-on.

Helping with homework. What should you do if your child asks for help with his homework? If he's puzzled and turns to you for clarification, there's no harm in straightening him out. But if your child wants you to do his work for him because he doesn't understand it, you're better off consulting the teacher. If the teacher is too busy to give your child some extra time, you may have to lend a hand. Even then, you should just help him to understand his work; you should not do it for him.

Sometimes a teacher will advise parents that their child

is falling behind and needs tutoring in a subject. If the school can recommend a good tutor whom you can afford, go ahead and hire him. Too often parents make poor tutors, not because they don't know enough or try hard enough, but because they care too much and become too upset when their child doesn't understand.

If a child is already mixed up in his lessons, an impatient parent may be the last straw. Another trouble is that a parent's method may be different from that of the teacher. If the child is already baffled by the subject as presented in school, the chances are that he will be even more baffled when it's presented in a different way at home.

It's not that a parent should never tutor a child, because in some cases it works very well. But it's wise to talk it over thoroughly with the teacher first, and then quit right away if it isn't going well. Whoever is tutoring the child should keep in touch with the teacher at regular intervals.

PROBLEMS IN SCHOOL

We should view school problems with the same urgency with which we view a high fever: it's an indication that something is wrong and that steps should be taken promptly to understand the problem and fix it. Whatever the cause, when problems persist, a child is bound to believe the worst about himself. Once a child becomes convinced that he is stupid, lazy or bad, it becomes much harder for him to change.

Causes of school problems. Many different problems, alone or in combination, may undermine a child's ability to make it in school. An average student may struggle in a class that is too high-powered and pressured; a bright student may find herself bored and unmotivated in a class that moves too slowly. A child who is being bullied may develop a sudden aversion to school and her grades may drop. Hearing or vision difficulties, chronic illness, learning disabilities (see page 1005) and ADHD (see page 820) may all lead to serious problems. Children with sleep disturbances may fail to pay attention because they are chronically overtired. An unforgivably high number of children still go to school hungry. Among psychological causes are worries about ill or angry parents, divorce or physical or sexual abuse.

It's very rare for a child to fail solely because of laziness, and a child who has given up trying isn't lazy. Children are naturally curious and enthusiastic. If they have lost their eagerness to learn, it's a sign that there is a problem that needs to be addressed.

School problems are not just a matter of grades. A child who gets all A's but is so perfectionistic and anxious that his stomach hurts and he dreads going to school has a problem. A child who gets B's only by working so hard that she has no time for friends or fun may also need help.

Sorting it out. Have a friendly, nonscolding discussion with your child about her school problem. Do this in a gentle and supportive manner. What does she think is causing the problem? Ask for details about what happens in school, and how she thinks and feels. Meet with the teacher and head. It's best to regard them as collaborators, not the enemy. Although the teacher or the school may be part of the problem, it is helpful to start out assuming that they are on your side. Talk with your doctor and make an appointment with a developmental and behavioural paediatrician, child psychologist or other professional who has experience in the area of school problems (see page 940). There should be one doctor – either your GP or a specialist – who helps you to put all of the information together to come up with a better idea of what the problem is and where to go next.

School intervention. Once you understand the problem, the solution is likely to suggest itself. When academic pressure is the problem, you may want to discuss the solutions with the head teacher. For learning disabilities, special education is often helpful (see page 1012), for ADHD, a combination of medication and behavioural therapy (see page 825). Better parent-teacher communication often helps with behaviour problems.

For problems of teasing or bullying, teachers need to intervene with the whole class, teaching that classmates are expected to take care of each other, never hurt one another's bodies or feelings, and always speak up if they see someone else being hurt. Positive education of this sort helps a great deal, particularly if it is done throughout the school (see page 203).

Helping children outside school. There is much that a parent can do outside the school setting to help a child who is having serious academic problems. Most children are curious about the world around them. When you share and encourage that curiosity, the child's interest in learning grows. Make regular excursion to parks, libraries and museums. Look in the local newspapers and check bulletin boards in libraries or on a nearby university campus for free concerts and lectures. Listen for signs of interest on your child's part, and follow those up with more exploration. When school is frustrating for a child, it is even more crucial that the child love learning.

Relations between parents and teachers. It's easy to get along with a teacher if your son is the star of the class. But if your child is having trouble, the situation is more delicate. It's natural for parents and teachers to develop possessive feelings towards the child. Each, no matter how reasonable, secretly feels that the child would be doing better if only the other would handle him a little differently. It's helpful to the parents to realize at the start that the teacher is just as sensitive on this point as they are, and that they will get further in a conference by being friendly and cooperative.

Some parents are afraid of facing a teacher, forgetting that just as often the teacher is afraid of them. The parents' main job is to give a clear history of the child's past, what his interests are and what he responds to well or badly, then to work with the teacher on how best to apply this information in school. Don't forget to compliment the teacher on those parts of the curriculum that are a great success with the child.

Occasionally a child and teacher just don't fit temperamentally, no matter how hard they both work at it. In these cases, the head teacher can be involved in the question of whether to move the child to another class.

Parents should avoid blaming the teacher if their child is unsuccessful in class. If the child hears the parents badmouthing his teacher, he will learn to blame others and to avoid taking responsibility for his contribution to his problems. You can be sympathetic without laying blame: 'I know how hard you are trying,' or 'I know how unhappy it makes you when your teacher is dissatisfied.'

LEARNING DISABILITIES

Children who are failing in school often assume that they are dumb; their parents and teachers are apt to assume that they are lazy. Most likely they are neither. A learning disability (LD) is a neurological condition that interferes with specific academic functions: reading, writing, calculating and others. As many as one child in seven is affected. Identifying a learning disability opens the door to accommodation, remediation and eventual success.

What is a learning disability? Learning disabilities are problems related to a child's brain development that interfere with school-related tasks. One way to think of this is in terms of the normal unevenness in talents (see page 963). One child is great in writing but poor in maths; another is strong in science but weak in foreign languages. Children whose abilities are extremely uneven may be so poor in certain subjects or academic processes that they are unable to do an adequate job; they are disabled.

As you might expect from their extreme unevenness, many children with LD are actually gifted in areas other than their disability. It's pretty common to see, for example, a child who is excellent in maths and has a fine artistic eye but whose reading skills are quite poor.

It's important to understand that LD and intelligence are very different issues. Children with LD can have IQ scores that are very high, average or below average. An older concept is that LD exists when there is a gap between IQ and ability or achievement in a particular subject. The problem with this idea is that children with low IQ scores may still have learning disabilities, even though there is no gap between their IQ and their achievement.

In learning disabilities, brain processes that are specific to academic learning are affected. There are many other reasons that children may have academic problems. Children who have serious problems with vision and hearing, muscular or movement disorders (such as muscular dystrophy or cerebral palsy) and severe mental health problems aren't counted as LD, although they, too, may have severe difficulties with academic skills.

What it feels like to have LD. Children with LD know that there is something wrong with them, but they have no way of knowing what it is. Their teachers and parents tell them to try harder. Sometimes, through very great effort, they have some success. For example, a child might spend five hours on a thirty-minute homework assignment. He does well, but he's simply not able to work that hard day after day (none of us can work full tilt for very long before we tire out). His teacher is pleased, but she doesn't see why he shouldn't always perform up to the level he is capable of. Instead of recognizing his extraordinary effort, she's likely to think that he's lazy. Understandably, the child might come to resent the teacher because she is impossible to please.

You can see how what starts as a learning disability can easily grow into an emotional or behavioural problem. Some children decide to be class clowns or to rebel against teacher discipline as a way of drawing attention away from their poor abilities. In their view, it is better to be bad than to be stupid. Other children suffer in silence. They forget (maybe intentionally) to turn in homework and never volunteer in class. They may act out their frustration or try to preserve their dignity by getting into fights in the playground.

Dyslexia. By far, the most common LD involves reading and spelling; it's often referred to as *dyslexia.* It makes up about 80 per cent of all LD, affecting as many as 15 per cent of all children – a very common problem indeed. Dyslexia is inherited: if both parents have it, chances are better than fifty-fifty that their child will, too. It's more common in boys, by about two to one.

The signs of dyslexia change over time, and vary somewhat from child to child. Very young children who begin to babble later or with less variety of sounds than average children may grow up to have dyslexia, as may toddlers who are late talkers. A child who is not talking well by age five has a high chance of showing reading problems.

In the early years of primary school, children with dyslexia struggle to connect letters with sounds. They may know the alphabet song, but they can't tell you the sounds that the different letters make (they often have a hard time remembering the names of the letters, too). Rhyming, which requires sensitivity to the sounds that make up words, is often very hard for them. If they do learn to read a few words, it's because they have memorized them whole; they don't have the ability to sound out the letters and then put the sounds back together to make words.

Children with dyslexia often reverse letters, and confuse letters that look alike (*b*'s and *d*'s and *p*'s, for example). It's a common misconception, however, that letter reversal is the key feature of dyslexia. Up to age seven, letter reversals are common in *all* children. Children with dyslexia also tend to mix up whole words when they are talking, or struggle to think of names for common objects (like doorknobs or nostrils).

Most children with dyslexia eventually learn how to read. However, they tend to read slowly and with difficulty. They often miss the point of what they've read, because it takes so much effort for them to decode the words. Tests are a special hardship because it takes them so long to read the instructions. If they go at their own pace, they complete the first half of the questions, then run out of time; if they rush to get through the whole test, they end up making lots of errors because they haven't read and understood the questions. However, if they're tested verbally, they often demonstrate a strong knowledge of the topic. Even as grown-ups, they rarely read for pleasure, although if they are very interested in something, they may plough through it.

Often, children and adults with dyslexia have special abilities, part of the uneven brain development I described on page 963. Frequently they are extremely creative and brilliant visual thinkers. There's a long list of outstanding scientists, entrepreneurs and artists who are thought to have had dyslexia, including Einstein and Picasso. (Where I live, children are always impressed that the world-famous heart surgeon who runs the Cleveland Clinic is widely known to have dyslexia.) There's a wonderful picture book about a girl with dyslexia and how she struggles in school. It's called *Thank You, Mr Falker*, written and illustrated by Patricia Polacco, who herself has dyslexia. Dyslexia doesn't have to limit a child's life chances; it may even expand them.

Most scientists agree that the problems underlying dyslexia are mainly in the parts of the brain that process the sounds of the language. Despite the fact that reading requires seeing, most children with reading problems see perfectly well. (Recently, more and more optometrists have been claiming that they can cure dyslexia with eye exercises, but there is no good evidence that this is so.) The treatments for dyslexia that have been shown to be effective all involve training the brain to connect speech sounds with letters, and to combine the individual sounds into words. The most well known of these programmes are probably Orton-Gillingham and Lindamood-Bell, but there are several others, all similar in their approach. If your child has dyslexia, it's worth seeking a tutor or school that uses one of these tried-and-true approaches.

With dyslexia, as with other learning disabilities, probably the most important first step is to recognize the problem, give it a name and help the child understand that it is not a matter of laziness or stupidity, but rather something that, with work, can be overcome. *Overcoming Dyslexia* by Sally Shaywitz, MD, is a readable and authoritative guide.

Other learning disabilities. Every ability needed to succeed academically has a corresponding disability. This is a partial list of academic abilities and what happens when they are lacking:

- *Reading.* Children need to be able to connect written symbols (letters and groups of letters) with the sounds they represent. Then they need to connect those sounds together and link them to words they know. Problems handling word sounds underlie most cases of dyslexia.
- *Writing.* Children have to be able to form all of the letters automatically – that is, without thinking about their shapes. If they have to stop and think about each letter, their writing will be slow and choppy and they will not be able to keep up with writing assignments.
- *Maths.* The ability to handle basic maths processes – addition and subtraction – is related to an underlying

ability to visualize things in space and gauge their quantity. Children with problems in this area may have what's called dyscalculia, a specific learning disability for maths.

- *Memory.* Skills involved in memory include taking information in, holding on to it and finding it again in response to an unspoken command, such as 'Who invented the lightbulb?' Problems with any of these memory processes – intake, storage or retrieval – can cause a learning disability.
- *Other skills.* There are many specific skills that can become problem areas, such as understanding or expressing spoken language, keeping things in order (sequencing), rapid recall, planning for movements and so on. Often a child has difficulty with more than one particular skill (and may have strengths in other areas).

LD assessments. If you suspect an LD, your first step should be to talk to your child's class teacher. Every school has a Special Educational Needs Co-ordinator (SENCO) who should be able to provide you with advice. Alternatively, you can arrange a private assessment. Most large hospitals have a learning clinic where a team of specialists provides comprehensive evaluations. The team usually includes a paediatrician with expertise in child development along with a learning specialist, psychologist and social worker. You should receive a detailed report that spells out your child's problems and diagnosis and gives suggestions for educational planning or treatment.

Treatments for LD. The first and most important treatment for a learning disability is for everyone to acknowledge that it exists. Once that happens, teachers and parents can recognize how hard the child is really working, and can praise the effort rather than criticizing the product. Children need to hear that they are not stupid; they have a problem that they need to work on, but they don't have to deal with it alone. With the help of parents and teachers, things can get better.

Specific educational treatments depend on the type of LD. For dyslexia, the most effective treatments centre on very intensive teaching of letters and the sounds they make. The child may use all of his senses, for example, feeling wooden letters, cutting them out of paper and making them out of biscuit dough and then tasting them. In addition to attacking the problem head-on, special educators teach children how to work around learning difficulties. A child who struggles with reading might listen to books on tape; a child with extremely poor handwriting might type some of his writing assignments on the computer. Just as critically, teachers also help children focus on and develop their strengths. For more information on LD, you can begin with the sources listed in the Resource Guide.

THE UNPOPULAR CHILD

Most children want to do well in school, but what matters most to them is having friends. Every child has days when he comes home and announces, 'Nobody likes me.' But the child who feels this way day after day is in real trouble. For the unpopular child, every day is torture. He's belittled and teased, victimized by bullies, the last to be picked for any game. He's apt to feel isolated, down on himself and depressed.

The unpopular child doesn't know how to fit in, or simply can't. He might not be aware of how his behaviour comes across to the other children. His efforts to make friends are often clumsy and drive his peers away even more. He gets labelled as 'weird' or 'unfriendly' (although he really desperately wants friends), and the other kids avoid him when they aren't actively tormenting him. An unpopular child often has developmental problems such as an autism spectrum disorder (page 930) or ADHD (page 820). The other children, of course, don't understand this. From their point of view, he simply doesn't know how to play, won't follow the rules or always insists on having things his way. The other children may be cruel, but doctors and psychologists have learned to respect their judgment as a sign that the unpopular child has serious problems.

Helping the unpopular child. If your child is very unpopular, don't shrug it off as unimportant. Watch him interact with the other children. It can be painful and very difficult to judge your child's behaviour objectively. Talk to his teachers and other caring adults who will be honest with you. If you're concerned, seek a professional evaluation by a child psychiatrist or psychologist sooner rather than later. A thorough evaluation will pinpoint not only your child's areas of difficulty but also his strengths.

As a tuned-in parent, you can do a lot to help your child make friends. Get involved in the school and get to know some of the other children and their parents. Ask the teacher to find a classmate who seems inclined to be friendly and seat him next to your child. Invite this classmate to your home to play, or to go with your child to a park, a film or some other place of mutual interest. Taking just one friend prevents your child from being the odd man out. For the first few times, make the play dates short so there's less time for things to go wrong. Remind your child ahead of time how to play nicely. You might say, for example, 'Remember, ask Johnny what he wants to play with; that way, he'll have a good time and want to come back.' Watch your child and praise him afterward for any positive behaviors he showed. If you have to, step in to get things back on the right track.

The unpopular child always is treated better when adults are around to supervise. For this reason, enroll your child in group activities such as sports, religious events or dance classes. Talk with the group leader ahead of time so she can give extra support. Your child's predicament will not be new or unusual to anyone who works with children.

When your child is having serious difficulties being accepted by other children, be available and listen empathetically; don't scold or reprimand. Every child needs comfort, love, and support; an unpopular child needs these most of all. An experienced doctor or psychologist can help work out if there is a diagnosis such as ADHD or depression that needs specific treatment. A therapist can help an unpopular child develop the skills needed to make and keep friends.

SCHOOL AVOIDANCE

A child cries and cries when his mother tries to leave him at preschool. An older child develops stomachaches every morning, which improve quickly as soon as he is allowed to stay home from school. Another child begins to vomit regularly in school but feels much better at home. Yet another shows such negative behaviours that he gets sent home; he may even arrange to get himself excluded. A child who has been at home for a few days begins to fret and complain at any mention of going back to school; when pressured, he throws a violent tantrum. School can be a difficult or scary place for a child; staying home can feel much more comfortable. School avoidance can begin for a specific reason and then continue as a habit, growing stronger with each passing day.

Preschool and Reception. For young children, the most common cause of school avoidance is separation anxiety. Many children have been going to day care since they were infants; for others, however, starting school may be a big adjustment. The building is intimidating, the hallways are a maze, the new room is full of children and adults they don't know, and the days seem to stretch on forever (remember, time goes very slowly for a four-year-old). For these children, the first education goal is simply to feel comfortable in school.

A child's discomfort at separating can mean different things. One child is temperamentally slow to warm up (see page 123), so any new situation takes time to feel right to him. Another child, who might otherwise be able to handle things well, reacts to his mother's anxious attempts to reassure him by becoming anxious himself. Sometimes it makes sense for a parent to sit in the classroom until the child is comfortable, even if it takes several days. Sometimes it makes sense for the parent to drop the child off, wave a cheerful good-bye, and depart. (It is never a good idea for a parent to sneak away; this only makes a child feel even more anxious, because now he has to worry that his mum or dad is apt to disappear the moment he looks the other way.)

Primary school. A school-age child may be afraid of being bullied or teased, or of the humiliation of being called on to read out loud if his reading skills are weak. A child who is very unpopular may feel so miserable and lonely in the lunchroom and in the playground that staying home is a relief. A child who has missed several days because of an illness may worry that he is too far behind to ever catch up.

Children may also avoid school because they are worried about what is happening at home. There may be domestic violence or a parent who is depressed. In other instances, a child's worries are less realistic. One child, for instance, worried constantly that his mother would get into a car accident if he wasn't there to prevent it. His dread grew all the while he was apart from her. Irrational fears like this may be a reaction to hostile thoughts a child harbours towards his parents but cannot openly express. This may sound unlikely, but psychiatrists have found it to be fairly common. A skilled therapist can help children handle their unacceptable feelings in a more direct and less destructive manner.

Secondary school. It's normal for teens to be uncomfortably self-conscious; many are painfully so. Girls who develop early and boys who develop late are particularly prone to these feelings, as are teens who are overweight or underweight or who have any other visible difference. One tall twelve-year-old girl was mortified when a male teacher casually mentioned that she was taller than he. This confirmed her own feelings that she was very unattractive and peculiar, and made going to school each day a torture.

Absenteeism may be higher on days when there is gym. For the child who is going through puberty and also struggling with other emotional issues that undermine his confidence, the thought of dressing and undressing in front of others, and of being forced to perform physical activities that will expose real or imagined inadequacies, may be more than he can bear. Trying to avoid school becomes, for him, the only solution.

What to do. A child's persistent avoidance of school, regardless of age, is an emergency. It often takes a team, including parents, educators and social workers, to determine the cause and put corrective measures in place. Professional help may be required in many instances. While all of this is going on, it's extremely important that the child continue to go to school, or that he return as soon as possible. Every day that a child stays home makes going back that much harder. School avoidance shrinks only when it is confronted. This doesn't mean that a child should be forced to face an overwhelming situation alone; rather, children need support as well as a parent's confident expectations that they will eventually master their fears.

PLANNING FOR UNIVERSITY

WHAT UNIVERSITY IS FOR

Ideally, university or college is an opportunity for young adults to stretch their intellectual wings, to explore the world of ideas, and to find themselves. A degree is the key to economic advancement for many, although not a guarantee of prosperity. Many college and university courses now offer opportunities for students to obtain specific technical or work-focused training.

University admissions seem to become more competitive with each passing year, even as the tuition becomes less affordable. For many, a university education seems increasingly out of reach; for others, getting ready to gain admission to university takes up an ever larger part of their adolescence. Of course, the actual education that a student acquires depends at least as much on the individual as it does on the college or university and its professors. Many highly educated people graduate from obscure colleges (or don't graduate at all), and some who earn degrees from famous universities take away very little else.

CHOOSING A UNIVERSITY

The process of choosing. As a parent, you care about the end result: you want your child to get on a good course, one where she'll be happy as well as successful. The process of decision making is also important. For most adolescents, choosing a college or university is the first major life decision in which they have a real say. It's an opportunity for them to examine their goals and weigh their priorities. You'd like your teen to take the decision seriously, but not so seriously that it becomes overwhelming.

Start by helping your teen get organized. The first step is to obtain a calendar of application deadlines from the school careers office. Your teen can then visualize the available time and plot what tasks to do when. It's easy to find out almost anything you want about any college or university in the United Kingdom. The standard prospectuses – available in many school careers offices and most public libraries – provide information about courses, students, campuses and financial aid for countless institutions. Every college, university and trade school has a website.

What if your child makes a mistake? Although choosing the right university can make for a happier, more successful experience, choosing the wrong university can be a learning experience as well. In fact, many students start at one university, find that it does not meet their needs and complete their degree at another institution. Changing universities is inconvenient, but it's not the end of the world. Knowing this should take some of the pressure off your teen and you.

Factors to consider. The main question when choosing a college or university is, 'What do I want to get out of university?' It helps to break down this big question into smaller, more manageable pieces. The list that follows is intended to introduce you to the range of issues involved in college and university selection and to help you in discussions you have with your teen. (But remember, the choice is your teen's to make.)

What type of course? Most students choose a three-year course leading to a BA (bachelor of arts) or BSc (bachelor of science) degree. But there are other options, such as the shorter programmes offered by many vocational schools. A three-year course offers the greatest amount of flexibility in future education and careers, but even so it's not always the best choice for every student. Also keep in mind that your child's decision is not carved in stone.

How big? Large universities offer a broad range of academic subjects and extracurricular activities. Although many big universities boast a number of top-rank professors, the average student may see them only in large lecture halls; most of the hands-on teaching is done by tutors. Smaller universities have fewer famous professors but may offer more access to them. Big universities provide a wider range of extracurricular and social activities, but it may be easier to get to know fellow students on smaller campuses. Some students feel lost at a big university; others feel too confined at a small one.

Location. Some students thrive in the excitement of a big city; others immerse themselves in their studies and pay little attention to the world outside their classroom walls. Your teen may have strong feelings about which part of the country she'll go to. Closeness to family is another key issue. How important is it to you and your teen to be able to spend time together at frequent intervals?

Extracurricular activities. Students who want a specific

athletic or extracurricular activity are often tempted to choose a university that excels in that area. It's better, however, if there are several areas where the school's strengths and the student's interests overlap. Otherwise, he may find himself unhappy for the many hours of each day when he is not pursuing his favourite activity.

Diversity. One of the virtues of a university education is the opportunity for students to learn from and about each other. Counterbalancing the benefit of diversity is the support some students derive from having peers with similar values and worldviews. This applies equally to racial or ethnic diversity, geographic and political diversity and sexual diversity (coeducational versus single sex or whether there is a sizable gay or lesbian community).

Reputation. Some universities have a reputation for being party places; others see themselves as serious or politically progressive. It is hard to determine this from the prospectus, but guidebooks note each school's special flavour – and this is, of course, one of the main things to look for on a campus visit.

Costs. The situation on tuition fees and maintenance loans and grants varies across England, Wales, Scotland and Northern Ireland. Scottish students studying in Scotland do not have to pay tuition fees, but unfortunately students in England now face costs of up to £9,000 per year for their tuition, depending on the university or college. In Northern Ireland and Wales, tuition fees are currently capped at £3,290. Living costs vary greatly depending on the location, as does the cost of transportation back and forth from home to school. It's best to find out well ahead of time what your child is entitled to – in terms of tuition fee loans, maintenance loans, maintenance grants and extra help – so that you can plan accordingly. All loans (but not grants) have to be paid back plus interest once your child has graduated and has hit an earnings threshold.

Other questions. In addition to the questions discussed on the preceding pages about personal values, it helps to have the answers to several factual questions:

- How many students apply, and how many of these are accepted?
- What are the required grades?
- Is the campus safe?
- What does the campus look like? Architecture that is inspiring to some may be gloomy to others.
- How is the campus housing? Some universities require first-year students to live in halls; some have mandatory meal attendance. It can be hard to assess the appearance of halls without actually visiting.
- What is the availability and cost of off-campus housing?
- How many students enroll, and how many complete their degrees, on average?
- How many who look for jobs in their chosen field get them? Ask about specific jobs, too.

Careers advisers. A good school careers adviser can help your teen assess her life goals and plan an academic course to reach them. Based on her goals, the adviser can help your child select the right courses and extracurricular activities, and can help her ask the questions and find the facts she needs to make the best choice. If this sounds precisely like the sort of help you yourself are planning on giving your child, it is. Professional careers advice shouldn't replace a parent's input, it should supplement it.

At the same time, your job is to help your child keep the whole process in perspective. Yes, it's important to think and plan ahead. But it's also important to enjoy life as you're living it. A sixth-former needs to follow his interests even if they don't lead to a better UCAS application, and he has to have some fun, too. He shouldn't sacrifice his adolescent years at the altar of university admissions.

SAVING FOR UNIVERSITY

It's true that the purpose of financial aid is to make university affordable to everyone. However, most financial aid comes in the form of loans, which means that most students finish university with a load of debt to go with their degree.

The key to university savings is to start putting money away early on to take advantage of compound interest. Putting money away in your child's name, perhaps in their Child Trust Fund, may save money in taxes, because your child's tax rate is likely to be lower than yours or nonexistent.

Make sure you know what grants and loans your child may be eligible for. Grants are dependent on your family income. Some universities and colleges also offer financial aid. Even though university is expensive, financial aid and loans should make it possible for every child to afford a college or university education.

COMMON MEDICATIONS FOR CHILDREN

At some point, almost every child runs a fever, gets a rash, has a cough or develops some other symptom that calls for medication. A basic knowledge of just a few frequently used drugs can help you treat these common complaints with confidence. But giving medication to a child can be a confusing business. Drug companies complicate things by giving medications multiple names. There's the trade name you probably know (Calpol, for instance) and the generic name – often unpronounceable – that identifies the active ingredient (paracetamol, in this case). Many over-the-counter drugs contain several active ingredients; each does something different. When you give your child a spoonful of medicine, it's not always easy to know just what you're giving.

To clear things up a bit, the guide that follows lists the generic names for some of the most common medications, tells what the medication is supposed to do and gives its most frequent side effects. Most prescriptions include the generic names and all over-the-counter drugs list the generic ingredients on the box under 'active ingredients'. Many commonly used medications fall into a few categories – antibiotics, antihistamines and anti-inflammatory medications, for example. Information about those drugs is grouped under the applicable categories.

The purpose of this guide is not to replace the advice of doctors or pharmacists. It is to help you better communicate with them. So when the doctor says, 'Let's give her some ibuprofen for that sore shoulder,' you can be thinking, 'Oh, Nurofen; we already tried that.'

A special word of caution about side effects is in order: this guide includes only *some* of the most common side effects. The package inserts that come with prescription drugs list many more. In fact, it is not possible to list every possible side effect for any medication, because individuals can have unusual reactions. Any unexpected, unpleasant symptom that pops up after taking a medication is a side effect until proven otherwise.

MEDICATION SAFETY

All medications should be treated with respect. Prescription drugs can have powerful side effects. But over-the-counter medications can also be dangerous, especially if a child takes an overdose. Notably, some very common cough and cold medicines have been found to be unsafe in children, sometimes even deadly – they should never be given to children under six. Some commonsense principles can lower the risk:

- Give medications, whether prescription or not, only on a doctor's advice.

- Keep medications in a locked cabinet or drawer. Even timid children have been known to climb up to high cabinets or shelves when curiosity drives them.
- Don't put your trust in childproof caps. They will slow a persistent child down, but they might not stop her.
- Pay special attention when you have visitors who might be carrying medications with them, or when you and your child visit others' homes. A handbag left sitting on a low table is a tempting target for a toddler.
- Tell your child that the medication is medicine, not sweeties.

At times of stress or when your daily routine undergoes a change, think about medications, cleaning supplies and other poisonous chemicals, and household hazards in general. Times of change are times of danger.

A WORD ON TERMINOLOGY

When doctors write prescriptions, they use a shorthand that can be confusing. When they say take one pill twice daily (BID in doctorese), they mean one pill every twelve hours. For example, you could take one dose at 8 am and another at 8 pm. Three times a day (TID) means every eight hours (for example, 8 am, 4 pm and midnight); four times a day (QID) is every six hours (for example, at 8 am, 2 pm, 8 pm and 2 am). PRN means 'as needed'. PO means

'by mouth'. A prescription that reads, 'take one tab PRN PO QID' means you *may* – but aren't required to – take one tablet as often as every six hours.

Measurements may also need translating. The instructions that come with over-the-counter medicines speak of teaspoons, tablespoons, millilitres or occasionally capfuls. But prescriptions are likely to be written in millilitres (ml) and milligrammes (mg). A standard teaspoon equals 5 millilitres and a tablespoon equals 15 millilitres. A doctor who instructs you to give 'one teaspoon three times a day' wants you to give 5 millilitres every eight hours. Since the teaspoons in your home may not hold exactly 5 millilitres, it's safer to use a medicine spoon with marked amounts or an oral syringe in order to get the dose right.

The reason it's good to be familiar with these terms is that you can ask questions. If the doctor tells you to take one tablet three times a day, then writes BID on the prescription, you should ask about that. If the doctor writes QID, and you're not sure whether you should give the medicine every six hours on the button, even if it means waking your baby, you should ask. Be sure you understand the instructions before you leave the surgery. Ask the pharmacist, too. You can't be too careful.

GLOSSARY OF COMMON MEDICATIONS

The following guide includes only a fraction of the drugs used today. For a more complete listing, look online at www.medicines.org.uk. Many of the medications following are sold under various trade names; only some examples are listed.

A short list like this one cannot include every possible side effect; there are many more that are not listed here. If you buy the medication over the counter, be sure to follow the dosing directions on the bottle. Just because a medication is sold without a prescription, there is no guarantee that it is safe. In general, the younger the child, the more cautious you need to be. The wisest course is to give medication *only* on the advice of a medical professional.

Acetylsalicylic acid (Aspirin)

(over the counter) *Trade name:* Disprin.

Effects: See Nonsteroidal anti-inflammatories.

Side effects: Use only under doctor's guidance. In children, aspirin can cause life-threatening liver disease (Reye's syndrome).

Amoxicillin

(prescription only) *Trade name:* Amoxil.

Effects: See under Antibiotics. Amoxicillin is the first-line treatment for ear infections.

Amoxicillin clavulanate

(prescription only) *Trade name:* Augmentin.

Effects: See under Antibiotics. Often the second choice if amoxicillin fails because of drug resistance.

Side effects: More likely than amoxicillin to cause stomach upset, diarrhoea.

Amoxil

(prescription only)

Effects: See Amoxicillin.

Antibiotics

(prescription only)

Effects: Antibiotics kill bacteria; not helpful in common viral infections, however.

Side effects: In infants especially, look for signs of thrush or candidal nappy rash (page 132); stomach upset, rashes are common.

Antihistamines

(over the counter or prescription)

Effects: These drugs block the action of histamine, a major component of allergic reactions. Used commonly to treat hay fever, hives, itching, etc.

Side effects: In young children, often cause hyper or overexcited response; in older children, sedation or drowsiness. Newer, more expensive drugs (Clarityn or Zirtec, for example) may have fewer such side effects. Antihistamines are often sold as part of combination medications containing decongestants and other medications: these medications are unsafe for young children.

Antivirals

(most are prescription only)

Effects: May shorten symptoms of some viral infections, such as oral herpes (cold sores) and influenza.

Side effects: Various, including stomach and intestinal upset, and allergic reactions that can be serious.

Azithromycin

(prescription only) *Trade name:* Zithromax.

Effects: See under Antibiotics; this drug is very similar to erythromycin but is given less frequently (and costs much more).

Side effects: Stomach upset, mainly.

Bacitracin ointment

(over the counter) *Trade name:* Neosporin.

Effects: A mild antibiotic that can be applied to the skin (topical).

Side effects: Rare.

Beclometasone nasal inhalation

(prescription only) *Trade name:* Qvar.

Effects: See under Corticosteroids, inhaled. Nasal corticosteroids, like Becotide and Qvar, reduce symptoms of hay fever.

Side effects: Rare when used as directed.

Benzocaine

(over the counter or prescription) *Trade name:* Lanacane.

Effects: Dulls pain sensation (anaesthetic). However, effects wear off with repeated use.

Side effects: Stinging or burning feeling. Overdose can cause heart rhythm disturbances.

Bisacodyl

(over the counter) *Trade name:* Dulco-Lax.

Effects: Stimulates the intestines to contract and propel faeces forwards.

Side effects: Cramping; diarrhoea.

Bronchodilators

(prescription only)

Effects: Combat tightness of the bronchial tubes caused by asthma.

Side effects: Increase in heart rate and blood pressure; nervousness, jitters, anxiety, nightmares and other behaviour changes.

Chlorphenamine

(over the counter) *Trade name:* Piriton.

Effects: See Antistamines.

Clemastine

(over the counter) *Trade name:* Tavegilo.

Effects: See Antihistamines.

Clotrimazole cream or ointment

(over the counter) *Trade name:* Canesten.

Effects: Kills the fungi that cause ringworm and some nappy rashes.

Side effects: Rare.

Corticosteroids, inhaled

(prescription only)

Effects: Inhaled corticosteroids are the best medications for reducing inflammation in the lungs caused by asthma.

Side effects: With overuse or misuse, enough corticosteroid is absorbed into the body to produce serious side effects; talk with the doctor about how to avoid them.

Corticosteroids, topical

(over the counter or prescription)

Effects: Corticosteroid creams, ointments and lotions reduce itching and inflammation of the skin; especially useful for eczema and some allergic reactions. There is a range of strengths.

Side effects: Thinning of the skin, lightening of pigment, absorption of medicine into the body; all worse with stronger corticosteroids used over larger areas for longer periods of time. Use of weaker types for short periods is usually safe.

Co-trimoxazole

(prescription only) *Trade name:* Septrin.

Effects: An antibiotic, often used for bladder infections; no longer used for ear infections (see Antibiotics).

Side effects: Stomach upset; call the doctor if paleness, rash, itching or other new symptoms appear.

Decongestants

(over the counter)

Effects: These medications cause blood vessels in the nose to contract so that the nose makes less mucus.

Side effects: Can be severe in young children under age six, or even deadly. Since these aren't effective in any case, avoid them. These medications often cause an increase in heart rate and blood pressure; nervousness, jitters, anxiety, nightmares and other behaviour changes. After a couple of days, the body often adjusts, so the medications no longer work. Be especially careful when taking with other medications that may have similar side effects, such as stimulants. Read the label: many are not for the use of children under twelve.

Dextromethorphan

(over the counter) *Trade names:* Robitussin Dry Cough and many others.

Effects: Supposed to suppress the cough reflex, but effectiveness is slight or perhaps nonexistent.

Side effects: Can be severe in young children; not safe under age six; use only under doctor's guidance in any child. Be aware, too, of other medications combined with the cough suppressant; all can have serious side effects.

Docusate
(over the counter) *Trade name:* Dulco-Ease.
Effects: A stool softener; not absorbed by the body.
Side effects: Diarrhoea, vomiting, allergic reactions.

Electrolyte solutions
(over the counter) *Trade name:* Dioralyte.
Effects: Used to prevent dehydration in children who are losing water through vomiting and diarrhoea, these solutions consist mainly of water, salt, potassium and different kinds of sugar in just the right proportions, so that as much water as possible is absorbed from the intestines into the bloodstream. Flavoured varieties and freeze-pops work well, too.
Side effects: None. However, a child who is having a lot of vomiting and diarrhoea should be under a doctor's supervision. It's possible to become dehydrated, even taking one of these rehydration solutions.

Erythromycin
(prescription only) *Trade name:* Erythroped.
Effects: An antibiotic, often used when penicillin allergy is present.
Side effects: Upset stomach, mainly.

Ferrous Fumarate, Ferrous Gluconate, Ferrous Sulfate
(over the counter or prescription) *Trade names:* Many.
Effects: Iron preparations; combat anaemia caused by iron deficiency.

Side effects: In overdose, iron is extremely dangerous, causing ulcers and other problems. Be careful with these medicines.

Flunisolide oral inhalation
(prescription only)
Effects: See Corticosteroids, inhaled.

Fluticasone nasal inhalation
(prescription only)
Effects: See Corticosteroids, inhaled.

Fluticasone oral inhalation
(prescription only)
Effects: See Corticosteroids, inhaled.

Guaifenesin
(over the counter) *Trade names:* Robitussin, Sudafed.
Effects: An expectorant, supposed to loosen mucus to make it easier to cough up.
Side effects: Not for the use of children under six years.

Hydrocortisone cream or ointment
(over the counter) *Trade name:* Hc45.
Effects: See Corticosteroids, topical. Hydrocortisone 0.5 per cent and 1 per cent are fairly weak; good for minor itching rashes, with few side effects.
Side effects: Like all corticosteroids, side effects increase with higher dose and longer use; check with the doctor.

Ibuprofen

(over the counter) *Trade names:* Calprofen, Ibuleve, Nurofen.

Effects: See under Nonsteroidal anti-inflammatories. Ibuprofen is good for aches and pains.

Side effects: Causes stomach upset, especially in high doses. Overdose is dangerous.

Ketoconazole lotion or cream

(over the counter) *Trade names:* Daktarin Gold, Nizoral.

Effects: Kills the fungi that cause ringworm and some nappy rashes.

Side effects: Rare.

Loperamide

(over the counter and prescription) *Trade names:* Diocalm, Imodium.

Effects: Reduces diarrhoea by reducing contractions in the intestines.

Side effects: Bloating, stomach pains. Not for children under twelve.

Loratadine

(over the counter) *Trade name:* Clarityn.

Effects: See Antistamines. Loratadine may cause less drowsiness than older (far cheaper) antihistamines.

Side effects: Rare headache, dry mouth, drowsiness or hyper behaviour.

Miconazole

(over the counter) *Trade name:* Daktarin.

Effects: Kills the fungi that cause athlete's foot and other rashes.

Side effects: Rare.

Montelukast

(prescription only) *Trade name:* Singulair.

Effects: Reduces inflammation in the lungs in asthma.

Side effects: Headache, dizziness, upset stomach.

Mupirocin

(prescription only) *Trade name:* Bactroban.

Effects: Kills bacteria that commonly cause skin infections.

Side effects: Rare.

Naproxen

(over the counter or prescription) *Trade name:* Naprosyn.

Effects: See Nonsteroidal anti-inflammatories. Naproxen is good for aches and pains.

Side effects: Causes stomach upset, especially at high doses. Dangerous in overdose. Take with food; talk to the doctor if taking for more than a day or two.

Nonsteroidal anti-inflammatories (NSAIDS)

(over the counter or prescription) Examples include paracetamol and ibuprofen.

Effects: These medications reduce inflammation in muscles and joints, lower fever, reduce pain.

Side effects: All can cause stomach upset, especially at higher doses; overdose can be very dangerous. Talk with your doctor if using at high doses or for long periods of time.

Nurofen
(over the counter)
Effects: See Ibuprofen.

Paracetamol
(over the counter) *Trade names:* Calpol, Panadol.
Effects: See under Nonsteroidal anti-inflammatories. Paracetamol reduces fever and pain.
Side effects: In large overdoses, causes serious liver disease. Ask the doctor if you are giving it for more than a couple of days.

Permethrin
(over the counter) *Trade name:* Lyclear.
Effects: This medication kills head lice.
Side effects: Rare.

Phenoxymethylpenicillin
(prescription only)
Effects: See Antibiotics. The treatment of choice for strep throat.
Side effects: Allergic reactions, usually a rash with little itchy bumps, are common; more serious allergic reactions are rare but do happen. Notify your doctor if you are allergic.

Phenylephrine

(over the counter) *Trade name:* Sudafed Blocked Nose.

Effects: See Decongestants.

Side effects: Not safe in children under twelve; use only on doctor's advice.

Polymyxin B

(over the counter) *Trade name:* Polyfax.

Effects: A mild antibiotic that can be applied to the skin (topical).

Side effects: Rare.

Pseudoephedrine

(over the counter) *Trade name:* Sudafed, Galpseud.

Effects: See Decongestants.

Side effects: Not safe in children under six; use only on doctor's advice.

Ranitidine

(prescription only) *Trade name:* Zantac.

Effects: Reduces stomach acid, reducing heartburn (a symptom of acid reflux).

Side effects: Headache, dizzines, constipation, stomach pain.

Salbutamol

(prescription only) *Trade names:* Salamol, Ventolin.

Effects: See Bronchodilators.

Sodium Cromoglicate

(prescription only) *Trade name:* Intal.

Effects: Reduces inflammation in the lungs in asthma; not as powerful as inhaled corticosteroids.

Side effects: Rare.

Triamcinolone oral inhalation

(prescription only)

Effects: See Corticosteroids, inhaled.

RESOURCE GUIDE

It's easy to be overwhelmed by the universe of online information and hard to know what to rely on. This guide lists reliable and informative government and nonprofit sites (website names ending in .gov and .org, rather than .co.uk). Most of the sites include articles for parents, guides to further reading and directories of local groups and professionals; many also have interactive discussion groups and special features for children and teens.

You'll need access to the Internet, which is available through most public libraries. For those who cannot go online, the guide includes telephone numbers as well: some are for hotlines; others are for the main office of the organization.

A word of caution: even for well-respected sites, there is no guarantee that all of the information on them will be accurate. A good plan is to look at the authorship before you read the article. Ideally, every article should list the author and his or her qualifications. Is the author someone you'd trust to advise you about your child? You should also be able to see when the article was last updated. Articles that are outdated or undated aren't as trustworthy. Finally, you have to use your own common sense: if something you read seems wrong or suspect, look at other sites and sources, or ask your doctor.

GENERAL INFORMATION

Citizens Advice Bureau
Myddleton House
115–123 Pentonville Road
London N1 9LZ
08444 111 444 (England)
08444 77 20 20 (Wales)
www.citizensadvice.org.uk
Details of your local office can be found in the phone book or by phoning the national office. CABs can help with a wide range of problems.

UK Advice (formerly Federation of Independent Advice Centres)
6th Floor
63 St Mary Axe
London EC3A 8AA
020 7469 5700
email: mail@adviceuk.org.uk
www.adviceuk.org.uk
A network of advice centres across the country.

Public Libraries
Useful starting points for finding out addresses of national and local organizations.

Social Services

A social worker at your local social services office will give you information on topics including benefits, housing, financial difficulties, employment, relationship problems, child care and useful organizations. Look up social services in the phone book under the name of your local authority.

ORGANIZATIONS FOCUSED ON FAMILY AND SOCIAL POLICY, CHILD DEVELOPMENT, CHILDBIRTH AND PARENTING

Adoption

Adoption Information Line

204 Stockport Road
Altrincham WA15 7UA
0800 883 8887
www.adoption.org.uk
A good starting point for information.

Bereavement

Child Death Helpline

York House
Great Ormond Street
London WC1N 3JH
0800 282986 (freephone helpline)
www.childdeathhelpline.org.uk
Help and support for parents whose child has died.

Compassionate Friends
53 North Street
Bristol BS3 1EN
0845 123 2304 (UK helpline)
0288 7788016 (Northern Ireland helpline)
www.tcf.org.uk
Help and support for parents whose child has died.

Breast-Feeding

Association of Breastfeeding Mothers
PO Box 207
Bridgewater
TA6 7YT
08444 122 949 (helpline)
abm.me.uk
Counselling helpline for breast-feeding mothers.

Breastfeeding Network
PO Box 11126
Paisley PA2 8YB
0300 100 0212 (helpline)
email: enquiries@breastfeedingnetwork.org.uk
www.breastfeedingnetwork.org.uk

Drugs in Breastmilk Helpline
Lactation Consultants of Great Britain
0844 4124665
email: info@lcgb.org
www.lcgb.org

La Leche League (Great Britain)
PO Box 29
West Bridgford
Nottingham NG2 7NP
0845 120 2918
email: lllgb@wsds.co.uk
www.laleche.org.uk

National Childbirth Trust
Alexandra House
Oldham Terrace
Acton
London W3 6NH
0300 330 0700 (general helpline)
0300 330 0771 (breast-feeding line)
www.nct.org.uk
Information about antenatal classes, breast-feeding and postnatal support.

Bullying
Bullying UK
0808 800 2222 (helpline)
www.bullying.co.uk
Advice for both children being bullied and their parents.

Child Abuse
Childline
42 Curtain Road
London EC2A 3NH
0800 1111 (24-hour helpline)

www.childline.org.uk
Free counselling service for children available 24 hours a day.

NSPCC (National Society for the Prevention of Cruelty to Children)
42 Curtain Road
London EC2A 3NH
020 7825 2500
0800 800 5000 (24-hour helpline for adults; children should call Childline, above)
email: help@nspcc.org.uk
www.nspcc.org.uk

Child Care

Day Care Trust/National Childcare Campaign
2nd Floor
73–81 Southwark Bridge Road
London SE1 0NQ
0845 872 6260
email: info@daycaretrust.org.uk
www.daycaretrust.org.uk
Charity campaigning to improve conditions for working parents and promoting high-quality, affordable child care for all.

4Children (formerly known as Kids' Club Network)
City Reach
5 Greenwich View Place
London E14 9NN
020 7512 2100 (information helpline)

email: info@4children.org.uk
www.4children.org.uk
Advice and information on all aspects of out-of-school child care.

National Childminding Association
81 Tweedy Road
Bromley
Kent BR1 1TG
0845 880 0044
www.ncma.org.uk
Advice on choosing a childminder or nanny.

National Day Nurseries Association
Longbow Close
Huddersfield
West Yorkshire HD2 1GQ
01484 407070
www.ndna.org.uk
Advice and information about registered day nurseries.

Working Families
1–3 Berry Street
London EC1V 0AA
0800 013 0313 (helpline)
email: office@workingfamilies.org.uk
www.workingfamilies.org.uk
Advice and information about childcare and employment issues relating to pregnancy and working parents.

Counselling

Your GP may be able to offer counselling or refer you for counselling.

British Association for Counselling and Psychotherapy
15 St John's Business Park
Lutterworth
Leicestershire LE17 4HB
01455 883300
email: bacp@bacp.co.uk
www.bacp.co.uk
Help with finding a counsellor.

Relate (Marriage Guidance)
0300 100 1234
email: enquiries@relate.org.uk
www.relate.org.uk
Has local branches around the country. Can be used by married or unmarried couples.

Samaritans
08457 909090 (UK)
email: jo@samaritans.org
www.samaritans.org

Domestic Violence

Refuge
0808 2000 247 (24-hour helpline)
refuge.org.uk

Emergency accommodation and advice for women and children experiencing domestic violence.

Women's Aid Federation of England
PO Box 391
Bristol BS99 7WS
01179 444411 (administration)
0808 2000 247 (24-hour helpline)
email: info@womensaid.org.uk
www.womensaid.org.uk

Doulas

Doula UK
1 Rockfield Business Park
Leckhampton
Cheltenham
Gloucestershire GL53 0AN
doula.org.uk

Education

Advisory Centre for Education
The Busworks
United House
North Road
London N7 9DP
0808 800 5793 (advice line)
www.ace-ed.org.uk
Advice for parents of children who are experiencing problems such as bullying, SEN and exclusion.

Family Mediation

Family Mediators' Association
Braeview House
9–11 Braeview Place
East Kilbride
G74 3XH
01355 244594
www.thefma.co.uk

National Family Mediation
Margaret Jackson Centre
4 Barnsfield Hill
Exeter
Devon EX1 1SR
0300 4000 636
www.nfm.org.uk
Has details of mediation services around the country.

Family Welfare

Family Action
501–505 Kingsland Road
London E8 4AU
020 7254 6251
www.family-action.org.uk
Provides social work and social care services to families and individuals.

Gay and Lesbian

Gay and Lesbian Legal Advice (GLAD)
020 7837 5212

A free phone line open in the evenings, providing free legal advice.

London Lesbian and Gay Switchboard
020 7837 6768
Helpline 0300 330 0630
www.llgs.org.uk
Provides details of local lesbian and gay support groups and switchboards.

Pink Parents UK
Unit 29
Hillier Road
Devizes
Wiltshire SN10 2FB
01380 727935
www.pinkparents.org.uk
Support for lesbian and gay parents and their families.

Stonewall Youth
08000 502020
www.youngstonewall.org.uk
Information and support for gay and bisexual teens.

Gifted Children
National Association of Gifted Children
01908 646433
www.nagcbritain.org.uk

Grandparenting

Children Need Grandparents
2 Surrey Way
Laindon West
Basildon
Essex SS15 6PS
01268 414607
Offers aid and advice to grandparents who are refused access to their grandchildren.

The Grandparents Association
Moot House
The Stow
Harlow
Essex CM20 3AG
01279 428040 (office)
0845 4349585 (helpline)
www.grandparents-association.org.uk

Learning Difficulties

National Association for Special Educational Needs (NASEN)
4/5 Amber Business Village
Amber Close
Amington
Tamworth
Staffs B77 4RP
01827 311500
www.nasen.org.uk
Information and advice about SEN.

Nutrition and Health

NHS Choices

www.nhs.uk

Advice on parenting, nutrition, health and fitness.

Parenting

Family Lives

49–51 East Road

London N1 6AH

0808 800 2222 (freephone)

www.familylives.org.uk

Parenting advice and support.

Racism

Equality and Human Rights Commission

3 More London

Riverside Tooley Street

London SE1 2RG

020 3117 0235

www.equalityhumanrights.com

Encourages good relations between people from different racial backgrounds, the elimination of racial discrimination and promotion of equal opportunities.

Safety, First Aid

Child Accident Prevention Trust

1–3 Brixton Road

London SW9 6DE

020 7608 3828

email: safe@capt.org.uk

www.capt.org.uk
Advice on accident prevention.

Child Car Seats
www.childcarseats.org.uk
Safety information and advice.

Directgov
think.direct.gov.uk
Road safety advice.

Red Cross
44 Moorfields
London EC2Y 9AL
0844 871 1111
www.redcross.org.uk
First-aid courses.

Royal Society for the Prevention of Accidents (ROSPA)
28 Calthorpe Road
Edgbaston
Birmingham B15 1RP
0121 248 2000
www.rospa.com
Provides information, advice, resources and training.

St John's Ambulance
27 St John's Lane
London EC1M 4BU
08700 10 49 50

www.sja.org.uk
First-aid courses.

Toys Advice
www.toysadvice.co.uk
Advice on toy safety.

Single Parents
Gingerbread
255 Kentish Town Road
London NW5 2LX
0808 802 0925 (freephone advice line)
www.gingerbread.org.uk
Local self-help groups for single parents and their children.

Single Parent Action Network (SPAN)
Millpond
Baptist Street
Easton
Bristol BS5 0YJ
0117 951 4231
email: info@spanuk.org.uk
www.spanuk.org.uk
Nationwide network of self-help organizations for single parents.

Toys
Playmatters National Association of Toy and Leisure Libraries (NATLL)
1A Harmood Street

London NW1 8DN
www.natll.org.uk
Provides information on local toy libraries.

INFORMATION ABOUT MEDICAL CONDITIONS AND SUPPORT GROUPS FOR SPECIFIC CONDITIONS

ADHD

National Attention Deficit Disorder Information and Support Service (ADDISS)
Premier House
112 Station Road
Middlesex HA8 7BJ
020 8952 2800
email: info@addiss.co.uk
www.addiss.co.uk
Advice and support for families with children who have attention deficit or hyperactivity disorder.

Alcohol and Drugs

Alcoholics Anonymous (AA)
0845 769 7555
www.alcoholics-anonymous.org.uk
Network of self-help groups whose members encourage each other to stop drinking and to stay off drink.

Drinkline
0800 917 8282 (alcohol helpline)

Narcotics Anonymous
0300 999 1212 (helpline 10 am–10 pm)
email: helpline@ukna.org
www.ukna.org

FRANK
0800 776 600 (freephone 24 hours)
frank@talktofrank.com
www.talktofrank.com
Advice on all aspects of drugs.

Asthma

Asthma UK
Summit House
70 Wilson Street
London EC2A 2DB
0800 121 62 44 (helpline)
www.asthma.org.uk
Information and advice on asthma.

Autism

National Autistic Society
393 City Road
London EC1V 1NG
0808 800 4104 (helpline)
email: nas@nas.org.uk
www.autism.org.uk
Information about resources and treatment of autism.

Bed-Wetting

Enuresis Resource and Information Centre (ERIC)
34 Old School House
Britannia Road
Kingswood
Bristol BS15 8DB
0845 370 8008 (helpline)
email: info@eric.org.uk
www.eric.org.uk

Blindness

See Visual Impairments, page 1075.

Cerebral Palsy

Scope
6 Market Road
London N7 9PW
0808 800 3333 (helpline)
email: response@scope.org.uk
www.scope.org.uk
Information and services for disabled people and people with cerebral palsy and their families.

Cleft Lip and Palate

Cleft Lip and Palate Association (CLAPA)
First Floor
Green Man Tower
332b Goswell Road
London EC1V 7LQ
020 7833 4883

email: info@clapa.com
www.clapa.com
Information and counselling for parents and contacts for local groups.

Cystic Fibrosis
Cystic Fibrosis Trust
11 London Road
Bromley
Kent BR1 1BY
0300 373 1010 (helpline)
www.cftrust.org.uk

Deafness
See Hearing Impairments, page 1066.

Depression
See Mental Health, page 1067.

Diabetes
Diabetes UK Careline
10 Parkway
London NW1 7AA
0845 120 2960 (9 am–5 pm, Mon–Fri)
www.diabetes.org.uk

Disabilities
Dial UK
St Catherine's Hospital
Tickhill Road

Doncaster DN4 8QN
01302 310123
www.dialuk.info
UK-wide disability information and advice services.

Disability, Pregnancy & Parenthood International
National Centre for Disabled Parents
Unit F9
89–93 Fonthill Road
London N4 3JH
0800 018 4730
email: info@dppi.org.uk
www.dppi.org.uk

Down's Syndrome
Down's Syndrome Association
Langdon Down Centre
2a Langdon Park
Teddington TW11 9PS
0845 230 0372
email: info@downs-syndrome.org.uk
www.downs-syndrome.org.uk

Dyslexia

British Dyslexia Association
Unit 8, Bracknell Beaches
Old Bracknell Lane
Bracknell RG12 7BW
0845 251 9002 (helpline)
email: helpline@bdadyslexia.org.uk
www.bdadyslexia.org.uk

Eating Disorders

Beat
0845 634 1414 (adult helpline)
0845 634 7650 (youth helpline)
www.b-eat.co.uk
Helplines, support and self-help groups.

Epilepsy

Epilepsy Action
0808 800 5050 (freephone helpline)
email: helpline@epilepsy.org.uk
www.epilepsy.org.uk

Haemophilia

Haemophilia Society
1st Floor
Petersham House
57A Hatton Garden
London EC1N 8JG
0800 018 6068 (helpline 9 am–5 pm, Mon–Fri)
email: info@haemophilia.org.uk
www.haemophilia.org.uk

Hearing Impairments

National Deaf Children's Society
15 Dufferin Street
London EC1Y 8UR
0808 800 8880 (freephone helpline)
email: helpline@ndcs.org.uk
www.ndcs.org.uk

SENSE (National Deaf-Blind and Rubella Association)
101 Pentonville Road
London N1 9LG
0845 127 0062
email: info@sense.org.uk
www.sense.org.uk

HIV/AIDS

My HIV
Terrence Higgins Trust
314–320 Gray's Inn Road
London WC1X 8DP
0808 802 1221
www.myhiv.org.uk
Advice on all aspects of HIV and AIDS as well as those related to parents.

Positively UK
345 City Road
London EC1V 1LR
020 7713 0222 (helpline 10 am–4 pm, Mon–Fri)
www.positively.uk.org

Information and practical advice for those with a positive AIDS diagnosis or who have ARC or AIDS, including women who are pregnant or who have children.

Intellectual Disability
MENCAP (Royal Society for Mentally Handicapped Children and Adults)
MENCAP National Centre
123 Golden Lane
London EC1Y 0RT
0300 333 1111
www.mencap.org.uk

Meningitis
National Meningitis Trust
Fern House
Bath Road
Stroud
Gloucestershire GL5 3JT
0800 028 1828 (helpline)
www.meningitis-trust.org

Mental Health
MIND (National Association for Mental Health)
Granta House
15–19 Broadway
London E15 4BQ
0300 123 3393 (information line 9.15 am–5.15 pm, Mon–Fri)
www.mind.org.uk

Young Minds
Baden Place
Crosby Row
London SE1 1YW
0808 802 5544 (parents' helpline)
www.youngminds.org.uk
Advice about children's and young people's emotional wellbeing and mental health.

Muscular Dystrophy
Muscular Dystrophy Campaign
61 Southwark Street
London SE1 0HL
0800 652 6352
www.muscular-dystrophy.org
Support and advice through local branches and a network of Family Care Officers.

Prematurity and Birth Defects
BLISS
9 Holyrood Street
London SE1 2EL
0500 618140 (helpline)
www.bliss.org.uk
Information and advice for parents of babies born prematurely.

New Life
Hemlock Way
Cannock

Staffordshire WS11 7GF
01543 462777
0800 902 0095 (nurse helpline)
email: info@bdfnewlife.co.uk
www.newlifecharity.co.uk
Charity for disabled and terminally ill children.

Tommy's, The Baby Charity
Nicholas House
3 Laurence Pountney Hill
London EC4R 0BB
020 7398 3400
www.tommys.org
Charity that raises funds for research into prematurity and provides advice on pregnancy and premature birth.

Selective Mutism
Selective Mutism Information and Research Association
email: lindsay@selectivemutism.co.uk
www.smira.org.uk

Sickle Cell Disease
Sickle Cell Society
54 Station Road
Harlesden
London NW10 4UA
020 8961 7795
www.sicklecellsociety.org

Spina Bifida

Shine (formerly the Association for Spina Bifida and Hydrocephalus)
42 Park Road
Peterborough PE1 2UQ
01733 555988
www.shinecharity.org.uk

Stuttering

British Stammering Association
15 Old Ford Road
London E2 9PJ
www.stammering.org

Sudden Infant Death Syndrome (SIDS)

Foundation for the Study of Infant Death (FSID)
11 Belgrave Road
London SW1V 1RB
0808 802 6868 (helpline)
email: helpline@fsid.org.uk
fsid.org.uk

Stillbirth and Neonatal Death Society (SANDS)
28 Portland Place
London W1B 1LY
020 7436 5881 (helpline)
020 7436 7940
email: support@uk-sands.org
www.uk-sands.org

Tourette's Syndrome
Tourettes Action
91–93 High Street
Camberley
Surrey GU15 3RN
0300 7778427 (helpline)
www.tourettes-action.org.uk

Twins
TAMBA (Twins and Multiple Births Association)
2 The Willows
Gardner Road
Guildford
Surrey GU1 4PG
0800 138 0509
www.tamba.org.uk

Multiple Births Foundation
Hammersmith House Level 4
Queen Charlotte's & Chelsea Hospital
Du Cane Road
London W12 0HS
020 3313 3519
email: mbf@imperial.nhs.uk
www.multiplebirths.org.uk

Visual Impairments

Action for Blind People
14–16 Verney Road
London SE16 3DZ
0303 123 9999 (RNIB helpline)
www.actionforblindpeople.org.uk

Royal National Institute for the Blind
105 Judd Street
London WC1H 9NE
0303 123 9999 (helpline)
www.rnib.org.uk

SENSE (National Deaf-Blind and Rubella Association)
101 Pentonville Road
London N1 9LG
0845 127 0062
email: info@sense.org.uk
www.sense.org.uk ndex

INDEX